PATRIOTIC GORE

PATRIOTIC GORE

STUDIES IN THE LITERATURE

OF THE AMERICAN CIVIL WAR

BY

EDMUND WILSON

———

Without the shedding of blood, there is no remission of sins

JOHN BROWN

> *The despot's heel is on thy shore,*
> > *Maryland!*
> *His torch is at thy temple door,*
> > *Maryland!*
> *Avenge the patriotic gore*
> *That flecked the streets of Baltimore,*
> *And be the battle-queen of yore,*
> > *Maryland! My Maryland!*

SONG OF THE CONFEDERATE SOUTH

NORTHEASTERN UNIVERSITY PRESS

Boston

Northeastern University Press edition 1984
Copyright © 1962 by Edmund Wilson
Reprinted by permission of Farrar, Straus and Giroux

Library of Congress Cataloging in Publication Data

Wilson, Edmund, 1895–1972.
Patriotic gore.
Reprint. Originally published: New York : Farrar,
Straus and Giroux, 1962. With new introd.
Includes index.
1. American literature—19th century—History and
criticism. 2. United States—History—Civil War, 1861–
1865—Literature and the war. 3. War in literature.
4. United States—Intellectual life—19th century.
I. Title.
PS211.W5   1984   810'.9'358   84-10118
ISBN 0-930350-61-8 (pbk.)

Poems by Frederick Tuckerman from *The Sonnets of
Frederick Goddard Tuckerman*, edited, with an Introduction,
by Witter Bynner, copyright 1931 by Alfred A. Knopf, Inc.
Renewed 1959 by Witter Bynner. Letters of Oliver Wendell
Holmes reprinted by permission of the Library of
Harvard University.

Printed and bound at the Murray Printing Co.,
Westford, Mass. The paper is Glatfelter Offset,
an acid-free sheet.

MANUFACTURED IN THE UNITED STATES OF AMERICA
95   94   93   92   91   90   5   4   3

Cover photo courtesy of Culver Pictures.

ACKNOWLEDGMENTS

I HAVE ACKNOWLEDGED in the course of the text most of my biographical sources. There are as yet no full-length biographies of Francis Grierson and John De Forest. For information about the former I am indebted to Mr. Shamus O'Sheel and Mr. Theodore Rousseau; about the latter to Mr. Gordon Haight of Yale, who has given me the benefit of his knowledge of the subject and supplied me with such printed materials as exist. Mr. Arlin Turner, the author of the admirable biography of George W. Cable, to which I am chiefly indebted for my detailed account of Cable's career, has been helpful in sending me material on Cable and on George Harris. I am grateful to Mr. Mark DeWolfe Howe, the editor and biographer of Justice Holmes, for reading and criticizing my chapter on Holmes and for putting at my disposal unpublished letters by him. I have also profited from my conversations with Mr. William Taylor of Harvard as well as from his brilliant book *Cavalier and Yankee*; and from my talks with my friend Mr. Chauncy Hackett, who, in the years during which I was writing this book, was able to give me tips and personal reminiscences that I found particularly valuable as coming from an old Washingtonian with a highly developed social and political sense of both the North and the South. To Mr.

Cecil Roth of Oxford I am indebted for pointing out to me the probable sources of the *Battle Hymn of the Republic*. I am grateful to Mr. William A. Jackson of the Houghton Library at Harvard for permission to include passages from unpublished letters by De Forest; and to Mr. Lyman Beecher Stowe and the Women's Archives at Harvard for permission to use unpublished letters by Calvin and Harriet Stowe. I should add that besides the works mentioned in the text on Harriet Beecher Stowe, I have drawn on a more recent study by Charles H. Foster of the University of Minnesota: *The Rungless Ladder: Harriet Beecher Stowe and New England Puritanism*. To my five students in a seminar at Harvard I am grateful for information derived from their own research in connection with papers which they wrote for me: Mr. Harvey G. Damaser, who traced the progress of the deification of Lincoln in the poetry published after the war; Mr. Barrie S. Hayne, who examined the works written in refutation of *Uncle Tom's Cabin*; Mr. Mark Irvin Whitman, who studied the scattered journalism as well as the books of George Fitzhugh; Miss Helen J. Sootin, who contributed some interesting discoveries to my section on American prose style; and Mr. Keith McKay Walker, who assessed the reliability of Harriet Beecher Stowe's book on Byron. I owe a special debt for checking documents, running down references and making editorial suggestions, to my secretaries Mr. Lowell Edmunds and Mrs. Philippe Radley. I am also especially grateful to Harvard and Yale Universities for allowing me the use of their libraries. The substance of some of these chapters first appeared in a different form in articles in the *New Yorker* magazine.

In quotations I have usually followed the spelling and punctuation of the writers, bad or old-fashioned though these sometimes are.

CONTENTS

FOREWORD

IT IS NOT EASY to say of an author who had as many diverse intellectual interests as Edmund Wilson just what his characteristic subject might be. Surely one of the more unlikely of them would be the Civil War period of American letters. And yet he could write of *Patriotic Gore,* "It will certainly be one of my best books." Published in 1962, in the last decade of his long life, it was his twenty-seventh book, and from the present perspective it does indeed seem to be one of his more valuable and durable works. It has long enjoyed a special and respected place as one of the most remarkable and readable books about the greatest tragedy in American history, and it still deserves the attention of anyone who is trying to understand the Civil War.

In his last years this Yankee-born world wanderer turned back to his native soil to rediscover his roots and locate his place on the family tree. The most absorbing object of this quest was the bloody family feud in which his people and those of his "Virginia cousins" had been involved a century earlier. He started his record of it with a series of essays on the literary remains of the Civil War generation; these early pieces were written for *The New Yorker,* where most parts of the book originally appeared. He wound up with some thirty studies of a biographical, speculative, and critical nature, about half of them on Yankees and half on Rebels, men and women.

Wilson's choice of characters will strike some readers as a bit erratic. With a cursory bow and the remark that the period "was not one in which belles lettres flourished," he nevertheless declares that he doubts there had "ever been another historical crisis of the magnitude of 1861–65 in which so many people were so articulate." They "did produce a remarkable literature which mostly consists of speeches and pamphlets, private letters and diaries, personal memoirs and journalistic reports." For him this informal outpouring often evoked the Civil War experience more poignantly and immediately than did the efforts of the professional men of letters. He offers as an example in his first paragraph, "the brilliant journal of Mary Chesnut, so much more imaginative and revealing than most of the fiction inspired by the war." Along with Chesnut he mentions as other examples the speeches of Lincoln, Sumner, and John Brown, the memoirs of Grant and Mosby, and the autobiographies of the Adams brothers. His distinct preference is for participants and combatants rather than what he called the "malingerers," on whom he is pretty hard. They only observed and contemplated. It is the *cri de coeur* of the anguished, the wounded, the desperately involved that fascinates him.

All very well. But for a work bearing the subtitle *Studies in the Literature of the American Civil War* there are some curious consequences of his bias. The three major poets of the period, Melville, Whitman, and Dickinson, get only passing attention, and three major fiction writers, Howells, Twain, and James, fare little better. He can spare more than sixty pages for John W. DeForest, but Emily Dickinson ("a little over rated," he suggests) gets only three. Blacks remain invisible. Some superficial scholarship and slipshod history occasionally mar his pages, and for all his promise to "avoid generalizations," he will indulge in pontifications on large subjects and venture questionable analogies when the mood is on him.

In spite of the somewhat raffish title he chose for the book (from "Maryland! My Maryland!") and the journalistic origins of the work, Wilson was perfectly serious about what he was doing. He read omnivorously and worked long and hard. Restraints tended to go by the board, however, in his "Introduction" about the meaning of it all. There he dismisses all talk of "morality," "justice," "principle," and "civilization" as "forms of warlike cant," and reduces the fratricidal struggle to the level of zoological phenomena such as the voracity of sea slugs and the fury of army ants. He swears in a letter written later that "the book is supposed to develop the theme I stated in the Introduction," and that there is no contradiction between them. His passionate identification with some of his subjects, however, does not bear out the claim. He fortunately reconsidered his declared intention (in a letter) "to compare Lenin, Lincoln, and Bismarck and show that they all had a good deal in common."

Wilson was blasphemously biased against patriotic pieties and partisan myths, but his prejudices were not regional. He remains identifiably Yankee, but those Virginia family connections of his are reflected in his statement that "the Southerners have a very good case for regarding the Northerners as treacherous aggressors." He goes on to say that "there is in most of us an unreconstructed Southerner who will not accept domination as well as a benevolent despot who wants to mold others for their own good." Those conflicting tendencies, he adds, "may also break the harmony of families and cause a fissure in the individual."

Patriotic Gore may not be the first book to open for a detached, measured, and reliable account of the most controversial period of American history and the literature it produced. Its author is too opinionated, prickly, erratic, and passionate for that. But if one seeks what Wilson called "the intimate essence of a conflict which, though fratricidal, was also incestuous," if the reader craves an understanding of the apocalyptic madnesses that set brothers tearing at each others' throats for four years, and if one must pick a sensitive intelligence deeply dedicated to communicating the collective experience of those involved in this tragedy, this book is indispensable.

New Haven   C. VANN WOODWARD
April, 1984

INTRODUCTION

THE PERIOD of the American Civil War was not one in which belles lettres flourished, but it did produce a remarkable literature which mostly consists of speeches and pamphlets, private letters and diaries, personal memoirs and journalistic reports. Has there ever been another historical crisis of the magnitude of 1861–65 in which so many people were so articulate? The elaborate orations of Charles Sumner, modelled on Demosthenes and Cicero; Lincoln's unique addresses, at once directives and elegies; John Brown's letters from prison and his final speech to the court; Grant's hard and pellucid memoirs and John Mosby's almost picaresque ones, together with the chronicles and apologetics of innumerable other officers of both the armies; the brilliant journal of Mary Chesnut, so much more imaginative and revealing than most of the fiction inspired by the war; the autobiographies of the Adams brothers, that cool but attentive commentary by members of the fourth generation of an historically self-conscious family — such documents dramatize the war as the poet or the writer of fiction has never been able to do. The drama has already been staged by characters who have written their own parts; and the peculiar fascination of this literature which leads one to go on and on reading it is rather like that of Browning's *The Ring and the*

Book, in which the same story is told from the points of view of nine different persons. We read in Mrs. Chesnut's diary of General Hood's unhappy passion for the beautiful girl "Buck" Preston; then we meet him in Sherman's memoirs protesting, at the taking of Atlanta, against the Northern invaders' harsh measures and engaging in polemics with him; then we discover that Hood has written his own memoirs. Charlotte Forten, the Negro school teacher from Philadelphia and the Boston Brahmin Thomas Wentworth Higginson turn out both to have left detailed records of the days that they spent together on the South Carolina Sea Islands. How very different Lincoln looks when he is seen by William Herndon, his law partner, by the Americanized Frenchman the Marquis de Chambrun, by Alexander H. Stephens, the Vice-President of the Confederacy, and by young Captain Oliver Wendell Holmes! How very different Grant appears to Henry and to Charles Francis Adams! And, as seems to have been natural in the nineteenth century so much more than it is in our own, everybody speaks in character in such a way that one can often almost hear their voices. It is as amusing to find McClellan writing home from the front to his wife, after a visit from Henry W. Halleck, who had displaced him as General-in-Chief, "He's a *bien mauvais sujet* — he is not a gentleman," as to remember General Forrest's reply, when asked how he had scored his success at Murfreesboro, that he had taken a short cut and "got there fustes' with the mostes'."

This book describes some thirty men and women who lived through the Civil War, either playing some special role in connection with it or experiencing its impact in some interesting way, and who have left their personal records of some angle or aspect of it. In dealing with them, I have mainly presented them in terms of their immediate human relations and of the values of their time and place, and I have tried to avoid generalizations and to allow the career and the character to suggest its own moral. I am, however, under some obligation to explain to the reader in advance the general point of view which gives shape to my picture of the war.

Having myself lived through a couple of world wars and having read a certain amount of history, I am no longer disposed to take very seriously the professions of "war aims" that nations make. I think that it is a serious deficiency on the part of historians and political writers that they so rarely interest themselves in biological and zoölogical phenomena. In a recent Walt Disney film showing life at the bottom of the sea, a primitive organism called a sea slug is seen gobbling up smaller organisms through a large orifice at one end of its body; confronted with another sea slug of an only slightly lesser size, it ingurgitates that, too. Now, the wars fought by human beings are stimulated as a rule primarily by the same instincts as the voracity of the sea slug. It is true that among the animals other than man it is hard to find organized aggression of the kind that has been developed by humanity. There are perhaps only the army ants which have mastered a comparable technique. But baboons travel in gangs; small birds will gang up on an owl; bees will defend a hive. The anthropoid gorilla, it seems, is now one of the least pugnacious of mammals: he lives in a family tree and does not molest the homes of others; but there is evidence that primitive man had to fight to defend his home. In any case, all animals must prey on some form of life that they can capture, and all will eat as much as they can. The difference in this respect between man and the other forms of life is that man has succeeded in cultivating enough of what he calls "morality" and "reason" to justify what he is doing in terms of what he calls "virtue" and "civilization." Hence the self-assertive sounds which he utters when he is fighting and swallowing others: the songs about glory and God, the speeches about national ideals, the demonstrations of logical ideologies. These assertions rarely have any meaning — that is, they will soon lose any meaning they have had — once a war has been got under way. The Germans have represented in our century the simplest kind of aggressive expansion. In the war of 1914, they invaded France and Belgium on the pretext that they needed *Lebensraum* and had a mission to spread *Kultur*; and when the disabling penalties of the Treaty of Versailles sent them out again rampaging through Europe, they called themselves the "master race," which had a mission to regiment humanity. In the case, however, of a people which has just had a successful revolution, the situation is a little more complicated. The slogans that such a people shouts may at first express a real exaltation on the part of some social group or country which has succeeded in escaping from the clutches of some other group or country that has been eating it, as well as enthusiastic hopes for the freer and happier society which it hopes to construct in the future. It may at first fight a civil war, and then when the once dominant power has been routed and dispossessed, still find itself under the necessity of defending the new society set up by the revolution against the return of the former regime, now supported perhaps by other still stable regimes which have made common cause with the power expelled. But once the insurgent party has succeeded in imposing its own authority, if it feels itself strong enough to go further, it will devour as much as it can, and its slogans will lose all meaning. The defense by the French of their revolution turned into Napoleon's conquests; the defense

by the Russians of theirs into the appetite for expansion
which has spurred them — while indignantly denouncing
"imperialism" — to swallow up the Balkan and the Baltic
countries and those of Central Europe, just as the Tsar's
Russia, by methods sometimes peaceful and sometimes
not, had swallowed up the innumerable peoples who
made up the old Russian Empire. The Napoleonic
French were boasting about *la gloire* as well as about
their revolutionary ideals, *Liberté, Egalité, Fraternité,* and
they made the *Marseillaise* do for both; the Russians have
been pretending to be the instruments of a relentless historical process which has chosen them to carry out the
mission of saving the rest of the world by converting it
into "people's democracies." And now we Americans of
the United States, we too the self-congratulatory grand-
children of a successful revolution but driven, also, by
the appetite for aggrandizement, have been adding such
terms as "the American dream," "the American way of
life" and "the defense of the Free World" to these other
forms of warlike cant.

It is, however, of course, very difficult for us to recognize that we, too, are devourers and that we, too, are
talking cant. If we would truly understand at the present
time the kind of role that our own country is playing,
we must go back and try to see objectively what our tendencies and our practice have been in the past.

Like modern France and the Soviet Union, we inaugurated our national existence with the expulsion of the
agents of a monarchic power; and as soon as that had
been accomplished, the process of expansion began. This,
except for our struggles with the Indians, to which I shall
later return, was for some time peaceful enough. We
bought Louisiana from the French and Florida from the
Spanish. In the case of Texas, we colonized it when it
was still a part of a Mexican province and under the rule

of Spain, and we made offers to buy it from Mexico, but the Mexicans would not sell. The colonists from the United States eventually drove the Mexicans out and set up an independent republic, which later became part of the United States. With the British we made a settlement to take over the Oregon Territory; but with the relatively incompetent Mexicans we continually became more high-handed. We demanded of Mexico the payment of a very large compensation for property belonging to Americans which had been lost in her revolutions and for Americans who had been shot in Mexico. We offered to cancel this debt if the Mexicans would cede to us that part of their territory which lay north of the Rio Grande and which we claimed as a part of Texas; and we tried to buy California, which was also a part of Mexico but which was already being settled, in the northern part, by pioneers from the United States. The Mexicans refused both these offers, and President Polk retorted by sending troops to occupy the territory north of the Rio Grande. The Mexicans defended it. The United States declared war, invaded Mexico and captured the capital city, and took over, by force of arms, New Mexico, California and all the rest of the unsettled West. This amounted to more than half the territory originally owned by Mexico. The government of Mexico was compelled to sign a treaty with us, by which it was agreed that, in compensation for the land that had been taken from it we should pay them fifteen million dollars and let them off from responsibility for the claims that the United States had pressed. The sentiment that justified the Mexican War may be illustrated by an extract from a letter written in 1847 by William Gilmore Simms, the South Carolinian novelist and publicist, to the South Carolinian senator James H. Hammond: "You must not dilate against military glory. War is the greatest element of modern civilization, and our destiny is conquest. Indeed the moment a nation ceases to extend its sway it falls a prey to an inferior but more energetic neighbour. The Mexicans are in the condition of those whom God seeks to destroy having first made mad. They are doing their best to compel us to conquer them. It is now impossible that it should be otherwise. Mark my words — our people will never surrender an inch of soil they have won. They are too certainly of the Anglo Norman breed for that. We will pay for it, perhaps, but only out of the assessed expense and damage of the conquest to us."

The next step was the repression of the Southern states when they attempted to secede from the Union and set up a republic of their own — in the course of which, it may be mentioned, the Canadians became so alarmed at the increasing aggressiveness of the Washington government that they for the first time began to take steps to consolidate their diverse provinces in a single federal system. The slave-owning Southern states and the rapidly industrializing North had by this time become so distinct from one another that they were virtually two different nations; they were as much two contending power units — each of which was trying to expand at the other's expense — as any two European countries. The action of the Washington government in preventing the South from seceding was not prompted by the motives that have been often assumed. The myth that it was fighting to free the slaves is everywhere except in the South firmly fixed in the American popular mind; and it is true, of course, that slavery in the Southern states was embarrassing to many people — in the South as well as the North; but many other people thoroughly approved of it — in the North as well as the South. Abolitionists like Whittier and Garrison were not in such mortal danger as they would have been in South Carolina, but both were mobbed in New England and the former, in Philadelphia, had the office of his paper burned down. These fanatics were handled rather gingerly by the anti-South Republicans, and exploitation of the wickedness of the planters became later a form of propaganda like the alleged German atrocities in Belgium at the beginning of the first World War. The institution of slavery, which the Northern states had by this time got rid of, thus supplied the militant Union North with the rabble-rousing moral issue which is necessary in every modern war to make the conflict appear as a melodrama. As for the wickedness of secession, New England itself had debated seceding when, at the time of the War of 1812, its trade with Great Britain was interrupted. But these pseudo-moral issues which aroused such furious hatred were never fundamental for the North; and it was possible for the Washington government to coerce and to crush the South not by reason of the righteousness of its cause but on account of the superior equipment which it was able to mobilize and its superior capacity for organization.

The North's determination to preserve the Union was simply the form that the power drive now took. The impulse to unification was strong in the nineteenth century; it has continued to be strong in this; and if we would grasp the significance of the Civil War in relation to the history of our time, we should consider Abraham Lincoln in connection with the other leaders who have been engaged in similar tasks. The chief of these leaders have been Bismarck and Lenin. They with Lincoln have presided over the unifications of the three great new modern powers. If one happens to belong to a class or to live in a part of the world which has reason to honor the memory of one of these statesmen but has been injured by the policies of another, one may find this grouping unexpected. Bismarck was detested by the French whom he defeated and humiliated; Lenin is widely detested by old regime Russians, by political heretics who have been outlawed by the Soviet government and by everyone who has been frightened by "Communism" as the enemy of old-fashioned *laissez-faire* (which can hardly be said now to exist in any of the so-called "capitalist" countries); Lincoln is detested by the American Southerners against whom he waged a four years' war and whom he reduced to unconditional surrender. But each became a hero for the people who gave their allegiance to the state he established. (I remember how shocked I was when, on a visit in my childhood to Virginia cousins, I heard them refer to Lincoln as "a bloody tyrant.") And they all had certain qualities in common. Lincoln and Bismarck and Lenin were all men of unusual intellect and formidable tenacity of character, of historical imagination combined with powerful will. They were all, in their several ways, idealists, who put their ideals before everything else. All three were solitary men, who lived with their concentration of purpose. None liked to deal in demagogy and none cared for official pomp: even Bismarck complained that he could not be a courtier and assured Grant and others — as he must have believed quite sincerely — that he was not really a monarchist but a republican. Each established a strong central government over hitherto loosely coördinated peoples. Lincoln kept the Union together by subordinating the South to the North; Bismarck imposed on the German states the cohesive hegemony of Prussia; Lenin — though contemptuous of bureaucracy, since he could not himself imagine that, once the old order was abolished, any decent person could want to be a bureaucrat — began the work of binding Russia, with its innumerable ethnic groups scattered through immense spaces, in a tight bureaucratic net.

Each of these statesmen risked everything for his object and each paid a heavy price. Lincoln was assassinated by a Confederate sympathizer at the end of hardly more than four years in office; Lenin did not last much longer — hardly more than seven years: he was shot by a political opponent, then suffered a series of strokes, which, in his last two years as head of the government, incapacitated him almost completely; Bismarck was not assassinated, but two attacks by social revolutionaries were made upon the life of his Emperor; and all of these acts of violence were gauges of the weight of repression which their objects had been imposing or were assumed to be responsible for imposing. Each of these statesmen was confident that he was acting out the purpose of a force infinitely greater than himself. Bismarck believed in God and thought that his successful strokes were guided by revelatory moments in which he could see where God was going; Lenin believed in "History," which had become, in the Marxist philosophy, a kind of substitute for the Protestant Providence; Lincoln talked sometimes, like Lenin, of History, sometimes, like Bismarck, of God, and he was always aware, like Lenin, of his destiny to play a decisive role in the drama of human development, although, unlike Lenin, he regarded himself as a simple human being, whereas Lenin identified himself with the "antithesis" of the dialectical process and, having dropped his real name in the underground, seems never to have thought of himself afterwa ds as a Russian named Vladímir Ulyánov.

Each of these men, through the pressure of the power which he found himself exercising, became an uncompromising dictator, and each was succeeded by agencies which continued to exercise this power and to manipulate the peoples he had been unifying in a stupid, despotic and unscrupulous fashion, so that all the bad potentialities of the policies he had initiated were realized, after his removal, in the most undesirable way. The generous program of Lincoln for readmitting the South to the Union was discarded by the Radical Republicans, who added every form of insult and injury to the bitterness of the Confederate failure. Bismarck was succeeded by a monarch who presided over a German defeat and debacle and then fled, by request, to another country, leaving his own in a situation which led inevitably to an even worse government, an even more outrageous aggression and an even more disastrous defeat; Lenin well before his death had been superseded by Stalin, who exterminated the old Bolshevik idealists, tormented the Russians with a reign of terror that made the French Revolution look moderate and let them in for a foreign invasion which laid waste the whole western part of their country and cost it seven million lives in addition to the several million that Stalin had already extinguished. We Americans have not yet had to suffer from the worst of the calamities that have followed on the dictatorships in Germany and Russia, but we have been going for a long time now quite steadily in the same direction. In what way, for example, was the fate of Hungary, at the time of its recent rebellion, any worse than the fate of the South at the end of the Civil War? The Russians put down this rebellion with brutality and tried to reduce the Hungarians to subjection just as we did with the Southerners, and they could protest the same justification: that the group they were forced to suppress was a retarded feudal society whose economy had become unworkable and was founded on social injustice.

These great modern federations that always speak with such horror of "imperialism" — for we do this as well as the Soviet Union — are continually put under a strain by the recalcitrance of the groups they have subjugated, and their revolts are likely to be stifled by their bureaucratic central governments as quickly as and often more quietly than they were by the old kings and emperors. In my account of the expansion of the United States, I did not dwell on our expulsion of the Indians from the lands that we had agreed they should occupy. In general, having ousted and cheated and murdered and demoralized this interesting people, we made haste to forget about them; and yet, so far as we know, there are now in North America about the same number of Indians that were here when Columbus arrived. These first natives still do not regard themselves as belonging to the United States; they have refused to accept American citizenship. They are resisting the efforts to deprive them of their lands in the interests of the truckroads and power projects which, in this centralizing age, in the United States and elsewhere, are usually given precedence over all individual or local interests; they are invoking their old treaties with our government — which are, after all, as recent as the end of the eighteenth century — treaties which we dare disregard for no more honorable reason than that we know that, in any given case, a few hundred or a few thousand Indians are helpless in a contest with our courts, our police and, if necessary, our armed forces. The Iroquois Indians of New York State and Canada have now organized a nationalist movement, and a general conference of Indians from all over the United States has, as I write, just been held in Chicago. This conference has drawn up a declaration demanding more assistance from the federal government for housing, education and health and a transference of the authority of the Indian Bureau, which they complain does not know much or care much about them, to reservation superintendents, who would be aware of their needs and make it possible for them to have access to Washington. All this has been going on at a time when we were priding ourselves on our loyalty to Chiang Kai-shek, a discarded Chinese nationalist whom we are keeping in comfort on Formosa, and lavishing millions of dollars on Laos and other distant countries, in which, for ridiculous reasons and with lavish ineptitude, we are supposed to be resisting Communism in the interest of the "freedom" of people who are often as primitive as those Indians whom we are constantly harassing at home.

This revival of resistance on the part of the Indians has hitherto seemed so feeble that we have not felt we needed to notice it; but the recent resistance of the South over the issue of school integration has been so violent and has continued for so long that we have been forced to take cognizance of it. In this case, there are two situations involved which work against one another in a way that makes it unrealistic for Northerners to talk, as they often do, in terms of a simple right and wrong. The Negroes are rebelling against the whites, who are afraid of them, as they have always been, and do not want them to better themselves because they do not want to have to compete with them; but the white Southerners themselves are rebelling against the federal government, which they have never forgiven for laying waste their country, for reducing them to abject defeat and for the needling and meddling of the Reconstruction. They have never entirely recognized the authority of the Washington government. It is possible to sympathize with both Negroes and whites, though not with the hoodlum and criminal methods employed by the latter against desegregation, which have left the Negro leaders, with their non-violent methods, in a position of moral superiority. Again, an analogy is useful. The relentlessness, it is said, of the color ban which is being imposed in South Africa by the white people of Dutch extraction is partly the result of their defeat by the British in the "imperialistic" Boer War. They take out their own humiliation on the blacks who are at their mercy, and the whites of the frustrated Confederacy take out theirs on the Negroes among whom they live. When the federal government sends troops to escort Negro children to white schools and to avert the mob action of whites, the Southerners remember the burning of Atlanta, the wrecking by Northern troops of Southern homes, the disfranchisement of the governing classes and the premature enfranchisement of the Negroes. The truth is that the South since the Civil War, in relation to the Washington government, has been in a state of mind that has fluctuated between that of Hungary and that of the Ukraine in relation to the government of Moscow. It was Lincoln who — though not without hesitation — decided to oppose secession and who reduced the South to total surrender; but he had disapproved of the Mexican War and had refused to endorse it in Congress, and he does not seem to have thought much about further expansion. Others, however, did, and we find in one of Stephen A. Douglas's speeches, in the course of his debates with Lincoln, a flight of prophecy which is a good illustration of this. Douglas had been the leader of the "Young America" movement in the Democratic Party, which had favored, if opportunity offered, the annexation of Mexico, Cuba and the countries of Central America.

"Let each State stand firmly," cries Douglas, "by that great constitutional right, let each State mind its own business and let its neighbors alone, and there will be no trouble on this question. If we will stand by that principle, then Mr. Lincoln will find that this republic can exist forever divided into free and slave States, as our fathers made it and the people of each State have decided. Stand by that great principle and we can go on as we have done, increasing in wealth, in population, in power, and in all the elements of greatness, until we shall be the admiration and terror of the world. We can go on and enlarge as our population increases, and we require more room, until we make this continent one ocean-bound republic. Under that principle the United States can perform that great mission, that destiny which Providence has marked out for us. Under that principle we can receive with entire safety that stream of intelligence which is constantly flowing from the Old World to the New, filling up our prairies, clearing our wildernesses and building cities, towns, railroads and other internal improvements, and thus make this the asylum of the oppressed of the whole earth. We have this great mission to perform, and it can only be performed by adhering faithfully to that principle of self-government on which our institutions were all established." Observe that the enlargement of the United States is supposed to be benevolent and beneficent, that our aim is to provide asylum for the oppressed of the rest of the world. To utter these altruistic professions has become our official policy. Whenever we engage in a war or move in on some other country, it is always to liberate somebody.

Let us follow our further expansion. Having occupied a broad strip of the continent, we purchased Alaska from Russia and began to reach out for the islands in the Pacific and the Caribbean. We acquired the Midway Islands and, in fear of having Hawaii and Samoa occupied by rival powers, we established naval bases on them. We had always had a yearning for Cuba, and in 1898, in spite of the fact that the Spanish were apparently ready to negotiate, we sent them an ultimatum demanding their withdrawal from the island. The immediate provocation for this was the sinking of the battleship *Maine* – though there was never any reason for believing that this had been done by the Spanish, and there is some reason for believing that it was engineered by William Randolph Hearst in order to set off a war. But before we invaded Cuba, we had sent Admiral Dewey to the Philippines, which also belonged to Spain, to destroy the Spanish warships in Manila Bay — a move that was apparently directed, with no official justification, by the expansionist Theodore Roosevelt, who was then Assistant Secretary of the Navy. We later sent troops to the Philippines and captured the city of Manila. The exploit had no relevance whatever to our quarrel with the Spaniards over Cuba, which was supposed to have been provoked by the struggle of the Cubans to get rid of them. This struggle had been going on since 1868 and had culminated in the ruthless suppression of a recent Cuban revolt. We dislodged the Spanish from the island at the cost of only three hundred of our own soldiers killed in battle but of three thousand who died from disease. We also took Puerto Rico, Guam and the Hawaiian Islands. But with the Philippines we had more trouble. The Filipino rebels against Spanish rule, who had assumed that our intervention was disinterested, turned their resistance against us when they discovered that we wanted to take over their islands. It took us more than two years to subdue them and cost us three and a half thousand lives among the seventy thousand soldiers we sent there. We established concentration camps of the kind which had aroused our indignation when the Spanish had resorted to them in Cuba, and the casualties of the Filipinos, mostly among civilians, were fifteen or twenty times ours. We paid Spain twenty million dollars. Later on, when Theodore Roosevelt was President, he arranged a revolution in Panama in order to break it off from Colombia, which was refusing to meet our terms for a lease on the Panama canal zone. We then leased the canal zone from Panama, which was given the half-subject status of a protectorate of the United States, as Cuba had already been and Haiti and the Dominican Republic were very soon to be. Colombia, resenting this, retorted by adopting a policy of making it difficult for American business men to obtain concessions there, so we eventually — not till 1921 — paid her twenty-five million dollars.

When the Germany that Bismarck had unified and turned into a great European power began to invade her neighbors in 1914, her chief rival, England, accepted the challenge and went to war with her on the Continent. Both England and Germany interfered with what the United States regarded as our neutral rights, the British by blockading our trade, by impounding American ships and by blacklisting American firms suspected of doing business with Germany, and the Germans by their submarine warfare, which, in spite of German warnings to Americans not to travel on the ships of Germany's enemies, resulted in the loss of American lives, and which later, when "unrestricted," was directed within certain zones against all kinds of merchant shipping. Bombarded by British propaganda and horrified by what we heard of the brutality of the Germans, with whom, nevertheless, we had a great deal in common and for whom throughout the nineteenth century we had expressed the highest admiration, we went in on the side of England and made her struggle for supremacy our struggle, when we might well by abstaining have shortened the war and left Europe less shattered and more stable. This cost us fifty thousand lives, about a sixth of the price of the war and a persecution of everything German in a country with an immense German population which had always been thought one of our more valuable elements, together with a hissing and hounding of every kind of opposition sentiment that far outdid the repressions of Lincoln. President Wilson had made a great effort to keep us out of the war, and when finally he took us in, he announced that we had no quarrel with the German people but only with the warlords who were inciting them to mischief; but, once involved with his European allies, he was dragged into subjecting the enemy to an unnecessary unconditional surrender and imposing on them such heavy penalties that a second war with Germany was inevitable. When this second war occurred — with, as George F. Kennan has said, a real "Beast of Berlin" directing it instead of the fatuous Kaiser, whom we had unfairly cast in this role — we were gradually and furtively brought into it by President Franklin D. Roosevelt, who had been making secret agreements with the British but pretending, in his public statements, that he had not committed himself. Roosevelt of course disliked Hitler just as Lincoln disliked slavery; but it was not the mass murders of Hitler that drove us into going to war, any more than it had been the wrongs of slavery that made us go to war with the South. The American Jews had the motive of wanting to save their own people: they had even stronger reasons for fighting him than had their ancestors for resisting the Greeks and the Romans, they were glad to have us go in against him. But the extermination of six million Jews was already very far advanced by the time the United States took action; and when the United States did take action, the occasion for intervention was supplied by the Japanese, whose depredations in China had been threatening our commercial interests there and who had become a new power unit expanding across the Pacific and making us uneasy about the Philippines. It is true that we were also fearful lest Germany might threaten us across the Atlantic if she succeeded in defeating England and managed, by way of Africa, to establish herself strongly in South America. In any case, we first declared war on Japan.

The attack on our fleet at Pearl Harbor has become, in

our popular history, an act of moral turpitude more heinous than the firing of the Confederates on Fort Sumter;
but it has been argued, to me quite convincingly, by
Charles A. Beard, Mr. Harry Elmer Barnes and others
that this act was foreseen by our government and — in
order to make our antagonists strike the first blow —
deliberately not forestalled at a time when a Japanese delegation was attempting to negotiate peace. As soon as we
declared war on Japan, the Germans declared war on us.
We sent our troops again to Europe and again into the
Pacific, and in this even larger-scale conflict three hundred and seventy-five thousand Americans were killed.
Unconditional surrender again, and the unnecessary
bombing of German cities. We used many of the most
horrible weapons of modern war and made a climax by
dropping atomic bombs on Hiroshima and Nagasaki —
though a Committee on the Social and Political Implications of using the atomic bomb, made up of physicists,
chemists and biologists, had recommended a harmless
demonstration, as a warning to the Japanese, in the
presence of representatives of the new United Nations.
"It may be very difficult to persuade the world," said
the report of this official committee, "that a nation which
was capable of secretly preparing and suddenly releasing
a new weapon, as indiscriminate as the rocket bomb
and a thousand times more destructive, is to be trusted
later in any proclaimed desire of having such weapons
abolished by international agreement. . . . It is not at
all certain that American public opinion, if it could
be enlightened as to the effect of atomic explosives,
would approve of our own country being the first to
introduce such an indiscriminate method of wholesale
destruction of civilian life. . . . Thus . . . the military
advantages and the saving of American lives achieved by
the sudden use of atomic bombs against Japan may be
outweighed by the ensuing loss of confidence and by a

wave of horror and revulsion sweeping over the rest of the world."

After the war, the troops and agents of the U.S.A. moved in all over Europe and Asia, from West Germany to South Korea, and we found ourselves confronted by the Soviet Union, which was also moving in. Neither the Soviet Russians nor we were very much beloved by the peoples in upon whom they had moved. The rivalry of power units had now reached an even more gigantic scale than that of the British and German Empires. The Russians and we produced nuclear weapons to flourish at one another and played the game of calling bad names when there had been nothing at issue between us that need have prevented our living in the same world and when we were actually, for better or worse, becoming more and more alike — the Russians emulating America in their frantic industrializing and we imitating them in our persecution of non-conformist political opinion, while both, to achieve their ends, were building up huge government bureaucracies in the hands of which the people have seemed helpless. We Americans, whose public officials kept telling us we were living in "the Free World," discovered that we were expected to pay staggering taxes of which it has been estimated that 70 per cent has been going not only for nuclear weapons capable of depopulating whole countries but also for bacteriological and biological ones which made it possible for us to poison the enemy with every abominable disease from pneumonia and encephalitis to anthrax, cholera, diphtheria and typhoid, as well as with such new devices as the chemical agent called "GB," which imitates the natural weapons of the Australian stone fish and the black widow spider in paralyzing the nerves of its victims so that a drop of it no larger than a dot can kill a man in fifteen minutes. We discovered that if we should refuse to contribute to these researches, we could be fined and clapped into jail — that we could even be clapped into jail if we protested against any of this by taking part in public demonstrations. We are, furthermore, like the Russians, being spied upon by an extensive secret police, whose salaries we are required to pay, as we are required to pay, also, the salaries of another corps of secret agents who are infiltrating foreign countries. And while all this expenditure is going for the purpose of sustaining the United States as a more and more unpopular world power, as few funds as possible are being supplied to educate and civilize the Americans themselves, and generations of young people are growing up who at worst live a life of gang warfare, the highest objectives of which are brawling and killing and robbing, in the buried crowded slum streets of cities outside of which they can imagine no other world, and at best find little spur to ambition when they emerge from four years in college to face two years in the armed services in preparation for further large-scale wars at the prospect of taking part in which they rarely feel the slightest enthusiasm.

I have said that the Americans discovered all this, but many of us have never discovered it. (Our research into bacteriological and biological weapons — which we are trying to make antibiotic proof — has, to be sure, been kept as secret as possible, though the men who have been conducting it, uncomfortable about what they were doing, at one time, in 1959, held an international conference in an effort to lift this secrecy and to curb the production of such weapons, and an issue of the *Bulletin of Atomic Scientists* [June, 1960] was recently devoted to the subject.) We do not want to know about it, we do not like to talk about it. We talk instead about the big bad Russia, of which we as a rule know nothing except the moral indignation of politicians and the name-calling of the popular press. We cannot imagine the figure that is presented to the rest of the world by the United States of

Hiroshima, which first used the atomic bomb and which is promising plague and annihilation if anybody treads on the tail of its coat — that inflated and centralized United States which, after rescuing Cuba, as we boasted, from the cruelties of Spanish tyranny, took quite calmly the regime of Batista with its tortures and executions, and which, when Fidel Castro overthrew it as it deserved to be overthrown, obstructed in every way possible his socialist revolution, misrepresented his aims and forced him to seek support from the Communists, whose influence we were supposed to be fighting. We wonder in a naïve way whether the Germans really knew about the gas chambers and the other mass killings of the Nazis, and if they did, how they could ever have stood for them. We have only to examine our own state of mind in regard to what the United States government is getting ready to do to a possible enemy — and the Nazis considered the Jews enemies — only a few years after Dachau and Belsen were emptied. We have tried to make up for our atomic bombs by treating and petting the Japanese women whom we disfigured or incapacitated. We like to read about this in the papers; but we do not like to realize, let alone resist, the exactions that our government is making of us in order to equip us for a warfare which would not merely blight but exterminate, or to confess the extent to which our own bristling attitude has brought this situation about.

I know very well, of course, all the arguments from expediency for our policies in the past and for our so-called preventive measures at present. The reluctance of the Washington government to allow the South to secede was partly due to the same sort of fear of the possible intervention of other powers — with which a seceded Confederacy might have decided to make its own arrangements — as was involved in our seizure of the Pacific islands, our uneasiness about the French in Mexico and our even more serious uneasiness about the Nazis in South America; but this kind of jockeying for position is itself an aspect of the power contest and inseparable from — since, unchecked, it must lead to — the competition for power for its own sake. I am not here making a moral criticism of the course of our foreign policy: I am trying to disregard the pretensions to moral superiority with which we have attempted to clothe it; I am trying — as in the book that follows — to remove the whole subject from the plane of morality and to give an objective account of the expansion of the United States. I want to suggest that — headed as we seem to have been, for a blind collision with the Soviet Union — we ought to stop talking in terms of defending and liberating the victims of "oppressors" and "criminals," our old patter of "right" and "wrong" and punishing the guilty party. We have forgotten the Mexican War — only historians ever think of it. We have tried to forget the Civil War, but we have had the defeated enemy on the premises, and he will not allow us to forget it. We continue, nevertheless, to make him as much the villain as we dare to. Everything, past, present and future, takes its place in the legend of American idealism. Mr. Robert Penn Warren, in his little book *The Legacy of the Civil War*, the most intelligent comment, so far as I know, that has yet been brought forth by this absurd centennial — a day of mourning would be more appropriate — has shown how two fraudulent traditions, in the South and in the North respectively, have been stimulated by the Civil War. In the South, it is, he says, the "Great Alibi," which enables the Southerners to put the blame for everything that is lazy, provincial, barbarous and degraded in the South on the damage that they suffered in the war; for the North, it is the "Treasury of Virtue," which has enabled us to carry along into all our subsequent wars — in which so far we have always won or enlisted on the winning side — the insufferable moral attitudes that appeared to us first to be justified by our victory over the Confederacy in 1865. This prevents us from recognizing today, in our relation to our cold-war opponent, that our panicky pugnacity as we challenge him is not virtue but at bottom the irrational instinct of an active power organism in the presence of another such organism, of a sea slug of vigorous voracity in the presence of another such sea slug.

This is the time to think what we are doing because, as soon as a war gets started, few people do any more thinking about anything except demolishing the enemy. It will be seen in the pages that follow how automatically, on both sides of the contest, as soon as it had come to war, a Southerner like Lee who had opposed secession and who did not approve of slavery was ready to fight to the death for both, and how a Northerner like Sherman who knew the South, who had always got on well with the Southerners and who did not much object to slavery, became more and more ferocious to devour the South. We have seen, in our most recent wars, how a divided and arguing public opinion may be converted overnight into a national near-unanimity, an obedient flood of energy which will carry the young to destruction and overpower any effort to stem it. The unanimity of men at war is like that of a school of fish, which will swerve, simultaneously and apparently without leadership, when the shadow of an enemy appears, or like a sky-darkening flight of grasshoppers, which, also all compelled by one impulse, will descend to consume the crops.

November, 1961

PATRIOTIC GORE

I

HARRIET BEECHER STOWE

LET US BEGIN WITH *Uncle Tom's Cabin.*

This novel by Harriet Beecher Stowe was one of the greatest successes of American publishing history as well as one of the most influential books — immediately influential, at any rate — that have ever appeared in the United States. A year after its publication on March 20, 1852, it had sold 305,000 copies in America and something like two million and a half copies in English and in translation all over the world. As for its influence, it is enough to remember the greeting of Lincoln to Mrs. Stowe when she was taken to call on him at the White House: "So this is the little lady who made this big war." Yet, in the period after the war, the novel's popularity steadily declined. Mrs. Stowe's royalty statements for the second half of 1887 showed a sale of only 12,225, and eventually *Uncle Tom* went out of print. Up to the time when it was reprinted, in 1948, in the Modern Library Series, it was actually unavailable except at secondhand.

What were the reasons for this eclipse? It is often assumed in the United States that *Uncle Tom* was a mere propaganda novel which disappeared when it had accomplished its purpose and did not, on its merits, deserve to live. Yet it continued to be read in Europe, and, up to the great Revolution, at any rate, it was a popular book in Russia. If we come to *Uncle Tom* for the first time today, we are likely to be surprised at not finding it what we imagined it and to conclude that the postwar neglect of it has been due to the strained situation between the North and the South. The Northerners, embarrassed by the memory of the war and not without feelings of guilt, did not care to be reminded of the issue which had given rise to so much bitterness. In the South, where before the war any public discussion of slavery had by general tacit agreement been banned, nothing afterwards was wanted less than Northern criticism of pre-war conditions. It was still possible at the beginning of this century for a South Carolina teacher to make his pupils hold up their right hands and swear that they would never read *Uncle Tom*. Both sides, after the terrible years of the war, were glad to disregard the famous novel. The characters did still remain bywords, but they were mostly kept alive by the dramatizations, in which Mrs. Stowe had had no hand and which had exploited its more obviously comic and its more melodramatic elements. These versions for the stage kept at first relatively close to the novel, but in the course of half a century they grotesquely departed from it. By the late seventies, *Uncle Tom's Cabin* was half a minstrel show and half a circus. The live bloodhounds that were supposed to pursue Eliza as she was crossing the ice with her baby — which did not occur in the novel — began to figure in 1879, and were typical of this phase of the play. The original characters were now sometimes doubled: you had two Topsys, two Lawyer Markses, two Uncle Toms. Topsy sang comic songs, and Uncle Tom was given minstrel interludes, in which he would do a shuffle and breakdown. In the meantime, on account of sectional feeling, the book could not be read in schools as the New England classics were, and it even disappeared from the home. It may be said that by the early nineteen-hundreds few young people had any at all clear idea of what *Uncle Tom's Cabin* contained. One could in fact grow up in the United States without ever having seen a copy.

To expose oneself in maturity to *Uncle Tom* may therefore prove a startling experience. It is a much more impressive work than one has ever been allowed to suspect. The first thing that strikes one about it is a certain eruptive force. This is partly explained by the author in a preface to a late edition, in which she tells of the oppressive silence that hung over the whole question of slavery before she published her book. "It was a general saying," she explains, "among conservative and sagacious people that this subject was a dangerous one to investigate, and that nobody could begin to read and think upon it without becoming practically insane; moreover, that it was a subject of such delicacy that no discussion of it could be held in the free states without impinging upon the sensibilities of the slave states, to whom alone the management of the matter belonged." The story came so suddenly to Mrs. Stowe and seemed so irresistibly to write itself that she felt as if some power beyond her had laid hold of her to deliver its message, and she said sometimes that the book had been written by God. This is actually a little the impression that the novel makes on the reader. Out of a background of undistinguished narrative, inelegantly and carelessly written, the characters leap into being with a vitality that is all the more striking for the ineptitude of the prose that presents them. These characters — like those of Dickens, at least in his early phase — express themselves a good deal better than the author expresses herself. The Shelbys and George Harris and Eliza and Aunt Chloe and Uncle Tom project themselves out of

the void. They come before us arguing and struggling,
like real people who cannot be quiet. We feel that the
dams of discretion of which Mrs. Stowe has spoken have
been burst by a passionate force that, compressed, has
been mounting behind them, and which, liberated, has
taken the form of a flock of lamenting and ranting,
prattling and preaching characters, in a drama that demands to be played to the end.

Not, however, that it is merely a question of a troubled
imagination and an inhibited emotional impulse finding
vent in a waking fantasy. What is most unexpected is
that, the farther one reads in *Uncle Tom,* the more one
becomes aware that a critical mind is at work, which
has the complex situation in a very firm grip and which,
no matter how vehement the characters become, is controlling and coördinating their interrelations. Though
there is much that is exciting in *Uncle Tom's Cabin,*
it is never the crude melodrama of the decadent phase
of the play; and though we find some old-fashioned
moralizing and a couple of Dickensian deathbeds, there
is a good deal less sentimentality than we may have been
prepared for by our memories of the once celebrated
stage apotheosis — if we are old enough to have seen
it: "Little Eva in the Realms of Gold." We may even
be surprised to discover that the novel is by no means
an indictment drawn up by New England against the
South. Mrs. Stowe has, on the contrary, been careful
to contrive her story in such a way that the Southern
states and New England shall be shown as involved
to an equal degree in the kidnapping into slavery of
the Negroes and the subsequent maltreatment of them,
and that the emphasis shall all be laid on the imprac-
ticability of slavery as a permanent institution. The
author, if anything, leans over backwards in trying to
make it plain that the New Englanders are as much to

blame as the South and to exhibit the Southerners in a favorable light; for St. Clare and Miss Ophelia, intended as typical products of, respectively, Louisiana and Vermont, are, after all, first cousins; they are the children of two New England brothers, both of whom are described as "upright, energetic, noble-minded, with an iron will," but one of whom had "settled down in New England, to rule over rocks and stones, and to force an existence out of Nature," while the other had "settled in Louisiana, to rule over men and women, and force existence out of *them*." The difference between the two cousins is, then, chiefly a difference of habitat: the result of the diverse effects of a society in which you have to do things for yourself and of a society in which everything is done for you. And as for Simon Legree — a plantation owner, not an overseer, as many people imagine him to be (due, no doubt, to some telescoping of episodes, in the later productions of the play, which would have made him an employee of St. Clare's) — Simon Legree is not a Southerner: he is a Yankee, and his harsh inhumanity as well as his morbid solitude are evidently regarded by Mrs. Stowe as characteristic of his native New England. Nor are these regional characterizations — though later, by the public, turned into *clichés* — of an easy or obvious kind. The contrasted types of the book, through their conflicts, precipitate real tragedy, and even, in some episodes, high comedy — the Sisyphean efforts, for example, of the visitor from Vermont, Miss Ophelia, to bring system into the St. Clare household, and her bafflement by the Negro-run kitchen, a place of confusion and mystery, out of which she is unable to understand how the magnificent meals are produced. There is, in fact, in *Uncle Tom,* as well as in its successor *Dred,* a whole drama of manners and morals and intellectual points of view which corresponds somewhat to the kind of thing that was then being done by Dickens, and was soon to be continued by Zola, for the relations of the social classes, and which anticipates such later studies of two sharply contrasting peoples uncomfortably involved with one another as the *John Bull's Other Island* of Bernard Shaw or E. M. Forster's *A Passage to India.*

But such a writer as Forster or Shaw is a well-balanced man of letters contriving a fable at his leisure. Mrs. Stowe's objectivity is taut, intent. She has nothing of the partisan mentality that was to become so inflamed in the fifties; and Lord Palmerston, who had read the book three times, was evidently quite sincere in complimenting her on the "statesmanship" of *Uncle Tom's Cabin.* She is national, never regional, but her consciousness that the national ideal is in danger gave her book a desperate candor that shook South and North alike, and a dramatic reverberation that, perpetuated by the run of the play, has outlasted the analysis of the novel. In what terms this ideal of the United States was conceived by Harriet Beecher Stowe appears very clearly from a passage in her autobiographical notes: "There was one of my father's books that proved a mine of wealth to me. It was a happy hour when he brought home and set up in his bookcase Cotton Mather's *Magnalia,* in a new edition of two volumes. What wonderful stories those! Stories, too, about my own country. Stories that made me feel the very ground I trod on to be consecrated by some special dealing of God's providence." And she tells of her emotions, in her childhood, on hearing the Declaration of Independence read: "I had never heard it before," wrote Mrs. Stowe, "and even now had but a vague idea of what was meant by some parts of it. Still I gathered enough from the recital of the abuses and injuries that had driven my nation to this course to feel myself swelling with indignation, and ready with all my little mind and strength to applaud the concluding passage, which Colonel Talmadge rendered with resounding majesty. I was as ready as any of them to pledge my life, fortune, and sacred honor for such a cause. The heroic element was strong in me, having come down by ordinary generation from a long line of Puritan ancestry, and just now it made me long to do something, I knew not what: to fight for my country, or to make some declaration on my own account." Her assumption, in writing *Uncle Tom*, is that every worthy person in the United States must desire to preserve the integrity of our unprecedented republic; and she tries to show how Negro slavery must disrupt and degrade this common ideal by tempting the North to the moral indifference, the half-deliberate ignorance, which encourages inhuman practices, and by weakening the character of the South through the luxury and the irresponsibility that the institution of slavery breeds. For Harriet Beecher Stowe, besides, the American Union had been founded under the auspices of the Christian God, and she could not accept institutions that did such violence to Christian teaching. One of the strongest things in the novel is the role played by Uncle Tom — another value that was debased in the play. The Quakers who shelter Eliza are, of course, presented as Christians; but not one of the other white groups that figure in *Uncle Tom's Cabin* is living in accordance with the principles of the religion they all profess. It is only the black Uncle Tom who has taken the white man's religion seriously and who — standing up bravely, in the final scene, for the dignity of his own soul but at the same time pardoning Simon Legree — attempts to live up to it literally. The sharp irony as well as the pathos is that the recompense he wins from the Christians, as he is gradually put through

their mill, is to be separated from his family and exiled;
tormented, imprisoned and done to death.

Another feature of the stage melodrama that is misleading in regard to the novel is the unity, or effect of
unity, imposed on its locale and chronology. The play
is made to center on New Orleans, and one sensational
scene is made to follow another so fast that we do not
have any idea of the actual passage of time. The two
distinct strands of the story have, furthermore, to be tied
up together in a way that they are not in the book. The
novel has a quite different pattern, for in it the Negro
characters — Uncle Tom and his family, on the one
hand; George Harris and Eliza, on the other — are involved in a series of wanderings which progressively
and excitingly reveal, like the visits of Chíchikov in
Gogol's *Dead Souls,* the traits of a whole society. One of
the main sources of interest, as in Gogol, is the variety of
Southern households to which, one after the other, we
are introduced; first, the bourgeois Kentuckian Shelbys,
who are naturally decent and kindly, but also essentially
conventional and very much attached to their comfort;
then the homelier Ohio Quakers, with their kitchen-
centered existence and their language based on the
Bible; then the St. Clares, in their villa on Lake Pontchartrain — their wastefulness and laxness and charm,
the whole family languishing with maladies that are
real or imaginary, full of bad conscience, baffled affections and unfulfillable longings; then, finally — in the
lowest circle — the nightmare plantation of Simon Legree, a prison and a place of torture, with its Negroes
set to flog other Negroes and its tensions of venomous
hatred between Simon Legree and his mistress — where,
amidst the black moss and the broken stumps of the
muddy and rank Red River, the intractable New England soul is delivered to its deepest damnation. The

creator of this long sequence, with its interconnecting episodes of riverboat, tavern and slave market, was no contemptible novelist. Even Henry James, that expert professional, is obliged to pay her his tribute when he tells us, in *A Small Boy and Others,* of a performance of the play that had been for him in childhood a thrilling "aesthetic adventure," which had first, he says, awakened his critical sense, and admits that the novel constitutes a perhaps unique literary case of a book which has made its impression without the author's ever having concerned herself with literary problems at all, "as if," as he says, "a fish, a wonderful 'leaping' fish, had simply flown through the air." One hardly knows, in this connection, to what other book of its period one can properly compare *Uncle Tom.* Turgenev's *A Sportsman's Sketches,* exactly contemporary with it, which is supposed to have had some effect in expediting the abolition of serfdom and which has sometimes been spoken of as "the Russian *Uncle Tom's Cabin,*" belongs so much more to the level of sophisticated literary art that it is difficult today to realize how subversive its implications once were. The Brontës have something in common with Harriet Beecher Stowe, but even they belong more to *belles lettres,* and their subjects are not social problems but passionate feminine daydreams. *Uncle Tom* is more closely akin to some such early novel of Dickens as *Oliver Twist,* and Dickens, who admired the book, was correct in detecting his own influence.

Uncle Tom was an explosive that had been shot into the world by a whole combination of pressures, personal as well as historical. Harriet Beecher had been born in Litchfield, Connecticut, but she had gone to live in Cincinnati, Ohio, in 1832, when her father Lyman

Beecher, a then famous Presbyterian preacher, had founded in that Western city Lane Theological Seminary. Four years later, when she was twenty-five, she married Calvin Ellis Stowe, the professor of Biblical literature at Lane, and, with widely spaced visits to New England, which were evidently blessed escapes, she remained eighteen years in Ohio. Cincinnati was then a pork-packing center, and the streets were obstructed with pigs; it was also a river-town, and the bar-rooms were full of bad characters. The situation across the state line was a constant source of disturbance. There were always desperate slaves fleeing from over the river, and some Ohioans wanted to help them while others wanted to hunt them down. Lyman Beecher was opposed to slavery but had not been converted to Abolition. On this subject, as in his theology, he tried to steer a politic course; but at the time of his absence one summer, the trustees of his new theological school provoked an Abolitionist movement by suppressing an Anti-Slavery Society and forbidding discussion of the subject "in any public room of the Seminary." A self-confident and brilliant student rallied and led a sedition of the whole student body, who left their buildings and encamped in a suburb, and eventually, in 1835, he carried away a large part of the seminary, students and faculty both, to Oberlin College, also in Ohio, which had just received an endowment for a theological department that was to be open to colored students. In the summer of 1836, a mob in Cincinnati wrecked the press of an Abolitionist paper, and this was followed by further riots, in the course of which Harriet Stowe, going into the kitchen one day, found her brother, Henry Ward Beecher, pouring melted lead into a mold. When she asked, "What on earth are you doing, Henry?" he answered, "Making bullets to kill men with." He faced the streets with two guns in his pockets. Both

Harriet and Henry, as a result of this experience, seem secretly to have become Abolitionists. The Stowes a little later took into their household a colored girl who said she was free but who was presently claimed by her master; Calvin Stowe and Henry Beecher, armed with pistols, arranged her escape at night. This girl was the original of Eliza Harris. In the meantime, another of Harriet's brothers, Edward, now the head of Illinois College, had encouraged Elijah Lovejoy, one of the most zealous of the Abolitionists, who had been publishing a paper in St. Louis and was threatened by the pro-slavery element, to transfer his operations to Alton, Illinois. In the November of 1837, the year after the Cincinnati riots, Lovejoy was shot to death while defending his printing press, which had just been unloaded from a Mississippi steamboat, and it was reported — though this turned out to be false — that Edward Beecher had also been murdered.

In this period, the issue of slavery was becoming involved with church politics. An exacerbated controversy was going on between the Princeton Theological Seminary and the Yale Divinity School, with Princeton on the unyieldingly conservative and Yale on the relatively liberal side. Lyman Beecher, who had studied at Yale, had found in Cincinnati a bitter opponent, a certain Dr. Joshua Wilson, the pastor of the First Presbyterian Church, a Calvinist fanatic so uncompromising that he refused to have pictures in his house on the ground that they were graven images. Dr. Wilson had occupied unchallenged the position of leader of the Church in the West, and he seems to have been jealous of Beecher. He succeeded — taking his cue, it is said, from Princeton — in having Lyman Beecher tried for heresy in 1835, first before the Presbytery, then before the Synod, but in both cases his victim had been acquitted.

Though rugged and open in manner, Lyman Beecher was a very astute politician. It is wonderful to find him declaring that he is sound on infant depravity by putting into solemn language his conviction that young children were badly behaved, exhibiting, as he says, "selfishness, self-will, malignant anger, envy and revenge," the evidence of "a depraved state of mind, voluntary and sinful in its character and qualities." (His denial that infant damnation had ever been an article of the Calvinist creed was evidently derived from Calvin's reservation in favor of children who belonged to the Elect.) When his son Henry Ward Beecher was about to be examined for ordination at Fort Wayne, Indiana — to which the old man rode seventy miles, arriving "besplashed and bespattered," as another of his sons has written, "with smoking steed and his saddle-bags crusted with mud" — the father admonished him as follows: "Preach little doctrine except what is of moldy orthodoxy; keep all your improved breeds, your short-horned Durhams, your Berkshires, etc., away off to pasture. They will get fatter and nobody will be scared. Take hold of the most practical subjects; popularize your sermons. I do not ask you to change yourself; but, for a time, while captious critics are lurking, adapt your mode so as to insure that you shall be rightly understood." Yet a split in the Church now took place. "The South," said Dr. Beecher in later years, "had generally stood neutral. They had opposed going to extremes in theology either way. Rice, of Virginia, was a noble fellow, and held all steady. It was Rice who said, after my trial, that I ought to be tried once in five years, to keep up the orthodoxy of the church. He was full of good humor, and did so much good. But they got scared about abolition. Rice got his head full of that thing, and others. John C. Calhoun was at the bottom of it. I know of his doing things — writing to ministers, and telling them to do this and do that. The South finally took the Old School side. It was a cruel thing — it was a cursed thing, and 'twas slavery that did it."

At the General Assembly in Philadelphia in 1838, Dr. Wilson had Beecher and Calvin Stowe read out of the Presbyterian Church. That same day in Philadelphia, a new building called Liberty Hall, which had just been dedicated to Abolition and to which white Quaker women had been seen going arm and arm with Negro men, was burned down by a mob, with the firemen refusing to put out the blaze. Dr. Beecher set out in the autumn on a kind of marauding expedition and persuaded several students from other colleges to transfer to Lane Seminary. In Louisville, he ran into a man he knew who was keeping a store in the city, and he induced him to give up his business and study for the ministry at Lane. When Beecher got back to the seminary, he found that his son-in-law, Calvin Stowe, who was a periodic hypochondriac, had succumbed to discouragement and taken to his bed. "Wake up!" cried Dr. Beecher. "I've brought ye twelve students. Get up and wash, and eat bread, and prepare to have a good class."

The Stowes had by this time four children — the first two of which were twins — and Harriet began to write stories in order to bring in some money. In the summer of 1841, several incidents of violence occurred. A man who was hiding a slave that had run away from Kentucky went so far as to attack the owner when the latter attempted to search his house; and at about the same time a local farmer was murdered by Negroes who were stealing his berries, and in the city a white woman was raped. In September, there were race riots that lasted a week, with several persons killed and wounded. A farmer with a Dutch name, who was to turn up in *Uncle Tom's Cabin* as Old John Van Trompe, made an effort to rescue nine slaves, only one of whom succeeded in getting away; but for the loss of this slave he was sued by the owner. He was defended by Salmon P. Chase, at that time a young lawyer in Cincinnati, who had played a courageous part in the 1836 riots and who was later to defend Dr. Beecher when the relentless Old School Presbyterians tried to oust him from the presidency of his seminary in order to take it over themselves. In Beecher's case, Chase was successful, but he failed in his defense of the farmer. He took it up to the Supreme Court at his own expense, but he lost on every decision. His client was finally ruined by having to pay the costs as well as fines and damages. A third brother of Harriet's, Charles, who was also to have entered the ministry, had been shaken in his faith at college by a treatise of Jonathan Edwards's, in which Edwards appeared to be arguing that man was completely deprived of the power of moral choice and yet that God held him accountable. Though Charles's resourceful father found it possible to interpret Edwards in a less discouraging way, the boy abandoned religion and became what he called a fatalist. Eventually, however, to Lyman's great joy, he emerged from this state of mind and, like his brothers, went into the ministry; but in the meantime he had been working as a clerk in New Orleans and, returning to Cincinnati at the time when mob violence was running high, he brought stories of plantation life in Louisiana that were later to be used by Harriet for the episode of Simon Legree. During the winter of 1842–43, there was a typhoid epidemic in the Seminary, and everybody turned out to nurse the sick. In July, just as Harriet Stowe was on the point of having another baby, her brother George, also a minister, accidentally shot himself. She was an invalid for months after the birth of the child; nor did the baby seem likely to live, and yet the little girl did survive. The Stowes, with their growing family, had no other means than Calvin's meager salary, and their life became rather sordid. A letter of Harriet's to Calvin, written on June 16, 1845, when Calvin is away at a ministers' convention, strikes the note of this dismal period:

"My dear Husband, — It is a dark, sloppy, rainy, muddy, disagreeable day, and I have been working hard (for me) all day in the kitchen, washing dishes, looking into closets, and seeing a great deal of that dark side of domestic life which a housekeeper may who will investigate too curiously into minutiæ in warm, damp weather, especially after a girl who keeps all clean on the *outside* of cup and platter, and is very apt to make good the rest of the text in the *inside* of things.

"I am sick of the smell of sour milk, and sour meat, and sour everything, and then the clothes *will* not dry, and no wet thing does, and everything smells moldy; and altogether I feel as if I never wanted to eat again.

"Your letter, which was neither sour nor moldy, formed a very agreeable contrast to all these things; the more so for being unexpected. I am much obliged to you for it. As to my health, it gives me very little solicitude, although it is bad enough and daily growing worse. I feel no life, no energy, no appetite, or rather a growing distaste for food; in fact, I am becoming quite ethereal. Upon reflection I perceive that it pleases my Father to keep me in the fire, for my whole situation is excessively harassing and painful. I suffer with sensible distress in the brain, as I have done more or less since my sickness last winter, a distress which some days takes from me all power of planning or executing anything; and you know that, except this poor head, my unfortunate household has no mainspring, for nobody feels any kind of responsibility to do a thing in time, place, or manner, except as I oversee it.

"Georgiana is so excessively weak, nervous, cross, and fretful, night and day, that she takes all Anna's strength and time with her; and then the children are, like other little sons and daughters of Adam, full of all kinds of absurdity and folly.

"When the brain gives out, as mine often does, and one cannot think or remember anything, then what is to be done? All common fatigue, sickness, and exhaustion is nothing to this distress. Yet do I rejoice in my God, and know in whom I believe, and only pray that the fire may consume the dross; as to the gold, that is imperishable. No real evil can happen to me, so I fear nothing for the future, and only suffer in the present tense.

"God, the mighty God, is mine, of that I am sure, and I know He knows that though flesh and heart fail, I am all the while desiring and trying for his will alone. As to a journey, I need not ask a physician to see that it is needful to me as far as health is concerned, that is to say, all human appearances are that way, but I feel no particular choice about it. If God wills I go, He can easily find means. Money, I suppose, is as plenty with Him now as it always has been, and if He sees it is really best, He will doubtless help me."

It was a very hard summer for both of them. Calvin, who was supposed to be raising money for the Seminary, stayed away till the beginning of October. He detested this money-raising, for which he was entirely unfitted. "This work," he writes Harriet on June 30, "is beyond measure irksome and trying to me, and the long absence from you and the children almost insupportable. And after all, it is not going to result in any immediate pecuniary *affluence* I can assure you. At most it will just enable us to struggle through another year, and give us hope that we shall not be obliged through excessive poverty to quit our post." And in September: "I am so nervous that any attempt to preach on the subject of raising money brings on neuralgic pains that are intolerable and lay me aside for a week or two . . . If I cannot live without begging money, I must die; the sooner the better." He is passing, besides, through a serious crisis. He fears that he is losing his faith, and he has been frightened by recent scandals created in the clerical world by certain "licentious hypocrites" into wondering whether it might not be possible for him, too, to disgrace his calling.

"I long to be with you once more," he writes in the letter first quoted. "I am a miserable creature without a wife, and having been blessed with such a wife as you are, it is the harder to be alone so much and so long, and in an employment so essentially disagreeable to me. Let me have a competent salary, let me be permitted to study and teach and lecture everyday, let me have my dear little children around me every evening, and let me sleep in my own bed with my own good wife every night, and Prince Albert himself is not so happy a man as I. Though I have, as you well know, a most enthusiastic admiration of fresh, youthful female beauty; yet it never comes anywhere near the kind of feeling I have for you. With you, every desire I have, mental and physical, is completely satisfied and filled up, and leaves me nothing more to ask for. My enjoyment with you is not weakened by time nor blunted by age, and every reunion after separation is just as much of a honey-moon as was the first month after the wedding. Is not your own experience and observation a proof of what I say? Does it not always *seem to be* just as I represent it? Just as it seems, so it is in reality. No man can love and respect his wife more than I do mine. Yet we are not as happy as we might be. I have many faults, and you have some failings, and Anna [the Stowes' maid and nurse], with all her good qualities, is rather aggravating sometimes — but the grace of God can mend all.

"I have thought much of our domestic happiness lately in connection with the melancholy licentiousness, recently detected, of several clergymen of high reputation in the east."

A bishop in Philadelphia, whom Calvin has admired as a writer for his effective refutation of the "historical argument against Christianity," "it now appears has long been addicted to intoxication, and while half boozled has caught young ladies who were so unfortunate to meet him alone, and pawed them over in the most disgusting manner, and actually attempted to do them physical violence. This has been going on for years until it could be borne no longer, and now it all comes out against him, to the dishonor of religion, his own unspeakable shame and anguish, and the distress unutterable of his wife and children." And: "Another distinguished high church episcopalian clergyman in Philadelphia, nearly 60 years old, is said to be in precisely the same predicament as his bishop. Bless the Lord, O my soul, that with all my strong relish for brandy and wine, and all my indescribable admiration and most overflowing delight in handsome young ladies, no offences of this kind have yet been written down against me in God's book. Next comes the most melancholy case of N. E. Johnson, lately editor of the N.Y. evangelists and recently pastor of the Meth. Church in Bloomfield, N.J. though he has been admired as an evangelical, spiritual, revival preacher of great talent and concentrated piety, and married to an intelligent, amiable and pious woman who has borne him children, though associating without suspicion with the most pious men and the most accomplished and Christian women, it now appears that for 8 or 9 years past he has been in the habit of not only visiting the theaters . . . but also the brothels and bawdy houses of the city of N.Y. where he would get beastly drunk and revel and swelter with the vilest harlots. . . .

"Last in this dreadful catalogue, J. H. Fairchild, formerly pastor of the Orthodox church in South Boston, and lately of Exeter N.H. a man 55 years old, twice married, and whose daughters are mothers. Circumstances have recently occurred, which show that he has for years been licentious, that while elder he seduced one of his own kitchen girls, committed adultery with a member of his own church; and lately he has cut his throat and killed himself in the agony of his shame, while pastor of one of the most respectable churches in Exeter. . . .

"Now what shall we think of all these horrid disclosures? Is there anybody we can trust? Are all ministers brutes? I confess I feel almost ashamed to go into a pulpit or ask anyone to contribute a cent for ministerial education. . . ."

Harriet's answer is prompt and firm: she takes the situation seriously, and that she and Calvin were quite right in doing so was to be proved by the later justification of a "presentiment" she speaks of here, in connection with a visit from her younger brother, Henry Ward Beecher, who was eventually to become involved in a similar, if less sordid, scandal: ". . . Yesterday Henry came from Crawfordsville uncommonly depressed and sober and spoke in church meeting of unexpected falls among high places in the church and the need of prayer for Christians. He seemed so depressed that a horrible presentiment crept over me. I thought of all my brothers and of

you — and could it be, that the great Enemy has prevailed against any of you, and as I am gifted with a
most horrible vivid imagination, in a moment I imagined — nay saw as in a vision all the distress and
despair that would follow a fall on your part. I felt weak
and sick — I took a book and lay down on the bed, but
it pursued me like a nightmare — and something seemed
to ask Is your husband any better *seeming* than so and
so! — I looked in the glass and my face which since
spring has been something of the palest was so haggard
that it frightened me. The illusion lasted a whole fore-
noon and then evaporated like a poisonous mist — but
God knows how I pity those heart wrung women —
wives worse than widows, who are called to lament that
the grave has *not* covered their husband — the father of
their children! Good and merciful God — why are such
agonies reserved for the children of men! I can conceive
now of misery which in one night would change the
hair to grey and shrivel the whole frame to premature
decrepitude! — misery to which all other agony is as a
mocking sound! What terrible temptations lie in the way
of your sex — till now I never realised it — for tho I did
love you with an almost *insane* love before I married
you I never knew yet or felt the pulsation which showed
me that I could be tempted in that way — there never
was a moment when I felt anything by which you
could have drawn me astray — for I loved you as I now
love God — and I can conceive of no higher love — and
as I have no passion — I have no jealousy, — the most
beautiful woman in the world could not make me jealous
so long as she only *dazzled the senses* — but still my
dear, you must not wonder if I want to warn you not
to look or *think* too freely on womankind. If your sex
would guard the outworks of *thought*, you would never
fall — and when so dizzying so astounding are the ad-

vantages which Satan takes it scarce is implying a doubt to say 'be cautious' . . ."

But Calvin's religious difficulties he confides to his father-in-law rather than to Harriet. "I wanted to tell you something of the state of my soul," he writes to Lyman Beecher on July 17. "Since I left Cleaveland I have suffered a great deal of mental agony, partly no doubt from physical causes. I feel that my heart is not right in the sight of God, that I do not yet know Christ as I ought to know him. I have been exceedingly distressed with skeptical doubts as to the reality of experimental religion, and whether the whole Bible is not after all a humbug; or at least merely the most simple and touching development of the religious sensibilities natural to man, which the human mind has yet been able to produce and whether in this state of things I ought not to leave the ministry and all studies connected with it, and devote myself to education, which is always a good, let the truth of religion stand as it may. I think with excessive pain of the great amount of exaggeration and humbug that exists in the so-called benevolent movement of the day, and of the great amount of selfishness and sectarianism in religious movements. I pray, and it is speaking to a dead wall and not to God — I call upon Christ, and he is a dead man who was buried 18 centuries ago — I try to be spiritually-minded, and find in myself a most exquisite relish, and deadly longing for all kinds of sensual gratification — I think of the revival ministers who have lived long in licentiousness with good reputation, and then been detested, — and ask myself, who knows whether there be any real piety on earth? O wretched man that I am! Who shall deliver me? . . . You are near the close of a long life spent in spreading the Gospel. Is the vail rent, and can you see through it into the holy of holies? Oh happy man if you can, and God grant me the same privilege, even at the expense of my life, O happy day when I and my wife and children are all in the quiet grave!"

To Harriet he writes three days later: "Though I can cheerfully trust the final salvation of my soul to Christ; yet I cannot now trust him for the temporal wants of my family and the institution. A strange inconsistency! Like Melanchthon, I have an unshaken hope of being forgiven and getting to heaven at last but everything else distresses me to death almost." He reproaches her on the 29th for not writing to strengthen his faith, to support his "feeble and tottering steps." " "*My soul is weary of my life,* and I feel it would be the greatest of mercies to take me out of the world . . . Still I have felt that I could have some hold on Christ through you, and I have longed for your letters to come that I might stay myself on those thrilling paragraphs with which they at first abounded — but there are lately no special religious views in them — no more than what I or any ordinary professor of religion might write. Perhaps it is because my letters have had so little of the spirit of Christ in them that they have chilled and discouraged you. Lean and barren they have been I do not doubt but I hope you will not allow my deathfulness to deprive you of life when you are capable of living and I am not." He did feel, however, that his paralyzing despair might prove to be merely a test, "a process of spiritual purification" through which the Lord was leading him; and by August 17, he seems to have emerged and recovered his faith: "My mind is now free," he writes from Portland, Maine, "and I can commune with my God and Saviour, but my nervous system has received such a shock that I am incapable of any serious exertion. My nerves in every part of my body feel sore, and there is danger of universal neuralgia unless I keep quiet . . . I had a grand sail the other day all around the harbor, and while some of the company were profane and rebellious enough to amuse themselves with catching fish which they did not want, and knew nothing what to do with them after they had got them, I left the boat and scrambled around on the rocks, and let the waves roar and dash all over me, and felt quite delighted." When he had spoken in the earlier letter of not being able to rely on Christ "for the temporal wants of my family and the institution," he meant that he was unsuccessful in raising funds for the Seminary; and Harriet — September 3 — tries heartily to reassure him that he can perfectly rely both on God and her: "My love you do wrong to worry so much about temporal matters — you really *do wrong*: You treat your Saviour *ungenerously* and you ought not to do it — Every letter of yours contains such unbelieving doubts 'Who will take care of us and keep us out of debt?' — My love if you were *dead* this day — and I feeble as I am with five little children I would not doubt nor despond nor expect to starve — tho *if* I *did* expect to starve I could bear it very well since Heaven is eternal. . . . It is all humbug — got up by Satan — this fussing about a temporal future — if you will put the affairs all into my hands and let me manage them my own way and not give a thought during winter only to be good and grow in grace *I'l engage* to bring things out right in spring . . . — Now do take me up on this — "

In Calvin's two last letters to Harriet — of September 29 and 30 — as the end of their separation draws near, we get for the first time a glimpse of what their life together had been. He is not looking forward now to a reunion which will be "just as much of a honey-moon as was the first month after the wedding." With a sudden return to the practical and a dropping of his valetudinarian tone, he explains to her all her faults, though admitting certain faults on his own part. She is slack and forbearing, he tells her, while he is methodical and irritable. He likes to have morning prayers and meals on time; she doesn't care when they have them. He likes to have the things in the house assigned to their places and left there; but it "seems to be your special delight to keep everything . . . on the move." He likes to have his newspapers "properly folded"; but she and Ann have vexed him "beyond all endurance" by "dropping them sprawling on the floor, or wabbling them all up in one wabble, and squashing them on the table like an old hen with her guts and gizzard squashed out."

But the next day a pang of compunction compels him to write her again: "The last letter I wrote you does not satisfy me, because it does not do you justice on a point on which you have seldom had justice done you, I mean your earnest and successful endeavour for self-improvement. In all respects in which both nature and an exceedingly defective or one-sided education have made you imperfect, I recognise and admire in you an earnest and Christian-like purpose to amend. Nature and bad education have done me great injury, and I know by my own experience how hard it is to get the better of such defects; and you have succeeded on your part far better than I have on mine." He cannot, however, refrain from enlarging on her shortcomings further: "Naturally thoughtless of expense and inclined to purchase whatever strikes your eye, without much reflection on the proportion of expenditure to be devoted to such objects, this propensity was indulged and greatly increased by your relations with Kate [her sister Catharine]. It can be corrected only by a rigid habit of keeping strict written accounts of all available income, of all absolute wants, and of all actual expense. . . . But there is another matter which needs care. When your mind is on any particular point, it is your nature to feel and act as if that were the only thing in the world; and you drive at it and make every thing bend to it, to the manifest injury of other interests. For instance, when you are intent on raising flowers, you are sure to visit them and inspect them very carefully every morning; but your kitchen would go for two or three days without any inspection at all, you would be quite ignorant of what there was in the house to be cooked, or the way in which the work was done. Your oversight of the flowers would be systematic and regular; of the kitchen, at haphazard, and now and then. You should be as regular in the kitchen as in the garden. — Again, you seldom hesitate to make a promise, whether you have ability to perform it or not, like your father and Kate, only not quite so bad; and promises so easily made are very easily broken. On this point Kate has no conscience at all, your father very little; and you have enough to keep you from making such promises, if you would only think beforehand whether you could fulfill them or not . . .

"Well, no more on this subject at present. I got your flower seeds and a pound of the guano. An ounce of the guano is to be dissolved in a gallon of water and applied to the plant once a week. This is the scientific direction so that a pound of guano will last a long time. I hope you will be content this winter with keeping a very few choice plants — for *labor* is a great article in our family; and we must adopt some plan to save labor and fuel. By the way, there is one other thing I will mention, because it has often vexed and irritated me intolerably. I must clean the stable, wash the carriage, grease the wheels, black my boots, etc. etc. but you scorn to sweep the carriage, you must always call your servant to do it, and not stoop yourself to so menial an act. This makes me mad, for you are not too good to do in your line what I am everyday obliged to do in mine. Now I believe I have opened my whole budget, and in these two letters given you all my grievances. I pray the Lord to strengthen me on my return to treat you with uniform tenderness, kindness, and love. I suffer amazingly every day I live. I hardly know what to make of it, unless it be the Lord's penance of our sin. You have suffered a great deal, but I doubt whether you have ever suffered as I have this summer.

"I will try to come home cheerful and confiding in God. By the good hand of God upon me I expect to be in Pittsburg Wednesday night, and then in Cincinnati as soon as I can get there — Probably I shall not write you again. Forgive me all the wrong I have ever done you, and give me credit for sincere endeavours to do better. I cannot tell you what admiration I have heard expressed of you wherever I have been, and not always in a way at all calculated to sooth my vanity. Good bye.

"affectionately C. E. S."

Harriet succeeded, the following spring, in getting away to Brattleboro, Vermont, where she took "the water cure" and remained for almost a year. But soon after she returned to the West, she found that she was pregnant again. And now Calvin, who, in Harriet's absence, had relapsed into hypochondria, decided that he, too, required a cure. He, too, had recourse to Brattleboro and remained away fifteen months. The completeness, during such absences, of Calvin's eclipse and the extent to which he unloaded on Harriet all the responsibility for the family may be gauged from a letter of July 29, 1855, written during another long absence: "I shall return as soon as possible after the meeting in N. York in Sept. — and until then you must manage all household matters in your own way — just as you would if I were dead, and you had never anything more to expect from me. Indeed, to all practical purposes I am dead for the present and know not when I shall live again. If I have the ability to do it, I will by and by write you a letter about household matters the coming season." A series of cholera epidemics had been added, in the years of their residence, to the other nerve-taxing elements of Cincinnati life; and while Harriet was handling the household alone, this series reached a terrible climax. At the peak of the new epidemic, a thousand people a week were dying. The city was filled with the fumes of the soft coal that was burned as a disinfectant, and everything was black with soot. There was general demoralization, and many people less austere than the Beechers and Stowes did their best to stay drunk all the time. Harriet wrote to her husband that he must not think of coming back. The Stowe children's pet dog died; then their old colored laundress died — the twins helped to make her a shroud. Then Harriet's most recent baby began to have convulsions, and in four days it, too, was dead. Harriet herself was attacked by cramps, and the doctor assumed she was dying; but her father, who had been away attending the Yale Commencement, was back now to give her support. The indomitable old preacher, now seventy, rubbed Harriet's hands, as he writes his wife, "with perseverance and vigor"; and he always remained by her side, spending the night "on a settee in the dining room, hot as an oven and thronged with mosquitoes, sleepless from their annoyance, and conscious of every noise and movement." He gave Harriet a dose of brandy, which made her at first delirious, but he seems to think it pulled her through. "The night of suspense passed safely, and she was better in the morning." "I am not sick," he adds, to reassure his wife,

" — never was better in my life, though last week I had to diet and abstain from corn and succotash; but this week I have studied and worked like Jehu every day, trimming up the trees, hoeing in the garden till my face was bathed and my shirt soaked, and yet I have not felt so well for a year past — so much like being young again."

So one's picture of this phase of Harriet's life is not really one of unrelieved horror. Such clerical New England families had a heritage of hearty vitality as well as of moral fortitude that prevented them from becoming pathetic. Yet, in the first sixteen years of her marriage, poor Harriet was suffering from miseries that must have been as little avowed — such complaints as the one I have quoted are rare — as the ever-rankling anxieties of slavery. *Uncle Tom,* with its lowering threats and its harassing persecutions, its impotence of well-meaning people, its outbreaks of violence and its sudden bereavements, had been lived in the Beecher home, where the trials and tribulations, as they used to be called, of the small family world inside were involved with, were merged in, the travail of the nation to which it belonged. This obscure personal anguish of Harriet Stowe went to energize her famous novel which had so strong an impact on public affairs, as did also the courage and faith, the conviction that God, after all, was just. And finally a turn does come in the fortunes of Calvin and Harriet Stowe: God does at last provide; a door of escape is unlocked; He is now at last giving them something which will offset their doubt, their ordeal, their self-imposed obligations, their self-control under His difficult exactions; the world will at last yield them something for what they have done and are. In the autumn of 1849, Bowdoin College in Maine offers Calvin a professorship, and though he knows that the chair is the worst-paid in the college — a thousand dollars a year — he is only too glad to accept. The Seminary tries to keep him by offering him fifteen hundred, and, immediately after this, the Theological Seminary at Andover makes him an even better offer. But he is definitely committed to Bowdoin, and the next spring the Stowes move to Maine. When they arrive, it is still very cold, and the house they are going to live in is shabby and bare and forlorn, but they light up a fire and set to work. Harriet spreads a long table on which the family can eat and she can write, and she repaints the woodwork and re-papers the walls, and this is the end of their long testing: they will never be so poor or so racked again.

At the end of the year 1850, the Fugitive Slave Bill became a law. Non-Southerners were now held respon-sible for Negroes who had fled from the South, and, as an inducement to the local officials who decided on the claims of ownership, a premium was put on returning them. When Harriet got a letter from a sister-in-law which said: "Hattie, if I could use a pen as you can, I would write something that will make this whole nation feel what an accursed thing slavery is," she read the letter to her chil-dren, then, crumpling it in her hand, stood up and said, "I will if I live." When her brother Henry Ward Beecher came to see her a little later, they talked about the odious law. He was now preaching Abolition from his pulpit in Plymouth Church, Brooklyn, and holding benevolent "auc-tions," in which he brought before his congregation slaves that had escaped from the South, and called for contribu-tions in order to buy their freedom. He, too, urged Harriet to write a book. She had met, a short time before, at the house of her brother Edward, who now had a church in Boston, a Negro preacher who had once been a slave and both of whose arms had been crippled by flogging, but who had succeeded in escaping to Canada and getting himself an education there; and one Sunday, when she had just taken Communion, the death of Uncle Tom was revealed to her "almost as a tangible vision." Scarcely able to restrain her emotion, she went home and wrote it down; and now the rest of Uncle Tom's story "rushed upon her with a vividness and importunity that would not be denied." She poured it out late in the evenings, after the demands of the household had been dealt with. She does not seem to have planned the story in advance, yet the course that it was taking imposed itself as something uncontrollable, unalterable. The novel appeared first as a serial in an anti-slavery weekly which was published in Washington, and it ran to such length — it continued from June 8, 1851, to April 1, 1852 — that the editor begged her to cut it short; but the story had taken possession of its readers as well as of Mrs. Stowe, and when the editor published a note suggesting that the public might have had enough, this elicited a violent protest, and Uncle Tom was spared none of the stages which were to lead him to the final scene which had come to Mrs. Stowe in church.

If there is something to be said for the author's claim that *Uncle Tom's Cabin* was written by God, it is evident that the nine novels which followed it were produced without divine intervention by Harriet Beecher Stowe herself.

The tremendous success of *Uncle Tom* as well as Calvin's eventual appointment to Andover rescued the Stowes for the rest of their lives. Mrs. Stowe became a public figure, and she was able to continue to the end of her life as a well-paid professional writer. She had, in these later years, her uncomfortable episodes and her family tragedies; but all of her subsequent books were written in comfort and security and in relative tranquillity of spirit, and none of them — perhaps for this reason — approaches the power of *Uncle Tom.* The absence of this power, in fact — the slackness of the narrative line, the failure in dramatic imagination and the wordiness that tends to blur contours — may come, as one explores these novels, to seem not merely disappointing but astonishing. The explanation of this, however, has been given with the utmost bluntness by one of Mrs. Stowe's closest friends, the wife of her Boston publisher, Mrs. James T. Fields: the truth was that Mrs. Stowe had in a sense no real interest in literature. "Books as a medium of the ideas of the age, as the promulgators of morals and religion, were of course like the breath of her life; but a study of the literature of the past as the only true foundation for a literature of the present was outside the pale of her occupations, and for the larger portion of her life outside of her interest." Mrs. Stowe did not much care to read novels; the sermon was undoubtedly the literary form by which she had been most deeply influenced; and in one of her late novels, *My Wife and I,* she complains, in a foreword, that it is "something of a trial" to have to put into "the form of a story" what she "wished to say respecting society and social ideals." It evidently bores her to contrive a plot, and she comes to depend more and more on conventional Victorian devices, which she handles in a more and more perfunctory way. She has a particularly exasperating habit of first narrating some episode at length, then telling it all over again in a letter or a conversation. The formula that she most relies upon for giving the reader his money's worth is to do him a pathetic deathbed — Little Eva's is not the worst — that derives from and outdoes Dickens. And though she sometimes creates situations that seem to have possibilities, and can even, from time to time, strike off an effectively dramatic scene, she never succeeds, after *Uncle Tom*, in building up a situation and carrying it through to an adequate climax. I say she never succeeds and she hardly even tries. One soon comes to understand that such things have simply flashed into her mind, and that she never gives a moment's thought to the problems of how to handle them. That is why she imagined that God was the author of *Uncle Tom's Cabin* — the flash had lasted all through the book.

The language of Mrs. Stowe, on its less prepossessing side, combines the clichés of her period with a certain amount of homely incorrectitude. As her father Lyman Beecher is reported to have used such forms as "creetur" and "Natur" even in the pulpit (pronunciations, however, which were perhaps old-fashioned rather than vulgar), so we find in Harriet's letters such expressions as "I admire to cultivate a taste for painting," "I don't know, I'm sure, as we shall ever get to Pittsburgh," "For a day or two we did not know but there would actually be war to the knife," and "In answer to your enquiries, I would say that I have never published but one book"; and if these are less common in her published works, it is only because her editors combed them out. Her writings flowed onto the paper with little more punctuation than Molly Bloom's meditations in *Ulysses*: she did not write either commas or periods, and she usually sent off her copy without having read it over. Yet these later books are not simply bad; only rarely does she write pure rubbish. Though it was true that Harriet Beecher Stowe was not really interested in literature in Mrs. Fields's high Bostonian sense, her literary gift was real. She can make us see a person and hear him talk, and she can render a scene or a landscape by a process that can only be likened to a flinging out of handfuls of words which succeed in conveying impressions with a precision that is rather surprising in view of the looseness of her language, of her having no sense whatever of the construction of a sentence or a paragraph, and hardly even a sense of syntax. The descriptions of the coast of Maine, in *The Pearl of Orr's Island* — which inspired Sarah Orne Jewett — are good examples of this. They, too, are showers of words — in this case bright and confetti-like; yet the seascapes are created, they take body on the page. It is as if she were communicating directly — that is, without the artist's deliberate skill — the perceptions of a sensitive woman. She had a natural mimetic gift, which is exhibited not merely in her dialogue but sometimes also in descriptions such as these through a poetic appropriateness of the language. And once one has ceased to expect of her fiction after *Uncle Tom's Cabin* anything comparable to it as a story, one comes to recognize that several of her books have considerable interest of another sort. Mrs. Stowe was a very observant and essentially realistic woman. Her intelligence was by no means limited, and of the subjects that most occupied her mind she had acquired a considerable grasp. She will not thrill you as a teller of tales, but she does throw a good deal of light on certain aspects of American society. As Arthur Schlesinger, Jr., once remarked, she may be regarded as "a great repository" which contains solid chunks of history.

Mrs. Stowe's second novel, *Dred: A Tale of the Dismal Swamp*, which was begun about the end of February, 1856, is a sequel to *Uncle Tom's Cabin* in the sense that it deals also with the problem of slavery, but, since it is supposed to take place in the Carolinas, it suffers — though scrupulously documented from newspapers, court records, etc. — more obviously than *Uncle Tom's Cabin*, which had behind it a visit to Kentucky and the sojourn in Cincinnati, from Mrs. Stowe's lack of firsthand knowledge of the region she is writing about. It suffers also from her habit of improvisation. You think at first that you are getting a love story. The heroine is a young-lady plantation owner, whose finishing-school frivolity does not conceal from the reader a courageous and generous nature, and she is evidently to fall into the arms of a serious-minded young lawyer who is making himself disliked for his championship of the Negroes. But in the May of that year, Charles Sumner, the Senator from Massachusetts and an ally of Mrs. Stowe's, was attacked in the Senate and beaten unconscious by a young Congressman from South Carolina who had resented, on behalf of a relative, a South Carolina Senator, an excoriating speech by Sumner on the Kansas-Nebraska Bill. It was proposed by the sponsors of this bill that the decision be left to the populations of these two newly created "territories" — which then extended to the Canadian border — as to whether their soil should be slave or free, and this had led to civil war in Kansas. A few days after the Sumner incident came the news of the Pottawatomie massacre. John Brown and his five sons had murdered in Kansas five pro-slavery men. The whole course of the story of *Dred* was apparently altered by these events. The heroine is quite unexpectedly, about two-thirds of the way through the book, made to die in a cholera epidemic; and the obvious purpose of this is to leave the situation clear for her brutal and drunken brother to run the plantation alone and to goad the slaves to rebellion. This villain is not to be punished so far as the story goes (Queen Victoria, who followed Mrs. Stowe with much interest, severely complained of this): at the end he is left still at large. The author wants, of course, to imply that that problem is yet to be dealt with; but in the meantime she has been preaching God's judgment through the character of Dred, the runaway slave, who, also to the reader's surprise, has superseded Nina, the heroine, as the principal character of the novel. Mrs. Stowe felt, no doubt, that her original idea that the South might be reformed from within, by the more enlightened elements of the planter class, had now been made to seem a mirage; that such elements were dying of the general contagion — for was not the mounting passion of the South also an epidemic? — and that the day for John Brown had arrived. The South had had its own black John Brown in the educated slave Nat Turner, who had become a religious fanatic and who, in 1831, had incited a slave rebellion and massacred fifty-one whites; and he served the disillusioned author as the principal model for Dred, who identifies himself with the Hebrew prophets and delivers interminable tirades. As Uncle Tom, in the previous book, is shown to understand the spirit of Christ as none of his masters do, so Dred is made to embody the Old Testament spirit of righteous wrath which the professional preachers in the story are too crass or too prudent to imitate, and to prophesy the downfall of the planter society. The ministers here play a prominent role, and long stretches of the book are devoted to their arguments on the subject of slavery: its theological implications and the Biblical sanction for it.

Of this clerical world Mrs. Stowe had, of course, the most intimate knowledge. We begin to see in *Dred* that her real preoccupation is not with slavery but with Christian morals. Even more than in Uncle Tom, she emphasizes here the contrasting ways in which her characters practice religion; and in the novel that follows, *The Minister's Wooing*, she plants in the center of her picture a problem that for the daughter of Lyman Beecher was of an importance more fundamental than slavery. It is probable that one of the crucial events of Harriet Beecher's life had been a tragedy in the life of her oldest sister, Catharine. When Harriet was about thirteen, the young man that Catharine was engaged to marry lost his life in a shipwreck. He was a brilliant professor at Yale, who taught natural philosophy and mathematics and had not shown any interest in religion; and Catharine, in addition to the pain of her loss, had to suffer from a terrible doubt as to whether he were saved or damned. Their father was not reassuring, and Catharine worked on the case in the hope of finding favorable evidence, but what she found instead was a journal which showed that her sweetheart had never repented. Oh, horror! he was doomed to an eternity of torment. Catharine fell into despair, and Harriet shared her anguish, but both of them, confronted with such a conclusion, began seriously to question the doctrine, to which their Presbyterian Church committed them, that God chooses only a few for Grace and consigns the rest to damnation, without either the condemned's or the saved's being able to influence the outcome. The older sister stood up boldly to this horror of an autocratic God who had punished the whole of humanity for Adam's sin and whom neither good works nor piety could hope to dissuade from His sentence. By 1840 she had got to the point of refuting Jonathan Edwards on the Will in an article defending "Free Agency," which was considered by theologians of her liberal way of thinking an exceptionally able performance, and by 1857 she had gone so far as to reject Original Sin itself. There occurred in this same year for Harriet a tragedy strangely similar to that which had so shaken her sister: her nineteen-year-old son was drowned. He had been still in an unregenerate state, but she could not believe he was damned.

The result of all this was the novel which — pale beside *Uncle Tom,* yet moving because deeply felt — really gives the main key to her work: *The Minister's Wooing* of 1859. Here Harriet is actually dramatizing both Catharine's ordeal and her own, but she has put her story back into the eighteenth century, at a time not long after the Revolution — which makes it possible for her to present the old doctrine in its most somber, most menacing form, and with the particularly baleful effects of the version of it expounded by Jonathan Edwards. A young man who has not been converted has supposedly been lost at sea, with the result that his mother and his fiancée are agonized, as Harriet and Catharine had been, by emotional and moral problems. One of the sections of *The Minister's Wooing* which is most worth reading today — *Views of Divine Government,* Chapter XXIII — is largely a critical account of the development of Calvinism in America. The author wants to show that the plight of her characters was typical and inevitable in a Calvinist society which lived constantly in fear of a God whose principles of selection were inscrutable — or, to put it as Jonathan Edwards did, who made one's salvation depend on a degree of illumination attainable only by those whom He had specially equipped to receive it. Communion, for Edwards, was not enough; what was usually called conversion was not enough. No matter how good a man seemed to be in the ordinary sense of the word — how unselfish, how kind, how correct — he could not qualify for Salvation. The psychological conflicts that arose from this doctrine are one of Mrs. Stowe's main themes. The mother who has been told that her son is in Hell first despairs, then revolts against God — she is tempted to conclude that a Deity who arranges the world in this way is a tyrannous and cruel monster. But, on the verge of this blasphemy — a denial of God's good-

ness that follows from the Calvinist conception of God —
she is rescued by the liberated black slave Candace, who
assures her that this doctrine cannot be true, since the
gospel of Christ contradicts it: "I'm clar Mass'r James is
one of de 'lect; and I'm clar dar's consid'able more o' de
'lect dan people tink. Why, Jesus didn't die for nothin', —
all dat love a'n't gwine to be wasted. De 'lect is more'n
you or I knows, honey! Dar's de *Spirit,* — He'll give it to
'em; and ef Mass'r James *is* called an' took, depend upon it
de Lord has got him ready — course He has, — so don't ye
go to layin' on your poor heart what no mortal creetur can
live under 'cause, so we's got to live in dis yer world, it's
quite clar de Lord must ha' fixed it so we *can,* and ef tings
was as some folks suppose, why, we *couldn't* live, and dar
wouldn't be no sense in anyting dat goes on." Here again
it will be seen that the Negro is made to intervene as a
moral guide, as corrector of the white man's religion.
If Uncle Tom is a kind of true saint, if Dred is a kind
of true prophet, Candace brings to bear upon Calvinism
a humanity and a common sense of which the Puritan
divines are incapable. It is evident that Mrs. Stowe has
been using her Negro characters to express her own
religious ideals. If these characters are open to criticism
from the point of view of strict plausibility, it is because
she cannot always refrain from making them think and
talk a little too much like preachers.

What is here worrying Mrs. Stowe, what is involved
in Uncle Tom and Candace, is the banishment of the
spirit of Jesus from the theology and practice of the
Calvinist faith. To read Calvin's *Institutes* today is to
be struck by the brutal audacity of his efforts to eliminate
this spirit from the Gospels. Christ's gospel of forgiveness quite disappears, as does his offering to all human
sinners the possibility of eventual repentance — since faith
must precede repentance and only those elected are given

faith. Christ's role is reduced to that of a special agent dispatched by God to the earth — since "so great was the discordance between our pollution and the perfect purity of God" that man could not rise to God — in order to deliver to him the message that a few would be saved, those few that, for inscrutable reasons, had been singled out by God as favorites, while — in view of the fact that "man, being enslaved by sin, can will nothing but what is evil" — they themselves no more than the damned could contribute to their own salvation. One feels that it would be easier for Calvin if the Gospels did not exist — he is obliged to explain so much of them away. It would be very much simpler for him if he had merely the Pauline epistles, with the emphasis they lay on Grace, upon which to erect his theology (though these, too, present certain embarrassments). Yet one could hardly, of course, read the Gospels without being exposed to the non-Calvinist Jesus, and the curious situation in which this landed the early New Englanders may be studied in the diaries of Cotton Mather. When anything goes wrong with Mather, from a toothache to the death of his wife, he is likely to fall into a panic lest he may not be, after all, elected, and to be stricken by a paroxysm of guilt. He attempts to pin down and confess his sin, and it is then, and only then, that he remembers the spirit of Jesus. "You are supposed to be merciful, to pardon," he says in effect to the Savior. "I beg you to forgive me. I grovel before you" — though if his fate is in any case predestinated, what is the use of appealing to this Savior? But otherwise the Jesus of the Gospels gets from Mather very little attention. At one point he does try to remember that he must hope for the salvation of his enemies. "In a wicked book," he once notes, "I readd a fling at clergymen, as a Revengful generation of men, who never Forgive such as have offended them.

I do not remember, for my part, that ever I designed the
Revenge of an Injury in my life. However, this Venomous Fling shall quicken my Watchfulness upon this
Article." But his bitterness against those who thwart him
long outlasts these self-admonitions. Disappointed in his
ambitions at the end of his life, he produces an effect
grimly comic by suddenly, in this hour of trial, identify-
ing himself with Christ: "I do most freely . . ." he
writes "consent unto the condition of a *crucified man.*"
When the obdurate Overseers of Harvard refuse to elect
him President, he calls himself, beating his breast, "a
Man of Sorrows and acquainted with Griefs." When he
is losing his congregation, "I shall enjoy a bright con-
formity to my Saviour . . . if, just before my Death, I
suffer a general withdrawal of my hearers from me." In
general, the figure of Jesus, sitting at the right hand of
the hanging God, had come to share the aspect of the
terrible Father, and in the case of some old-fashioned
Americans, this conception was carried along well to the
end of the nineteenth century. The uncle of a friend
of the writer's from St. Louis — sometime in the seventies or eighties — was sent to college at Yale, and there he
came under the influence of the non-fundamentalist
views of the Yale Divinity School. His mother got wind
of this and, when he next returned for the holidays,
attacked him the moment he entered the house. "I understand," she said to the boy, "that since you've been away
to college, you're beginning to doubt the divinity of our
Lord Jesus Christ." "Why, mother," the young man replied, "I believe that Jesus was a very good man — "
" 'Good man'!" the mother cracked down. "You think
Jesus Christ was just a 'good man'? You wait until after
you die and you'll find out how *good* he is!"

It was precisely this odious cult of the Father as omnip-
otent Bugaboo — which alternated abjection with arro-

gance — that Harriet Beecher Stowe and her sisters were attempting to disprove and discredit; and it was Harriet's especial concern to substitute the Jesus of the Sermon on the Mount for the Calvinist "Mediator" at the center of what was called the Christian religion. We shall see later where this finally led her; but in the meantime it might be mentioned that a similar enthusiasm for a God of Love, in reaction against the Calvinist Hangman, must partly account for the unashamed amours — so embarrassing to his sister Harriet — of the eloquent Henry Ward Beecher. He was eventually to go so far as to preach the non-existence of Hell.

Old Town Folks, published ten years later, when the Civil War was over — in 1869 — was considered by the author, after *Uncle Tom's Cabin,* the most important of her novels, and it has usually been accepted as such. With this estimate I should agree, though I should join with it *Poganuc People,* a shorter book of a similar kind, which came out in 1878. This should not, however, be thought to imply that these novels are successful as works of art or even effective as stories. The love affairs of the characters in these chronicles — Mrs. Stowe was never strong in the romantic department — are rarely in the least exciting; the plots would become preposterous if the author did not treat them so cavalierly; and the narratives are far from compelling. But the two books, taken together, make a kind of encyclopedia of old New England institutions, characters, customs and points of view. If you want to find out how Thanksgiving or the Fourth of July was observed when the whole day involved a ritual, you will find a chapter on each; or if you want to know what life was like in a parsonage at the beginning of the nineteenth century, at the time when

the Puritan clergy were losing their old power and forced
to compete with the Episcopalians, or in one of those
old-fashioned academies where the students seem to
have got such sound training, these novels will take you
there. But *Oldtown Folks,* at any rate, should not
probably have been a novel at all. It would have been better as a series of essays, or of sketches like Washington
Irving's *Sketch-Book,* of the type that — in the days
before *Uncle Tom's Cabin* — Mrs. Stowe had begun by
writing. One of the most valuable chapters of *Oldtown
Folks* (XXIX) is introduced by the following words:
"Reader, this is to be a serious chapter, and I advise all
those people who want to go through the world without
giving five minutes' thought to any subject to skip it.
They will not find it entertaining, and it may perhaps
lead them to think on puzzling subjects . . ." This
chapter returns to the problems of religion, and it begins
by discussing the paradox — in connection with the narrator's grandmother — of the persistence of amiable qualities: tolerance, affection and mercy, in people who sub-
scribe to the Calvinist creed and who have scrupulously
studied its doctrine. He goes on — this narrator is a
man — to attempt an interpretation of the development
of Protestantism in America. "When the Puritans arrived," he says, "at a perception of the political rights of
men in the state, and began to enunciate and act upon
the doctrine that a king's right to reign was founded
upon his power to promote the greatest happiness of
his subjects, and when, in pursuance of this theory, they
tried, condemned, and executed a king who had been
false to the people, they took a long step forward in
human progress. Why did not immediate anarchy follow,
as when the French took such a step in regard to their
king? It was because the Puritans transferred to God
all those rights and immunities, all that unquestioning

homage and worship and loyalty, which hitherto they had given to an earthly king . . . The Puritans had still a King. The French Revolutionists had nothing; therefore, the Puritan Revolution went on stronger and stronger. The French passed through anarchy back under despotism." The rigor of early New England in both its moral and its physical life brought them through the American Revolution. "They were a set of men and women brought up to *think,* — to think not merely on agreeable subjects, but to wrestle and tug at the very severest problems. Utter self-renunciation, a sort of grand contempt for personal happiness when weighed with things greater and more valuable, was the fundamental principle of life in those days. They who could calmly look in the face, and settle themselves down to, the idea of being resigned and thankful for an existence which was not so good as non-existence, — who were willing to be loyal subjects of a splendid and powerful government which was conducted on quite other issues than a regard for their happiness, — were possessed of a courage and a fortitude which no mere earthly mischance could shake. They who had faced eternal ruin with an unflinching gaze were not likely to shrink before the comparatively trivial losses and gains of any mere earthly conflict. Being accustomed to combats with the Devil, it was rather a recreation to fight only British officers."

But once the agents of the Crown had been beaten, the militant spirit of republicanism went on to attack theology, to rebel against the Calvinist monarch — that is, the Presbyterian Deity — who had been oppressing his soul. This movement was gathering momentum during the lifetime of Harriet Stowe. Her father, the politic Beecher, had been trying to maintain the Calvinist faith by softening its worst implications, and he found himself embattled on opposite fronts, with, on the one hand, the Old

Presbyterians, who accused him, as one of them said, of "exalting *human agency,* so as virtually to lose sight of its correlate, *human dependence,* and thus make regeneration a result of *means* and instrumentality, so that the sinner is born rather of blood, or of the will of man, than of God"; and, on the other hand, the Unitarians, who had thrown over creeds altogether and who professed only a general allegiance to "the fatherhood of God, the brotherhood of man, the leadership of Jesus, salvation by character, and the progress of mankind upward and onward forever."

In reading the history of the Beechers, one comes better to understand what Oliver Wendell Holmes, Sr., meant when he said that *The One-Hoss Shay* was a parable of the break-up of Calvinism. You can here see it going fast. The central subject in Mrs. Stowe's novels is the crisis in Calvinist theology — with its effects on social life and morals — in New England in the last century. The whole Beecher family were steeped in theology, and they constantly debated religious questions. Not only did Harriet Beecher know the insides of ministers' households — how they dressed, what they ate, how the housework got done, what kind of furniture they had, how they behaved in their family relations — in such a way that she was able to describe it as no other native novelist has done; she had also a close understanding, which must have been rather unusual for an American woman of her time, of the theological questions with which the minds of the ministry were occupied. Harriet Stowe had church history at her fingertips, and she knew all the ins and outs of contemporary church controversy and politics; she had studied the Catholic Church as well as the various forms of Protestantism; and these matters are never abstract for her: she never ceases for a moment to be conscious of their implications for practical personal conduct, and their relation to the tumultuous events of American secular history. Her unique, her invaluable picture of American clerical life extends from the end of the eighteenth century, just after the Revolution, when Newport (*The Minister's Wooing*) is the home of Jonathan Edwards's follower, the Reverend Samuel Hopkins, and the doctrine of Predestination hangs over the pious world, to the seventies (*Pink and White Tyranny, We and Our Neighbors*), when Newport has become a playground for the conspicuous-wasters of New York, and old rock-bound Congregationalism is troubled, and sometimes melted, by the charms of Episcopalianism and even of Roman Catholicism. There is not, so far as I know, any other writer in English who has produced, in the form of fiction, such a chronicle of religious history. In these books, the sharp observation of social and regional traits which had already, in *Uncle Tom's Cabin,* resulted in the projection of typical figures so vivid that, forgetting a novelist invented them, we tend to accept them today as myths — this sharp observation of Mrs. Stowe's always comes into play to present the varieties of religious experience in terms of milieu and character. The conversations in Mrs. Stowe's novels are likely to become rather boring because they go on too long — verbosity is one of her most serious faults — but they always show a very strong sense of what human beings are as well as of what they think or what they think they think. The feature of Harriet Beecher Stowe which prevents us from reading her today and doing justice to her exceptional intelligence is not only, however, this verbosity but our reflex shying away from the accents of the old-fashioned parsonage in which she habitually addresses us: the earnestness and fervor of the minister's wife who sympathizes so much with sorrow, who mimics the humble so charmingly, who does hope so very sincerely that the weak and the misguided will mend their ways. The best way to read Mrs. Stowe — except, of course, *Uncle Tom's Cabin* — would be probably in a volume of extracts which gave specimens of her social criticism, her intimate historical insights and the scattered reminiscences of her own life which she wrote down in various connections.

One should also preserve, if possible, those flashes of dramatic genius which occasionally enliven her narratives. One of these is her conception of Aaron Burr, who seems greatly to have excited her imagination. He turns up not only in *The Minister's Wooing* but also in *Old-town Folks*. The "Minister" of the title of the first of these is a real man, Samuel Hopkins, the pupil of Jonathan Edwards. Edwards's daughter was the mother of Burr, and Burr is made to visit Newport, where Dr. Hopkins is living. He is first introduced in the company of one of Lafayette's French officers, whose young wife he is trying to seduce, and he has also an eye on the glowing young girl whom the old theologian is supposed to marry. This spiritual and earnest young girl befriends and comforts the Frenchwoman when she has become disillusioned with Burr; Burr himself she reduces to tears by appealing, in a final interview, to "the diviner part" of his nature, though she does not succeed in shaking his infidel rationalism. In the later novel — rather surprisingly, but it is characteristic of the author's insouciance — we find ourselves encountering the very same personage, who is presented as the grandson of Jonathan Edwards but given an imaginary name, and he plays an almost exactly similar role. He is elegant, rationalistic and coldbloodedly immoral with women, and he is killed in a political duel. But Mrs. Stowe, in connection with Burr, has got hold of a promising idea. She seems more conscious of what she is after in the second

attempt than the first, and she succeeds with it somewhat better. Her point is that Jonathan Edwards, in his
overweening spiritual pride, had put the Calvinistic
qualifications for Election and Salvation so high, at a
level so unattainable by the ordinary man — this matter
had been much on Harriet's mind ever since her brother
Charles had been driven to despair by reading the treatise
by Jonathan Edwards — that Aaron Burr, also the son
of a clergyman and brought up in his grandfather's
shadow, had from the start been discouraged with religion and led by a powerful intellect completely to discard morality in furthering his own career. This picture
of Aaron Burr is thus a part of Mrs. Stowe's exposé of
the pernicious effects of Calvinism. She stops just short
of the clear implication that the self-serving logic of Burr,
which allows him to abandon his mistresses, only reflects the same qualities in Edwards which led him to
prove without flinching the predestinated damnation of
the non-elect. Oh, if Harriet could only have shown
him the prime fallacy of all this logic! "No man," she
says, "ever demonstrated more forcibly the truth that it
is not a man's natural constitution" — as the Calvinists,
she thinks, believed — "but the *use* he makes of it, which
stamps him as good or vile." In the meantime, she is at
her best — on the level of high comedy she sometimes
touched — in depicting the guile of Burr in imposing on
his godly acquaintances. Perfectly versed in all questions
of doctrine, always respectful of the memory of his
grandfather, he never plays the insolent rake, but exhibits a consummate tact in dealing with ministers'
households and invariably, while pursuing his wicked
designs, is able to say the correct theological thing.

The truth is that this sort of character — sophisticated,
clever and fearless — rather piques and excites Mrs.
Stowe. We have already become aware, in *Uncle Tom's
Cabin* and *Dred*, of a similar attraction exerted on her

by the nonchalant Southern gentleman, of whose way of life she also disapproves. We are later to feel it again in her writings on the Byron affair. Lady Byron, whom she had known in England, had told her the then horrifying story of the poet's relations with his half-sister and had convinced her that Byron, in the first year of their marriage, had treated his wife brutally and had afterwards worked systematically to present her in an odious light and himself as the injured party.* Her

---

* A recent book by Mr. G. Wilson Knight, *Lord Byron's Marriage: The Evidence of Asterisks,* makes this problem appear more complicated. Mr. Knight has attempted to show that the homosexual tendencies of Byron were stronger than had been supposed and that he scandalized his wife's family by forcing her to submit to the equivalent of homosexual practices. The story of incest, he thinks, was a myth created by Lady Byron as a substitute for the then unprintable truth — a story which could serve the same purpose by putting all the blame on Byron. Mr. Knight is, however, such a partisan of Byron and has been so carried away by his homosexual explanation that he hardly does justice to the indications which would seem to bear out Lady Byron. There is no certain evidence for either theory; but both offenses may well have been involved, and Mrs. Stowe's general picture of the relations of the Byrons could really be made to cover them both: he neglected her, treated her with cruelty, made it plain that he did not want to be married to her, and behaved more and more like a madman. He wrote covertly about incest in *Manfred;* but it seems obvious that, as Mrs. Stowe says but as Mr. Knight will not recognize, the great romantic, for all his bravado, his invitations to Lady Byron to make public her charges against him, was made uneasy to the end of his life by the fear that she might reveal something. He might have counted on her not bringing the second charge, but he could not, as events later indicated, have been perfectly certain about the first. Many people were shocked by *Don Juan,* and, in spite of the fact that incest was fashionable in romantic literature, the exposure of an incestuous relationship would certainly have done him harm with his public. It is a curious sign of the change in our attitude toward sexual matters that Mrs. Stowe's story of incest in 1869 should have brought down on her the bitterest abuse, but that a theory based on homosexuality should elicit in 1957, on the part of the British reviewers, almost nothing but cordial approval.

article on this subject in the *Atlantic Monthly*, *The True Story of Lady Byron*, published in 1869, lost the magazine fifteen thousand subscribers, and the book, *Lady Byron Vindicated*, in which she dealt with it at greater length, intensified the clamor against her. Yet her handling of the Byron affair is not in the least hysterical: she shows a good deal of sympathetic insight into both Lady Byron and Byron. She never lost her admiration for the latter. Byron and Walter Scott had been the only imaginative writers that her father had let the children read. She tells us, in her reminiscences, of the impression that Byron had made on her youth: "I remember hearing father relate the account of his [Byron's] separation from his wife; and one day, hearing him say, with a sorrowful countenance, as if announcing the death of someone very interesting to him, 'My dear, Byron is dead — gone.' After being awhile silent, he said, 'Oh, I'm sorry that Byron is dead. I did hope he would live to do something for Christ. What a harp he might have swept.'" The next Sunday Dr. Beecher preached a sermon on the poet's death; and "Father," the daughter continues, "often said, in after years, that he wished he could have seen Byron, and presented to his mind his views of religious truth. He thought 'if Byron could only have talked with Taylor and me [Dr. Taylor was his lifelong ally at the Yale Divinity School], it might have got him out of his troubles.'" And Harriet's view was similar. For her, Lady Byron's story of her husband's affair with Augusta Leigh — which she decided to make public when, following Lady Byron's death, a book by the Countess Guiccioli put the blame for all of Byron's mishaps on his wife — was not, as it was for the press, which reviled Mrs. Stowe so outrageously, a scandal that would blacken him forever but a sin that deserved forgiveness. She could help to clear up the mystery of Byron's married life precisely because she could understand how it was possible for Anabella to love him and even to be friendly with Augusta, and to take in, after the latter's death, their illegitimate child. She was impressed by the diagnosis that Lady Byron had by that time made of her complicated husband's case, and it gratified Mrs. Stowe that the evil effects of Calvinism should be a part of this diagnosis. She suggests that an image of the Calvinist God, imposed during his childhood in Scotland, had bedevilled Byron's whole life, either driving him to believe in his own damnation or goading him to rebel against it. It is a pity that Harriet Stowe was never entirely successful in dramatizing Aaron Burr as a tragic damned soul of this sort — that is, a soul needlessly lost through a monstrous misconception of God.

Three of Mrs. Stowe's later novels — *Pink and White Tyranny, My Wife and I, We and Our Neighbors* — deal with life in New York City and society and social reform; and they have few, perhaps none, of her flashes. The experience of reading them seems to become more and more like grasping an unwieldy bath sponge; you squeeze out a gallon of words and then find that you have in your hands the diminished but resistant residuum of a dry and fibrous substance, which the author will re-dip for another novel. Yet at last, at the end of her life, she succeeds in writing another not uninteresting book. The comparative success of *Poganuc People* (1878) is due to its being the story of Harriet Beecher herself; and it is a relief to get back to old New England — Poganuc is Lyman Beecher's Litchfield — from the contemporary social world which Mrs. Stowe did not know so well. This is the only one of her books that is at all

pulled together, that is relatively short and compact, and
it is made memorable by solidly remembered scenes —
of candlemakings, quiltings and apple bees, chestnuttings
and huckleberryings: the whole life of a country parsonage, with the children playing at town meetings or
preaching and singing hymns, the minister laying in
an equipment of Latin and Greek quotations for use in
next Sunday's sermon, while his wife packs the dough-
nuts for a picnic; with the trumpet-blossomed squash-
vines in the garden, the spinning wheels and corn in the
garret, the cider barrels and rats in the cellar. Or a scene
from another interior, the household of a granitic Connecticut farmer. It is four o'clock in the morning. The
season is March, but "the snowbank still lay in white
billows above the tops of the fences. . . . The feeble
light of a tallow dip seemed to cut but a small circle into
the darkness of the great kitchen. The frost sparkled
white on the back of the big fireplace, where the last
night's coals lay raked up under banks of ashes. An
earthquake of tramping cowhide boots shook the rafters
and stairs." This sound is the farmer's four full-grown
sons marching down to breakfast. Their father, Zeph
Higgins, holds morning prayers, reading from Zechariah
"with a voice as loud and harsh as the winds that were
blowing out of doors." They devour their heavy breakfast
of sausages, Indian bread, pork and beans, and tea. They
are going to town to vote, and as soon as the first faint
red streaks appear in the wintry sky, they start off,
against a cutting wind, in a sled drawn by well-fed
oxen and heavily loaded with cordwood (which they are
taking this occasion to deliver), whose runners creak in
the snow. The father would like to control his boys'
votes, but he does not dare to ask them their intentions,
and at the polls he will not tell anyone how he is going
to vote himself.

It is the election of 1818, at which the Jeffersonian Republicans defeated the conservative Federalists and, in adopting a new constitution that separated Church and State, succeeded in abolishing in Connecticut forever the old theocratic system. The Episcopal Church, in the meantime, which had once been the Church of England and was still associated in people's minds with the tyranny of the British Crown, had been taking advantage of the vacancy created by the lapse of Calvinism to slip quietly back into New England. There is now a new Episcopal church in Poganuc, and the Christmas before the election — the church hung with holiday greens and an enormous gold-tinsel star — the first Christmas celebration is held there. The Puritans did not celebrate Christmas — John Calvin having abolished at Geneva both Christmas and Easter festivities — and the children of the parsonage are very much excited by what is going on in the rival church. The minister's little girl — who represents Harriet herself — sneaks in and attends the service. Her father, learning of this, buys her a sugar dog, but explains to the children that nobody knows on what day Christ was born, that "if we are going to keep any day on account of the birth of Christ, the best way to keep it is by doing all our duties on that day better than any other," and he sends them off to school. But the family becomes further demoralized on receiving a package of presents from a Tory aunt in Boston who has remained an Episcopalian. "Mother worries," writes this aunt, "because she thinks you Presbyterians won't get any Christmas presents." The family in Connecticut are of course Congregationalists, but their relatives make no distinction between the two barbarous branches of the Calvinist faith.

Some years later, "our little friend Dolly [Harriet] had shot up into a blooming and beautiful maiden —

warm-hearted, enthusiastic, and whole-souled as we have seen her in her childhood." She is adored by a young man named Abner, one of Zeph Higgins's sons, who is now a theological student studying with Dolly's father. Abner Higgins now looms as the "menace": the reader is deadly afraid that Dolly will become reconciled to marrying him. But again the Tory aunt intervenes to rescue the Congregationalist heroine. She invites the girl to visit her in Boston, and there Dolly meets a young cousin from England, who has been brought over by a childless uncle to succeed him in the family business. It is just before Christmas, and the visitor has a chance, for the first time in her life, to put up Christmas decorations. "I made garlands and wreaths and crosses, and all sorts of pretty things," she writes home, "and Cousin Alfred put them up, and Aunty said that really, 'for a blue Presbyterian girl,' I showed wonderful skill and insight in the matter." But she has never been told anything about mistletoe, and she gets kissed by Cousin Alfred. "A bright flush of amazement and almost resentment" passes over her face, but then Cousin Alfred explains that kissing under the mistletoe is an old Christmas custom. He is soon writing a friend in England that he hopes to "succeed in pleasing this little American princess." They are married the following spring, on "a radiant June morning, when the elms of Poganuc were all alive with birds, when the daisies were white in the meadows, and the bobolink on the apple-tree was outdoing himself."

"Years have passed since then," the story ends. "Dolly has held her place among the matronage of Boston; her sons have graduated at Harvard, and her daughters have recalled to memory the bright eyes and youthful bloom of their mother." This conclusion departs completely from Harriet's own career. She *had* had a Tory Episcopalian aunt, with whom she had liked to stay in her youth and who had exercised over her a considerable influence, and she had herself repudiated the Calvinist creed in 1864 by becoming an Episcopalian. But it is curious that Harriet Beecher Stowe, writing in her middle sixties, should have arranged for her heroine a destiny which was really a young girl's dream, which exempted her from all the circumstances that had molded her own personality and given her work its importance — the ordeal of Cincinnati, the lifetime of clerical associations, the responsibilities of a public figure — that, as if with a certain wistfulness, she should have married her "little American princess" to an affluent business man and assigned her to a comfortable position among the cultivated "matronage of Boston."

And yet not even *Poganuc People* is somehow quite satisfactory as a novel of New England family life. Something in the picture is lacking — something that is present in the more popular stories of Louisa M. Alcott. What is it? Perhaps some sort of sense of intimate human relations. As a girl, Harriet Beecher had been thought rather plain, and she had never had many admirers. She had been shy, and she had done, in the course of her life, a good deal of sitting around while she listened to people and watched them. She could mimic the way people talked, and she had developed a sharp sense of character, intellectual, social and moral. "Richly as her nature was endowed," Forrest Wilson, her biographer, writes of her, "in her early life, at least, she was critical of people. She did her best to correct her social attitude and at any rate succeeded in veneering it over. But behind the affectionate terms [sic] which she could eventually address even to strangers, one feels her blue eyes weighing and appraising. Her bitterest critics were to attack her knowledge of character, especially Southern character. They could not have assailed her at a stronger point. Character was what she *did* know, for she spent her life reading character." Henry James, who had met Mrs. Stowe at the Oliver Wendell Holmeses', speaks, in his notes for an essay on Mr. and Mrs. James T. Fields, of "her extraordinary little vaguely observant, slightly woolgathering, letting her eyes wander all over the place kind of little way." This lifelong habit of detachment made her strength as a social critic but it insulated her somewhat from her fellows. She was so much tied into the network of her enormous and complicated family, she was so imperturbably loyal to her father and her husband and her sisters and brothers, she obviously suffered so much from the loss of two of her children and from the moral collapse of a son who had fought in the Civil War, and she is able so to make one's blood boil by using the grief of bereavement to drive home the knife in *Uncle Tom*, that we may not be aware at first of a certain absence of warmth. But when we come to read her in bulk, we are obliged to conclude that the tragic deaths she inflicts on so many of her heroines are not merely due to literary fashion, to the attempt to supply a demand created by Little Eva. The author, we realize, is happiest when — as in *Dred* and *The Pearl of Orr's Island* — she can irrevocably separate her lovers by arranging to have one of them die. Each one of her deaths is accompanied by a curious sublimation, by which it is invariably suggested that the posthumous influence of her heroine — as a permanently uplifting ideal — will be of more real benefit to her lover than she could ever have been in the flesh if she had lived to be his earthly bride. This theme is no doubt connected with Harriet's loss of her mother, who died when Harriet was five, and with the cult that Harriet devoted to her memory. But it is difficult to sympathize with a cult of this kind when it appears in a work of fiction as an element in the relation between two lovers; and the majority of Mrs. Stowe's characters, in all their earthly relations, are complete non-conductors — to the reader — of the emotions they are supposed to be feeling. This is probably one of the factors that have kept most of her novels from being much read, while *Little Women* — though a good deal inferior in intellectual and social interest — has been a favorite ever since it was written and has become a kind of national legend.

Mrs. Stowe had got rid of Calvinism; she had dramatized the teaching of Jesus. Yet her God was still a God of Justice rather than a God of Love. Her pity runs to sentimentality, which is to say that it sometimes seems false; but she is never an obnoxious moralist: her judgment of men is quite sober and her judgment of ideas quite sound.

II

CALVIN STOWE; FRANCIS GRIERSON; THE BATTLE HYMN OF THE REPUBLIC; THE UNION AS RELIGIOUS MYSTICISM

MRS. STOWE, after the drowning of her son, had resorted to spiritualistic séances, but she had found the communications supposed to be elicited from the other world disappointing and unconvincing. "If the future life," she wrote, "is so weary, stale, flat and unprofitable as we might infer from these readings, one would have reason to deplore an immortality from which no suicide could give an outlet. To be condemned to such eternal prosing would be worse than annihilation." She continued to be contemptuous of professional mediums and ridiculed them in *My Wife and I;* yet she did incline to believe that some intercourse with another world was possible, and she argued in favor of the supernatural, as "an uncommon working of natural laws," with George Eliot and Oliver Wendell Holmes. She was undoubtedly much influenced in this by her husband, Calvin Stowe, who had been visited since boyhood by apparitions, and who suggests, in a letter to George Eliot, that it is not "absurd to suppose that some peculiarity in the nervous system, in the connecting link between soul and body, may bring some more than others into an almost abnormal contact with the spirit-world (for example, Jacob

Boehme and Swedenborg), and that, too, without correcting their faults or making them morally better than others." It is said that these experiences of Calvin's were decisive in reconciling Harriet — when she was trying to get rid of the old theology — to the miraculous element in religion.

Calvin Stowe is an odd Yankee character, who — in spite of his hypochondria — inspires respect and sympathy. He was a mixture of New England hardheadedness and New England idealism, and he lived on intimate terms with the devils of a Calvinist fantasy, among whom his sensitive nature had introduced some more beneficent spirits. Calvin Ellis Stowe had been a poor boy in Natick, Massachusetts — son of the village baker, who had died when Calvin was six — and he had worked during his teens in a paper mill, but had got himself an education and graduated from Bowdoin College and Auburn Theological Seminary. His appetite for study was immense, and he became a considerable Semitic scholar and an authority on education. But there was always something rustic about him. He was full of New England stories from the days of his childhood in Natick, and Harriet's *Oldtown Folks* owes so much to the material he gave her that it represents in some sense a collaboration. In his sermons and other writings, he loved to use homely examples, to call in the prosaic and practical in order to prop the divine. Here is the typical opening of his once very popular book, *The Origin and the History of the Books of the Bible*:

"The purpose of this volume can best be shown by a familiar illustration: I purchase several different parcels of real estate in the city of Hartford, and wish to ascertain the validity of my title to each one of the parcels. I take the deeds to the register's office and there trace each one by itself through all the preceding purchasers till I come to the title derived from the original proprietors. If there is no break in this chain of documentary evidence, the title is perfect.

"So each one of the books of the New Testament must be traced up to the Apostles, who only had authority to deliver inspired books to the churches. This is what the present volume professes to do. It is a book of authorities and testimonies; it is the tracing and verifying of title deeds.

"But there are some deeds in which the chain is broken before we get to the original proprietors; there are some which are forgeries and were not given by the men whose name they bear; and there are others which were given by the persons whose names they bear, but these persons had no authority to make the sales. All such deeds are invalid and confer no title.

"These latter deeds represent the apocryphal books. . . ."

In the often rather feverish atmosphere created by Harriet's activities, Calvin Stowe sometimes came to her rescue with a devastating common sense. Soon after the publication of *Uncle Tom* — in 1853 — the Stowes visited Scotland and England, where Harriet was much applauded. The climax of this triumph was a meeting in Exeter Hall in London, at which four thousand people were present and for which they had been queueing up for twenty-four hours. Calvin was sitting on the platform, and Harriet, to a violent ovation, arrived with the Duchess of Sutherland and occupied a private gallery. What followed rather frightened Harriet: "There were hoarse surgings and swellings of the mighty mass, who were so closely packed that they moved together like waves. Some began to rise in their seats, and some cried, 'Order! Order!'" "I am afraid," said the Duchess of Sutherland, "that we are going to have one of our

genuine Exeter Hall 'brays.' " The Stowes came to
realize, when the speeches began, that the meeting was
an anti-American demonstration. The English had controlled at one time more than half the Western slave
trade, and had continued to pour slaves into the American colonies at a time when the latter wanted to end
this traffic; but almost twenty years before the Stowes'
visit — in 1834 — slavery had been abolished in all British
possessions, and the Londoners were now delighted to
give vent, under the pretext of moral indignation, to the
bitterness of their resentment against their former enemies and present rivals. The situation for Harriet, as the
speeches went on, became more and more uncomfortable;
and the excitement was brought to a boil when Lord
Shaftesbury told the audience of the President's assurance, in his recent inaugural address, that the Fugitive
Slave Law would be enforced. There were hisses and
cries of "Shame!" Now, the President at this time was
Franklin Pierce, an old classmate from Bowdoin of Calvin Stowe's, and this may, as Forrest Wilson suggests in
his biography of Mrs. Stowe — though no special explanation is needed — have had something to do with
what followed. Calvin Stowe rose and answered the
speaker. He told the audience that in view of the fact
that England provided the market for four-fifths of the
American cotton, she had the power of ending slavery
at once: she had only to refuse to buy cotton that was
cultivated and picked by slave labor. "Are you willing
to sacrifice one penny of your own profit for the sake
of doing away with this accursed business?" They had
just been invoking, he reminded them, the conscience of
the growers of cotton, but "has the cotton-consumer no
conscience? The receiver is as guilty as the thief." He
afterwards wrote of his speech that it was "heard by some
with surprise and by others with extreme displeasure."

Edouard de Stoeckl, the Tsar's Minister at Washington, was later to write his government (March 2, 1863), that he had been assured by Lord Lyons, the English Minister, that "the English want cotton and want it as cheaply as possible, and it is only by the toil of slaves that they can obtain it thus. They would therefore be loath to see emancipation come about, no matter what the orators of Exeter Hall may say." But the London press, hitherto fulsome in its praise of the visiting Stowes, now diverted its indignation from the American slaveholders to Calvin. His challenge was characterized by the *Morning Advertiser* as "an insult to the head and heart of the country, an outrage on Christianity itself, and especially unpardonable in a man placed in Professor Stowe's circumstances."

Calvin's tendency, like that of his wife, was all to eliminate the rigors of the merciless and terrifying doctrine after whose founder he had been christened; and in the recovery of faith after his crisis of doubt in 1844, he had not lost his common sense. But though he held that the account of creation in Genesis could make no claim to scientific accuracy and that it did not discredit the findings of geology, he believed and attempted to demonstrate that the Pentateuch was written by Moses; and though he took cognizance of Renan and the German "higher critics," it was only to brush them off. He accepted at face value the testimony of the early Church Fathers as to the authenticity of the Gospels. But he was also quite unconventional, as a Presbyterian scholar, in his interest in rabbinical literature. He even produced a study of the Talmud, which Harriet attempted without success to have published by the *Atlantic Monthly*. And as Harriet turned Episcopalian, so Calvin, in his later years, seems to have been attracted toward Judaism — which had always had a high prestige for the New England Puritan mind. He is said to have been very much pleased when George Eliot remarked that he looked like a rabbi, and — as a result, it is said, of this — he ceased to shave or to have his hair cut. He contributed further to this role by wearing a black skullcap. For the frontispiece of his book on the Bible, he had himself photographed in a solemn pose, holding in his hand an object which, though labelled in Greek "The New Testament," suggests rather the scroll of the Torah that is read in the synagogue; and even in an informal family picture, in which you see him and Harriet and some of the children sitting on their lawn in Florida, you find Calvin, among these ladies in their conventional costumes of the seventies, incongruously playing Moses, as he exhibits, propped up on his knee and supported by his right hand, something that looks so much like the Tables of the Law that one is at a loss to imagine what it could really have been. Harriet, in writing to her friends, got to referring to Calvin as "my poor rabbi," or simply "my old Rab."

Yet side by side with Calvin Stowe's shrewd realism and his non-apocalyptic Judaizing — and as if in a separate compartment — there existed a close contact with the supernatural: a lifelong sequence of hallucinations which seems to have been as real to him as anything else in his experience. He had been visited since early childhood by a race of otherworldly beings that appeared to him so distinctly and gave so much the illusion of solidity that he admitted their insubstantiality only after he had come to realize that other people did not see them. The story of these visions is included by Harriet in her novel *Oldtown Folks,* but it is better read in Calvin's own words, as he wrote it in the 1830's for a literary club in Cincinnati and as it is printed in the *Life of Harriet Beecher Stowe* by her son Charles Edward Stowe.

"As early as I can remember anything, I can remember observing a multitude of animated and active objects," which "exhibited all possible combinations of size, shape, proportion and color, but their most usual appearance was with the human form and proportion, but under a shadowy outline that seemed just ready to melt into the invisible air, and sometimes liable to the most sudden and grotesque changes, and with a uniform darkly bluish color spotted with brown, or brownish white." These beings were preyed upon by "a sort of heavy clouds floating about overhead, of a black color, spotted with brown, in the shape of a very flaring inverted tunnel without a nozzle, and from ten to thirty or forty feet in diameter. They floated from place to place in great numbers and in all directions, with a strong and steady progress, a tremendous, quivering internal motion that agitated them in every part. Whenever they approached, the rational phantoms were thrown into great consternation; and well it might be, for if a cloud touched any part of one of the rational phantoms it immediately communicated its own color and tremulous motion to the part it touched.

"In spite of all the efforts and convulsive struggles of the unhappy victim, this color and motion slowly, but steadily and uninterruptedly, proceeded to diffuse itself over every part of the body, and as fast as it did so the body was drawn into the cloud and became a part of its substance. It was indeed a fearful sight to see the contortions, the agonizing efforts, of the poor creatures who had been touched by one of these awful clouds, and were dissolving and melting into it by inches without the possibility of escape or resistance."

But at one period of Calvin's boyhood, "Every night,

after I had gone to bed and the candle was removed, a very pleasant-looking human face would peer at me [through an unfinished place in the wall] . . . and gradually press forward his head, neck, shoulders, and finally his whole body as far as the waist, through the opening, and then, smiling upon me with great good-nature, would withdraw in the same manner in which he had entered. He was a great favorite of mine; for though we neither of us spoke, we perfectly understood, and were entirely devoted to, each other. It is a singular fact that the features of this favorite phantom bore a very close resemblance to those of a boy older than myself whom I feared and hated; still the resemblance was so strong that I called him the same name, Harvey.*

"Harvey's visits were always expected and always pleasant; but sometimes there were visitations of another sort, odious and frightful. One of these I will relate as a specimen of the rest.

"One night, after I had retired to bed and was looking for Harvey, I observed an unusual number of the tunnel-shaped tremulous clouds already described, and they seemed intensely black and strongly agitated. This alarmed me exceedingly, and I had a terrible feeling that something awful was going to happen. It was not long before I saw Harvey at his accustomed place, cautiously peeping at me through the aperture, with an expression of pain and terror on his countenance. He seemed to warn me to be on my guard, but was afraid to put his head into the room lest he should be touched by one of the clouds, which were every moment growing thicker and more numerous. Harvey soon withdrew and

* One wonders whether the play called *Harvey* by Mrs. Mary Chase, which opened on November 1, 1944, and ran for over four years, may not have owed something to Calvin Stowe. The Harvey of the play is an imaginary man-sized rabbit, who appears to and befriends the alcoholic hero.

left me alone. On turning my eyes toward the left-hand wall of the room, I thought I saw at an immense distance below me the regions of the damned, as I had heard them pictured in sermons. From this awful world of horror the tunnel-shaped clouds were ascending, and I perceived that they were the principal instruments of torture in these gloomy abodes. These regions were at such an immense distance below me that I could obtain but a very indistinct view of the inhabitants, who were very numerous and exceedingly active. Near the surface of the earth, and as it seemed to me but a little distance from my bed, I saw four or five sturdy, resolute devils endeavoring to carry off an unprincipled and dissipated man, in the neighborhood, by the name of Brown, of whom I had stood in terror for years. These devils I saw were very different from the common representations. They had neither red faces, nor horns, nor hoofs, nor tails. They were in all respects stoutly built and well dressed gentlemen. The only peculiarity that I noted in their appearance was as to their heads. Their faces and necks were perfectly bare, without hair or flesh, and of a uniform sky-blue color, like the ashes of burnt paper before it falls to pieces, and of a certain glossy smoothness.

"As I looked on, full of eagerness, the devils struggled to force Brown down with them, and Brown struggled with the energy of desperation to save himself from their grip, and it seemed that the human was likely to prove too strong for the infernal. In this emergency one of the devils, panting for breath and covered with perspiration, beckoned to a strong, thick cloud that seemed to understand him perfectly, and, whirling up to Brown, touched his hand. Brown resisted stoutly, and struck out right and left at the cloud most furiously, but the usual effect was produced, — the hand grew black, quivered, and seemed to be melting into the cloud; then the arm, by slow degrees, and then the head and shoulders. At this instant Brown, collecting all his energies for one desperate effort, sprang at once into the centre of the cloud, tore it asunder, and descended to the ground exclaiming, with a hoarse, furious voice that grated on my ear, 'There, I've got out; dam'me if I haven't!' This was the first word that had been spoken through the whole horrible scene. It was the first time I had ever seen a cloud fail to produce its appropriate result, and it terrified me so that I trembled from head to foot. The devils, however, did not seem to be in the least discouraged. One of them, who seemed to be the leader, went away and quickly returned bringing with him an enormous pair of rollers fixed in an iron frame, such as are used in iron-mills for the purpose of rolling out and slitting bars of iron, except instead of being turned by machinery, each roller was turned by an immense crank. Three of the devils now seized Brown and put his feet to the rollers, while two others stood, one at each crank, and began to roll him in with a steady strain that was entirely irresistible. Not a word was spoken, not a sound was heard; but the fearful struggles and terrified, agonizing looks of Brown were more than I could endure. I sprang from my bed and ran through the kitchen into the room where my parents slept, and entreated that they would permit me to spend the remainder of the night with them."

It is not difficult to recognize in these images the damnations and salvations of the Calvinist theology. But Calvin Stowe saw other visions, also, which must have been summoned before him by the promptings of sexual appetite: "a very large Indian woman and a very small Indian man," who disputed about "a huge bass viol"; "a charming little female figure . . . eight inches high and exquisitely proportioned," who "would smile upon me, raise her hands to her head and draw them down on each side of her face, suddenly turn round and go off at a rapid trot," disclosing "a good-looking mulatto man, rather smaller than herself, following directly in her wake and trotting off after her." He awoke "one bright moonlight night," and found, he says, lying in bed with him, "a large full-length human skeleton of an ashy-blue color." At this time he was solitary and lonely, would wish himself annihilated, would run home to see whether "my friends at home" were not "suffering some dreadful calamity," would experience "fits of corroding melancholy, irritation and bitter remorse" — which were evidently the forerunners of the prolonged and abysmal depressions from which he suffered in later life. These feelings of guilt and despair would seem to have been especially stimulated by the theology of Original Sin and uncertain elusive Grace, as the beings that came to frighten him must have derived from Cotton Mather's *Magnalia* and Jedidiah Morris's *History of New England,* which he tells us were among the first books that he read or had read to him in boyhood. The appearance of the phantoms, he says, "was always attended with considerable effort and fatigue on my part; the more distinct and vivid they were, the more would my fatigue be increased; and at such times my face was always pale and my eyes unusually sparkling and wild. This continued to be the case after I became satisfied that it was a delusion of the imagination, and it so continues to the present day."

For he never ceased to see these phantoms. On one occasion, when Harriet had missed a train and returned when he did not expect her, he came into her room but did not speak and behaved as if she were not there. When she finally began to laugh, he exclaimed, "Why, is that you? I thought it was one of my visions." In his old age, the Devil returned to plague him. The Stowes had now lost three sons, and the only surviving boy was at that time studying in Germany. The Devil, disguised as a horseman, would visit Calvin night after night and shout to him that Charley was dead, then ask whether he still believed in the goodness and wisdom of God. But Calvin found the way to rout him. "I was ready for him last night," he said. "I had fortified myself with passages of Scripture. I found some things in *Ephesians* which were just what I wanted, and when he came . . . , I *hurled* them at him. I tell you it made him bark like a dog, and he took himself off. He won't trouble me again."

These hauntings must have acted as a brake upon Calvin's curiosity as a scholar. How could one who had the Devil on the premises be seduced by the sweet words of Renan?

There were many such household devils and super-natural visitants — a heritage, as in Stowe's case, from the old theology — still alive in the practical North on the eve of the Civil War. The enterprising breed of New England, with their shipping and banking and mills, had still remained in quite close touch with what Mather called "the Wonders of the Invisible World"; and this world, as we shall see, was present to the Westerner Francis Grierson as well as to Calvin Stowe; and the politician Lincoln, like Grierson, was visited by prophetic visions. This was the age of the spiritualist David Home, who had come from the same New England town as the family of Calvin Stowe and whose career, on his lower level, somewhat resembled Grierson's. He, like Grierson, conquered Europe. He refused to take money for his spiritualist séances — though he was always living on someone — and he impressed many members of the Eng-

lish aristocracy. He must have been an accomplished
magician, for he was able to persuade his clientèle, often
in broad daylight, that the furniture in a room was being
lifted and pushed about by invisible forces and that they
saw and clasped spirit hands. He once convinced several persons that he had floated out the window of a London hotel and back in at the window of an adjoining
room — though when the American magician Houdini,
in the course of his investigation of alleged spiritualistic
phenomena, came to analyze the testimony of these
"witnesses," he discovered that nobody present had actually seen Home float. Houdini discovered, also, on
visiting the rooms in question, that it was possible to get
into the adjoining room by way of the window-ledges.
There was enough of the artist in Home — he did sculp-
ture and gave public readings — to produce an illusion
of refinement of character, and he managed to be taken
seriously by John Ruskin, Sir William Crookes, Alexei
Tolstoy and Alexander II of Russia. He twice married
Russian ladies of property, and he was at one time a
member of the household of the Empress Eugénie.
Mrs. Stowe, during a sojourn in Italy, discussed spirit-
ualism with Elizabeth Barrett Browning, and both the
Brownings and the Stowes discussed Home. Mrs. Browning was enchanted by him, and he became between her
and Robert something of a sore issue. Browning was
piqued by Home into writing his monologue *Mr. Sludge,
the Medium,* in which, though he makes the spiritualist
a shoddy enough figure, he allows him to be not quite
sure that there are not certain chinks of his own perception through which supernatural influence has occasionally entered. Calvin Stowe, though he did not
like Home and said that he had been, in his childhood,
"a disagreeable nasty boy," was inclined to think there
was something in his claims. "He certainly has quali-

ties," he wrote to George Eliot, "which science has not yet explained, and some of his doings are as real as they are strange."

Francis Grierson's real name was Jesse Shepherd. He was the son of an Irish father and a Scottish mother, who had come to this country in 1849, when the boy was six months old, and had lived for a time in a log cabin in Sangamon County, Illinois. Later they moved to Alton on the Mississippi, and still later down to St. Louis, where Francis commenced a musical career by singing in the choir of a Catholic church. In 1869, when he was twenty, he somehow made his way to Paris. With a minimum of technical training — he seems never to have learned to read music and said that he never practised — the boy had developed an astonishing gift for piano improvisation, a gift which so dazzled the Parisian writers, the ladies who had artistic salons, and even, to some extent, the musicians, that, arriving unknown and with little means, he soon became a well-known figure, much in demand for his musical performances. The next year he tried London, which chilled him, and moved on to St. Petersburg, arriving there, as he says, "possessed of twenty francs and a feeling of security that bordered on indifference"; he stayed something less than a year. A portrait of him painted in Russia shows a face almost incredibly beautiful in its dreaminess, refinement and elegance — though he is said to have had enormous hands that could stretch to an octave and a half, and big feet that he stumbled over and about which he was self-conscious. Thereafter, for a couple of years, returning to western Europe, he seems to have enjoyed a triumph, singing and playing the organ in cathedrals on great occasions, giving recitals before crowned heads.

Mallarmé and Sully-Prudhomme both expressed themselves extravagantly about him. Mallarmé went so far as to say that Grierson achieved "with musical sounds, combinations and melodies what Poe did with the rhythm of words"; and of his voice, which had a range of four octaves, that it was not a voice but a choir.

No beginning could seem more brilliant, yet it is characteristic of Grierson's strange career that after this he should drop out of sight and his movements remain obscure for something like fifteen years, during which it is known of him only that he revisited the United States, passed again through Paris and London and spent a year in Australia. There is no biography of Grierson, and we are obliged to depend for our information on scattered incomplete sources. The late Theodore Spencer of Harvard, who had made a special study of Grierson with a view to writing a long poem about him and who contributed an introduction to a reprint of his best-known book, tells us that in 1887 "some art-loving citizens of San Diego, California, anxious to give cultural publicity to their town, presented Grierson . . . with a city block . . . and some money to help build a house on it. Grierson drew the plans himself and called the house the Villa Montezuma." He lived there with a German friend named Lawrence Waldemar Tonner, whom he had met in 1885 and who was to remain with him all the rest of his life. Tonner wrote, after Grierson's death, that he and Grierson had given "large receptions to all celebrities who came to San Diego," but, that later, "when the boom died out of San Diego in 1889," they had had "to sell for what we could get."

Now Grierson returned to Europe, and his literary career commenced. He had apparently long had the ambition to write, and he referred to his books as his "serious work," as distinguished from his public performances, and signed them "Francis Grierson" with his mother's family name, because he did not want his writings, as he said, to be associated with a "mere musician." His first volume was written in French — *La Révolte Idéaliste* — and was privately published in Paris in 1889, where it seems to have made an impression, particularly on Maeterlinck, who called Grierson "the supreme essayist of the age" and said that the book had influenced him more than any other he had ever read. Ten years later, a good deal of *La Révolte Idéaliste* appeared in an English version in a collection of his essays called *Modern Mysticism*. This book and the half dozen similar volumes with which Francis Grierson followed it were praised by some distinguished men of letters and enjoyed a certain vogue; but when we read Grierson's essays today, their virtues seem partly to have evaporated. His work in this form may be said to stand halfway between Maeterlinck and Emerson, and one no longer feels the same kind of interest — the appetite for "spiritual" nutriment — that the serious reading public formerly did in this kind of sententious essay. But Grierson also imitated with a certain success, in a book called *La Vie et les Hommes* (1911), the pellucid and abstract aphorisms of the classical French moralists. In this vein he is sometimes witty, sometimes penetrating, sometimes insipid. In another book, *Parisian Portraits,* published the same year, he collected a number of personal sketches, in which — along with the work of Verlaine, Mallarmé and Leconte de Lisle — he celebrated the banalities in prose and verse of certain aristocratic ladies in whose salons he had been asked to perform; and the fact that he seems at that time to have felt an almost equal enthusiasm for Mallarmé and for Sully-Prudhomme shows how eagerly he had swallowed French culture. Yet he wrote about Yvette Guilbert a subtle and

accurate essay that gave her the place she deserved — far
above the level of the *café chantant,* where, in spite
of her vogue in the nineties, the French have as a rule
liked to leave her.

These essays make a curious impression. They combine a very Scottish common sense with the aloofness
of a disembodied spirit. The language seems always
precise, and it is always fastidiously chosen, yet the paragraphs may leave one blank. Francis Grierson had
lived in so many countries that his point of view was
truly international, or rather, perhaps, supernational, and
he undoubtedly enjoyed an advantage in being able to
approach Poe and Emerson, Goethe and Wagner, Tolstoy
and Ibsen, Zola and Flaubert, Carlyle and George Eliot,
with a minimum of national prejudice. Except for his
occasional weakness, under the influence of his fashionable hostesses, for the elegantly second-rate, he had a
sound and even bold perception of what was important
and what was not, and on the subject of music, especially,
he could be quite independent and sharp, as when he resisted the spell of Bayreuth, which he regarded as a
species of mass hypnotism, and wrote a damaging essay
called *Parsifalitis.* He was also, as a general critic, quite
unusual in being able to appreciate that such statesmen
as Lincoln, Napoleon and Bismarck should be judged,
like the artists, as creative forces. Yet there is also a certain disadvantage in being quite so far up above everything as Grierson usually is in these essays, in not intimately participating, as he does not here, in any of the
cultures he appraises. We are always being stopped on
the threshold; we are never taken inside anything. And
even in his chosen realm, the universal realm of spirit,
he continues to be unsatisfactory. He regarded himself
as a mystic, but his mysticism was queerly limited. He
does not seem to have committed himself to either the

Protestant or the Catholic church, and he rarely refers to God. He usually appears to assume that the human world which we know has behind it invisible forces whose impulses and aims can be read by those who are sensitive enough; yet he sometimes expresses himself in terms that are closer to modern psychology, as when he said to the American composer Arthur Farwell: "We are only beginning to get a glimpse of our secret selves as through a glass darkly. What we took for supernaturalism is beginning to be revealed as natural law working up from the secret springs of the subconscious"; and, "The artist who believes himself under the domination of some invisible power is to be pitied. The soul is either master or slave." In a good deal of the writing of Grierson, neat and even though it always is, we have continually a queer impression that the visible and apprehensible are fading and losing their meaning, that the concrete image and the definite word are ready at any moment to turn into mere verbalizing. We begin to feel baffled as, for some puzzling reason, we fail to gain access to the author's mind — cannot find out who he is or where he lives. It was this that made A. R. Orage, the London editor of the weekly *New Age,* who, for two years — 1909–11 — published Grierson's articles regularly, confess at the end of this time that he could not be perfectly sure that Grierson was not a charlatan; and it was this that made Arnold Bennett, a fellow contributor to the magazine, describe him as the "most enigmatic personality of our day." Bennett, who was always much interested in how people got their money and how much they got, had, in this case, the special frustration of never having been able to find out — since it appeared that Orage did not know — who it was that paid Grierson for his articles. "Somebody else pays me," was all that Grierson would say.

Yet Francis Grierson, though unquestionably enigmatic, was — as Orage, in spite of his doubts, was on the whole disposed to believe — no charlatan, or not consciously and intentionally one. One's impression is, in fact, that Grierson was himself never quite able to account for the mysterious resources, subconscious or extra-human, on which he was able to draw. One decides that his speculations on "the psychic action of genius," "the artistic faculty in literature," "the Celtic temperament," etc., represent to a large extent an attempt to explain to himself his strange gift of improvisation, as well as, since this gift did not satisfy him and he was nothing if not critically minded, his impulse to acknowledge its weaknesses. One gathers, from descriptions of his playing, that his music was a visitation which seemed to arrive from another world, to make itself heard through his mediumship, and then, shy of the craftsman's discipline, to go back to a realm of mist. "On the one occasion when I heard him play," Mr. Shaemas O'Sheel has written, "he passed from music that voiced the soul of modern Europe, the Europe whose cosmopolitan and introspective and somewhat weary culture also produced Chopin, to exotic melodies evocative of the Orient, whose subtlety lies just beneath the surface of bland simplicity. It was distinguished music; it held haunting suggestions; it seemed weirdly to well up from a remote interior source, or to crystallize from uncanny presences in the air. At one hearing, that was all one could say." Arthur Farwell, then the editor of *Musical America,* who had been trying to find materials for a native music in the chants of the American Indians, reports a conversation with Grierson in 1913, when the latter had returned to the United States, and describes him in extravagant terms — though he had apparently not heard him play — as "this new musical liberator — the most authentically psychic and most daringly and far-seeingly critical musical personality of the time."

On Theodore Rousseau, a young Franco-American, who had been sent by the *Evening Post* to interview Grierson when he landed, he made an impression rather disconcerting. "I had never," writes Mr. Rousseau (in a private letter to the author), "seen a man with lips and cheeks rouged and eyes darkened. His hair was arranged in careful disorder over his brow, his hands elaborately manicured and with many rings on his fingers; he wore a softly tinted, flowing cravat."

Such an observer, if he had not known Grierson's work, might have supposed that the mystic had quite left behind his native Sangamon County and the log cabin in which he had lived as a child. But this would have been an error. Francis Grierson had published in 1909 a book called *The Valley of Shadows*, a memoir of the Middle West on the eve of the Civil War, which is by far the best thing he wrote. It was the book over which he had taken most pains. He had been occupied with it ten years, polishing every sentence with a solicitude that was almost Flaubertian. In this late evocation of backwoods Illinois, so different from anything else that Grierson wrote, every word has a solid value and every detail sounds real. For his memories of his boyhood in the wilderness would appear, in the long run, to have come quite to outweigh for Grierson all the other experiences of his far-ranging life. He had grown up in the excitement of the war years and of the era of Western expansion. His father had supported Lincoln, and the boy had heard Lincoln and Douglas debate; he had served as a page on the staff of the explorer John C. Frémont, when Frémont, in 1861, was military commander of St. Louis and he had heard from men who had shared them the stories of Frémont's adventures, sometimes fantastic or gruesome, among cannibal Indians and frozen heights. Francis Grierson was a cousin of that General Grierson who, with a single brigade of Western cavalry, some of them men and boys whom Francis had known on the prairies, had brought off a spectacular coup in connection with the Vicksburg campaign. He had made an audacious raid on the South that had covered six hundred miles from Lagrange, Tennessee, to Baton Rouge, Louisiana. The musician and man of letters who had taken the Grierson name had been always very proud of this family connection; and he had been proud of whatever in America — the work of Lincoln, Whitman, Poe — had achieved intensity of thought or dignity of imagination. The prophets and poets of the United States were to remain fundamental to his culture; but when, at twenty, he had come to Paris, these had hardly been enough to sustain him; he had been conquered by the French tradition and his style had lost something of the savor of English. Now he tackles an American subject, and his training in the clearness and precision of French is to stand him in good stead. Dealing here with illiterate pioneers, a life often crude and brutal, he presents it with qualities exceedingly rare in our literature of the Middle West: a fine pointedness and an elegant lucidity. The landscapes as seen by a child, the special sensations of night and day, moonrise and sunset, winter and summer, in a lonely log cabin beyond civilization, are created with all the skill that a high civilization can teach; and the rude people on their little farms are differentiated and understood with a cultivated sensitivity that never patronizes or caricatures them. The clairvoyance, the vivid perception of moral and aesthetic forces, that Grierson had always possessed is also here to serve him well, for it enables him to light up from inside these bearish men and these pious women, and to reveal the apprehension of great events — only half comprehended and hardly expressed — awaking in the consciousness of a scattered community. No other book so gives us the sense of the imminence of the national crisis for which people dimly felt they were being prepared without having been given the power to control it — not so much a storm that was going to burst as a drama, a sacred drama, in which they would have to perform.

In another respect, too, the mediumistic side of Grierson appears to advantage in *The Valley of Shadows*. The impression produced by the book is the opposite of that which we so often receive from the naturalistic method in fiction: the impression that the writer is reconstructing, by careful observation and research, an experience outside himself. We feel, on the contrary, with Grierson, that the experience has imposed itself on him, that a great moment of history has lived itself through him. The events — most of which had taken place when the author was about ten and which were described when he was over fifty — can hardly have been reproduced with anything like a photographic or phonographic fidelity, for they include long narratives and conversations that could not have been reported verbatim. It is suggested by Bernard De Voto, in a preface to *The Valley of Shadows*, that, in the case of one of its episodes, the author has got an old dime novel mixed up with a story he had actually heard. Yet the effect is never that of fiction, and the narrative is full of details that must be authentic memories — for example, in the episode in question, the chapter called *The Regulators*, the incident that occurs in the courtroom when "one o' the Sawyer boys let his rifle fall plumb across the paws of a big dog layin' on the floor beside him" and "an awful howl went up, in which all the other dogs joined, and 'twixt the dogs, the robbers, an' the honest settlers, it was confusion worse confounded."

Francis Grierson thus makes an exception to the usual procedure of American artists in the period after the war. He did, like so many others, find in Europe a more favorable environment in which to cultivate his talents, and these talents, as a result of transplanting, did become a little etiolated; but, instead of first dealing with American subjects and then dropping them for foreign ones, he began as a European writer who hardly rose above the second-rate and then reverted to the United States for the subject of a first-rate book. One of the oddest anomalies in our literary history is the spectacle of this rather pale fashioner of classical French *pensées* at last breaking out in the dialects of Mark Twain and Uncle Remus, and rivalling these storytellers in their own line. The appreciator of the modern French poets, the critic of Wagner and Nietzsche, proved, after all, to feel himself closer to Lincoln than he did to any of these. The celebrator of the Duchesse de La Roche-Guyon, the Comtesse de Beausacq and the Princesse Bonaparte-Rattazzi turned out to write a good deal more eloquently about Silas Jordan's wife, Kezia, than he had about any of these ladies, and his description of Kezia Jordan may well come to be counted among the noblest successes in describing the early American character:

"The sentiments she inspired in me were like those produced by the motion of clouds on a calm, moonlight night, or the falling of leaves on a still, dreamy day of Indian summer. There were moments when her presence seemed to possess something preternatural, when she imparted to others an extraordinary and superhuman quietude. Her spirit freed forever from the trammels and tumults of the world, seemed heedless of the passing moments, resigned to every secret and mandate of destiny;

for hers was a freedom which was not attained in a single battle — the conflict was begun by her ancestors when they landed at Plymouth Rock. In the tribulations that followed the successive generations were stripped of the superfluities of life. One by one vanities and illusions fell from the fighters like shattered muskets and tattered garments. Each generation, stripped of the tinsel, became acquainted with the folly of plaints and the futility of protests. Little by little the pioneers began to understand, and in the last generation of all there resulted a knowledge too deep for discussion and a wisdom too great for idle misgivings.

"Where was the hurried visitor from foreign lands who could sound the depths of such a soul?"

The Valley of Shadows is thus unique, and I agree with Bernard De Voto, that — so strangely disregarded by historians and by writers on American literature — the book fills "a niche . . ." — as De Voto says — "which no other book quite fits, and deserves to become a classic. It is true, as De Voto points out, that the interest of the story lapses when the family leave the log house and go to live in Alton and St. Louis. Up to then, we have been given a consecutive narrative and a constantly tightening tension, but this does not build up to a climax, to the dramatic revelation we have been led to expect. The war itself, when it comes, is shown only in a chapter on Grierson's raid and in the author's boyhood memories of Frémont.

But *The Valley of Shadows* was supplemented — even, one may say, completed — by Grierson's later essay on Lincoln in the volume called *The Humor of the Underman,* published in 1911, and by the small book called *Abraham Lincoln, the Practical Mystic* which he brought out in 1918. These ought to be read with *The Valley of Shadows.* In the latter, the author develops at length his special conception of Lincoln as the designated and conscious instrument through which larger forces were working. He had always had a cult of Lincoln, for whom perhaps his own combination of ungainliness — his enormous unmanageable hands and feet — with aesthetic and moral refinement had given him a particular sympathy. And here for the first time in his writings, in connection with this chief of his political heroes, the American religious spirit takes full possession of Grierson. We have had intimations before of its vigorous persistence in him. We may have been somewhat surprised to find in the volume called *The Celtic Temperament*, published in 1901, when we had thought him in his Francophile phase, two essays called *Hebraic Inspiration* and *Practical Pessimism*, with quotations from the Bible in Hebrew, which glorify the Jewish tradition at the expense of the Graeco-Roman. One wonders whether Tonner, his closest friend and his companion of forty-two years, may not have been himself Jewish and have supplied him with his Hebrew texts. But the insight of these two essays, which contain some of Grierson's best pages, is evidence of a natural affinity on the part of this half-Scottish American with Old Testament literature and thought. "Hebrew," he writes, "is the principal tongue in the hierarchy of languages, the mother of profound and exalted emotions, the most primitive and authoritative medium for the expression of transcendent praise and ineffable sorrows." And then, after an invidious description of the Greeks: "The grandeur of Israel is that the prophets and the singers all spoke with one voice. There are no discords, discussions, contradictions or schisms. [This is, of course, not true.] From the time that Moses descended from Sinai with the ten commandments, to the last recorded prophecy, there is but one spirit, one impulsion, one source and aim animating the whole." And: "The Jews on the one hand, and the Celts on the other, are awakening to a fresh appreciation of the realities of life. But the Israelite never lost the sense of unity embodied in the sacred writings of his ancestors. Here, and nowhere else, lies the explanation of the cohesive power of the modern followers of the Prophets. For in spite of the decadence of Jewry, from covetousness, there exists a vital spark of the old inspirations which has helped to enlighten and illuminate the remnants of Israel everywhere."

With the little book on Abraham Lincoln, Grierson becomes frankly millennial. The mood of apocalyptic expectation that he had known in the West in his childhood and had described in *The Valley of Shadows* has been stimulated in Grierson again — the *Lincoln* was published in 1918, toward the close of another war — and is carried here even further than when he wrote in the earlier book, as he reminds us now in the later, that the birth of the Republican party was accompanied by the appearance of a comet. It has been said by Dr. Paul Tillich, the émigré German theologian, that the cultural vocation of the United States was to realize the Kingdom of Heaven on earth, that the motive behind the American Dream and the American Way of Life — to use the current propaganda phrases — was primarily a religious one. It is somewhat surprising to hear that this expectation still survives as a phenomenon sufficiently general to be noticeable to a foreign theologian. Yet this vision, brought over to New England by the Pilgrims and carried on by the New England divines, had blazed up against the twilight of the Calvinist faith, at the beginning of the Civil War. We find it described as follows in the *Poganuc People* of Mrs. Stowe: "After the singing came Dr. Cushing's prayer — which was a recounting of God's mercies to New England from the beginning, and of her deliverances from her enemies, and of petitions for the glorious future of the United States of America — that they might be chosen vessels, commissioned to bear the light of liberty and religion through all the earth and to bring in the great millennial day, when wars should cease and the whole world, released from the thraldom of evil, should rejoice in the light of the Lord. The millennium was ever the star of hope in the eyes of the New England clergy; their faces were set eastward, towards the dawn of that day, and the cheerfulness of those anticipations illuminated the hard tenets of their theology with a rosy glow. They were children of the morning." And we now hear Francis Grierson still prophesying much in this vein. One can indicate the tenor of his *Lincoln* by a sequence of brief quotations: "Abraham Lincoln, the greatest practical mystic the world has known for nineteen hundred years, is the one man whose life and example ought to be clearly set before the English-speaking peoples at this supreme climax in the history of civilization. . . . His whole existence was controlled by influences beyond the ken of the most astute politicians of his time. His genius was superhuman. And since this world is not governed by chance, a power was at work which foreordained him for his unique mission . . . The renaissance of practical mysticism is now apparent both in and outside the churches but its greatest influence is exerted on that large class which, before the war [that is, the first World War], had no religious convictions of any kind. We have arrived at a climax in history. . . . That Lincoln possessed intuition and illumination without resorting to human aid is clear and irrefutable. His words were simple and his actions were simple, like those of the Hebrew seers . . . The universe was created by a Supreme Mind and the direction of affairs is in the hands of this All-Seeing Power, manifesting in all forms — sometimes personal, sometimes collective. In Lincoln's case it took a pronounced individual form, isolated and unique, as in Moses." This Supreme Mind, this All-Seeing Power, is not often mentioned by Grierson — though he sometimes, in these later writings, deplores what he calls agnosticism, so prevalent, he says, in his day, and insists upon the cardinal importance of a revival of religion through the churches. It is more characteristic of him that he should try to define in the following terms the "Destiny" which, as he says, "created," in Lincoln's case, "the man and the crisis at the same time, as always happens." "Destiny," he says, "is the collective conscience acting through elective genius." The *Lincoln* concludes as follows: "The principles enunciated by Abraham Lincoln are abiding examples, not only for the English-speaking peoples but for the whole world. Out of what seems universal confusion, tending towards chaos, there arises a new era. A material transformation had to occur before the uprising of the spiritual, and the truth is beginning to dawn in the minds of thousands that behind all material phenomena there dwells the divine idea. Before the gates of oblivion closed on civilization we were plucked from the gulf in accordance with the Divine purpose. Amidst the strife of contending factions the thunder of upheaval reverberates from continent to continent, heralding the close of a dispensation that has known the trials and triumphs of nearly two thousand years, from which is emerging the mystical dawn of a new day."

Francis Grierson, after *The Valley of Shadows*, wrote three inferior books: *The Invincible Alliance* in 1913, *Illusions and Realities of the War* in 1918, and *Psycho-Phone Messages* in 1921. All of these deal entirely or mainly with social and political problems, and all have an element of the apocalyptic, though the tendency of the prophecies shifts in response to current events. We see Grierson at his weakest in politics, but here, too, he is not without his intuitions. He had become by 1913 so thoroughly convinced that there was going to be a war between England and Germany that he brought his friend Tonner to the United States. He had a comprehensive view of the world and a touch of that practical shrewdness which he so much admired in Lincoln; but his realism that always stops short, his mystic glowings which do not quite reach intensity, make a less impressive showing here than they do in the field of the arts. His prophecies were in some cases accurate, in others entirely mistaken.

The last book that Grierson wrote — he was by this time seventy-three — was privately printed in Los Angeles, where Tonner and he were then living, and it shows signs of that exalted lightheadedness which is likely to seize prophets in that part of the world. It purports to be a series of messages, communicated by means of "the psycho-phone" — a device which is never explained — from the spirits of Jefferson, Franklin, Lincoln, Grant, John Marshall, Robert Ingersoll and other illustrious Americans, who warn the United States against her danger both from foreign aggression and from revolutionary ferment at home. Francis Grierson and his friend were now terribly poor. The pamphlet has a preface by Tonner, in which he explains to a public that could hardly have heard Grierson's name, what a celebrated and brilliant star his companion had formerly been: the oracle of the London *New Age*, "the central figure," as he puts it, of "the artistic and literary circles of Europe as well as the most intellectual of the royal courts." He quotes what Sully-Prudhomme had said about Grierson the first time he heard him play: "You have placed me on the threshold of the other world.

There are not words in the French language to express what I have felt tonight!"; and what Edwin Bjorkman had written: "As we read essay after essay, it is as if we beheld the globe of life revolving slowly between us and some unknown source of light." Six years later, when Grierson was seventy-nine, he and Tonner invited an audience to hear him play. They were going to take up a collection. When the pianist had finished his last improvisation, he continued to sit without turning around, his large hands resting still on the keys. "He often did that," says Tonner, "but it lasted too long, and I went up to him — he was gone." Tonner had been a tailor when he first made the acquaintance of Grierson, and now that he had been left by that elusive spirit with whom he had passed more than four decades, he applied to a Los Angeles relief agency, which set him up in a dry-cleaning shop.

Uncle Tom's Cabin and *The Valley of Shadows* have certain striking features in common. Each is unique in its author's career, for both were forced into being — almost, it would seem, accidentally — by the pressures of the ominous fifties. *Uncle Tom* is a *product* of this period, a dramatization of its conflicts; *The Valley of Shadows* is a kind of poem, an attempt to convey to a subsequent age an essence and an atmosphere. In both books, a sensitive consciousness, susceptible in Mrs. Stowe's case to undercurrents, in Grierson's, perhaps rather, to overtones, has registered the moment when the Civil War was looming as something already felt but not yet clearly foreseen: an ambiguous promise and menace, the fulfillment of some awful prophecy which had never quite been put into words. Grierson's *Proem* to *The Valley of Shadows* is colored by his own peculiar fantasy, yet — as we learn, also, from other sources — the climate of emotion it communicates was experienced by others, too.

"In the late 'Fifties,'" Grierson writes, "the people of Illinois were being prepared for the new era by a series of scenes and incidents which nothing but the term 'mystical' will fittingly describe.

"Things came about not so much by preconceived method as by an impelling impulse. The appearance of *Uncle Tom's Cabin* was not a reason, but an illumination; the founding of the Republican party was not an act of political wire-pulling, but an inspiration; the great religious revivals and the appearance of two comets were not regarded as coincidences, but accepted as signs of divine preparation and warning. [Mrs. Stowe also thought that the wave of revivals was a portent of the Judgment to come.]

"The settlers were hard at work with axe and plough; yet, in spite of material preoccupation, all felt the unnameable influence of unfolding destiny. The social cycle, which began with the Declaration of Independence, was drawing to a close, and during Buchanan's administration the collective consciousness of men — that wonderful prescience of the national soul — became aware of impending innovation and upheaval.

"It was impossible to tell what a day might bring forth. The morning usually began with new hope and courage; but the evening brought back the old silences, with the old, unsolved questionings, strange presentiments, premonitions, sudden alarms. Yet over and around all a kind of subconscious humor welled up, which kept the mind hopeful while the heart was weary. Dressed in butternut jeans, and swinging idly on a gate, many a youth of the time might have been pointed out as a likely Senator, poet, general, ambassador, or even President. Never was there more romance in a new

country. A great change was coming over the people
of the West. They retained all the best characteristics
of the Puritans and the settlers of Maryland and Virginia, with something strangely original and characteristic of the time and place, something biblical applied
to the circumstances of the hour.

"Swiftly and silently came the mighty influences.
Thousands labored on in silence; thousands were acting
under an imperative spiritual impulse without knowing
it; the whole country round about Springfield was being
illuminated by the genius of one man, Abraham Lincoln, whose influence penetrated all hearts, creeds, parties, and institutions."

And he tells, in his book on Lincoln, an anecdote to
demonstrate that Lincoln himself was aware of his destined role. As a young man of twenty-three, he attended,
says Grierson, a camp meeting at which "Dr. Peter Akers,
one of the greatest Methodist preachers of the time, was
about to preach a sermon on 'The Dominion of Christ.'"
The minister "declared that the Dominion of Christ could
not come in America until slavery was destroyed. His sermon lasted three hours, and he showed that a great civil
war would put an end to human bondage. 'I am not a
prophet,' he said, 'but a student of the Prophets.' . . .
When at last he cried out: 'Who can tell but the man who
shall lead us through this strife may be standing in this
presence!' a solemn silence fell over the assembly." When
Lincoln was asked later what he thought of the sermon, he
is supposed to have said to his friends: "Gentlemen, you
may . . . think it strange, but when the preacher was
describing the civil war, I distinctly saw myself, as in
second sight, bearing an important part in that strife."
The next morning Lincoln came late to his office. "Why,
Lincoln, what's the matter?" his law partner, William
Herndon, is supposed to have asked when he saw Lin-

coln's haggard face. "I am utterly unable," he answered, "to shake myself free from the conviction that I shall be involved in that terrible war."

The real causes of war still remain out of range of our rational thought; but the minds of nations at war are invariably dominated by myths, which turn the conflict into melodrama and make it possible for each side to feel that it is combatting some form of evil. This vision of Judgment was the myth of the North. If we study the Civil War as a political or an economic phenomenon, we may fail to be aware of the apocalyptic aspect it wore for many defenders of the Union; but this myth possessed the minds of the publicists, the soldiers and the politicians to an extent of which the talk about "Armageddon" at the time of the first World War can give only a feeble idea, and the literature of the time is full of it. Though Calvinism was being displaced by more liberal forms of religion — Unitarianism in New England dates from 1820 — the old fierceness, the old Scriptural assertiveness of the founders of the New England theocracy had not yet been wholly tamed by their children, and were ready to spring out at a challenge. William Lloyd Garrison, the leader of the Boston Abolitionists, had since 1834 been preaching in his paper, the *Liberator*, his intransigent crusade against slavery. Though he had broken with the traditional New England church, he exhibited all the old fanaticism, and when faced with the argument that the Constitution did guarantee property in slaves and provided no way of freeing them, he denounced it, in the language of Isaiah, as "a covenant with death and an agreement with hell." And this semi-religious fervor is felt in the passionate enthusiasm — a spirit that has not been displayed in any of our subsequent wars — with which the more idealistic of the Northern youth threw themselves into the regional conflict.

The songs these soldiers sang were like psalms. It is significant that in *John Brown's Body,* the Federals' favorite song, John Brown should be "a soldier in the army of the Lord"; and that Julia Ward Howe, when asked to provide for the popular tune a more dignified set of words, should have produced, in *The Battle Hymn of the Republic,* a more exalted version of the same idea. It will be worthwhile to scrutinize this poem, which, carried along by the old rousing rhythm, has persisted so long and become so familiar that we have ceased to pay attention to its sense. The *Battle Hymn* seems to have burst into life as uncontrollably as *Uncle Tom's Cabin.* The day after the suggestion was made, says Mrs. Howe in her *Reminiscences,* she woke in the early dawn, and "the long lines of the desired poem began to twine themselves in my mind." Fearing she might forget them, she made herself get out of bed and write them down "in the dimness" with "an old stump of a pen which I remembered to have used the day before. I scrawled the verses almost without looking at the paper."

Now, there were probably two influences at work in the just-awakened mind of Mrs. Howe when she composed *The Battle Hymn of the Republic.* She must certainly have taken her cue from Isaiah 63.1–6:

"1. Who is this that cometh from Edom, with dyed garments from Bozrah? this that is glorious in his apparel, travelling in the greatness of his strength? I that speak in righteousness, mighty to save. 2. Wherefore art thou red in thine apparel, and thy garments like him that treadeth in the winefat? 3. I have trodden the winepress alone; and of the peoples there was none with me: for I will tread them in mine anger, and trample them in my fury; and their blood shall be sprinkled upon my garments, and I will stain all my raiment. 4. For the day of vengeance is in mine heart, and the year of my redeemed is come. 5. And I looked, and there was none to help; and I wondered that there was none to uphold: therefore mine own arm brought salvation unto me; and my fury, it upheld me. 6. And I will tread down the people in mine anger, and make them drunk in my fury, and I will bring down their strength to the earth."

Macaulay had already made use of this passage in one of his *Songs of the Civil War*:

THE BATTLE OF NASEBY, BY OBADIAH BIND-THEIR-
KINGS-IN-CHAINS-AND-THEIR-NOBLES-WITH-LINKS-
OF-IRON, SERJEANT IN IRETON'S REGIMENT 1824

Oh! wherefore come ye forth, in triumph from the North,
    With your hands, and your feet, and your raiment all red?
And wherefore doth your rout send forth a joyous shout?
    And whence be the grapes of the wine-press which ye tread?

Oh, evil was the root, and bitter was the fruit,
    And crimson was the juice of the vintage that we trod;
For we trampled on the throng of the haughty and the strong,
    Who sat in the high places, and slew the saints of God.

.   .   .   .

Down, down, forever down, with the mitre and the crown,
    With the Belial of the Court, and the Mammon of the Pope;

There is woe in Oxford Halls; there is wail in Durham's
    Stalls:
  The Jesuit smites his bosom; the Bishop rends his cope.

And She of the seven hills shall mourn her children's
    ills,
  And tremble when she thinks on the edge of Eng-
    land's sword;
And the Kings of earth in fear shall shudder when they
    hear
  What the hand of God hath wrought for the Houses
    and the Word.

That Mrs. Howe, in what was doubtless unconscious
memory, went back directly to Isaiah is proved by her
writing "the grapes of wrath" instead of merely Macaulay's "grapes," and the meter of the *Battle Hymn* is
different from Macaulay's; but the *Hymn* does have
something in common with the poem on the Battle of
Naseby and may well have been suggested by it. In
this case, the cause of the North was associated by
Julia Ward Howe not merely with God's punishment of
the enemies of Israel but also with the victory over the
Royalists and Papists of Ireton's Cromwellian army.

Let us examine now the *Battle Hymn* itself:

Mine eyes have seen the glory of the coming of the Lord:
He is trampling out the vintage where the grapes of
    wrath are stored;
He hath loosed the fateful lightning of his terrible swift
    sword:
  His truth is marching on.

The advent of the Union armies represents, then, the
coming of the Lord, and their cause is the cause of God's
truth.

I have seen Him in the watch-fires of a hundred circling
    camps;
They have builded Him an altar in the evening dews
    and damps;
I can read His righteous sentence by the dim and flaring
    lamps.
    His day is marching on.

I have read a fiery gospel, writ in burnished rows of
    steel:
"As ye deal with my contemners, so with you my grace
    shall deal;
Let the Hero, born of woman, crush the serpent with
    his heel,
    Since God is marching on."

The Confederacy is a serpent, which God's Hero must
slay, and in proportion to the punishment inflicted by
this Hero on God's enemies, who are also his own, the
Deity will reward the Hero.

He has sounded forth the trumpet that shall never call
    retreat;
He is sifting out the hearts of men before his judgment-
    seat:
Oh! be swift, my soul, to answer Him! be jubilant, my
    feet!
    Our God is marching on.

The Lord is apparently checking on those who do and
those who do not enlist, so hurry up and join the Lord's
army!

In the beauty of the lilies Christ was born across the sea,
With a glory in his bosom that transfigures you and me:
As he died to make men holy, let us die to make men
    free,
    While God is marching on.

This stanza is particularly interesting on account of its treatment of Jesus, so characteristic of Calvinism. As is often the case with Calvinists, Mrs. Howe, though she feels she must bring Him in, gives Him a place which is merely peripheral. He is really irrelevant to her picture, for Christ died to make men holy; but this is not what God is having *us* do: He is a militant, a military God, and far from wanting us to love our enemies, He gives "the Hero" orders to "crush the serpent with his heel." The righteous object of this is to "make men [the Negroes] free," and we must die to accomplish this. Note that Christ is situated "across the sea"; he is not present on the battlefield with His Father, yet, intent on our grisly work, we somehow still share in His "glory." I have not been able to guess where Julia Ward Howe got these lilies in the beauty of which Jesus is supposed to have been born. The only lilies mentioned in the Gospels are those that toil not neither do they spin. Was she thinking of Easter lilies? But these are associated not with Christ's birth but with His resurrection. In any case, they serve to place Him in a setting that is effeminate as well as remote. The gentle and no doubt very estimable Jesus is trampling no grapes of wrath. And now come on, New England boys, get in step with the marching God! If you succeed in crushing the serpent, God will reward you with "grace." (This cheats on Predestination, but Mrs. Howe, "brought up," as she says, "after the strictest rule of New England Puritanism," had afterwards become more liberal.) It is probable that Abraham Lincoln is transformed into a Biblical patriarch in Stephen Foster's popular recruiting song: "We are coming, Father Abraham, three hundred thousand more." He was, in any case, by the end of the war, to be treated by the Northern crusaders with a reverence that was semi-religious. This was a feeling that had been gradually generated by the relation between Lincoln and his public. Alexander H. Stephens, the Vice-President of the Confederacy, said of Lincoln that, "the Union with him in sentiment rose to the sublimity of a religious mysticism" — an opinion which Francis Grierson quotes with approval. After Lincoln's assassination, when the great crusade had been successful, when Mrs. Howe's militant God was no longer needed and Lincoln's martyrdom had made him a saint, he was often assimilated to Jesus. This is made very clear in such poems about Lincoln as the two pieces by Herman Melville and Christopher Pearse Cranch which are both entitled *The Martyr* and have references to Good Friday and Calvary, and by a sonnet of Edmund Clarence Stedman's, which begins with the words of the crucified Jesus, "Forgive them, for they know not what they do." James Branch Cabell, the Virginian novelist, watched this process with irony and wonder, and in a volume of epistles to historical characters makes the most of the parallel with Jesus in congratulating John Wilkes Booth on having brought about the deification of Lincoln:

"It is not profitless, Sir, in this place to summarize our accredited knowledge of Lincoln as, the more thanks to your artistry, it survives in man's general belief. Abraham Lincoln was born in humble circumstances, in a mere barn, thitherto used as a stable. His nominal father was a carpenter: it is contended that, in point of fact, his real father was a person of considerably higher station. Abraham Lincoln was a reformer, maligned and abused by his perverse people. He was a seer and a prophet, foreknowing his own cruel doom, yet remaining always calm and meek and patient. He was saddened by the knowledge that he, who labored through self-immolation to redeem mankind from its sins, had come to bring not peace but a sword. He was killed, treacherously, upon

Good Friday: and was duly buried. A little while afterward his sepulchre was found to be vacant."

This last must refer to the removal of Lincoln's body from a burial vault in Springfield to the monument there. Cabell, of course, is having fun with these analogies, but his fundamental point is sound: the war leader has taken his place as a kind of martyred Messiah and become the central figure of the Northern myth.

Let us see how far Lincoln himself contributed to this Northern myth.

III

ABRAHAM LINCOLN

WHAT PRECISELY did Alexander Stephens mean when he said that for Lincoln the Union had risen to the sublimity of religious mysticism?

Whether or not it is true that Lincoln was troubled by the eloquence of the Methodist preacher mentioned by Francis Grierson, there is no evidence that, in early maturity, he ever saw the approaching crisis as an apocalyptic judgment or the possible war as a holy crusade. He was not a member of any church, and it is plain that in his earlier days, before he had become a great public figure, he was what was called a free-thinker. William Herndon, his law partner in Springfield, tells us that the young Lincoln had been associated, during his years at New Salem, with persons who had been strongly influenced by the skepticism of the eighteenth century, and that he had read Voltaire, Volney and Tom Paine. Later, in Springfield, when Herndon had brought to the office the books of Darwin, Spencer and Feuerbach, Lincoln had dipped into these. "He soon grew into the belief," says Herndon, "of a universal law, evolution, and from this he never deviated. Mr. Lincoln became a firm believer in evolution and [in] law. Of the truth of this there is no doubt and can be none. Mr. Lincoln believed in laws that imperiously ruled both matter and mind. With him there could be no miracles outside of law; he held that the universe was a grand mystery and a miracle. Nothing to him was lawless, everything being governed by law. There were no accidents in his philosophy. Every event had its cause. The past to him was the cause of the present and the present including the past will be the cause of the grand future and all are one, links in the endless chain, stretching from the infinite to the finite. Everything to him was the result of the forces of Nature, playing on matter and mind from the beginning of time," which would continue to do so "and will to the end of it . . . giving the world other, further, and grander results." Herndon says that Lincoln did not believe "that Jesus was . . . the son of God any more than any man," or "that the Bible was the special divine revelation of God as the Christian world contends," and he goes on to tell us that Lincoln, at some point in his middle twenties, before he had left New Salem, had even composed a long essay setting forth his views on religion, which he wanted to bring out as a pamphlet. But when he read it to the proprietor of the general store in which he was then working, his scandalized employer asked to look at it, then quickly thrust it into the stove. In 1842, when the thirty-three-year-old Lincoln delivers a remarkable address before the Springfield Temperance Society, it is quite evident that his hopes for the world are still confined to a human utopianism which does not yet embody the will of God. "Of our political revolution of '76 we are all justly proud," he says. "It has given us a degree of political freedom, far exceeding that of any other of the nations on the earth. In it the world has found a solution of the long mooted problem, as to the capability of man to govern himself. In it was the germ which has vegetated, and still is to grow and expand into the universal liberty of mankind." The march of this cause of political freedom, "cannot fail," he continues, "to be on and on, till every son of earth shall drink in rich fruition, the sorrow quenching draughts of perfect liberty. Happy day, when, all appetites controlled, all passions subdued, all matters subjected, *mind*, all conquering *mind*, shall live and move the monarch of the world. Glorious consummation! Hail fall of Fury! Reign of Reason, all hail!"

But when Lincoln was running for Congress in 1846, his Democratic opponent, a Methodist preacher, denounced him for infidelity. The candidate then made a point of writing and publishing in a local paper a statement of his religious views, the only one he ever made, which seems to have satisfied his public. When, however, we examine this closely, we discover that the supposed clarification is not really a confession of faith: it does not commit Lincoln to anything. Lincoln says that he has "never denied the truth of the Scriptures," but he does not say that he affirms this truth. "I have never spoken with intentional disrespect of religion in general, or of any denomination of Christians in particular" — which, of course, does not imply agreement. "It is true that in early life I was inclined to believe in what I understand is called the 'Doctrine of Necessity' — that is, that the human mind is impelled to action, or held in rest, by some power over which the mind itself has no control"; but he adds that he has only discussed this "with one, two or three, but never publicly," and has "entirely left off for more than five years." "I have always understood this same opinion to be held by several of the Christian denominations" — with which denominations, however, it is plain that he does not associate himself. He ends by remarking that he would not care to support any man for office "whom I know to be an open enemy of, and scoffer at, religion" — on the ground that no man "has the right to insult the feelings, and injure

the morals, of the community in which he may live."
There is nothing, so far, to conflict with Herndon's version of Lincoln's views. Herndon admits that Lincoln's
"Doctrine of Necessity" had a conception of divinity behind it. "He firmly believed in an overruling Providence,
Maker, God, and the great moral of Him written in the
human soul. His — late in life — conventional use of the
word God must not by any means be interpreted that he
believed in a personal God. I know that it is said Mr.
Lincoln changed his views. There is no evidence of this."
This overruling Providence, this Deity, which we find,
in the degree to which Lincoln advances to political
prominence, taking the place of such words as *Reason*
and *mind* in such an utterance as the Temperance Society speech, wears sometimes the more secular aspect of
the creative or the fatal operation of "history."

This conception of history as a power which somehow
takes possession of men and works out its intentions
through them is most familiar today as one of the characteristic features of Marxism, in which "history" has become the object of a semi-religious cult and has ended by
supplying the stimulus for a fanaticism almost Moham-
medan. But it was very widespread in the nineteenth
century, and appeared in other contexts, at the time
when the scientific study of the past had not yet disen-
tangled itself from the doctrine of divine Providence.
When we find Lincoln speaking as follows, in 1858, in
the course of his debates with Stephen A. Douglas, we
are made to feel the menace of "history" as a kind of
superhuman force that vindicates and overrides and that
manipulates mankind as its instruments: "Accustomed
to trample on the rights of others, you have lost the
genius of your own independence, and become the fit
subjects of the first cunning tyrant who rises among you.
And let me tell you that all these things are prepared

for you with the logic of history, if the elections shall promise that the next Dred Scott decision and all future decisions will be quietly acquiesced in by the people." And again, in his message to Congress of December 1, 1862: "Fellow-citizens, *we* cannot escape history. We of this Congress and this administration, will be remembered in spite of ourselves. No personal significance, or insignificance, can spare one or another of us. The fiery trial through which we pass, will light us down, in honor or dishonor, to the latest generation." But he needed something more in keeping than this doctrine of historical necessity with the Scriptural religious conceptions of most of his fellow Americans. His Methodist competitor for Congress had come close to injuring his reputation (just as Herndon's account in his *Life* of Lincoln's early skepticism was to give rise to such an outcry on the part of the clergy that the book on its first appearance, as a result of their influence, was virtually banned; though several times reprinted, it has never been popular). But it was not really easy for Lincoln's public to suspect him of a critical attitude toward the Scriptures, for the Bible was the book he knew best; he had it at his fingertips and quoted it more often than anything else. And he must now have deliberately adopted the practice of stating his faith in the Union and his conviction of his own mission in terms that would not be repugnant to the descendants of the New England Puritans and to the evangelism characteristic of his time. In this he went much further than Herndon, with his confidence in Spencer and Darwin, was willing to recognize. Lincoln's speeches, on the eve of his inauguration, are full of appeals to the Deity. "A duty devolves upon me," he says in his farewell address at Springfield, "which is, perhaps, greater than that which has devolved upon any other man since the days of Washington. He

never would have succeeded except for the aid of Divine
Providence upon which he at all times relied. I feel that
I cannot succeed without the same Divine aid which
sustained him, and on the same Almighty Being I place
my reliance for support, and I hope you, my friends, will
all pray that I may receive that Divine assistance without
which I cannot succeed, but with which success is certain." He continues in this vein in his subsequent
speeches; and we find him at last in his inaugural address describing the situation in the following terms: "If
the Almighty Ruler of nations, with his eternal truth
and justice, be on your side of the North or on yours of
the South, that truth, and that justice, will surely prevail, by the judgment of this great tribunal, the American people"; and, "Intelligence, patriotism, Christianity,
and a firm reliance on Him who has never yet forsaken
this favored land, are still competent to adjust, in the
best way, all our present difficulty."

He is to revert several times in the years that follow to
the attitude of God toward the war; and as the struggle
continues undecided, he becomes a good deal less sure that
the moral issue is perfectly clear, that the Almighty Ruler
of nations is committed to the side of the North. "The
will of God prevails," we find him writing in a document to which Nicolay and Hay gave the title *Meditation on the Divine Will*, a note found after his death,
which dates from the autumn of 1862, at a time when
he was much discouraged by the failures of George Mc-
Clellan, his General-in-chief. "In great contests each party
claims to act in accordance with the will of God. Both
may be, and one must be, wrong. God cannot be for
and against the same thing at the same time. In the
present civil war it is quite possible that God's purpose
is something different from the purpose of either party;
and yet the human instrumentalities, working just as

they do, are of the best adaption to effect his purpose. I am almost ready to say that this is probably true; that God wills this contest, and wills that it shall not end yet. By his mere great power on the minds of the now contestants, he could have either saved or destroyed the Union without a human contest. Yet the contest began. And, having begun, he could give the final victory to either side any day. Yet the contest proceeds." Two years later, in a letter to a Quaker lady, "we hoped," he writes, "for a happy termination of this terrible war long before this; but God knows best, and has ruled otherwise. . . . Surely he intends some great good to follow this mighty convulsion, which no mortal could make, and no mortal could stay." This line of anxious speculation is to culminate in the Second Inaugural Address. "Both," he writes there of the North and the South, "read the same Bible, and pray to the same God; and each invokes His aid against the other. It may seem strange that any men should dare to ask a just God's assistance in wringing their bread from the sweat of other men's faces; but let us judge not that we be not judged. The prayers of both could not be answered; that of neither has been answered fully. The Almighty has his own purposes. 'Woe unto the world because of offences! for it must needs be that offences come; but woe to that man by whom the offence cometh!' If we shall suppose that American Slavery is one of those offences which, in the providence of God, must needs come, but which, having continued through His appointed time, He now wills to remove, and He gives to both North and South this terrible war, as the woe due to those by whom the offence came, shall we discern therein any departure from those divine attributes which the believers in a Living God always ascribe to Him? Fondly do we hope — fervently do we pray — that this mighty scourge of war

may speedily pass away. Yet, if God wills that it continue, until all the wealth piled by the bond-man's two
hundred and fifty years of unrequited toil shall be sunk,
and until every drop of blood drawn with the lash, shall
be paid by another drawn with the sword, as was said
three thousand years ago, so still it must be said 'the judgments of the Lord are true and righteous altogether!' "

We are far here from Herndon's office, closer to Harriet Beecher Stowe. If the need on Lincoln's part, as a
public man, to express himself in phrases congenial to his
public may have had some part in inducing him to
heighten and personify the formulas of his eighteenth-
century deism, if it is true that as the war went on and
gave rise to more and more disaffection, it became more
and more to his interest to invoke the traditional Lord of
Hosts, it is nevertheless quite clear that he himself came
to see the conflict in a light more and more religious,
in more and more Scriptural terms, under a more and
more apocalyptic aspect. The vision had imposed itself.

And now let us put aside this Scriptural phraseology
and examine Lincoln's view of the war as a crisis in
American history and his conception of himself as an
American leader. Both of these emerge very early. Lincoln had always felt himself very close to the American
Revolution. He had been seventeen when Jefferson died;
his great hero was Henry Clay, who, in putting through
the Missouri Compromise, had averted a break with the
slave interests. He has from youth been acutely aware
that the survival of the Union may still be threatened,
and he has already had dreams of defending it. In a
speech on *The Perpetuation of Our Political Institutions,*
made before the Young Men's Lyceum of Springfield in
1838, when Lincoln was twenty-nine, he mounts up to

the following impassioned climax. At the time of the American Revolution, he says of its heroes and leaders, "all that sought celebrity and fame, and distinction, expected to find them in the success of that experiment. . . . They succeeded. The experiment is successful, and thousands have won their deathless names in making it so. . . . This field of glory is harvested, and the crop is already appropriated. But new reapers will arise, and *they,* too, will seek a field. It is to deny what the history of the world tells us is true to suppose that men of ambition and talents will not continue to spring up amongst us. And when they do, they will as naturally seek the gratification of their ruling passion as others have so done before them." You may assume that the young Lincoln is about to exhort his auditors to follow the example of their fathers, not to rest on the performance of the past but to go on to new labors of patriotism; but the speech takes an unexpected turn. "The question, then, is, can that gratification be found in supporting and maintaining an edifice that has been erected by others? Most certainly it cannot." He has been, it seems, preparing to deliver a warning: "Towering genius," he tells them, "disdains a beaten path. It seeks regions unexplored. . . . It *denies* that it is glory enough to serve under any chief. It scorns to tread in the footsteps of *any* predecessor, however illustrious. It thirsts and burns for distinction; and, if possible, it will have it, whether at the expense of emancipating slaves or enslaving freemen. Is it unreasonable then to expect that some man possessed of the loftiest genius, coupled with ambition sufficient to push it to its utmost stretch, will, at some time, spring up among us? And when such a one does, it will require the people to be united with each other, attached to the government and laws, and generally intelligent, to successfully frustrate his designs." Now, the effect of this is somewhat ambiguous: it is evident that Lincoln has projected himself into the role against which he is warning them. And a little less than two years later we find one of his political speeches winding up with the following peroration: "The *probability* that we may fall in the struggle *ought not* to deter us from the support of a cause we believe to be just: it *shall not* deter me. If ever I feel the soul within me elevate and expand to those dimensions not entirely unworthy of its Almighty Architect, it is when I contemplate the cause of my country, deserted by all the world beside, and I standing up boldly alone and hurling defiance at her victorious oppressors."

The young Lincoln, then, was extremely ambitious; he saw himself in an heroic role. He is aware in the earlier of these two speeches that the political tug-of-war going on between the two sections of the country gives a chance for "some man possessed of the loftiest genius" to perform a spectacular feat. Such a man would "thirst and burn for distinction . . . whether at the expense of emancipating slaves or enslaving freemen." And which was Lincoln to choose? He was not unsympathetic with the South. His father had come from Kentucky, and he told Herndon that his mother's father had been "a well-bred Virginia planter." He has started his political career with the party of the propertied interests, the Whigs, and he never shows anything of the animus of the leader who has come up from poverty. He did not approve of slavery, but he did not much resent the slaves' masters, and he was accustomed to say that if they of the North had found themselves in their opponents' situation they would undoubtedly have behaved like the planters. He is at first philosophic about slavery. Lincoln was once taken by a Springfield friend, Joshua F. Speed, for a visit to the latter's family on their plantation near Louisville, Kentucky, and on his return he wrote to Speed's half-sister (letter to Mary Speed, September 27, 1841) telling of their journey back: "By the way, a fine example was presented on board the boat for contemplating the effect of *condition* upon human happiness. A gentleman had purchased twelve negroes in different parts of Kentucky and was taking them to a farm in the South. They were chained six and six together. A small iron clevis was around the left wrist of each, and this fastened to the main chain by a shorter one at a convenient distance from, the others; so that the negroes were strung together precisely like so many fish upon a trot-line. In this condition they were being separated forever from the scenes of their childhood, their friends, their fathers and mothers, and brothers and sisters, and many of them, from their wives and children, and going into perpetual slavery where the lash of the master is proverbially more ruthless and unrelenting than any other where; and yet amid all these distressing circumstances, as we would think them, they were the most cheerful and apparantly happy creatures on board. One, whose offence for which he had been sold was an over-fondness for his wife, played the fiddle almost continually; and the others danced, sung, cracked jokes, and played various games with cards from day to day. How true it is that 'God tempers the wind to the shorn lamb,' or in other words, that He renders the worst of human conditions tolerable, while He permits the best, to be nothing better than tolerable." Years later, in a letter to the same friend (August 24, 1855), in which he discusses their political disagreements, he gives this incident a somewhat different emphasis: "You suggest that in political action now, you and I would differ. I suppose we would; not quite as much, however, as you may think. You know I dislike slavery; and you fully admit the abstract wrong of it. So far there

is no cause of difference. But you say that sooner than
yield your legal right to the slave — especially at the bidding of those who are not themselves interested, you
would see the Union dissolved. I am not aware that *any
one* is bidding you to yield that right; very certainly *I* am
not. I leave that matter entirely to yourself. I also acknowledge *your* rights and *my* obligations, under the
constitution, in regard to your slaves. I confess I hate to
see the poor creatures hunted down, and caught, and
carried back to their stripes, and unrewarded toils; but I
bite my lip and keep quiet. In 1841 you and I had
together a tedious low-water trip, on a Steam Boat from
Louisville to St. Louis. You may remember, as I well do,
that from Louisville to the mouth of the Ohio there
were, on board, ten or a dozen slaves, shackled together
with irons. That sight was a continual torment to me;
and I see something like it every time I touch the Ohio,
or any other slave-border. It is hardly fair for you to assume, that I have no interest in a thing which has, and
continually exercises, the power of making me miserable.
You ought rather to appreciate how much the great body
of the Northern people do crucify their feelings, in order
to maintain their loyalty to the constitution and the
Union."

But in the critical year of 1858, the forty-nine-year-old
Lincoln, now a public figure, who has served in Congress and is running against Stephen A. Douglas for the
Senate, takes definitely a new stand. The struggle over
slavery in Kansas and Nebraska was intensifying political antagonisms. The new Republican party had already
been organized — in 1854 — by Democratic and Whig
opponents of the Kansas-Nebraska Act, and northern
Democrats who had not become Republicans were now
being alienated by the efforts of the Democratic President, James Buchanan, to forestall secession by appeasing

the South. The debates, in their campaign for the Senate, between the Republican Lincoln and one of these anti-Buchanan Democrats drove Lincoln to make bold statements and to formulate a point of view which still exerts a very strong authority over the Northerner's conception of the Civil War. He had already in Springfield, on June 16, made his "House Divided" speech which reverberated all through the political world and which is echoing still in our minds: " 'A house divided against itself cannot stand.' I believe this government cannot endure, permanently half *slave* and half *free*. I do not expect the Union to be *dissolved* — I do not expect the house to *fall* — but I *do* expect it will cease to be divided. It will become *all* one thing, or *all* the other." How much Lincoln had staked on this speech is attested by W. H. Herndon, who tells Weik, in one of his letters, that Lincoln "was a good while preparing it . . . he was at it off and on about one month." When he read it to Herndon, "I emphatically said to him: 'Lincoln, deliver and publish your speech just as you have written it.' " This speech figured constantly in the debates with Douglas, and after Lincoln was defeated by him, "hundreds of friends," says Herndon, "flocked into the office and said to Lincoln, 'I told you that speech would kill you.' "

While the Lincoln-Douglas debates were going on, Senator W. H. Seward of New York State, taking his cue from Lincoln, delivered in Rochester, on October 25, another anti-slavery speech, which was also to have long reverberations:

"Russia yet maintains slavery, and is a despotism. Most of the other European states have abolished slavery and adopted the system of free labor. It was the antagonistic political tendencies of the two systems which the first Napoleon was contemplating when he predicted that Europe would ultimately be either all

Cossack or all republican. Never did human sagacity utter a more pregnant truth. The two systems are at once perceived to be incongruous. But they are more than incongruous — they are incompatible. They never have permanently existed together in one country, and they never can. It would be easy to demonstrate this impossibility, from the irreconcilable contrast between their great principles and characteristics. . . .

"Hitherto, the two systems have existed in different states, but side by side within the American Union. This has happened because the Union is a confederation of states. But in another aspect the United States constitute only one nation. Increase of population, which is filling the states out to their very borders, together with a new and extended net-work of railroads and other avenues, and an internal commerce which daily becomes more intimate, is rapidly bringing the states into a higher and more perfect social unity or consolidation. Thus, these antagonistic systems are continually coming into closer contact, and collision results.

"Shall I tell you what this collision means? They who think that it is accidental, unnecessary, the work of interested or fanatical agitators, and therefore ephemeral, mistake the case altogether. It is an irrepressible conflict between opposing and enduring forces, and it means that the United States must and will, sooner or later, become either entirely a slaveholding nation, or entirely a free-labor nation. Either the cotton and rice-fields of South Carolina and the sugar plantations of Louisiana will ultimately be tilled by free labor, and Charleston and New Orleans become marts for legitimate merchandise alone, or else the rye-fields and wheat-fields of Massachusetts and New York must again be surrendered by their farmers to slave culture and to the production of slaves, and

Boston and New York become once more markets for trade in the bodies and souls of men."

This social-political issue was thus dramatized by the rising and militant Republicans as presenting sensational alternatives, a choice which would affect all history; but the issue had also to be shown as fundamentally a moral one. In the last of his debates with Douglas (October 15), Lincoln speaks with a frankness and a vehemence which, in the previous ones, he has hardly released: his answer to his opponent becomes a sermon. Slavery is a *wrong*, and not merely "social and political" but "moral." "That is the real issue. That is the issue that will continue in this country when these poor tongues of Judge Douglas and myself shall be silent. It is the eternal struggle between these two principles — right and wrong — throughout the world. They are the two principles that have stood face to face from the beginning of time; and will ever continue to struggle. The one is the common right of humanity and the other the divine right of kings. It is the same principle in whatever shape it develops itself. It is the same spirit that says, 'You work and toil and earn bread, and I'll eat it.' [Loud applause.] No matter in what shape it comes, whether from the mouth of a king who seeks to bestride the people of his own nation and live by the fruit of their labor, or from one race of men as an apology for enslaving another race, it is the same tyrannical principle."

In his more famous Cooper Institute speech of February 27, 1860, on the eve of his campaign for the presidency, he reiterates this with even more eloquence: "If slavery is right, all words, acts, laws, and constitutions against it, are themselves wrong, and should be silenced, and swept away. If it is right, we cannot justly object to its nationality — its universality; if it is wrong, they cannot justly insist upon its extension — its enlargement.

All they ask, we could readily grant, if we thought slavery right; all we ask, they could as readily grant, if they thought it wrong. Their thinking it right, and our thinking it wrong, is the precise fact upon which depends the whole controversy. Thinking it right, as they do, they are not to blame for desiring its full recognition, as being right; but, thinking it wrong, as we do, can we yield to them? Can we cast our votes with their view, and against our own? . . . Neither let us be slandered from our duty by false accusations against us, nor frightened from it by menaces of destruction to the Government nor of dungeons to ourselves. LET US HAVE FAITH THAT RIGHT MAKES MIGHT, AND IN THAT FAITH, LET US, TO THE END, DARE TO DO OUR DUTY AS WE UNDERSTAND IT."

Now, Lincoln — as he explains in his debates with Douglas — did not think that, aside from his right to be free, the Negro deserved to be set on a basis of equality with the white man. "I have no purpose," he says, "to introduce political and social equality between the white and black races. There is a physical difference between the two, which, in my judgment, will probably forever forbid their living together on the footing of perfect equality, and inasmuch as it becomes a necessity that there must be a difference, I as well as Judge Douglas am in favor of the race to which I belong having the superior position. [Cheers, 'That's the doctrine.']" Nor had he approved of the Abolitionists. He believed that their furious agitation only made the situation worse; and even later, when the Republican party included a strong Abolitionist element, he took pains to dissociate himself from it. Yet his declarations that slavery was a *moral* issue, his talk about "right" and "wrong," made a connection between his policies and the spirit of the New England crusaders who were to turn the conflict of interests between the Northern and Southern states into a Holy War led by God. Though Lincoln was defeated in his contest with Douglas, his rivalry had prodded the latter into giving full expression to views sufficiently unfavorable to slavery to be quite inacceptable to the slave-owners and had thus deepened the split in the Democratic party which was to give the Republicans their chance; and Lincoln himself now stood out as a formidable public figure. He had indeed his heroic role, in which he was eventually to seem to tower — a role that was political through his leadership of his party; soldierly through his rank of commander-in-chief of the armies of the United States; spiritual — for persons like Grierson — as the prophet of the cause of righteousness. And he seems to have known that he was born for this.

Now, aside from this self-confident ambition, what kind of man was Lincoln? There has undoubtedly been written about him more romantic and sentimental rubbish than about any other American figure, with the possible exception of Edgar Allan Poe; and there are moments when one is tempted to feel that the cruellest thing that has happened to Lincoln since he was shot by Booth has been to fall into the hands of Carl Sandburg. Yet Carl Sandburg's biography of Lincoln, insufferable though it sometimes is, is by no means the worst of these tributes. It is useless if one tries to consult it for the source of some reported incident, but it does have its unselective value as an album of Lincoln clippings. It would, however, be more easily acceptable as a repository of Lincoln folk-lore if the compiler had not gone so far in contributing to this folk-lore himself. Here is Sandburg's intimate account of the behavior of Lincoln's mother, about whom almost nothing is known:

"She could croon in the moist evening twilight to the shining face in the sweet bundle, 'Hush thee, hush thee, thy father's a gentleman!' She could toss the bundle into the air against a far, hazy line of blue mountains, catch it in her two hands as it came down, let it snuggle to her breast and feed, while she asked, 'Here we come — where from?' And after they had both sunken in the depths of forgetful sleep, in the early dark and past midnight, the tug of a mouth at her nipples in the grey dawn matched in its freshness the first warblings of birds and the morning stars leaving the earth to the sun and dew." And here is his description of Lincoln in the days when, according to Herndon, he was in love with Ann Rutledge, about whom we know hardly more than we do about Lincoln's mother: "After the first evening in which Lincoln had sat next to her and found that bashful words tumbling from his tongue's end really spelled themselves out into sensible talk, her face, as he went away, kept coming back. So often all else would fade out of his mind and there would be only this riddle of a pink-fair face, a mouth and eyes in a frame of light corn-silk hair. He could ask himself what it meant and search his heart for an answer and no answer would come. A trembling took his body and dark waves ran through him sometimes when she spoke so simple a thing as, 'The corn is getting high, isn't it?'" The corn is getting high, indeed! To one of the most vigorous passages in Lincoln's debates with Douglas, his biographer has added the following comment: "He [Lincoln] was a sad lost man chanting a rhythm of the sad and lost."*

Carl Sandburg is not obnoxious when he is strumming his homely guitar and singing American ballads or in his chunks of Middle Western rhapsody that com-

---

* It should be noted that in a new edition of Sandburg's *Lincoln* a good deal of this matter has been removed.

bine the density of a Chicago block with the dryness of a Kansas drought; but Lincoln took him out of his depth, and the result was a long sprawling book that eventually had Lincoln sprawling. The amorphous and coarse-meshed Sandburg is incapable of doing justice to the tautness and the hard distinction that we find when, disregarding legends, we attack Lincoln's writings in bulk. These writings do not give the impression of a folksy and jocular countryman swapping yarns at the village store or making his way to the White House by uncertain and awkward steps or presiding like a father, with a tear in his eye, over the tragedy of the Civil War. Except in the debates with Douglas and some of his early productions, there is very little humor in these writings, and only the gravest sentiment. The dignity of the public utterances and the official correspondence of the Presidency is only infrequently varied by some curtly sarcastic note to a persistently complaining general or an importunate office-seeker. This is a Lincoln intent, self-controlled, strong in intellect, tenacious of purpose.

The raw realities of Lincoln's origins — the sordidness of his childhood environment, the boorishness of his first beginnings — are unflinchingly presented by Herndon, and the public has always found them repellent; but Herndon brings into the foreground Lincoln's genius and his will to succeed as the more romantic writers do not. From those who knew Lincoln best, we learn that he was naturally considerate, but essentially cold and aloof, not really caring much, Herndon tells us, about anyone but his wife and children. He seems always to have had the conviction of his own superiority. The legend of the log-cabin, the illiterate father, the rail-splitting, the flat-boat and all the rest has vulgarized Lincoln for the vulgar even in making him a backwoods saint. Aside from the possibility of his finding himself sustained by his belief that he came from good stock, he was able to derive self-confidence from knowing that, through physical strength, through sound character, through active brains and through personal charm, he had been able, with no other advantages,. to establish himself as a person of importance in rude pioneer Illinois, where most people started from scratch and where one had to have sound qualifications in order to command respect. Though Henry Adams makes a point of telling us that Lincoln, at his Inaugural Ball, had difficulty in managing his gloves, we never feel that he is seriously ill at ease or that he finds himself with others at any sort of disadvantage. "Mr. Lincoln was a curious being," says Herndon in a letter to Weik. "He had an idea that he was equal to, if not superior to, all things; thought he was fit and skilled in all things, master of all things, and graceful in all things," — adding, however, that he "had not good judgments; he had no sense of the fitness, appropriateness, harmony of things." "With all [Lincoln's] awkwardness of manner," wrote Don Piatt, a journalist who had seen a good deal of him, "and utter disregard of social conventionalities that seemed to invite familiarity, there was something about Abraham Lincoln that enforced respect. No man presumed on the apparent invitation to be other than respectful. I was told at Springfield that this accompanied him through life. Among his rough associates, when young, he was a leader, looked up to and obeyed, because they felt of his muscle and its readiness in use. Among his associates at the bar it was attributed to his wit, which kept his duller associates at a distance. But the fact was that this power came from a sense of reserve force of intellectual ability that no one took account of save in its results." John Hay, who was Lincoln's secretary and observed him at close range all the time he was in the White House, insisted that it was "absurd to call him a modest man. No great man is ever modest. It was his intellectual arrogance and unconscious assumption of superiority that men like Chase and Sumner could never forgive." It was this, too, that made it possible, even in suppressing opponents, for him to exercise a magnanimity unusual for a politician, especially in a period of crisis — as when he continued to keep Salmon P. Chase in his cabinet at the time when the latter was working against him and allowing Chase's followers to attack him in leaflets which he refused to read.

Two other descriptions of Lincoln by persons who had closely observed him insist upon his intellectual qualities. "Mr. Lincoln's perceptions," said Herndon, in a speech after Lincoln's death, "were slow, cold, clear and exact. Everything came to him in its precise shape and colour. To some men the world of matter and of man comes ornamented with beauty, life and action, and hence more or less false and inexact. No lurking illusion or other error, false in itself, and clad for the moment in robes of splendour, ever passed undetected or un-challenged over the threshold of his mind — that point that divides vision from the realm and home of thought. Names to him were nothing, and titles naught — assump-tion always standing back abashed at his cold, intellec-tual glare. Neither his perceptions nor intellectual visions were perverted, distorted or diseased. He saw all things through a perfect mental lens. There was no diffraction or refraction there. He was not impulsive, fanciful, or imaginative, but calm and precise." Add to this the following passages from the letters of the Marquis de Chambrun, writing to his mother from America. "Mr. Lincoln," he says, "stopped to admire an exceptionally tall and beautiful tree growing by the roadside and ap-plied himself to defining its particular beauties: powerful trunk, vigorous and harmoniously proportioned branches, which reminded him of the great oaks and beeches under whose shade his youth had been passed. Each different type he compared, in technical detail, to the one before us. His dissertation certainly showed no poetic desire to idealize nature; but if not that of an artist, it denoted extraordinary observation, mastery of descriptive language and absolute precision of mind. . . . No one who heard him express personal ideas, as though thinking aloud, upon some great topic or incidental question, could fail to admire his accuracy of judgment and rectitude of mind. I have heard him give opinions on statesmen and argue political problems with astounding precision. I have heard him describe a beautiful woman and discuss the particular aspects of her appearance, differentiating what is lovely from what might be open to criticism, with the sagacity of an artist. In discussing literature, his judgment showed a delicacy and sureness of taste which would do credit to a celebrated critic."

It must have been the Frenchman who turned Lincoln's attention to literature and beautiful women. But it is true that his sense of style was developed to a high degree. His own style was cunning in its cadences, exact in its choice of words, and yet also instinctive and natural; and it was inseparable from his personality in all of its manifestations. This style pervades Lincoln's speeches, his messages to Congress, his correspondence with his generals in the field as well as with his friends and family, his interviews with visitors to the White House and his casual conversation. Lincoln's editor, Mr. Roy P. Basler, in a study of Lincoln's style prefixed to a volume of selections from his writings, explains that the literary education of Lincoln was a good deal more thorough than used to be thought. "A careful examination," he says, of the books on elocution and grammar "which Lincoln studied both in and out of school will not impress anyone with Lincoln's poverty of opportunity for the study of grammar and rhetoric. It is safe to say that few children today learn as much through twelve years of formal schooling in these two subjects as one finds in the several textbooks which Lincoln is supposed to have studied." For it is true that the schoolbooks of the early nineteenth century taught not only the mechanics of writing — that is, of grammar and syntax — but also the art of rhetoric — that is, of what used to be called "harmonious numbers" and of dramatic and oratorical effectiveness. Here is a passage from a private letter dealing with personal matters which was written by Lincoln in his thirty-third year: "The second [cause of his correspondent's melancholy] is, the *absence* of *all business* and *conversation of friends,* which might divert your mind, and give it occasional rest from that *intensity* of thought, which will sometimes wear the sweetest idea threadbare and turn it to the bitterness of death." Here, in the final phrases, the balance of vowels and consonants, the assonance and alliteration, the progression from the long "e"s of "sweetest idea," over which one would want to linger, to the short and closed vowels of "bitterness of death," which chill the lyrical rhythm and bite it off at the end — all this shows a training of the literary ear that is not often taught in modern schools. The satirical *Letter from the Lost Townships,* written in 1842, which nearly cost Lincoln a duel, handles colloquial language with a similar sense of style: it is quite a successful experiment in the vein of homely frontier humor that Mark Twain was to bring to perfection; and the poems that Lincoln wrote four years later, when he revisited his old home in Indiana, show even a certain skill in a medium in which he was

less at home. He is describing a neighbor who had gone
insane and whose daft doleful singing he now remembers:

> I've heard it oft, as if I dreamed,
>   Far-distant, sweet, and lone;
> The funeral dirge it ever seemed
>   Of reason dead and gone.
>
> To drink its strains, I've stole away,
>   All silently and still,
> Ere yet the rising god of day
>   Had streaked the Eastern hill.
>
> Air held his breath; the trees all still
>   Seemed sorr'wing angels round.
> Their swelling tears in dew-drops fell
>   Upon the list'ning ground.

In his *Eulogy on Zachary Taylor*, delivered in 1850,
in striving for a loftier eloquence, he resorts, with less
successful results, to a kind of constricted blank verse.
Yet in prose, as in verse, he is working for the balance of
eighteenth-century rhythms, and he learns to disembarrass
these of eighteenth-century pomposity. He will discard
the old-fashioned ornaments of forensic and congressional
oratory, but he will always be able to summon an art
of incantation with words, and he will know how to
practice it magnificently — as in the farewell to Springfield, the Gettysburg speech and the Second Inaugural
Address — when a special occasion demands it. Alone
among American Presidents, it is possible to imagine Lincoln, grown up in a different milieu, becoming a distinguished writer of a not merely political kind. But actually the poetry of Lincoln has not all been put into his
writings. It was acted out in his life. With nothing of the

deliberate histrionics of the Roosevelts or of the evangelical mask of Wilson, he created himself as a poetic figure, and he thus imposed himself on the nation.

For the molding by Lincoln of American opinion was a matter of style and imagination as well as of moral authority, of cogent argument and obstinate will. When we put ourselves back into the period, we realize that it was not at all inevitable to think of it as Lincoln thought, and we come to see that Lincoln's conception of the course and the meaning of the Civil War was indeed an interpretation that he partly took over from others but that he partly made others accept, and in the teeth of a good deal of resistance on the part of the North itself. If you are tempted to suspect that the Lincoln myth is a backward-reading invention of others, a closer acquaintance with the subject will convince you that something like the reverse is true. Though Lincoln is not responsible for the element of exaggeration, humorous or sentimental, with which he himself has been treated, we come to feel that the mysticism of a Grierson in his *Lincoln* and *The Valley of Shadows,* as well as the surprising nobility, at once classical and peculiarly American, of the Grant of the *Personal Memoirs,* are in some sense the creations of Lincoln, and that Lincoln has conveyed his own legend to posterity in an even more effective way than he did to the America of the sixties.

Should we, too, have accepted this vision if we had lived at the time of the Civil War? Can an American be sure he would have voted for Lincoln, that he would even have wanted him as a candidate, in the election of 1864? The war was then in its fourth year, and hundreds of thousands of men had been killed without, as it seemed to many, having brought a decision nearer. Lincoln had just called for a draft of half a million more, though the draft of the summer before had set off in New York City a series of riots in which a thousand people had been killed or injured: Negroes had been shot and lynched, and Unionists' houses had been burned to the ground. The writ of habeas corpus had been suspended by Lincoln in spite of much public disapproval and an obstinate filibuster in Congress, and one of Lincoln's bitterest critics, the Democratic Congressman Clement L. Vallandigham, who had demanded that the fighting be stopped and the quarrel submitted to foreign arbitration, had been sent to jail for the duration of the war (though his sentence was later commuted to banishment behind the Confederate lines). To the Albany Democratic Convention, which had passed a set of resolutions condemning the suppression of civil liberties, the President had addressed a retort which asserted his uncompromising policy and showed his argumentative style at its most compelling: "The man who stands by and says nothing when the peril of his government is discussed, cannot be misunderstood. If not hindered, he is sure to help the enemy; much more if he talks ambiguously — talks for his country with *buts* and *ifs* and *ands*" (he should have said *ans*). Could this nasty situation have been averted? Should the war not have earlier been brought to an end? Could it not, in fact, have been prevented? Should Fort Sumter have been relieved? Would it not have been a good deal less disastrous if the South had been allowed to secede? All these questions have been debated; and yet — except, of course, in the South — the ordinary American does not often ask them. He does not doubt now that Lincoln was right. Did he not, by reducing the Confederacy to an unconditional surrender, save the Union and liberate the slaves? Lincoln's conduct of the Civil War is usually now accepted as one of the most conclusive and most creditable exploits of our history. If the war left a lasting trauma, and resulted in, not an apocalypse, but, on the one hand, a rather gross period of industrial and commercial development and, on the other, a severe disillusionment for the idealists who had been hoping for something better, these are matters about which we in the North have rarely thought and even less often spoken. We have, in general, accepted the epic that Lincoln directed and lived and wrote. Since it was brought to an end by his death the moment after the war was won, we are able to dissociate him entirely from the ignominies and errors of the Reconstruction and to believe he would have handled its problems better.

But let us see what Lincoln's epic leaves out. Of the strategy of the economic interests at work in the Civil War, which has been analyzed by Charles A. Beard in *The Rise of American Civilization* — a highly unconventional book when it was published in 1927 — you will get no inkling from Lincoln, for the reason that he had none himself. The tariff for the benefit of the Northern manufacturers — which prevented the South from buying goods from England more cheaply than they could from the North and had constituted one of their grievances — was raised higher during the years of the war than it ever had been before; the government presented enormous grants to the various railroad companies; and a prospect of high wages for labor encouraged by the absence of men in the army was averted, on behalf of the employers, by the Immigration Act of 1864, which authorized the importing of labor under terms that could compel the immigrant to pay for the cost of his journey by pledging his wages for as long as twelve months. At the end of the Civil War, the industrialists were firmly in the saddle, but of what this implied for the future Lincoln had had no idea.

He refers on several occasions to the relations of capital and labor, and does not seem to be aware how completely the Republican party is already the champion of the former, for he always arrives at the conclusion that capital overrates its importance, since labor can get along without capital whereas capital cannot get along without labor, and is, in fact, as he says, "the fruit of labor, and could never have existed if labor had not first existed." Though he examined the mechanical devices that were brought to him in the years of his Presidency and is reported to have understood them, he does not seem to have been much impressed by the development of machinery in America or even much interested in it. In a speech before the Wisconsin State Agricultural Society, in 1859, he takes rather a dubious view of the prospects of the steam plow, and a lecture delivered in the same year on the subject of "Discoveries, Inventions, and Improvements" is a curious production for its period and was quite comprehensibly not a success, since most of the speech was devoted to extolling the value to humanity of language and the art of writing, the only discovery, invention or improvement that appears to have excited his enthusiasm. This was perfectly natural for Lincoln, since he evidently felt that the use of the Word was the only technique he needed; and for him, in his impoverished youth, it had been also a discovery and an improvement. Nor did he compensate for his indifference to industry by a sympathetic solicitude for agriculture. He does not seem to have looked back with pleasure on his labors in his boyhood on his father's farm, much publicized though these were, and when he writes to a friend who is working the land, it is usually in the vein of "I am so glad it is you and not I who are trying to run that farm." Though he tells his Wisconsin audience that, since the farmers in the United States constitute the largest occupational group, they are "most worthy of all to be cherished and cultivated," he hopes that he will not be expected to flatter them "as a class" or "to impart to you much specific information on agriculture," because, as he says, "you have no reason to believe, and do not believe, that I possess it."

Lincoln begins as a provincial lawyer and soon becomes a politician of more than provincial importance. His real vocation was for what we call statesmanship, and, as a statesman, he was entirely absorbed by the problems created by secession — though, under pressure of the necessity of winning the war, he was forced to become something of a military strategist. From the moment of his advent to the Presidency just after the withdrawal of seven states, he had of course little opportunity to occupy himself with anything else.

It is partly these limitations that give Lincoln's career its unity, its consistency, its self-contained character. He is not tempted to dissipate his energies; he has no serious conflicts of interest. Everything hangs together. He is conscious from the first of his public role, not only in relation to the history of his country but also in relation to the larger world, for which all the old values will be modified, the social relations altered, if it is possible to prove to it the practicability of the principles of our revolutionary documents. With conviction and persistence he performs this role, and he is always articulate in it. He has always had a sense of drama, as appears in the debates with Douglas, which seem actually to have proved effective when they were recently put on the stage, and now every word that he utters belongs to his part as President. In order to appreciate Lincoln's lines, you have, of course, to know the whole drama. A foreigner who did not know our history might be able to hear the music of the Second Inaugural and the Gettysburg Addresses yet at the same time not fully grasp the reasons for the powerful emotional effect that they have on Lincoln's fellow-Americans; and as for the letter to Mrs. Bixby, such a visitor might be quite at a loss to account for the elaborate trouble that has been taken to track Mrs. Bixby down and to authenticate that the letter is really by Lincoln and not by his secretary John Hay. These things must be felt in their contexts, where they speak to us with all the power of Lincoln's inspired conception of his role in the Civil War.

The dreams and premonitions of Lincoln are also a part of this drama, to which they contribute an element of imagery and tragic foreshadowing that one finds sometimes in the lives of poets — Dante's visions or Byron's last poem — but that one does not expect to encounter in the career of a political figure: Lincoln's recurrent dream of a ship on its steady way to some dark and indefinite shore, which seemed to prophesy that the war would be going well, since it had always been followed by a victory; his ominous hallucination, after the election of 1860, when, lying exhausted on a sofa, he saw in a mirror on the wall a double reflection of his face, with one image paler than the other, which his wife had taken as a sign that he would be elected to a second term but that he would not live to complete it. He repeated this story to John Hay and others the night of his second election, and a few days before his death he had spoken of a more recent dream, in which he had seen a crowd of people hurrying to the East Room of the White House and, when he followed them, found his own body laid out and heard voices saying, "Lincoln is dead."

Herndon tells us that in the early days in Springfield, Lincoln would say to him, "Billy, I fear that I shall meet with some terrible end." But although he had been shot at in '62 when he was riding in the streets of Washington, he would not have a bodyguard; he explained that he wanted the people to know that "I come among them without fear." He would take walks in the middle of the night alone. It was only in the November of 1864 that four plain-clothesmen were posted at the White House. On his way back to Washington from his visit to Richmond just after the city's surrender, he read to his companions on the boat the scene from *Macbeth* that contains the lines:

> Duncan is in his grave;
> After life's fitful fever he sleeps well;
> Treason has done his worst: nor steel, nor poison,
> Malice domestic, foreign levy, nothing,
> Can touch him further.

The night before Lincoln was murdered, he dreamed again of the ship approaching its dark destination. He had foreseen and accepted his doom; he knew it was part of the drama. He had in some sense imagined this drama himself — had even prefigured Booth and the aspect he would wear for Booth when the latter would leap down from the Presidential box crying, '*Sic semper tyrannis!*' Had he not once told Herndon that Brutus was created to murder Cæsar and Cæsar to be murdered by Brutus? And in that speech made so long before to the Young Men's Lyceum in Springfield, he had issued his equivocal warning against the ambitious leader, describing this figure with a fire that seemed to derive as much from admiration as from apprehension — that leader who would certainly arise among them and "seek the gratification of [his] ruling passion," that "towering genius" who would "burn for distinction, and, if possible . . . have it, whether at the expense of emancipating slaves or enslaving freemen." It was as if he had not only foreseen the drama but had even seen all around it with a kind of poetic objectivity, aware of the various points of view that the world must take toward its protagonist. In the poem that Lincoln lived, Booth had been prepared for, too, and the tragic conclusion was necessary to justify all the rest.

It is not to be doubted that Lincoln, in spite of his firm hand on policy, had found his leadership a harrowing experience. He had himself, one supposes, grown up in pain. The handicaps imposed by his origins on his character and aspirations must have constrained him from his earliest years, and his unhappy relations with women, the tantrums and pretensions of his rather vulgar wife, and the death of two of his sons must have saddened and worried and humiliated him all through his personal life. The humorous stories and readings that his cabinet sometimes found so incongruous only served, as he once explained, as a relief from his fits of despondency, his constant anxiety about the war. Though not warm in his personal relationships, he was sensitive to the pain of others. He had remembered from fourteen years before that the sight of the slaves on the steamboat had been "a continual torment," and though he had pardoned, whenever it was possible, the soldiers who had been sentenced to death, he had been compelled by his office to authorize the executions of two hundred and sixty-seven men. He must have suffered far more than he ever expressed from the agonies and griefs of the war, and it was morally and dramatically inevitable that this prophet who had crushed opposition and sent thousands of men to their deaths should finally attest his good faith by laying down his own life with theirs.

IV

NORTHERN SOLDIERS: ULYSSES S. GRANT

When Mark Twain, in 1881, first met ex-President Grant, he tried to persuade him to write his memoirs. Grant, says Mark Twain, "wouldn't listen to the suggestion. He had no confidence in his ability to write well; whereas we all know now that he possessed an admirable literary gift and style. He was also sure that the book would have no sale, and of course that would be a humility, too. I argued that the book would have an enormous sale, and that out of my experience I could save him from making unwise contracts with publishers, and would have the contract arranged in such a way that they could not swindle him, but he said he had no necessity for any addition to his income."

Three years later, however, Grant was ruined by the colossal swindle in which he had lost almost all his money as well as that of several of his relatives and a large loan that William H. Vanderbilt had made him; and he agreed to write a book for the Century Company. When Mark Twain heard about this, he went to talk to Grant about it. He discovered that the Century people had been telling Grant that they expected to sell only from five to ten thousand copies, and that they were offering him only ten percent royalties. The successful humorist insisted to Grant that he ought to try for better terms elsewhere. The old general had been made the victim, both as President and in his recent speculation, of a whole ghastly series of confidence games, but he had still so little head for business that, since the Century Company had asked him first, he did not want to take the book to another publisher. Mark Twain replied that, in that case, Grant ought to give the book to him — he was at that time himself a publisher — since it was he who had suggested it first. Grant was struck by the justice of this, but thought Mark Twain was going too far, taking far too great a risk out of kindness, in offering him twenty percent on the list price or seventy percent of the net returns. The first of these arrangements he would not allow, but he was finally persuaded to accept the second. If the book made no money, he said, Mark Twain would not owe him anything. And he set out to write the memoirs under handicaps as serious as any that he had faced in the Civil War. Grant was ill: he was suffering from cancer of the throat. But he dictated the first part of the manuscript, and when it became impossible to use his voice — in increasing discomfort or pain, which, alleviated by doses of cocaine, he bore with his usual fortitude — he wrote out the rest of the story. He finished it in eleven months, and died about a week later, July 23, 1885. The book sold three hundred thousand copies in the first two years after publication, a little less than half as many as *Uncle Tom's Cabin*, and made $450,000 for Grant's impoverished family. The thick pair of volumes of the *Personal Memoirs* used to stand, like a solid attestation of the victory of the Union forces, on the shelves of every pro-Union home. Today, like *Uncle Tom*, they are seldom read by anyone save students of the Civil War; yet this record of Grant's campaigns may well rank, as Mark Twain believed, as the most remarkable work of its kind since the *Commentaries* of Julius Cæsar. It is also, in its way — like Herndon's *Lincoln* or like *Walden* or *Leaves of Grass* — a unique expression of the national character.

Owen Wister has said truly, in his little book on Grant, that Grant's was an even odder case than Lincoln's. For Lincoln had been always ambitious: he had passionately desired to distinguish himself as a political figure, he had a "call" to lead the country in its crisis. Even during his years of obscurity, he had always been hardworking, effective; there are in Lincoln's career no real slumps. But Grant — the son of a tanner, born in Ohio in a two-room cabin — had never given people the impression that he had any very high ambition. He did not want to work in his father's tannery, and he said that he much preferred farming to any other occupation. When his father shipped him off to West Point, he went there without enthusiasm. "If I could have escaped West Point without bringing myself into disgrace at home," he once told John Russell Young, his companion on his journey around the world, "I would have done so. I remember about the time I entered the academy there were debates in Congress over a proposal to abolish West Point. I used to look over the papers, and read the Congress reports with eagerness to see the progress the bill made, and hoping that the school had been abolished." When he graduated, he tells us in his *Memoirs*, he had had no idea of remaining in the army and had wanted to prepare himself for a professorship of mathematics "in some college." He was, however, ordered off to the Mexican War, of which he did not approve. "I do not think," he said to Young, in his later years, "there was ever a more wicked war than that waged by the United States on Mexico. I thought so at the time, when I was a youngster, only I had not moral courage enough to resign: I had taken an oath to serve eight years, unless sooner discharged, and I considered my supreme duty was to my flag. I had a horror of the Mexican War, and I have always believed that it was on our part most unjust." He served in the quartermaster department, and when the war was over, he spent six years in a succession of dreary posts. He eventually took to drink and was made to resign from the army. The seven years that followed were equally depressing: he tried several occupations — selling real estate, clerking in a custom house, running for county engineer — and failed in every one. He was regarded at one point, in St. Louis, as so hopeless a down-and-outer that, fearing they would be asked for a loan, people sometimes crossed the street in order not to meet him. He ended by working in a leather store — in Galena, Illinois — which was run by his two younger brothers.

But it was characteristic of Grant that a period of moral collapse should have been followed by a period of intense concentration. When Fort Sumter was fired upon, he immediately volunteered. He was at that time thirty-nine. I shall not retrace his campaigns nor show how, through the exercise of this power of concentration, he came to be assigned by Lincoln to the top leadership of the Union armies. But since he does not in his *Personal Memoirs* either emphasize his own exceptional qualities or celebrate his own achievements, one must cite, in connection with the *Memoirs,* the testimony of such close associates as his military secretary Adam Badeau and his aide-de-camp Horace Porter to Grant's poise and detachment in the field — the qualities which also distinguish his writing. Badeau says of Grant that he "never braved danger unnecessarily; he was not excited by it, but was simply indifferent to it, was calm when others were aroused. I have often seen him sit erect in his saddle when everyone else instinctively shrank as a shell burst in the neighborhood. Once he sat on the ground writing a dispatch in a fort just captured from the enemy, but still commanded by another near. A shell burst immediately over him, but his hand never shook, he did not look up, and continued the dispatch as calmly as if he had been in camp." Horace Porter tells similar stories. "Ulysses don't scare worth a damn," was said of him by one of his soldiers. When he was writing dispatches at Petersburg, exposed to the enemy's fire, and this fire "became hotter and hotter, several of the officers, apprehensive for the general's safety, urged him to move to some less conspicuous position; but he kept on writing and talking, without the least interruption from the shots falling around him, and apparently not noticing what a target the place was becoming or paying any heed to the gentle reminders to 'move on.' After he had finished his dispatches he got up, took a view of the situation, and as he started toward the other side of the farmhouse said with a quizzical look at the group around him: 'Well, they do seem to have the range on us.'" "This calmness was the same," says Badeau, "in the greatest moral emergencies. At the surrender of Lee, he was as impassive as on the most ordinary occasion; and until some of us congratulated him, he seemed scarcely to have realized that he had accomplished one of the greatest achievements in modern history."

But this constant attentiveness and self-control put Grant under a terrible strain, and whenever there was a break in the tension of war, he was likely to revert to the bottle. During the winter of 1862–63, when he was waiting to capture Vicksburg, he indulged in a private spree on a boat on the Mississippi. The facts about these aberrations had always been kept rather dark and very little had been known about them till the recent publication of a memoir — *Three Years with Grant* — by a man

named Sylvanus Cadwallader, a correspondent for the
New York *Herald,* who had been very close to the General and come to occupy a kind of privileged position.
He could not bring himself to put these memories on
paper till he was seventy years old, in the middle nineties
— "To speak the whole truth," he writes, "concerning
General Grant's periodical fits of intemperance has required all the courage I could summon" — and the Illinois State Historical Library, which had acquired the
manuscript, did not get to the point of publishing it till
1955. Cadwallader was, it seems, on the boat with Grant
at the time of his Vicksburg debauch. He says that Grant
— making no concealment — simply stupefied himself
with whisky. Cadwallader first made an effort to induce
the officers aboard to do something to restrain the General, but they felt that this would amount to insubordination, and it developed upon the civilian Cadwallader to "take the General in hand." "I . . . enticed him
into his stateroom, locked myself in the room with him,
and commenced throwing bottles of whiskey . . .
through the windows . . . into the river. Grant soon
ordered me out of the room, but I refused to go . . . I
said to him that I was the best friend he had in the
Army of the Tennessee; that I was doing for him what
I hoped someone would do for me, should I ever be in
his condition." Eventually, "after much resistance," he
got Grant to take off his clothes and lie down, and "soon
fanned him to sleep." The next day they landed, and the
General, having had too much whisky again, began putting the spurs to his horse "the moment he was in the
saddle, and the horse darted away at full speed before
anyone was ready to follow. The road was crooked and
tortuous, following the firmest ground between the
sloughs and bayous. . . . Each bridge had one or more
guards stationed at it, to prevent fast riding or driving

over it; but Grant paid no attention to roads or sentries. He went at about full speed through camps and corrals, heading only for the bridges, and literally tore through and over everything in his way. The air was full of dust, ashes, and embers from campfires; and shouts and curses from those he rode down in his race." Cadwallader pursued him, caught up with him, and again had to get him to sleep, this time "on the grass, with the saddle for a pillow." The next day he dreaded seeing Grant, thinking he would be embarrassed, and "purposely kept out of his way," but when he did meet the General again, Grant did not, to Cadwallader's surprise, "make the most distant allusion" to the incident. "But there was a perceptible change in his bearing towards me. I was always recognized and spoken to as if I had been regularly gazetted as a member of his staff. My comfort and convenience was considered; a tent pitched and struck for me whenever and wherever I chose to occupy it."

It was difficult, Cadwallader says, for people who had only seen Grant in the aspect he usually wore to credit these dissipations. Unlike a Sherman or a Sheridan, he never used profanity or betrayed excitement; his habitual coolness and self-restraint were always an important factor in keeping up the morale of his men. Cadwallader adds a notable instance to the many already recorded. Grant, he says, at the siege of Vicksburg, "had gone into the cramped exposed redoubt to see how the work was progressing and, noticing the reluctance with which the men could be brought to the open embrasure, deliberately clambered on top of the embankment in plain view of the sharpshooters, and directed the men in moving and placing the guns. The bullets zipped through the air by dozens, but strangely none of them touched his person or his clothing. He paid no attention to appeals or expostulations, acting as though they were not heard; and smoked quietly and serenely all the time, except when he removed his cigar to speak to the men at work. His example shamed the men into making a show of courage; but several were wounded before he left the place."

There occurred, as Sherman tells us, after Vicksburg, "a general relaxation of effort, a desire to escape the hard drudgery of camp: officers sought leaves of absence to visit their homes, and soldiers obtained furloughs and discharges on the most slender pretexts"; and Grant himself was not proof against this. He was drunk on dress parade in New Orleans and afterwards fell off his horse. He spent twenty-one days in bed and had to go limping to Chattanooga, the scene of the next of his victories.

But when the effort of the war was over, he did not again go to pieces. His wife was now constantly with him, and she always had a stabilizing effect on him. Detached from the troops that he manipulated as well as from his fellow officers, living alone with his responsibility, he had required a close human relationship, and Julia Grant had been brought on, when possible, in the lulls of her husband's campaigning.

Before one goes on to the *Personal Memoirs*, it is worthwhile to call attention to one of Grant's notes to his doctor, written just before his death when he could not speak: "If I live long enough I will become a sort of specialist in the use of certain medicines, if not in the treatment of disease. It seems that man's destiny in this world is quite as much a mystery as it is likely to be in the next. I never thought of acquiring rank in the profession I was educated for; yet it came with two grades higher prefixed to the rank of General officer for me. I certainly never had either ambition or taste for political life; yet I was twice President of the United States. If anyone had suggested the idea of my becoming an author, as they frequently did, I was not sure whether they were making sport of me or not. I have now written a book which is in the hands of the manufacturers. I ask that you keep these notes very private lest I become an authority on the treatment of diseases, I have already too many trades to be proficient in any. Of course I feel very much better for your application of cocaine, the first in three days, or I should never have thought of saying what I have said above."

But the book that Grant had written turned out to be another of his victories. The *Personal Memoirs of U. S. Grant* has had a number of distinguished admirers who were primarily interested in literature rather than war. I have spoken of Mark Twain's appreciation. Matthew Arnold devoted a long essay to the *Memoirs* in his *Civilization in the United States,* written after his trip to America. "I found in [the *Personal Memoirs*]," he says, in his lofty way, after explaining that when he had met Grant in England, he had thought him a dull fellow: "a man, strong, resolute and business-like, as Grant had appeared to me when I first saw him; a man with no magical personality, touched by no divine light and giving out none. I found a language all astray in its use of *will* and *shall, should* and *would,* an English employing the verb *to conscript* and the participle *conscripting,* and speaking in a dispatch to the Secretary of War of having *badly whipped* the enemy; an English without charm and without high breeding. But at the same time I found a man of sterling good-sense as well as of the firmest resolution; a man, withal, humane, simple, modest; from all restless self-consciousness and desire for display perfectly free; never boastful where he himself was concerned, and where his nation was concerned seldom boastful, boastful only in circumstances where nothing but high genius or high training, I suppose, can save an American from being boastful. I found a language straightforward, nervous, firm, possessing in general the high merit of saying clearly in the fewest possible words what had to be said, and saying it, frequently, with shrewd and unexpected turns of expression."

It may perhaps seem stranger that the *Personal Memoirs* should have been one of the favorite books of Gertrude Stein, and that, in her volume called *Four in America,* she should have written about the author at length. But it is not really difficult to understand what Gertrude Stein admired in Grant, what she must have felt she had in common with him: his impassivity, his imperturbability, his persistence in a prosaic tone combined with a certain abstractness which she regarded as essentially American and which was also, I think, one of the reasons for her enjoyment of Frank Stockton and Henry James. She must have found in him a majestical phlegm, an alienation in the midst of action, a capacity for watching in silence and commanding without excitement. The impression produced by her curious portrait is that Miss Stein has been led by this aloof side of Grant to fancy that in other circumstances he might have become a religious leader, or rather, perhaps, that there was an aspect of Grant which had something in common with the leaders of religions. Grant did certainly present like Miss Stein a mask that was hard to penetrate, did share with her some quality that was not of this world but which yet did not seem to relate itself to the other world of the mystic. It is interesting in this connection to note a passage in a letter to Gertrude Stein by Lloyd Lewis, one of Grant's biographers: "My mind harps on Grant and religion ever since I began reading your MS. . . . Morale was stiffened upon his every advent. This is not much different than a conviction of salvation. People didn't star him as a savior, nor perhaps as the worker of miracles at all. But they did begin to believe in themselves . . . He could do this without sermons or oratory of any kind. I don't know how he did it . . . Your religious concepts of the situation are the best I have read on this puzzling point." Yet in any literal sense Grant was not religious at all. Though he thoroughly believed in the Union cause as he had not in our war with Mexico, it is evident that the war did not wear for him that aspect of Armageddon, the heritage of the older Puritanism, that excited the Abolitionists and that came to influence Lincoln. Only rarely did Grant express himself in terms of the New England mythology, as when, for example, on one occasion, he said to John Russell Young that "it was only after Donelson that I began to see how important was the work that Providence devolved upon me," or to Lincoln, in his speech of acceptance of his commission of lieutenant general: "I feel the full weight of the responsibilities now devolving on me, and I know that if they are met it will be due to those armies, above all, to the favor of that Providence which leads both nations and men." When a clergyman complained to Grant that too many battles were taking place on Sunday, he replied: "You see, a commander, when he can control his own movements, usually intends to start out early in the week so as not to bring on an engagement on Sunday; but delays occur often at the last moment, and it may be the middle of the week before he gets his troops in action. Then more time is spent than anticipated in manœuvring for position, and when the fighting actually begins it is the end of the week, and the battle, particularly if it continues a couple of days, runs into Sunday." "It is unfortunate," commented the clergyman. "Yes, very unfortunate," admitted Grant. "Every effort should be made to respect the Sabbath day, and it is very gratifying to know that it is observed so generally throughout our country." On his deathbed, when a preacher came to pray with him, Grant said he did not mind how much praying he did if it made his wife and children feel better. And yet in what Grant did and in what he wrote, it is true that there is something of the driving force, the exalted moral certainty, of Lincoln and Mrs. Stowe. The completely non-religious Sherman once paid him the very strange compliment of writing to Grant that his feeling about him, at the time when he had been fighting under the General's command, could be likened "to nothing else than the faith a Christian has in his Savior." Alexander H. Stephens, the Vice-President of the Confederacy, whose remark about Lincoln I have already quoted, said of Grant when he had seen him, near the end of the war, at the time of the Confederate peace mission: "He is one of the most remarkable men I have ever met. He does not seem to be aware of his powers."

This capacity for inspiring confidence, this impression Grant gave of reserves of force, comes through in the *Personal Memoirs* without pose or premeditation. Grant faltered a little in the later chapters — sometimes repeating himself — when his sufferings blur the text; but, in general, the writing of the *Memoirs* is perfect in concision and clearness, in its propriety and purity of language. Every word that Grant writes has its purpose, yet everything seems understated. We see the reason for his special admiration for the style of Zachary Taylor: "He knew how to express what he wanted to say in the fewest well-chosen words, but would not sacrifice meaning to the construction of high-sounding sentences." That no one can have tampered much with the original text of the *Memoirs* — it was rumored that Mark Twain had ghosted it and Badeau, after Grant's death, made a claim to have written most of it — is proved by the complete uniformity of their style with that of Grant's dispatches, his letters and his recorded conversations. "In conversation," says Young, "he talks his theme directly out with care, avoiding no detail, correcting himself if he slips in a detail, exceedingly accurate in statement, always talking well, because he never talks about what he does not know." "His voice," says Horace Porter, "was exceedingly musical, and one of the clearest in sound and most distinct in utterance that I have ever heard. It had a singular power of penetration, and sentences spoken by him in an ordinary tone in camp could be heard at a distance which was surprising. . . . In his writing, his style was vigorous and terse, with little of ornament; its most conspicuous characteristic was perspicuity. General Meade's chief of staff once said: 'There is one striking thing about Grant's orders: no matter how hurriedly he may write them on the field, no one ever had the slightest doubt as to their meaning, or ever had to read them over a second time to understand them. . . . He rarely indulged in metaphor, but when he did employ a figure of speech, it was always expressive and graphic. . . . His style inclined to be epigrammatic without his being aware of it." Even Henry James, reviewing a volume of Grant's letters, speaks of "a ray of the hard limpidity of the writer's strong and simple Autobiography."

These literary qualities, so unobtrusive, are evidence of a natural fineness of character, mind and taste; and the *Memoirs* convey also Grant's dynamic force and the definiteness of his personality. Perhaps never has a book so objective in form seemed so personal in every line, and though the tempo is never increased, the narrative, once we get into the war, seems to move with the increasing momentum that the soldier must have felt in the field. What distinguished Grant's story from the records of campaigns that are usually produced by generals is that somehow, despite its sobriety, it communicates the spirit of the battles themselves and makes it possible to understand how Grant won them. Humiliated, bankrupt and voiceless, on the very threshold of death, sleeping at night sitting up in a chair as if he were still in the field and could not risk losing touch with developments, he relived his old campaigns; and one finds confirmed in these memoirs everything that has been said about Grant by those who were associated with him. One is impressed by the clairvoyance, coolness, the consistency of purpose, the endurance that, subject to occasional relapses, were able to sustain themselves in a kind of dissociation from ordinary life and yet to marshal men, to take cities and to break down the enemy's strength. The magnitude of Grant's command, which, says Porter, has "seldom been equalled in history," his will, which "was almost supreme in all purely military questions," his authority, which "was usually unquestioned," are reflected in the scope and the sureness of his descriptions of his complicated operations; and he has also, without conscious art, conveyed the suspense which was felt by himself and his army and by all who believed in the Union cause. The reader finds himself involved — he is actually on edge to know how the Civil War is coming out. We grow anxious, we imagine the anxiety of Lincoln, we are aware of the quick intensity with which he must be watching the dispatches. At the moment when the drop in morale that preceded Lincoln's second election seems endangering the cause of the Union, the pressure on Grant in the field, the desperate need for victories, make the early months of 1864 seem a turning-point in the destiny of the United States. Then with spring we get the hardly hoped successes. Retracing in his narrative the steps of his movements, Grant carries the reader along with his army — as it were, almost without impediment. A fiasco like the Petersburg mine, which Horace Porter, in his book *Campaigning with Grant*, describes as so horrible and so daunting a disaster, is noted by Grant as "a stupendous failure" but is made to seem an obstacle quickly surmounted. We are here with a plan and a power which do not admit serious obstacles.

The action of the *Memoirs* mounts up to two climaxes: the taking of Vicksburg and Lee's surrender. The same moral is pointed by both. "The enemy had been suffering," writes Grant, "particularly towards the last. I myself saw our men taking bread from their haversacks and giving it to the enemy they had so recently been engaged in starving out." And later: "The prisoners were allowed to occupy their old camps behind the intrenchments. No restraint was put upon them, except by their own commanders. They were rationed about as our own men, and from our supplies. The men of the two armies fraternized as if they had been fighting for the same cause. When they passed out of the works they had so long and so gallantly defended, between the lines of their late antagonists, not a cheer went up, not a remark was made that would give pain. Really, I believe there was a feeling of sadness just then in the breasts of most of the Union soldiers at seeing the dejection of their late antagonists.

"The day before the departure the following order was issued: 'Paroled prisoners will be sent out of here tomorrow. They will be authorized to cross at the railroad bridge, and move from there to Edward's Ferry, and on by way of Raymond. Instruct the commands to be orderly and quiet as these prisoners pass, to make no offensive remarks, and not to harbor any who fall out of ranks after they have passed.' "

Grant had not then met Lincoln and was not to do so till March of the following year, when he received his commission as Lieutenant General. I believe, as I shall presently explain, that he was strongly influenced by reasons of his own in the direction of generosity toward the enemy; but, once he had talked with Lincoln, his understanding with him seems to have been complete, and their frequent conversations together must have strengthened him in this disposition. "Lincoln, I may almost say," John Russell Young reports Grant's telling him, "spent the last days of his life with me. I often recall those days. He came down to City Point in the last days of the war, and was with me the whole time. . . . He was a great man, a very great man. The more I saw of him, the more this impressed me. He was incontestably the greatest man I ever knew." At the surrender at Appomattox, it is obvious that Grant is doing his best to carry out the Lincolnian policy of no bitterness and no reprisals, a policy for which Lincoln had had to contend with those powerful elements in his own party who wanted to reduce the South to the status of a subjugated province.

In connection with the Civil War, in general, it is astonishing to what extent the romantic popular legend has been substituted for the so much more interesting and easily accessible reality. It is not, of course, true that Robert E. Lee surrendered underneath an apple tree, and that he presented his sword to Grant, who immediately handed it back to him. Grant himself makes a point of explaining that none of this ever happened, yet many people still think it did. The reality was far more dramatic and more characteristic of the actors. The pursuit of Lee, in Grant's *Memoirs*, creates from its beginning a peculiar interest. I do not want to add to the bizarre interpretations already offered for *Moby-Dick* by suggesting that it anticipates the Civil War, but there are moments, in reading the *Memoirs,* when one is reminded of Captain Ahab's quest. Grant had served with Lee in Mexico and, as he says, knew that Lee was mortal. He makes it plain that for him the Virginian had never had the same prestige that he did for a good many Northerners as well as for his fellow Southerners; and he afterwards told John Russell Young that he had been far more afraid of Joe Johnston. Yet we cannot help feeling that Lee represents for Grant a challenge that is always at the back of his mind. "His praise," Grant tells us, "was sounded throughout the entire North after every action he was engaged in: the number of his forces was always lowered and that of the National forces exaggerated. He was a large, austere man, and I judge difficult of approach to his subordinates. To be extolled by the entire press of the South after every engagement, and by a portion of the press of the North with equal vehemence, was calculated to give him the entire confidence of his troops and to make him feared by his antagonists. It was not an uncommon thing for my staff-officers to hear from Eastern officers, 'Well, Grant has never met Bobby Lee yet.'" It would seem that the Confederate leader, too, felt something of a personal challenge. He regretted the dismissal of McClellan and the substitution of Grant because, as he said, he had always understood pretty well how McClellan was going to act but he could not be sure of Grant. At the end of the war, he declared, "There is nothing left for me to do but go and see General Grant, and I would rather die a thousand deaths." He would hardly have spoken thus of McClellan. We look forward to the eventual encounter as to the final scene of a drama — as we wait for the moment when Ahab, stubborn, intent and tough, crippled by his wooden leg as Grant had sometimes been by his alcoholic habits, will confront the smooth and shimmering foe, who has so far eluded all hunters — and the meeting does at last take place. The great Southerner appears with his jewelled sword, presented by some ladies in England; his handsomely spurred new boots, stitched at the top with red silk; his new uniform, buttoned to the throat; his silver-gray hair and beard and his long gray buckskin gauntlets; while Grant, not expecting to meet him so soon, has arrived in an unbuttoned blue flannel blouse, swordless and spattered with mud and with nothing but his lieutenant-general's shoulder-straps to show that he is not a private. "I remember now," he said to Young, "that I was concerned about my personal appearance. . . . I was afraid Lee might think I meant to show him studied discourtesy by so coming — at least I thought so. But I had no other clothes within reach, as Lee's letter found me away from my base of supplies." Yet the simplicity of Grant's costume is not only characteristic but significant. His indifference to the badges of rank has already been brought out, in the *Memoirs,* by his comments on other generals who cared more about such things than he did; and this ideal of the powerful leader, with no glamor and no pretensions, who is equally accessible to everybody and who almost disclaims his official rank, though never explicit with Grant, is implicit in his story of Lee's surrender. It is an ideal that he shared with Lincoln, and that was perhaps something new in the world. It was to reappear in Russia with Lenin, and in the young Red Army in its Leninist phase, before the restoration of epaulettes. And in Grant there was a genuine diffidence. His state of mind at Appomattox was not in the least exultant, but, he tells us, "sad and depressed. I felt like anything rather than rejoicing at the downfall of a foe who had fought so long and valiantly, and had suffered so much for a cause."

It is impossible to summarize this scene. One would have to quote it entire. The note of the whole encounter is struck by the unexpected beginning:

"We soon fell into a conversation about old army times. He remarked that he remembered me very well in the old army; and I told him that as a matter of course I remembered him perfectly, but from the difference in our ranks and years (there being about sixteen years' difference in our ages), I had thought it very likely that I had not attracted his attention sufficiently to be remembered by him after such a long interval." Horace Porter, who was present at the interview, says that Lee replied, "Yes, I met you on that occasion, and I have often thought of it, and tried to recollect how you looked, but I have never been able to recall a single feature." "Our conversation," Grant continues, "grew so pleasant that I almost forgot the object of our meeting. After the conversation had run on in this style for some time, General Lee called my attention to the object of our meeting, and said that he had asked for this interview, for the purpose of getting from me the terms I proposed to give his army. I said that I meant merely that his army should lay down their arms, not to take them up again during the continuance of the war unless duly and properly exchanged. He said that he had so understood my letter. Then we gradually fell off again into conversation about matters foreign to the subject which had brought us together."

What follows is still, I believe, not too well known to be quoted. Grant had written out brief terms of surrender: the Confederates to give their paroles and turn over their army, artillery and public property, with the exception of the officers' sidearms and their private horses and baggage; then to return to their homes, where they were "not to be disturbed by United States Authority" so long as they observed their paroles and the laws in force where they might reside.

"When I put my pen to the paper I did not know the first word that I should make use of in writing the terms. I only knew what was in my mind, and I wished to express it clearly, so that there could be no mistaking it. As I wrote on, the thought occurred to me that the officers had their own private horses and effects, which were important to them, but of no value to us; also that it would be an unnecessary humiliation to call upon them to deliver their side arms.

"No conversation, not one word, passed between General Lee and myself, either about private property, side arms, or kindred subjects. He appeared to have no objections to the terms first proposed; or if he had a point to make against them he wished to wait until they were in writing to make it. When he read over that part of the terms about side arms, horses and private property of the officers, he remarked, with some feeling, I thought, that this would have a happy effect upon his army.

"Then, after a little further conversation, General Lee remarked to me again that their army was organized a little differently from the army of the United States (still maintaining by implication that we were two countries); that in their army the cavalrymen and artillerists owned their own horses; and he asked if he was to understand that the men who so owned their horses were to be permitted to retain them. I told him that as the terms were written they would not; that only the officers were permitted to take their private property. He then, after reading over the terms a second time, remarked that that was clear.

"I then said to him that I thought this would be about

the last battle of the war — I sincerely hoped so; and I said further I took it that most of the men in the ranks were small farmers. The whole country had been so raided by the two armies that it was doubtful whether they would be able to put in a crop to carry themselves and their families through the next winter without the aid of the horses they were then riding. The United States did not want them and I would, therefore, instruct the officers I left behind to receive the paroles of his troops to let every man of the Confederate army who claimed to own a horse or mule take the animal to his home."

This scene has the same effect as the quick easing-off after the capture of Vicksburg. The long effort for victory at last succeeds, but the victory itself is presented with complete and deliberate flatness. (It is amusing that an English review should have said of the *Personal Memoirs* that they did not contain "a battle piece worth quoting.") Grant hated the kind of vindictiveness exhibited by Andrew Johnson in the early months of his presidency, when, as Grant tells us, he was always denouncing the South and saying, "Treason is a crime and must be made odious." Though Grant's own policy had largely been directed by Lincoln, it is plain from his handling of his subordinates that he disliked to humiliate people. He had himself known humiliation, in the days after the Mexican War when his drinking had cost him discharge from the Army. He had known it again after Shiloh, that uncoördinated free-for-all scrimmage at an early stage of the war, when neither officers nor men had yet learned their business. Grant's strange unreadiness here — perhaps due, as Lew Wallace, who was present, suggests, to the ineptitude and jealousy of Halleck, who had more or less tied his hands — had given Halleck a pretext to shelve him. At that time, it had been only the confidence of Lincoln which had prevented Grant's being removed from command and only the exhortations of Sherman which had prevented him from resigning. Sherman, in his own memoirs, has recorded how Grant had suffered from "the indignity, if not insult, heaped upon him" then. (The rumor was quick to spread that Grant had been drinking again, but everyone who was at Shiloh and has written about it says that Grant was completely in control of himself. "He spoke," says Lew Wallace, "in an ordinary tone, cheerful and wholly free from excitement. From his look and manner, no one could have inferred that he had been beaten in a great battle only the day before. If he had studied to be un-dramatic, he could not have succeeded better.") The fact was, I think, that Grant did not care to pass humiliation on.

If the purified fervor and force that still come through the *Personal Memoirs* may still exhilarate the reader and fill the Northerner with moral pride, it is only because the book makes it possible for him to forget a good deal of the Civil War. In the first place, the victory of the Union cause is made, by a literary illusion, to seem a great deal easier than it actually was — because Grant is here concerned only with those operations in which he himself figured. He has almost nothing to say of those early Northern defeats that were so discouraging to Lincoln, and he minimizes his own mistakes at Shiloh and at Cold Harbor. In the second place, the very objectivity of Grant's method of describing the war always works to eliminate its tragedy. His mind seems so firm and clear that no agony or horror can cloud it. I have noted only two brief passages — these, however, have their quiet force — in which he mentions the sufferings of the soldiers. One night it comes on to rain when he has been lying under a tree in pain from a swollen ankle, and he goes into a log house for shelter. But "this," he says, "had been taken as a hospital, and all night wounded men were being brought in, their wounds dressed, a leg or an arm amputated as the case might require, and everything being done to save life or alleviate suffering. The sight was more unendurable than encountering the enemy's fire, and I returned to my tree in the rain." Later on, after the victory of Champion's Hill, he assembles his staff on the porch of a house "which had been taken," as he says, "for a rebel hospital and which was filled with wounded and dying who had been brought from the battlefield we had just left. While a battle is raging one can see his enemy mowed down by the thousand, or the ten thousand, with great composure; but after the battle these scenes are distressing, and one is naturally disposed to do as much to alleviate the suffering of an enemy as a friend."

Actually, we learn from Badeau that, although, "after the fiercest fighting and the most awful destruction, [Grant] still knew and felt that only by fresh effort of the same sort could he conquer, and gave orders grimly but unbroken still," he had not, in civilian life, been able to stay through a hurdle race because he could not bear "to see men risk their necks needlessly," and that "he came away from one of Blondin's exhibitions at Niagara, angry and nervous at the sight of one poor wretch in gaudy clothes crossing the whirlpool on a wire." And we learn from Horace Porter, in his account of the battle of the Wilderness, that "it was noticed that he [Grant] was visibly affected by his proximity to the wounded, and especially by the sight of blood. He would turn his face away from such scenes, and show by the expression of his countenance, and sometimes by a pause in his conversation, that he felt most keenly the painful spectacle presented by the field of battle." In diet he was virtually a vegetarian. He could not bring himself to eat any kind of fowl, saying, "I never could eat anything that goes on two legs," and the only meat he cared for was beef, which "he could not eat unless it was so thoroughly well done that no appearance of blood could be seen. If blood appeared in any meat which came on the table, the sight of it seemed to destroy his appetite." One remembers that Viscount Montgomery has confessed that he could not visit field hospitals because they distressed him too much.

We must, in fact, go to Horace Porter, a vigorous and vivid writer of a more "literary" kind than Grant, for the human actualities of Grant's campaign. His remarkable narrative *Campaigning with Grant* is needed to supplement the *Personal Memoirs,* for we find here all the horrors which Grant has omitted, which the strainer of his chaste style keeps out. The terrible battle of the Wilderness, at which Grant was "visibly affected," is described by Porter as follows:

"There were features of the battle which have never been matched in the annals of warfare. For two days nearly 200,000 veteran troops had struggled in a death-grapple, confronted at each step with almost every obstacle by which nature could bar their path, and groping their way through a tangled forest the impenetrable gloom of which could be likened only to the shadow of death. The undergrowth stayed their progress, the upper growth shut out the light of heaven. Officers could rarely see their troops for any considerable distance, for smoke clouded the vision, and a heavy sky obscured the sun. Directions were ascertained and lines established by means of the pocket-compass, and a change of position often presented an operation more like a problem of ocean navigation than a question of military manœuvers. It was the sense of sound and of touch rather than the sense of sight which guided the movements. It was a battle fought with the ear, and not with the eye. All circumstances seemed to combine to make the scene one of unutterable horror. At times the wind howled through the tree-tops, mingling its moans with the groans of the dying, and heavy branches were cut off by the fire of the artillery, and fell crashing upon the heads of the men, adding a new terror to battle. Forest fires raged; ammunition-trains exploded; the dead were roasted in the conflagration; the wounded, roused by its hot breath, dragged themselves along, with their torn and mangled limbs, in the mad energy of despair, to escape the ravages of the flames; and every bush seemed hung with shreds of blood-stained clothing. It was as though Christian men had turned to fiends, and hell itself had usurped the place of earth. . . .

"The battle near the 'angle' was probably the most desperate engagement in the history of modern warfare, and presented features which were absolutely appalling. It was chiefly a savage hand-to-hand fight across the breastworks. Rank after rank was riddled by shot and shell and bayonet-thrusts, and finally sank, a mass of torn and mutilated corpses; then fresh troops rushed madly forward to replace the dead, and so the murderous work went on. Guns were run up close to the parapet, and double charges of canister played their part in the bloody work. The fence-rails and logs in the breastworks were shattered into splinters, and trees over a foot and a half in diameter were cut completely in two by the incessant musketry fire. A section of the trunk of a stout oak-tree thus severed was afterward sent to Washington, where it is still on exhibition at the National Museum. We had not only shot down an army, but also a forest.

The opposing flags were in places thrust against each other, and muskets were fired with muzzle against muzzle. Skulls were crushed with clubbed muskets, and men stabbed to death with swords and bayonets thrust between the logs in the parapet which separated the combatants. Wild cheers, savage yells, and frantic shrieks rose above the sighing of the wind and the pattering of the rain, and formed a demoniacal accompaniment to the booming of the guns as they hurled their missiles of death into the contending ranks. Even the darkness of night and the pitiless storm failed to stop the fierce contest, and the deadly strife did not cease till after midnight. Our troops had been under fire for twenty hours, but they still held the position which they had so dearly purchased."*

In all this morass of agony, the misery of a single soldier, accidentally subjected to indignity, could move Grant to an impulse of pity: "General Grant had ridden over to the right to watch the progress of this attack. While he was passing a spot near the roadside where there were a number of wounded, one of them, who was lying close to the roadside, seemed to attract his special notice. The man's face was beardless; he was evidently young; his countenance was strikingly handsome, and there was something in his appealing look which could not fail to engage attention, even in the full tide of battle. The blood was flowing from a wound in his

---

* Horace Porter was something of a pioneer in the non-romantic treatment of war. An article of his called *The Philosophy of Courage* in the *Century Magazine* of June, 1888, a study of the behavior of soldiers in battle based on his own observations, was laid under contribution by Bernard Shaw for his early play *Arms and the Man* and adduced as evidence by him when he was scolded for belittling the heroism of the military. See *A Dramatic Realist to His Critics* included in *Shaw on Theatre*, a recently published volume of hitherto uncollected pieces.

breast, the froth about his mouth was tinged with red, and his wandering, staring eyes gave unmistakable evidence of approaching death. Just then a young staff-officer dashed by at a full gallop, and as his horse's hoofs struck a puddle in the road, a mass of black mud was splashed in the wounded man's face. He gave a piteous look, as much as to say, 'Couldn't you let me die in peace and not add to my sufferings?' The general, whose eyes were at that moment turned upon the youth, was visibly affected. He reined in his horse, and seeing from a motion he made that he was intending to dismount to bestow some care upon the young man, I sprang from my horse, ran to the side of the soldier, wiped his face with my handkerchief, spoke to him, and examined his wound; but in a few minutes the unmistakable death-rattle was heard, and I found that he had breathed his last. I said to the general, who was watching the scene intently, 'The poor fellow is dead,' remounted my horse, and the party rode on. The chief had turned round twice to look after the officer who had splashed the mud and who had passed rapidly on, as if he wished to take him to task for his carelessness. There was a painfully sad look upon the general's face, and he did not speak for some time. While always keenly sensitive to the sufferings of the wounded, this pitiful sight seemed to affect him more than usual."

The sight of a suffering animal had excited him perhaps even more. In this case he had someone to blame, and it was possible for him to rescue the victim. "Rawlins [Grant's principal staff officer] rode with the general at the head of the staff. As the party turned a bend in the road near the crossing of the Totopotomoy, the general came in sight of a teamster whose wagon was stalled in a place where it was somewhat swampy, and who was standing beside his team beating his horses brutally in the face with the butt-end of his whip, and swearing with a volubility calculated to give a sulphurous odor to all the surrounding atmosphere. Grant's aversion to profanity and his love of horses caused all the ire in his nature to be aroused by the sight presented. Putting both spurs into 'Egypt's' flanks, he dashed toward the teamster, and raising his clenched fist called out to him: 'What does this conduct mean, you scoundrel? Stop beating those horses!' The teamster looked at him, and said coolly, as he delivered another blow aimed at the face of the wheel-horse: 'Well, who's drivin' this team anyhow — you or me?' The general was now thoroughly angered, and his manner was by no means as angelic as that of the celestial being who called a halt when Balaam was disciplining the ass. 'I'll show you, you infernal villain!' he cried, shaking his fist in the man's face. Then calling to an officer of the escort, he said: 'Take this man in charge, and have him tied up to a tree for six hours as a punishment for his brutality.' The man slunk off sullenly in charge of the escort to receive his punishment, without showing any penitence for his conduct. He was evidently a hardened case. Of course he was not aware that the officer addressing him was the general-in-chief, but he evidently knew that he was an officer of high rank, as he was accompanied by a staff and an escort, so that there was no excuse for the insubordinate and insolent remark. During the stirring scenes of that day's battle the general twice referred to the incident in vehement language, showing that the recollection of it was still rankling in his mind."

All the cost of the Civil War can, in fact, not be learned from Grant, and though he presided over the country in the White House for eight years after the war

(1869-77), the consequences of Northern victory, with its unleashing of the money-grabbing interests, were quite beyond his grasp. Grant's *Memoirs*, like the writings of Lincoln, are, after all, a literary creation, an intellectual construction with words. They are a part of that vision of the Civil War that Lincoln imposed on the nation, and we accept them as firsthand evidence of the actualization of that vision. Yet if we stand outside this construction, we find ourselves facing a vista for which we have not been prepared. The prospect of the future presented by Grant in the final pages of the *Memoirs* has a character almost utopian: "The war has made us a nation of great power and intelligence. We have but little to do to preserve peace, happiness, and prosperity at home, and the respect of other nations. Our experience ought to teach us the necessity of the first; our power secures the latter. I feel that we are on the eve of a new era, when there is to be great harmony between the Federal and Confederate. I cannot stay to be a living witness to the correctness of this prophecy; but I feel it within me that it is to be so. The universally kind feeling expressed for me at a time when it was supposed that each day would prove my last, seemed to me the beginning of the answer to 'Let us have peace.' "

Yet Grant had, without being aware of it, quite walked out of Lincoln's vision, and he was living in a different world. The murder of Lincoln had ended this vision. The intellectual and moral slump that followed the assassination, and the slackening from the strain of the war, brought down with them the whole idealistic edifice that the nobler Union supporters had built. When the former Vice-President Andrew Johnson — after his brief phase of bitterness against the South — tried to carry out the generous policies of Lincoln, he was opposed by the Radical Republicans, who even tried to remove him as

President and who, in the period of "Reconstruction,"
humiliated and exploited the South. This period would
certainly have been difficult for Lincoln. He was dead
and safely out of it, but Grant was still alive and only
forty-three. He lived on in this world of the Republican
party, to which he was not native, and, playing in it a
different role, he came to wear a different aspect.

The contrast between the General and the President
may be illustrated by the almost comic contrast between
two descriptions of Grant, one by the younger Charles
Francis Adams and the other by his brother Henry. Just
after the battle of the Wilderness, Charles Francis, at
that time on Grant's staff, wrote to his father the following characterization: "Things meanwhile work in the
Army charmingly. Grant is certainly a very extraordinary
man. He does not look it and might pass well enough
for a dumpy and slouchy little subaltern, very fond of
smoking. Neither do I know that he shows it in his conversation, for he never spoke to me and doesn't seem to
be a very talkative man anyhow. They says his mouth
shows character. It may, but it is so covered with beard
that no one can vouch for it. The truth is, he is in appearance a very ordinary looking man, one who would
attract attention neither in the one way or the other.
Not knowing who it is, you would not pronounce him
insignificant, and knowing who it is, it would require
some study to find in his appearance material for hero
worship, though there is about his face no indication of
weakness or lack of force. He has not nearly so strong
a head and face as Humphreys', for instance, who at
once strikes you as a man of force. In figure Grant is
comical. He sits a horse well, but in walking he leans
forward and toddles. Such being his appearance, however, I do not think that any intelligent person could
watch him, even from such a distance as mine, without

concluding that he is a remarkable man. He handles those around him so quietly and well, he so evidently has the faculty of disposing of work and managing men, he is cool and quiet, almost stolid and as if stupid, in danger, and in a crisis he is one against whom all around, whether few in number or a great army as here, would instinctively lean. He is a man of the most exquisite judgment and tact. See how he has handled this Army. He took command under the most unfavorable circumstances — jealousy between East and West; the Army of the Potomac and the Army of the Southwest; that general feeling that the officers from the West were going to swagger over those here and finally that universal envy which success creates and which is always ready to carp at it. The moment I came to Head Quarters I saw that, though nothing was said, yet the materials were all ready for an explosion at the first mistake Grant made. All this has passed away and now Grant has this army as firmly as ever he had that of the Southwest. He has effected this simply by the exercise of tact and good taste. He has humored us, he has given some promotions, he has made no parade of his authority, he has given no orders except through Meade, and Meade he treats with the utmost confidence and deference. The result is that even from the most jealously disposed and most indiscreet of Meade's staff, not a word is heard against Grant. The result is of inestimable importance. The army has a head and confidence in that head. It has leaders and there is no discord among those leaders. We seem to have gotten rid of jealousy and all now seem disposed to go in with a will to win."

And here are Henry Adams's impressions of the presidential Grant from the chapter on him in the *Education*:

"Badeau took Adams to the White House one evening and introduced him to the President and Mrs. Grant.

First and last, he saw a dozen Presidents at the White House, and the most famous were by no means the most agreeable, but he found Grant the most curious object of study among them all. About no one did opinions differ so widely. Adams had no opinion, or occasion to make one. A single word with Grant satisfied him that, for his own good, the fewer words he risked, the better. Thus far in life he had met with but one man of the same intellectual or unintellectual type — Garibaldi. Of the two, Garibaldi seemed to him a trifle the more intellectual, but, in both, the intellect counted for nothing; only the energy counted. The type was pre-intellectual, archaic, and would have seemed so even to the cave-dwellers. Adam, according to legend, was such a man.

"In time one came to recognize the type in other men, with differences and variations, as normal; men whose energies were the greater, the less they wasted on thought; men who sprang from the soil to power; apt to be distrustful of themselves and of others; shy; jealous; sometimes vindictive; more or less dull in outward appearance; always needing stimulants, but for whom action was the highest stimulant — the instinct of fight. Such men were forces of nature, energies of the prime, like the *Pteraspis* [a prehistoric fish], but they made short work of scholars. They had commanded thousands of such and saw no more in them than in others. The fact was certain; it crushed argument and intellect at once.

"Adams did not feel Grant as a hostile force; like Badeau he saw only an uncertain one. When in action he was superb and safe to follow; only when torpid he was dangerous. To deal with him one must stand near, like a Rawlins, and practice more or less sympathetic habits. Simple-minded beyond the experience of Wall Street or State Street, he resorted, like most men of the

same intellectual calibre, to commonplaces when at a
loss for expression: 'Let us have peace!' or, 'The best way
to treat a bad law is to execute it'; or a score of such
reversible sentences generally to be gauged by their sen-
tentiousness; but sometimes he made one doubt his good
faith; as when he seriously remarked to a particularly
bright young woman that Venice would be a fine city if
it were drained. In Mark Twain, this suggestion would
have taken rank among his best witticisms; in Grant it
was a measure of simplicity not singular. [Henry Adams
seems to assume that Grant meant removing the water
from Venice, but he must actually have been speaking
of sewage disposal, the desirability of which in Venice
has occurred to many Americans.] Robert E. Lee betrayed
the same intellectual commonplace, in a Virginian form,
not to the same degree, but quite distinctly enough for
one who knew the American. What worried Adams was
not the commonplace; it was, as usual, his own education. Grant fretted and irritated him, like the *Terebratula*
as a defiance of first principles. [The *Terebratula* was a
kind of shellfish of which Adams had been told that it
"appeared to be identical from the beginning to the end
of geological time."] He had no right to exist. He should
have been extinct for ages. The idea that, as society grew
older, it grew one-sided, upset evolution, and made of
education a fraud. That, two thousand years after Alexander the Great and Julius Cæsar, a man like Grant
should be called — and should actually and truly be —
the highest product of the most advanced evolution, made
evolution seem ludicrous. One must be as commonplace
as Grant's own commonplaces to maintain such an absurdity. The progress of evolution from President Washington to President Grant, was alone evidence enough
to upset Darwin."

What is involved in the striking contrast that these

characterizations present is, of course, the contrasting situations of the Adams brothers themselves. Charles Francis had been in the war: he had acted in the Unionist drama; whereas Henry was quite outside it: he had been working with his father in the Embassy in London while the fighting was going on, and he had hardly been touched by the Lincolnian vision. He somewhere implies a doubt as to the wisdom of Lincoln in launching the war. Though he had thought for a moment that he ought to enlist after the Northern defeat at Bull Run, one feels that the effect of the war had been simply to make him uncomfortable. When he came back home to the States — in the summer of 1868 — he was to find himself a horrified spectator of the scandals of the Grant administration, and he could not really see Grant as he was since he was able to conceive of him only as the dupe of financial swindlers. It was actually true that Grant appears in two quite different lights in his capacity as a soldier and in his capacity as — what should one say? One cannot call him a politician, for Grant hated politicians and had not the least aptitude for politics. Nor can one possibly call him a statesman. Whenever, as President, he did anything wise, it had the look of a happy accident. In the field, as commanding general, he could be patient, far-seeing, considerate, adroit at handling complicated situations. But in Washington he had no idea of what it meant to be President of the United States; he did not even, it soon appeared, understand constitutional government.

Many instances might be given of Grant's almost unbelievable attempts to take action on his own initiative — as if he were an officer commanding troops — and running up against the limits of his office. His first impulse on these occasions was to say, "Let the law be changed." He had had the idea, for example, that it might be an excellent thing to send some of the freed Negroes to Haiti, and he had taken advantage of a situation created by two rival governments there to draw up with one of its Presidents a treaty for the annexation of the whole island of Santo Domingo. He came smiling to a cabinet meeting and announced with the air of a man who was producing a delightful surprise that a treaty was ready to be signed and that all that was necessary now was to send it back to Haiti and get somebody in the consulate to attend to it. The Cabinet was indeed surprised. Grant was asked by the Secretary of the Interior whether it really had been decided that they wanted to annex Santo Domingo. The President flushed and made no reply; he proceeded to the next business and went away from the meeting furious. The Secretary of State, who had not been consulted, came to Grant and offered to resign. The President persuaded him to support the plan, but he then ran aground on Charles Sumner, the chairman of the Senate Foreign Relations Committee, who had not been consulted either. He could no doubt have put through his project if he had had the smallest capacity for that kind of political trickery which was later to make it possible for Theodore Roosevelt to take over Panama; but Grant could not even have imagined this.

His appointments to his Cabinet were often fantastic: he had no judgment about people in civil life, and he appointed as Secretary of the Treasury the proprietor of a large New York dry-goods store, unaware that anyone in foreign trade was debarred from holding this office; for Minister to France he selected a half-illiterate Illinois Congressman. Henry Adams's charge of vindictiveness was prompted by Grant's petulant reprisals on occasions when he found that his wishes had not been obediently carried out — a practice which was entirely at variance with his habit, when Lieutenant General, of shifting his difficult generals to commands in which he thought they and he would not be likely to come into conflict.

Under Grant's two administrations, there flapped through the national capital a whole phantasmagoria of insolent fraud, while a swarm of predatory adventurers was let loose on the helpless South. There was the Crédit Mobilier affair, in which the promoters of the Union Pacific Railroad, who had obtained an immense government loan and twelve million acres of government land, made a contract with themselves under another name and paid themselves three times more than the cost of building the railroad, in the meantime bribing the congressmen with shares in the imaginary company. There was the gold conspiracy of Jim Fisk and Jay Gould, in which Grant was persuaded by these two financiers, without in the least understanding their aims, to assist them in cornering the gold market by causing the United States Treasury to shut off the circulation of gold. There was the Whisky Ring, a group of distillers who evaded the internal revenue tax by bribing the Treasury agents — a scandal that landed at the President's door when his secretary, a General Babcock who had been with him at Appomattox, was shown to have been taking the distillers' money and to have used it in financing Grant's campaign. Grant testified that he believed in the innocence of Babcock, but later he quietly sacked him. One can hardly even say that Grant was President except in the sense that he presided at the White House, where the business men and financiers were extremely happy to have him, since he never knew what they were up to. His sole idea about business, expressed in the *Personal Memoirs*, was that all the big industrial and money people were doing great things for the country by making it more prosperous and more important. It was the age of the audacious confidence man, and Grant was the incurable sucker. He easily fell victim to their trickery and allowed them to betray him into compromising his office because he could not believe that such people existed.

Even after his retirement from the Presidency, he fell for what would seem to us nowadays — when our crooks have had to become more sophisticated — the most implausible goldbrick of all. Grant was ruined by a swindler named Ferdinand Ward, who succeeded, with no other devices than a small bogus bank and a double set of books, in collecting from Grant and his family and a good many other people, under the pretense of investing their money, a sum that seems to have run into millions. When the crash came, poor Grant, who had imagined that his interest in this firm of which his son was a partner and to which he had lent his prestige, was worth about two million and a half, found himself, in a compromising position, with a hundred and eighty dollars in cash. When Mark Twain discussed this swindle with Grant, he himself, he says, was "inwardly boiling — scalping Ward — flaying him alive — breaking him on the wheel — pounding him to a jelly"; but "never at any time," writes Mark Twain's biographer Albert Bigelow Paine, "did [Grant] betray any resentment toward Ward." He "characterized him as one might an offending child." Ward had been a friend of his son's, and now he had been sent to prison, and Grant had never liked to see people humiliated.

He does not deal with his Presidency in the *Personal Memoirs,* or with the events of his later years, but this period is to some extent filled in by the series of conversations recorded by John Russell Young in his book *Around the World with General Grant.* Immediately on the expiration of Grant's second term in the Presidency, he embarked on extensive travels, which lasted over two years (from May 17, 1877 to September 20, 1879) and in the course of which he managed to visit almost all the European countries, some of them more than once — Anglo-Saxon, German, Scandinavian, Latin and Balkan — as well as Egypt, the Middle East, Russia, India, Siam, China and Japan. The General, in his middle fifties, seems still to have been as indefatigable as he had been in his military campaigns, and he dragged his family and his retinue through some very rough explorations. He would be up early every morning and, at an hour announced the night before, would depart on a sight-seeing tour: if his companions were tardy, they were left behind.

John Young was a friend of Grant's, an Irish-American journalist who had lived a good deal in Europe. He accompanied Grant on his trip and became its official chronicler. The chapters are especially interesting which deal with their adventures in the Orient: China, Japan and Siam, countries which were then little visited by foreigners and where the General was everywhere received by the emperors, viceroys and kings with apparently unprecedented honors. Young himself became interested in Chinese affairs, and Grant later got President Chester Arthur to appoint him Minister to China. His book — two gigantic volumes, with eight hundred illustrations, the kind of thing that in those days was sold by subscription — contains hundreds of pages of padding: historical and travelogue material which has nothing to do with Grant. But Young was a rather intelligent man, and some of this stuff is worth reading: there is an amusing disquisition on Americans in Paris — Bohemians and permanent sojourners who put the touch on compatriot tourists, the kind of people that Grant himself never saw — which shows that such expatriates have changed very little since the seventies of the last century.

But the book is only really important for its report on Grant's meeting with Bismarck and for its record of the author's conversations with Grant. In these latter, Grant expresses himself on the characters and capacities of the Civil War generals with more candor than he will later allow himself when he comes to write the *Personal Memoirs,* and he discusses, in a naïve way, some of the incidents of his administrations. "I did not," he told Young, "want the Presidency, and I have never quite forgiven myself for resigning the command of the army to accept it; but it could not be helped. I owed my honors and opportunities to the Republican Party, and if my name could aid it, I was bound to accept. The second nomination was almost due to me — if I may use the phrase — because of the bitterness of political and personal opponents. My reëlection was a great gratification, because it showed me how the country felt." And he describes his struggle with his conscience over signing an inflation bill. This was the only occasion, he says, on which he "ever deliberately resolved to do an expedient thing for party reasons, against my own judgment. . . . I never was so pressed in my life to do anything as to sign that bill, never." He wrote a message defending the bill and trying to show that it would not mean inflation. But "when I finished my wonderful message, which was to do so much good to the party and country, I read it over and said to myself: 'What is the good of all this? You do not believe it. You know it is not true.' Throwing it aside I resolved to do what I believed to be right — veto the bill!"

Grant's conversations with Bismarck, whom he met in Berlin — written down by John Russell Young — are of interest in showing how this small-town American who had disapproved so strongly of our policy with Mexico had become one of the staunchest supporters of the Unionist policy of force, the most illustrious living representative of the powerful political organism which the United States had now become. He and Bismarck had much in common, and their agreements were fraternal and emphatic. Each had played a critical role in the unification of his country, and both felt the necessity of maintaining that unity by the exercise of a strong hand. The one had directed the armies which had defeated Jefferson Davis's Confederacy; the other had directed the Reich which had defeated Louis Napoleon's France. The one had seen his president assassinated by a fanatic of the dissident conquered South who had also wished to take Grant's own life; the other, two attempted attacks on the life of his sovereign Wilhelm I by members of the radical movement. The second of these attacks on the Emperor, in which he had been seriously injured, had taken place just before Grant's visit, and Wilhelm was unable to receive him. "Here is an old man," says Bismarck, — "one of the kindest old gentlemen in the world — and yet they must try and shoot him!" The General answers that Lincoln had been "a man of the kindest and gentlest nature." Bismarck — who had once told Sheridan that he tended toward republicanism in his youth but had decided now that Germany was not up to it — goes on to say that Emperor Wilhelm was "so republican in all things that even the most extreme republican if he did his character justice would admire him." The General replies "that the influence which aimed at the Emperor's life was an influence that would destroy all government, all order, all society, republics and empires," and this leads him to declare that "although at home there is a strong sentiment against the death penalty, and it is a sentiment which one naturally respects, I am not sure but it ought to be made more severe rather than less severe." " 'That,' said the prince, 'is entirely my view.

My convictions are so strong that I resigned the government of Alsace because I was required to commute sentences of capital nature. I could not do it in justice to my conscience.' . . . 'All you can do with such people,' said the General quietly, 'is to kill them.' 'Precisely so,' answered the prince."

Their conversation about the aims of the United States exposes in a striking way the psychology of the champions of the Union cause. The Prussian was quite realistic in stating the situation: "What always seemed so sad to me . . . was that you were fighting your own people. That is always so terrible in wars, so very hard." " 'But it had to be done,' said the General. 'Yes,' said the prince, 'you had to save the Union just as we had to save Germany.' 'Not only save the Union, but destroy slavery,' answered the General. 'I suppose, however, the Union was the real sentiment, the dominant sentiment,' said the prince. 'In the beginning, yes,' said the General; 'but as soon as slavery fired upon the flag it was felt, we all felt, even those who did not object to slaves, that slavery must be destroyed. We felt that it was a stain to the Union that men should be bought and sold, like cattle.' " Bismarck changes the subject. The General is quite unaware that, by putting the thing in this way, he has indicated that slavery, on the part of the Unionists, has at the last moment been recruited to justify their action in the struggle for power.

"General," says the prince, at the end of their talk, "the pleasure and the honor are mine. Germany and America have always been in such friendly relationship that nothing delights us more than to meet Americans, and especially an American who has done so much for his country, and whose name is so much honored in Germany as your own." "The guard presented arms, the General lit a fresh cigar, and slowly strolled home. 'I am glad I have seen Bismarck,' the General remarked. 'He's a man whose manner and bearing fully justify the opinions one forms of him. What he says about the Emperor was beautifully said, and should be known to all the Germans and those who esteem Germany."

At that time the people of the United States held Germany in the highest esteem. The developments of the two big countries were to some extent now running parallel. Both were expanding geographically and constructing great industrial plants and railroads. Both were up-and-coming nations of vigorous Teutonic stock. The Germans who immigrated to the United States adapted themselves more readily to American life and distinguished themselves more frequently than any other immigrant group between the Revolution and the Civil War; and Americans went to Germany rather than to the British universities for the purpose of studying medicine, music, philology, philosophy and the natural sciences. Bismarck kept in touch with American affairs and was usually on very cordial terms with our official representatives in Berlin. John L. Motley, the historian of the Dutch Republic, was one of his closest friends, and Andrew D. White, the President of Cornell University, who was for eight years our minister or ambassador to Germany, also knew Bismarck well and had a great admiration for him. When Sheridan, in 1870, had got Grant to send him to Europe as an observer of the Franco-Prussian War, and the latter had asked Sheridan to which army he wished to be attached, he had answered, "The German" — for the reason, as he explains in his own *Personal Memoirs*, "that I thought more could be seen with the successful side, and that the indications pointed to the defeat of France. My choice evidently pleased him greatly, as he had the utmost contempt for

Louis Napoleon, and had always denounced him as a usurper and charlatan."

For the boy from the two-room cabin, who had not wanted to go to West Point and who had hoped that it would be abolished in order that he might not have to finish there, who had had, he said, "a horror" of the Mexican War in which he had been forced to serve, believing it to be "most unjust," who had taken to drink and, discharged from the army, had gone to clerking in his brothers' leather store, who could not bear the sight of blood nor even face a steak not well done, and who said that he much preferred farming to fighting — this man had found himself, in his forties, the most conspicuous figure in what had been up to that time the most destructive war in history and afterwards at the head of the formidable state which this war had consolidated; the equal, the sympathetic colleague, of the master of that other great new state which had consolidated the German principalities.

NORTHERN SOLDIERS: WILLIAM T. SHERMAN

THE *Memoirs of General William T. Sherman* was published — in 1875 — before Grant's *Personal Memoirs*. The book has an interest quite equal to Grant's, and an almost equal importance, but is as different from the *Personal Memoirs* as Sherman's personality was from Grant's. Grant is lucid and simple, but in this very lucidity and simplicity there is something a little uncanny. We feel that he is sensitive and shy, and that a good deal is left untold. Sherman, in one of his letters to Grant, speaks of him as "guarded" and "prudent," in contrast to himself: "outspoken" and "careless." The writer of the *Personal Memoirs* is the aloof and dispassionate Grant, and the book reflects the clairvoyant vision of a mind unexcited by whisky and unclouded by the shadow of failure. The emotions and sensations of Grant, his personal problems, his political opinions are hardly allowed to impinge on the record. But Sherman makes a quite different impression. The man is all there in his book; the book is the man speaking.

For Sherman was a good deal better educated than Grant — as he once took occasion to remind him — and from a somewhat higher social stratum. Sherman's father had been a lawyer and one of his grandfathers a judge, and, after the death of his father, William was brought up in the household of Thomas Ewing, the "Logician of the West," who had been senator from Ohio in the thirties and then served in the cabinets of Harrison and Taylor. He had a trained gift of self-expression and was, as Mark Twain says, a master of narrative. His dispatches and reports to Washington had already given evidence of this, but his memoirs are quite amazing. The vigorous account of his pre-war activities and his conduct of his military operations is varied in just the right proportion and to just the right degree of vivacity with anecdotes and personal experiences. We live through his campaigns, as we do not do Grant's, in the company of Sherman himself. He tells us what he thought and what he felt, and he never strikes any attitudes or pretends to feel anything which he does not feel. His frankness and self-dependence, his rectitude in whatever he undertakes — in the panic of 1855, he was almost the only banker in San Francisco who managed to remain solvent — and his contempt for petty schemes and ambitions, together with a disregard for many conventional scruples, make Sherman, in spite of his harshness, a figure whom we not only respect but cannot help liking. Though he declared that war was "all hell" and though the Southerners thought him a devil, his soldiers called him "Uncle Billy," and he was popular both before and after the war as a talker and dancer and diner-out. He is supposed to have been strongly attractive to women. Like Eisenhower, Churchill and Hitler, Sherman was an amateur painter — in water color. He had also a great appetite for the theater and was always quoting from Shakespeare, and he read Dickens over and over again.

William Tecumseh Sherman — he was named after the great Shawnee chief, whom the elder Sherman admired — was characterized by Henry Adams, correctly if a little superciliously, as fundamentally "a transplanted New Englander; a variety grown in ranker soil." The

family had been in New England from the early seventeenth century, but Sherman's father had moved from
Connecticut to Ohio, and the son combined with a
Pilgrim rigor the large ease and free movement of the
West. The first two hundred pages of the *Memoirs* are
occupied with Sherman's adventures as a young officer
in California during and after the Mexican War — voyages and shipwrecks, rough overland journeys, Sutter's
Fort and the Gold Rush; then banking in St. Louis and
San Francisco (also, at that time, a precarious business),
and an attempt, as the officer responsible for order, to
prevent in the latter city the murderous activities of lynch
law. Do not believe for a moment, says Sherman, that
the Vigilance Committee, as they tell you, was justified
by the lawlessness of those days; "they were recruiting
the worst elements in San Francisco, but they had succeeded in capturing our arsenal, and, unarmed, we were
helpless against them."

In 1860, after many wanderings, Sherman thought he
was settling down as head of a military academy that
had been newly established in Louisiana. But the war
put an end to this. When Louisiana seceded from the
Union in January, 1861, he announced that he could no
longer hold his post and, though strongly urged to stay,
resigned. In May he was appointed a colonel of infantry,
and he saw his first action at Bull Run in July. In spite
of his service in the West, he had never been in battle
before, and he writes of it with his usual candor. The
rereading, he tells us in his *Memoirs*, of one of his old
reports brought back to him "the whole scene of the
affair at Blackburn's Ford, when for the first time in my
life I saw cannon-balls strike men and crash through
trees and saplings above and around us, and realized the
always sickening confusion as one approaches a fight
from the rear; then the night-march from Centreville, on

the Warrenton road, standing for hours wondering what was meant; the deployment along the edge of the field that sloped down to Bull Run, and waiting for Hunter's approach on the other side from the direction of Sudley Springs, away off to our right; the terrible scare of a poor negro who was caught between our lines; the crossing of Bull Run, and the fear lest we should be fired on by our own men; the killing of Lieutenant-Colonel Haggerty, which occurred in plain sight; and the first scenes of a field strewed with dead men and horses. Yet, at that period of the battle, we were the victors and felt jubilant."

When the day turns against them, an incident occurs which, in retrospect, one can see to have had its significance: "A slow, mizzling rain had set in, and probably a more gloomy day never presented itself. All organization seemed to be at an end . . . Some of [the men] were so mutinous, at one time, that I had the battery . . . unlimber, threatening, if they dared to leave camp without orders, I would open fire on them." An officer said to him, "Colonel, I am going to New York today. What can I do for you?" "I answered: 'How can you go to New York? I do not remember to have signed a leave for you.'" He replied that he had engaged to serve for only three months and had already served longer than that. He was a lawyer and had neglected his business and now proposed to go home. "I noticed that a good many of the soldiers had paused about us to listen, and knew that, if this officer could defy me, they also would. So I turned on him sharp, and said. . . , 'If you attempt to leave without orders, it will be mutiny, and I will shoot you like a dog! Go back into the fort *now*, instantly, and don't dare to leave without my consent.'" The man obeyed.

On the same day, President Lincoln arrived in a carriage for the purpose of stimulating the morale of the troops. He would invite them at the end of a speech "to appeal to him personally in case they were wronged." The officer whom Sherman had rebuked — with pale face and lips compressed — "forced his way through the crowd to the carriage, and said: 'Mr. President, I have a cause of grievance. This morning I went to speak to Colonel Sherman, and he threatened to shoot me.' Mr. Lincoln, who was still standing, said, 'Threatened to shoot you?' 'Yes, sir, he threatened to shoot me.' Mr. Lincoln looked at him, then at me, and stooping his tall, spare form toward the officer, said to him in a loud stage-whisper, easily heard for some yards around: 'Well, if I were you, and he threatened to shoot, I would not trust him, for I believe he would do it.' The officer turned about and disappeared, and the men laughed at him. Soon the carriage drove on, and, as we descended the hill, I explained the facts to the President, who answered, 'Of course, I didn't know anything about it, but I thought you knew your own business best.' I thanked him for his confidence, and assured him that what he had done would go far to enable me to maintain good discipline, and it did."

This is the characteristic note of Sherman, which sets him off — in the early phase of the war — from certain of the generals of the North as well as from those of the South. It is impossible to read of this phase without getting the impression that there was a certain amount of comedy in the first squaring-off of the combatants. They did not really want to fight; it was something of a gentlemen's game. The South took the thing as a tournament, and in the North the inactive McClellan, General-in-chief till March, 1862 — though he, too, had to behave with severity in suppressing the mutinies that followed Bull Run — did much to encourage this spirit. "The trouble with many of our generals in the beginning," said Grant to John Russell Young, "was that they did not believe in the war. I mean that they did not have that complete assurance in success which belongs to good generalship. They had views about slavery, protecting rebel property, State rights — political views that interfered with their judgments." It was Sherman and Grant who changed this.

Let us accompany Sherman on his famous campaign, which begins in the spring of 1864, when Lincoln has just had Grant made General-in-chief of the Union armies and when Grant has turned over to Sherman, now a brigadier general in the regular army, the Division of the Mississippi. Sherman's pursuit of General Joseph Johnston has brought him by July to Atlanta, and he is launched upon an independent exploit which is to open a new age in tactics and to set a new record for ruthlessness in the conduct of the Civil War.

A British expert on military matters and the author of a book on Sherman, Captain B. H. Liddell Hart, has discussed Sherman's innovations in a recent introduction to a reprint of the *Memoirs*.* Liddell Hart acknowledges his own indebtedness for his "theory of strategy and tactics in mechanized warfare" to his study of Sherman's campaigns, and he asserts that the methods of Rommel and other German commanders in World War II were influenced by translations of his, Liddell Hart's, writings. The perpetrator of "the march to the sea" does

---

* This reprint is not, however, otherwise to be recommended. It reproduces the text of the first edition and lacks the first and the final chapters which Sherman afterwards added, as well as Sherman's revisions and the copious appendix of letters, contesting or supplementing his statements, that he received when the book first appeared.

seem to have invented the *Blitzkrieg*. He successfully broke away from the old-fashioned battle in form, in which one side is lined up against the other. While Grant engaged the enemy in Virginia, Sherman made a grand tour of the South, cutting loose from his base of supplies, reducing his transport and equipment to a minimum, and feeding his troops on the country. It was in the course of Sherman's campaigns that engineering first became important as a factor in modern warfare. Sherman's troops were so adept in rebuilding bridges and in repairing the railroads which they needed that one of the inhabitants, says Sherman, exclaimed of a blown-up tunnel which had been meant to block the invaders: "Oh, hell! Don't you know that old Sherman carries a *duplicate* tunnel along?"

Sherman's story of his march on the South must be one of the most articulate and engrossing ever written by an important general. It creates the appalled suspense of a kind of Grand Guignol horror, as we follow this intrepid and disciplined man, in many ways so sympathetic, going further and further in destructiveness, and recounting the process with the utmost exactitude and without the slightest compunction. The personality of Sherman was rather complex; he alternated between contradictory impulses, but he was passionate in everything he did. His love of his men was real, his devotion to his family touching. He wept when General James McPherson was killed and the news had to be communicated to the girl whom Sherman, by forbidding him furlough, had just prevented McPherson from marrying, as he had wept when he heard the news of South Carolina's secession, and he had been so much overcome by the tears of his Louisiana cadets when he had to resign from the seminary that, unable to make them a farewell speech, he had simply, an onlooker reports, "put his hand on his heart, saying 'You are all here,' wheeled on his heel" and left the room. He had very much liked the Southerners in his early days, when he was stationed in South Carolina, and the spontaneous affection toward old Southern friends which continues to manifest itself throughout the war as a natural generosity, will afterwards, in his policy toward the enemy, come to conflict with such previous expressions as the following in a letter to Sheridan, on the eve of the march to Atlanta: "The problem of war consists in the awful fact that the present class of men who rule the South must be killed outright rather than in the conquest of territory." But he was given, when severely taxed, to morbid apprehensions and obsessions. He had become so despairing of success in Kentucky in the autumn of 1861, so irrationally convinced that the enemy outnumbered the Federal forces, that his superiors had grave misgivings and sent him home for a rest. For a time he was suicidal, and his wife, in much anxiety, wrote to his brother John, then Senator from Ohio, "If there were no kind of insanity in your family and if his feelings were not already in a marked state, I would feel less concern about him, but as it is, I cannot bear to have him go back to St. Louis haunted by the specter and reading the effects of it in any apparent insubordination of officers or men. It will induce and fasten upon him that melancholy insanity to which your family is subject." Three years later, after the success of the Atlanta campaign, Sherman was to write to Halleck: "I owe you all I now enjoy of fame, for I had allowed myself in 1861 to sink into a perfect slough of despond, and do believe I would have run away and hid from dangers and complications that surround us."

But in the course of the Atlanta campaign it is evident that a "manic" elation is coming to compensate for his earlier demoralization. He was later to demand of the enemy whether it had not been the Southern soldiers who had begun "to burn the houses of Union men in Kentucky and carry off the slaves of Union men in Kentucky" at a time when "I, poor innocent, would not let a soldier take a green apple, or a fence rail to make a cup of coffee," and it was not Sherman but Grant who had inaugurated the policy of "living off the country." Grant had instructed Sheridan to strip the Shenandoah Valley of "crops, animals, negroes, and all men under fifty years of age capable of bearing arms." Houses, however, were not to be burned. But already, in the Vicksburg campaign, it was obvious that Sherman, then one of the two heads of the Division of the Mississippi, was beginning to show ominous signs of pursuing a more brutal policy. When Confederate guerrillas had opened fire on certain Mississippi steamboats that were not involved in Union operations, he warned Memphis that for every such incident ten families would be expelled from the city, and when this happened again a few days later, he had a village burned near the place where the attack had occurred, and threatened to fill some boats with captive guerrillas and use them as targets for his cannon.

One has already been struck, reading Sherman's account of the incidents of the Vicksburg campaign, by a certain ineffectiveness and a certain insouciance in his efforts to protect property. When he has entered on one occasion a fine house by Lake St. Joseph and discovered a Federal soldier with his feet on the keys of "a magnificent grand piano," after sending the soldier about his business, he orders the Negroes on the place to bring back some furniture they have taken away and orders an old servant to stand on the porch and tell any marauding soldiers that "the property belonged to Mr. Bowie, who was the brother-in-law of our friend Mr. Reverdy Johnson, of Baltimore." He sent a wagon to rescue two portraits, "but before the wagon had reached Bowie's, the house was burned, whether by some of our men or by negroes I have never learned." A hotel in Jackson had burst into flames a few moments after Sherman had assured the owner that he had no intention of burning it. And now we are chilled as we realize that this once over-anxious and panicky but now firm and clearheaded man is about to let his ruthlessness rip. Yet we cannot help sharing his excitement, we cannot help being swept along. This is the true exhilaration of conquest, something that gets away out of bounds of the checks of civilian society. This is the real exaltation of leadership. "It is related of Napoleon," says Sherman, "that his last words were, 'Tête d'armée!' Doubtless, as the shadow of death obscured his memory, the last thought that remained for speech was of some event when he was directing an important 'head of column.' I believe that every general who has handled armies in battle must recall from his own experience the intensity of thought on some similar occasion, when by a single command he had given the finishing stroke to some complicated action. . . . To be at the head of a strong column of troops, in the execution of some task that requires brain, is the highest pleasure of war — a grim one and terrible, but which leaves on the mind and memory the strongest mark; to detect the weak point in the enemy's lines; to break through with vehemence and thus lead to victory; or to discover some key-point and hold it with tenacity; or to do some other distinct act which is afterward recognized as the real cause of success. These all become matters that are never forgotten. Other great difficulties, experienced by every general, are to measure truly the thousand-and-one reports that come to him in the midst of conflict; to preserve a clear and well-defined purpose at every instant of time, and to cause all efforts to converge to that end. . . . Some men think that modern armies may be so regulated that a general can sit in an office and play on his several columns as on the keys of a piano; this is a fearful mistake. The directing mind must be at the very head of the army — must be seen there, and the effect of his mind and personal energy must be felt by every officer and man present with it, to secure the best results. Every attempt to make war easy and safe will result in humiliation and disaster."

We are aware, as we read the *Memoirs*, that an appetite for warfare is emerging, and that it grows as it feeds on the South. "War is cruelty, and you cannot refine it," he was to write to the people of Atlanta; but later, to one of his generals, that Sheridan, if the latter came to join him, would be "a disturbing element in the grand and beautiful game of war." And there was evidently, for Sherman, a certain relation between the cruelty and the beauty. He was quite different in this from Grant, who told Young that he "never went into a battle willingly or with enthusiasm. I was always glad when a battle was over. I never want to command another army. I take no interest in armies. When the Duke of Cambridge asked me to review his troops at Aldershot, I told his Royal Highness that the one thing I never wanted to see again was a military parade. When I resigned from the army and went to a farm I was happy. When the rebellion came I returned to the service because it was a duty."

Neither Sherman nor Grant for a moment questioned the paramount importance of saving the United States; it was not to free the slaves they were fighting, in spite of what Grant was to tell Bismarck, but inspired by the political ideal which Walt Whitman and others called "Unionism." In Sherman's case, we feel that he is constantly sustained by a genuine indignation against the "disloyalty" of the "rebels." "He could not comprehend or tolerate," says the writer of the posthumous chapter of the *Memoirs,* "any minimizing of the principles of Supreme National Authority, or of the absolute right of the government to the use of force in vindicating the supremacy of the nation." And a demon possesses him now to abase and lay waste the Confederacy. Yet of course it is the enemy whom he sees as demonic. "It will be," he wires to Grant, "a physical impossibility to protect the roads, now that Hood, Forrest, Wheeler, and the whole batch of devils, are turned loose without home or habitation. . . . I propose that we break up the railroad from Chattanooga forward, and that we strike out with our wagons for Milledgeville, Millen, and Savannah. Until we can repopulate Georgia, it is useless for us to occupy it; but the utter destruction of its roads, houses, and people will cripple their military resources. By attempting to hold the roads, we will lose a thousand men each month, and will gain no result. I can make this march, and make Georgia howl! We have on hand over eight thousand head of cattle and three million rations of bread, but no corn. We can find plenty of forage in the interior of the State."

Now, Sherman was not religious. He has moments when he falls into the Biblical language that so often sets the tone for the North: "God himself," he declared to the Tennesseans when they protested at his cruel reprisals for the firing on Mississippi steamboats, "has obliterated whole races from the face of the earth for sins less heinous"; but he admitted in his later years that he "guessed he did not believe in anything," and he was far from sharing the common New England delusion of the apocalyptic character of the war. He had no use for the Abolitionists and had thoroughly disapproved of John Brown. He said that "if the people of the South had

stood by the Constitution, I for one would have fought
for the protection of the slave property, just as much as
for any other kind of property." (The Southerners, as
will be seen, had a different interpretation of the Constitution.) When invited in Louisiana, at the time of
his residence there, to give his views on the Negro problem, he recommended a prohibition against the splitting-
up of families by sale and a repeal of the statute that
made it a crime to teach Negroes to read and write
(opinions, in fact, very similar to those of the Virginia
plantation owner in John Pendleton Kennedy's novel
Swallow Barn, published in 1832). In letters to his
brother-in-law, Sherman was expressing himself even
more strongly than this: "I would not if I could abolish
or modify slavery. I don't know that I would materially
change the actual political relation of master and slave.
Negroes in the great numbers that exist here must of
necessity be slaves. Theoretical notions of humanity and
religion cannot shake the commercial fact that their labor
is of great value and cannot be dispensed with," and
he discusses the advisability, when his wife shall be
joining him there, of "buying a nigger" for the household. "But it is inevitable," he adds, as if to anticipate
objection. "Niggers won't work unless they are owned,
and white servants are not to be found in this parish."
He regrets the institution of slavery, but for the reason
that the fear of revolt is unsettling to Southern society.
He incurred the disapprobation of the Abolitionist North
by driving away the Negroes who attempted to follow
his army, except in the case of such males as he thought
could render useful service, and he was horrified and
astounded when, just before the end of the war, he
heard for the first time from Stanton that there was serious question in Washington of giving the Negro the
vote. He wrote to his brother, when the war was over,

that the problem before the country was not to "enlarge" the privilege of voting but "gradually" to "curtail it, in order to have stability and security."

It cannot even be thought that Sherman was fighting in any sense for democracy. The man who said "Vox populi, vox humbug" and who wrote to his wife, at the time when he was becoming famous, "Read history, read *Coriolanus*, and you will see the true measure of popular applause," the great soldier who described himself as "almost a monarchist" and who is said to have asserted repeatedly that, in the interest of winning the war, every newspaper in the country should be suppressed, can hardly be regarded as a democrat. He had been all for abolishing the governments of the "rebellious" Southern states and, by depriving them of a voice in their own affairs, reducing them to virtual subjection "for years to come" after victory. He even at one point believed that the South should be recolonized by the North and that a first step toward this should be made by sending four million Northerners south of the Ohio River to live on confiscated farms and plantations.

So Grant, after his two terms as President, was to admit, "Looking back over the whole policy of reconstruction, it seems to me that the wisest thing would have been to have continued for some time the military rule. Sensible Southern men see now that there was no government so frugal, so just, and fair as what they had under our generals. That would have enabled the Southern people to pull themselves together and repair material losses. As to depriving them, even for a time, of suffrage, that was our right as a conqueror, and it was a mild penalty for the stupendous crime of treason." Grant, as we have seen, was as little preoccupied with the ways of God as Sherman was; but both had the power of the Union behind them and were being driven by it, and we can catch from the pages of Sherman the strong throb of the lust to dominate and the ecstasy of its satisfaction which in the past has made people believe that they were fighting as instruments of God and in our own time as instruments of "History."

On September 7, 1864, after taking Atlanta, the now confident and towering Sherman announces to General John B. Hood, commander of the Confederate Army of Tennessee, that he "deemed it to the interest of the United States" to banish from their city the entire population. The reasons he submits to Halleck, then Chief of Staff at Washington, are that he needs the houses of the city for military storage and occupation; that the continued residence of the population would eventually compel him to feed them, which he cannot afford to do; that it is dangerous to have them around and a nuisance to have to guard them, that "listening to [their] ever-lasting complaints and special grievances" would take up too much of his officers' time; and that he wants to contract his lines so as not to include "the vast suburbs," which "will make it necessary to destroy the very houses used by families as residences." Hood replies that, in the situation, he cannot refuse to comply. "And now, sir, permit me to say that the unprecedented measure you propose transcends, in studied and ingenious cruelty, all acts ever before brought to my attention in the dark history of war. In the name of God and humanity, I protest, believing that you will find that you are expelling from their homes and firesides the wives and children of a brave people."

An extraordinary polemic ensues. Sherman slangs back at Hood. He declares that the Confederates had burned their own houses when they found it convenient for their purpose and that they had "defended Atlanta on a line so close to town that every cannon-shot and many musket-shots from our line of investment, that overshot their mark, went into the habitations of women and children." And he goes on to a political indictment: "In the name of common-sense, I ask you not to appeal to a just God in such a sacrilegious manner. You who, in the midst of peace and prosperity, have plunged a nation into war, dark and cruel war — who dared and badgered us to battle, insulted our flag, seized our arsenals and forts that were left in the honorable custody of peaceful ordnance-sergeants, seized and made 'prisoners of war' the very garrisons sent to protect your people against negroes and Indians, long before any overt act was committed by the (to you) hated Lincoln Government; tried to force Kentucky and Missouri into rebellion, spite of themselves; falsified the vote of Louisiana; turned loose your privateers to plunder unarmed ships; expelled Union families by the thousands, burned their houses, and declared, by an act of your Congress, the confiscation of all debts due Northern men for goods had and received! Talk thus to the marines, but not to me, who have seen these things, and who will this day make as much sacrifice for the peace and honor of the South as the best-born Southerner among you! If we must be enemies, let us be men, and fight it out as we propose to do, and not deal in such hypocritical appeals to God and humanity. God will judge us in due time, and he will pronounce whether it be more humane to fight with a town full of women and families of a brave people at our back or to remove them in time to places of safety among their own friends and people."

To this Hood replies that such houses as the Confederates had had to destroy had been sacrificed in self-defense, and that the danger to the civilians in Atlanta had been due to the failure of Sherman to give notice "of your purpose to shell the town, which is

usual in war among civilized nations. . . . The residue
of your letter is rather discussion. It opens a wide field
for the discussion of questions which I do not feel are
committed to me. I am only a general of one of the
armies of the Confederate States, charged with military
operations in the field, under the direction of my superior
officers, and I am not called upon to discuss with you the
causes of the present war, or the political questions which
led to or resulted from it. These grave and important
questions have been committed to far abler hands than
mine, and I shall only refer to them so far as to repel
any unjust conclusion which might be drawn from my
silence. You charge my country with 'daring and badger-
ing you to battle.' The truth is, we sent commissioners
to you, respectfully offering a peaceful separation, before the first gun was fired on either side. You say we
insulted your flag. The truth is, we fired upon it, and
those who fought under it, when you came to our doors
upon the mission of subjugation. You say we seized
upon your forts and arsenals, and made prisoners of the
garrisons sent to protect us against negroes and Indians.
The truth is, we, by force of arms, drove out insolent
intruders and took possession of our own forts and arsenals, to resist your claims to dominion over masters,
slaves, and Indians, all of whom are to this day, with a
unanimity unexampled in the history of the world, warring against your attempts to become their masters. You
say that we tried to force Missouri and Kentucky into
rebellion in spite of themselves. The truth is, my Government, from the beginning of this struggle to this hour,
has again and again offered, before the whole world, to
leave it to the unbiased will of these States, and all
others, to determine for themselves whether they will
cast their destiny with your Government or ours; and
your Government has resisted this fundamental principle

of free institutions with the bayonet, and labors daily, by force and fraud, to fasten its hateful tyranny upon the unfortunate freemen of these States. You say we falsified the vote of Louisiana. The truth is, Louisiana not only separated herself from your Government by nearly a unanimous vote of her people, but has vindicated the act upon every battle-field from Gettysburg to the Sabine, and has exhibited an heroic devotion to her decisions which challenges the admiration and respect of every man capable of feeling sympathy for the oppressed or admiration for heroic valor. You say that we turned loose pirates to plunder your unarmed ships. The truth is, when you robbed us of our part in the navy, we built and bought a few vessels, hoisted the flag of our country, and swept the seas, in defiance of your navy, around the whole circumference of the globe. You say we have expelled Union families by thousands. The truth is, not a single family has been expelled from the Confederate States, that I am aware of; but, on the contrary, the moderation of our Government toward traitors has been a fruitful theme of denunciation by its enemies and well-meaning friends of our cause. You say my Government, by acts of Congress, has confiscated 'all debts due Northern men for goods sold and delivered.' The truth is, our Congress gave due and ample time to your merchants and traders to depart from our shores with their ships, goods, and effects, and only sequestrated the property of our enemies in retaliation for their acts — declaring us traitors, and confiscating our property wherever their power extended, either in their country or our own. Such are your accusations, and such are the facts known of all men to be true. . . . You say, 'Let us fight it out like men.' To this my reply is — for myself, and I believe for all the true men, ay, and women and children in my country — we will fight you to the death!

Better die a thousand deaths than submit to live under you or your Government and your negro allies!"

Sherman retorts to this that he was not bound — "see the books" — by the laws of war to give notice of the shelling of Atlanta, a fortified town, with magazines and arsenals, and that "we have no 'negro allies' in this army; not a single negro soldier left Chattanooga with this army, or is with it now." But though Hood, Sherman says, has begun the dispute "by characterizing an official act of mine in unfair and improper terms," he agrees that "this discussion by two soldiers is out of place, and profitless."

This browbeating was part of a policy of deliberate intimidation. Sherman was anticipating the *Schrecklichkeit* exploited by the Germans in the first World War as well as the *Blitzkrieg* of the second. "My aim . . . was to whip the rebels, to humble their pride, to follow them to their inmost recesses, and make them fear and dread us. 'Fear of the Lord is the beginning of wisdom.'" And he explains that he has come to realize that terrorization itself is "a weapon."

Some idea of the consternation created by Sherman's invasion — and even for a professional soldier like Hood — may be formed from reading the writings of the once popular novelist John Esten Cooke. John Esten Cooke was an amiable Virginian, who inhabited a world of chivalry that was partly perhaps real but was in any case very much colored by the fantasies of chivalric fiction. It was said of him that, by marrying a Page, he had allied himself to all the first Virginia families to which he was not already related. His war novel, *Surry of Eagle's-Nest,* published in 1866, which was once in every Southern library, combines his own firsthand experience as officer of horse artillery with an absurd melodramatic story, which is all in the following vein: "When, drying her eyes, she [the heroine] turned and looked at me with a smile, those great violet orbs made my pulses leap"; "He [the villain] became livid, and uttered the hoarse growl of a tiger at bay. 'Who are you?' he cried, with a flash of fury in his bloodshot eyes. . . . And, grinding his teeth audibly, he left the room." But, in spite of the authenticity of a good deal that Cooke relates in the chapters that deal with the war — the pages of which are studded with asterisks referring to notes: "His words," "Historical," "A real incident" — these glimpses of Stonewall Jackson and the other Southern generals and of the engagements in which Cooke had taken part seem almost as dreamlike as the imagined romance. In typical Southern fashion, Cooke had served under his own "kin," his cousin-in-law "Jeb" Stuart, whom he regarded as the "Flower of Cavaliers" and who is represented in *Surry* and in a biographical sketch as the jolliest fellow in the world, performing prodigies of gallantry but always ready for a good hearty laugh. He will not stand for drinking or swearing but he incurs the disapproval of one of the sterner generals by recruiting two well-known minstrels, who perform on the banjo and violin and whose presence or even the mention of whom will set Stuart's feet a-shuffling. The dashing Confederates in *Surry* are always capturing Federal wagons full of champagne and lobster salad, and feasting on them with roguish delight. When the hero is captured by McClellan — whom, apparently on account of his gentlemanliness, the author calls the greatest soldier on the Union side — he is hospitably received by the Northern general and converses with him at length in a scene which is a model of punctilious deportment. Surry, the narrator-hero, has a brother on the Union side — as

Cooke had a West Point uncle — and they occasionally meet in the course of the war, fraternally embracing on the battlefield and talking about the family and the old plantation.

In a volume of non-fictionized memoirs — *Wearing of the Gray* — published the year after the novel, Cooke is somewhat more realistic, and he protests against the current tendency to idealize the Southern generals. "The 'picturesque,'" he says, "is a poor style of art, when truth is sacrificed to it. To represent General Lee decked out in a splendid uniform bedizened with gold lace, on a 'prancing steed,' and followed by a numerous and glittering staff, might 'tickle the ears of the groundlings'; but the picture would be apt to 'make the judicious grieve.' The latter class would much prefer the actual man, in his old gray cape and plain brown coat, riding, unattended, on his sober iron-gray along the lines; would rather hear him say amid the storm of Gettysburg, in his calm brave voice, 'Never mind; it is not your fault, General; I am to blame,' than read the most eloquent sentences which the imagination could invent for him." But no more than Cooke's novels do these memoirs ever depart from the ideals of chivalry. This chivalry of course existed. I do not intend to imply that the Confederate leaders did not sometimes possess the qualities he attributes to them. The portrait of Jeb Stuart in *Wearing of the Gray* is consistent with that in the novel, and is confirmed by the testimony of others; but the mention of Stonewall Jackson's "gay and elegant form" and the statement that "his soldiers adored him" are somewhat at variance with other evidence and seem an example of the author's tendency to represent all his heroes as charmers. The good John Esten Cooke, in any case, whether recording his firsthand impressions or concocting Arthurian romances, hardly lives on the same planet as Sherman.

Yet the knightly companions of Cooke are recognizable in Sherman's picture. "The enemy had no infantry nearer than the Tallahatchee bridge, but their cavalry was saucy and active, superior to ours, and I despaired of ever protecting a railroad, presenting a broad front of one hundred miles, from their dashes." And in Sherman's remarkable analysis of the elements that compose the Confederacy which is contained in his report to Halleck of September 17, 1863, he lists: "Fourth. The young bloods of the South: sons of players and sportsmen, men who never did work and never will. War suits them, and the rascals are brave, fine riders, bold to rashness, and dangerous subjects in every sense. They care not a sou for niggers, land or anything. They hate Yankees, *per se,* and don't bother their brains, about the past, present, or future. As long as they have good horses, plenty of forage, and an open country, they are happy. This is a larger class than most men suppose, and they are the most dangerous set of men that this war has turned loose upon the world. They are splendid riders, first-rate shots, and utterly reckless. Stuart, John Morgan, Forrest, and Jackson, are the types and leaders of this class. These men must all be killed or employed by us before we can hope for peace."

Cooke had once been detailed in Maryland to search the house of a Union captain for United States Post Office money. This officer had taken to his bed and was ostensibly in violent pain, with his anxious wife at his bedside. A little daughter guided Cooke through the house, and he was overcome with embarrassment at having to ransack the ladies' wardrobes. He began to suspect that the captain had the money hidden under his mattress and was playing at illness to protect it, but he was unable to bring himself to make the other officer move, and he refused to search any more houses in which the ladies would be discommoded. One can imagine how the methods of Sherman — unexpected, implacable, outraging — would have affected such a man as Cooke. It is not at all surprising to read in the *Recollections* of George Cary Eggleston that poor Cooke had declared to him after the war that fighting was "fit work for brutes and brutish men," and confessed that, in modern warfare, "where men are organized in masses and converted into insensate machines, there is nothing heroic or romantic or in any way calculated to appeal to the imagination."

Sherman occupied Atlanta two months; then, restless and eager for action, he set the city on fire and started out on his terrible march to Savannah. "Behind us," he writes of his morning of departure, in a lyrical mood rather rare with him, "lay Atlanta, smouldering and in ruins, the black smoke rising high in the air, and hanging like a pall over the ruined city." The soldiers sang *John Brown's Body*. "We turned our horses' heads to the east; Atlanta was soon lost behind the screen of trees, and became a thing of the past. Around it clings many a thought of desperate battle, of hope and fear, that now seem like the memory of a dream; and I have never seen the place since. The day was extremely beautiful, clear sunlight, with bracing air, and an unusual feeling of exhilaration seemed to pervade all minds — a feeling of something to come, vague and undefined, still full of venture and intense interest. Even the common soldiers caught the inspiration, and many a group called out to me as I worked my way past them, 'Uncle Billy, I guess Grant is waiting for us in Richmond!' Indeed, the general sentiment was that we were marching for Richmond, and that there we should end the war, but how and when they seemed to care not; nor did they measure the distance, or count the cost in life, or bother their brains about the great rivers to be crossed, and the food required for man and beast, that had to be gathered by the way. There was a 'devil-may-care' feeling pervading officers and men, that made me feel the full load of responsibility, for success would be accepted as a matter of course, whereas, should we fail, this 'march' would be adjudged the wild adventure of a crazy fool." Though their foraging, he tells us, "was attended with great danger and hard work, there seemed to be a charm about it that attracted the soldiers. . . . No doubt, many acts of pillage, robbery, and violence were committed by these parties of foragers, usually called 'bummers'; for I have since heard of jewelry taken from women, and the plunder of articles that never reached the commissary; but these acts were exceptional and incidental. I never heard of any cases of murder and rape."

But later, in South Carolina, he writes Grant that he "will burn the houses where the people burn their forage"; and he will threaten Hardee at Savannah that unless he surrenders the city, he, Sherman, will "feel justified in resorting to the harshest measures" and will "make little effort to restrain my army." He laughs when one of his generals speaks of a town called Barnwell as "Burnwell." "If the people raise a howl," he writes Halleck, "about my barbarity and cruelty, I will answer that war is war and not popularity-seeking. If they want peace, they and their relatives must stop the war." This is the Attila Sherman of Mathew Brady's horrendous and bristling photograph, taken just after the end of hostilities, to pose for which the General either could not or would not relax his fierce and obdurate frown or subdue the almost animal hackles of his fiery red hair and beard.

In the memoirs of Grant, we have seen, one is almost

never permitted to look upon the dreadful results of carnage and devastation. These are among the things screened off, made invisible. Sheridan, too, in his account of his battles, in his own *Personal Memoirs*, never speaks of the débris of battle. It is said that he could not bear to look at a corpse, and it is only when he is writing later of the Franco-Prussian War of 1870, to which he had persuaded President Grant to send him as an observer, that he surprises us by describing the results of the carnage and expressing the utmost horror at the sights and smells of the battlefield which, in his record, he has hitherto ignored. But with Sherman the actualities, the chaos and violence and mess, are there with us all the time, along with his own personal attitude toward them, which mingles at moments with its grimness a passing expression of human regret or a brief note of admiration for the audacity of the enemy. He will speak of a "poor" farmer whom they had to rob of his cattle, of the "poor" starving mules which he had had to have shot, of "poor Columbia," South Carolina, which he had not really meant to destroy.

While Sherman was occupying Columbia, before it had gone up in flames, a message was brought to the invading general that there was a lady in town who had known him in the forties, at the time when he had been stationed in South Carolina. He walked to her house and was rather surprised to discover that her chickens and ducks had not been carried off by his soldiers, and to find about the place "a general air of peace and comfort that was really pleasant to behold at that time of universal desolation; the lady in question met us at the head of the steps and invited us into a parlor which was perfectly neat and well furnished." He inquired about her family and said that he was pleased to see "that our men had not handled her house and premises as roughly as

was their wont. 'I owe it to you, general,' she answered.'"
"Not at all," he replied. "I did not know you were here
till a few minutes ago." She produced for him a treatise
on water color that he had given her with an inscription
in the days when they had both tried to paint. By producing this old gift, she had kept off the troops, who,
says Sherman, "in five minutes more, would have rifled
her premises of all that was good to eat or wear. I made
her a long social visit, and, before leaving Columbia,
gave her a half-tierce of rice and about one hundred
pounds of ham from our own mess-stores." Sherman's
soldiers, though he does not mention it, deliberately burned
the library and destroyed the scientific collections of a very
distinguished scholar, Dr. R. W. Gibbes of Columbia,
and, though some effort was made to protect it, the Revolutionary historical library, probably unequalled in the
South, of William Gilmore Simms, its most famous contemporary writer, was eventually burned by the "bummers."

But only rarely, in describing his exploits, does the
writer strike a false note — as when he castigates as
"wanton mischief" the shelling of his troops by the enemy
when the Federals were encamped just outside Columbia,
though he himself had been firing what he minimizes as
"a few shells near the depot, to scare away the negroes who
were appropriating the bags of corn and meal which we
wanted" and "three shots at the unoccupied State-House";
or when he becomes excessively indignant over the plant-
ing of "torpedoes" in his route. "This was not war, but
murder, and it made me very angry. I immediately ordered
a lot of rebel prisoners to be brought from the provost-
guard, armed with picks and spades, and made them march
in close order along the road, so as to explode their own torpedoes, or to discover and dig them up. They begged hard,
but I reiterated the order, and I could hardly help laughing

at their stepping so gingerly along the road, where it was supposed sunken torpedoes might explode at each step." It is noteworthy as throwing into special relief the uninhibited reactions of Sherman and his frankness in giving them expression that Sheridan, in telling of a similar incident — a mined road and Confederate prisoners compelled to dig out the torpedoes — is neither amused nor indignant. Yet Sherman had the instincts of a statesman and knew how to put the brakes on his depredations. When Savannah readily surrendered, he of course confiscated its cotton, but he treated the inhabitants with leniency and even fed them out of his stores. The terror had been successful. Two of the Confederate generals entrusted their families to Sherman's protection. They knew very well, says Sherman, that the newspaper reports in Savannah had been wildly exaggerated.

When Sherman had finally established himself, in March, 1865, in Goldsboro, North Carolina — after a march, he says, even more arduous, from swampland, bad weather and difficult rivers, than his progress from Atlanta to the sea — he and Grant met with the President for a conference at City Point, Virginia. Here Lincoln explained his policy of offering the enemy liberal terms — presumably along the lines that he was to lay down, on April 11, in the last of his public addresses: state governments loyal to the Union were to be encouraged in the Southern states, and the vote for the time being granted only to "the very intelligent" Negroes or to "those who serve our cause as soldiers."

The second part of this program was more acceptable to Sherman than the proposal of the Radical Republicans to give the franchise to the Negroes indiscriminately, and though the first part of it, as we have seen, was contrary to the views that he had sometimes expressed in certain of his harsher moods, he was now having one of his *revirements* in the direction of generous feeling. He was writing his wife that the suffering of the South was already "beyond comprehension. People who talk of further retaliation and punishment, except of political leaders, either do not conceive the suffering endured already, or they are heartless or unfeeling"; and to Grant's right-hand man Rawlins: "The South is broken and ruined and appeals to our pity. To ride the people down with persecutions and military exactions would be like slashing away at the crew of a sinking ship." A few days after Appomattox, Sherman held conferences in North Carolina with General Joseph E. Johnston and with General John C. Breckinridge, then Confederate Secretary of War, for the purpose of arranging a truce. He and Johnston, though they had not met before, addressed one another as "Cump" and "Joe," their nicknames from West Point days. When Johnston suggested having Breckinridge present, Sherman objected, "No, no. We don't recognize any civil government among you fellows, Joe." Johnston reminded Sherman that Breckinridge was a major general, and as an officer had a right to be received by Sherman, and Sherman assented to this. But Breckinridge, "a huge Kentuckian," says Sherman's biographer Lloyd Lewis, who "had for days gone without his quota of whisky," badly needed a drink before he could unlimber his legal lore, and Sherman, perceiving this, said, "Gentlemen, it occurred to me perhaps you were not overstocked with liquor, and I procured some medical stores." Everybody had a drink, and Breckinridge proved very helpful. But then Sherman, becoming thoughtful, poured another drink for himself without offering one to the others and, putting the bottle back into his saddlebags, drank it silently while he looked out the window. "What do you think of Sherman?" asked Johnston when the conference was over and the two Southerners were riding away. "He is a bright man and a man of great force," said Breckinridge; but then burst out: "General Johnston, General Sherman is a hog. Yes, sir, a hog! Did you see him take that drink by himself?" Johnston attempted to defend him: Sherman was "a royal good fellow, but the most absent-minded man in the world." "Ah, no Kentucky gentleman," cried Breckinridge, "would ever have put away that bottle. He knew we needed it." When this was later repeated to Sherman, he said that he did not remember it, "but if Joe Johnston told it, it is so. Those fellows hustled me that day; I was sorry for the drink I did give them."

For Sherman's position was difficult, and it was later to become even more so. The terms he was offering the Confederates — in consequence of his interview with Lincoln — included recognition by the Federal Government of the ex-Confederate states when they should have taken the oath of loyalty, and a Federal guarantee of the "political rights and franchises" of the Southerners as well as of "their right of person and property" as citizens of the United States. He assumed that it would be only a question of referring this agreement to Washington and having it approved by the War Department. But in the meantime Lincoln had been murdered, and in the leaderless confusion that followed, these magnanimous terms were overruled by Secretary of War Stanton, who absurdly attributed to Sherman the ambition of becoming a dictator and seems even to have been fearing a coup d'état. Stanton, with no Lincoln to guide him, went to the lengths of arousing the press by publishing a garbled version of the peace terms proposed by Sherman and suggesting that the wrecker of Georgia had connived at letting Jefferson Davis escape with a considerable amount of gold. This charge was entirely false, but even if it had been true, it would not have been contrary to the policy of Lincoln — so far as Davis's escape was concerned — as he had intimated to Sherman and Grant in one of his humorous parables in the course of the conference at City Point. Sherman, of course, was furious, and thereafter, during the period of the Reconstruction, when the Radical Republicans in Congress were having it all their own way, found himself in the strange situation of having earned popularity in the South as its champion against Federal oppression.

He had come to loathe politicians and was never at home in Washington. Much shrewder than Grant in a worldly way and self-willed to the point of truculence, he managed to keep clear of the mess which was created, after Lincoln's death, in Washington, as a result of the duel between Andrew Johnson, who was now trying to rescue the South from the faction that wanted to crush it, and the Radical Congress which tried to remove him — a contest in which Stanton's retention of the office of Secretary of War when the President wanted to get rid of him was to become one of the principal issues. Grant found himself rather perplexed between the head of his department and the President, and the latter made a desperate effort to get Sherman to come to Washington and act as an intermediary. He offered to promote him to the rank of Grant; but Sherman flatly refused, explaining that, during the years of the war, he had spent, on an average, with his wife and children only about thirteen days out of the three hundred and sixty-five and that he wanted to "make the acquaintance of his family."

When Grant became President in 1869, he made Sherman "General of the Army," but at the same time appointed as Secretary of War his guardian angel Rawlins, one of whose chief duties had been to stand between Grant and the bottle. The opinionated and obstinate

Rawlins issued orders without consulting Sherman, but he died at the end of six months, and was succeeded, at Sherman's suggestion, by General W. W. Belknap, who constantly went over Sherman's head and gradually usurped his functions. Sherman protested to Grant, but could not persuade him to take any action; then, accepting the situation with unusual equanimity, he indulged himself in a year abroad and on his return moved the headquarters of his department to St. Louis, where he discharged at his ease the routine of his office and worried as little as possible about what was going on in Washington. Belknap was forced to resign in March, 1876, as a result of having been exposed as a trafficker in sutlerships, and Sherman now agreed to move back to the capital, "if assured of decent treatment." He retired as General of the Army in April, 1884, in the summer of which the heaviest possible pressure was brought to bear by the Republican party to induce him to run for the Presidency. Understanding himself and politics so much better than Grant had done, he emphatically wired the convention, "I will not accept if nominated and will not serve if elected."

One day, Sherman tells us, when, after the war, he was riding along Pennsylvania Avenue with Grant, his companion "inquired of me in a humorous way, 'Sherman, what special hobby do you intend to adopt?' I inquired what he meant, and he explained that all men had their special weakness or vanity, and that it was wiser to choose one's own than to leave the newspapers to affix one less acceptable, and that for his part he had chosen the 'horse,' so that when any one tried to pump him he would turn the conversation to his 'horse.' I answered that I would stick to the 'theater and balls,' for I was always fond of seeing young people happy, and did actually acquire a reputation for 'dancing,' though I had not attempted the waltz, or anything more than the ordinary cotillion, since the war."

If the General's dancing had somewhat lapsed, his passion for the theater survived the war. At Nashville in 1863, when Sherman was visiting headquarters, he had persuaded Grant and two other generals to attend a performance of *Hamlet*, at which they sat in the first row of the balcony. Sherman, as one of his companions reports, became "so indignant at the butchery of the play [that is, the bad production] that he could not keep still" and kept making loud complaints. This caused so much embarrassment to the others, who were afraid that the audience of soldiers would recognize them and give them an ovation, that Grant, his superior officer, was obliged to make him leave the theater before the performance was over.

When at last he was released from the strain of the war, Sherman thoroughly enjoyed his freedom and his prestige as a national figure — though he developed an extreme antipathy to the war song *Marching Through Georgia*, which so often greeted his appearance, and was heard to curse softly when on one occasion a chorus of colored porters, on a Pullman car in which he was travelling, tried to pay him a tribute by singing it. He loved attending Army reunions, constantly dined out, and was much in demand for after-dinner speeches. Even Chauncey Depew said of Sherman that he was "the readiest and the most original talker in the United States." Typical is his comment on his critics in the preface to the second edition of his *Memoirs*: "I am publishing my own memoirs, not theirs, and we all know that no three honest witnesses of a simple brawl can agree on all the details. How much more likely will be the difference in a great battle covering a vast space of broken ground, when each division, brigade, regiment, and even company, naturally and honestly believes that it was the focus of the whole affair! Each of them won the battle. None ever lost. That was the fate of the old man who unhappily commanded." Good also are his descriptions of "military fame": "to be killed on the field of battle and have our names spelled wrong in the newspapers"; and his program for visiting Europe: "Uncle Cump was travelling abroad," one of his nieces wrote, "and such an odd tour, not going first to England as was the custom, but first through the Continent, then even to Egypt, saving England for the last, as he explained, so that he might be equal to those Englishmen when they mentioned their travels abroad." As was often the case with Westerners who had had the range of the early West, he liked to revisit those canyons and coasts, those communities of struggling settlers, and take account of what had happened since his youth. St. Louis in the long run bored him, and he came to live in New York, where he frequented the Union League Club, chafed at dinners which were making him late for the theater and became one of the founders of the Players Club.

Sherman's life in his later years was, however, in one very important respect, sadly unsatisfactory: he was not fully to realize his hope of establishing close relations with his family. One is struck, in reading his memoirs, by the relatively little amount of time which, even before the war, he seems to have spent with his wife and children. They are always either just about to join him or have just been obliged to return to Lancaster, Ohio, the common birthplace of Ellen Sherman and

Sherman. Their reunions were invariably fruitful — they had eight children through a period of as many years — but one wonders about Ellen Sherman, and one may have one's curiosity gratified, or partially gratified, by the copiously documented biography, *Sherman, Fighting Prophet,* by the late Lloyd Lewis.

Ellen Sherman was the daughter of that Thomas Ewing, the senator and Cabinet member, who, at the time of their father's death, had made himself responsible for "Cump" and had taken him into his household. The boy had grown up with the Ewing children almost as if with sisters and brothers (while his mother still lived in the same block), and Cump had married Ellen when he was thirty. Mr. Lewis believes that her relations with Sherman were to remain always more or less sisterly. In some sense, she was perhaps not impressed by him in the way that his troops and the public were. She had been close to him from earliest childhood; she knew that he was rather erratic; she had seen him through his breakdown at the beginning of the war. Certainly their letters show that Ellen did not allow herself to be very much influenced by him, and her career was semi-independent. Her tendency seems always to have been — rather, one gathers, to Sherman's annoyance — to gravitate back to Lancaster, where her family were still living. Thomas Ewing, says Mr. Lewis, was as important to Ellen as her husband — she eventually, after his death, wrote a biography of him — and she seems to have been one of the few people closely associated with Sherman who never came under his domination.

Thomas Ewing was a Presbyterian, but Ellen's mother had been Irish and a Catholic. Ellen had been brought up in her mother's religion, and her intensifying activities as a Catholic were to come more and more to figure as a barrier between her and her husband. When at one point he had shown irritation with her for taking some Catholic line, she had protested, "Why Cump, why should you be surprised? You knew when you married me that I was a Catholic." "Of course I did," he replied, "but I didn't know that you would get worse every year." In the teeth of the annoyance of Sherman, who could ill afford the extra expense yet was unable to prevail against Ellen, she sent the children to parochial schools. During the war, she worked for Catholic charities, and her husband once wrote her rebuking her for selling things at a bazaar — not, he said, on account of the Catholic auspices but because it was no role for a lady to serve customers behind a counter. When he discovered that she was bringing her influence to bear on General Dodge in St. Louis to set free some political prisoners, Sherman wrote him, "You must not issue these orders and release these people simply because Mrs. Sherman requests you to do so. . . . I appreciate fully what you are doing and why you do it, but, my dear general, you know you must cling to a soldier's duty." At the time when he was being urged to accept the Republican nomination for President, he gave as one of his reasons for refusing that Mrs. Sherman would keep the White House "full of priests."

One of the tragedies of Sherman's life had been the loss of his eldest son. "He seemed," writes the father, "more than any of the children to take an interest in my special profession"; but Willie had died at nine in Memphis of typhoid, in the autumn after the Vicksburg campaign. "Willie was, or thought he was," wrote his father, in reply to a letter of condolence on behalf of the Thirteenth Battalion, "a sergeant in the Thirteenth. I have seen his eye brighten, his heart beat, as he beheld the battalion under arms, and asked me if they were not *real* soldiers." And Sherman's plans, after the war, for a younger son were to be frustrated in a different way. "One day," reports a niece of Ellen's, "the General came in to dinner full of spirits, sparkling and happy. 'I was talking to Grant today,' he said. 'He's going to send Fred to such and such a preparatory school, and I'll have Tom go there too; so Grant's boy and mine can be together. Later on, they can go to West Point together. That will be splendid. And Senator Blank wants Ellie and Rachel to go to such and such a school with his little girls. . . .' Aunt Ellen broke in: 'Cump, tomorrow morning at 8 o'clock Tom's going to Georgetown to the Jesuit College, and tomorrow morning the girls are going to the Sisters' school around the corner — or tomorrow morning at 10 o'clock I'll take them all back to my father.' The General was terribly hurt, got up and left the table. He was mum for several days. But by the end of the week Aunt Ellen said he was reconciled to it and was helping Tom with his lessons as though nothing had happened. He was tremendously loving with his family, very close to them and affectionate."

Tom later on graduated from law school, but then, to the bitter disappointment of his father, decided to enter the priesthood. "He was the keystone of my Arch," Sherman wrote to an old friend, "and his going away lets down the whole structure with a crash." The General was even driven to try to formulate a theological position. "I believe God governs this world," he wrote to the same friend, "with all its life, animal, vegetable and human, by invariable laws, resulting in the greatest good, though sometimes working seeming hardships. The idea of a vocation from God seems to me *ir*religious and I would look for the inspiration of a vocation in the opposite quarter (the Devil). When anybody assumes 'vocation' their reason and all sense ceases and man becomes simply a blind animal. My idea of God is that he has given man reason, and he has no right to disregard it." And eleven years after this he writes to a member of the family: "I can't get over Tom. Why should they have taken my splendid boy? They could have brought over thirty priests from Italy in his place." He did not attend Tom's ordination, and when the latter had finished his noviceship in a Jesuit college in England, he wrote his father, after seeing him in Washington, that he had not been able to help seeing "that it cost an effort on your part to overcome the repugnance my strange dress naturally excited." Relations between them were never the same.

One may sympathize with Sherman in his disappointment; one may even feel resentful of Ellen. Yet one guesses that there was something more than an accelerating Catholic fanaticism in her resolute and zealous devotion. She was perhaps trying to expiate a little the horrors and griefs of Georgia, and her son's dedication to the priesthood was perhaps the price paid by his father for the reckless elation of his March to the Sea. In the remarkable painting of Ellen by G. P. A. Healy, the cross that hangs on her bosom, unobtrusive though it is at first sight, comes inevitably, as one looks, to draw attention as the center of the picture.

Ellen died in 1888. When her husband was called to her bedside, he came running upstairs, calling out, "Wait for me, Ellen: No one ever loved you as I love you!" He fell immediately after her death into one of his abysmal depressions and survived her only three years. He died in February, 1891; he had collapsed just after his seventy-first birthday, which he had spent in the room in which Ellen had died. He had been sitting in a rocking chair in front of the fire, rereading *Great Expectations*.

Tom Sherman was, however, very proud of his father. His biographer, Father Joseph T. Durkin, must surely be right in believing that the attraction he felt toward the Jesuit Order was partly due to its discipline, which allowed him to think of it as a kind of army. He was to say of the Jesuits later: "We are regulars in the army of Christ." And the key to his determination to get away from his family in St. Louis and pass his novitiate in England, which so much annoyed his father, is probably to be found in a passage from a letter of the General's to one of his daughters: "Tom's course . . . has embittered me more than I ought to write. I try to check my feelings against him personally but cannot against the cause of his action, the Catholic Church. I realize that all I held most dear and whom I have tried hard to provide for literally are not mine, but belong to a power that heeds no claim but its own; who takes unfeelingly . . . my son whom I had trained to assist me in the care of a large and expanding family." It seems clear that, if Tom had not left home, he would have been more or less under his father's orders, and that if, even as a Jesuit, he had remained in St. Louis, his duties in his calling would have come into conflict with his father's demands upon him. Yet he thought of his father with tenderness and was troubled by the estrangement between them. "I think," he wrote him many years later, "you and I have been very sensible, everything considered. We have agreed to differ and what better can men do who are set each in his own way? The remembrance of the chat I had with you in St. Louis will be one of my most cherished recollections through life, though I suppose all of your children will be inclined to dwell on the thought of their father as he came back to the fireside in '65 with a nation's blessing and unsullied honor fixed upon him, when he read to them from Dickens, Scott, and Irving, with the sim-

plicity and tenderness of one of those old Roman heroes —
a Fabius, Cincinnatus or a Scipio." And so powerful was
the pull of the General in Tom's blood and imagination
that he eventually became obsessed by him and confused
his own career with his father's.

First of all, Father Sherman, the Jesuit priest, was to
become a public figure, and it is significant that his
emergence into celebrity should have begun — in 1891 —
just after his father's death. From then on, for almost
five years, he was to attain as a preacher and a public
lecturer a popularity that seems astonishing for a member of this very private order who had begun as a priest
and a scholar. His audiences grew bigger and bigger,
and he travelled from coast to coast. On the platform,
says Father Durkin, "he looked like nothing so much as
a field commander addressing his troops. It was always
noted that his spare, militarily erect figure of medium
height, his snapping blue eyes, aggressive jaw, and decisive — almost impatient — gestures recalled his father's
appearance. The lines of his pale face were clear-cut and
refined. His voice had usually a metallic ring and great
carrying power; but he had a trick of modulating it to a
tense softness."

Undoubtedly he dramatized himself: the father's love
of the theater seems to have come out in the son — and
also the father's harshness. With his pupils, in connection with the Civil War, he had always been cutting
about the South, and he now delivered fierce orations
against Socialism and anti-Catholicism, which he regarded as allied conspiracies. He eventually, on a visit to
Chicago, went so far as to allow to be quoted in print a
statement that, "the father who slays the corrupter of his
child must be left to God Almighty, the man who shoots
an anarchist at sight is a public benefactor." There was
a bad public reaction to this, and his superiors felt that

he had got out of hand. He was rebuked by the Father Provincial of Missouri for the sensationalism of his lectures and ordered to discontinue them. This was followed by what was then called a "nervous breakdown," and Father Sherman asked for permission to recuperate outside the Jesuit house. He had come to feel a certain discomfort in the restrictions imposed by the Order, and believed that his only hope was "to live for awhile as if he were not a Jesuit." This request was refused by the Provincial. But our war with Spain then broke out, and Father Sherman's superiors had the happy idea of sending him as a chaplain to Puerto Rico, where he was able to wear a uniform and to act as an observer for the War Department. He turned in what was evidently a thorough and quite realistic report, in which he explained with intelligence the differences between the Spanish Puerto Ricans and ourselves, described the degraded life of many of the native population and pointed out the prime importance of our winning the support of the educated classes; and he somewhat alarmed his own church by calling the island "a Catholic country without a religion," though he added that Faith was "not dead, but dormant."

He spent a night in a hacienda in which he found the household on edge: a band of rebels had been burning plantations. Three civil guards had come to defend them, and all the men on the place had been armed. Father Sherman took a revolver, too. He posted himself at the gate and held up some unknown persons approaching the house, who, however, turned out to be friendly. This experience evidently thrilled him, and he afterwards wrote about it in an article called *A Month in Porto Rico*: "When I saw the smouldering ruins of an erst flourishing plantation, where a general officer of our army had been invited to take breakfast that very morning, when I saw the sky reddened with the flames of other buildings burning in the near distance, when I heard the pistol shot which seemed to us to be the signal for an attack, when I felt the keen alarm of those about me, guards and servants and all, then for the first and only time in my life did I realize the intense pleasure which there is in exposure to danger, a pleasure which the psychologist may analyze as he chooses, the moralist may classify as he may, but a pleasure still, and one that leads all the world of manhood to concede that fighting is the best fun in the world. Yet the bravest men are the first to admit that they soon get enough of it."

When he returned, he was again able to work for the Order and became a travelling missionary. He founded, in 1901, the Catholic Truth Society of Chicago — Chicago was now his headquarters — in connection with which, through his lectures and pamphlets, he did what the Jesuits regarded as immensely valuable work. His specialty was preaching to the Protestants, and he is supposed to have made a good many converts. But the morale of the Jesuit son of the manic depressive General was more precarious than that of his father. This period of ardent activity was to end in a terrible collapse, brought on in a curious way. In the spring of 1906, a statue of Tom's father was unveiled in Washington, and President Roosevelt gave a dinner for the Sherman children. Father Sherman attended in his uniform. It was mentioned that a group of West Point cadets was being sent to study his father's campaigns by retracing on horseback the March to the Sea. The President, with his indiscreet expansiveness, invited Father Sherman to go along. He accepted, and the results were disastrous. The South of course flew into a rage. "Father Sherman," said a Georgia Congressman, "may have trouble tracing the line of march now, but some time ago crumbling chimneys and smouldering homes would have made the path plain"; and a veteran of the Confederate Army declared, "I wish no one harm, but I would not regret at all if someone killed young Sherman should he attempt to march through Georgia." The mayor of Savannah said: "If it were left to me, I'd have him caught and hung before he reached Savannah." Others took the line that, if he had come alone, as his father had done after the war, he would have been as well received as the General. "But when this clerical son," wrote the Atlanta *Georgian*, "of the South's greatest devastator comes to the South as to a hostile or belligerent country, with a military escort furnished by the government, it makes a reflection upon our people which is not creditable either to the government or to the officials who furnished the escort." "Sentiment," wrote the Atlanta *Evening News*, "is a powerful spring in the heart of all self-respecting people and to us in Georgia it is savored of gratuitous remembrance to have the son of General Sherman make a miniature reproduction of one of the most ghastly and repulsive features of the civil war for the delectation of his personal pride, and do it with the aid and consent of army attendants whom our own money is now helping to support for other and national purposes." As in the case of Father Sherman's statement that anyone who shot an anarchist was a public benefactor, his behavior was ill-advised also for the reason that it was highly inappropriate for a man in Christian orders to be retracing the General's frightfulness rather than the Christian Passion. In the conflict between father and mother, the cross of Ellen Sherman was losing. The party was recalled by Roosevelt before it had got very far. But this does not seem to have embarrassed Father Sherman: he was simply indignant with the government by whom he thought he had been insulted. But he did not proceed farther.

And now, when he returned to Chicago, he got himself into serious difficulties with the discipline of his Order. He had been handling in rather an irregular way the finances of the Catholic Truth Society — borrowing money from laymen and using funds that were intended for other purposes. He feared that he had violated his vow of poverty, "which forbids," Father Durkin tells us, "the free use of money in one's possession." He asked his Father Provincial to allow him to go to Rome in order to explain himself to the Jesuit Father General. He had frequently used the expression, "Always go to the Commander-in-Chief." This request the Provincial refused and told him not to worry about the funds. But Father Sherman was getting quite out of hand. In preparation for a Christmas entertainment, he closeted himself with a "lady secretary"; he ordered the house servants around in disregard of the Father Minister; and he demanded a telephone. A Brother Donaghy wrote to the Father Provincial that "at the concert [Father Sherman] made himself very conspicious [sic] by escorting the lady singers or players off the stage by catching their hand and accompanying them back of the curtain separately. As many as three or four prominent ladies afterward sayed [sic]: 'It is too bad Father Sherman so far forgot his dignity.' A few other people of prominence who were there asked, 'What was his lecture on? Was it on Porto Rico or was it a lecture of compliments to General and Mrs. Grant?'" The man of the world had been coming out, and it was not quite a Jesuit man of the world. After Christmas, Father Sherman left the Jesuit house for a visit to his family in St. Louis, locking the door of his office but failing to turn off the lights. When he came back, he found that the room had been opened, and in a fury raised a cry of burglary. He dismissed from the Catholic Truth Society the Brother who had informed against him.

He retired at first to a hospital, then took a vacation in Santa Barbara and stayed in the West two years. But he was now becoming quite insane and was eventually removed to a mental hospital in the suburb of Boston called Brookline, which turned out to be expensive and in which he began worrying again about breaking his vow of poverty. He was troubled by delusions of persecution and a sense of inferiority, as the General had apparently been when he imagined that his army was outnumbered in Kentucky and his superiors made him go home for a rest. Father Sherman was convinced that he had lost his faith, that he had sinned in escaping to California. "No hope whatever of eternal salvation," he wrote to the Father Provincial, " — continual effort to choke back blasphemies against God. Blind obedience has brought no amelioration. I will have no instant of peace in time as in eternity. Of this I am most positive. Still my vows press on me and I will continue to obey blindly." He had become for the Jesuits a serious problem, and they seem to have handled his case with tact and consideration. When he emerged from medical care, he announced that he was leaving the Order but would still remain a practising priest. It was impossible, according to Jesuit law, to dismiss an insane member, but, fearing he would make a scandal — he was already denouncing the Jesuits — they allowed him to think he had left the Order.

The story of his last twenty years is most painful. He was able to travel and to live alone, and he engaged in a whole forlorn series of self-invented ministries and projects. Father Sherman first set out to organize a Catholic Colonization Society, designed to resettle, in the state of Washington, recent immigrants of Catholic faith from the big American cities (he also at one time believed that he had founded and was head of an organization called the Chevron Order for the Defence of the Catholic Faith); then he made a journey to Spain for the purpose of kneeling, in the country of Loyola, before the holy crucifix at Limpias; then spent several years in Santa Barbara, in a bungalow equipped with an altar, at which he said Mass for himself; then returned to Puerto Rico with the intention of working among the poor, whose misery he had never forgotten, but found himself too lonely in the country village to which he had been assigned and stuck it out for only a few months. He came back to Santa Barbara, but his retirement there was disrupted by fits of insane violence, and one of his nieces was finally obliged to go out and bring him East to a sanitarium. This was a Catholic hospital in New Orleans, and at first the Jesuits there, having heard that he had left the Order, did as little as possible for him. The niece made an appeal to an American assistant of the Jesuit Father General in Rome, and he cabled to the people in New Orleans. Father Sherman was offered Communion but always said to the nursing Sisters, "It is too late, it is too late." When sitting in a wheelchair in the garden, he always wore his military cloak.

When at last Father Sherman was dying — in April, 1933 — he told the Sister to "call Father Provincial — I wish to renew my vows." Three members of the Order were summoned. They knelt beside the poor old fighter's bed, and Father Sherman repeated in their presence the long formula to which he had sworn.

VI

WE HAVE SO FAR been dealing with Unionists and have hardly explored the South except through the novels of Mrs. Stowe and in company with Sherman's invaders. Let us examine it through the eyes of two Northerners who, before and after the war, went to study and report on a region that was little understood in the North.

Frederick Law Olmsted, born in Hartford, Connecticut, in 1822, had a remarkable double career. During the latter part of the century, he came to figure in the United States as our leading landscape architect. He invented, in fact, the American park at a time when large public gardens had been thought to be "too aristocratic to be sanctioned in America, too artistic to be respected by the American populace." The project for Central Park in New York was regarded as "an unrepublican waste of money . . . for only the rich would use it; or, if the poor used it, they would quickly destroy its beauty." Olmsted was, however, recruited for this project in 1856 and, assisted by a professional architect, which Olmsted himself was not, took it over from the originally appointed planner and, in the teeth of much opposition on the part of the politicians and the resistance of the rocky site itself, put it through in about four years' time. He first showed here the extraordinary resourceful-ness — he constructed sunken road-ways for the transverse traffic — which enabled him to deal with the problems of the most varied American localities. He afterwards built Riverside Drive and Morningside Drive in Manhattan and Prospect Park in Brooklyn; created out of tidal marshes the Back Bay Fenway in Boston; laid down the marble ter-races of the Capitol at Washington; summoned up the World's Fair grounds in Chicago; and had the Yosemite and Niagara Falls set aside as national reservations. He designed any number of rich men's estates, college cam-puses and smaller parks.

But in the years before 1856, Frederick Olmsted was mainly known as a magazine editor and journalist. He published during the fifties a number of books, and he left one work of permanent importance.

In December, 1852, Olmsted was sent by the New York *Times* on a three months' trip through the South-ern states to report on conditions there. He later col-lected his articles into a volume, and this was followed by two similar volumes, the products of a trip of at least eight months made in 1853 and 1854, when he visited first Texas, then what he called the "back country" of Mississippi and the Appalachian highlands. At the be-ginning of the Civil War, it was suggested by Olmsted's English publisher that a one-volume abridgment of all three of these books would be of interest to the British public, and Olmsted, then busy with Central Park, ar-ranged to have this condensation made by an anti-slavery writer from North Carolina. Olmsted himself contrib-uted to it a new introduction on *The Present Crisis*.

This book, called *The Cotton Kingdom*, had in its time a good deal of influence on the Northern point of view toward the South. Of Olmsted's reports on the South, Charles Eliot Norton said, "They have permanent value, and will be chief material for our social history whenever it is written," and James Russell Lowell wrote him, "I have learned more about the South from your books than from all others put together, and I valued them the more that an American who can be patient and accurate is so rare a phenomenon." John Stuart Mill, to whom *The Cotton Kingdom* was dedicated, described Olmsted as "calm and dispassionate" and relied upon his account of the South in formulating his own attitude toward the Civil War.

The Cotton Kingdom has been compared to Arthur Young's account of his travels in France before the French Revolution, and it has certainly for historians a comparable interest. Olmsted, in the literary sense, was a very bad writer; when he is generalizing, he often has difficulty, on account of the clumsiness of his syntax, in expressing what he wants to say, and he is always entirely pedestrian. The only knack that sometimes makes his pages vivid is a remarkably accurate ear for the accent and the language of the people he meets (he tells us that he was able so accurately to imitate Southern speech that he was never, unless he revealed himself, identified as a man from the North). The conversations reported by Olmsted give the impression of all having been reproduced, without any art of selection, precisely as Olmsted remembered them, and he seems to have remembered everything. He tenaciously and patiently and lucidly made his way through the whole South, undiscouraged by churlish natives, almost impassable roads or the cold inns and uncomfortable cabins in which he spent most of his nights. He talked to everybody and he sized up everything, and he wrote it all down.

Frederick Olmsted, at the time of these travels, was himself a highly successful farmer, with a hundred and thirty acres on Staten Island, and he had already published a study of English agriculture called *Walks and Talks of an American Farmer in England*. His interest was primarily economic, but to explain the economic aspects of life in the South involved also a detailed account of the habits of Southern society. Olmsted's object, as he told a friend, was to produce "a valuable book of observations on Southern agriculture and general economy as affected by slavery . . . matter of fact to come after the deluge of spoony fancy pictures now at its height shall be spent," and Olmsted's reporting today can provide an indispensable antidote to the later crop of spoony fancy pictures that had already reached ripeness in the eighties with the fiction of Thomas Nelson Page, and which has more or less continued into our own day.

The new ironists and realists and poets of the South have, of course, themselves criticized this legend. James Branch Cabell in *The Rivet in Grandfather's Neck* amusingly parodied Page, and he played some mischievous tricks on the pretensions of the first Virginia families; William Faulkner, with tragic scorn, stripped away the pretensions of the Mississippians. Both aroused the indignation of their neighbors, yet with both the real basis for the legend was still solidly there in the background: the Big House, the fine plantation, the romantic and feudal ideal. The popular novelist in *Grandfather's Neck* is promptly rebuked by a friend for making fun of "the vitality of the legend," with its "prattle of 'ole Marster' and 'ole Miss,'" and its "sprinkling of 'mockinbuds' and 'hants' and 'horg-killing time,' and of sweeping animadversions as to all 'free niggers,'" and of "how 'de quality use ter cum' — you spell it c-u-m because that looks so convincingly like dialect — 'ter de gret house'"; and he confesses that, in spite of the "sardonic imp" that makes him behave with irreverence, it is still true that "when I am writing of those tender-hearted, brave, and gracious

men and women, and of those dear old darkies," it is
often "with tears in my eyes." The drama of *The Rivet
in Grandfather's Neck* derives from the chivalry of the
principal character, the family-proud Colonel Musgrave,
toward the young wife whom he regards as a social inferior; and in the Faulkner of *Intruder in the Dust* we
find the remnants of this antiquated chivalry rallying
against the upstart mob in order to defend a mulatto who
is known to have some of the best white blood.

I do not mean thus to suggest that the whole ideal implied by these writers is a delusion that Olmsted punc-
tures, or that there did not exist in the South individuals
who tried to live up to it. On the contrary, the power of
such books as these, which deal with the Southern gentry
in its later dispossessed and diluted state, is the proof that
there must once have flourished certain qualities of a very
rare kind. We have already had a glimpse of them in
John Esten Cooke, and we shall later return to the question of the reality and the legend of the pre-war South.
The point to be made here is simply that the Big House,
with its graces and splendors, hardly figures in *The
Cotton Kingdom* at all. In a newspaper article by Olmsted, an article on "the Northern and Southern characters" (included by Mr. Arthur M. Schlesinger as an
appendix in his edition of *The Cotton Kingdom*), Frederick Olmsted does pay his respects — though in some
of his most awkward writing — to "the honest and un-
studied dignity of character, the generosity and the real
nobleness of habitual impulses, and the well-bred, manly
courtesy which distinguish" the Southern gentleman "in
all the relations and occupations of life, equally in his
business, in his family, and in general society," and which
"are sadly rare at the North." But in the author's social-
economic survey these qualities scarcely count. "The traditional 'old family,'" he says, "stately but condescending,

haughty but jovial, keeping open house for all comers on the plantations of Virginia or South Carolina, is not wholly a myth. There really was something which, with some sort of propriety, could be termed a gentry in Carolina and Virginia in their colony days." Yet of such real " 'old families' . . . I think it will be difficult for most readers who have not studied the matter at all to form a sufficiently small estimate; call them a dozen or a hundred, what does it matter in a region much larger than the old German empire?"

What, then, is Olmsted's own picture of the society of the rest of this region? *The Cotton Kingdom* runs to three hundred thousand words and does not lend itself easily to summary, for it is mostly a record of innumerable incidents — journeys, conversations, night's lodgings; people who are courteous and people who are oafish, men who think slavery a curse and men who think it ordained by Heaven, masters who mistreat their slaves and masters who take excellent care of them; many gradations of misery and squalor, and a few of relative comfort. Nor does Olmsted deal only with the cotton country: he visits also the rice fields of Georgia and the tobacco plantations of Virginia. But all these impressions combine to bring the traveller to one general conclusion: that the economy of the ante-bellum South is fundamentally, inescapably impractical; that slavery not only degrades the slaves but demoralizes the masters and prevents agricultural progress; that the South, once involved in the system, has been steadily degenerating; and that, if it cannot be found possible in time to get rid of or modify this system, the whole region is bound to regress to a point where it will almost lose contact with the rest of the civilized world.

The Negro, first of all, has no interest whatever in working for the white man who has made him a slave.

He is always sabotaging, dawdling, malingering, revolting or running away. A small group of farmhands in New York or New England, who have a real grasp of what they are doing and who are earning money by it, are able to get through more work than a whole plantation of Negroes, and — in New York as compared with Virginia — they cost twenty-five percent less per man. The slaves must be constantly goaded and supervised very closely — "nigger-driving" was, it seems, not an opprobrious term but an accepted technical expression — and when the planter, as is always the case if he owns any large number of slaves, is unable to do this himself, he must hire an overseer, who will get out of them as many bales of cotton as possible. This leads to a human disregard of the Negroes; and the high rate of turnover in overseers, who rarely remain on a plantation more than a year or two, would seem to show that the slaves make it difficult, once they have got onto their driver's tricks, for him to keep on overworking them effectively. Since the overseer is aiming at quantity, he does not, furthermore, care how the cotton is picked and may allow it to become so dirty from the sloppy handling of the Negroes that it is worth from one to two cents less a pound than the cotton more carefully picked by the free German labor of Texas. The impression of Northern visitors that the Negroes on the big plantations are devoted to their masters and beloved by them is due to the fact that the visitor sees only the household servants, of whom this is often true, and never has the least idea of the condition or state of mind of the army of workers in the field on whom the whole system depends. The relation of the master to his working crew — unless he is exceptionally brutal — can never be clear or certain. Since they are slaves, he can never treat them like other human beings, whose rights he would have to respect, yet since they *are,* after all, human beings, he cannot use them up like tools. This is bad for the morale of the master, since he is always obliged to choose between inefficient production and inhuman methods.

The planter must also live in continual apprehension of a Negro insurrection, and has been led in several states by this fear to pass laws which make it a criminal offense to teach Negroes to read and write. Olmsted, who was no Abolitionist, tells us that when he first went South he believed that the advantages to the Negro of living in contact with a superior race must outweigh the disadvantages, and that it was only after long observation that he was forced to come to the conclusion that the slave had been degraded, not elevated. Not merely was the slave kept illiterate, but it was not at all true, as the Southerners asserted, that the average slave in the South lived better than the average Northern laborer. "The fact is," Olmsted estimates, "that ninety-nine in a hundred of our free laborers . . . live, in respect to food, at least four times as well as the average of the hardest-worked slaves on the Louisiana sugar-plantations. And for two or three months in the year I have elsewhere shown that these are worked with much greater severity than free laborers at the North ever are. For on no farm, and in no factory, or mine, even when double wages are paid for night-work, did I ever hear of men or women working regularly eighteen hours a day." Side by side with the blacks, there exists the wretched class of poor whites, who live as badly or worse, who are despised by the other whites and who in turn detest the Negroes, because so long as the latter are slaves, the whites cannot compete with them in the labor market.

As for the planters, in the case of the less well-to-do, "I have seen," Olmsted asserts, "many a workman's lodging at the North, and in England, too, where there was double the amount of luxury that I ever saw in a regular cotton-planter's house on plantations of three cabins," and he describes with depressing monotony a succession of such lower-grade households, with their windowless log cabins and their families sleeping on the floor, gulping down corn bread and bacon for three meals a day, and occupying their leisure in the evenings by sitting dumbly in front of the fireplace, which provides their only light, and spitting tobacco-juice into the fire. Even the families of a higher standard — isolated, loutish, morose — sound more like the landowners of Gogol's *Dead Souls* than like those of Page's *In Ole Virginia.* But the economic system of the South does not favor the moderate-sized plantation. There is hardly any educated middle class. It is only through large-scale production that cotton can be made very profitable, since it is only the large-scale planter who can maintain his own press and gin, his mules and his plows and other implements, whereas the small one must pay for the use of all these; and it is only the large-scale planter who can afford the journey to the seaboard to deal with the exporter directly, while the poorer man must do this through middlemen.

What is the life of the wealthy planters? Olmsted finds that it is almost completely devoid of any of the things he regards as the essentials of civilization. The children are brought up by illiterate Negroes, and if the parents themselves are intelligent enough to want them to have something better, they have to send them away to school or to bring in for them tutors and governesses. This, however, of course, does nothing, from the point of view of education, to benefit the community at large. There is no way of getting schools, just as there is no incentive for building roads or bridges. The traveller finds that one family he visits is putting through a road in a certain direction in order to establish communication with neighbors whom they happen to like, but doing nothing in the other direction, because they do not like the people who live there. He is astonished at the lack of "improvements" of the kind that are always being made in the North, and he eventually becomes appalled at the deficiency of the South in that "culture" which means so much to New England. There are few newspapers, and few people read them. Almost no books are published. The press is under virtual censorship, since no discussion of slavery is possible. The people rarely talk about anything except narrowly local matters. They have almost no interest in literature or art, science or foreign affairs. If their manners are more elegant than those of the North, it is only because social gatherings are their sole form of recreation, and, with ceremony and gracefulness and gallantry, they make out of them all that they can. But in general they have nothing else — neither sports nor debating societies, military companies nor libraries, theaters nor concert halls, singing societies nor amateur theatricals. There are no civic bodies to sit on — no school boards or church corporations, no benevolent or agricultural societies, no bridge or water companies.

Observing this state of things, the traveller is brought to the conclusion that the classical argument that the bondage of an inferior class of laborers is justified by the use of his leisure that the liberated master may make has not been proved in the South. Nor have the planters had the energy or foresight to develop their peculiar economy along its own lines. Since large-scale production is profitable, why have they never organized any joint-stock cotton plantations to correspond to the joint-stock mills of Massachusetts? And why, in the middle of the nineteenth century, when, no further away than Ohio, the spinning wheel and the hand-loom have already become curiosities, does the South produce nothing but homespun? The Southerners will not even take care of their soil but simply use it up and move on, leaving whole areas sterile and desolate. The Northerner Olmsted can demonstrate, by a statistical contrast with Pennsylvania, New York and Massachusetts, how Virginia, with its magnificent natural resources, has declined from its once brilliant civilization and its first place among the states to a place far below the three others in agriculture, industry and education. He might have mentioned that, even in Charlottesville, Jefferson's Monticello had been left to neglect and ruin, with the drawing room used as a granary, that when the patriotic Jewish veteran of the War of 1812 Uriah P. Levy rescued the place by buying it and tried to induce Virginia to make it into a national shrine, he failed to arouse any interest; he might also have mentioned that the only two living Southerners who commanded respect outside the South by reason of their intellectual attainments — as Lowell says in his *Biglow Papers* — were William Gilmore Simms, the novelist, who complained that he was never read in his native South Carolina, and Matthew Fontaine Maury, the oceanographer, both born at the beginning of the century.

The large generosity of the planter, the tradition of hospitality, this far-ranging traveller has been reduced, after months of the most varied experience, to dismissing as an all but complete myth— a conclusion which, Olmsted says, he has confirmed in comparing notes with other travellers who know the South well. He was denounced by a Southern critic as one of those "lying, sneaking, cowardly knaves" who "defamed the characters of the unsuspecting patrons at whose hospitable boards their miserable carcasses are each day filled with abundance of every species of good cheer." But according to

Olmsted's account, this would be an exaggeration. He often found it difficult, he tells us, to get anyone to put him up at all when he was not within range of the very few inns (themselves sufficiently primitive), and he usually had to pay for his entertainment. "Only twice," he says, "in a journey of four thousand miles, made independently of public conveyances, did I receive a night's lodging or a repast from a native Southerner without having the exact price in money which I was expected to pay for it stated to me by those at whose hands I received it."

He elsewhere describes the minimum that a traveller in New York or New England would be likely to be offered by his host, and continues, "In what civilized region after such advice [to seek shelter with certain householders reputed to be exceptionally hospitable and well-equipped to entertain him], would such thoughts [as to what ought to constitute that minimum of hospitality] be preposterous unless in the Southern States? Not but that such men and such houses, such family and home comforts may be found in the South. I have found them — a dozen of them, delightful homes. But then in a hundred cases where I received such advice, and heard houses and men so described, I did not find one of the things imagined above, nor anything ranging with them. In my last journey of nearly three months between the Mississippi and the Upper James River, I saw not only none of those things, received none of those attentions, but I saw and met nothing of the kind. Nine times out of ten, at least, after such a promise, I slept in a room with others, in a bed which stank, supplied with but one sheet, if with any; I washed with utensils common to the whole household; I found no garden, no flowers, no fruit, no tea, no cream, no sugar, no bread (for corn pone — let me assert in parenthesis, though possibly, as tastes differ, a very good thing of its kind for ostriches — is not bread: neither does even flour, salt, fat, and water, stirred together and warmed, constitute bread); no curtains, no lifting windows (three times out of four absolutely no windows), no couch — if one reclined in the family room, it was on the bare floor — for there were no carpets or mats. For all that, the house swarmed with vermin. There was no hay, no straw, no oats (but moldy corn and leaves of maise), no discretion, no care, no honesty; at the ——— [the deletion is Olmsted's] there was no stable, but a log-pen; and besides this no other outhouse but a smoke-house, a corn house and a range of nigger houses."

Not only did Olmsted's reports, in the form in which they appeared before the war, make a considerable impression in the North, but their justice was sometimes acknowledged even by writers in the South. At that time, he was still attempting to suggest that there might be ways out for the South, but in the wartime abridgment of *The Cotton Kingdom* he takes the view that the South is doomed: constrained by the meshes of slavery, the Southerners will be powerless to advance or even to hold their own except through having these meshes broken. But, in the meantime, the opinion of Olmsted that the economy of the South is an anachronism, that it obstructs the course of history, is being by others pressed into the service of a passionate religious conviction that the weakness of this feudal system implies somehow an essential turpitude, and that the cause of the North is the cause of God. We have seen how it grew upon Lincoln in proportion as it grew upon his public. We have seen also that he came to wonder whether the values of the war could be quite so simple. But the lengths to which this idea could be carried by other Northerners may be traced in a successor of Olmsted's, the author of another report on the South, which possibly derives from *The Cotton Kingdom* and may be read as a supplement to it.

Just after the fighting had stopped, in the summer of 1865 and again in the following winter, John T. Trowbridge, a New Yorker who lived in Boston, the once popular author of books for boys and a friend of Whitman and Emerson, visited the former Confederate states, and he published in 1866 a detailed account of what he found. His book — called *The South: A Tour of Its Battlefields and Ruined Cities, A Journey Through the Desolated States, and Talks with the People* — is somewhat less searching than Olmsted's, but his travels were almost as extensive. In the very first pages of Trowbridge, we meet the suggestion that the hand of God is to be seen in the battle of Gettysburg, that direct intervention by the Deity may account for the negligence of the Southerners in failing to secure a strategic hill and thus laying themselves open to defeat; and this is followed, in other connections, by what can only be called boasts of divine backing. John T. Trowbridge is not unintelligent and not insensitive to suffering. In setting down what he sees and is told, he is quite as impartial as Olmsted — that is, as impartial as was possible after a conflict in which almost everyone had been forced to take definite sides. He gives us examples of Negroes who stuck to their Confederate masters and circumvented the plundering Yankees as well as of a callous master who turned away his aged ex-slaves, though they had served him all their lives, when the younger ones asked for wages. He chronicles the atrocities committed by Federals at the time of Sherman's invasion as well as the Dachauesque horrors of the Andersonville prison in Georgia. Though he gives way, as Olmsted does not, to occasional passages of rhetoric, his narrative is not melodramatic, and, like Olmsted's, it carries conviction through its realistic observation and its patient setting-down of detail.

This, we find, is the same semi-feudal society that Olmsted has described in the decade before. Trowbridge talks with the same stupid planters, who tell him that the Negro will never work unless he is driven to it, with the same Negro-hating poor whites, who are now, however, rejoicing in the liquidation of slavery; he is horrified by the same lack of interest in improving or preserving the soil, disgusted by the same log cabins, and even by some of the houses of the relatively well-to-do, in which he finds that in the coldest weather the doors are left open till the sun goes down for the reason that the dim-witted inhabitants have not yet got used to having windows and persist in habits acquired in the days when they depended for light on their doorways; and he is struck, as Olmsted was, by the fewness of schools and churches. But now this whole limping, impoverished, this speculating, pretentious society has been desolated and levelled by war. Where battles have recently occurred, the farmers are now plowing among corpses; the hogs are rooting up old graves; the trees have been shot to splinters, sometimes they have been cut clean off. The houses of the farmers have often been burnt, their stock slaughtered and their household goods stolen; the planters' big mansions are empty, the glass of their windows smashed and Yankee names scratched on the walls – one house that Trowbridge tried to enter proved to be a mere façade: he met the sky on the other side — and such railroads as the South has possessed are now mostly a litter of rails twisted into horseshoes or wound around trees. Atlanta, Savannah and Charleston have been partly reduced to ruins almost as gruesome, it would seem, as any since achieved by our more modern methods, and the inhabitants, Trowbridge reports, are sheltering in hovels like Indians. He sometimes sees Negroes who have been turned away or have refused to work without wages camping out around fires in the fields, but he also sees and hears of many, sometimes with farms of their own, who are upsetting the assumptions of the planters by exhibiting a new energy and initiative.

"The great trouble in this country is," he is told by one young man in Georgia, who has just taken over his father's plantation, "the people are mad at the niggers because they're free. They always believed they wouldn't do well if they were emancipated, and now they maintain, and some of them even hope, they won't do well — that, too, in the face of actual facts. The old planters have no confidence in the niggers, and as a matter of course the niggers have no confidence in them. They have a heap more confidence in their young masters, and they work well for us. They have still more confidence in the Yankees, and they work still better for them." For the Negroes, the moment seems hopeful. The Yankees remain on the ground, with their military commandants and their Freedmen's Bureaus, to which the ex-slaves can come with their grievances and problems. The religious and benevolent societies of the North have established many Negro schools. Yet it is plain that Mississippi and South Carolina are already putting through new codes designed to restore serfdom, and the government of Andrew Johnson is confusing the situation on the Sea Islands of Georgia and South Carolina by giving back to the white planters, who have taken the oath of allegiance to the Union, extensive properties on which Negro freedmen have been encouraged to settle and on which they have been comfortably farming.

But Trowbridge is optimistic, and he predicts a big

cotton crop. His Northern conviction that the Union cause has represented the will of God is strong with him throughout his travels. There are moments when — like Lincoln in certain of his speeches — his conception of recent events appears to have something in common with the Hegelian-Marxist philosophy which describes the vicissitudes of humanity in terms of the conflict of historical forces. "Here let them rest together," he says of the Union and Confederate soldiers, who are to be buried side by side at Antietam, "they of the good cause and they of the evil. . . . For neither was the one cause altogether good, nor was the other altogether bad: the holier being clouded by much ignorance and selfishness, and the darker one brightened here and there with glorious flashes of self-devotion. It was not, rightly speaking, these brothers that were at war. The conflict was waged between two great principles — one looking towards liberty and human advancement, the other madly drawing the world back to barbarism and the dark ages. America was the chessboard on which the stupendous game was played, and those we name Patriots and Rebels were but as the pawns."

But we may find rather hard to accept, for example, Trowbridge's notion that the defeat of the Union forces at the earlier battle of Bull Run was deliberately planned by God in order to bring about, later on, a more crushing defeat of the South: "Temporary success to the bad cause was necessary to draw it irretrievably into the currents of destruction." And we may feel that the Southerners, defeated, might well have been infuriated by Trowbridge's explanation of the burning of Charleston in 1861: "It [the fire] is looked upon as one of the disasters of the war, although it cannot be shown that it had any connection with the war. When Eternal Justice decrees the punishment of a people, it sends not War alone, but also its sister terrors, Famine, Pestilence and Fire."

Yet so deeply theocratic was that age, in which Stonewall Jackson, the Confederate general, felt himself to have been taken into the confidence of God hardly less than the New York State crusader John Brown, that a young South Carolinian with whom Trowbridge fell in on a train ride could say to the Northern visitor, "I think it was in the decrees of God Almighty that slavery was to be abolished in this way, and I don't murmur." And he added, "I had never thought much about politics, though I believed our state was right when she went out. But when the bells were ringing, and everybody was rejoicing that she had seceded, a solemn feeling came over me, like I had never had in my life, and I couldn't help feeling there was something wrong. I went through the war; there were thousands like me. In our hearts we thought more of the Stars and Stripes than we did of the old rag we were fighting under."

So one of the former professors of the Louisiana military academy over which Sherman had presided before the war wrote him from Baton Rouge in 1875: "Mr. Jefferson Davis, whatever else may be said of him, is a humane Christian gentleman. He was really opposed to the war, thought secession premature, but, as a states-rights man, went along with Mississippi into the Confederacy, and became, without his seeking, its president. He entered into the great struggle with his whole soul, and *failed* simply because God seems not to have meant us [of the South] to break up the Union! How else can you account for the death of Albert Sidney Johnston, from a mere *scratch,* just in the height of his victory at Shiloh; and the calling back of Jackson, by Lee, when in the act of making his final rush on McClellan at Harrison's Bar, when McClellan says (under oath) he expected to surrender his whole army? And the killing of Jackson, by *his own men*, when Hooker's condition was so desperate at Chancellorsville? And Ewell standing still in the streets of Gettysburg and quietly looking on at Meade slowly and timidly crowning the heights with men and guns? And a *commissioned officer five days* slow in carrying to Dick Taylor and Kirby Smith the terrible straits of General Banks's army and Admiral Porter's fleet at Grand Ecore, after the defeat at Mansfield? And, that army captured and that fleet destroyed, would not the blockade of the Mississippi River have been raised, and Nashville fallen to Hood, and Jubal Early have taken Washington? The issues of war turn often upon trifles too small for man to see or consider; but God observes them all, integrates all such differentials, and uses them for His own wise purposes. He never meant us of the Confederacy to succeed, and it is the duty of every true Confederate soldier to acquiesce in *His* decision; to thank Him for the abolition of slavery, and the preservation of the American Union."

One may find a place here in conclusion for one of the bitterest and oddest of these theocratic interpretations of the events of the Civil War — in this case, on the part of a Northerner. Garth Wilkinson James, the younger brother of William and Henry, who had enlisted in Colonel Shaw's Negro regiment and been twice wounded in the assault on Fort Wagner, wrote to his father after the assassination of Lincoln: "You no doubt see something a great deal higher and better than I do in this murder, yet I see something a good deal higher than I ever thought I should. I see God's wise Providence and justice ridding the sinner of a too pure-minded and clement judge, and putting over him a less worthy and more competent and timely one. He knew that Lincoln never would give the hell to these men that they had been preparing themselves for, and consequently arranged this aright."

VII

NORTHERNERS IN THE SOUTH: CHARLOTTE FORTEN
AND COLONEL HIGGINSON

CHARLOTTE FORTEN was the granddaughter of James Forten, a Philadelphia Negro, whose grandfather, the son of a slave, had succeeded in obtaining his freedom and who, at the time of the Revolution, had volunteered to fight for the colonists. After the war, he returned to his native city and there became a prosperous sailmaker. In his championship of Negro causes, he was something of a public figure. He advocated abolition and fought against the Fugitive Slave Act of 1793, but he strongly opposed the movement which aimed to have American Negroes shipped off to colonize Liberia. Like everyone else in America who had fought in the Revolution — his father had also served — he felt that he had the right to enjoy the advantages and the privileges of a citizen of the United States, and he asked whether he could really be expected to find himself at home in that Africa from which his great-grandfather had been brought and to "run at once to the old hut where my forefathers lived a hundred years ago." His sons carried on this tradition as well as the sailmaking business. A daughter of James Forten married a well-educated mulatto, partly English, partly Moorish, and nearly white, who became one of William Lloyd Garrison's lieutenants and President of the American Anti-Slavery Society.

239

Charlotte Forten, the granddaughter of James, who modestly wrote a little and sometimes appeared in print, kept in her youth a diary, which was published in 1953 as *The Journal of Charlotte L. Forten* and which fills in a curious corner of the complicated Civil War picture. Charlotte Forten, as will be seen from the above family history, was the product of a special milieu. Not admitted to the white schools of Philadelphia, she was educated by tutors at home, then sent by her father to Salem, Massachusetts, where there was no discrimination in the schools and where she could live with the family of Charles L. Remond, another able mulatto, who also worked for the Anti-Slavery Society. This was in 1854, and it was then that Charlotte Forten commenced her diary. At school she excelled in her studies. She won a poetry prize at her graduation, and she was offered a job as teacher, which she accepted and filled till her health broke down (she was tubercular, like many Negroes).

She was evidently very well-liked, and in her journal she gives the impression of being naturally affectionate and gentle. She read a good deal, and her favorite writers were Emerson and Mrs. Browning. She constantly attended lectures, and she was most proud to make the acquaintance of the great New England Abolitionists — Whittier and Garrison, Parker and Phillips. There are pages which, as one reads them, might make one take her for a Boston girl eager for "culture" or a conventional and rather shy Philadelphian of the well-to-do white bourgeoisie, but on other pages the paradox of her social position makes itself painfully felt. Respected by a number of distinguished men, a star at her Salem school, she finds that she is likely to be cut on the street by girls who have been friendly with her in class, and this rouses in her a constant distrust and an impulse to retaliation which are discordant with her other instincts.

"Oh! it is hard," she exclaims, "to go through life meeting contempt with contempt, hatred with hatred, fearing, with too good reason, to love and trust hardly anyone whose skin is white — however lovable, attractive, and congenial in seeming. In the bitter passionate feelings of my soul, again and again there rises the question 'When, oh! when shall this cease?' . . . Conscience answers it is wrong, it is ignoble to despair; let us labor earnestly and faithfully to acquire knowledge, to break down the barriers of prejudice and oppression."

It is certainly an unlucky, an unhealthy fate to find oneself thus condemned to have no intercourse on equal terms with any white people except reformers, and at home, in Philadelphia, Miss Forten has no longer even these. It is a nuisance and hard on one's nerves never to know, in one's native town, that one will not be put out of a restaurant. To face social exclusion in a white community, to live constantly with the color problem, to expend upon it so much despairing thought, so much festering helpless emotion — this has sometimes had the effect of goading a Negro of exceptional character or abilities to distinguish himself and compete with the whites. But Miss Forten is no genius or heroine; she is simply a young girl who likes poetry and who thirsts to see something of the world, who longs to know other people who share her tastes, who needs a husband on her own level. Will she not deteriorate if she is given no chance to develop?

Charlotte Forten was saved by the war when she was still only twenty-five. When the forces of the federal government had captured the Sea Islands south of Charleston and the Port Royal region of South Carolina, and when all the white inhabitants had left, the Northerners found themselves confronted with a dense population of liberated Negroes, who sometimes spoke only Gullah and had never been off their islands, and a project was got under weigh to educate the new freedmen and to help them to cultivate the big estates from which the masters had fled. Miss Forten very soon applied to teach school among these Negroes. She first got a letter from Whittier to the Boston Educational Commission, who kept her waiting for weeks and finally turned her down, telling her that they were "not sending women at present." Disappointed, she then went back to what she calls "old abominable Philadelphia," where she was fortunate enough to find in the secretary of the Port Royal Relief Association an Abolitionist who was glad to send her. She sailed for South Carolina in October, 1862.

For Miss Forten, a strange new experience, both idyllic and exacting, began. She had her troubles with the Gullah children, who had never been subjected to school discipline and whose speech she had difficulty in understanding, but she loved to hear them sing their spirituals and got Whittier to write them a Christmas hymn. They must have seemed almost as remote from her as they were from the white invaders, but her close association with these latter she evidently found inspiring.

The most distinguished of Charlotte Forten's white associates was Colonel Thomas Wentworth Higginson of Boston, whose lectures she had attended before the war and whom, when the war began, she had watched with admiration in the streets of Worcester drilling his white troops. He had, however, come to South Carolina as a leader of Negro troops, the First South Carolina Volunteers, who were also the first black regiment. A wholehearted Abolitionist as well as something of a scholar and something of a man of the world, he combined with a critical and dry intelligence of the kind characteristic of Boston a capacity for direct action not often to be found at that date in the New England idealists and reformers. After being ordained, in his twenties, as a Unitarian minister, he had, as he said, preached himself out of his Newburyport pulpit by his sermons on the slavery question. He had taken a leading part in a couple of attempts at jailbreaks when runaway slaves had been arrested in Boston, and — what was unheard of there on the part of a representative of one of its first families — had got himself clubbed by the Boston police.

He had led a migration to Kansas at the time when, as a result of the conflict between freesoil and proslavery settlers, there was as yet no authoritative government there and the two elements were actually fighting. In that then remote western territory, Higginson had risked a lynching by delivering a sermon on a text which had been rendered for him particularly sacred on account of its having been employed by a revolutionary New England clergyman the Sunday after he had fought at Bunker Hill: "Be not ye afraid of them; remember the Lord, which is great and terrible, and fight for your brethren, your sons, and your daughters, your wives, and your houses."

He had got to know John Brown and had helped him raise money for his project of organizing a movement of runaway slaves who were to make themselves a stronghold in the Allegheny Mountains — a project, it seems, later abandoned for the equally chimerical one of an invasion of the Southern states by John Brown and his handful of followers and a rallying of rebellious slaves. Knowing little of the actual South, these men had been convinced by the Abolitionists, who knew as little as they, that the Negroes would come flocking to their summons and that their owners would be helpless to restrain them. When, in consequence of his futile first step of capturing the arsenal at Harper's Ferry, John Brown was caught and put on trial, Thomas Higginson had been unique among this madman's secret backers in not becoming panicky or running away but in seeing to it that Brown had counsel and, even after the latter was executed, attempting to rescue his followers.

There can be no more striking evidence of the semi-religious character of the idealism of the Northern crusade than Thomas Higginson's relations with Brown. Brown himself was of New England stock, and there was about him, as has often been said, something of the Cromwellian Covenanter, which persuaded the militant reformers to regard him as their great man of action. He had the gift of establishing authority and, all through his crack-brained exploits, he maintained an indestructible dignity, a stoical fortitude, which compelled the admiration of even the pay master of the Harper's Ferry Armory, who, though captured and confined there by Brown, having talked with him and watched him defend himself, said he "could not go to see him hanged." Brown's speech to the court, his last letters to his wife, his Roman deportment at the gallows continue to impress us today if we come to them knowing nothing of Brown save the myth of Old John Brown the martyr, which, embodied in the famous song, did so much to inspire the Union armies.

Yet it is plainly on record today that Brown's family was riddled with insanity — that his mother and her mother both died insane, that many of his maternal aunts and uncles as well as his sister, her daughter, one of his brothers and six first cousins are known to have been more or less deranged and in some cases confined in asylums; that his first wife and one of his sons died insane; and that, at the time when it was a question of saving him from the gallows, his relatives and others who knew him signed nineteen affidavits declaring that they believed him mad. These included a former business associate, and it is true that Brown's schemes to make money appear to have been quite unsound — they invariably resulted in failure — and to have brought him under suspicion of dishonesty. They were visionary, like his other projects, and, unable to support his family, he had risen above these problems to devote himself to the grandiose vision of recruiting and governing, in the mountains, his new kingdom of liberated Negroes.

It was an article of John Brown's creed that "without the shedding of blood, there is no remission of sins," and he had already directed in Kansas the murder of three men and two boys, whom — assisted by a boorish band that included two of his sons — he had got out of their beds at night. The murdered boys and their father were part of a family of illiterate poor whites who had emigrated from Tennessee in order to get away, precisely, from the competition of slave labor, and none of these people owned slaves. But Brown, who had circulated among them in his role of land surveyor, had previously satisfied himself that "each one had committed murder in his heart, and, according to the Scriptures . . . were guilty of murder, and I felt justified in having them killed." The slaughter of these five men, which, said Brown, had been "decreed by Almighty God, ordained from Eternity," was enacted in retaliation for the murder of five freesoilers by the pro-slavery immigrants. One of these latter had been hacked to pieces, and, in Brown's Pottawatomie massacre, he made a point of chopping up all his victims. The five Southerners were not merely shot but were stabbed and gashed in the face, and their fingers and arms were lopped away with old-fashioned two-edged broadswords which Brown had

been allowed, by connivance, to acquire from the abandoned equipment of a filibustering expedition.

Now, the news of what had happened in Kansas did,
of course, reach New England at first in a dim or distorted form, and the evidence that Brown was a lunatic
no doubt never reached his admirers at all. It is possible,
then, to understand how Emerson could have compared
John Brown's speech in court to Lincoln's Gettysburg
Address — though Brown's statements about his actions
are as revealing of his unreliability as his handling of
his business affairs — and that Thoreau should have
compared his hanging to Jesus's crucifixion. (Edouard
de Stoeckl, the Russian Minister, wrote his government
after Harper's Ferry: "When the sad results of this foray
became known, John Brown was proclaimed from the
very roof-tops as the equal of our Savior. I quote these
facts to point out how far Puritan fanaticism can go.
Little by little, the extreme doctrines of New England
have spread throughout the land.") But Higginson had
himself been in Kansas in the autumn of 1856 and he
ought to have known the truth about the massacre of
the previous May. In one of his volumes of memoirs —
characteristically called *Cheerful Yesterdays* — he says
simply that he "heard of no one who did not approve
of the act, and its beneficial effects were universally admitted" — making later only the slight demurrer, in connection with someone else's defense of Brown, that "personally, I have never fully reconciled myself to this vin-
dication of the blow." It was true that the Northerners
had some reason for believing that the federal government was falling completely into the hands of the
Southerners; it was true that the Kansas-Nebraska Act
had done away with the former demarcation between
free and slave-holding territory and made the system
that should predominate in these areas dependent on

the votes of the settlers, with the result that the pro-slavery people had been faking the election of their candidates by bringing in bogus voters from over the border in Missouri; it was, in fact, true that recently the forces opposed to slavery had been getting all the worst of it. But nothing except the latent ferocity that stimulates the militant moralist, the capacity for self-delusion of the Bible-drugged New England idealist (even though Thomas Wentworth Higginson himself was not a Calvinist but a Unitarian) can account for the readiness of so "high-minded" a man to gloss over the Kansas horrors — which had *not* had "beneficial effects" but only led to more bloody reprisals — and, by supplying John Brown with money, virtually to give him *carte blanche* to go on and do the same thing elsewhere, with the result that the fiasco in Virginia alarmed the whole of the South with the menace of a Negro uprising and made the bad situation worse. It is strangest of all to find Higginson — in his essay *A Visit to John Brown's Household in 1859* — writing of his expedition to interview John Brown's widow in her bleak little Adirondack farm with a piety that could not have been more reverent if Mrs. Brown had been the widow of Emerson.

Colonel Thomas Wentworth Higginson had, in any case, arrived, at the time I write of — the second year of the war — on the coast of South Carolina as a com-mander of colored troops, and was skirmishing and raid-ing on the Sea Islands at the moment that Miss Forten arrived. When Miss Forten first encountered the Colonel, in camp at Beaufort on St. Helena Island, she was "so much overwhelmed," she writes, "that I had no reply to make to the very kind and courteous little speech with which he met me. I believe I mumbled something, and grinned like a simpleton, that was all."

She met there, also, by an exciting coincidence, a certain Dr. Seth Rogers, who had done her "a world of good — spiritually as well as physically," when he had treated her, during one of her breakdowns, at the water cure in Worcester, Massachusetts. Of both gentlemen she saw a good deal, and it is interesting to find their existence, so Spartan in some respects and yet so often delightful, described in very much the same terms — they sometimes record the same incidents — in both Miss Forten's and Colonel Higginson's diaries. The latter was to be included in a book that he later published, *Army Life in a Black Regiment,* for Thomas Wentworth Higginson was a man of letters, and a rather accomplished one, as well as a fighting reformer. He was interested in Emily Dickinson, who had sent him some of her poems, though it was not till after her death that he encouraged the publication of her poetry. His volumes of autobiography and of his memoirs of his New England contemporaries have survived as something more than documents. His limpid and elegant style has a flavor of artistic personality; he was sensitive to aesthetic impressions, and he could render them with a certain delicacy. "I pressed no flowers," he writes of his days on the Sea Islands, "collected no insects or birds' eggs, made no notes on natural objects, reversing in these respects all previous habits. Yet now, in the retrospect, there seems to have been infused into me through every pore the voluptuous charm of the season and the place; and the slightest corresponding sound or odor now calls back the memory of those delicious days. Being afterwards on picket at almost every season, I tasted the sensations of all; and though I hardly then thought of such a result, the associations of beauty will remain forever." Both he and

Charlotte Forten were recording the magnolias and the
moonlight nights, the boat trips between the islands
and the horseback rides through the pine-woods, the
rousing Negro "shouts" they attended, and especially a
big New Year's barbecue at which ten oxen were roasted.

Of this New Year's celebration in the Sea Islands at
the beginning of 1863, Colonel Higginson writes as
follows: "The services began at half past eleven o'clock,
with a prayer by our chaplain, Mr. Fowler, who is always, on such occasions, simple, reverential, and impressive. Then the President's Proclamation was read by
Dr. W. H. Brisbane, a thing infinitely appropriate, a
South Carolinian addressing South Carolinians; for he
was reared among these very islands, and here long since
emancipated his own slaves. Then the colors were presented to us by the Rev. Mr. French, a chaplain who
brought them from the donors in New York. All this
was according to the programme. Then followed an incident so simple, so touching, so utterly unexpected and
startling, that I can scarcely believe it on recalling,
though it gave the keynote to the whole day. The very
moment the speaker had ceased, and just as I took and
waved the flag, which now for the first time meant anything to these poor people, there suddenly arose, close
beside the platform, a strong male voice (but rather
cracked and elderly), into which two women's voices
instantly blended, singing as if by an impulse that
could no more be repressed than the morning note of
the song-sparrow. —

> My Country, 'tis of thee,
> Sweet land of liberty,
> Of thee I sing!

"People looked at each other, and then at us on the
platform, to see whence came this interruption, not set

down in the bills. Firmly and irrepressibly the quavering voices sang on, verse after verse; others of the colored people joined in; some whites on the platform began, but I motioned them to silence. I never saw anything so electric; it made all other words cheap; it seemed the choked voice of a race at last unloosed. Nothing could be more wonderfully unconscious; art could not have dreamed of a tribute to the day of jubilee that should be so affecting; history will not believe it; and when I came to speak of it, after it was ended, tears were everywhere. . . . Just think of it! — the first day they had ever had a country, the first flag they had ever seen which promised anything to their people, and here, while mere spectators stood in silence, waiting for my stupid words, these simple souls burst out in their lay, as if they were by their own hearths at home! When they stopped, there was nothing to do for it but to speak, and I went on; but the life of the whole day was in those unknown people's song."

That evening, returning from Camp Saxton, where the celebration had taken place, Miss Forten, on her side, reports, "We had a good time on the *Flora*. L. [a white Quaker girl] and I promenaded the deck, and sang *John Brown*, and Whittier's *Hymn*, and *My Country 'Tis of Thee*. And the moon shone bright above us, and the waves beneath, smooth and clear, glistened in the soft moonlight. At Beaufort we took the row boat, and the boatmen sang as they rowed us across."

Both Higginson and Charlotte Forten mention the chains and handcuffs which were brought by the Colonel from a local plantation, on which there had been found a wealthy lady "living in solitary splendor." "She spent a long time," says Charlotte, "trying to convince Dr. Rogers that she and her husband had devoted themselves to the good of their slaves, and lamented

their ingratitude in all deserting her — as they have all
done except one or two petted house servants." Colonel
Higginson had appeared there with one of her Negroes,
who had run away from her service and was now a
corporal in the Colonel's regiment. "I never saw," he
writes, "a finer bit of unutterable indignation than came
over the face of my hostess, as she slowly recognized
him. She drew herself up, and dropped out the monosyllables of her answer as if they were so many drops of
nitric acid. 'Ah,' quoth my lady, 'we called him Bob!'
. . . [Bob] simply turned from the lady, touched his hat
to me, and asked if I would wish to see the slave-jail,
as he had the keys in his possession." This turned out
to be "a small building, like a Northern corn-barn," in
the middle of the door of which was fixed "a large staple
with a rusty chain, like an ox-chain, for fastening a
victim down. When the door had been opened after the
death of the late proprietor, my informant said, a man
was found padlocked in that chain. We found also three
pairs of stocks of various construction, two of which
had smaller as well as larger holes, evidently for the
feet of women or children. In a building near by we
found something far more complicated, which was perfectly unintelligible till the men explained all its parts:
a machine so contrived that a person once imprisoned in
it could neither sit, stand nor lie, but must support the
body half raised, in a position scarcely endurable."

These estates the invading visitors were exploring with
keen curiosity. Of an abandoned plantation on Edisto
Island, Charlotte Forten writes, "This must once have
been a beautiful place. The grounds were evidently laid
out with great taste and are filled with beautiful trees,
among which I noticed particularly the magnolia tree,
with its wonderful white blossoms, large, pure, dazzlingly
white, as they shone among the rich, dark, shining

leaves. . . . We explored the house but found nothing but rubbish, and an old bedstead, and a very good bathing tub — which Lieut. R. graciously consented to my appropriating. It is quite a treasure in these regions."

Both Higginson and Charlotte Forten admired young Colonel Shaw, another New England crusader in command of another colored regiment, and both mourned his death when he fell in the unsuccessful attack on Fort Wagner. He had, says Higginson, "already got beyond the commonplaces of inexperience, in regard to colored troops. . . . For instance, he admitted the mere matter of courage to be settled, as regarded the colored troops, and his whole solicitude bore on this point — Would they do as well in line-of-battle as they had already done in more irregular service, and on picket and guard duty?" "It is too terrible, too terrible to write," Miss Forten cries when the bad news has reached them. "That our noble, beautiful young Colonel is killed, and the regiment cut to pieces! . . . The 54th put in advance; fought bravely, desperately, but was finally overpowered and driven back after getting into the Fort. Thank Heaven! they fought bravely!"

Charlotte Forten was evidently popular; she seems even to have been something of a belle. Her relations with Dr. Rogers, discreetly although she records them, decidedly give us the impression of verging on a genuine love affair. The need for more intimate companionship has taken the odd form, in her diary, of impelling her to create an imaginary confidante to whom she can recount her sensations. This phantom is addressed as "dear A." In Charlotte's first difficult days on the islands, she is able to relieve her mind by confessing to "dear A." such moods of depression as the following: "Had my first regular teaching experience, and to you and you only, friend beloved, will I acknowledge that it was *not*

a very pleasant one. Part of my scholars are very tiny —
babies, I call them — and it is hard to keep them quiet
and interested while I am hearing the larger ones," etc.
Dear A. becomes more and more real: "Was there ever
a lovelier road than that through which part of my way
to school lies? Oh, I wish you were here to go with me,
cher ami": "Old friend, my good and dear A., a very,
very happy New Year to you!"

But by February of 1864, she is able to report to her
imaginary friend the progress of intimacy with a real
one. Dr. Rogers takes her by surprise by dropping in on
her school one day. He hears the children read. "They
sang beautifully, too, which delighted him. He came to
dine with us, and then we — just he and I — had the
loveliest horseback ride to Thorpe's place. It was lovely
through those pines, and we found the most exquisite
jessamine. . . . Dr. R. broke off long sprays and twined
them around me. I felt as grand as a queen. . . . Dear
A., I can give you no idea of the ride homeward. I know
only that it was the most delightful ride I ever had in
my life. The young moon — just a silver bow — had a
singular, almost violet tinge, and all around it in the
heavens was a rosy glow, deepening every moment,
which was wonderfully beautiful. I shall never forget
how that rosy light, and the moon and stars, looked to
us as we caught them in glimpses, riding through the
dark pines. How wild and unreal it all seemed and
what happiness it was, as we rode slowly along, to
listen to the conversation of the dear friend who is
always so kind, so full of sympathy, and of eager enthusiasm in the great work in which he is engaged. No
wonder the soldiers love him so much. . . . There is a
magnetism about him impossible to resist. I can never
be thankful enough that he came here. But oh, I do not
want him to be ill, or to die. Most gladly would I give

my life that one so noble, so valuable might be preserved. He brought me a note from Col. Higginson. So very kind! I shall not say anything about its contents or about what Dr. Rogers said to me relating to it, even to you yet, my dear A., for it is a profound secret, which I must not trust to paper. But rest assured you will know all about it ere long."

The Colonel had invited Charlotte to go with his regiment to Florida, but the expedition never took place. Dr. Rogers had written her from there, when he had had to go away for a time, and sent her "a very light pretty rocking chair." Of another delightful ride with him, she writes, "It is very pleasant to know he cared so much for me, even although I know he *thinks* far better of me than I deserve."

But the Mr. Thorpe, whose place is mentioned above, a school superintendent from Rhode Island, "intelligent and agreeable," she says, seems also to be taking an interest in her. In May, returning from a visit to him, in company with the Quaker girl and with Mr. Thorpe himself, she describes still another enchanting ride: "I rode Mr. Thorpe's horse, a splendid, swift, high spirited creature. Could hardly hold him. But enjoyed the ride exceedingly. I like Mr. Thorpe. Report says that he more than likes me. But I *know* it is not so. Have never had the least reason to think it. Although he is very good and liberal, he is still an *American,* and would, of course, never be so insane as to love one of the proscribed race. The rumor — like many others — is entirely absurd and without the shadow of a foundation. How strange it seemed riding to-night through the woods — often in such perfect darkness we could see nothing — how strange and wild! I liked it."

But what happened after that? What is hidden behind this entry of a couple of months later? "Had a pleasant morning under the trees, near the water, while Dr. R. read Emerson to us. Then had a long talk with him, after which came the very sudden determination to go North in the next steamer. It is necessary for my health; therefore, it is wise to go."

Colonel Higginson, too, was very soon to return. He had sustained some sort of injury the summer before, "a knock on the side, not breaking the skin," he explains in a letter to his mother, "I don't know from what, which still lames me somewhat but it doesn't amount to the dignity of a wound." "No pain, no dressings or doses, a pleasant languor, nothing to do and no wish to do anything, a beautifully kept house and nobody but Dr. R. and myself in it, the hostess herself absent . . . to lie all day on a breezy balcony with green leaves and floating clouds, — why it is Arcadia, Syrian peace, immortal leisure. I blush to have bought it so cheaply as by a mere black and blue spot on the side, to show where a bombshell did *not* touch me." After a furlough of a month, he had returned to his regiment, but he was never quite well again, and he was allowed to resign on account of ill health in the spring of 1864, and went comfortably to recover in Newport. In a book on the St. John's River, James Branch Cabell gives a scathing account of Higginson's campaign in Florida, contrasting the delicious sensations which the Colonel describes in his diary with the robbing and burning of farms committed under his orders by his colored troops. The climax of Cabell's story comes when Higginson, having set fire to Jacksonville and about to leave it to the flames, puts the bud of a white tea-rose in his buttonhole, regretting that this is "the end of our brilliant enterprise" and noting that this is "the only time since I entered the service when I have felt within the reach of tears." And it is true that there is something about Higginson which instinctively cuts itself off from alien associations and which is not far removed from smugness — in Kansas, on the Sea Islands, in Florida, in his attitude toward Emily Dickinson when he went to see her at Amherst and, aware of "an excess of tension," felt that Emily was "much too enigmatical a being for me to solve in an hour's interview" and confined himself thereafter to correspondence. We can imagine his attitude toward Charlotte Forten: sympathetic, approving, instructive, very sure of his own benevolence. This had all been a beautiful experience for Charlotte Forten and Colonel Higginson and Dr. Seth Rogers — those days when the Negro's deliverers and a cultivated Negro woman who wanted to work for the advancement of her race were meeting in a common mission on the plantation of the vanished enslaver, when they rode through the pines in the moonlight and sang their patriotic songs. But the moment was soon to pass, the contact was not to last long. Colonel Higginson and Dr. Rogers were to leave the delightful South and go back home to their Massachusetts, and Charlotte Forten to the Philadelphia which could hardly be called hers; and thereafter, one imagines, they ceased to meet.

But Charlotte's story had a happy ending. The Grimkés of South Carolina were an old Revolutionary family of French and German blood. John Faucheraud Grimké was a wealthy judge. His two sisters became active Abolitionists and champions of women's rights, and one of them wrote, in 1836, an anti-slavery *Appeal to the Christian Women of the South*. They eventually went to live in New England, where they were freer to work for their cause but where there reached them, in 1868, from the South they had left behind, a revelation that was rather upsetting. One of the sisters had noticed in a Northern anti-slavery paper that a literary meeting at Lincoln University, a new institution of learning for Negroes, was to be addressed by a Francis Grimké. She knew well that there was only one family of Grimkés and, after wondering and worrying a month, she finally wrote to this unknown person. She then learned that one of her brothers in Charleston had had three sons by one of his slave girls. This brother, on his death, had bequeathed his slaves to the eldest of his white sons but had ordered that his own mulatto children should be freed. The white heir, however, in contempt of this, had threatened, when one of these boys was ten, to sell him to another master, and the boy, whose name was Francis, had run away during the war and served as valet to a Confederate officer. In ill health, after two years of this, he had returned to his home in Charleston, where his half-brother, still legally his owner, treated him as a runaway slave, sending him, first, to jail and then selling him to another officer. He was rescued, after the fall of the Confederacy, by the United States Sanitary Commission, and, with one of his brothers, sent North, where they got themselves an education and graduated from Lincoln. Both the boys were unusually able. Archibald went on to Harvard Law School, served as consul in Santo Domingo, and wrote lives of Sumner and Garrison and books on the Negro problem. Francis Grimké studied for the ministry. He graduated from Princeton Theological Seminary and preached in Presbyterian churches, first in Washington, D.C., then in Jacksonville. Both were active in the cause of Negro rights. And Francis, the bar-sinister scion of this old Carolinian family, met Charlotte Forten and married her.

VIII

THREE CONFEDERATE LADIES: KATE STONE, SARAH MORGAN, MARY CHESNUT

OLMSTED AND TROWBRIDGE both were, after all, outsiders in the South. A Southerner might well have complained that neither was in any position to enter into the mind of the South, to convey the point of view of the men who rushed to arms in defense of the Confederacy without calculating the chances or counting the cost, of the women who so passionately backed them; that, small in proportion to the population though the educated upper class might be, they had generated, nevertheless, the conceptions that dominated the Southern cause; and that Olmsted, with his economist's scrutiny and his flat factual tone, having never shared these Southerners' experience, could have no notion how their feudal world appeared to them, in what terms their own lives were conceived.

Let us now look into this experience. We shall first consult the diaries of the women of this cultivated upper class, in which it finds its most spontaneous and most intimate expression. In presenting three Confederate ladies, I shall proceed from the simpler to the more complex.

Kate Stone of Louisiana — whose diary was published in 1955, under the title *Brokenburn: The Journal of*

Kate Stone, 1861-1868 — is the typical Dixie heroine, as approved by the Southern tradition. In her opinions, she is perfectly orthodox. When the Federal fleet arrives, she declares that the Yankee gunboats "are polluting the waters of the grand old Mississippi." "Is the soul of Nero reincarnated in the form of Butler?" she asks, when General Ben Butler in New Orleans has a Louisiana gentleman shot for tearing down the flag of the Union. "I wonder what will be the result of this diabolical move," she writes of the Emancipation Proclamation. "I think there is little chance of a happy hereafter for President Lincoln." And of Lincoln's assassination she writes, "All honor to J. Wilkes Booth, who has rid the world of a tyrant and made himself famous for genera-tions. Surratt has also won the love and applause of all Southerners by his daring attack on Seward, whose life is trembling in the balance. How earnestly we hope our two avengers may escape to the South, where they will meet with a warm welcome."

Kate Stone was twenty years old when the war began, and was living with her widowed mother about thirty miles northwest of Vicksburg, at Brokenburn, a rich Louisiana cotton plantation of over a thousand acres, worked by a hundred and fifty slaves. She had been educated by a tutor and looked forward to a visit to Europe in 1862. When Grant's army closed in on Vicks-burg, the Stone ladies were forced to flee. They had been frightened, on a visit to a neighbor's, when the house was robbed by Negroes while a Negro held them up with a gun. There follow the usual incidents of insolence from Yankee soldiers, disillusion with trusted slaves. In Texas, where Kate and her mother and sister are obliged to spend two and a half years, she finds herself for the first time in her life in contact with the squalor and the boorishness of that Southern back coun-

tryside with which Olmsted was so well acquainted but
with which Miss Stone had had no acquaintance whatever. On her way there, but still in her native State,
she records that "at house after house, dark and unin-
viting with a host of little towheads and forlorn-looking
women, generally spinning, amid the barking of a pack
of dogs, would come the response, 'Naw, we don't take
in travellers,' in a tone of contempt, as though the very
name of traveller was a disgrace." In Texas, "the table
was set on a low, sunny gallery, and half a dozen dirty,
unshaven men took their seats in their shirt sleeves at
the dirtiest tablecloth and coarsest ware. We saw the
Negro girl wash the dishes at the *duck pond* right out
in the yard. That was too much for me, but Mamma and
Mr. Smith managed to swallow down something." And
later, in another place: "I despair of giving any idea of
the dirt. We tried to eat without seeing or tasting and
to sleep without touching the bed. They gave us coffee,
a horrid decoction of burnt wheat and milk without
sugar, in saucers, and water in the halves of broken
bottles. The table was set in the dirtiest of kitchens with
a dirt floor and half a dozen half-naked little Negroes
and numberless cats and dogs scampering through the
room and under the table. The rafters were festooned
with old hoop skirts and worn-out, rough boots. It surpassed any place we have been in yet. We certainly have
found the dark corner of the Confederacy." Once settled
in Tyler, Texas, they are comfortable but lack diversion.
At one point, she writes in her diary that she has "nearly
memorized Tennyson," and that they have read and re-
read their "favorite plays in Shakespeare . . . We hope
Mr. McGee will be able to get *Harper's* to us. We wrote
to him for it. That would keep us stirred up for awhile
at least. The literature of the North is to us what the
'flesh pots of Egypt' were to the wandering Israelites —

we long for it." Yet there were many Louisianians in Tyler, and they managed to amuse themselves with the inevitable private theatricals. Kate makes the inevitable comparison of the planters expelled from their homes with the dispossessed French nobility at the time of the Revolution.

All the miseries of the war years are here. The Negroes threaten them and the Yankees molest them. The silver has to be buried in order that it may not be stolen. One of Kate's young brothers is killed in battle, and another dies of fever. When Kate and her mother at last — in November, 1865 — return to their old estate, "It does not seem the same place," she writes. "The bare echoing rooms, the neglect and defacement of all — though the place is in better repair than most — and the stately oaks and the green grass make it look pleasant and cheerful, though gardens, orchards, and fences are mostly swept away. But if the loved ones who passed through its doors could be with us again, we might be happy yet. But 'never, never, never more' echoes back to our hearts like a funeral knell at every thought of the happy past. We must bear our losses as best we can. Nothing is left but to endure." Even in her courage and grief, poor Kate is rather wooden. Yet one of her reactions is interesting: "How still and lifeless everything seems," she writes on her return to Brokenburn. "How I fear that the life at Tyler has spoiled us for plantation life. Everything seems sadly *out of time*. [italics mine]" Time is after all a function of the life of a society, and as to pass from one to another is to shift one's perception of time, so to have one's society destroyed is to find oneself "out of time."

It is difficult for the menfolks to adapt themselves to their changed relations with the Negroes. Kate's nineteen-year-old-brother Johnny "had a fight with a young Negro in the field, shot and came near killing him, and

was mobbed in return. Johnny would have been killed
but for the stand one of the Negroes made for him, and
Uncle Bo's opportune arrival just as the Negroes brought
him to the house — a howling, cursing mob, with the
women shrieking 'Kill him!' and all brandishing pistols
and guns. . . . Johnny had to be sent away . . . and
the Negroes quieted down, and after some weeks the
wounded boy recovered, greatly to Johnny's relief. He
never speaks now of killing people as he formerly had a
habit of doing."

Kate's journal contains no comment on the problems
of the institution of slavery. It was only in 1900, when
she wrote a foreword for her diary, that she frankly
expressed her feelings. Though, as she says, she had
generations of planters behind her, "my first recollection
is of pity for the Negroes and desire to help them. Even
under the best owners, it was a hard, hard life: to toil
six days out of seven, week after week, month after
month, year after year, as long as life lasted; to be
absolutely under the control of someone until the last
breath was drawn; to win but the bare necessaries of
life, no hope of more, no matter how hard the work,
how long the toil; and to know that nothing could change
your lot. Obedience, revolt, submission, prayers — all
were in vain. Waking sometimes in the nights as I grew
older and thinking it all over, I would grow sick with
the misery of it all. As far as Mamma could, the Negroes
on our place were protected from cruelty and well cared
for; they were generally given Saturday evening and had
plenty to eat and comfortable clothes. Still there were
abuses impossible to prevent. And constantly there were
tales circulated of cruelties on neighboring plantations,
tales that would make one's blood run cold. And yet we
were powerless to help. Always I felt the moral guilt of
it, felt how impossible it must be for an owner of slaves

to win his way into Heaven. Born and raised as we were, what would be our measure of responsibility?" And though the war has "swept from us everything," she has never regretted the freeing of the slaves. "The great load of accountability was lifted."

A considerably more interesting young woman is Kate Stone's sister Louisianian, Sarah Morgan of Baton Rouge, whose journal, with the title *A Confederate Girl's Diary*, was published in 1913. Sarah Morgan was twenty when the war broke out. Her father, a local judge, died in the autumn of 1861. Three of her brothers were away from home, fighting in the Confederate Army and Navy, and she found herself the strongest character in a family of three sisters — one of them a married woman with five children — and a weak and frightened mother. Her diary begins on March 9, 1862, with the reflections of a sensitive young girl on her relations with one of her sisters by whom she feels she has always been outshone. There follows an account of the killing in a duel of another of her brothers, who is not in the services — one of those ridiculous affairs of honor which Olmsted regards as a manifestation of the lack of self-restraint that results from the owning of slaves. It is evident that this reckless hot-headedness, this readiness to call people out, was a very important element in the action of South Carolina itself in seceding from the Union and firing on Fort Sumter. In the case of Sarah Morgan's brother Harry, the whole affair sounds quite puerile and, in her account of it, is hardly intelligible. One of the young men who came to the Morgans' house had, in the course of an apparently convivial evening, been called upon by the company to sing, and had obliged them with a song which Sarah says was "not nice" — though in reviewing her diary years later, she adds, with an exclamation point, that this song was merely *Annie Laurie*. An old gentleman got up to leave, and this old gentleman's son, an obnoxious outsider to the Morgans' world, who may or may not have been under the influence of opium, imagined that the song had offended his father. Harry Morgan denied this, and the outsider called him a liar. "That is a name that none of our family has either merited or borne with; and quick as thought Hal sprang to his feet and struck him across the face with the walking-stick he held. The blow sent the lower part across the balcony in the street, as the spring was loosened by it, while the upper part, to which was fastened the sword — for it was father's sword-cane — remained in his hand. I doubt that he ever before knew the cane could come apart. Certainly he did not perceive it, until the other whined piteously he was taking advantage over an unarmed man; when, cursing him, he [Harry] threw it after the main body of the cane, and said, *'Now* we are equal.' The other's answer was to draw a knife, and he was about to plunge it into Harry, who disdained to flinch, when Mr. Henderson threw himself on Mr. Sparks and dragged him off." A duel followed, and Harry was killed.

That April Admiral Farragut, at the cost of a stiff battle, succeeded in running the Confederate forts along the Mississippi and, still with fourteen of his seventeen ships, arrived at and captured New Orleans. On May 9, the Federal officers took over Baton Rouge, with the order that all Confederate flags were immediately to be "suppressed." "*Good,*" Sarah Morgan exclaims. "As soon as one is confiscated, I make another, until my ribbon is exhausted, when I will sport a duster emblazoned in high colors, 'Hurrah! for the Bonny Blue Flag!'" (*The Bonny Blue Flag* was a Confederate song.) But she adds: "This is a dreadful war, to make even the hearts of women so bitter! I hardly know myself these last few weeks. I, who have such a horror of bloodshed, consider even killing in self-defense murder, who cannot wish them [the Union soldiers] the slightest evil, whose only prayer is to have them sent back in peace to their own country — talk of killing them! For what else do I wear a pistol and carving-knife? I am afraid I *will* try them on the first one who says an insolent word to me. Yes, and repent for it ever after in sackcloth and ashes. *Oh!* if I was only a man! Then I could don the breeches, and slay them with a will! If some few Southern women were in the ranks, they could set the men an example they would not blush to follow. Pshaw! there are *no* women here! We are *all* men!"

The last part of this outburst is typical of one type of Southern woman, the proud and spirited kind, who were behaving, in New Orleans, with such insolence toward the Union troops that General Ben Butler — whom they called "Beast" Butler — had been goaded to issue the order which so much inflamed them further: "Hereafter, when any female shall by mere gesture or movement insult or show contempt for any officers or soldiers of the United States, she shall be regarded and held liable to be treated as a woman about town plying her avocation." Yet Miss Morgan was not merely a fierce little Confederate who stood up to the infamous Yankees. Her father the judge had opposed secession till his state had voted to secede; and another of her brothers, also a judge, married and living in New Orleans, had continued to support the Union even after war was declared, though he refused to bear arms against the Confederacy. An older sister of Sarah's had married a Union army officer, who was stationed in California and had exercised an influence that was probably decisive in checking secession there. Thus the sympathies of Miss Morgan

were somewhat divided; and in this she is representative
of a certain minority in the South that differed from the
group to which Kate Stone belonged: the professional
or mercantile non-planter class, with a tradition of public
service that had come down from the Revolution and a
habit of thinking in terms of the principles and welfare
of the country as a whole. Such people had no great stake
in the planters' economy; they were likely to own few
slaves or none.

Sarah Morgan, like many such Southerners, was
shocked by the intolerant sectionalism of the South and
its venomous hatred of the Northerners. "I insist," she
writes on June 16 of 1862, "that if the valor and chivalry
of our men cannot save our country, I would rather have
it conquered by a brave race than owe its liberty to the
Billingsgate oratory and demonstrations of some of these
'ladies.' If the women have the upper hand then, as they
have now, I would not like to live in a country governed
by such tongues. Do I consider the female who could
spit in a gentleman's face, merely because he wore
United States buttons, as a fit associate for me? Lieutenant Biddle assured me he did not pass a street in New
Orleans without being most grossly insulted by *ladies*.
It was a friend of his into whose face a lady *spit* as he
walked quietly by without looking at her. (Wonder if
she did it to attract his attention?) He had the sense to
apply to her husband and give him two minutes to
apologize or die, and of course he chose the former. Such
things are enough to disgust anyone. 'Loud' women, what
a contempt I have for you! How I despise your vulgarity! . . . O women! into what loathsome violence
you have abased your holy mission! God will punish us
for our hard-heartedness. Not a square off, in the new
theater, lie more than a hundred sick soldiers. What
woman has stretched out her hand to save them, to give

them a cup of cold water? Where is the charity which should ignore nations and creeds, and administer help to the Indian and Heathen indifferently? Gone! All gone in Union versus Secession!"

Sarah Morgan is unquestionably a girl of unusual intelligence and character. She is able to think for herself and to stick to her opinions and principles; in the confusion and uncertainty of the war years, she applies herself, whenever it is possible, to systematic self-education, and though she has had only ten months of schooling, she has learned a good deal of history, and she works hard at music and French. She shows a strong taste for literature, and her journal is distinguished not only by naturalness and vivacity but by something of a sense of style. Yet there is nothing in her situation to contradict Olmsted's assertion that such people were rare in the South. One of the things that are most vividly brought home to us is the social isolation of the Morgans. There exists for her, of course, the prime Southern distinction between "gentlemen" and "ladies," on the one hand, and everybody else, on the other, and of course she identifies herself with the former. Of an inferior who has presumed on his uniform to try to speak to her on terms of equality, "I was quite familiar," she writes, "with the cart of De J——— *pére*, as it perambulated the streets. My first impressions are seldom erroneous. From the first, I knew that man's respectability was derived from his buttons. That is why he took such pride in them, and contemplated them with such satisfaction. They lent him social backbone enough to converse so familiarly with me; without the effulgence of that splendid gold, which he hoped would dazzle my eyes to his real position, he would have hardly dared to 'remember me when I was a wee thing, so high.' Is he the only man whose coat alone entitles him to respectability?

He may be colonel, for all I know; but still, he is A＿＿
de J＿＿ to me." Of a Mr. Harold, whom she later met,
she writes: "I need not describe him, beyond this slight
indication of his style. Before half an hour was over, he
remarked to Anna that I was a *very* handsome girl, and
he addressed me as — *Miss Sally!* That is sufficient." "Our
vivid imaginations," she is to note of the Confederate
prisoners in New Orleans, "are constantly occupied in
depicting their sufferings, privations, heroism, and manifold virtues, until they have almost become as demigods
to us. Even horrid little Captain C＿＿ has a share of
my sympathy in his misfortune! Fancy what must be my
feelings where those I consider as gentlemen are concerned!"

Yet, even among those she accepts, she is conscious of
belonging to some better breed. Sarah's ideal of manhood seems based on some superior standard established
by her father and her brothers; and one gets the impression that, in Baton Rouge, there are hardly, among
the "ladies" and "gentlemen," even any of their own
neighbors whom the Morgans quite regard as equals. "I
am beginning to believe that we are of even more importance in Baton Rouge than we thought we were. It is
laughable to hear the things a certain set of people, who
know they can't visit us, say about the whole family . . .
When father was alive, they dared not talk about us
aloud, beyond calling us the 'Proud Morgans' and the
'Aristocracy of Baton Rouge' . . . But now father is
gone, the people imagine we are public property, to be
criticized, vilified, and abused to their hearts' content
. . . And now, because they find absurdities don't succeed, they try improbabilities. So yesterday the town was
in a ferment because it was reported the Federal officers
had called on the Miss Morgans, and all the gentlemen
were anxious to hear how they had been received . . .

I suppose the story originated from the fact that we were unwilling to blackguard — yes, that is the word — the Federal officers here, and would not agree with many of our friends in saying they were liars, thieves, murderers, scoundrels, the scum of the earth, etc. Such epithets are unworthy of ladies, I say, and do harm rather than advance our cause. Let them be what they will, it shall not make me less the lady; I say it is unworthy of anything except low newspaper war, such abuse, and I will not join in. . . . Shall I acknowledge that the people we so recently called our brothers are unworthy of consideration, and are liars, cowards, dogs? Not I! If they conquer us, I acknowledge them as a superior race; I will not say that we were conquered by cowards, for where would that place us? It will take a brave people to gain us, and that the Northerners undoubtedly are. I would scorn to have an inferior foe; I fight only my equals." What is interesting here is an aristocratic sense that has detached itself from planter solidarity.

Sarah Morgan, under stress of the war, is to develop a fortitude and a self-control, an ability to take the initiative, which are conscious but never theatrical. The family, in Baton Rouge, are living in a constant state of apprehension. When a Union officer is shot, the Unionists shell the city. At the sound of the first cannon, Mrs. Morgan begins screaming. "What awful screams!" comments Sarah. "I had hoped never to hear them again after Harry died [the brother who had been shot in the duel]." She liberates her pet canary, and the Morgan family flee, with most of the rest of the town, to a nearby place of safety. Later on, they return to their house, but they are still obliged to beware of the possible arrival of their own Confederate soldiers, who, if they retake the town, will burn it. They are awakened in the night by the roll of drums, and they smell burning cot-

ton. They get the children up and snatch together some
warm clothes, but this proves to be a false alarm. Two
days later, however, they all decamp and take refuge in
a Deaf and Dumb Asylum, from which, since nothing
has happened, they are glad to return again. Sarah hears
"a well-known cheep in the streets," and gets her canary
back. It has been caught by a Negro and turned over to
a neighbor. Hundreds of wounded Unionists are unloaded from boats on the docks. "Cousin Will saw one
lying dead without a creature by to notice when he
died. Another was dying, and muttering to himself as he
lay too far gone to brush the flies out of his eyes and
mouth, while no one was able to do it for him. Cousin
Will helped him, though. Another, a mere skeleton, lay
in the agonies of death, too; but he evidently had kind
friends, for several were gathered around holding him up
and fanning him, while his son leaned over him, crying
aloud. Tiche says it was terrible to hear the poor boy's
sobs. All day our *vis-à-vis*, Baumstark, with his several
aids, plies his hammer; all Sunday he made coffins, and
says he can't make them fast enough. Think, too, he is
by no means the only undertaker here! Oh, I wish these
poor men were safe in their own land! It is heartbreaking
to see them die here like dogs, with no one to say God-
speed. The Catholic priest went to see some, sometime
ago, and going near one who lay in bed, said some kind
thing, when the man burst into tears and cried, 'Thank
God, I have heard *one* kind word before I die!' In a few
minutes the poor wretch was dead."

On the eve of the battle of the fifth of August, they escape to a plantation across the river. When one of
Sarah's sisters makes an excursion to Baton Rouge, she
finds that their house has been wrecked: "Ours was the
most shockingly treated house in the whole town. We
have the misfortune to be equally feared by both sides,

because we will blackguard neither . . . It was one
scene of ruin. Libraries emptied, china smashed, side-
boards split open with axes, three cedar chests cut open,
plundered and set up on end; all parlor ornaments carried off — even the alabaster Apollo and Diana that Hal
valued so much. Her [the sister's] piano, dragged to the
center of the parlor, had been abandoned as too heavy
to carry off; her desk lay open with all letters and notes
well thumbed and scattered around, while Will's last
letter to her was open on the floor, with the Yankee
stamp of dirty fingers. Mother's portrait half-cut from
its frame stood on the floor. Margaret, who was present
at the sacking, told how she had saved father's. It seems
that those who wrought destruction in our house were
all officers. One jumped on the sofa to cut the picture
down (Miriam saw the prints of his muddy feet) when
Margaret cried, 'For God's sake, gentlemen, let it be! I'll
help you to anything here. He's dead, and the young
ladies would rather see the house burn than lose it!' 'I'll
blow your damned brains out,' was the 'gentleman's'
answer as he put a pistol to her head, which a brother
officer dashed away, and the picture was abandoned for
finer sport. All the others were cut up in shreds.

"Upstairs was the finest fun. Mother's beautiful
armoire, whose single door was an extremely fine mirror,
was entered by crashing through the glass, when it was
emptied of every article, and the shelves half-split and
half-thrust back crooked. Letters, labeled by the boys
'Private,' were strewn over the floor; they opened every
armoire and drawer, collected every rag to be found and
littered the whole house with them, until the wonder
was where so many rags had been found. Father's
armoire was relieved of everything; Gibbes's handsome
Damascus sword with the silver scabbard included. All
his clothes, George's, Hal's, Jimmy's, were appropriated.

They entered my room, broke that fine mirror for sport, pulled down the rods from the bed, and with them pulverized my toilet set, taking also all Lydia's china ornaments I had packed in the wash-stand. The debris filled my basin, and ornamented my bed. My desk was broken open. Over it was spread all my letters, and sundry tokens of dried roses, etc., which must have been *very* funny, they all being labeled with the donor's name, and the occasion. Fool! How I writhe when I think of all they saw; the invitations to buggy rides, concerts, 'Compliments of,' etc. — ! Lilly's sewing-machine had disappeared; but as mother's was too heavy to move, they merely smashed the needles.

"In the pillaging of the armoires, they seized a pink flounced muslin of Miriam's, which one officer placed on the end of a bayonet and paraded around with, followed by the others, who slashed it with their swords, crying, 'I have stuck the damned Secesh! that's the time I cut her!', and continued their sport until the rags could no longer be pierced. One seized my bonnet, with which he decked himself, and ran in the streets. Indeed, all who found such, rushed frantically around town, by way of frolicking, with the things on their heads. They say no frenzy could surpass it. Another snatched one of my calico dresses and a pair of vases that mother had when she was married, and was about to decamp when a Mrs. Jones jerked them away and carried them to her boarding-house and returned them to mother the other day. Blessed be Heaven! I have a calico dress! Our clothes were used for the vilest purposes and spread in every corner — at least those few that were not stolen.

"Aunt Barker's Charles tried his best to defend the property. 'Ain't you 'shamed to destroy all dis here, that belongs to a poor widow lady who's got two daughters to support?' he asked of an officer who was foremost in the destruction. 'Poor? Damn them! I don't know when I have seen a house furnished like this! Look at that furniture! *They* poor!' was the retort, and thereupon the work went bravely on, of making us poor, indeed.

"It would have fared badly with us had we been there. The servants say they broke into the house crying, 'Where are those damned Secesh women? We know they are hid in here, and we'll make them dance for hiding from Federal Officers!' And they could not be convinced that we were not there, until they had searched the very garret. Wonder what they would have done? Charles caught a Captain Clark in the streets, when the work was almost over, and begged him to put an end to it. The gentleman went readily, but though the devastation was quite evident, no one was to be seen and he was about to leave, when, insisting that there was someone there, Charles drew him into my room, dived under the bed and drew from thence a Yankee captain by one leg, followed by a lieutenant, each with a bundle of the boys' clothes, which they instantly dropped, protesting they were only looking around the house. The gentleman captain carried them off to their superior."

On the way to Baton Rouge in a buggy, she has passed some Yankee camps that the Confederates have taken over. There are corpses lying in the ditches, skeletons of men and horses with the flesh still hanging on them. Yet, in spite of the fear and the horror, the sense of responsibility, she manages, from time to time, quite girlishly to enjoy herself. There are moments when her high spirits as well as her passionate feelings remind us of Natasha in *War and Peace*. Her good sense and her self-imposed coolness curb, but they are far from inhibiting, the romantic and heroic ideas of a young Louisianian brought up on Walter Scott. She was evidently too proud for flirtation, but her relations with the various young men she meets, Confederate and Union alike, unfailingly stimulate gallantries, to which she is alert and challenging. It is amusing, after the battle of Baton Rouge, when the Yankees are holding the town, to find her dreaming she is to marry a Federal officer: "That was in consequence of having answered the question, whether I would do so with an emphatic 'Yes! if I loved him,' which will probably ruin my reputation as a patriot in this parish. Bah! I am no bigot! — or fool either."

With the young men of their own kind, wherever she may happen to be perched, Sarah and her sisters and their girl-friends enjoy a good deal of jollity. There are taffy-pulls and Puss Wants a Corner. They amuse themselves with a romp of Puss on a visit to a cane-sugar purgery. As soon as the game is suggested, "all flew up to the second staging, under the cane-carrier and by the engine. Such racing for corners! Such scuffles among the gentlemen! Such confusion among the girls when, springing forward for a place, we would find it already occupied! All dignity was discarded. We laughed and ran as loud and fast as any children, and the General enjoyed our fun as much as we, and encouraged us in our pranks. Waller surpassed himself, Mr. Bradford carried all by storm, Mr. Enders looked like a schoolboy on a frolic, Mr. Carter looked sullen and tried lazily not to mar the sport completely, while Mr. Harold looked timidly foolish and half afraid of our wild sport. Mrs. Badger laughed, the General roared, Anne flew around like a balloon, Miriam fairly danced around with fun and frolic, while I laughed so that it was an exertion to change corners. Then forfeits followed, with the usual absurd formalities, in which Mr. Bradford sentenced himself unconsciously to ride a barrel, Miriam to make him a love speech going home, Mr. Enders to kiss my hand, and I to make him (Mr. Enders) a declaration, which

I instantly did, in French, whereby I suffered no inconvenience, as Miriam alone comprehended. Then came more sugar-cane and talk in the purgery, and we were horrified when Mrs. Badger announced that it was twelve o'clock and gave orders to retire."

She is reckless and will not keep out of danger. "By the time the little *émeute* had subsided, determined to have a frolic, Miss Walters, Ginnie, and I got on our horses and rode off down the Arkansas Lane, to have a gallop and a peep at the gunboats from the levee. But mother's entreaties prevented us from going that near, as she cried that it was well known they fired at every horse or vehicle they saw in the road, seeing a hundred guerrillas in every puff of dust, and we were sure to be killed, murdered, and all sorts of bloody deaths awaited us; so, to satisfy her, we took the road about a mile from the river, in full view, however. We had not gone very far before we met a Mr. Watson, a plain farmer of the neighborhood, who begged us to go back. 'You'll be fired on, ladies, sure! You don't know the danger! Take my advice and go home as quick as possible before they shell you! They shot buggies and carriages, and of course they won't mind *horses* with women! Please go home!' But Ginnie, who had taken a fancy to go on, acted as spokeswoman, and determined to go on in spite of his advice, so, nothing loath to follow her example, we thanked him and rode on." And the next day: "Again I had to notice this peculiarity about women — that the married ones are invariably the first to fly, in time of danger, and always leave the young ones to take care of themselves. Here were our three matrons, prophesying that the house would be burnt, the Yankees upon us, and all murdered in ten minutes, flying down the Guerilla Lane, and leaving us to encounter the horrors they foretold, alone.

"It was a splendid gallop in the bright moonlight, over the fields, only it was made uncomfortable by the jerking of my running-bag, until I happily thought of turning it before. A hard ride of four miles in about twenty minutes brought us to the house of the man who so kindly offered his hospitality."

But one day, as she is riding past a camp, a gun goes off and scares her horse. She is thrown, and her back is severely injured; she remains a cripple for months. Her slowness of recovery suggests that she has also at last broken down under the continual strain on her nerves. Now the Yankees are occupying the Morgan house, and her family decide that there is nothing to do but to retreat to captured New Orleans, where her Unionist brother will protect them. Having accomplished the arduous journey, they are faced with the oath of allegiance, which — Sarah with self-controlled qualms, her mother after futile protestations — they must force themselves now to swear. Two of Sarah's combatant brothers are killed in the same week, and their deaths make her feel more than ever alone in a world to which she cannot be reconciled. When Lincoln is assassinated, she writes: " 'Vengeance is mine; I will repay, saith the Lord.' This is murder. God have mercy on those that did it! . . . Charlotte Corday killed Marat in his bath, and is held up in history as one of Liberty's martyrs, and one of the heroines of her country. To me, it is all murder. Let the historians extol blood-shedding; it is woman's place to abhor it." But when, two or three days later, she happens to meet a Yankee officer, a cousin of Mrs. Lincoln's, who in her childhood was one of her beaux, she treats him coolly and discourages his efforts to be friendly. When he has left her, "I returned," she writes, "to my own painful reflections. The Mr. Todd who was my 'sweetheart' when I was twelve and he twenty-four, who was my brother's friend, and daily at our home, was put away from our acquaintance at the beginning of the war. This one I should not know. Cords of candy and mountains of bouquets bestowed in childish days will not make my country's enemy my friend now that I am a woman."

Sarah Morgan, nine years after this entry, was to marry Francis Warrington Dawson, an Englishman who at twenty-one, romantically aroused by the Confederacy, had come to this country to fight for the South and had figured in a dozen engagements. After the war, he remained in the United States and became a newspaper man, who exercised a considerable influence as editor of the Charleston *News and Courier*. He had the courage to advocate that Negroes be permitted to run for municipal office and he succeeded in having enacted a statute that made duelling unlawful; but, in the end he fell victim, like his wife's brother Harry, to the inveterate quarrelsomeness of the Southerners: he was shot, in the typical Carolinian fashion, by a gallant gentleman of Charleston, who resented Dawson's resentment of what the latter regarded as an insult to the Dawsons' family governess.

———

Sarah Morgan was no doubt, in her girlhood, in her provincial town on the Mississippi, a more or less isolated phenomenon among people she regarded as social inferiors and to whom she was unquestionably superior in intellect. Mrs. James Chesnut, on the other hand, whose journal has been published as *A Diary from Dixie*, also a woman of exceptional intelligence, was surrounded by all that the Confederacy could show of most cultivated and most distinguished. The father of Mary Chesnut's husband was a rich South Carolinian, who owned

five square miles of plantations, but the son had studied
law and gone into politics. Like his father, he had been
educated at Princeton, and he had travelled with his
wife in Europe. He had served in the United States
Senate from 1858, stoutly defending slavery, and, in the
autumn of 1860, even before the secession of his State,
had been the first Southern senator to resign from the
Senate. He had, the following year, taken part in the
convention that drafted the ordinance of secession and
in the Congress of the Confederate States that drafted
their constitution. It was he who had been sent to Major
Anderson to demand the surrender of Fort Sumter, and,
as an aide with the rank of colonel on the staff of Jefferson Davis, he was close to the Confederate government
all through the Civil War and was entrusted with many
missions which brought him in touch with the military
as well as with the political aspects of the conflict.

Mrs. Chesnut had thus the advantage of living much
at the headquarters of the Confederacy, first in Montgomery, Alabama; then, when its capital was shifted, in
Richmond, Virginia, where she had for her daily associates the Davises and the Lees, all sorts of incapacitated
or visiting army officers — the "first families" of South
Carolina and Virginia — and such literary men as the
South had produced, the novelist William Gilmore
Simms and the poet Paul Hamilton Hayne. Yet we are
struck, as we read these two diaries, Miss Morgan's and
Mrs. Chesnut's, as well as other Southern documents of
the period, by the recurrence of the same family names.
Sarah Morgan in Baton Rouge is related to and knows
the same families as the Chesnuts in Richmond a
thousand miles away. The world that we have here to
deal with — the world of that fraction of the ruling class
that is at all public-spirited and well-educated — is, as
Olmsted says, extremely limited; and how far this ele-

ment was from being capable of influencing the policy or saving the fortunes of the South may be seen in an appalling and a heartbreaking way in the chronicle of Mrs. Chesnut's diary.

This diary is an extraordinary document — in its informal department, a masterpiece; and on that account, one cannot do it justice by merely running through its record as we have done with that of Sarah Morgan. Mrs. Chesnut is a very clever woman, who knows something of Europe as well as of Washington and who has read a good deal of history as well as of other kinds of literature. Not only is she fully aware of the world-wide importance of the national crisis at one of the foci of which she finds herself; she has also, it would seem, a decided sense of the literary possibilities of her subject. The very rhythm of her opening pages at once puts us under the spell of a writer who is not merely jotting down her days but establishing, as a novelist does, an atmosphere, an emotional tone. A hundred and fifty thousand words of the four hundred thousand words that Mrs. Chesnut wrote were first published in 1904, and this book was read many years after by the late Ben Ames Williams, in preparation for a novel he was writing — *House Divided* — which was to deal with the Civil War. For his purposes, Mr. Williams, as he tells us, laid it heavily under contribution, and even introduced a character that was based on Mrs. Chesnut herself. It would seem to have been injudicious to attempt to exploit for fiction a work that is already a work of art; but Mr. Williams was not at that time in a position to appreciate fully how much a work of art it was. When his interest in Mrs. Chesnut led him to look up her original fifty notebooks, he discovered whole episodes, including the important one of "Buck" Preston and General Hood, as well as elements of the social picture — the ignominies and cruelties of slav-

ery — which the editors had suppressed; and he now tried
to do the writer justice by bringing out, in 1949, a new
edition of her diary twice as long as the original one.
This still left a hundred thousand words unpublished,
and the interest of the document as we know it suggests
that it might be worth while eventually to print the
whole text.

Mr. Williams, in thus cutting down this text, has perhaps, however, pointed it up, and his instincts as a writer
of fiction may have led him, by pulling it together, to
help the large canvas compose. Yet the diarist's own
instinct is uncanny. Starting out with situations or relationships of which she cannot know the outcome, she
takes advantage of the actual turn of events to develop
them and round them out as if she were molding a
novel. One of her most effective performances is her
handling of the episode mentioned above — the affair of
"Buck" Preston and General Hood. The teen-age belles
of the South had sometimes incongruous nicknames. The
elaborate chivalric gallantry of young gentlemanhood
and young ladyhood was likely to have been preceded by
a somewhat rough-and-tumble plantation childhood.
Buck Preston had been given this nickname because
one of her middle names was Buchanan (another beauty
was known as "Boozer"). She was actually a lovely young
girl, who had, Mrs. Chesnut tells us, "a mischievous
gleam in her soft blue eyes; or are they gray, or brown,
or black as night? I have seen them of every color varying with the mood of the moment." (Another Southern
lady who knew the Prestons — Mrs. Burton Harrison, in
her *Recollections Grave and Gay* — describes Buck and
her two sisters as "like goddesses upon a heaven-kissing
hill, tall and stately, with brilliant fresh complexions, altogether the embodiment of vigorous health.") Buck,
Mrs. Chesnut says, was "the very sweetest woman I ever

knew, had a knack of being fallen in love with at sight, and of never being fallen out of love with." But so many of her soldier lovers have been killed in battle or fatally wounded — "Ransom Calhoun, Bradly Warwick, Claude Gibson, the Notts," Mrs. Chesnut enumerates them — that people are beginning to feel that it is bad luck to fall in love with her. Colonel "Sam" Hood from Kentucky (his real name was John Bell Hood), a West Pointer just turned thirty, has already served in Texas and California and has been seriously wounded in fighting the Indians. He has been put in command of the "Texas Brigade" and, as the result of distinguishing himself at Gaines's Mill and Antietam, has been advanced to the rank of major general. But he has lost his right leg at Chickamauga, and he is obliged to retire to Richmond. He had "won his three stars," says Mrs. Chesnut, under the eye of the uncouth and formidable Stonewall Jackson, and it was Jackson who had requested his promotion. "When he came in with his sad face," she writes, " — the face of an old crusader who believed in his cause, his cross and his crown — we were not prepared for that type as a beau ideal of wild Texans. He is tall, thin, shy, with blue eyes and light hair, a tawny beard and a vast amount of it, covering the lower part of his face. He wears an appearance of awkward strength. Someone said that his great reserve of manner he carried only into the society of ladies. Mr. Venable added that he himself had often heard of the light of battle shining in a man's eyes, but he had seen it only once. He carried orders to Hood from General Lee, and found him in the hottest of the fight. The man was transfigured. 'The fierce light of his eyes,' said Mr. Venable, 'I can never forget.' "

Hood, too, falls in love with Buck Preston, and his long and adoring suit becomes a great subject of interest to their friends and a source of suspense for the reader.

Will she or will she not marry him? Her parents are opposed to the match, for reasons which are not made clear, though one gathers that he is somehow not suitable, certainly not "first family." "He does not," says a fellow officer, "compare favorably with General Johnston, who is decidedly a man of culture and literary attainments." And, besides, he has only one leg. There follows a scene in which the girls of the neighborhood, rather gruesomely, complain of their mutilated lovers: "After some whispering among us, Buck cried: 'Don't waste your delicacy! Sally is going to marry a man who has lost an arm, so he is also a maimed soldier, you see; and she is proud of it. The cause glorifies such wounds.' Annie said meekly: 'I fear it will be my fate to marry one who has lost his head!' 'Tudy has her eye on one who lost an eye!' What a glorious assortment of noble martyrs and heroes! The bitterness of this kind of talk is appalling." Yet everybody has to respect Sam Hood, who, with his tough Texas training, contrasts with many other of the Confederate officers by reason of his professional pertinacity — what the officer quoted above speaks of as his "simple-minded directness of purpose"; and this he brings, also, to the courtship of Buck.

One gets, in general, from Mrs. Chesnut an impression that is not reassuring of the leaders of the army of secession. She quotes General Winfield Scott, the hero of the Mexican War, a Virginian who had stood by the Union, on the qualities of Southern soldiers: Scott feels, she says, that "we [the Southerners] have courage, woodcraft, consummate horsemanship, and endurance of pain equal to the Indians, but that we will not submit to discipline. We will not take care of things, or husband our resources. Where we are, there is waste and destruction. If it could all be done by one wild desperate dash, we would do it; but he does not think we can stand the long blank months between the acts, the waiting! We can bear pain without a murmur, but we will not submit to being bored."

Even the high officers share these qualities: they have carried into the army the same disposition that has made the young men fight so many duels. They mostly belong to the same social world, and they know each other too well. They are touchy and jealous of one another. If they don't like the way they are treated, they are apt to get angry and sulk, and to try to get themselves transferred. The rich planter Wade Hampton, who is not a West Pointer, complains to Mrs. Chesnut that one of his brigades has been taken from him and given to Fitzhugh Lee, Robert E. Lee's nephew, and that when he had appealed to Robert E., threatening to resign from the service, the latter had "told him curtly: 'I would not care if you went back to South Carolina with your whole division.' Wade said that his manner made this speech immensely mortifying . . . It seems General Lee has no patience with any personal complaints or grievances. He is all for the cause, and cannot bear officers to come to him with any such matters as Wade Hampton had come about." She does not approve of this pettiness; yet she betrays, in an account of a visit to the Richmond fortifications, how difficult it is for the Southerners of the stratum to which she belongs to realize their responsibilities, as members of a collective enterprise, to take one another seriously: "Mr. Mallory offered me his arm, and we set off to visit and inspect the fortifications of this, our 'Gibraltar of the Jeems,' of whose deeds they are so proud. It holds its own against all comers. Everywhere we went, the troops presented arms, and I was fool enough to ask Mr. Mallory why they did that. With a suppressed titter he replied: 'I dare say because I am at the head of the Navy Department.'"

General Hood's adoration of Buck Preston and the uncertainty of her final acceptance of him become, in this situation, a kind of symbol for the general failure of the South; and it is significant that Mrs. Burton Harrison, the wife of Jefferson Davis's secretary and a friend of Mrs. Chesnut's, should also treat the wooing of Buck Preston, a "fair and regal being," as a subject of major interest. Fascinated, like these ladies, we follow Mrs. Chesnut's account of Buck's vacillations between hot and cold. "Buck saw me sending a rice pudding to the wounded man — it seems he cares for no other dainty — whereupon she said, in her sweetest, mildest, sleepiest way: 'I never cared particularly about him, but now that he has chosen to go with those people [we are not told who they were], I would not marry him if he had a thousand legs, instead of having just lost one.'" Yet somehow she becomes engaged to him: "Such a beamingly, beautiful, crimson face as she turned to me, her clear blue eyes looking straight in mine. 'Do you believe I like him now?' 'No.' She did not notice my answer." But Buck long continues to sustain her role: "Mrs. Preston was offended by the story of Buck's performance at the Iveses'. General Breckenridge told her 'it was the most beautifully unconscious act I ever saw.' The General was leaning against the wall, Buck standing guard by him. The crowd surged that way, and she held out her arm to protect him from the rush. After they had all passed, she handed him his crutches, and they, too, moved slowly away. Mrs. Davis said: 'Any woman in Richmond would have done the same joyfully, but few could do it so gracefully.' Buck is made so conspicuous by her beauty, whatever she does cannot fail to attract attention." Their story runs all through the frivolities — the dinners and the suppers and the amateur theatricals — with which, at once desperate as their situation worsened and unwilling to face its dangers, they continue to amuse themselves. As the result of an evening party cut short by the cook's getting news that her son has just been killed at the front — "Instead of a tray of good things, came back that news to the Martins!" — Mrs. Chesnut, like Kate Stone, is reminded of the French Revolution and says that they now understand the French prisoners who continued to flirt and dance while they were waiting for the tumbril to come for them.

But the devotion of the crippled Hood still persists through all the intrigue and quarrelling which, in the final phases of the war, demoralize the Confederate government. In this government, the fatal incapacity of the Southerners for agreeing or working together becomes even more apparent than in the conduct of the war itself. The passion for independence which with masters of a subject race so often takes the form of wrongheadedness, of self-assertion for its own sake, of tantrums, this self-will that has made an issue, and that is now making a cult, of states' rights, is now provoking certain elements to rebel against the Confederacy itself. President Davis is constantly opposed and denounced in a way that Mrs. Chesnut thinks scandalous, and the various departments of the government have now become quite insubordinate. The great irony is that the recalcitrance of the Southerners against any sort of central control, which has led them to secede from the Union, is also — since they refuse to submit to the kind of governmental coercion that will enable the North to win — obstructing their success with the war. President Davis is doing his best to put through the same war measures as Lincoln — conscription, the suspension of habeas corpus, and even, in the final year, the emancipation of the slaves — but all these are either burked or evaded. The big planters will not allow the government to inter-

fere in any way with their Negroes, even to send them,
as James Chesnut advocates, to work on the fortifications.
When the crisis becomes alarming, when the need for
taking a stronger line is a matter of life or death, the
cry goes up at once that Jefferson Davis wants to make
himself a dictator, a despot like Abraham Lincoln.

We come to feel that Hood's patient unwavering purpose to induce Buck Preston to marry him is doomed as the
Confederacy is. It is like one of those relationships in
Chekhov that we know can never come to anything and
that, with Chekhov — and we cannot be sure that Mrs.
Chesnut is not just as much aware of what her story
implies — are meant to imply the impotence and the impending ruin of Russian society. General Hood is sent
back to the Army at the beginning of 1864, and he is
obliged to retreat, under Johnston, before Sherman, who
is marching on Atlanta. When the insecure Jefferson
Davis, against the advice of Hood, decides to remove
Johnston and put Hood in his place, the latter is left
to face Sherman alone. We have already seen him, helpless but proud, exchanging polemics with his terrible
opponent over the latter's deportation of the people of
Atlanta. The supplies that are needed do not arrive, and
the morale of the army is lost. After defeat in a couple
of battles, the General is obliged to give up the campaign, and he resigns his command in January, 1865.
"The Hood melodrama is over," Mrs. Chesnut ambiguously writes in March, "though the curtain has not fallen
on the last scene. Hood stock going down. When that
style of enthusiasm is on the wane, the rapidity of its
extinction is marvellous, like the snuffing out of a candle;
one moment here, then gone forever."

In May, after Appomattox, Buck Preston makes a
rather queer attempt to explain things to Mrs. Chesnut —
"The music and the moonlight, and that restful feeling

of her head on my knee, set her tongue in motion" — though she cautions the older lady that if she should write about the affair in her diary, she must say, "This is translated from Balzac." It had begun with "those beautiful, beautiful silk stockings." Buck had exposed them to view by warming her feet at the fender. Her admirer had always raved about his mistress's foot and ankle (*mistress* in the gallant old sense), but up to now he had treated her with reverence, had never gone further than to kiss her hand. Now he seized her and kissed her throat. She was shocked, and poor Hood had been humble. "He said it was so soft and white, that throat of mine," and put "a strong arm" around her waist so tight that she could not leave the room. "He said that, after all, I had promised to marry him, and that that made all the difference." But the girl could not see it that way, and now she makes a point of wearing boots and never warming her feet, and she wears, also, "a stiff handkerchief close up around my throat." "You see," she says to Mrs. Chesnut, "I never meant to be so outrageously treated again . . . Yet now, would you believe it, a sickening, almost an insane longing comes over me just to see him once more, and I know I never will. He is gone forever. If he had been persistent, if he had not given way under Mamma's violent refusal to listen to us, if he had asked *me!* When you refused to let anybody be married in your house, well, I would have gone down on the sidewalk, I would have married him on the pavement, if the parson could be found to do it. I was ready to leave all the world for him, to tie my clothes in a bundle and, like a soldier's wife, trudge after him to the ends of the earth."

But now it is too late. When we get our last glimpse of Buck Preston, she is travelling in Europe with her married sister; they are going to spend the winter in Paris.

Another of Mrs. Chesnut's main subjects is the plantation of her husband's parents at Camden, South Carolina, where she is sometimes obliged to stay and where she suffers acutely from boredom. She suffers also from the irking constraint imposed upon her by her ninety-year-old father-in-law, an opinionated austere old man who, even when deaf and blind, still keeps such a strong hand on his immense domain that he never has trouble with his slaves. This household of the old-world Chesnuts reminds one of the Bolkónskys of *War and Peace* (comparisons with Russia seem inevitable when one is writing about the old South). The father, presiding at dinner, as "absolute a tyrant as the Tsar of Russia," with his constantly repeated axioms and his authoritarian tone, is a less piquant Bolkónsky *père*. James, Jr., is an equally distinguished and equally conscientious, if not equally dashing, André; Miss Chesnut, his sister, may figure as a cool-headed and penurious, a less sympathetic Princess Marie. But there is also a dowager Mrs. Chesnut, originally from Philadelphia, who was married in 1796 and falls easily into telling people about "stiff stern old Martha Washington" and describing the Washingtons' drawing room. The younger Mrs. Chesnut likes her mother-in-law, who has evidently more human warmth than the other members of the family and who, though never buying books herself, borrows them from other people and reads them in enormous quantities; but, in general, the younger woman finds Mulberry, the Chesnut estate, both oppressive and melancholy. "My sleeping apartment is large and airy, with windows opening on the lawn east and south. In those deep window seats, idly looking out, I spend much time. A part of the yard which was once a deer park has the appearance of the primeval forest; the forest trees have been unmolested and are now of immense size. In the spring, the air is laden with perfumes, violets, jasmine, crab apple blossoms, roses. Araby the blest never was sweeter in perfume. And yet there hangs here as on every Southern landscape the saddest pall. There are browsing on the lawn, where Kentucky bluegrass flourishes, Devon cows and sheep, horses, mares and colts. It helps to enliven it. Carriages are coming up to the door and driving away incessantly."

The Chesnut Negroes are faithful; they have been well trained and well treated. Yet everyone is rather uneasy. Mrs. Chesnut the younger herself has, like Kate Stone, a horror of slavery. When she sees a mulatto girl sold at auction in March, 1861, "My very soul sickened," she writes, and a few days later, when, with a visiting Englishwoman, she is again passing the auction block, "If you can stand that," she says to her companion, "no other Southern thing need choke you." And "I wonder," she is soon reflecting, "if it be a sin to think slavery a curse to any land. Men and women are punished when their masters and mistresses are brutes, not when they do wrong. Under slavery, we live surrounded by prostitutes, yet an abandoned woman [a white one, she means] is sent out of a decent house. Who thinks any worse of a Negro or mulatto woman for being a thing we can't name? God forgive us, but ours is a monstrous system, a wrong and an iniquity! Like the patriarchs of old, our men live all in one house with their wives and their concubines; and the mulattoes one sees in every family partly resemble the white children. Any lady is ready to tell you who is the father of all the mulatto children in everybody's household but her own."

This problem of the mixture of white and black blood,

so systematically suppressed by Southern writers — "the ostrich game," Mrs. Chesnut calls this — she treats with remarkable frankness and exclaims at the hypocrisy of the Chesnuts in locking up the novels of Eugène Sue, and even a Gothic romance by the Carolinian Washington Allston, when the colored girls of the household are more or less openly promiscuous. "I hate slavery," she writes at the beginning of the war. "You say there are no more fallen women on a plantation than in London, in proportion to numbers; but what do you say to this? A magnate who runs a hideous black harem with its consequences under the same roof with his lovely white wife, and his beautiful and accomplished daughters? He holds his head as high and poses as the model of all human virtues to these poor women whom God and the laws have given him. From the height of his awful majesty, he scolds and thunders at them as if he never did wrong in his life. Fancy such a man finding his daughter reading *Don Juan*. 'You with that immoral book!' And he orders her out of his sight. You see, Mrs. Stowe did not hit the sorest spot. She makes Legree a bachelor."

Encountering such passages, we wonder whether the prudery of Buck Preston with her fiancé may not be something more than a curious local development of the nineteenth-century proprieties, something more than a romantic convention derived from the age of chivalry. That Buck Preston was not unusual in her reluctance to let men see her feet is shown by another anecdote, this time about James Chesnut's young nephew: "Today he was taking me to see Minnie Hayne's foot. He said it was the smallest, the most perfect thing in America! Now, I will go anywhere to see anything which can move the cool Captain to the smallest ripple of enthusiasm. He says Julia Rutledge knew his weakness, and would not show him her foot. His Uncle James had told him of its arched instep and symmetrical beauty. So he followed her trail like a wild Indian, and when she stepped in the mud, he took a paper pattern of her track, or a plaster cast; something that amazed Miss Rutledge at his sagacity." And Mrs. Chesnut herself, though she is not disinclined to flirt as the younger ladies do and occasionally provokes jealous scenes on the part of Mr. Chesnut, is offended by risqué stories and horrified by current French novels (which, nevertheless, she continues to read); will not allow legs to be mentioned; and cannot digest the news, brought back by a traveller from Europe, that the sternly moralistic George Eliot has been living in sin with George Henry Lewes.

One is forced to the conclusion that the pedestalled purity which the Southerners assigned to their ladies, the shrinking of these ladies themselves from any suggestion of freedom, were partly a "polarization" produced by the uninhibited ease with which their men could go to bed with the black girls. There is an atmosphere of tittering sex all through Mrs. Chesnut's chronicle, yet behind it is a pride that is based on fear and that sometimes results in coldness. Mrs. Chesnut, who was married at seventeen, has obviously no passionate interest in her husband, yet though Chesnut has, we gather, amused himself with occasional love affairs — not, so far as one is told, with blacks but with white women of inferior social status — she has never dared to take a lover. To allow oneself to weaken in this direction would be to associate oneself with the despised and dreaded slave girls who were bearing their masters' half-breeds, to surrender one's white prestige. The gaiety and ease of these ladies must have always masked a fundamental, a never-relaxing tension.

Mrs. Chesnut, in this intimate record, drops the mask

and expresses herself with more candor than was usual
for Southern ladies, even, as one imagines, in the working of their own minds. Her attitude toward Harriet
Beecher Stowe is strikingly different, for example, from
that of most Southerners of Mrs. Chesnut's own day or,
indeed, of any day. Grace King, the New Orleans historian and novelist, born in 1852, writes in her autobiography of the "hideous, black, dragonlike book that
hovered on the horizon of every Southern child" but
which in her own family was never allowed to be mentioned. Mrs. Chesnut takes this horror more coolly and
shows a strong interest in *Uncle Tom's Cabin*. In March
of 1862 she rereads it, and at any instance of cruelty to
slaves she is likely to mention that Mrs. Stowe would be
delighted to hear of it. "I met our lovely relative," she
writes in May, 1864, "the woman who might have sat
for Eva's mother in *Uncle Tom's Cabin*. Beautifully
dressed, graceful, languid, making eyes at all comers, she
was softly and in dulcet accents regretting the necessity
of sending out a sable Topsy to her sabler parent, to be
switched for some misdemeanor. I declined to hear her
regrets as I fled in haste." She says of the grandfather
of one of her friends that he used to "put Negroes in
hogsheads, with nails driven in all round, and roll the
poor things downhill."

Her own point of view is vigorously expressed in
November, 1861, in an outburst against Mrs. Stowe.
Mrs. Stowe, she declares, and Greeley and Thoreau and
Emerson and Sumner "live in nice New England homes,
clean, sweet-smelling, shut up in libraries, writing books
which ease their hearts of their bitterness against us.
What self-denial they do practice is to tell John Brown
to come down here and cut our throats in Christ's name.
Now consider what I have seen of my mother's life, my
grandmother's, my mother-in-law's. These people were

educated at Northern schools, they read the same books as their Northern contemporaries, the same daily papers, the same Bible. They have the same ideas of right and wrong," while they of the South are doomed to "live in Negro villages," the inhabitants of which "walk through their houses whenever they see fit, dirty, slatternly, idle, ill-smelling by nature. These women I love have less chance to live their own lives in peace than if they were African missionaries. They have a swarm of blacks about them like children under their care, not as Mrs. Stowe's fancy painted them, and they hate slavery worse than Mrs. Stowe does. . . . The Mrs. Stowes have the plaudits of crowned heads; we take our chances, doing our duty as best we may among the woolly heads. My husband supported his plantation by his law practice. Now it is running him in debt. Our people have never earned their own bread. Take this estate, what does it do, actually? It all goes back in some shape to what are called slaves here, called operatives or tenants or peasantry elsewhere. I doubt if ten thousand in money ever comes to this old gentleman's hands. When Mrs. Chesnut married South, her husband was as wealthy as her brothers-in-law. How is it now? Their money has accumulated for their children. This old man's goes to support a horde of idle dirty Africans, while he is abused as a cruel slave-owner."

In this she is unfair to the New Englanders: she forgets that Elijah Lovejoy has been murdered for his Abolitionist agitation, that Garrison has been dragged through the streets of Boston and Whittier stoned by a mob in New Hampshire, and that Sumner has had his head broken and been incapacitated for two years by a furious South Carolinian; and she of course had not the least idea of the years of anxiety and hardship which, in the case of Harriet Beecher Stowe, had produced her explosive book. Yet there is plenty of evidence in Mrs. Chesnut's diary that slavery had become to the Southerners a handicap and a burden. At one point she makes the assertion that "not one third of our volunteer army are slave-owners" and that "not one third of that third fail to dislike slavery as much as Mrs. Stowe or Horace Greeley."

Mrs. Chesnut notes again and again the apparent impassivity of the Negroes in relation to what is going on. "We have no reason to suppose a Negro knows there is a war," she is still able to write in November, 1861. "I do not speak of the war to them; on that subject, they do not believe a word you say. A genuine slave-owner, born and bred, will not be afraid of Negroes. Here we are mild as the moonbeams, and as serene; nothing but Negroes around us, white men all gone to the army." Yet one of their neighbors, a Cousin Betsey, has been murdered only a few weeks before. This old lady, whose domestic servants are said to have been "pampered" and "insubordinate," has been smothered in her bed by two of them after her son has promised them a thrashing. The elder Mrs. Chesnut, a Northerner, had been frightened in her youth by the stories of the Haiti rebellion, and, as a result, now treats every Negro "as if they were a black Prince Albert or Queen Victoria." She makes her daughter-in-law uneasy by incessantly dwelling, as the younger woman says, "upon the transcendent virtues of her colored household, in full hearing of the innumerable Negro women who literally swarm over this house," then by suddenly saying to the family at dinner, "'I warn you, don't touch that soup! It is bitter. There is something wrong about it!' The men who waited at table looked on without a change of face." But the staff of the Chesnut household finally begins to crack in an unexpected place. James Chesnut is very much dependent on his Negro valet Lawrence, who is always at his side, always, says Mrs. Chesnut, with "the same bronze mask," who darns socks and has made Mrs. Chesnut a sacque, who is miraculous in his resourcefulness at producing, despite wartime shortages, whatever is wanted in the way of food — even to that special rarity, ice for mint juleps and sherry cobblers. But in February, 1864, while the Chesnuts are living in Richmond, Lawrence turns up at breakfast drunk. When he is ordered to move a chair, he raises it over his head and smashes the chandelier. His master, whose self-control is always perfect, turns to his wife and says, "Mary, do tell Lawrence to go home. I am too angry to speak to him!" But Lawrence "will soon be back," Mrs. Chesnut confides to her diary, "and when he comes he will say: 'Shoo! I knew Mars' Jeems could not do without me!' And indeed he cannot."

In the meantime Colonel Higginson and his fellow Yankees were exploring the abandoned plantations of the South Carolinian Sea Islands. We hear something from Mrs. Chesnut of the families to which these had belonged. Of the Middletons, on whose place Charlotte Forten had admired the magnolia tree and from whose house she had taken the bathtub, Mrs. Chesnut writes as follows: "Poor Mrs. Middleton has paralysis. Has she not had trouble enough? . . . Their plantation and house at Edisto destroyed [it had actually been plundered but not destroyed], their house in Charleston burned, her children scattered, starvation in Lincolnton, and all as nothing to the one dreadful blow — her only son killed in Virginia. Their lives are washed away in a tide of blood. There is nothing to show they were ever on earth." And of another expropriated family from the coastland taken over by the Northerners: "Captain Barnwell came to see us," she writes. "We had a dinner for them at Mulberry. Stephen Elliott was there. He gave us an account of his father's plantation at Beaufort, from which he has just returned: 'Our Negroes are living in great comfort. They were delighted to see me, and treated me with overflowing affection. They waited on me as before, gave me beautiful breakfasts and splendid dinners; but they firmly and respectfully informed me: "We own this land now. Put it out of your head that it will ever be yours again."'"

The Negroes on the Chesnut plantation, with the exception of one boy who goes off with the Yankees, all, however, remain loyal to the family when Sherman's army comes through Camden. This has not always been the case with the slaves of their neighbors, and an annoying problem presents itself when the black women run away and drop off their children beside the road. It is with somewhat mixed feelings that their former owners greet the efforts of a well-meaning person who has collected these abandoned babies and brought them back in a cart. The soldiers of the Northern army have bayoneted the runaway women if they proved to be an encumbrance; eighteen corpses are found. And the Chesnuts have been fortunate, also, in that their house has not been burned down. Neither James nor his wife was then at home. He had sent her to North Carolina to be out of the line of Sherman's march, and they had been fully prepared to lose everything. But when at last they make their way back to Camden, through a countryside with no sign of habitation except the "tall, blackened chimneys," they find that the house is still standing, though the horses have all been driven off and the road to Charleston is strewn with their books and letters and papers. One side of the house has been badly damaged: every window broken, every bell torn down, every door smashed in, and every piece of furniture demolished.

But this wreckage had been arrested when Sherman, in one of his relentings, decided that it had gone far enough. "It was a sin," he had told his soldiers, "to destroy a fine old house like this, whose owner was over ninety years old." Miss Chesnut has behaved splendidly. When a Yankee officer entered and sat down at the fire to warm himself, she said to him "politely," " 'Rebels have no rights. But I suppose you have come to rob us. Please do so and go. Your presence agitates my blind old father.' The man had jumped up in a rage: 'What do you take me for? A thief?' " Miss Chesnut is proud of the fact that they have lost, aside from the horses, the smashed furniture and the scattered books, only two gold-headed canes and two bottles of champagne.

The old man survived everything with dignity. His wife, also over ninety, had died before the final disaster. His daughter-in-law remembers having seen him in the mornings sauntering down the wide corridor from his own to his wife's bedroom, with a large hairbrush in his hand. He would take his stand on the rug before the fire in her room and, as he brushed his few remaining white locks, would roar out to her his morning compliments so loudly that it shook the panes in the windows of the room above. One morning, after her mother-in-law's death, Mary Chesnut, passing the door of Mrs. Chesnut's room, saw her father-in-law kneeling and sobbing beside the empty bed. When we hear of him last, he is ninety-three, but "apparently as strong as ever and certainly as resolute of will." His Negro servant Scipio has never deserted old Chesnut: "six feet two, a black Hercules and as gentle as a dove in all his dealings with the blind old master, who boldly strides forward, striking with his stick to feel where he is going." "Partly patriarch, partly *grand seigneur*," his daughter-in-law sums him up, "this old man is of a species that we will see no more; the last of the lordly planters who ruled this Southern world. His manners are unequalled still, but underneath this smooth exterior lies the grip of a tyrant whose will has never been crossed."

On the eve of Lee's surrender, when Mary Chesnut has taken refuge in North Carolina, her husband comes to see her and tells her that many of their own fellow-Southerners are rejoicing over the ruin of the planter class. "They will have no Negroes now to lord it over!" he says he has heard one of them say. "They can swell and peacock about and tyrannize now over only a small parcel of women and children, those only who are their very own family."

IX

SOUTHERN SOLDIERS: RICHARD TAYLOR, JOHN S.

MOSBY, ROBERT E. LEE

NEAR THE END of Mrs. Chesnut's chronicle we find the following entry (May 10, 1865): "Said Henrietta: 'That old fool Dick Taylor will not disband and let his nasty Confederacy smash and be done with it.' I rose. 'Excuse me. I cannot sit at table with anybody abusing my country.' So I went out on the piazza, but from the windows came loud screams of vituperation and insult. 'Jeff Davis's stupidity, Joe Johnston's magnanimity, Bragg's insanity.' So I fled. Next day she flew at me again, and raved until I was led out in hysterics, and then I was very ill. They thought I was dying, and I wish I had died."

This Dick Taylor was General Richard Taylor, the son of Zachary Taylor, one of the heroes of the Mexican War, who had been elected President in 1848 but had died in his second year of office. Richard Taylor wrote a volume of memoirs called *Destruction and Reconstruction: Personal Experiences of the Late War*, first published in 1879, which is perhaps the masculine document that, from the point of view of realistic intelligence, is most nearly comparable to Mary Chesnut's diary.

Richard Taylor was a handsome, high-mettled young

man — thirty-five at the beginning of the war — who had had, for a Southerner of the period, an exceptionally good education: he had studied at Edinburgh and Paris and had been graduated from Yale. He had never before been a soldier, and had had only a glimpse of the Mexican War, when he had visited his father's camp. His first occupation after college had been managing his father's Mississippi plantation; later, after Zachary's death, he bought a larger one in Louisiana. He collected a considerable library and was famous for the success of his race horses and the brilliance of his conversation. He had been more or less active in politics and, though not a strong defender of the Southern system, had voted for secession in the senate of his state. He was bitter about the carpetbaggers, after the war, and excoriated the Grant regime, but declared that "the extinction of slavery was expected by all and regretted by none." As a soldier, he was full of audacity, sharp-tongued and rather arrogant with his equals, with his men rather undemocratic. He was evidently feared by the latter, and on one occasion had several shot in order to correct their slack discipline, but he trained them to a degree of efficiency that seems to have been rare among the Confederate forces. He criticizes what he regards as "the vicious system of election of officers [by the ranks]," which, he says, "struck at the very root of that stern discipline without which raw men cannot be converted into soldiers," and he later makes a similar point when he says that the difficulty of this — "converting raw men into soldiers" — is greatly increased when the men are mounted: "Living on horseback, fearless and dashing, the men of the South afforded the best possible material for cavalry. They had every quality but discipline, and resembled Prince Charming, whose manifold gifts, bestowed by her sisters, were rendered useless by the malignant fairy."

Better educated than most of his fellow officers and with more experience of the world, he sees everything in a larger context. His book is full of allusions to "the witty Dean," "honest Dick Steele," Rabelais's *mauvais quart d'heure* and Walpole's correspondence with Mme. du Deffand, as well as comparisons of recent events with French, English and German military history, that show a wide range of reading. Like Mrs. Chesnut, not approving of slavery and not much believing in victory, he is not intellectually committed to the struggle in which his pride — as a vindicator of Southern honor — has spurred him to take so active a part, and the effect of this is rather peculiar. Richard Taylor is conscious, and a little vain, of being a *rara avis*; he is a connoisseur of soldiers and battles; he plays his fine role with a shade of disdain, even, perhaps, with a shade of enjoyment — vain, also, and almost perverse — of its gratuitousness and ultimate futility.

When Dick Taylor was early promoted to the rank of brigadier general, he tried at first to decline this honor on the ground that there were several colonels who deserved it through right of seniority; but, persuaded to accept it by his fellow officers, he took part with this rank under Stonewall Jackson in the Shenandoah Valley campaign of the spring of 1862. Jackson came to think highly of Taylor and Taylor to admire Jackson — though they could hardly have been, temperamentally, more unlike and more uncongenial; and this mixture of esteem with unlikeness makes Dick Taylor's portrait of Jackson, as it is gradually filled in, stroke by stroke, a unique and a piquant one. The only thing the two men had in common was that both of them inspired in their troops a respect that was tinged with fear. But Jackson was more alien to his people than his dashing young brigadier general; he had nothing of the spirit of chivalry or of playing the game for the game's sake. "He impressed me always," said Grant of him, "as a man of the Cromwell stamp, a Puritan — much more of the New Englander than the Virginian. If any man believed in the rebellion, he did."

The son of a bankrupt lawyer from Virginia beyond the Alleghenies, Jackson had been left an orphan at three; he had had to work hard for an education and had become at fourteen a devout attendant at the Presbyterian church. He was close to those types of the North, those single-track embodiments of will, whom these gentlemanly Southerners dreaded: the impassive indefatigable Grant, the Jehovah-led avenger John Brown. Thomas Jackson (not yet called "Stonewall") seems indeed to have had some fellow feeling with Brown when he presided as major of militia at Brown's hanging at Charlestown. He had prayed for the mad Brown's soul the night before the execution, and when it was over had written his wife that the fanatic "had behaved with unflinching firmness . . . I was much impressed with the thought that before me stood a man in the full vigor of health, who must in a few moments enter eternity. I sent up the petition that he might be saved. Awful was the thought that he might in a few minutes receive the sentence, 'Depart, ye wicked, into everlasting fire!' I hope that he was prepared to die, but I am doubtful. He refused to have a minister with him." Thomas Jackson himself was sometimes thought a little mad.

Mrs. Chesnut had listened with interest to a characterization of Jackson by one of his generals: "Jackson's men had gone half a day's march before Pete Longstreet waked and breakfasted. . . . I think there is a popular delusion about the amount of praying Jackson did. He certainly preferred a fight on Sunday to a sermon. Failing to manage a fight, he loved next best a long Presbyterian sermon, Calvinistic to the core. He had no sympathy with human infirmity. He was a one-idea man . . . He classed all who were weak and weary, who fainted by the wayside, as men wanting in patriotism. If a man's face was white as cotton and his pulse so low that you could not feel it, he merely looked upon him impatiently as an inefficient soldier, and rode off out of patience. He was the true type of all great soldiers. He did not value human life where he had an object to accomplish. He could order men to their death as a matter of course. Napoleon's French conscription could not have kept him supplied with men, he used up his command so rapidly. Hence, while he was alive there was more pride than truth in the talk of his soldiers' love for him. They feared him, and obeyed him to the death; faith they had in him. . . . But I doubt if he had their love . . . Be ye sure, it was bitter hard work to keep up with Stonewall Jackson, as all know who ever served with him. He gave orders rapidly and distinctly, and rode away without allowing answer or remonstrance. When you failed, you were apt to be put under arrest. When you succeeded, he only said 'good.'" His certainty that his army was the instrument of God was as strong as that of any Northerner. "General Lee is very kind," he said when his commanding general had congratulated him on a victory, "but he should give the praise to God"; and, concluding that one of his operations had been blocked by divine interference, on account of its having been attempted on Sunday, he forbade any use, for a second attempt, of powder procured on the Sabbath. Jackson accepted slavery, says his sister-in-law in a memoir, "as it existed in the Southern States, not as a thing desirable in itself, but as allowed by Providence for ends which it was not his business to determine." Distressed by the ignorance of the Negroes, he had established, "by much personal effort and under some obloquy, a Sunday school for them in Lexington, which he kept up with assiduous diligence till the breaking out of the war."

But Richard Taylor, incapable of hero worship, was not at all frightened of Jackson and observed him with a critical eye. "An ungraceful horseman," he writes, "mounted on a sorry chestnut with a shambling gait, his huge feet with out-turned toes thrust into his stirrups, and such parts of his countenance as the low visor of his stocking cap failed to conceal wearing a wooden look, our new commander was not prepossessing." Jackson was taciturn, implacable, unable to joke; he lived on hardtack and water and was always sucking a lemon — this seems to have been his only indulgence. He was as obstinate a Spartan as any New Englander. Mrs. Chesnut reports him as having said, "in his quaint way: 'I like strong drink, so I never touch it.'" On one occasion, Taylor tells us, when some of his Creole soldiers were waltzing to the music of their band, General Jackson remarked "after a contemplative suck at a lemon, 'Thoughtless fellows for serious work!'" and once, when Taylor swore at his troops, "he placed his hand on my shoulder" and "said in a gentle voice, 'I am afraid you are a wicked fellow.'" The only moment, says Taylor, when Jackson appeared to brighten was at a battle in which his own troops were being shot up by the enemy at a time when they "were advancing steadily, with banners flying and arms gleaming in the sun. . . . Jackson was on the road, a little in advance of his line, where the fire was hottest, with reins on his horse's neck, seemingly in prayer. Attracted by my approach, he said, in his usual voice, 'Delightful excitement.' I replied that it was pleasant to learn he was enjoying himself, but thought he might

have an indigestion of such fun if the six-gun battery
was not silenced." Later on, Taylor made an attempt
to intervene with his formidable chief in behalf of a
General Winder, who had asked leave to go to Richmond, had been refused by Jackson and in pique had resigned from the service. "Holding Winder in high esteem, I hoped to save him to the army, and went to
Jackson, to whose magnanimity I appealed, and to
arouse this dwelt on the rich harvest of glory he had
reaped in his brilliant campaign. Observing him closely,
I caught a glimpse of the man's inner nature. It was but
a glimpse. The curtain closed, and he was absorbed in
prayer. Yet in that moment I saw an ambition boundless
as Cromwell's, and as merciless. . . . I have written
that he was ambitious; and his ambition was vast, all-
absorbing. . . . He loathed it, perhaps feared it; but he
could not escape it. . . . He fought it with prayer, constant and earnest — Apolyon and Christian in ceaseless
combat."

This last observation of Taylor's and his tone in regard
to this trait of his chief's brings out an important difference. The Southerners, as a rule, did not entertain
this kind of ambition. Though touchy and competitive
among themselves, they were defending an ancient ideal,
a traditional kind of society, in which each wanted merely
to maintain his place; the roles they aimed to play were
knightly. Even Lee, the idol of his people, when his fortune had been lost in the war, made no effort to enrich
himself or to exercise political influence, but accepted,
with the utmost modesty, the Presidency of Washington
College, once a "classical school" of distinction, but by
that time left a ruin by the Federal troops, with a student
body of forty and a faculty of four. Elsewhere than in the
South the men who had got to be public figures were
looking forward to a dynamic future. The Union was

strong and could now move ahead, and the Northerners plunged after money and power.

Stonewall Jackson was killed by accident in May, 1863, at the battle of Chancellorsville, in which he had defeated the Unionists; he was shot by his own men, who had mistaken him, in the moonlight, for a Yankee. Mrs. Chesnut went to see him lying in state in the Confederate Capitol in Richmond — "Shall I ever forget," she asks, "the pain and fear of it all?"; and at the time that Grant is carrying all before him, she continually utters such cries as "Stonewall, if he could only come back to us here!"; "One year more of Stonewall would have saved us!"; "If we had Stonewall or Albert Sidney Johnson where Joe Johnston and Polk are, I would not give a fig for Sherman's chances"; "Chickamauga is the only battle we gained since Stonewall was shot by Malone's brigade." Richard Taylor, writing of Jackson after the war, exhibits a characteristic detachment: "Fortunate in his death, he fell at the summit of his glory, before the sun of the Confederacy had set, ere defeat and suffering and selfishness could turn their fangs upon him." In a less romantic and rhetorical vein, Grant doubted whether Jackson would have been equally successful in the later phase of the war. Such "sudden daring raids" as his "might do against raw troops and inexperienced commanders, such as we had at the beginning of the war, but not against drilled troops and a commander like Sheridan."

That other effective and untypical Southern general, Nathan Bedford Forrest of Tennessee, who "got there fustest with the mostest," is not mentioned by Mrs. Chesnut. He was liked and respected by Taylor, who saw him often in the final weeks of the war. Taylor notes that Forrest "read with difficulty" and that his father had been "a poor trader in Negroes and mules."

With Taylor and with Mrs. Chesnut, we are always
in the world of the Confederate gentry, and the weakness
of its situation is brought out for us all the more vividly
by the brilliance of the minds that describe it.

———

No other figure of the Civil War became during his
lifetime such a storybook legend as Colonel John Single-
ton Mosby, the audacious and resourceful Confederate
soldier who, operating in sight of the Capitol dome with
a handful of undisciplined guerrillas, performed prodigies
in breaking up Union communications and capturing or
putting to flight detachments of Union troops that were
often far larger than his own. His legend has even survived to make him the hero of a television series — *The
Gray Ghost* — for which Mosby himself has supplied
much of the material by writing two books about his own
career. These are *Mosby's War Reminiscences and
Stuart's Cavalry Campaigns* and *The Memoirs of Colonel
John S. Mosby*. The first of them is based on a series of
lectures, and here Mosby is a story-teller amusing his
audience. The *Reminiscences* reads almost like the imaginary adventures of some character of the Conan Doyle
era — Raffles or Brigadier Gerard. But, aside from a careful study of "Jeb" Stuart's activities at Gettysburg, it
does not contain much more than these exploits. The
Colonel, however, in his later years, set out to write a
genuine autobiography which would include some account of his early life, his recollections of Lee and
Grant, and presumably some record of his fifty-one years
of civilian life after the war. He did not live to finish
this, but what he left of it was edited and published after
his death by his brother-in-law, Charles W. Russell.

It is fascinating, in these memoirs, to meet face to
face the actual human being who created in the minds

of his enemies the impression of a will-o'-the-wisp, of a lurking and mocking spirit, an unseizable force of frustration that might turn up at any moment in any place and interfere with any operation.

An unexpected feature of Mosby, as we see him at close range in his writings, is an appetite for literature and a range of historical reading that seem even to surpass Dick Taylor's. The imaginative liveliness of his actual adventures, his train-stoppings, his commissary-robbings, his bluffings and masqueradings, his unexpected poppings-up and his ominous playings of possum, is embellished by constant quotations from the poets — each chapter of the *Reminiscences* has an epigraph, as in one of Scott's or Cooper's novels — and dignified by constant reference to ancient, medieval and modern wars. The ideal of education that Jefferson had hoped to encourage in founding the University of Virginia was sometimes to realize itself in unpredictable ways through temperaments quite alien to Jefferson's. Edgar Allan Poe had been such a case, and Mosby was another. Coming to the university from a farm outside Charlottesville, he had a brilliant academic career — particularly excelling in Latin and Greek — up to the moment when he got into trouble for shooting a fellow student who imagined that Mosby had insulted him and came to his lodgings to attack him. It was a typically absurd Southern quarrel. Mosby's enemy, who was bigger and stronger than he, had already slashed one boy with a knife and had almost killed another with a rock. He had threatened to eat Mosby "blood raw," and Mosby received him with a pistol. He shot at the aggressor and wounded him, and was sentenced to a fine and a year in jail; but the attorney who had sent him there found him one day reading Milton in his cell and, when he learned that the young man wanted to study law, he supplied him with legal works. Public sentiment was much in his favor, and he was released before he had served his full term. The young Mosby was rather frail and was thought to be disposed to "consumption."

He continued to study law, and eventually set up in practice in the small town of Bristol, Virginia. He married the daughter of a prominent lawyer. John Mosby was in his late twenties when the War between the States broke out. He had been almost alone in his community in resolutely opposing secession. But when Lincoln, after the fall of Fort Sumter, had called for troops to suppress the rebellion and Virginia had voted to secede, "Nobody cared," Mosby writes in the *Memoirs*, "whether it was a constitutional right they were exercising, or an act of revolution. At such times reason is silent and passion prevails." "I went along with the flood like everybody else," he says in the *Reminiscences*. "A few individuals here and there attempted to breast the storm of passion, and appeared like Virgil's shipwrecked mariners, '*Rari nantes in gurgite vasto.*' Their fate did not encourage others to follow their example, and all that they did was to serve 'like ocean wrecks to illuminate the storm.'"

I do not know the source of this last quotation, but in the first twenty-one pages of the *Reminiscences* one notes quotations from or references to Homer, Virgil, Gibbon, Sterne, Byron, Moore, Macaulay and Longfellow. This bold and tough man of action, who lived constantly in movement, without even a camp, had always the classics about him. One finds, for example, "We dashed after them [the Federal soldiers]. I was riding a splendid horse — a noble bay — Job's warhorse was a mustang compared to him — who had now got his mettle up and carried me at headlong speed right among them. I had no more control over him than Mazeppa had over the

Ukraine steed to which he was bound." "Everywhere above the storm of battle could be heard the voices and seen the forms of the Dioscuri — 'Major' Hibbs and Dick Moran — cheering on the men as they rode headlong in the fight. . . . Sam, to give more vigor to his blows, was standing straight up in his stirrups, dealing them right and left with all the theological fervor of Burly of Balfour. I doubt whether he prayed that day for the souls of those he sent over the Stygian river. I made him a captain for it." "The deliberations of the [United States] Senate were frequently distracted by the cry that the Gauls were at the gate." "When, after my rout, I appeared at Warrenton, attended by a single companion, where I had passed the night before with my command, I was apparently as forlorn as Charles,

> After dread Pultowa's day,
> When fortune left the royal Swede.

But I felt no discouragement. My faith in my ability to create a command and continue my warfare on the border was still as unwavering as Francis Xavier's when he left the Tagus, to plant the cross on the shores of Coromandel." "The Rev. Sam Chapman had passed through so many fights unscathed that the men had a superstition that he was as invulnerable as the son of Thetis. His hour had come at last, and a bullet pierced the celestial armor of the soldier-priest; but he fought with the rammer of his gun as he fell. He lived to pay the debt he contracted that day. 'For time, at last, sets all things even.' The victors now held the howitzer, and barred the only way for my escape; but I held in my hand a more potent talisman than Douglas threw into the Saracen ranks. My faith in the power of a six-shooter was as strong as the Crusader's was in the heart of the Bruce." In the *Memoirs*, we find "I felt a good deal like Hercules did when he put on the shirt of the Centaur and couldn't pull it off." A letter, after the war, to an old comrade-in-arms ends with a passage in which Caesar's *Commentaries* and the incidents of the *Iliad* almost crowd into the background the more recent events in which they have taken part. In December, 1862, at the beginning of his activities as a partisan, he asks his wife to send him "some books to read. Send Plutarch, Macaulay's *History* and *Essays, Encyclopedia of Anecdotes,* Scott's Works, Shakespeare, Byron, Scott's Poems, Hazlitt's *Life of Napoleon,* — if you can get me a copy of *My Novel,* send it, also *Memoirs of an Irish Gentleman* (for Fount Beattie), *Corinne,* and *Sketch Book.*" One wonders how, travelling as light as he did, he expected to transport this library.

Yet for all his Virginian upbringing and his love of romantic reading, John Mosby had none of the gratuitous gallantry, the tournament ceremonial, that sometimes bemused and hampered the other Confederate officers. "I confess my theory of war was severely practical — one not acquired by reading the Waverley novels — but we observed the ethics of the code of war. Strategy is only another name for deception and can be practised by any commander. The enemy complained that we did not fight fair; the same complaint was made by the Austrians against Napoleon" (*Memoirs*). "In one sense the charge that I did not fight fair is true. I fought for success and not for display. There was no man in the Confederate army who had less of the spirit of knight errantry in him, or took a more practical view of war than I did. The combat between Richard and Saladin by the Diamond of the Desert is a beautiful picture for the imagination to dwell on, but it isn't war, and was no model for me. . . . Grant, Sheridan, and Stonewall Jackson had about the same ideas that I had on the subject of war" (*Reminiscences*). Depending entirely on "the remorseless revolver," he laughed at the old-fashioned sabres, "as harmless as the wooden sword of harlequin." He said that he believed he was "the first cavalry commander who discarded the sabre as useless and consigned it to museums for the preservation of antiquities." He was as impatient with the formalities of the Richmond government as Sherman ever was with the political machinations of Washington: "Although a revolutionary government, none was ever so much under the domination of red tape as the one at Richmond. The martinets who controlled it were a good deal like the hero of Molière's comedy, who complained that his antagonist had wounded him by thrusting him in *carte,* when, according to the rule, it should have been in *tierce.* I cared nothing for the form of a thrust if it brought blood. I did not play with foils." (Yet it was after all only this toughness that Mosby shared with the men of the North. He, too, was a knight errant in the sense that his audacious successes were in the nature of individual exploits. Mosby was more fortunate or cleverer than some of his Confederate fellows in getting partially free of a higher command and acting on his own inspiration.)

It was Mosby's unexpected ruthlessness as well as his mysterious ubiquity that made the Northern Army so nervous. For them, he was a different kind of Southerner, a fighter who could never be counted upon to behave in the traditional Southern way. Of one of the trains he shelled, he writes, "There was nobody but soldiers on this train, but, if there had been women and children, too, it would have been all the same to me." As a private at the beginning of the war, he had been "so depressed at parting with my wife and children that I scarcely spoke a word," and at Manassas he wrote to his wife, "There was scarcely a minute during the battle that I did not think of you and my sweet babes. I had a picture of May [his daughter] which I took out once and looked at"; but two years later, when he was warned by the enemy that women and children would be travelling on certain of the Union trains, he replied that he "did not understand that it hurts women and children to be killed any more than it hurts men." If the enemy took refuge in a building, he immediately set fire to it and reduced them to escaping at the price of surrender, and on one occasion, capturing a train with a carful of immigrant Germans, he gave the order, "Set fire to the car and burn the Dutch, if they won't come out." He was led to hang prisoners — whom he chose by lot — in reprisal for executions by the enemy. Grant had given the order, "When any of Mosby's men are caught, hang them without trial," and General George Custer, in the autumn of 1864, had had six of Mosby's followers executed. Three were shot, two were hanged, and a seventeen-year-old boy, who had borrowed a mount to join Mosby, was dragged through the streets by two horsemen and shot in the presence of his mother, who was begging them to treat him as a prisoner of war.

His own action, says Mosby, was justified, since it put a stop to such executions. But though he does not discuss the subject in the *Reminiscences*, intended for popular consumption, he seems to worry about it somewhat in the *Memoirs*. In any case, even in the latter account, written in his old age, when the exhilaration of youth has lapsed, we are caught by his insolent daring, his agile movement, his sense of humor. "A great many ludicrous incidents occurred," he remarks in connection with the capture of the train already mentioned above. "One lady ran up to me and exclaimed, 'Oh, my father is a Mason!' I had no time to say anything but, 'I can't help it.' One passenger claimed immunity for himself on the ground that he was a member of an aristocratic

church in Baltimore." At the end of 1862, when he set
out as an independent ranger, he had, he says, only
nine men (though his biographer, Mr. Virgil C. Jones,
says, there were actually six), and he had always, till
he was given a colonelcy at the end of the following
year, to depend on haphazard recruits, who made up,
he says, "almost as motley a crowd as Falstaff's regiment."
There were stragglers from "nearly all the cavalry regiments," along with "a sprinkling of men from the infantry," who had been disabled by wounds but could
still be useful if mounted; some had to carry their
crutches tied to their saddlebows. When the news reached
their former commanders that these men had been re-
claimed by Mosby and were functioning as soldiers
again, they would at once insist on having them back.
And this company of strayed guerrillas had to be rec-
ompensed with loot and horses — the latter of which the
Confederate government did not supply to its cavalry
— and once they had got their mounts, after serving in
a raid or two, they would be likely to disappear. He had
then no subordinate officer, and his authority over his
men was so "transitory" that he "disliked to order them
to do anything but fight" and was afraid that if he dispersed them at any point without promising them immediate action, he "would never see them again." Yet,
though some of them could not be counted on, though
there were always men coming and going, Mosby did
maintain a hold on his troops that was astonishing, he
says, to others. "The true secret was that it was a fascinating life, and its attractions far more than counter-
balanced its hardships and dangers. They had no camp
duty to do, which, however necessary, is disgusting
to soldiers of high spirit." When he was later given authority to raise a command but was not allowed to re-
cruit among those who were subject to conscription, he

had difficulty in collecting the requisite quota of sixty competent men.

Yet Mosby, with these oddly assembled troops, was able to keep the Northern cavalry in a continual state of anxious vigilance: "I have often thought that their fierce hostility to me was more on account of the sleep I made them lose than the number we killed and captured." By attacking them from the rear, he would distract them from their main objectives. He would dismay them by assuming the offensive when immediate surrender was expected. Since he had no fixed lines to guard or definite territory to hold, they never knew where to find him, and the rapidity of his attacks at different points far distant from one another led them wildly to overestimate his forces. It was characteristic of Mosby that he should maintain this extreme mobility. "He is slender, gaunt, and active in figure," writes John Esten Cooke in *Wearing the Gray*; "his feet are small, and cased in cavalry boots, with brass spurs; and the revolvers in his belt are worn with an air of 'business' which is unmistakable. The face of this person is tanned, beardless, youthful-looking and pleasant. He has white and regular teeth, which his habitual smile reveals. His piercing eyes flash out from beneath his brown hat, with its golden cord, and he reins in his horse with the ease of a practiced rider. A plain soldier, low and slight in stature, ready to talk, to laugh, to ride, to oblige you in any way — such was Mosby, in outward appearance. Nature had given no sign but the restless, roving, flashing eye, that there was much worth considering beneath. The eye did not convey a false expression. The commonplace exterior of the partisan concealed one of the most active, daring, and penetrating minds of an epoch fruitful in such."

Mosby sometimes took far more prisoners than he himself had men, and he enjoys, in the *Reminiscences*, subjoining at the end of a chapter the dispatches of the other side, which exhibit the fantastic notions that the Federals had of his numbers. On one occasion, single-handed, he captured a whole company of Yankee cavalry simply by riding up to them, demanding their surrender at the point of his pistols, and shouting "Charge 'em, boys! Charge 'em!" to imaginary followers behind him. This was one of the incidents in his celebrated feat of ascertaining the position of McClellan's army by riding completely around it. Among his other achievements were carrying off from a raid on a train a hundred and sixty-eight thousand dollars in greenbacks, which were being transported by Federal paymasters, and kidnapping General Stoughton with a hundred men and their mounts: "A light was quickly struck, and on the bed we saw the general sleeping as soundly as the Turk when Marco Bozzaris waked him up. There was no time for ceremony, so I drew up the bedclothes, pulled up the general's shirt, and gave him a spank on his bare back, and told him to get up." Mosby's account of this incident is amplified by John Esten Cooke, who says that the general sat up and demanded, "Do you know who I am, sir?" "Do you know Mosby, general?" said Mosby. " 'Yes,' was the eager response, 'have you got the _____ rascal?' 'No, but he has got you!' " Another of the Federal officers was forced to escape in the nude.

One of the most sensational of Mosby's escapades — told at length in the *Memoirs* and making a kind of climax which fiction could hardly surpass — occurred toward the end of December in the final winter of the war. He had one evening gone to the house of a farmer to celebrate the wedding of his ordnance sergeant, but he there received the report that a detachment of the enemy's cavalry had been sighted not far away. "Not caring to interrupt the wedding festivities, with one man . . . I rode off to reconnoitre." Two cavalrymen fired at them, but did not pursue, "and we soon saw the whole column in blue moving on the road to Rectortown." He notified his officers that they would have to attack in the morning, and, hungry and chilly now, not returning to the wedding, he dropped in at "the house of a citizen . . . who was famous for always setting a good table"; but while Mosby was at the table "enjoying some good coffee, hot rolls, and spareribs," the tramp of horses was heard; a group of Federals arrived, and before he could get away, walked into the room where he was. "I was better dressed that evening than I ever was during the war. Just before starting to Richmond I got through the blockade across the Potomac a complete suit from head to foot. I had a drab hat with an ostrich plume, with gold cord and star; a heavy, black beaver-cloth overcoat and cape lined with English scarlet cloth, and as it was a stormy evening, over this I wore a gray cloak, also lined with scarlet. My hat, overcoat, and cape were lying in the corner. I wore a gray sack coat with two stars on the collar to indicate my rank as lieutenant-colonel, gray trousers with a yellow cord down the seam, and long cavalry boots." (This panache was also a trait of the romantic Southern officer. Though Mosby so scorned such a "light French saber" as Cooke says Jeb Stuart always wore, this ostrich plume and scarlet-lined cape were quite in the manner of Stuart, under whom Mosby had served and whose costume, as Cooke tells us, included "a beautiful yellow sash" and "bright patent leather boots decorated with gold thread" and who "never moved on the field without his splendid red battle-flag.")

In this costume, then, Mosby was trapped by the Federals. "As the Northerners entered the room, I placed my hands on my coat collar to conceal my stars, and a few words passed between us. The situation seemed desperate, but I had made up my mind to take all the chances for getting away. I knew that if they discovered my rank, to say nothing of my name, they would guard me more carefully than if I were simply a private or a lieutenant. But a few seconds elapsed before firing began in the back yard. One of the bullets passed through the window, making a round hole . . . and striking me in the stomach. . . . My self-possession in concealing the stars on my collar saved me from being carried off a prisoner, dead or alive. The officers had not detected the stratagem, when I exclaimed, 'I am shot!' The fact was that the bullet created only a stinging sensation, and I was not in the least shocked. My exclamation was not because I felt hurt, but to get up a panic in order that I might escape."

There were three hundred Union cavalrymen outside; they kept shooting, and the panic occurred; but Mosby now found himself in no situation for taking advantage of it. The wound "was having its effect; I was bleeding profusely and getting faint. . . . I determined to play the part of a dying man." Going into the next room, he took off his coat with the insignia of his rank and tucked it under the bureau. The soldiers found him lying on the floor "with the blood gushing from my wound." When they asked who he was, he invented a name. A doctor examined his wound and declared that it was mortal: he had been shot through the heart. (The Federals, Mosby says, had had a good deal of liquor.) "He located the heart rather low down, and even in that supreme moment I felt tempted to laugh at his ignorance of human anatomy. I only gasped a few words and affected to be dying." The soldiers now went away, and Mosby was put into an ox-cart and carried to the house of a neighbor, two miles away, through "a howling storm of snow, rain, and sleet. . . . When we reached there, I was almost perfectly stiff with cold, and my hair was a clotted mass of ice."

In a few days the Federals found out that the man who had been shot was Mosby. They searched for him but could not find him — he had been moved again, to his father's house — and they gave out the report that he had died of his wound, an idea that the Confederates were careful to encourage. Philip Sheridan, then fighting in the Shenandoah Valley, was delighted to hear of his death. But, in spite of a bad relapse, a hemorrhage caused by laughing at his doctor's jokes, he was back with his command by the twentieth of February, and continued his successful raids. He had already been given his colonelcy before he had fully recovered, and he was put in command, at the end of March, of the whole of Northern Virginia. Appomattox came two weeks later.

All this is the TV Mosby. But growing out of these astonishing exploits, there is also a mythical Mosby, possessed of supernatural powers, who, as a creature of the "folk" imagination, has a certain curious interest. The great ranger, in his *Reminiscences,* makes a point of discussing this folklore.

"When the struggle was over," he writes of his men, "they relapsed into the habits of their former life, and like the Puritan soldiers of Cromwell, became as marked for devotion to their civil duties as they had ever been to war. As for myself, it was for a long time maintained that I was a pure myth, and my personal identity was as stoutly denied as that of Homer or the Devil. All historic doubts about my own existence have, I believe, been settled; but the fables published by the Bohemians who followed the army made an impression that still lives in popular recollection. . . . Among the survivors

of the Army of the Potomac there are many legends
afloat, and religiously believed to be true, of a mysterious
person — a sort of Flying Dutchman or Wandering Jew
— prowling among their camps in the daytime in the
garb of a beggar or with a pilgrim's staff, and leading
cavalry raids upon them at night. In popular imagination,
I have been identified with that mythical character." He
was supposed, he says, to have been seen in the theater
the night that Lincoln was shot, and "I recently heard
an officer of the United States army tell a story of his
being with the guard for a wagon train, and my passing
him with my command on the pike, all of us dressed as
Federal soldiers, and cutting the train out from behind
him. I laughed at it, like everybody who heard it, and
did not try to unsettle his faith. To have corrected it
would have been as cruel as to dispel the illusion of
childhood that the story of *Little Red Riding Hood* is
literally true, or to doubt the real presence of Santa
Claus. It was all pure fiction about our being dressed
in blue uniforms, or riding with him. . . . I can now
very well understand how the legendary heroes of
Greece were created. I always wore the Confederate uniform, with the insignia of my rank. So did my men."
But it *had* been one of Mosby's tricks to insinuate himself, with members of his band, their uniforms hidden
by raincoats or darkness, among a group of Union officers, who would quickly be made to surrender, or a
marching column of Union troops which would enable
them to move unnoticed. This happened again and
again. Since he sometimes conversed with the Federals
before presenting his pistols, one wonders why none of
these Northerners should have noticed his Virginia accent. But Mosby had a special genius for misleading the
people he met.

One day in April, 1864, when Mosby was not far from

Washington, he met a woman who was driving a wagon and who told him that she was on her way to join her husband in the capital. He was a Virginia man loyal to the Union, who had gone for refuge there. Mosby cut off a lock of his hair and told her to take it to Lincoln with the message that he was coming for a lock of his. It was reported in a newspaper that this had been done and that Lincoln had laughed about it.

Between Mosby and Grant there grew up, without their ever having seen one another, a peculiar relationship based on mutual respect and interest that was to realize itself after the war in an actual personal friendship. Grant tells in his own *Memoirs* how Mosby — in the spring of 1864, when Grant was making weekly trips between Culpeper, Virginia, and Washington — came within an ace of capturing the train in which the Union lieutenant general was travelling. (Mosby was afterwards to say to him that if this capture had taken place, he, Mosby, might well have been in Grant's place as President.) "Since the close of the war," adds Grant, "I have come to know Colonel Mosby personally, and somewhat intimately. He is a different man entirely from what I had supposed. He is slender, not tall, wiry, and looks as if he could endure any amount of physical exercise. He is able, and thoroughly honest and truthful. There were probably but few men in the South who could have commanded successfully a separate detachment, in the rear of an opposing army and so near the border of hostilities, as long as he did without losing his entire command."

"I had strong personal reasons," writes Mosby, "for being friendly with General Grant. If he had not thrown his shield over me, I should have been outlawed and driven into exile." When Lee had surrendered at Appomattox, Mosby, by order of Stanton, was the only

Confederate officer excluded from parole, but Grant had corrected this. The great ranger, as we have seen, had at first been an opponent of secession, and he had never approved of slavery; he was to write after the war, in the *Memoirs*, that "we now thank Abraham Lincoln for abolishing it." He much admired Grant, and he decided to support him against Horace Greeley, when Grant ran for President the second time, on the ground, as he said, that the South had been fighting Greeley for forty years but had fought Grant for only four. He was invited by Grant to the White House, and was able, after the reëlection, to secure government jobs for his sister and for some of his former followers. He would not accept office for himself, but this abstention did not protect him against vehement attack from the South as a turncoat seduced by self-interest. He found it necessary to carry a revolver, and someone in the town where he lived took a shot at him in the darkness one night. President Grant, just retiring from office, became alarmed at this incident and induced his successor, Rutherford B. Hayes, to offer Mosby the consulship at Hong Kong, a post which he was willing to accept but from which, after seven years, the advent of Grover Cleveland displaced him. When asked what he thought of China, he answered, "Better fifty years of Europe than a cycle of Cathay."

After Mosby's return to the States, he worked for the Southern Pacific Railroad till, as the result of a reorganization, he was laid off in 1901. He spent three years as an agent at the Land Office, then was appointed by Theodore Roosevelt to a post of assistant attorney in the Department of Justice. He was dropped in 1910, at the age of seventy-seven, and reduced to extreme poverty: "I was up against it," he said, "during the war and did not take it seriously to heart. I shall endeavor to do so now." He had not even tea to offer his visitors and would walk around Washington in his bedroom slippers. He had lost his wife in childbirth in 1876, and the use of one of his eyes when, in 1896, he was kicked by a horse he was driving. He had always kept in touch with his veterans, but most of them now were dead. He had become in his later years rude, irritable and dictatorial; he would lay down his opinions in conversation and then abruptly leave the room to show that no reply was possible or get up from the dinner table before the others had finished. It was said of him by one of his sons that the war had "ruined a good father." Five years after losing his post, he died. Just at the end a delegation from his old university had brought him a bronze medal and an embossed address. He spoke of his imprisonment in Charlottesville for the shooting of his fellow student, and added, "My chief regret is that I could not do for my prison what Tasso did for his dungeon at Ferrara — confer immortality upon it."

The mythical aspect of Mosby of which I have spoken above so seized upon the imagination of Herman Melville that he made it the subject of a narrative poem. This poem — *The Scout toward Aldie* — was included in a book of verse published in 1866, but it belongs with Melville's short stories in prose, especially *Benito Cereno* and *Billy Budd,* and it seems rather strange that, with all the attention that has recently been paid to Melville, this piece should never, so far as I can find, have been dealt with in connection with his other fiction. In the April of 1864, Herman Melville paid a brief visit to a cousin much younger than he, who was encamped in Virginia with the Army of the Potomac. Mosby was by this time in command of eight companies, and the country in which he operated had become known as Mosby's Confederacy. It had been said of him, he tells us in the *Memoirs*, before a Congressional committee, "that the planks on the bridge across the Potomac were taken up every night to prevent us from carrying off the Government." At the time of Herman Melville's visit, a special determined effort was being made to put an end to this maddening harassment, and the subject of *The Scout toward Aldie* is the adventures of a detachment of Federal cavalry who have gone into the forest to capture Mosby.

This is one of Melville's most ambitious pieces in verse, and, as a poet, he is not quite up to it. His complicated stanza form, his knotted and jolting style and his elliptical way of telling his story — which seem somewhat to derive from Browning — are really the kind of thing that requires a master to bring it off. But, as a story, *The Scout toward Aldie* is tightly organized and well contrived, and it effectively creates suspense. The young colonel who is leading the detachment is eager for military glory, and he has brought his young bride to camp. They are spending their honeymoon in a "bannered tent." But his men, from the moment they enter the wood, feel themselves to be in Mosby's country, and though "The sun is gold, and the world is green" and "Opal the vapors of morning roll," everything they encounter seems ominous: a spring beside which one of their men has been shot; an apparently haunted house in which the ghosts have turned out to be rebels; a strip of dangling bark which reminds them of how Mosby and they have been hanging one another's prisoners. Mosby pervades the whole place. "As glides in seas the shark, / Rides Mosby through green dark," writes Melville, reverting to his maritime imagery. The obsession with Mosby of the scouting party is conveyed by the recurrent repetition of his name, which is made to pop up at some point in the last couplet of every stanza. (The real Mosby was on one occasion supposed to have escaped recognition by having his face covered with lather in a barber's chair, and, on another, to have avoided capture, when surprised at night with his wife and children, by escaping through the bedroom window to the branch of a tree outside.) The Federals take prisoner five enemy soldiers, who are standing in plain sight on a hill. One of them is groaning: he cannot walk, he has evidently an internal injury. The Federals give him some brandy and eventually leave him in a house with people whom they know to be Confederate sympathizers. They also waylay a wagon, driven by a humpbacked Negro, in which a veiled lady is riding. The Negro begs for his freedom, and they let him go, but they detain the lady and take from her a letter which they see sticking out of her dress. This turns out to be an invitation to a party to be given in a nearby town in celebration of Mosby's last victory. Now, they think, they know where to find him: he will certainly attend the party. They joke with their Confederate captives, exchanging taunts and boasts, and at evening both factions sing grisly songs, with the grisliness disguised as gaiety. The young colonel converses with an elderly major, who has his doubts about the lady and the letter and who somewhat dampens the young colonel's ardor. The latter takes a nip of brandy, and their feeling of uncertainty grows. They soon find they have been caught in a trap. The lady and her driver were Mosby's men; the crippled soldier was Mosby. (These incidents were evidently suggested by an actual exploit of Mosby's, in which his wife, an old Negro and a carriage figured, and by his device of making use of convalescent cripples, who would emerge from their hospitals, take part in a raid, then return to their invalids' bed and thus become quite unidentifiable as the marauders who, the previous night, had created such alarm in the Federal camp.) He had been with them without their knowing it, directing their expedition, and now they are in Mosby's hands. Some of the Yankees are wounded, others are taken prisoner; the ambitious young colonel is killed.

> The weary troop that wended now —
>   Hardly it seemed the same that pricked
> Forth to the forest from the camp:
> Foot-sore horses, jaded men;
>   Every backbone felt as nicked,
>   Each eye dim as a sick-room lamp,
>   All faces stamped with Mosby's stamp.

They carry back the young colonel's body, and when they come within sight of his tent, they see his young bride outside it, waiting for them and waving her handkerchief.

What we recognize, of course, in this story is Melville's familiar theme: the pursuit or the persecution by one being of another, with an ambivalent relation between them which mingles repulsion and attraction but which binds them inescapably together: Captain Ahab and Moby Dick, Claggart and Billy Budd, Babo and Don Benito. For though the death of the young colonel is a tragedy and though Mosby plays the role of menace, the whole poem, in a way characteristic of Melville, involves a glorification of Mosby. We are made to feel that the colonel has a kind of fatal rendezvous with the sinister ranger, that he is drawn to his opponent by a kind of spell that is somehow a good deal more powerful than the attraction which has drawn him to his bride.

Yet the story, though so personal a product of Melville's imagination, has also its historical significance in its insight into one aspect of the Civil War. What Melville has revealed in the fanciful tale inspired by his visit to his cousin is a mutual fascination of each of the two camps with the other, the intimate essence of a conflict which, though fratricidal, was also incestuous. One is continually being reminded, in reading the military memoirs of the war, how often — from West Point or Mexico or even through family ties — the officers on both sides of the lines had been closely associated with one another. I have already called attention to the Melvillean aspect of Grant's pursuit of Lee; and Mosby's peculiar knack of infiltrating the Federal Army and getting himself mistaken for a Northerner, this myth of the false Northerner who is out to destroy the real ones, is evidently a symptom of the same situation. This peculiar entanglement with one another of the American North and South was, after the war, to give rise to a formula of romantic fiction which continued to be popular for decades and which produced all those novels and plays in which two lovers, one Northern, one Southern, though destined for one another, are divided by their loyalties to their different flags.

An astonishing late product of this aspect of the war is the recent play called *Sud* by Julian Green, an American of Southern parentage, who was born in France and grew up there and who now lives in Paris and writes in French. This play, first produced in Paris in 1953 and afterwards done in Germany, sounds as if it might have been based on a reminiscence of Bronson Howard's once famous *Shenandoah*. *Shenandoah* was first produced in 1888, and Green was born in 1900, but this very full-value melodrama continued to be popular for many years, and Green may perhaps have seen it when he came to the United States to attend the University of Virginia. Green's play exploits the same situation of the dilemmas of Civil War lovers of which one party is

Northern, the other Southern, and it builds up, like the first act of *Shenandoah*, to the firing on Fort Sumter.

The novelty of *Sud*, however, is that the central North-South relationship is a homosexual one. There was perhaps something of this kind already latent in *The Scout toward Aldie*; but it is odd to see the whole polarization of 1861 transposed into terms of André Gide's Paris. The fable is also much more complex. Here a young Polish American, the son of a Polish aristocrat who has been hanged in 1848 by the Prussians, finds himself a Federal officer stationed at Fort Sumter on the eve of the Civil War. By a dramatic *coup de foudre*, he is made to conceive a passion for a twenty-year-old plantation owner, who has proved his high-mindedness by freeing his slaves. Realizing that this passion is hopeless, he provokes the young planter to a duel and — having just been recalled to his post to defend the Federal fort — allows the young man to kill him. The situation is further complicated by a young girl, a New England cousin who has been living with the Charleston family in whose house the action takes place. She is a conscientious Unitarian, a young woman of moral principle, and when she sees that the war is inevitable, she announces that she is going back North. But though she fears and disapproves of the Pole, who represents aristocracy as well as, by family tradition, the struggle of a minority for freedom, she also admires him so much that she cannot help falling in love with him. When Wiezewski is carried in dead, the girl gives a terrible cry, "Ian, come back!" and collapses beside the body. The first firing on Fort Sumter is heard. This play, not without its power, is perhaps a little touch too Proustian for the America of the eighteen-sixties. One is rather surprised to learn that the old plantation owner who figures in it also shares the tastes of Charlus, so is able to guess

Wiezewski's secret. But the play is a curious piece of evidence — written in an alien language and acting only on alien audiences — of the persistence and reverberation of the drama of the Civil War.

It is true that such exciting figures as Dick Taylor and Jeb Stuart and Mosby are typical of one element of the Confederate Army. Its most celebrated soldier, however — though popular romance has extended to him something of the glamor of the Southern legend — really represents a different tradition. Robert E. Lee has left no apologia. Though his records were mostly destroyed by his clerks on the retreat from Petersburg or burnt up in the fire when Richmond fell, he was collecting in his later years the materials for a book on his Virginia campaigns; but he did not live to write it. We can only come at all close to Lee through the volume of personal documents compiled by his son, Captain Robert E. Lee: *Recollections and Letters of General Robert E. Lee,* which shows him in his relations with his family and as President of Washington College. As a letter-writer, Lee is monotonous. Though occasionally playful with his children, when he is talking of their love affairs or the family pets, his tone is extremely sober, and these letters have in common with his military dispatches that they are occupied mainly with practical arrangements, about which he issues the most precise instructions. During the period after the war, he exercises an admirable restraint — in view of the policies of the Reconstruction — in not commenting on current events. These injustices, he says, must be left to time: the animosity of the North will subside; and, in the meantime, agreeing with intelligent critics in the South as well as in the North that what the South most needs is education, he is quietly and conscientiously devoting himself to this end.

As always, his life is an exemplification of principles rarely expressed — among which are fundamental the assumptions of the Church of England, hardly altered by transplantation, which have little in common with the religion of New England, the agonies of sin and salvation. Nor does Lee speak directly with God, irrespective of time or place, as Stonewall Jackson had done. He is punctilious in going to church, where he sits in the family pew, humble before his Maker but the cornerstone of the congregation. He respectfully trusts in God; there is no drama in his intercourse with Heaven. "You will, however, learn before this reaches you that our success at Gettysburg was not so great as reported — in fact, that we failed to drive the enemy from his position, and that our army withdrew to the Potomac. Had the river not unexpectedly risen, all would have been well with us; but God, in His all-wise providence, willed otherwise, and our communications have been interrupted and almost cut off. The waters have subsided to about four feet, and, if they continue, by to-morrow, I hope, our communications will be open. I trust that a merciful God, our only hope and refuge, will not desert us in this hour of need, and will deliver us by His almighty hand, that the whole world may recognize His power and all hearts be lifted up in adoration and praise of His unbounded loving-kindness. We must, however, submit to His almighty will, whatever that may be. May God guide and protect us all is my constant prayer." And everything that happens in his family is confidently referred to the divine authority. "I am so grieved, my dear daughter," he writes to his daughter-in-law, "to send Fitzhugh to you wounded. But I am so grateful that his wound is of a character to give us full hope of a speedy recovery. . . . I know that you will unite with me in thanks to Almighty God, who has so often sheltered him in the hour of danger, for his recent deliverance, and lift up your whole heart in praise to Him for sparing a life so dear to us, while enabling him to do his duty in the station in which He has placed him." When he learns that this daughter-in-law has died, he writes his wife of their eventual reunion: "What a glorious thought it is that she has joined the little cherubs and our angel Annie in Heaven. Thus is link by link the strong chain broken that binds me to earth, and our passage soothed to another world." To his wife, on a wedding anniversary, not long after the end of the war: "Do you recollect what a happy day thirty-three years ago this was? How many hopes and pleasures it gave birth to! God has been very merciful and kind to us, and how thankless and sinful I have been. I pray that He may continue his mercies and blessings to us, and give us a little peace and rest together in this world, and finally gather us and all He has given us around His throne in the world to come."

There is nothing about Lee that is at all picturesque, but his dignity and distinction are impressive, and this memoir helps us better to understand the reasons for his lasting prestige in the North as well as the South — why a New Englander who had served in the Union army like the younger Charles Francis Adams should have wanted to have a statue of him in Washington. The point is that Lee belongs, as does no other public figure of his generation, to the Roman phase of the Republic; he prolongs it in a curious way which, irrelevant and anachronistic though his activities to a Northerner may seem to be, cannot fail to bring some sympathetic response that derives from the experience of the Revolution. The Lees had been among the prime workers in our operations against the British and the founding

of the United States. Robert's father, "Light-Horse
Harry," had been one of the most brilliant heroes of our
war against the Crown, a favorite of George Washington,
with the privilege of direct communication with him,
and afterwards Governor of Virginia for three successive
terms. Robert Lee himself had married the daughter of
a grandson of Martha Washington, which grandson had
been adopted by the Washingtons, and she and Robert,
after they married, went to live in the old Custis mansion at Arlington, which was full of Washington relics.
To say the American Revolution was always present in
the Lee background would be perhaps to understate the
situation: the Lees had never really emerged from the
world of the Thirteen Colonies. Robert was born on
the Lee estate at Stratford in Westmoreland County,
in a huge old H-shaped brick house, built in 1730,
which, with its widely spaced double pair of chimneys,
its broad floor-beams, its great kitchen, great attic, great
hall, its accounting room, its farmyard, its stables that
made it supreme in its countryside, unneighbored and
self-sustaining, was a profoundly serious place, a headquarters of responsibility. That the Lees' responsibility
somewhat lapsed when Light-Horse Harry returned from
the wars and ruined himself in grandiose speculations
and when the Henry Lee who was Robert's half-brother
and inherited the family place ruined his political career
by creating a scandal with his wife's sister and getting
himself into such financial difficulties that he was eventually obliged to sell Stratford, undoubtedly acted on
Robert — who had neither his father's extravagance nor
his brilliance — as a stimulus to return to the Roman
ideal. He was under an obligation to restore the slipping
status of the Lees, and the sense of responsibility, displaced later not merely from Stratford but also from
the Arlington mansion, which the Federals took over in

the Civil War (including the Washington relics the return of which the Radical Congress forbade in 1869 and
which were only given back to the family in the early
nineteen-hundreds) — this sense of responsibility is evident
in everything he does: both in the field during the Civil
War and afterwards, when the cause was lost, in his
patient administration of Washington College, his supervision of the care of his invalid wife, his advice to his son
about running a farm.

What is especially interesting and of fundamental
importance is the transference by Lee of the spirit that
accomplished the Revolution from the earlier crisis to
the later. It is likely to seem strange to the Northerner
that this upright and scrupulous man who had taken
the oath to the United States and had served as superintendent of West Point, who wanted to abolish slavery,
who did "not believe in secession as a constitutional right,
nor that there is sufficient cause for revolution," who
detested the boasting of the "Cotton States," their habitual truculent arrogance and their threats against the
"Border States" for their reluctance to go along with
them, should have become the commander of the Confederate Army and have led it through four years of the
bitterest fighting when he did not even hope that the
South could win: "I have never believed," he told
General Pendleton, a day or two before his surrender, that
"we could, against the gigantic combination for our subjugation, make good in the long run our independence unless foreign powers should, directly or indirectly, assist us
[he had made it clear at an early stage that no such intervention was to be expected]. . . . But such considerations
really made with me no difference. We had, I was satisfied, sacred principles to maintain and rights to defend, for
which we were in duty bound to do our best, even if we
perished in the endeavor." Nor was Lee the only Southern

soldier who did not expect to win: such paladins were too proud to need hope. This was partly, as has been said, in the spirit of the traditional gentlemen's duel, their heritage from the eighteenth century; but in Lee's case, as to some extent in theirs, it was an instinctive emulation of his ancestors, the manifestation of a regional patriotism more deeply rooted than loyalty to the United States. Virginians regarded Virginia as itself an autonomous country, which, with the help of certain New Englanders and certain Philadelphians, had expelled the monarchical forces and established in America a republican society, and it was not going to be interfered with by those now rather unfamiliar elements inhabiting the rest of the country to whom Lee, who had not sat with them in Congress, always referred as "those people." The same sense of honor and independence which stimulated Virginia to stand up to the Crown later spurred them to stand up to the Yankees. With Lee this was almost automatic: he had no real understanding of politics, no interest in economics. He had only the ancient valor and the tradition of a certain sort of role which the Lees were appointed to play.

His biographer Douglas Southall Freeman has shown that just before Lee's decision to resign from the Union Army, he had been reading a life of Washington, and his comment in a letter home is significant and characteristic: "How his spirit [Washington's] would be grieved could he see the wreck of his mighty labors! I will not, however, permit myself to believe till all ground of hope is gone that the work of his noble deeds will be destroyed, and that his precious advice and virtuous example will so soon be forgotten by his countrymen. As far as I can judge by the papers, we are between a state of anarchy and Civil War. May God avert us from both. It has been evident for years that the country was doomed to run the full length of democracy. To what a fearful pass it has brought us. I fear that mankind will not for years be sufficiently Christianized to bear the absence of restraint and force." Washington was a great Virginian, the enemy of disorder and anarchy; he had tried to save America from this, but when the structure he had founded broke down, one naturally remained with Virginia. The classical antique virtue, at once aristocratic and republican, had become a national legend, and its late incarnation in Lee was to command a certain awed admiration among Northerners as well as Southerners.

X

DIVERSITY OF OPINION IN THE SOUTH: WILLIAM
J. GRAYSON, GEORGE FITZHUGH, HILTON R.
HELPER

THE SENSATION caused by *Uncle Tom's Cabin* in the
North brought a vehement retort from the South. In
the three years following its publication in 1851, no less
than fourteen novels were written with the purpose of
obliterating the picture of slavery presented by Mrs.
Stowe; and in other departments of letters a similar
attempt was made to retort to the Abolitionist press of
the North by a counterblast of moral reprobation. What
about the iniquities in the Northern states of the ruthless industrial system? What about the New England
wage-slaves? The hardships involved in factory labor and
the helplessness of the working class had long been a
matter of concern to students of contemporary society,
and certain Southerners who had kept in touch with
what was going on in the rest of the world were goaded
by the nagging of the Northerners to make out a moral
case of their own.

One of the writers that took this line who — by reason
of his literary ability — is best remembered today was the
South Carolinian William John Grayson. He had a
wider horizon than most Southerners, for he had been
educated in New York and New Jersey and in the

South by New England teachers. A scholar who had inherited no estate, he was first schoolmaster and then lawyer, edited a local paper, sat for a term in Congress and served in Charleston as Collector of Customs. In his late sixties, he applied himself to literature: became a regular contributor to a Charleston periodical and published in Charleston, in 1856, together with some other poems, a longish piece in heroic couplets called *The Hireling and the Slave*. I have indicated, in connection with Sarah Morgan as well as with John Mosby, the relative indifference toward the slavery issue of the non-planter class of professional men in Louisiana and Virginia. In South Carolina, however, says Grayson in his memoir of his friend Judge Petigru, who had "engaged in the ordinary and legitimate proceeding of investing his professional profits in a plantation and negroes," this was "the approved Carolina custom in closing every kind of career. No matter how one might begin, as lawyer, physician, clergyman, mechanic or merchant, he ended, if prosperous, as proprietor of a rice or cotton plantation. It was the condition that came nearest to the shadow of the colonial aristocracy which yet remained." And William Grayson himself purchased "Fair Lawn" plantation the same year that he composed his pro-slavery poem.

His opinions on the subject of slavery were not, however, extreme. He explains in his preface to *The Hireling* that he does not want to create more slaves — that is, presumably, to renew the slave-trade, as some Southerners wanted to do — but simply to justify the slave-owners' right to continue to hold those Negroes who have already been reduced to the status of slaves; that he does "not say that slavery is the best system of labor, but only that it is best for the Negro in this country"; that "all cruelty is an abuse; does not belong to the

institution; is now punished, and may in time be prevented." It may perhaps be true, he goes on, that "in
a nation composed of the same race or similar races,
where the laborer is intelligent, industrious, and provi-
dent, money-wages may be better than subsistence"; but
in England, under the factory system, the "hireling" will
be left to starve if the employer does not give him employment at a time when the market is low, whereas the
slave is a permanent value and must always be kept
alive by his owner.

The poem itself begins with a tragic and well-turned
picture — in the nail-driving style of Pope — of the present condition of the people in Britain and on the Continent. Serfdom has been abolished but the liberated
serfs are worse off than before, since nobody any longer
is obliged to take responsibility for them, and they are
nonetheless paupers for what they produce. Beside the
"lordly halls" of their masters, they now live in "squalid
huts." When unemployed, they take to drunkenness and
prostitution. The mothers murder their children. The
peasants are conscripted for foreign wars, in which, "half
fed, half clad, the tentless earth their bed," they are
slaughtered or die of disease or exposure. The poet
knocks off one by one the champions of the anti-slavery
cause: "mad Garrison," who "carnage and fire . . . invokes"; Sumner the "supple," who "grieving at a brother's
woe, / Spits with impartial spite on friend and foe";
Seward, who "smiles the sweet perennial smile, / Skilled
in the tricks of subtlety and guile"; and, last and at greatest length, "Stowe," who, "with prostituted pen, assails /
One half her country in malignant tales." He contrasts
her with Florence Nightingale, who "tends the suffering
sick with woman's care," and describes her as "a moral
scavenger, with greedy eye. . . . On fields where vice
eludes the light of day, / She hunts up crimes as beagles

hunt their prey" . . . With hatred's ardor gathers New-
gate spoils, / And trades for gold the garbage of her
toils."

After staging this procession of horrors, Grayson shows
us the life of the slave, and his picture is entirely idyllic.
You get a series of charming descriptions of the South
Carolina Sea Islands, on one of which, at Beaufort, the
poet was born and of which he had delightful boyhood
memories — the islands on which Colonel Higginson and
his freedom-bringing Federal companions are later to dis-
port themselves. There is no presentation of the status
of the slave that derives from mature firsthand knowledge; there is only the invidious comparison. If the
Negroes are occasionally whipped, what is this beside
the flogging of British soldiers?; and are the peasantry
of Europe more literate than the Negroes of Southern
plantations? The Negro slave in his old age is well cared
for; the white peasant is sent to die in the poor-house.
The real aim of the gentle poet is to recreate the glamor
of childhood, and his becoming a plantation-owner at
sixty-seven is evidently part of a fantasy in which he returns to his youth: to hunting possum and wild turkey
in autumn, when "light hoar-frost sparkles on the fallen
leaf"; to fishing and boating in early June, by the "light
of the full-orbed moon," which "shines on the billows
tremulously bright," among the "sandy islets" where the
terrapin lays her eggs; to the feasts of shrimp, oyster and
mullet, when they cook and eat the catch out of doors,
where "camp-fires glimmer through the trees," and discuss "the fish and fortunes of the day, / How sly the
bite, how beautiful the play; / Tell, with grave fact, the
superstitious charm / That wrought the fisherman success or harm." With scorn for the contemporary dema-
gogues, who "have won, with brazen throat, / The loudest
cheer and most triumphant vote," the poet exalts the

tradition of Washington, who "Turned from the noisy hall, the coarse debate, The curse of patronage and frauds of state" to "happier scenes than office can supply"; and he remembers "the vanished Indian," whom, "If slavery guard his subject race no more," the Negro must follow to oblivion.

In a sense, the Negro for Grayson is already half a phantom like the Indian — not a man with a life of his own but a figment, along with the moon-light, the soft waterways, the flora and fauna of Beaufort, an element lightly woven into the texture of the poet's impressions. What is most curious in this elegant work is the author's assimilation of the Negro's condition of servitude to the attractiveness of the luxuries he helps to provide. Though the point has been made so sharply that the hireling is never allowed to derive any satisfactions from the "rich fabrics wrought by his unequalled hand," the poet ten pages later appears to be unaware that the Negro is unable to participate except to a limited extent — which does not include the refinements that the white man particularly prizes — in the products of the sugar-cane or tobacco plantation. He has been celebrating the beauties of cotton and maize, and he continues thus, in celebrating the lot of the slaves:

> Nor these alone they give; their useful toil
> Lures the rich cane to its adopted soil —
> The luscious cane, whose genial sweets diffuse
> More social joys than Hybla's honey dews;
> Without whose help no civic feast is made,
> No bridal cake delights — without whose aid
> China's enchanting cup itself appears
> To lose its virtue, and no longer cheers,
> Arabia's fragrant berry idly wastes
> Its pure aroma on untutored tastes,

Limes of delicious scent and golden rind
Their pungent treasures unregarded find,
Ices refresh the languid belle no more,
And their lost comfits infant worlds deplore.
　　The weed's soft influence too, his hands prepare,
That soothes the beggar's grief, the monarch's care,
Cheers the lone scholar at his midnight work,
Subdues alike the Russian and the Turk,
The saint beguiles, the heart of toil revives,
Ennui itself of half its gloom deprives,
In fragrant clouds involves the learned and great,
In golden boxes helps the toils of state,
And, with strange magic and mysterious charm,
Hunger can stay, and bores and duns disarm.

If it were not, then, for Negro slavery, the mistress
would have no sugar for her imported tea and the languid belle no sweetening for her ices; nor — what is most
amusing — would the strenuous saint have his friendly
pipe to relax him, nor would the debtor, with no cheroot
to offer, be equipped to disarm his creditors.

———

A much more important apologist was George Fitzhugh of Virginia, a lawyer of very old family, who, by
marriage, had come into possession of a five-hundred-acre
plantation at the little town of Port Royal between the
Potomac and the Rappahannock. The author of two
books on the Southern system, he eventually became a
more or less professional journalist and the most influential pro-slavery propagandist of the decade before the
war. Fitzhugh had not much formal education: he was
to visit the North only once, and he seems never even
to have travelled in the South outside his native state of
Virginia; but he kept in touch with the larger world

through the British periodicals which he got from New York: the *Edinburgh* and *Westminster Reviews, Blackwood's Magazine,* etc.; and he evolved, in his provincial privacy, an original political philosophy which, though messy and amateurish, had pretensions to historical perspective and showed a broader intellectual scope than the views of most of his fellow Southerners. This philosophy he most substantially expounded in two once-provocative volumes, which he had published in Richmond in 1854 and 1857: *Sociology for the South* — George Fitzhugh was one of the first to use the word *sociology* in English — and *Cannibals All! or Slaves without Masters.*

These works present a problem of summarization. George Fitzhugh, unlike the neat Grayson, is a rather confused writer — inconsecutive and repetitious, often self-contradictory and full of extreme statements, condemnatory or eulogistic, which ring out with the full intonations of expansive after-dinner drinking over the generous Virginia board. It would be possible to give in three pages a more plausible as well as a far straighter statement of George Fitzhugh's case than Fitzhugh himself was capable of. But to do so would be in some degree to misrepresent him. You must also have the flush of the wine, the drowsy atmosphere of Tidewater Virginia, the gentlemanly old-fashioned eloquence and the ornaments of classical learning. One should blur and embellish the argument with specimens of the author's style. "The reader," writes Fitzhugh, "must have remarked our propensity of putting scraps of poetry at the head of our chapters or of interweaving them with the text. It answers as a sort of chorus or refrain, and, when skillfully handled, has as fine an effect as the fiddle at a feast, or the brass band on the eve of an engagement." These quotations from the poets, he says, are his answer to the hymns of the Abolitionists. And he apologizes pleasantly for his "manner," "discursive, immethodical and unartistic," partly on the ground that "we practiced as a jury lawyer for twenty-five years, and thereby acquired an inveterate habit of cumulation and iteration, and of various argument and illustration. . . . We admire not the pellucid rivulet, that murmurs and meanders, in cramped and artificial current, through the park and gardens of the nobleman; but we do admire the flooded and swollen Mississippi, whose turbid waters, in their majestic course, sweep along upon their bosom, with equal composure, the occupants of the hen-roost and poultry yard, the flocks, the herds, the crops, the uprooted forest, and the residences of man. . . . A continuous argument, without pause or break, on a subject profoundly metaphysical, equally fatigues the writer and the reader. Nobody likes it, and very few read it." We are not surprised to learn that Fitzhugh was not remarkably successful in his law practice or to find him confessing that he hated "listening to clients," which, "if persevered in, would make a man idiotic. No possible amount of fee can compensate a lawyer for the agonies he suffers from the needless reiteration of useless details by clients. This horror at the approach of clients is as natural and universal as the dread of snakes." In undertaking to boil down Fitzhugh, one must not boil him down to the bone.

The main leverage for Fitzhugh's case for slavery as expounded in *Sociology for the South* and *Cannibals All!* — which more or less hang together and represent a phase of his thought — is obtained by using as a fulcrum the same view of the industrial system as that of *The Hireling and the Slave*; but Fitzhugh goes much farther than Grayson. He has learned from the British reviews and from Carlyle's *Latter-Day Pamphlets* of the conditions of the working class in Britain, and he devotes a good deal of space to quotations from these foreign sources. (Both the title and the subtitle of *Cannibals All!* were borrowed from the *Latter-Day Pamphlets*.) This heavy documentation recalls Karl Marx. Fitzhugh had not read *Das Kapital*: it had not been published yet; but his conception of value as determined by labor suggests that he may have known something of the earlier writings of Marx which were then available in English. He tells us that he did have, at secondhand, some acquaintance with the socialist ideas of Fourier, Robert Owen, Louis Blanc and Proudhon, and he lays them under contribution for his arguments against what he calls "Free Society" — that is, laissez-faire capitalism. These prophets and planners, he says, have unanimously come to the conclusion that modern Free Society is a failure, and their proposals for correcting its evils all tend in the direction of more control. Though the Socialists will not quite admit it, the real goal of their efforts is enslavement. It is true that the miseries of industrialism have not yet been felt in the United States to the extent that they have in Europe; but Fitzhugh was not dealing here with doctrines that were merely exotic.

In the forties, the United States, with its unencumbered spaces and its freedom, had become the great field of experimentation for the Fourierists, the Owenites and others. Albert Brisbane was, in fact, even propagandizing for Fourier's communist "phalansteries" in Horace Greeley's New York *Tribune,* which Fitzhugh attentively read. More than forty such groups were recruited; and this also was the era of the New England Brook Farm and the New York State Oneida Community, of the Shaker and Mormon communities. George Fitzhugh regarded as utopian the ideal of the Fourierist phalanstery, in which everybody's interests and abilities were to be made to fit together perfectly in such a way that it would run like clockwork. Actually, Fitzhugh explains, no such perfect arrangement is possible. Such a community may function successfully so long as it is directed by "a despotic head" — he is thinking of the Shakers' Mother Ann and the Mormons' Brigham Young. "Socialism, with such [a] despotic head, approaches very near to Southern slavery, and gets along very well so long as the despot lives." "Add a Virginia overseer to Mr. Greeley's Phalansteries, and Mr. Greeley and we would have little to quarrel about."

The domination of a master class, a whole system of despotic directors, is, in fact, for a stable society, the indispensable primary condition. Is not the family, in any society, the fundamental unit, and must not the father keep his dependents in order? Are not wives and children slaves in the sense that they are under restraint and obliged to obey a superior? It is true that in the North at present there is a movement for Women's Rights and Free Homes which, if successful, would destroy the home; but this is merely an advanced symptom of the general disintegration there which is already resulting in chaos — a chaos to which the only corrective, as Free Society must find out in time, is enslavement for the majority of white men as well as for all the blacks. The socialists have been groping toward this, but they have not thought their problem through. Yet all history has established this principle: the great ancient civilizations that were based on slavery, Egypt and Greece and Rome; the taking for granted of servitude by the New Testament as well as the Old. And the success of these civilizations was due to what would be called in our own day their development as "organic" entities. "The great men of [any] day but show larger portions of the common thought. Men, and all other social and gregarious animals, have a community of thought, of motions, instincts, and intentions. The social body is of itself a thinking, acting, sentient being. This is eminently observable with the lower animals. Bees and herds perform their evolutions with too much rapidity and precision to leave any doubt but that one mind and one feeling, either from within or without, directs their movements. The great error of modern philosophy is the ignorance or forgetfulness of this fact. The first departure from it was not the Reformation — for that was preëminently a social idea and a logical movement — but the doctrine of the right of private judgment, which speculative philosophers and vain schismatics attempted to engraft upon it, or deduce from it. Human equality, the social contract, the let-alone and selfish doctrines of political economy, universal liberty, freedom of speech, of the press, and of religion, spring directly from this doctrine, or are only new modes of expressing it. Agrarianism, Free Love, and No Government, are its logical consequences: for the right to judge for ourself implies the right to act upon our judgments, and that can never be done in a world where the private appropriation of all capital and the interference of government restricts our free agency, and paralyzes our action on all sides." For Fitzhugh is on the side of the government restrictions; and, later on, again echoing Carlyle, he formulates his position as follows: the "riots, mobs, strikes, and revolutions" characteristic of modern society have demonstrated that "the mass of mankind cannot be governed by Law. More of despotic discretion, and less of Law, is what the world wants. We take our leave by saying 'THERE IS TOO MUCH OF LAW AND TOO LITTLE OF GOVERNMENT IN THIS WORLD.'" It is thus logical that the horrors of the French Revolution, with its heresies of Liberty and Equality, should have led to the paternalism of Louis Napoleon. The republic which was set up in Paris after the Revolution of 1848 had promised "employment and good wages to everybody. The experiment is tried and fails in a week. No employment, except transplanting trees and levelling mounds could be found, and the Treasury breaks. After struggling and blundering and staggering on through various changes, Louis Napoleon is made Emperor. He is a socialist, and socialism is the now fashionable name of slavery. He understands the disease of society, and has nerve enough for any surgical operation that may be required to cure it. His first step in socialism was to take the money of the rich to buy wheat for all. The measure was well-timed, necessary and just. He is now building houses on the social plan for working men, and his Queen is providing nurseries and nurses for the children of the working women, just as we Southerners do for our negro women and children."

Now compare the anarchic North, distracted by its innumerable "Isms," with the self-confident and comfortable South. "An unexplored moral world stretches out before us, and invites our investigation; but neither our time, our abilities, nor the character of our work, will permit us to do more than glance at its loveliness." For in this atmosphere of patriarchal good feeling we are safe from the inhumanities of what Fitzhugh calls "political economy" — by which he means the school of Adam Smith, whose doctrines, so contrary to the Christian ones, he wants to see "banished from our schools." "It is pleasing . . . to turn from the world" in which this political economy prevails, and "in which 'might makes right,' and strength of mind and of body are employed to oppress and exact from the weak, to that other and better, and far more luminous world, in which weakness rules, clad in the armor of affection and benevolence. It is delightful to retire from the outer world, with its competitions, rivalries, envyings, jealousies, and selfish war of the wits, to the bosom of the family, where the only tyrant is the infant — the greatest slave the master of the household. You feel at once that you have exchanged the keen air of selfishness, for the mild atmosphere of benevolence. Each one prefers the good of others to his own, and finds most happiness in sacrificing selfish pleasures, and ministering to others' enjoyments. The wife, the husband, the parent, the child, the son, the brother and the sister, usually act towards each other on scriptural principles. . . . The dependent exercise, because of their dependence, as much control over their superiors in most things, as those superiors exercise over them. Thus, and thus only, can conditions be equalized. This constitutes practical equality of rights, enforced not by human, but by divine law. Our hearts bleed at the robbing of a bird's nest; and the little birds, because they are weak, subdue our strength and command our care. We love and cherish the rose, and sympathize with the lily which some wanton boy has bruised and broken. Our faithful dog shares our affections, and we will risk our lives to redress injustice done him."

Our relation to our slaves is, of course, the same. They, also, "belong to the family circle. Does their common humanity, their abject weakness and dependence, their great value, their ministering to our wants in childhood, manhood, sickness and old age, cut them off from that affection which everything else in the family elicits? No; the interest of master and slave are bound up together, and each in his appropriate sphere naturally endeavors to promote the happiness of the other. The humble and obedient slave exercises more or less control over the most brutal and hard-hearted master." "Slaves too," he has already explained in *Sociology for the South*, "have a valuable property in their masters.

Abolitionists overlook this — overlook the protective influence of slavery, its distinguishing feature . . . Infant negroes, sick, helpless, aged and infirm negroes, are simply a charge to their master; he has no property in them in the common sense of the term, for they are of no value for the time, but they have the most invaluable property in him. He is bound to support them, to supply all their wants, and relieve them of all care for the present or future. And well, and feelingly and faithfully does he discharge his duty. What a glorious thing to man is slavery, when want, misfortune, old age, debility and sickness overtake him." But the owning class in Free Society get their labor at cheaper rates since they need not maintain their hands in the periods when business has slumped; and thus they are "cannibals all," and the laborers are "slaves without masters."

In America, Fitzhugh admits, it is true that the pressure is not yet so severe as it has now become in industrial Europe, since it has always been possible for the unemployed to resettle further West; but eventually there will be no more frontier, and in the meantime Fitzhugh, like most Southerners, is strongly opposed to the Homestead Act, which was intended to relieve such distress as was caused by the panic of 1857, the year when *Cannibals All!* was published, by offering to the settler in the West the use of a tract of the public land, which, at the end of five years' occupation, he could purchase for a nominal fee. This provision was vetoed in 1860 by the South-appeasing President Buchanan and was not passed until 1862 by the Republican administration of Lincoln; and it was regarded by George Fitzhugh as an outrageous and inadmissible device for allowing the preëmption by free soilers, in the interest of the non-slave-holding states, of land which had originally been acquired at the expense of the United States and the disposition of which the Southerners — though they did not have the same spur to migration — had as much right to control as the Northerners.

George Fitzhugh, a spokesman for the South, was in several ways, however, unconventional. It was not necessarily characteristic of Virginia, which did not depend on slavery to the same extent as the cotton states, so wholeheartedly to justify the institution. It is striking that the pre-war Virginians of most intellectual or moral stature, in contrast to the corresponding South Carolinians, were likely to be outspokenly opposed to it. The attitude of John Randolph had been self-contradictory: though he declared himself against slavery on principle and called himself "an ardent *ami des noirs*," he insisted on its constitutionality and opposed the prohibition of the slave trade. Randolph made a will in which he liberated his nearly four hundred slaves, then later on made another ordering that they should be sold — which latter was eventually set aside on the ground that he had no longer been mentally responsible. Other slave-owners liberated their slaves, and in Virginia by the middle of the century there were almost 55,000 free Negroes. Matthew F. Maury, the great oceanographer, wanted to send the Negroes off to Brazil to work at developing the Amazon. Moncure D. Conway, the Unitarian preacher and biographer of Tom Paine, who had been told by his father that slavery was "a doomed institution," first attempted, in an effort to reconcile it with the Declaration of Independence, to convince himself that the Negro was not a human being, but then became an Abolitionist, as a result of which he was driven out of his native town and spent most of the rest of his life in Washington, Massachusetts and England; the Lexington physician, William A. Caruthers, who wrote romantic novels about old Virginia, thought that slavery was not so bad in his native state, where the slaves were "more in the tradition of tenants to their landlords" but that it had become "intolerable" in the Carolinas, where the Negroes were "plantation livestock," and that the institution ought to be got rid of — though not, to be sure, by simply freeing the slaves, since this "would set at defiance all laws for the protection of life, liberty and property, either among them or the whites."

Robert E. Lee himself had always so disapproved of slavery that, on a visit to Baltimore, not long before his death, he complained to a visitor that the Northern press "insisted that the object of the war had been to secure the perpetuation of slavery. On this point he seemed not only indignant but hurt. . . . He declared . . . that he had emancipated most of his slaves years before the war, and had sent to Liberia those who were willing to go"; and reminded his interviewer that the Virginia legislature had come within an ace of abolishing slavery in 1832. "So far," he went on, "from engaging in a war to perpetuate slavery, I am rejoiced that slavery is abolished. I believe it will be greatly for the interests of the South. So fully am I satisfied of this, as regards Virginia especially, *that I would cheerfully have lost all I have lost by the war, and have suffered all I have suffered, to have this object attained.*" And even, as Fitzhugh says, when slavery — in Virginia and elsewhere in the South — had been justified by people of education, it had been usually as "an exceptional institution," with the admission — from Fitzhugh's point of view, hypocritical or merely stupid — that "slavery, in the general and in the abstract, is morally wrong, and against common right." Yet Fitzhugh, though he had seen so much less of the world than Maury or Conway or Caruthers or Lee, had the audacity, on the basis of his desultory reading and his squirely cogitations, to declare in *Cannibals All!* that "if we mean not to repudiate all divine, and almost all human authority in favor of slavery, we must vindicate that institution in the abstract."

In regard to the question of tariff — which had also become a sore issue between the South and the North — his position was quite at variance with the orthodox Southern one. It was held in the South that the Northerners, in maintaining a high tariff on imports from abroad, put the Southerners at a disadvantage by making it difficult for them to buy foreign products and thus keeping them dependent on the goods of the North. The ideal of Fitzhugh, on the contrary, was for the South to develop its own industries, in which event it would have to protect its own products by tariff. It ought not to be dependent upon England any more than upon the North. What was needed — here he partly rejoined the conventional thinking of the South, with its emphasis on regional autonomy — was a cluster of Southern states which would be really in effect small nations. The Union was a league of such nations, adopted for no other purpose than mutual support and defense against menacing foreign enemies, and, "treated as a league or treaty," it may yet have a long and useful existence; but in the meantime the new states and territories were getting out of control of the federal government, and state sovereignty was the thing to encourage. Each one of the Southern states should "condone within its boundaries all the elements of separate independent nationality . . . Each state must not only have within itself good lawyers, doctors and farmers, but also able statesmen, learned philosophers, distinguished artists, skillful mechanics, great authors, and every institution and pursuit that pertain to high civilization." Only so could they supply all those lacks — schools, newspapers, libraries, etc. — of which Olmsted had complained in the South;

only so could they stand up to New England. "Do these things and she [the South] will be rich, enlightened and independent, neglect them and she will become poor, weak and contemptible. Her State Rights doctrines will be derided, and her abstractions scoffed at."

To create a sound civilization it was necessary, needless to say, that property and social tradition should remain in the hands of the same set of families from generation to generation; but Fitzhugh here again departed from the typical ideal of the planter. He does not approve of the rich, who, he says, are "all absentees. Some go off for pleasure, some to religious conventions and associations, some for education and those who remain at home, do so not to spend money and improve the country, but to save it, in order that they too may hereafter visit other regions. The latter are no less absentees, in effect, than the former classes." And such a defecting landlord may be master of "twenty thousand acres of illy cultivated lands and five hundred idle negroes. . . . When farms are too large, they occasion a sparse population, absenteeism of the rich, and a sort of colonial or plantation life." But it must not be supposed, on the other hand, that small farms are a desirable alternative to these: small farms do not promote civilization. "Lands divided minutely, depress all pursuits; for small farms want only coarse and cheap articles, quack doctors, illiterate parsons, and ignorant attorneys." What, then, is the solution? Why, entailed estates of about five hundred acres, with limitations on reducing them by sale. A community of such estates would, presumably, perpetuate the standards and permit the freedom and leisure which are necessary for a highly developed society while at the same time keeping the owner at his post, making it hard for him to leave or neglect it. Now, it happened that Fitzhugh's own place, which had belonged to the family of his wife — described by Moncure Conway as "a rickety old mansion, situated on the fag-end of a once noble estate" — was exactly five hundred acres.

But Fitzhugh's most serious heresy was — consistently with his authoritarian principles — his throwing overboard of the Constitution, the Declaration of Independence and the ideas of Thomas Jefferson. The Declaration itself was all nonsense. "We do not agree with the authors . . . that governments 'derive their just powers from the consent of the governed.' The women, the children, the negroes, and but a few of the non-property holders were consulted, or consented to the Revolution, or the governments that ensued from its success. As to these, the new governments were self-elected despotisms, and the governing class self-elected despots. Those governments originated in force, and have been continued by force. All governments must originate in force, and be continued by force. The very term, government, implies that it is carried on against the consent of the governed." Nor were all men created equal. They were "endowed by their Creator with certain inalienable rights" only in the quite non-Jeffersonian sense that they were entitled, without disturbance, to occupy their proper places of authority or subordination. "We conclude that about nineteen out of every twenty individuals have 'a natural and inalienable right' to be taken care of and protected, to have guardians, trustees, husbands, or masters; in other words, they have a natural and inalienable right to be slaves." We may expect from his refusal to insist on state rights that he will not defend his case by invoking the Constitution; and he was later to call it "the most absurd and contradictory paper ever penned by practical men." He had, in fact, nothing but scorn for constitutions in general. "If government on paper were really useless and harmless, we should say nothing about it. But it is fraught with danger, first because it rarely suits the occasion. Men and societies are endowed by Providence generally with sufficient knowledge and judgment to act correctly or prudently under circumstances as they arise; but they cannot foresee or provide for the future, nor lay down rules for other people's conduct. All platforms, resolutions, bills of rights and constitutions are true in the particular, false in the general. Hence all legislation should be repealable, and those instruments are but laws." As for the Jeffersonian idealism: "The true grandness of Mr. Jefferson was his fitness for revolution. He was the genius of innovation, the architect of ruin, the inaugurator of anarchy. His mission was to pull down, not to build up." He was useful against the British, but otherwise simply a crank — "useless, if not dangerous in quiet times" — who fed his horses on potatoes and recommended that growing boys should be brought up, without schoolmasters, on the philosophy of laissez faire and the morality of Laurence Sterne.

George Fitzhugh's extreme positions, which he went on reiterating interminably in the Richmond *Enquirer* and *De Bow's Review,* gave him a certain intersectional importance and even to some extent affected the course of events. He was invited to visit New Haven after the appearance of *Sociology for the South,* and he lectured there on "The Failure of a Free Society" and listened to a counter-lecture by Wendell Phillips, which he afterwards described as "an eloquent tirade against Church and State, Law and Religion . . . flat treason and blasphemy — nothing else." He was in general horrified by what he regarded as the "infidelity" of New Haven, and when he took the opportunity to visit Gerrit Smith, the wealthy New York State reformer, who had married a

cousin of Fitzhugh's, he found him full of all the "Isms"
— pacifism, vegetarianism, religious nationalism, temperance and women's rights — which he regarded as sympto-
matic of the breakdown of modern society. (The quixotic
Gerrit Smith was four years later to contribute to John
Brown's raid and eight years after this to contribute to
the bail demanded for the release from prison of Jefferson
Davis.) With William Lloyd Garrison, George Fitzhugh exchanged a whole series of polemics, and when
Cannibals All! was published, it is said to have received more attention in the *Liberator* than any other
book ever had. Fitzhugh, in *Cannibals All!*, had made a
point of baiting Garrison, and had quoted from him a
violent passage certainly as extreme and absurd in its
repudiation of government as Fitzhugh had ever been
in the other direction: "Indeed, properly speaking, there
is but one government, and that is not human, but divine;
there is but one law, and that is 'the Higher Law'; there
is but one ruler, and that one is God, 'in whom we live
and move, and have our being.' What is called human
government is usurpation, imposture, demagoguism, pecu-
lation, swindling, and tyranny, more or less, according
to circumstances, and to the intellectual and moral condition of the people. Unquestionably, every existing government on earth is to be overthrown by the growth of mind
and moral regeneration of the masses. Absolutism, limited
monarchy, democracy — all are sustained by the sword;
all are based upon the doctrine, that 'Might makes right';
all are intrinsically inhuman, selfish, clannish, and opposed to a recognition of the brotherhood of man. They
are to liberty, what whiskey, brandy and gin are to
temperance. They belong to the 'Kingdoms of this
World,' and in due time are to be destroyed by the
Brightness of the coming of Him, 'whose right it is to
reign'; and by the erection of a Kingdom which cannot

be shaken. They are not for the people, but make the people their prey; they are hostile to all progress; they resist to the utmost all radical changes. All history shows that Liberty, Humanity, Justice, and Right have ever been in conflict with existing governments, no matter what their theory or form."

But the forcing of the issue by Fitzhugh — as between "free society" and universal slavery — had its most important repercussion in its effect upon Republican campaigning. William Herndon, in a letter to Jesse Weik, the compiler of Herndon's *Life of Lincoln,* explains that Lincoln and he subscribed to the Charleston *Mercury* and the Richmond *Enquirer* as well as to the Northern anti-slavery papers. "Lincoln was well posted on both sides. I had a Southern work called *Sociology* by Fitzhugh, I think. It defended slavery in every way. This aroused the ire of Lincoln more than most pro-slavery books." Later on, at the time of the election of 1856, a pro-Lincoln paper in Illinois reprinted some of Fitzhugh's articles, to provide ammunition against the South by showing to what scandalous lengths its spokesmen were willing to go, and Herndon, for the same purpose, even induced a pro-slavery paper in Springfield to publish one of Fitzhugh's recommendations that whites should be enslaved as well as blacks.

Now, already, in *Sociology for the South,* Fitzhugh had declared that, "Our set of ideas will govern and control after awhile the civilized world." He was to make this more explicit in *Cannibals All!,* in a letter addressed to Horace Greeley: " 'Tis not possible that our two forms of society can long coexist. All Christendom is one republic, has one religion, belongs to one race, and is governed by one public opinion. Social systems, formed on opposite principles, cannot coendure." And he wrote elsewhere: "Two opposing and conflicting forms of soci-

ety *cannot,* among civilized men, coexist and endure.
The one *must* give way, and cease to exist; the other become universal." Now, Lincoln in a letter to Judge
Robertson of the following year, 1855, expresses the
opinion that "Our political problem now is 'Can we, as a
nation, continue together *permanently — forever —* half
slave, and half free?'" But when Lincoln had made his
famous "house divided" speech at Springfield in 1858,
and it had been seconded in Rochester, New York, by
Seward with his "irrepressible conflict," and this idea
had become a *leit motif* throughout the debates with
Douglas, Lincoln explained, in reply to a voice from
the crowd, that neither Seward nor he was "entitled to
the enviable or unenviable distinction of having first
expressed that idea. That same idea was expressed by
the Richmond *Enquirer* in Virginia in 1856; quite two
years before it was expressed by the first of us."

Lincoln thought that the anonymous article in which
this statement appeared had been written by the editor
of the *Enquirer,* but actually it had been written by
Fitzhugh; and when Fitzhugh found the Republicans
echoing him, he was stimulated to further assertion and
added Seward's famous phrase to his repertoire: "There
is an irrepressible conflict of ideas, thoughts, opinions,
philosophies, impending Reformation has run mad, liberty has run into licentiousness. . . . We must raise
the issue of conservatism against anarchy."

The writings of Fitzhugh were pernicious in very
much the same way — though on the opposite side — as
the activities of John Brown. They embarrassed the
moderate Southerners and exacerbated the Northerners
against them. One cannot, in spite of this, refuse a certain respect to a man who argues with consistency so

bold and unconventional a case. But the Fitzhugh of the late fifties and the sixties and seventies — even in that period of swift events, when people often changed their positions — seems to become, in his political articles, too much the all too pliable journalist who, responding to current pressures, contributing opinions from week to week and in Fitzhugh's case often anonymously, soon ceases to expect to be held to account for his previously expressed opinions.*

His earlier ideas about capitalists and socialists underwent startling modifications. At one point he declared that the planters and the capitalists must unite to suppress socialism, which, instead of being destined, as he had said before, to realize the ideal of slavery, was now "the enemy with which we have to contend." By 1869, he had come to believe that the capitalists of the North shared with the Southern slaveholders the great merit of subjecting "the many to the dominion, taxation and exploitation of these few"; and in the meantime he had thought up a way of combining his old assumptions with his new conclusions: it was true that, by promoting competition, the modern capitalist system became the generator of civilization, but, "in densely settled countries," it would reduce its working class to such misery that they would have to be rescued by slavery. Yet he did not recommend any longer that the Southerners should build their own industries. He now believed that they should stick to their agriculture and not be "in haste to become, like Englishmen, shopkeepers, cobblers and common carriers."

* In what follows, I am indebted for most of my quotations from the articles and speeches of Fitzhugh and his editor De Bow to Mr. Harvey Wish's biography, *George Fitzhugh, Propagandist of the Old South* (Louisiana State University Press, 1943), and to an unpublished paper on Fitzhugh by Mr. Mark I. Whitman.

As for the Negro, though in *Cannibals All!* Fitzhugh had rejected as un-Christian and inconsistent with the Biblical account of our common human parentage, the assumption that the black man, because of his race, could have no common footing with the white, he later became converted — in 1861 — to the position maintained by his editor, De Bow, that the Negro could be shown scientifically to belong to an entirely different breed and to be doomed to inferiority. And though Fitzhugh had in 1857 been all against the disruption of the Union and had declared that "a civil war in America would be a potato-rot for Christendom" (that is, as much of a disaster as the potato famine had been in Ireland), he told his audience in a lecture of March, 1860, that "the South must soon have to take care of itself," and returned to his emphasis of *Cannibals All!* on the status of the federal government as "a mere league between small nations, to give them ability to cope with stronger nations. Like all such leagues, it lasts so long as there is a common danger, an outside pressure, and from habit, a little while longer. It is not a government, because it has neither a people nor a territory"; and in February of the following year, on the eve of the war itself, he announced that "Dissolving the union will be attended with little difficulty. *It is a natural operation;* the Union had served its purpose, and expires in gentle euthanasia. The apple is ripe, and drops from its present stem." And though at the time he had written *Sociology for the South,* he had opposed a revival of the slave trade on the ground that it would mean a renewal of cruelty: "hunting and catching Africans like beasts, and then exposing them to the horrors of the middle passage," he later — by 1859 — was supporting a movement for such a revival. He now declared that the rigors of the middle passage were no worse than those of the first settlers in America or of white immigrants, coming here from Europe. His editor, James De Bow, took an even tougher line, and one fears that Fitzhugh, in changing his mind, may have been influenced by the attitude of his chief. "We do not," wrote De Bow, "admit this trade to have less of humanity than other kinds of individual exportation. The foreign immigration trade, the Coolie trade, the Liberia settlement affair, the early conquest of America from the savage, the present reclamation of the backwoods, the opening of Texas and California, the pioneering of Walker [William Walker, the Tennessee adventurer, who filibustered in Mexico and Nicaragua], all have their horrors, their frightful hecatombs of human lives, their violent and coerced sunderings of domestic relations, their crimes, and their groanings. The car of civilization, like that of Juggernaut, demands all this."

Between 1858 and 1860, the slave trade had actually been started again, and — with the usual ghastly results — thousands of Negroes were brought from Africa and smuggled in through the Southern ports. When this was discovered by the federal authorities, the slavers were brought before the federal courts, but no jury in the South would convict them. The sentiment in favor of renewing the trade was denounced by certain prominent Southerners on the ground that it would lead to secession, and that the Union must not be sacrificed. A Whig congressman from Tennessee, declaring that the utterances of George Fitzhugh were doing as much harm to the South as those of any Boston Abolitionist, proposed in the House and carried a resolution condemning any advocacy of a revival of the slave trade as "shocking to the moral sentiment of the enlightened portion of mankind." Fitzhugh had by this time convinced himself that the original purpose of the slave trade had been to convert the heathen and that one had to accept the fact that this could not be accomplished in any other way.

On the eve of the war, when hostilities seemed certain, Fitzhugh decided that war itself was an ennobling and beneficent institution. "Wars seem unnecessary and unnatural, but God, who is wiser than we, has instituted them for salutary purposes, and prompted mankind to prepare for them. . . . The most perfect system of government is to be found in armies, because in them there is least of liberty, and most of order, subordination, and obedience." During the war, Fitzhugh's mansion was shelled, but he and his family had left for Richmond, where he worked in the Treasury Department of the Confederate administration. Even after the defeat of the South, he was continuing, in 1866, to celebrate the salutary effects of war: "The war has purified and elevated our natures, taught us to respect ourselves, and has won for us the respect of foreign nations. . . . War draws men closer together, makes them dependent on each other, allays domestic strife and competition, in a great measure equalizes conditions, banishes selfishness, and makes men live, labor and fight for each other; and continually seeing and feeling their mutual inter-dependence, it begets brotherly love."

He had become, in fact — despite the devastation of the South — so passionately devoted to the idea of war that he now found it rather difficult to discover the merits of peace, and decided that if peace had any merit, it was because it was eventually "needed to repair the damages of war." He served in the Freedmen's Bureau as associate judge of the Freedmen's Court and, while drugging himself with innumerable pipes, felt "pretty much, we suppose," he says, "as Sancho Panza felt while distributing justice in the island of Barretaria." He ran true to his lack of respect for the law by assuming that "our jurisdiction was almost unlimited, and that we were bound by no system of laws, and therefore ought to decide each case according to our notions of right and wrong," and John T. Trowbridge, whose travels in the South have been described in an earlier chapter, was struck, when he visited the Richmond court in which George Fitzhugh was presiding, by what he calls the "admirable directness" with which justice was administered there.

George Fitzhugh before his death did a certain amount of work on another book, which was to deal with his theory of "antinomic pathology." This system — though no evidence exists that Fitzhugh had ever read Hegel — seems to have had something in common with the workings of the Hegelian dialectic. Fitzhugh had picked up from Proudhon the conception of economic and social contradictions, and he combined it with the Newtonian conception of the centrifugal and centripetal forces that govern the heavenly bodies. He applied this conception to the North and the South, Aristotle and Thomas Jefferson, traditionalism and experimentalism. But one could never, he insisted, grasp the basic reality of the conflicts between these antitheses. One could only "follow the promptings of feeling and instinct, and the diverse and shifting lights of human experience." One could sense it when the forces were out of balance, and the "pathology" consisted of a diagnosis and the effort to correct what was wrong, not by taking theoretical measures but by simple empirical remedies. The struggle against a centralized government would continue to be one of these, and the principle of subjection for the Negro was still balanced against free labor of the whites. But by this time George Fitzhugh had come to admit that an able white laborer was superior to a slave, and the issue which he had forced on the opposition of a union all slave or all free had thus been allowed to lapse when his opponents had settled it, at least to the extent of an amendment to the Constitution, in contradiction of Fitzhugh's principles. Dealing with Negroes in the Freedman's Bureau and deciding their problems for them with no fixed policy or appeal to law, he knew that the elements of the situation were not now so much different as they seemed to the North from what they had been before. Fitzhugh's "antinomic" philosophy is a good deal more realistic than his categorically stated alternatives. He had written long ago in *Sociology for the South* that, "Total changes, which revolutions propose, are never wise or practicable, because most of the institutions of every country are adapted to the manners, morals and sentiments of the people. Indeed, the people have been moulded in character by those institutions, and they cannot be torn asunder and others substituted, for none others will fit. Hence reforms result in permanent change and improvement. Revolutions, after a great waste of blood and treasure, leave things soon to return to the 'status quo ante bellum.'" In Fitzhugh's instinctive empiricism is his true, his only wisdom.

William Grayson's defense of slavery derived mainly, then, from his nostalgia for his boyhood, and Fitzhugh's from a patriarchal fantasy which he had elaborated without much real knowledge of the society in which he lived and which he wished to extend to the world. But in the year in which *Cannibals All!* appeared, a sudden and astonishing counterblast came out of North Carolina — "that vale of humility," as the old saying was (at-

tributed to a North Carolinian), "between two mountains of conceit" (Virginia and South Carolina) — which
excited the North and enraged the South. The son of
an illiterate farmer, whose parents had died early and
left him nothing, who had first clerked in a local bookstore, then gone to California in search of gold and
returned, after three years, with nothing to show for it,
Hinton Rowan Helper (originally Helfer: his grandparents had come from Heidelberg) published a book
called *The Impending Crisis* which was a documented
attack on slavery as the economic ruin of the South. In
a previous book on the Gold Rush, he had attempted to
tell, incidentally, of his discovery in the course of his
travels that slave labor was less profitable than free labor
and in Baltimore, where the book was to be published,
he had run into a Maryland statute, dating from 1831,
which made it a felony with a penalty of not less than
ten years in jail knowingly to write or print anything
"having a tendency to excite discontent . . . amongst
the people of color of this state, or of either of the other
states or Territories of the United States." Compelled
to excise these comments, Hinton Helper — an irascible
man — resolved to speak out his whole mind in a book
devoted entirely to this subject. This work, called *The
Impending Crisis of the South: How to Meet It,* turned
out to be almost as difficult to get published in New York
as in Baltimore. Neither Appleton nor Harper's nor Scribner's wanted to risk losing its Southern market, and Helper
was obliged at last to resort to a New York book agent,
who insisted on a guarantee against possible financial loss.
Helper himself went to live in New York. He thought
it quite possible, as he explains in his book, that, if he
continued to stay in the South, he might not merely
"encounter opposition" but "even be subjected to physical

violence" at the hands of the "conceited and cruel oligarchy."*

The Impending Crisis is even today to some extent a usefully informative book. It includes a comprehensive chapter on anti-slavery opinion in the South from Washington, Jefferson and Madison to the author's contemporaries; and a good part of it consists of statistical tables which show, as Olmsted had done, that the slave-owning states of the South had long ago lost their old position and fallen behind the North, as the result of a system which exhausted the soil and reduced the value of property in a reckless and unnecessary way and which, depending as it did on workers who had no interest in efficiency or diligence, could never compete with free labor. It is not at all true, says Helper, that — as George Fitzhugh had tried to believe when he made his expedition to New Haven — "agriculture is not one of the leading and lucrative pursuits of the free states, that the soil there is an uninterrupted barren waste, and that our Northern brethren, having the advantage in nothing except wealth, population, inland and foreign commerce, manufactures, mechanisms, inventions, literature, the arts and sciences, and their concomitant branches of profitable industry, — miserable objects of charity — are dependent on us for the necessaries of life." As for the treatment of the virgin forests: "the difference is simply this: At the North everything is turned to advantage. When a tree is cut down, the main body is sold or used for lumber, railing or paling, the stump for matches and shoepegs, the knees for shipbuilding, and the branches for fuel. At the South everything is either neglected or

---

* For the details of Helper's career, I am indebted to *Southern Sketches, Number 1: Hinton Rowan Helper, Advocate of a "White America,"* by Hugh Talmage Lefler, 1953, Historical Publishing Company, Charlottesville, Virginia.

mismanaged. Whole forests are felled by the ruthless hand of slavery, the trees are cut into logs, rolled into heaps, covered with the limbs and brush, and then burned on the identical soil that gave them birth. The land itself next falls a prey to the fell destroyer, and that which was once a beautiful, fertile and luxuriant woodland, is soon despoiled of all its treasures, and converted into an eye-offending desert." As for the mineralogical resources of the South — in contrast to "the gold and quicksilver of California, the iron and coal of Pennsylvania, the copper of Michigan, the lead of Illinois" and "the salt of New-York" — they have hardly been touched or explored. "The marble and freestone quarries of New England" alone are, "incredible as it may seem . . . far more important sources of revenue than all the subterranean deposits in the slave States." For no one in those states really wants to work. The "freemen regard labor as disgraceful" while the "slaves shrink from it as a burden tyrannically imposed upon them," so "half a million of your population can feel no sympathy with the society in the prosperity of which they are forbidden to participate, and no attachment to a government at whose hands they receive nothing but injustice." He dwells much, like Fitzhugh, on the desirability of developing Southern industries and cities. People say that "Cotton is king," but its products are all manufactured by New England and Old England. "It is carried in their ships, spun in their factories, woven in their looms, insured in their offices, returned again in their own vessels, and with double freight and cost of manufacturing added, purchased by the South at a high premium. Of all the parties engaged or interested in its transportation and manufacture, the South is the only one that does not make a profit. Nor does she, as a general thing, make a profit by producing it."

And in fact almost everything that is used in the South — including food for man and beast — has originally come from the North. He delivers a tirade on this subject: "Reader! would you understand how abjectly slaveholders themselves are enslaved to the products of Northern industry? If you would, fix your mind on a Southern 'gentleman' — a slave-breeder and human-flesh monger, who professes to be a Christian! Observe the routine of his daily life. See him rise in the morning from a Northern bed, and clothe himself in Northern apparel; see him walk across the floor on a Northern carpet, and perform his ablutions out of a Northern ewer and basin. See him uncover a box of Northern powders, and cleanse his teeth with a Northern brush; see him reflecting his physiognomy in a Northern mirror, and arranging his hair with a Northern comb. See him dosing himself with the medicaments of Northern quacks, and perfuming his handkerchief with Northern cologne. See him referring to the time in a Northern watch, and glancing at the news in a Northern gazette. See him and his family sitting in Northern chairs, and singing and praying out of Northern books. See him at the breakfast table, saying grace over a Northern plate, eating with Northern cutlery, and drinking from Northern utensils. See him charmed with the melody of a Northern piano, or musing over the pages of a Northern novel. See him riding to his neighbor's in a Northern carriage, or furrowing his lands with a Northern plow. See him lighting his segar with a Northern match, and flogging his negroes with a Northern lash. See him with Northern pen and ink, writing letters on Northern paper, and sending them away in Northern envelopes, sealed with Northern wax, and impressed with a Northern stamp. Perhaps our Southern 'gentleman' is a merchant; if so, see him at his store, making an unpatriotic use of his time in the miserable traffic of Northern gimcracks and haberdashery; see him when you will, where you will, he is ever surrounded with the industrial products of those whom, in the criminal inconsistency of his heart, he execrates as enemies, yet treats as friends. His labors, his talents, his influence, are all for the North, and not for the South; for the stability of slavery, and for the sake of his own personal aggrandizement, he is willing to sacrifice the dearest interests of his country."

Nor has the South any literature to speak of. We have seen how Kate Stone, the plantation lady, fleeing from the Union armies and inveighing against the North, is reduced to hoping that a friend can send her *Harper's Magazine*, and how the Charleston novelist William Gilmore Simms complained that only Northerners read him. Hinton Helper, by his statistical method applied to the field of publishing, exposes the extreme disproportion between literacy in the North and in the South. *Harper's Monthly Magazine*, he says, has a circulation of two million copies, only twenty per cent of which is in the Southern states; and of the three hundred publishing houses now functioning nine-tenths are in the non-slave states. The Southerners, even in the literature that defends their "patriarchal institution," "have their books printed on Northern paper, with Northern types, by Northern artizans, stitched, bound and made ready for the market by Northern industry; and yet fail to see in all this, as a true philosophical mind *must* see, an overwhelming refutation of their miserable sophisms in behalf of a system against which humanity in all its impulses and aspirations, and civilization in all its activities and triumphs, utter their perpetual protest."

It is all very well for the Southerners to talk about having a literature of their own, but how on earth can they ever have it when, in the first place, the attitude toward plantation labor prevails also in the literary field and leads the more or less well-to-do and educated class to "expect to get talent without paying for it" and to refuse to invest its money in Southern publishing or to support Southern magazines; and when, further — what is of primary importance — so many people cannot read and so many of those who can do not care to. He gives a graduated table of illiteracy from which it appears that in Connecticut, at the top, only one person out of five hundred and sixty-eight was illiterate and that at the bottom, in North Carolina — Helper's own state — the proportion was one to seven. At that time Indiana and Illinois were the only free states whose literacy was surpassed by that of any of the slave states: by two, Louisiana and Maryland.

But among the literate class themselves, no new literature can be created for the reason that the ban on the discussion of slavery has made freedom of the press impossible. "The entire mind of the South either stultifies itself into acquiescence with slavery, succumbs to its authority, or chafes in indignant protest against its monstrous pretensions and outrageous usurpations. A free press is an institution almost unknown at the South." This impediment to free expression has served further to slow up the sluggishness natural to a slave society. "Mental activity — force — enterprise — are requisite to the creation of literature"; but "where free thought is treason, the masses will not long take the trouble of thinking at all. Desuetude begets incompetence — the *dare-not* soon becomes the *cannot*. The mind, thus enslaved, necessarily loses its interests in the processes of other minds; and its tendency is to sink down into absolute stolidity or sottishness. Our remarks find melancholy confirmation in the abject servilism in which multitudes of the non-slave holding whites of the South are involved. In them, ambition, pride, self-respect, hope, seem alike extinct. Their slaveholding fellows are, in some respects, in a still more unhappy condition — helpless, nerveless, ignorant, selfish; yet vain-glorious, self-sufficient and brutal. Are these the chosen architects who are expected to build up 'a purely Southern literature'?" He points out that not only is Simms usually published and mainly read in the North but even the literary executors of Calhoun have had to go to the North for a publisher.

In all this there is apparent, on Helper's part, a militant social bias. He is seething with class resentment. Coming himself from all but the lowest stratum, Helper is arguing the case of what he calls the "non-slaveholding whites," who, he says, though they make up seven-tenths — that is, five million — of the white population of the South, are entirely at the mercy of the 347,000 planters and persons engaged in the commerce in slaves. "The magistrates in the villages, the constables in the districts, the commissioners of the towns, the mayors of the cities, the sheriffs of the counties, the judges of the various courts, the members of the legislatures, the governors of the states, the representatives and senators in Congress — are all slaveholders." "The lords of the lash are not only absolute masters of the blacks, who are bought and sold, and driven about like so many cattle, but they are also the oracles and arbiters of all non-slaveholding whites, whose freedom is merely nominal, and whose unparalleled illiteracy and degradation is purposely and fiendishly perpetuated. How little the 'poor white trash,' the great majority of the Southern people, know of the real condition of the country is, indeed, sadly astonishing. The truth is, they know nothing of public measures, and little of private affairs, except what their imperious masters, the slave-drivers, condescend to tell, and that is but precious little, and even that little, always garbled and one-sided, is never told except in public harangues; for the haughty cavaliers of shackles and handcuffs will not degrade themselves by holding private converse with those who have neither dimes nor hereditary rights in human flesh."

Nor does it matter whether these whites are not "trash" but decent and industrious men. "In the South, unfortunately, no kind of labor is either free or respectable. Every white man who is under the necessity of earning his bread, by the sweat of his brow, or by manual labor, in any capacity, no matter how unassuming in deportment, or exemplary in morals, is treated as if he was a loathsome beast, and shunned with the utmost disdain. His soul may be the very seat of honor and integrity, yet without slaves — himself a slave — he is accounted as nobody, and would be deemed intolerably presumptuous, if he dared to open his mouth, even so wide as to give faint utterance to a three-lettered monosyllable, like yea or nay, in the presence of an august knight of the whip and the lash." And these men are made to serve in local guards for the purpose of protecting against slave revolt a class with whom they have no interests in common.

How, then, should these white men act? Though an individual slaveholder here and there might be moved to liberate his slaves, one had to face the fact that the planter class could no more be expected to abolish slavery than one might "expect to hear highway men clamoring for a universal interdict against travelling." But "Ye are many, they are few." We can unite on the following program: refusal to vote for slaveholders in office; "no affiliation with them in society" (though Helper is to declare a few pages on that "long since, and in the most unjust and cruel manner, have they socially outlawed the non-slaveholders"); complete boycott of slaveholding merchants, doctors, lawyers, ministers of religion, newspapers which support slavery and hotels which are served by slaves; "no more hiring of slaves by non-slaveholders" — a practice which he says is due partly to the foolish prestige attached to having slaves on one's place; a tax of sixty dollars for every slave in a planter's possession between now and Independence Day, 1863 — to be applied to the slaves' transportation to Liberia or Central or South America or to their "comfortable settlement" in the United States, and a fine of forty dollars on every slave kept beyond that date.

The book attracted some attention and sold 13,000 in the year of its publication, but in the spring of 1859 the Republicans took it up, had an abridgment made and circulated a hundred thousand copies. Many more than this were printed later, and the *Crisis* became the most disturbing work contributed to the anti-slavery cause since the publication of *Uncle Tom's Cabin*. In December of 1859, after the hanging of John Brown, when antagonisms had been further exacerbated, the *Crisis* came to figure as a decisive factor in the contest for the speakership of the House of Representatives. The Republican candidate was John Sherman, the General's brother, and he was fiercely opposed by John B. Clark, a Representative from Missouri, on the ground that the candidate from Ohio had commended *The Impending Crisis*. The gentleman from Missouri was supported by Millson of Virginia, who declared that "one who consciously, deliberately, and of purpose lent his name and influence to the propagation of such writings is not only not fit to be speaker, but is not fit to live." The debate went on for two months, and the members on both sides and their friends in the gallery carried pistols and bowie-knives. One of the members from Illinois got to the

point of drawing a gun on an opponent, with the words,
"By God, if I can't talk, I can do something else!" John
Sherman — though he protested he had not read the
book at the time he had expressed his approval of it —
lost the speakership by seven votes. He finally withdrew
his name, and a member from New Jersey was elected.
In the South, it was made a penal offense to read or to
circulate the *Crisis*. In Washington, a boat club requested
the withdrawal of a member who had endorsed the book;
in Baltimore, no "Black Republican or indorser or sup-
porter of the Helper book" was allowed to be a police-
man or to work on the new street railroad; in Virginia, a
farmer was sent to jail for having purchased four copies
of the *Crisis;* in Helper's own North Carolina, ten copies
were publicly burned, one minister was sent to jail and
three others were driven out of their churches for having
the book in their possession; in Arkansas, three men were
hanged.

As in the case of *Uncle Tom's Cabin,* the rebuttals
from the South were prompt. Helper's critics attempted
to show that the statistics of the *Crisis* were juggled, as
in a few cases they seem to have been, to give results
unfavorable to the South — though a good many of the
facts produced had been derived from a report by James
De Bow, Fitzhugh's fierce pro-slavery editor, who had
been superintendent of the Federal census — and that
actually the Southern states were richer and more productive than those of the North. But Helper was vulnerable on other counts. There was a matter of $300 of
which he had robbed the till in the days when he had
clerked in the bookstore. When this was brought up in
the South, Helper answered through Horace Greeley's
New York *Tribune* that he had long ago confessed to
the man who had employed him this old misdemeanor,
committed in his teens, "misled by bad advice, and the

assurance that it was usual with clerks to do so," and that he had paid him back from California. But, according to his own account, he had made almost nothing in the West, and his book on his adventures there was furthermore compromising by reason of its complaints of the effect on the West of the "meddling abolitionists" and an opinion that Nicaragua, which he had visited on his way home, "can never fulfill its destiny until it introduces negro slavery."

It is easy, reading Helper today, to understand why his book made so deep an impression. In contrast to the rambling Fitzhugh, the sensitive and gentlemanly Grayson — repetitious though the *Crisis* is, like so much of this Southern writing — the author sweeps the reader along through his canyons of apparently granite statistics on a stream of exhilarated invective whose directness and outspokenness seem bracing after the sophistries of Southern apologetics. Yet a further acquaintance with Helper and a knowledge of his subsequent career make one realize that already in the *Crisis* he is exhibiting the symptoms of a rabid crank with delusions of persecution. I have summarized his case above in such a way as to show it at its strongest; but one realizes there is something wrong when one reads that "all the pro-slavery slaveholders . . . deserve to be at once reduced to a parallel with the basest criminals that lie fettered within the cells of our public prisons," and that they must be made to pay the difference in dollars between the present value of their lands and the estimated value of these after slavery shall have been abolished: a sum, he insists, of almost four billions, minus the "putative value" of the slaves — which would leave for the reforming beneficiaries $2,333,535,520. When we examine Helper's whole career, we discover that he has always had a grievance, that he was never to succeed anywhere and that he was always to blame society for his failure. He had already denounced the West as a fraud and a sink of iniquity before he turned his fury against the South; and when the slaves have been freed by the war — though he has previously deplored in the *Crisis* the inhumanity with which they were treated — he proceeds to denounce the Negroes. The purpose of his next book, *Nojoque: A Question for a Continent* (No Joke? — I cannot find that the title is anywhere explained by the author), published in 1867, is "frankly and categorically," as he says in his preface, "to write the Negro out of America." "We should," he says, "so far yield to the evident designs and purposes of Providence, as to be both willing and anxious to see the negroes, like the Indians and all other effete dingy-hued races [including all men of mixed blood, and there had been, by a minimum estimate of the census of 1860, 588,000 mulattoes in the United States] gradually exterminated from the face of the whole earth." The Negroes should be sent to Africa or some other remote place. They are quite unfit to live with the whites. With his usual show of documentary evidence and lumping together all the dark-skinned groups as if their various peculiarities were typical of the whole black world, he tries to demonstrate anatomically, part by part, organ by organ — from the meager convolutions of Negro brains and the presence in them of certain brown spots "never found in the brain of a European" to the steatopygous behinds of the Hottentots — that the Negro is physiologically inferior. He then proceeds to two long chapters which deal respectively with "Black: A Thing of Ugliness, Disease," and "White: A Thing of Life, Health, and Beauty," and in which he tries to show that the first of these colors has always been associated with sinister things such as mourning, the Devil, the darkness of night, while the second is associated with the light of day, divine trans-figuration, the beneficent moon and stars, the durability and nobility of marble, the fair complexions of romantic ladies, the costumes of Romans and angels, and the white of the American flag so beautifully combined with blue and red and without ever a touch of the black that has been chosen for the flag of pirates. The next chapter — which runs to over seventy pages, partly made up of lists, is a parade of the great figures in every department who have unquestionably belonged to the white race. Where are the blacks to match them? Next, a chapter on "Spanish and Portuguese America," which shows that this part of the world has been ruined by the Catholic Church and by the use of the Spanish and Portuguese tongues, since, unlike good Protestant English — which the South Americans ought to be speaking instead — these have been deeply polluted by the Catholicism of the Latin peoples; and this leads to a drastic program for the reorganization of humanity, under "Caucasian-blooded" domination, into twenty-one "sovereign and independent nationalities," all republican and with no state religion. *Nojoque* is the book of an exalted racist much madder than George Fitzhugh the "fascist" — as he is nowadays sometimes called — who was, in the old sense, hardly more than maggoty. Was there something of his lower-class German blood in the doctrine of his later years? He reminds one — with his cult of the white man, his congenital ineradicable grievance, the readiness with which he shifts from the attack on his white superiors to establishing his own superiority by assigning the Negro to a lower place — of the Hitler of *Mein Kampf*. If Helper had had a little more practical shrewdness and had appealed to the religious instinct, he might conceivably have founded a movement like Mormonism.

The fantastic *Nojoque* was followed by other similar

works, always heavy with documentation. These books had very little sale. Hinton Helper never had the knack of doing well for himself in any reliable way. Even *The Impending Crisis*, in spite of its wide circulation for purposes of campaign propaganda, had made him very little money. When his penury, in 1861, was brought to the attention of Lincoln, he was given the consulship in Buenos Aires, where he married a rich Argentinian wife and remained for five years. When he resigned, it turned out that he was short in his accounts by something like $6000, but this deficit was expunged by the Grant administration. He devoted the last part of his life to, and wasted a good deal of money on, a project for a railroad to connect the "three Americas." This money had been partly his wife's, and she eventually went back to Argentina.

Yet Helper had always, it would seem, possessed a certain power of imposing himself. That he could still in these last years of failure present an impressive appearance is attested by a correspondent of the Louisville *Courier-Journal*, who saw a good deal of Helper in Washington. He describes him as "a very athletic man, about six feet in height, straight as an arrow, and broad shouldered as a giant, and long armed as Bob McGregor. His face wore the florid complexion of an Englishman, his eyes were sky blue, and his hair as white as cotton, but a vigorous, ivory cotton. His beard was the same. He would have been a distinguished presence in any company, though his physique was suggestive of the coarse. His features were large and heavy, but there was an expression of unmistakable resolution written all over his countenance, and an air of manifest destiny in his every utterance. Every one paid the closest attention to what he said, and all accorded him something very nearly like deference." He now expressed the positive opinion that the reason why "humanity was going to the dogs" was its addiction to novel-reading. "He contended that it was a crime for a teacher to depart from fact in the instruction of youth or for anyone to deal in fancy discourse, written or spoken, with his fellow men." He was evidently convinced that the amassed quotations, the towering lists and the blocks of statistics that made up so large a part of his books established the soundness of the conclusions he drew.

By 1909, when Helper was eighty, he had apparently become quite insane, and he ended by killing himself in a cheap rooming house in Washington, where he had given a false name. When he was last seen alive by his friends, the last thing he had been heard to say was, "there is no justice in this world."

———

To such mental and moral confusion were the thinkers of the South reduced by their efforts to deal rationally with the presence among them of four million kidnapped and enslaved Africans of a different color of skin and on a different cultural level from their own.

XI

ALEXANDER H. STEPHENS

"Fort Warren, Near Boston, Mass., May 27, 1865. — This book was purchased this day of A. J. Hall, Sutler at the Post, by Alexander H. Stephens, a prisoner at the Fort, with a view of preserving in it some regular record of the incidents of his imprisonment and prison life. It may be of interest to himself hereafter, should he be permitted to refer to it; and if his own life should not be spared, it may be of interest to some of his relatives and friends."

So begins one of the most remarkable personal documents of the period of the Civil War: the diary in prison of Alexander H. Stephens, the former Vice-President of the Confederacy.* Like all books about prison, it is dismal, but it is also, like some, heroic. Stephens had been arrested while calmly attending to his correspondence at his home in Crawfordville, Georgia, on May 11, 1865 — "Master! more Yankees have come! a whole heap are in town galloping all about with guns!" — and first taken to Atlanta, where he saw with chagrin, remembering his efforts to prevent the war, the ruins which Sherman had left. Stephens was given his choice of travelling by train or boat to a destination and a fate — perhaps, he thought, execution — of which he was not

* Published in 1910 as *Recollections of Alexander H. Stephens.*

380

told, and he preferred to go by sea. On his way to Augusta by train, he was allowed to stop off at Crawfordville, to collect some clothing and bedding. He had an estate there of a thousand acres, with a mansion called Liberty Hall, and was revered as a statesman and sage. There was a crowd at the depot to say farewell, made up of blacks as well as whites, since he had always been liked by the Negroes; and his friends and his servants wept. From Augusta to Savannah, he was transported on a tug, still waited on by two of his Negro man-servants; but when he changed to a steamer at Hampton Roads, these servants were sent away, and, in company with Judge J. H. Reagan, who had been Postmaster-General of the Confederacy, he was taken to Fort Warren on George's Island in Boston Harbor.

In this fortress Alexander Stephens was imprisoned for four months and nineteen days — May 25 to October 13 — and till almost the end of July was held incommunicado. He was allowed to write letters and send them out, but these had to be cleared by the Governor of New York, and he was always kept in suspense as to when or even whether they had been received. He and Reagan were taken out regularly for walks on the parapets, but separately, in such a way that conversation between them was impossible. Stephens was confined between the "white sepulchral walls" of a cell that was partly underground but which had little windows high in the wall, through which visitors, leaning down, could stare at the captive Confederate. This cell was furnished with a table and chair and a narrow bunk of a bed. It was warmed by a coal grate, but this hardly met the chill of the thick stone blocks of which the floor was made.

Stephens, then fifty-three, had always been extremely frail; though tall, he was very lean, had seldom weighed a hundred pounds. He had suffered, in the course of his life, from more or less disabling attacks of pneumonia, abscess of the liver, bladder stones, kidney trouble, facial neuralgia and migraine; and he had now caught cold on his journey, and his uncertain digestion was taxed by the rather rude prison fare, which seems to have consisted mainly of bacon and beans and tough beef. But he boiled himself tea in a tin cup and was able to buy vegetables from Boston. He had brought with him a bottle of whisky, which the authorities, after some demur, allowed him to keep in his cell, and since he had never, he estimated, in the whole of his life, consumed more than three gallons of liquor, and since he rarely took more than a tablespoonful a day — "I finished with a pretty stiff drink" . . . he writes of one of his dinners, "about two tablespoonfuls" — we find him still drinking it at the end of August. He had to live with his pail of slops and with the stench that arose from the sink; but he was able to buy a wooden bucket from which to bathe. He was humiliated and ill, sometimes wept. It was possible, for all he knew, that he was still to be tried and hanged. "In my judgment," he wrote, "the authorities have no settled purpose. I and the others are held only as political capital out of which they will make the most they can. They have probably not reached any conclusion as to the best market to operate on. We are kept as hostages for the good conduct of our friends and sympathizers at large, and as an example *in terrorem* over them. That is the present political market in which we are speculated upon. When that closes, what new enterprises may open up for bold strikes, time must determine. . . . We are held, as captives were by the old Aztec tribes, to be disposed of in such a way as will most promote the interest of the captors. The main thing is the ransom, the political advantage to follow the disposition determined upon. Little thought or care

about the captives is indulged in. Whether they shall
be graciously set at large, or be piously delivered over
as victims to the eager priest at the public sacrificial
altar, is a matter which depends upon which course
will pay best."

He had read in a Boston paper that "Mr. Davis has
been put in irons at Fortress Monroe. This I deeply
grieve .to learn. Most profoundly do I sympathize with
him in his present condition. Widely as I differed from
him on public policy before and after secession, ruinous
to our cause as I have thought his aims and objects,
much as I attribute the condition of our country to his
errors, yet I do now most deeply pity him and com-
miserate his condition." Stephens and Davis by the end
of the war — for reasons to be later explained — had been
hardly on speaking terms; and Stephens had requested at
Atlanta that he be not made to travel with Davis. They
had, however, been compelled to make the boat-trip together from Augusta to Hampton Roads, and they had
managed to be civil to one another. "Mr. Davis came
out on deck," writes Stephens, "soon after I got up.
It was our first meeting since our parting the night
after my return from Hampton Roads Conference to
Richmond [that is, since his peace talk with Lincoln].
. . . His salutation was not unfriendly, but it was far
from cordial. We passed but few words; these were commonplace." Yet Stephens and his companion Judge
Reagan were to dine every day with the Davises: the
ex-President presided at the head of the table and all remained standing till Mr. and Mrs. Davis were seated.
The parting of Davis and Stephens had been something
more than commonplace: "On my taking leave of Mr.
Davis, he seemed more affected than I had ever seen him.
He said nothing but good-bye, and gave my hand a cordial squeeze; his tone evinced deep feeling and emo-

tion." And the news that reached Stephens now that Davis had been put in chains may well have distressed and disturbed him.

The treatment of the accomplished Mississippian who had accepted rather reluctantly the office of President of the Confederacy — graduate of West Point and veteran of the Black Hawk and Mexican Wars, who had served in both the House and the Senate and as Secretary of War under Pierce — was as harsh, short of execution, as anything that Stephens could have feared. Andrew Johnson only a little while before, on the basis of false information, had announced that Jefferson Davis had been involved in the murder of Lincoln and had offered a reward of $100,000 for his capture. The feeling against him after his capture had been further intensified by the rumors, equally false, that he had tried to get away in a woman's hoopskirt and had carried off the Confederate funds. And there was also the public indignation over the horrors of the Andersonville prison camp, for which the camp commander Wirz had been executed, and for which Davis was ultimately blamed, though, as Stephens was later to argue, they had been due partly to the general lack at that time of medicine and food in the South and partly to the unwillingness of the Union authorities to consent to an exchange of prisoners which would augment the enemy's forces. All the vindictive animosity of the North was now being visited on Davis and — in a way that today suggests Stalinist Russia — also on his wife and the rest of his family. When Mrs. Davis with her sister and four children, one of them a baby, had been separated from Davis at Hampton Roads, they were not allowed to go to Richmond or Charleston in order to be with friends, but had been forced to return in the same ship to Savannah. Their baggage was raided by an officer, who took most of the children's clothes and all of the provisions they had brought with them, giving them hardtack instead, and they had thereafter to run a gauntlet of insult. Men and women came out on tugs to jeer at them from the water, and their cabins were invaded by officers, who did not knock to come in. When the wife of a Confederate Senator who was also believed to have been implicated in the assassination of Lincoln and so had also had a price on his head said, "Gentlemen, do not look in here — it is a ladies' stateroom," one of them threw the door open and replied, "There are no *ladies here!*" — to which the indomitable Southern woman retorted, "There certainly are no gentlemen there."

In the meantime, Jefferson Davis — consigned to Fortress Monroe, which was itself surrounded by a wide moat and guarded by seventy men — had been locked in a casemate with only one aperture, made impenetrable with iron bars, and two armed sentinels inside his prison that paced back and forth night and day; yet as soon as he was incarcerated, two blacksmiths appeared, with an, it must be said, reluctant officer, to rivet shackles and a chain on his ankles. Davis, a high-strung and high-spirited man, declared that he was a soldier and a gentleman, stood with his back to the wall and said, "Let your men shoot me at once." One of the smiths stooped down to put on the irons, and Davis knocked him over. The blacksmith threatened Davis with his hammer, but the officer intervened and summoned a reinforcement. Four men held the prisoner down while the shackles were fastened upon him. He had already been ill when captured and was weak and emaciated, and the leg-irons immobilized him completely. He could only pull the blanket over them.

This story was given to the newspapers, where it was read by Varina Davis as well as by Alexander Stephens.

Mrs. Davis was not allowed to leave Savannah and was constantly watched by detectives. Most of her money had been taken away, so she was not able to stay in a hotel but huddled with her children in a rented room. The baby had the whooping-cough, and when she let the other children go out, they were ragged by the Federal soldiers, who told them that their father had "stolen eight millions," put them up to stealing apples from fruit-stands and made the two-year-old boy sing, "We'll hang Jeff Davis to a sour-apple-tree," one of the stanzas of *John Brown's Body* — the effect of which constant baiting was to make him declare himself a Yankee. Two ladies from Maine tried to whip him, but somebody came to his rescue.

The prison doctor at Fortress Monroe was afraid that Davis would die. He prevailed on the commanding officer to have the leg-irons removed at the end of five days and to allow the prisoner a daily outing; but this officer, a low-grade young man of twenty-six, who referred to Davis as "Jeff," either was a natural sadist or hoped that severity would win him promotion. It afterwards appeared that it was his own idea to put leg-irons on his prisoner, and he now for a year tormented him in every possible way. He would forget or neglect till it was almost night to take him for walks on the ramparts, and when he did so would needle him in various ways. He took away all but a minimum of Davis's clothes, suppressed letters and gifts from his family, would at first allow him nothing but the Bible to read and later only papers that denounced the South. The casemate was dark and damp; a light was always kept burning, and this with the tramping and talk of the guards — he was never let alone for a moment — made it almost impossible for the prisoner to sleep. Nor could he eat; he came out with erysipelas. Devoured by bedbugs, of which he had had no experience, he thought that this was a skin-disease, too. His wife was not allowed to see him till he had been in prison a year, when she had reason to believe that her husband was dying and got Johnson to let her visit him. The doctor, who feared again for the prisoner's life, gave her a letter to this effect. Hugh Mac-Culloch, Johnson's Secretary of the Treasury, was sent to investigate the situation, and the brutal young officer was now removed, and the prisoner given more freedom.

Mrs. Davis went to the President, who received her reluctantly and told her that he could not do anything for her husband: "We must wait, our hope is to mollify the public toward him." Why, then, Mrs. Davis asked, did the President not deny his proclamation that her husband had been implicated in the murder of Lincoln? By this time it was perfectly well known that the man who had produced the evidence against Davis and other Southern leaders was a professional suborner of perjury who had been paid by the Bureau of Military Justice for testimony as unconvincing as any brought into court at the Moscow trials, and the President admitted to Varina Davis that he had never believed in this evidence, but explained that, a Southerner himself, under fire from the Radical Republicans for his supposed excessive leniency to the South, he could not now afford to defend the ex-President of the Confederacy against even such a false charge as this. He did not say that he had himself been accused by the same aggressive group of Republicans of having engineered the murder of Lincoln in order to succeed to the Presidency, nor that he always expressed the opinion that a few of the top men of the Confederacy ought to be executed as a deterrent example. Having risen like Helper from the nether stratum of the country people of North Carolina, he was prejudiced against the planters. He declined to pardon the former landowner because Davis was too proud to plead for clemency, which he held would imply an admission of guilt. He demanded to be tried for the charges against him; but the government, in its very weak position, would not allow the matter to be brought into court. The second year of Davis's imprisonment was not nearly so bad as the first, and at the end of it the embarrassed authorities, influenced by the decency of Grant, who so disliked to see people humiliated, allowed him to be liberated on the bail which was offered by two old Abolitionists, Horace Greeley and Gerrit Smith.

When Alexander Stephens, in Fort Warren, had learned what was happening to Davis, he was evidently much depressed. "Got from sutler, Greeley's *American Conflict*. Read it till time to put out lights, nine-thirty," he writes; but the next day: "Sunday — the horrors of imprisonment, close confinement, no one to see or to talk to, with the reflection of being cut off for I know not how long — perhaps forever — from communication with dear ones at home, are beyond description. Words utterly forsook me. O God, if it be possible, let this cup pass from me! Yet Thy will be done."

For Stephens the greatest of hardships was to be separated from his half-brother Linton. Alexander was eleven years older than Linton. His mother had died when he was only a month old, and her successor, his stepmother, had died when Alexander was fourteen and her own son Linton three. They lost their father in the same year, and Alexander, who first worked on an uncle's farm, then taught school and practised law, had paid for Linton's schooling and, when he himself came of age, had legally adopted his half-brother. Their grandfather Stephens, a Jacobite, had come over in 1746, when the Stuart Young Pretender was defeated at Culloden, and the tradition of tenacity to a hopeless cause was to contribute perhaps to the steadfastness with which both the brothers were to stick, after the defeat of the South, to their political principles. This grandfather, after whom Alexander was named, had fought, besides, in the Revolution. Their father had been a schoolmaster, and both the sons had vigorous intellects and a stern sense of public duty. In the case of Alexander, his moral force, his ratiocinative passion, were stimulated by physical weakness to extraordinary feats of assertion, of endurance, of inspired longevity. In February, 1851, at the time when he is representing Georgia in the House, we find him writing as follows to Linton: "Man's life is but a dreary pilgrimage through an inhospitable clime. . . . Sometimes I have thought of all men I was most miserable — That I was particularly doomed to misfortune, to melancholy, to sorrow and grief — That my pathway of life was not only over the same mountains and heaths and deserts with others but that an evil genius was . . . following at my side and forever mocking and grinning and making those places which in the lives of others are most happy . . . most miserable. No it is useless — The misery — the deep agony of spirit and soul I have suffered no mortal on earth knows. . . . The torture of body is severe. . . . But all these are slight when compared with the pangs of an offended or wounded spirit. . . . I am tempted to tell you a secret — It is the secret of my life. . . . The secret of my life has been *revenge*. . . . Not revenge in the usual acceptation of that term — But a determination to war over against fate — To meet the world in all its forces, to master evil with good. . . . My greatest courage has been drawn from the deepest despair! . . . I have often had my whole soul instantly aroused with the fury of a lion and the ambition of a Cæsar by . . . as *slight* a thing as a *look!* Oh what have

I suffered from a look! What have I suffered from the tone of a remark . . . from a supposed injury? an intended injury? But each . . . such pang was the friction that brought out the latent fires. . . ."

Mrs. Jefferson Davis, in writing of the ascendancy of Alexander Stephens over that other Southern leader, the magnificent and trumpeting Robert Toombs, as she had known them in the forties in Washington, describes him as "not small, but he looked so from the shortness of his body. The shape of his head was unpolished and immature. His arms were disproportionately long, and his beardless, wrinkled face gave him the look of one born out of season. His eyes were clear hazel, and had a fine, critical, deliberate expression that commanded attention. His voice was thin, and piercing like a woman's, but there the resemblance ended. His was a virile mind sustained by an inflexible will; and, in all matters of importance, Mr. Toombs came up, in the end, on Mr. Stephens's side." Though in certain ways so different in temperament from these other politicians of Georgia, who were likely to be blustering and overblown, he could show himself sensitive on matters of honor to the point of provoking a quarrel. When he was told that a local judge, who disapproved of Stephens's policy in Washington, had called him a political traitor, Stephens was not content, on meeting this man at a Whig rally, to accept his opponent's denial but declared that, if it *had* been true, he would have slapped the Democrat's face. The latter, goaded on by the taunts of gossip, wrote Stephens and demanded a retraction, to which Stephens merely replied that the remark had been contingent. When the two men met later by chance on the piazza of an Atlanta hotel, the judge did call Stephens a traitor, and Stephens hit him across the face with his cane. The judge attacked with a knife, and Stephens snatched away an umbrella which his opponent was holding in his other hand and tried to defend himself; but the judge, who weighed three hundred pounds, threw himself upon Stephens and knocked him down, and stabbed him between the ribs, crying, "Now, damn you, retract or I'll cut your damned throat!" "No, never! Cut!" cried Stephens. He caught the knife as it was aimed at his throat and managed to get to his feet. He was eventually rescued by the spectators, but by this time his hand had been so badly cut and he was losing so much blood from a severed artery that it was thought he could never live; yet he recovered, as he always did from his apparently shattering disasters and ailments.

The physical handicaps of Stephens seem also to have impeded his relations with women. There is evidence that he sometimes admired certain ladies to the verge, if not beyond it, of passion, and he was able to exercise upon them the attraction that such dedicated men sometimes do; but he was either incapacitated for marriage or — discouraged by his invalidism — self-condemned to a lifelong privation. His capacity for affection was great, and he seems to have found objects that could satisfy it fully in Linton and Linton's family. But especially in Linton — he once said that he knew that there was a strong element of the feminine in his character; he had guided his half-brother's career, and Linton had lived up to his hopes. Like Alexander, Linton had studied law, and he had sat in the state legislature; afterwards he had served in the United States Senate. But in other ways he supplemented Alexander. In the photographs of the half-brothers, we see that they both had sharp and lively eyes and firm faces of a certain nobility. But where Alexander is somewhat withdrawn and skeletal, Linton is outgoing, well-fleshed and obviously full of a charm that perhaps has a shade of the rakish. The younger Stephens

was married twice (he had suffered tortures of guilt
after the death of his first wife in childbirth) and, unlike
the fragile Alexander, he had been able to serve in the
war. The relationship between the half-brothers was intimate and became indispensable to both. They talked
everything over together, and when they were not near
enough to meet they wrote long letters to one another.
It was only Alexander's imprisonment that, by inter-
rupting his intercourse with Linton, had driven him to
keeping a diary. He continually fretted and grieved
about these broken communications. It was worse, perhaps, than being cut off from a wife, for Linton was his
younger lieutenant, his companion-in-arms in politics.
He was almost a lobe of Alexander's brain.

But the self-sufficient first citizen of Crawfordville,
squire and scholar and Vice-President of the Confederacy,
repressed his tormenting anxieties, presented his complaints with dignity and accepted his fate like a philosopher. When he learned that a Proclamation of Amnesty
and Pardon had been made by Andrew Johnson at the
end of May, he wrote to the President requesting parole
in accordance with the terms of a proviso "that special
application might be made . . . for pardon by any person belonging to the excepted classes." When ten days
later he read in the paper — a statement which proved
untrue — that the President would agree to pardon him
on condition that he leave the country, he wrote in his
journal: "I will not accept pardon on those terms. I am
willing to die if I cannot return to my home and be
with Linton while our joint lives last. As for dreading
trial for treason, or its consequences, I care but little.
My conscience is void of offense toward God and man.
I should feel no shame in being executed for anything
I have done; and if I cannot be permitted to spend the
balance of my days at home, with the dear ones there,

in my farm, in my gardens, orchards, and vineyards, and amongst my books, then let me die, even on the gallows though it be." The Confederate generals had all been paroled; a politician who had advocated secession when Stephens was still opposing it had just been appointed Provisional Governor of South Carolina, and others had been pardoned or paroled. But Stephens received no reply, and on June 29 he wrote again, withdrawing his appeal to the President and asking to be put on trial if any charge was to be brought against him. He quoted the Constitution, which provided that no person should "be deprived of life, liberty, or property without due process of law."

But, in the meantime, Alexander Stephens had settled down to the solitude and silence — the latter broken only by the guns and the bugles — to read Cicero, the Bible (the New Testament in Greek), Prescott's histories and Bacon's essays, Silvio Pellico's book on his prisons, Burns and Coleridge and the first series of Matthew Arnold's *Essays in Criticism,* just published and sent him by a lady in Boston, of which he found the morality dubious; and to comment upon them in his diary. He reads the Boston papers intently, trying to make out, behind the meager news, what is really going on in Washington. He is courteous and friendly toward everyone — though the lieutenant who guards him on his walks will shake hands with him only at the end of two months. He offers to teach the orderly Latin and advises him to study law. He sings a hymn on arising every morning. He reflects on his relations with the bedbugs and mice:

"Since my last big row with bedbugs, I have made it a business every day or two to search for and break them up. I have just been at this work of self-preservation.

"As for my mouse, I have never, since the instance given, got a sight of it. But I have kept up my dropping of crumbs; they disappear when I am out or when my eyes are off the spot; I suppose the little creature is about but keeps close, not knowing that I would not hurt it. It may see from its hiding-place, what I do with the chinches, and draw conclusions which prompt it to keep out of my power. I have often felt sorry for what I have to do to these blood-suckers. Most willingly would I turn them loose and let them go away if they would go and stay, but this they will not do. Between them and me, therefore, there is 'an irrepressible conflict.' Either I or they must be extinguished. This seems to be fixed in the laws of our nature. I am sorry it is so, but so it is. Toward the mouse I feel very much as Burns expressed himself to one in his day:

> I doubt na, whyles, but thou may thieve;
> What then? Poor beastie, thou maun live;
> A daimen icker in a thrave
>   'S a sma' request;
> I'll get a blessin' wi' the lave,
>   And never miss 't.

Not so with these vermin that feed on my blood. Of that I have not a drop to spare without missing it, to say nothing of the torture of having it sucked out as they do it. I would willingly let them alone if they would let me alone, and I would even contribute something to their support and sustenance. But to live and let live is not in accordance with the laws or their existence. Hence they justly bring their death upon themselves."

He was transferred on August 20 — by the order of President Johnson, whom Linton had been to see — to a larger room higher up, and was allowed to receive visitors. At last — on September 1 — Linton arrives at the fort and stays in the prison with him. "Sunday Sept. 3. — After midnight, the fever I had had all day passed off.

Read in Ezra. Linton read me portions of this journal. He read the first pages yesterday. To-day, he read on from where he left off yesterday. When he got to the second day's imprisonment here, I told him to stop. It made me sad. For some cause, his emotions overpowered him and he wept aloud. I, too, wept, but told him not to grieve. It was all over I hoped. I had suffered greatly, but did not now. The doctor called soon; called again before noon, and again this evening. Linton and I spent the day in talking. How pleasant a day it was to me!"

Alexander Stephens and Reagan were released on October 12, under a general order from Washington, and they left the fort the next day. The Stephenses spent a few days in Boston, where many people came to see them. Alexander Stephens and Reagan went out for a night to Topsfield, where they were entertained by a millionaire, who, says Stephens, "had large interests in the South and may lose a good deal there. . . . All the persons I saw or met on this trip, common people and all, seemed delighted to see me out of prison." But in the meantime his hair had grown white.

But the most important passages in Alexander Stephens's diary are those that are written in justification of his policy in connection with the war. He cast them sometimes in the form of imaginary dialogues with an old Georgian lawyer friend, and these must have suggested to him the larger-scale dialogues which make up the full apologia to which Stephens addressed himself almost immediately after his release. The complete title of this apologia is *A Constitutional View of the Late War Between the States; Its Causes, Character, Conduct and Results Presented in a Series of Colloquies at Liberty Hall.* It came out in two huge volumes — in 1867 and

1870 — and it runs, exclusive of its indices, to 1455 pages. The first volume, by the beginning of November, 1870, had sold over 67,000 copies, and it excited a certain amount of controversy; but when the readers discovered that what they were being given by the former Vice-President of the Confederacy did not consist of inside revelations of the official affairs of the Confederacy — which were more or less mysterious to Northerners and to the Southerners a subject of impassioned debate — but was a work of political philosophy, in which the whole history of the United States from the Declaration of Independence on was methodically reviewed and analyzed, with no gossip and no picturesque narrative, they were not so eager for the second volume, and this did not do nearly so well. This was quite incomprehensible to Stephens, who blamed its lack of success on his publisher. He inhabited too high an intellectual sphere even to think about popular appeal. The eloquence of his early speeches is considerably sobered here, and he aims to be accurate and lucid, without heat to explain and persuade; but, in doing so, he quite fails to take into account the convenience of the ordinary reader: he argues his case step by step through an impossible succession of dialogues on the scale, if not with the subtlety, of the longest Platonic ones.

These dialogues take place between Stephens himself and a set of three imaginary Unionists, of whom he insists, however, that they are typical of three categories of Northerners who have come to see him at Liberty Hall. The Unionists are Judge Bynum of Massachusetts, who represents the Radical wing of the Republicans; Professor Norton of Connecticut, who represents the Conservative wing; and Major Heister of Pennsylvania, who represents what were called the War Democrats. The Professor, the Judge and the Major are allowed to ex-

press themselves, to counter the statements of Stephens
with their Unionist versions of recent events, and these
versions with Stephens's rebuttals — since they are not
all Aunt Sallies set up by the author but actual legends
accepted in the North — have their interest in illustrating
the readiness with which the partisans in any conflict
come to falsify the actualities; but these Unionists are
always outtalked and outargued by the master of Liberty
Hall, who is unanswerably able to show that their notions
of what has been happening have been derived from
incorrect information, and to compel them to admit their
mistakes. Stephens spares neither them nor the reader
in the thoroughness of his documentation. He reads
them long passages from old speeches and from the proceedings of the *Congressional Record,* and he adds no
less than twenty-six appendices, which include more
speeches, given *in toto,* the Declaration of Independence,
the Articles of Confederation, the Constitution of the
United States, the text of Supreme Court decisions and
of legislative resolutions, letters on public matters, the
documents of the Southern surrender and the complete
words of *Maryland! My Maryland!* The book thus becomes much too long: it is not only overdocumented but
repetitious. The *Constitutional View* is — in form as well
as in format — too unwieldy to be easily read. When you
see the same argument unfolding again, you skip to
the end of the paragraph, or even through several pages.
You wonder that none of Stephens's Northern guests
ever interrupts his long expositions with, "Yes, yes:
you have made that point." Their host is unfailingly
friendly in the best tradition of Southern courtesy, and
he is punctilious in dropping politics in the intervals between the colloquies, when he is "doing the honors of
the table" or taking them for country drives; but as soon
as these reprieves are over, they must all be herded back

to the library and made to listen again to the merciless old ideologue. We sympathize with the Radical Judge Bynum, at the end of the fourteenth session, when the host says, "We will, if you please, return to [these matters] after a little rest and refreshment," adding, "Well, Judge, what say you to an iced lemonade for us, while the Major and the Professor indulge in something stronger, if they prefer?" The Judge unexpectedly replies — unexpectedly, since he is supposed to be a blue-nosed New Englander — that he, too, is ready for something stronger (though it is evident that Stephens the author means that Stephens the Socratic interlocutor has so shaken the Judge by his arguments that he now feels the need of a drink in order to keep up his morale).

Nor could Stephens resign himself to rest his case when he had published his gigantic book. He added to it in 1872 a "supplement" called *The Reviewers Reviewed,* in which he answered in the same systematic way the attacks or dissents of his critics; and he included in this collection not merely his own replies but his opponents' replies to these, his "rejoinders" to these rebuttals, "surrejoinders" to his "rejoinders" and refutations by Stephens of the "surrejoinders." He relentlessly reprints long extracts from the *Constitutional View* and repeats the old demonstrations; no opponent is allowed the last word.

Yet throughout these years of passionate debating, the master of Liberty Hall is continually in very bad health; he becomes more and more of an invalid. Since prison he has complained that he is always fatigued: "I can hardly walk about." He accomplishes his prodigies of literary production on coffee and chicken wings. At the time that he was working on the second volume of the *Constitutional View,* he was crippled by a serious accident — an injury to his hip, on which a heavy iron gate had fallen — and he was never to be able to walk without

crutches again; yet he survived still for fourteen years and
retained almost to the end the full vigor of his tireless intellect. He even lived to publish, in 1882, the year before his death, *A Comprehensive and Popular History of
the United States,* an expansion to over a thousand
double-columned pages of a school history written ten
years earlier. (Its bulk is, to be sure, partly due to the
inclusion of many illustrations and of long excerpts from
a Northern historian that deal with the military events
of the War, in which Stephens had never been very
much interested and which he was willing now to leave
to the outargued opponent whose success had been
merely on the battlefield.) In this history, he restates
his position, and he ends with his invariable moral,
which has become the burden of all his work and with
which we must presently deal.

Stephens's history has been quite forgotten, but his
great work, the *Constitutional View,* has endured as a
great, cold, old monument which few people have cared
to visit but which no one has succeeded in demolishing.
Bound in calf, with black strips for the titles, it resembles an old-fashioned law book, and it has remained in
the libraries of Southern homes, never touched and
often deep in dust, as a sustaining reassuring presence,
as if it were an authority that could always be summoned
to provide legal justification for the action of the Southern Confederacy and the attitude it has left behind it.
When one tackles the *View,* however, one finds it a
work of much interest, which may provoke today a
franker sympathy on the part of the Northern reader
than any Northerner could admit to at the time it was
written. One is tempted at first to imagine that the book
might not have so been lost sight of, that it might have
been respected as a classic, if it had been cast in the
form of a tract, closely argued, incisive, emphatic; but

then one remembers that, at the time it was written, such a tract could have had no function: the war was over, the South was beaten, the forensic give and take was finished. Such a defense, which took so lofty a tone, could hardly sway public policy — even to modify the despotism of Reconstruction — as the utterances of Calhoun and Stephens's own had once been able to do. It had to stand as a monument or nothing: a compendium, a packed repository, even a mausoleum perhaps, but a mausoleum some day to be opened. It had to contain — to be found there, laid away by the last traditionalist of the eighteenth-century South — The Declaration of Independence and all the rest; even the words of *Maryland! My Maryland!,* which have had to be disregarded or which substitutes have had to be found for when the song has been sung in the North: "The despot's heel is on thy shore . . . Avenge the patriotic gore that flecked the streets of Baltimore . . . Dear Mother, burst the tyrant's chain . . . Virginia should not call in vain . . . *She* needs her sisters on the plain — '*Sic semper,*' 'tis the proud refrain . . . That baffles minions back amain . . . Arise, in majesty again, Maryland! My Maryland!"

This lyric had been composed — like the *Battle Hymn of The Republic,* in an outburst of emotion in the middle of the night — by James R. Randall, a young man from Baltimore, then tutor in a Louisiana Creole school, on hearing of the wounding of a classmate when, in April, 1861, the Sixth Massachusetts regiment had, while marching through the Baltimore streets, been attacked by and had fired on a crowd. The metrical pattern of *Maryland! My Maryland!* had evidently been taken over from a poem called *The Karamanian Exile* by the Irish poet James Clarence Maugan, which Randall had just read; but it was fitted — by way of *Lauriger Horatius,* an American college song — to the melody of the old German Christ-

mas carol *Tannenbaum, O Tannenbaum* by a young
lady of Baltimore, who sang it to Beauregard's Maryland
troops; and the solemnly rejoicing old tune had been
turned by the memory of that anguish, first defiant and
afterwards helpless, into something sweet, brave and
sad, so that even the *"Sic semper tyrannis!"* echoed by
Booth when he jumped from the box in which he had
murdered Lincoln takes its place in a pathetic perspective.
With Stephens, the song becomes a kind of hymn that
consecrates the sealing of the tomb.

And now, what is Stephens's philosophy of government and what is the "invariable moral," of which I
have spoken above, to which his arguments always lead
him? One should begin by explaining that the Vice-
President of the Confederacy had a somewhat eighteenth-
century mentality and a kinship with the French political
theorists of the revolutionary period and after, who aimed
at the construction of a perfect society. In the modern
sense, Alexander Stephens is not at all historically
minded. He makes comparisons with ancient societies, as
everyone after Montesquieu did; but for him the great
"principles" are always the same: he puts as an epigraph
on his title-page the statement that "Times change and
men often change with them, but principles never!" At
the beginning of the long discussion in the *Constitutional
View,* Judge Bynum declares that his principles are
founded upon "the impregnable position of Truth, Justice and Right," and Stephens replies that, "Our ideas of
Truth, Justice and Right, in political as well as social
matters, and all the relations of life, depend very much
upon circumstances. This seems to be owing partly to the
infirmities of human nature. There ought, however, to be
no difference between intelligent minds as to Truth,
which rests simply and entirely upon matters of fact; but,

in practical life, there are great and wide differences, even on this, owing to a disagreement or a different understanding of the facts merely."

The implication is that, once the facts are established, the correct principles follow. These principles unarguably lead one to the republican form of government, and — Stephens's conception of the Union is the same as that of Fitzhugh — where several republican units have come into existence side by side, it may, under certain circumstances, prove convenient for these to form an alliance. This was what had occurred when the colonies were breaking away from Great Britain: they simply made a combination against her; they were not opposing a centralized government to another centralized government. The states were all sovereign powers and they never, in their agreements among themselves, surrendered their sovereignties as states. This is shown very clearly in the language of the Declaration of Independence of 1776, in which the United Colonies are referred to not as a state but as "free and independent states"; of the Articles of Confederation of 1778, in which it is said that "Each State retains its sovereignty, freedom and independence, and every Power, Jurisdiction and right, which is not by this confederation expressly delegated to the united states, in congress assembled"; and of the treaty with Great Britain of 1783, in which "His Britannic Majesty acknowledges" the thirteen units "to be free, Sovereign and Independent States." The omission of any mention of sovereignty in the Constitution of 1787 does not mean that the states had surrendered it: this silence must imply, on the contrary, that state sovereignty was taken for granted; and in an amendment it was afterwards made clear that "The powers not delegated to the United States by the Constitution, nor prohibited by it to the States, are reserved to the States, respectively, or to the people." These powers, insists Stephens, are meant to include sovereignty, "which is the source of all powers, those delegated as well as those re served." And this sovereignty of the states is guaranteed by the provision in the Constitution itself that "no meas ure can be passed, no law can be enacted, if a majority of the States oppose it." "But, no sirs! This is not a Gov ernment of the People of this country as one Nation." Why, then, asks Professor Norton, does the Constitution begin by saying, "We the People of the United States, in order to form a more perfect Union," etc.? It would have been incorrect, answers Stephens, to enumerate all the states at a time when Rhode Island and North Carolina had not yet ratified the Constitution. It was better to say "We the people," which could stand for those states which had ratified it already and could also include those who might ratify it later. "Is there any such thing," then, asks Stephens, "as citizenship of the United States, apart from citizenship of a particular State or Territory of the United States? To me it seems most clearly that there is not. We are all citizens of par ticular States, Territories, or Districts of the United States, and thereby only, citizens of the United States." What about naturalized foreigners? asks Bynum. Their situation, says Stephens, is the same as that of everyone else, except that, in the case of foreigners, the states have agreed to make uniform rules — the same in all the states — by which foreigners may be permitted to become citi zens of the several states or territories.

In defending this view, the intrepid Stephens has to wrestle with some formidable opponents: Supreme Court Justice Story, the historian John Motley, Daniel Webster, Horace Greeley. The crisis over Nullification in 1833 is analyzed at enormous length. The theory of the right of any state, in its capacity as a sovereign power, to

nullify any law that it held to be unconstitutional had
been formulated first by Calhoun in 1831, in connection
with the protective tariff which was thought to discriminate against the planters. A tariff bill put through
Congress in the summer of 1832 provoked in November
an ordinance passed by South Carolina in a special
convention, declaring this Act "null and void, and no
law, nor binding upon this State, its officers and citizens."
The President, Andrew Jackson, retorted, at the beginning of the following year, with a Force Bill which
should give him the power "to use the land and naval
forces for suppressing any resistance to the execution
of the revenue laws too powerful to be overcome by the
civil officers of the general Government." This bill was
signed on March 2, but in the meantime a compromise
tariff bill, which removed the objections of the South, had
been put through by Henry Clay, and it was signed on
the same day as the Force Bill, so that a resort to arms
was averted.

Stephens gives us almost a hundred pages of the debates at this time between Calhoun and Webster. The
fundamental question is whether the Constitution is to
be regarded — as Calhoun claims it must be — as a compact between sovereign states or as an overall national
government that may tax individuals "in any mode and
to any extent," that may demand of them military service
and that may punish them for treason against that government. It is possible for Webster to cite to his purpose
the minutes of the constitutional convention of 1785,
which records a resolution to the effect "that a National
Government ought to be established, consisting of a
Supreme Legislature, Judiciary and Executive." The
phrase "National Government" was, to be sure — as
Webster admits — altered to "Government of the United
States," as a compromise with those representatives who

wanted to call it a "Confederation"; but "the substance of this resolution was retained." To this Calhoun could reply that Jefferson, in his Resolutions for the Legislature of Kentucky of 1798, begins with *"Resolved,* that the several States composing the United States of America, are not united on the principle of unlimited submission to their General government; but that by Compact under the style and title of a Constitution for the United States, and of amendments thereto, they constituted a General Government for special purposes," etc.; and he is able to point out that Webster, in an earlier speech of 1830, had followed the language of Jefferson and referred to the "Constitutional Compact." What is useful in all this is that Stephens brings out as no Northerner at that point would have done the uncertainty of the meaning of the "United States," and the wavering between different interpretations which took place under varying pressures. We see also how the two conceptions become more and more explicit and partisan, and more and more antagonistic — till it has come to seem to Stephens "a conflict, fierce and bitter . . . for seventy years . . . between those who were for maintaining the Federal character of the Government, and those who were for centralizing all power in the Federal Head. . . . It was a conflict between the true supporters of the Federal Union of States established by the Constitution, and those whose object was to overthrow this Union of States established by the Constitution, and by usurpations to erect a National Consolidation in its stead."

If Calhoun and Stephens are right, any one of the American states was as free to detach itself from the Union as any member of a European alliance to decline to renew a treaty. If it had been possible for eleven states to withdraw from the Confederation of 1788, which had been declared to be "perpetual," and "enter into the new Union . . . leaving North Carolina and Rhode Island out . . . why," Stephens asks, "could not the same eleven, or any other eleven, in 1861, just as rightfully withdraw from the Union of 1788, which was not declared to be perpetual?" There was no question of "Insurrection or Rebellion, or even Civil War in any proper sense of the terms." The proper description of the conflict — since these states were sovereign powers — was the War between the States, as one would speak of a war between the old Balkan countries or the South American republics. And the states, by reason of their sovereignty, could exercise, each within its own jurisdiction, the right of eminent domain. Fort Sumter was within the jurisdiction of the State of South Carolina, and although the fort itself belonged partly to the other states, it had been built for the protection of South Carolina, and once she had withdrawn the powers that had been delegated to the federal government, it would no longer, in the hands of that government, be serving South Carolinian interests, so, on payment of a "just compensation," she could perfectly well demand to possess it. In the same way, the Negroes were the property of their masters. The right to hold property in slaves was provided for by the Constitution, which recognized the obligation on the part of the non-slaveholding states, though they might themselves have laws against slavery, to return, upon the "Claim" of his master, any "Person held to Service or Labour," if he escaped from a slaveholding state; and this had been reinforced, under pressure of the Southern States, by the Fugitive Slave Law of 1850, which deprived any Negro who claimed to have been freed of the right to a trial by jury; which imposed a heavy penalty on anyone who impeded the arrest of a fugitive or who hid him or helped him to escape; and which put a premium on catching fugitives by providing for a $10 payment to the commissioners in charge of arresting them if they issued a certificate of ownership to the person who claimed the slave and only $5 if his claim was not recognized. But the officials of non-slave-holding states had been unwilling to comply with this law. They had even, as in the case of Vermont, passed laws that ran counter to it, by which it was attempted to rule that former slaves who might enter those states should be free; and the Governors of Ohio, New York and Maine had, in certain cases, openly refused to deliver up runaway slaves. Since the governments of these Northern states had thus violated the Constitution, it was they who were the rebels, not the Southerners; it was they who had offered the provocation – so why should not the South, then, withdraw from a compact which the other party no longer honored?

The institution of slavery, however, does require some special justification in Stephens's ideal system. This justification is, first, the familiar argument that slavery is sanctioned by the Bible, in both the Old Testament and the New. Abraham and Isaac and Jacob and all the rest of the patriarchs were slaveholders. Job was "a large slaveholder," and "certainly one of the best men we read of in the Bible." Jesus has nothing to say against slavery, any more than Moses does. And did not Paul send the runaway slave Onesimus – after converting him to the Christian faith – back to his master Philemon? Lincoln had once answered this argument, a favorite one in the South, by pointing out that if the Bible was to be used for precedents, the defenders of Negro slavery ought to advocate white slavery, too. Now, Alexander Stephens, to be sure, does not accept this logical next step as George Fitzhugh had done; but he does not have the slightest difficulty in passing from Paul and the patriarchs to the assumption that the Negro race is so much inferior to the white that it ought to be subordinate to it. There is a hierarchy among human beings which is based on natural differences, and these differences have been ordained by God. It had sometimes happened that the men of the Confederacy had expressed themselves on this subject before the War in a sense that was somewhat inconsistent with the line they took after secession. We find John Esten Cooke, for example, in his novel *The Virginia Comedians,* published in 1854, making one of his pre-Revolutionary characters refer to Negro slavery as one of the hateful burdens that England had imposed on the colonists: "She cursed us with this race of Africans who are eating us up and ruining us, and some day, in the blind convulsions of her rage, she will taunt us bitterly for asking what we do not grant ourselves — for demanding freedom, when our arms are holding down a race human as ourselves!" (It was true that, as Jefferson Davis insists in *The Rise and Fall of the Confederacy,* Virginia had done her best as early as 1761 to prevent the importation of slaves but had been overruled by the Crown, and that South Carolina and Georgia had made similar unsuccessful attempts to avoid being inundated with Africans.) And so Stephens, in 1846, brooding on the iniquities of the human race — "the baseness, the meanness and brutality that abound everywhere" — had asked himself how it was possible that man could "turn upon his own species . . . and make beasts of burden of them."

But after the War, when he is writing the *View,* he has come to accept the relation between white master and Negro servant as something inherent in nature, which may well remain forever unchangeable. This relation has, however, Stephens now asserts, never really been describable as slavery: "What was called Slavery amongst us, was but a legal subordination of the African to the

Caucasian race. This relation was so regulated by law as to promote, according to the intent and design of the system, the best interests of both races, the Black as well as the White, the Inferior as well as the Superior. Both had rights secured, and both had duties imposed. It was a system of reciprocal service, and mutual bonds."

Stephens's recent biographer, Mr. Rudolph von Abele, believes that his opinions on this subject may well have been affected, between these two utterances, by his acquisition of slaves for his own estate. He had bought his first slave, a man, in 1841, and the next year, a woman and two children. In 1850, he had thirteen slaves; in 1860, thirty-two. He says in the *Recollections* that he believes he has owned "about thirty-five." In his acceptance of the status of the Negro, Stephens had had, however, certain reservations. "Education was denied," he wrote in his prison diary. "This was a wrong that I condemned. Many things connected with it did not meet my approval but excited my disgust, abhorrence and detestation." But, he adds, "the same I may say of things connected with the best institutions in the best communities in which my lot has been cast." And this theorist of the perfect system for organizing human beings in relation to one another must admit a precarious element introduced by our relation to God. It is not, he says, the institution of slavery itself for which the South has been punished but the abuse of this institution: "I looked on the institution recognized amongst us by our laws . . . as sanctioned by God, yet I thought great wrongs had been perpetrated under it; as with all human institutions in accordance with the sanction of the Creator, there were reciprocal duties and obligations . . ."; but "the Negro had been made to perform his part of the obligation while the white man had failed to fully perform his: this was, in my judgment, one of the great sins for which our people were brought to trial."

Yet in his speech of retirement from Congress in 1859, he had assured his Georgia constituents that "African slavery rests upon principles that can never be successfully assailed by reason or argument. . . ." There follows an extraordinary vision in which the servitude of the Negro is represented as one of the "immutable features of the harmony and order of the universe: I, too believe in the 'higher law' [Seward, in his public speeches, had invoked against slavery a higher law] — the law of the Creator, as manifested in his works and his revelation. Upon this, our cause eminently rests. I claim nothing barely upon the ground that 'thus it is nominated in the bond.' I recognize to the fullest extent, the doctrine that all human laws and constitutions must be founded upon the Divine law. And if there is any right secured, or any obligation imposed in our constitution, inconsistent with this law, underlieing and overruling all others, such right and such obligation must be yielded. I would not swear to support any constitution inconsistent with this higher law. Let us not deceive ourselves — this question has to be grasped and comprehended in all its vast dimensions — on it, we need not be orators so much as thinkers, nor declaimers so much as reasoners. We must stand on the higher law, as well as upon the constitution. The latter must be subordinate to the former. But as I read the inscriptions upon the canvass of the universe about us and around us, and over us, as well as the teachings of inspiration, 'Order is nature's first law'; with it, come graduation and subordination; this principle extends from the throne of the Creator to the utmost limits of his works. We see it in the heavens above — in the greater and lesser lights — in the stars that differ from each other in magnitude and lustre; we see it in the earth below — in the vegetable and animal kingdoms — ranging from the stateliest trees of the forest to the rudest mosses and ferns. From the magnolia grandiflora gloriosa, the rose, and the japonica, down to the most uncouth flower we tread under foot — from the hugest monsters of life in the air, on the land, or in the ocean, to the smallest *animalcule* to be found in them all. We see similar distinctions and gradations in the races of men — from the highest to the lowest type. These are mysteries in creation which are not for us to explain. It is enough to know that they work out in a grand harmony through the whole; and that in our system of government, which, in my judgement, is the best in the world, we do but conform to these immutable principles of nature. Who, then, is warring against the higher law? We who conform to it, or those who are striving to reverse the decrees of the Almighty?

"In politics and morals, as in mechanics, it is impossible to war successfully against principle. The principle will ultimately prevail. The wickedest of all follies, and the absurdest of all crusades, are those which attempt to make things equal which God in his wisdom has made unequal. It is a struggle against a principle which can never succeed, where reason has sway, until 'the leopard can change his spots and the Ethiopian his skin.'"

From the moment this man of principles has established a principle that makes slavery obligatory, every step of the course of the South follows logically from his previous postulates. He reviews the Missouri Compromise of 1820, which legalized the owning of slaves below the line of 36°30', and the Kansas-Nebraska Bill of 1854, which did away with this convenient demarcation and made the holding of slaves in the newly created territories dependent on a popular vote. Stephens himself, who represented Georgia in the House from 1834 to 1859, had succeeded, by resorting to an adroit device, in getting this measure put through when it had been held up for months by debate; and he blames the bloody brawling that followed entirely on the Abolitionists who had subsidized John Brown and contributed to the Emigrant Aid Societies. Again, all the trouble had been made by the North.

When Lincoln was elected President and many Georgians were ready for secession on the ground that the government was now dominated by a man whom they believed to be hostile to their interests, Stephens had done his best to discourage them, and, in January, 1861, he had attempted to hold up the Ordinance of Secession; when it went through in spite of his efforts, he felt, however, that he had to sign it. He was chosen then as one of the delegates to the Congress of Seceded States, but he did not want to go and did his best to refuse: his extremely individualistic "principles" almost never coincided with popular opinion or the policy of any group. In the present situation, says von Abele, he "was in a position, it seemed to him, of extreme impotence"; and "he allowed himself to be persuaded . . . only after the convention had pledged the delegates to organize a permanent government for the seceded states on the basis of the old Constitution" — of which he repeatedly said that it represented the best government the world had known. This reluctance to take part in the Congress is one of a number of matters on which — minimizing his differences with his colleagues — he does not touch in the *Constitutional View*. He goes on now to tell how the Commissioners from the seven seceded states were sent on to confer with Washington; how they received no reply from a note which they addressed to

Secretary Seward, but were told by Supreme Court Justice John A. Campbell, a Unionist from Alabama, who acted as an intermediary between the Commissioners and Seward, that he, Campbell, "felt entire confidence that Fort Sumter will be evacuated in the next few days" and "that no measure changing the existing *status,* prejudiciously to the Southern Confederate States, is at present contemplated." The Commissioners were given to understand that the fort would be evacuated within ten days, but after more than ten days had elapsed, they got a telegram from General Beauregard telling them that the fort was still occupied and that Major Anderson was making repairs. They reported this to Judge Campbell, who assured them "that the failure to evacuate Sumter was not the result of bad faith." They then learned that a relief squadron had sailed from New York and again appealed to Judge Campbell, who received a message from Seward saying, "Faith as to Sumter fully kept — wait and see." But this was April 7, when the fleet had already been sent "for the purpose of provisioning and reinforcing Fort Sumter 'peaceably,' if permitted; 'otherwise by force.'" On the ninth, the Commissioners addressed to Seward an indignant and reproachful note: "'Your Government has not chosen to meet the undersigned, in the conciliatory and peaceful spirit in which they are commissioned. . . . Had you met these issues with the frankness and manliness with which the undersigned were instructed to present them to you and treat them, the undersigned had not now the melancholy duty to return home and tell their Government and their countrymen, that their earnest and ceaseless efforts in behalf of peace had been futile, and that the Government of the United States meant to subjugate them by force of arms.'" The attack on Fort Sumter followed. Stephens believes that Lincoln, in the course of these negotiations, had changed his mind about evacuating Sumter, but he declares that this "can in no way excuse or palliate the duplicity and fraud practiced afterwards on the Confederate Commissioners."

This is how the affair looked to Stephens, and it is important, if we would understand the Civil War, to know that the Southerners have a very good case for regarding the Northerners as treacherous aggressors. In popular opinion in both the North and the South — the kind of catchword version of history, derived from no other reading than textbooks studied in school, which was satirized for the British in 1066 and All That — it is believed by either side that it was first attacked by the other. We now know that the newspaper stories which alarmed the Southern Commissioners were in some cases inaccurate reports of what was actually happening in Washington; that the ships sent by Lincoln to Fort Sumter, though they carried troops as well as supplies, had been ordered to resort to arms only if the South Carolinians should attempt to prevent provisioning. We know that the inconsistency between the steps that were eventually taken and the assurances that had been given the Commissioners was due to a conflict of policy between Seward's determination to avoid hostilities and Lincoln's growing conviction, under pressure of various forces, that Fort Sumter would have to be held — though, since Virginia had not yet decided on secession, it was still possible for him to hope to avert this by conceding the evacuation. The whole story of these confused and decisive days has just been told — with much new documentation — in the chapter of Allan Nevins's *The War for the Union* called *Contest for Power: Seward and Lincoln*. Besides making the points above, the historian shows that if the messages from Seward were misleading to the Southern Commissioners, the Southerners were themselves something less than ingenuous in encouraging the impression that a conciliatory policy on the part of Washington would bring back to the Union the seceded states. Yet, given the Southerners' conviction of their right to withdraw from the Union, they could claim, as Stephens does, that they had been attacked, that an effort was being made to coerce them into submission to such a strongly centralized government as they had never accepted or contemplated.

This fear of the centralized state, of the empire which is no longer a federation, as the eventual product of Unionist policy is one of the principal themes of the writings of Alexander Stephens, and it gives the *Constitutional View* a certain importance which is not merely that of a plea for a lost cause. "What may be called a Union," cries Stephens at the close of his Volume I, "may spring from the common ruins, but it would not be the Union of the Constitution! — the Union of States! By whatever name it might be called, whether Union, Nation, Kingdom, or any thing else, according to the taste of its dupes or its devotees, it would, in reality, be nothing but that deformed and hideous Monster which rises from the decomposing elements of dead States, the world over, and which is well known by the friends of Constitutional Liberty, everywhere, as the Demon of Centralism, Absolutism, Despotism! This is the necessary reality of that result, whether the Imperial Powers be seized and wielded by the hands of many, of few, or of one!"

From the moment of the relief of Fort Sumter, almost every measure that Lincoln takes is for Stephens a step in the direction of despotism: conscription, the suspension of habeas corpus, searches and seizures without warrant, the suppression of free speech. He reminds his Unionist opponents of the arrest and imprisonment in

Baltimore of the Mayor and the municipal officials, as well as of many other citizens, with no formal charges against them, and the incarceration for months in Fort Lafayette, with no charge and no hearing, of "Ex-Governor Charles S. Morehead, the lifelong personal and political friend of Henry Clay, as well as one of the most devoted adherents to the Union under the Constitution who ever lived, who was arrested at his residence near Louisville, for nothing but his denunciations of the flagrant usurpations of the Washington Authorities." He reminds them of the boast of Seward reported by the British Minister to Washington: " 'I can touch a bell on my right hand and order the arrest of a citizen of Ohio. I can touch the bell again and order the arrest of a citizen of New York. Can Queen Victoria do as much?' He well knew that she could not, and that no Crowned Head in Europe, not even the Czar of Russia, could do more!"* Lincoln's calling for seventy-five thousand men to suppress the "insurrectionary combinations" was itself an unconstitutional act, since Congress had by that time adjourned, and a war could not be declared without the approval of Congress. The Emancipation Proclamation was also unconstitutional, since the powers assigned to the President were executive not legislative, and the proclamation was really an edict — to say nothing of the fact that the Constitution still guaranteed the right to own slaves. This latter was followed two days later (January 3, 1863) by an edict of martial law, which created, "by Imperial orders through the War Department," "a new class of officers under military commission for the execution of this high-handed measure, unknown to the laws and the Constitution."

* One is reminded of the boast attributed to Robert Moses, New York Commissioner of Parks and head of the New York State Power Authority: "I can take your house away from you and arrest you for trespassing if you try to go back to it."

It is possible also for Stephens to demonstrate that these actions of Lincoln's — even apart from recalcitrant New York State — were in some quarters unpopular in New England itself by citing the objections of Benjamin R. Curtis, a former United States Supreme Court Justice of Boston, who can hardly be suspected of pro-Southern sentiment, since he had resigned from the Court in protest against the Dred Scott decision and was afterwards one of the defense counsel in the impeachment trial of Andrew Johnson. Justice Curtis, though a follower of Story and Webster, had expressed himself strongly in a public address, which was circulated afterwards as a pamphlet:

"No citizen," Curtis declared, "can be insensible to the vast importance of the late Proclamations and Orders of the President of the United States. . . . It has been attempted by some partisan journals to raise the cry of 'disloyalty' against anyone who should question these Executive acts. But the people of the United States know that loyalty is not subserviency to a man, or to a Party, or to the opinions of newspapers; but that it is an honest and wise devotion to the safety and welfare of our country, and to the great principles which our Constitution of Government embodies, by which alone that safety and welfare can be secured. And when those principles are put in jeopardy, every true loyal man must interpose according to his ability, or be an unfaithful citizen. This is not a Government of men. It is a Government of laws. . . . I do not propose to discuss the question whether the first of these Proclamations of the President, if definitively adopted, can have any practical effect on the unhappy race of persons to whom it refers; nor what its practical consequences would be, upon them and upon the white population of the United States, if it should take effect, nor through what scenes of bloodshed, and worse than bloodshed, it may be, we should advance to those final conditions; nor even the lawfulness, in any Christian or civilized sense, of the use of such means to attain *any* end.

"If the entire social condition of nine millions of people has, in the providence of God, been allowed to depend upon the Executive decree of one man, it will be the most stupendous fact which the history of the race has exhibited. But, for myself, I do not yet perceive that this vast responsibility is placed upon the President of the United States. I do not yet see that it depends upon his Executive decree, whether a servile war shall be invoked to help twenty millions of the white race to assert the rightful authority of the Constitution and the laws of their country, over those who refuse to obey them. *But I do see that this Proclamation* asserts the power of the Executive to make such a decree! . . .

"The second Proclamation, and the Orders of the Secretary of War, which follow it, place every citizen of the United States under the direct military command and control of the President. They declare and define new offences not known to any law of the United States. They subject all citizens to be imprisoned upon a military order, at the pleasure of the President, when, where, and so long as he, or whoever is acting for him, may choose. They hold the citizen to trial before a Military Commission appointed by the President, or his representative, for such acts or omissions as the President may think proper to decree to the offences; and they subject him to such punishment as such Military Commission may be pleased to inflict. They create new offices, in such number, and whose occupants are to receive such compensation, as the President may direct; and the holders of these offices, scattered through the States, but with one chief inquisitor at Washington, are to inspect and report upon the loyalty of the citizens, with a view to the above described proceedings against them, when deemed suitable by the central authority. . . .

"It must be obvious to the meanest capacity, that if the President of the United States has an *implied* Constitutional right, as Commander-in-Chief of the Army and Navy in time of war, to disregard any one positive prohibition of the Constitution, or to exercise any one power not delegated to the United States by the Constitution, because, in his judgement, he may thereby 'best subdue the enemy,' he has the same right, for the same reason, to disregard each and every provision of the Constitution, and to exercise all power, *needful, in his opinion* to enable him 'best to subdue the enemy.' "

But the powers of the President are "executive merely. He cannot make a law. He cannot repeal one. He can only execute the laws. He can neither make, nor suspend, nor alter them. He cannot even make an article of war. He may govern the army, either by general or special orders, but only in subordination to the Constitution and laws of the United States, and the Articles of War enacted by the Legislative power.

"The time has certainly come when the people of the United States *must* understand, and *must* apply those great rules of Civil Liberty, which have been arrived at by the self-devoted efforts of thought and action of their ancestors, during seven hundred years of struggle against arbitrary power."

Stephens adds that at the fall elections of 1862, "The Centralists . . . lost the great State of New York," and that "Pennsylvania, New Jersey, Ohio, Indiana, and Illinois gave strong indications that a majority of their people were in full sympathy with the sentiments of Judge Curtis." (It may be noted that Charles Francis Adams the elder had been of the same opinion as Curtis.

"The President's proclamation," he said, "as well as most of the plans of reconstruction of the state authorities which were offered in Congress seem to me to rest upon a mistaken idea of the powers vested by the Constitution. As President, Mr. Lincoln unquestionably had no power to emancipate a single slave. Neither had Congress the smallest right in my mind to meddle with the reconstruction of a single state.")

A discussion of the character of Lincoln, whom Stephens had known in Congress, is one of the most interesting things in the *View*. One can come to understand well enough from other Southern sources why the South regarded Lincoln as a bloody tyrant and even why Booth should have wanted to kill him; but Stephens is too philosophical for hateful and railing rancor. He can see how the passion of expanding power may communicate itself to a public official and compel him to impose this power in a way that he had never expected and be responsible for rigors and brutalities that did not seem to be in his nature. As a corrective to the immense amount of mush that has been written about Lincoln in the North, it is useful to read the reflections of Stephens. Professor Norton, in Colloquy XXI, is made to express surprise at his host's severe judgment of the late President: "I always understood that you entertained for him not only a good opinion, but even high regard. Besides the rumor to which I referred of his having offered you a place in his Cabinet, I know in a way that gives me full assurance of the fact, that he frequently expressed himself as entertaining for you sentiments not only of kindness, but of the highest esteem. . . . I do not see how you could entertain sentiments of esteem towards one, whom you look upon as a public usurper — disre-

garding his oath, and even wanting in humanity. . . .
I always considered Mr. Lincoln, whatever may have been
the defects of his character, and no one is exempt from
defects of some sort or other, as eminently distinguished
for his frankness, good nature and general kindness of
heart." "So were many men," answers Stephens, "who
have figured in history, and who have brought the greatest sufferings and miseries upon mankind. Danton and
Robespierre, the bloodiest monsters in the form of men
we read of in history, were distinguished for the same
qualities. They both had the personal esteem as well as
the strong attachment of some of the best men in France,
who were utterly opposed to their public acts and
policy. . . .

"A man may possess many amiable qualities in private
life — many estimable virtues and excellencies of character, and yet in official position commit errors involving
not only most unjustifiable usurpations of power, but
such as rise to high crimes against society and against
humanity. This, too, may be done most conscientiously
and with the best intentions. This, at least, is my
opinion on that subject. The history of the world abounds
with apt instances for illustration. Mr. Lincoln, you say,
was kind-hearted. In this, I fully agree. No man I ever
knew was more so, but the same was true of Julius
Cæsar. All you have said of Mr. Lincoln's good qualities,
and a great deal more on the same line, may be truly said
of Cæsar. He was certainly esteemed by many of the
best men of his day for some of the highest qualities
which dignify and ennoble human nature. He was a
thorough scholar, a profound philosopher, an accomplished orator, and one of the most gifted, as well as
polished writers of the age, in which he lived. No man
ever had more devoted personal friends, and justly so,
too, than he had. And yet, notwithstanding all these

distinguishing, amiable and high qualities of his private character, he is by the general consent of mankind looked upon as the destroyer of the liberties of Rome!

"The case of Cæsar illustrates to some extent my view both of the private character of Mr. Lincoln, and of his public acts. In what I have said of him, I have been speaking only of his official acts — of their immediate effects and ultimate tendencies. I do not think that he intended to overthrow the Institutions of the country. I do not think he understood them or the tendencies of his acts upon them." And there follows the illuminating passage quoted by Francis Grierson: "The Union with him in sentiment, rose to the sublimity of a religious mysticism; while his ideas of its structure and formation in logic, rested upon nothing but the subtleties of a sophism! His many private virtues and excellencies of head and heart, I did esteem. Many of them had my admiration. In nothing I have said, or may say, was it, or will it be my intention to detract from these. In all such cases in estimating character, we must discriminate between the man in private life, and the man in public office. The two spheres somehow, and strangely enough too, appear to be totally different, and men in them, respectively, usually seem to be prompted and governed by motives totally different. Power generally seems to change and transform the characters of those invested with it. Hence, the great necessity for 'those chains' in the Constitution, to bind all Rulers and men in authority, spoken of by Mr. Jefferson."

One remembers this passage in connection with the chapter in Allan Nevins's *The War for the Union* to which I have referred above. As one follows the fluctuations of policy between Lincoln's inauguration on March 4 and his sending on April 6 of the relief expeditions to Forts Sumter and Pickens, one can trace step by step the stimuli which impelled this melancholy and humorous man, whose ambition had led him to the Presidency, to become an implacable war president. There were the threat of resignation from the Cabinet of the Postmaster-General Montgomery Blair (though he seems to have been the only member who was opposed to surrendering the forts), who told him that a failure to stand up to the Southerners would give them confidence and make the situation worse; the blast administered on a visit to Washington by Montgomery Blair's father Francis, a veteran politician, who told Lincoln that he would run the danger of being impeached on the ground of treason — both contributing, no doubt, to a fear of incurring the charge of weakness just after he had taken office — the unanimity of sentiment, on the occasion of a recent Republican caucus, in favor of relieving Fort Sumter and a crystallization of opinion revealed at a meeting of the Cabinet that had taken place on March 9. Immediately after this meeting, the President gave orders for ships to be got ready — though he cherished still the bare possibility that the expedition might be withheld if that would prevent Virginia from joining the seceded states. The next day, says Mr. Nevins, Lincoln "had a bad sick-headache," and, as Mrs. Lincoln put it, for the first time in years "keeled over." The process of transformation which filled Stephens with horror had now begun.

The "Monster," as he calls it, that Stephens fears is "the Demon of Centralism, Absolutism, Despotism"; and the warning against the danger of this is the burden of all his post-war writing. Here is a passage from the peroration of the *Constitutional View*. "It affords me pleasure," he declares to his guests, "to say, in winding up, that, while in our long and social interchange of views, and discussions of the various questions

. . . in which we here occasionally so widely differed upon some points, yet upon one we are at last all so fully agreed; and that is, in our abhorrence of anything like Imperialism in this Country! Perfect agreement on this point is the more agreeable to me, because this presents the only real *living issue* of paramount importance before the Peoples of the several States. The great vital question now is: Shall the Federal Government be arrested in its progress, and be brought back to original principles, or shall it be permitted to go on in its present tendencies and rapid strides, until it reaches complete Consolidation!

"Depend upon it, there is no difference between Consolidation and Empire; no difference between Centralism and Imperialism. The consummation of either must necessarily end in the overthrow of Liberty and the establishment of Despotism. . . . But without further speculation upon this subject or any other, let me, in conclusion, barely add: If the worst is to befall us; if our most serious apprehensions and gloomiest forebodings as to the future, in this respect, are to be realized; if Centralism is ultimately to prevail; if our entire system of free Institutions as established by our common ancestors is to be subverted, and an Empire is to be established in their stead; if that is to be the last scene in the great tragic drama now being enacted: then, be assured, that we of the South will be acquitted, not only in our own consciences, but by the judgement of mankind, of all responsibility for so terrible a catastrophe, and from all the guilt of so great a crime against humanity!"

And here is the peroration to his history of the United States: "Now, therefore, that the chief cause which led to the late war between them is forever removed, if they shall adhere to the principle of the sovereign right of local self-government, on the part of the States respectively, which lies at the foundation of the whole fabric, then there is no perceived reason why they should not go on in a still higher career in all that constitutes true greatness in human development and achievement. But if this principle shall be abandoned, then all that is so glorious in the past and so hopeful in the future will, sooner or later, be lost in the same inevitable despotism of a Consolidated Centralized Empire, which eventuated in the overthrow and destruction of the liberties of Rome."

If you should assume that Stephens's case against Lincoln as the founder of a centralized state is a mere piece of partisan rationalizing, you would greatly mistake Stephens's character and underestimate the force of his "principles." He had resisted the "despotism" of Jefferson Davis as uncompromisingly as he had that of Lincoln, and this had put him in a very queer position. It was obvious that if the Confederacy was really to stand up to the Federal Government, it would have to have recourse to Lincoln's methods, to organize an efficient machine and accept a wartime discipline; but the Southerners did not care for discipline and, unlike the industrial North, they were not used to organization. They were fighting for state rights, and they were not willing to sacrifice these even to their own central government. And none was more intransigent than Stephens himself. He had opposed, as he tells his guests, "the impressment of provisions at arbitrary prices — the suspension of the Writ of *Habeas Corpus,* and the raising of the necessary military forces by conscription. These last I considered not only radically wrong in principle, but as violative of the Constitution, and as exceedingly injurious to our Cause in their effects upon the people." Major Heister, the War Democrat of the dialogues, expresses surprise at this, and remarks that he had "thought it was

generally conceded that this prompt and judicious measure [conscription] was what actually saved Richmond in
1862, and sustained the Cause as long as it was." Not a
bit of it, Stephens retorts: the great battles that prevented the taking of Richmond were fought mostly by
volunteers; and almost all the deserters were conscripts.
Stephens had, it was true, been obliged, in the long run,
to accept the suspension of habeas corpus, but even when
this measure was being put through, he did his best to
reduce it to nullity by insisting that "this by no means
interferes with the administration of justice so far as to
deprive any party arrested of his right to a speedy and
public trial by a jury after indictment, etc. It does not
lessen or weaken the right of such party to redress for an
illegal arrest. It does not authorize arrests except upon
oath or affirmation upon probable cause." In a speech
of November 1, 1862, he is reported to have closed with
the exhortation, "Away with the idea of getting independence first, and looking after liberty afterward. Our
liberties, once lost, may be lost forever." When in December, 1864, the Confederacy was near defeat, and it was
necessary to pass a new bill to renew the suspension of
habeas corpus, Stephens still fought it tooth and nail
and, when he lost, walked out of the Senate, over which,
as Vice-President, he had to preside, intending to resign
his office.

In the meantime, in his resistance to martial law,
Stephens had replied to the mayor of Atlanta, whom
the military had appointed its civil governor and who
had written for directions in regard to his duties: "The
truth is your office is unknown to the law. General Bragg
had no more authority for appointing you civil governor
of Atlanta, than I had; and I had, or have, no more
authority than any street-walker in your city. Under his
appointment, therefore, you can rightfully exercise no

more power than if the appointment had been made by a street-walker." And the Vice-President of the Confederacy, with his close ally Governor Joseph E. Brown of Georgia, who maintained himself four terms in office, deliberately practised throughout the war a systematic sabotage against Jefferson Davis's demands for troops. Brown would not allow the Richmond government to accept volunteers from Georgia but insisted on its applying to him, and he tried, though the armies were inadequately equipped, to prevent Georgia soldiers from taking arms out of the state as well as to require that twelve-month volunteers who were not going to reënlist be allowed to bring their arms back home with them; and he claimed that he, the Governor, and not Davis's Secretary of War had the right to commission officers. Stephens and his half-brother and Governor Brown disapproved of Richmond's conduct of the war, and Alexander, in letters to Linton, expressed himself so strongly on the subject that he took the precaution of mailing them with no signature and no return address. At one point the Vice-President of the Confederacy did not visit Richmond for a year and a half. Hence his difficult relations with Davis.

At the end of December, 1864, Francis P. Blair the elder — one of the founders of the Republican party and one of those who had brought pressure on Lincoln not to abandon Fort Sumter — asked permission of Jefferson Davis to come to Richmond for an unofficial interview. This took place on January 12. Lincoln had not only not authorized Blair to speak for him but had avoided seeing him before he left, and Blair admitted to Davis that the suggestions he was about to make "were perhaps merely the dreams of an old man." He proposed that the

Confederacy and the United States should give over
their conflict with one another and unite in the common
purpose of expelling Maximilian and the French from
Mexico — an exploit which may today seem chimerical
but which had already, before Sumter was fired on, been
suggested by Secretary Seward as a possible device for
averting war. Blair also told Jefferson Davis that Lincoln
was now being pressed by the Radicals in Congress who
wanted to humiliate and ruin the South, by reducing it
to the status of a conquered nation, and that he, Blair,
thought the time had come when the President would
be ready to negotiate peace. Lincoln did indeed, when
Blair had returned, signify through the latter to Davis
his willingness to talk with a peace commission, and the
President of the Confederacy sent Alexander Stephens
and two others. On January 30–31, Lincoln, accompanied by Seward, conferred with them at Fort Monroe.
This episode is described at length in the *Constitutional
View,* and Stephens also gives an interesting description
of the impression made upon him by Grant, whom he
met when he first arrived. He says that he was disappointed, but that this "disappointment . . . was in every
respect favorable and agreeable. I was instantly struck
with the great simplicity and perfect naturalness of his
manners, and the entire absence of every thing like
affectation, show, or even the usual military air or *mien* of
men in his position. He was plainly attired, sitting in a
log-cabin, busily writing on a small table, by a Kerosene
lamp. It was night when we arrived. There was nothing
in his appearance or surroundings which indicated his
official rank. There were neither guards nor aids about
him. Upon Colonel Babcock's rapping at his door, the
response, 'Come in,' was given by himself, in a tone of
voice, and with a cadence, which I can never forget.

"His conversation was easy and fluent, without the

least effort of restraint. In this, nothing was so closely noticed by me as the point and terseness with which he expressed whatever he said. He did not seem either to court or avoid conversation, but whenever he did speak, what he said was directly to the point, and covered the whole matter in a few words. I saw before being with him long, that he was exceedingly quick in perception, and direct in purpose, with a vast deal more of brains than tongue, as ready as that was at his command."

Lincoln received the commission in the saloon of a steamer at Hampton Roads. When Stephens had stripped off his shawls and revealed his emaciated figure — Stephens himself does not report this incident — the President, shaking hands with him and smiling, said, "Never have I seen so small a nubbin come out of so much husk." This remark was not meant to be unfriendly, but it must have had behind it a consciousness of the shrinkage of the once boastful Confederacy. Lincoln had admired Stephens ever since 1847, when he had written to his law partner Herndon that "Mr. Stephens of Georgia, a little, slim, pale-faced consumptive man . . . has just concluded the very best speech of an hour's length I ever heard. My old, withered, dry eyes are full of tears yet." This speech had been directed against President James Polk for waging an unconstitutional war on Mexico, and Lincoln was, like Stephens, in the opposition. Their relations now were strangely altered. Through the ironies of time, it had come about that Stephens, that man of principle, was condemning Lincoln himself for waging an unconstitutional war, and this second unconstitutional war was turning out to be as successful as the one against Mexico. Yet, meeting at Hampton Roads, they talked for a time about the old days in Congress, days when they had been working together for the election of Zachary Taylor, and inquired about old former colleagues on the other side of the lines. Then, "Well, Mr. President," said Stephens, "is there no way of putting an end to the present trouble?" They discussed the situation at length, and Stephens expounded to Seward his doctrine of sovereign states. The Secretary of State replied to him that the theory sounded plausible enough but that practically it would never work. Suppose, for example, that Louisiana, which had been bought at such cost by the United States, should, "holding the mouth of the Mississippi and controlling the commerce of its immense valley," withdraw from the United States and go over to a foreign enemy. The other characteristically answers that "it was not my intention to argue the general principles as matters of fact"; but that in such an hypothetical case as that of Louisiana, if the other states "would so act towards her as to make it to her interest to remain in the Confederation" — by which he means the United States — "as it was when she joined it, she would never think of leaving it, or forming any alliance with a foreign inimical Power."

When Stephens asked Lincoln what the status would be, in the event of peace being agreed upon, of those slaves who should be outside the areas then occupied by Federal forces and who thus would not have been affected by the Emancipation Proclamation — which had freed only about 200,000 out of the almost four million Negroes in the South — Lincoln answered that that was a matter which the courts would have to decide; that he himself regarded the Proclamation as "a *war measure*," which, "as soon as the war ceased . . . would be inoperative for the future," but that the courts might decide otherwise. "He then went into a prolonged course of remarks about the Proclamation. He said it was not his intention in the beginning to interfere with Slavery in the States; that he never would have done it, if he had not been compelled by necessity to do it, to maintain the Union; that the subject presented many difficult and perplexing questions to him; that he had hesitated for some time, and had resorted to this measure, only when driven to it by public necessity; that he had been in favor of the General Government prohibiting the extension of Slavery into the Territories, but did not think that the Government possessed power over the subject in the States, except as a war measure; and that he had always himself been in favor of emancipation, but not immediate emancipation, even by the States. Many evils attending this appeared to him." Seward had already explained that an amendment to the Constitution was at that time pending in Congress which was intended to invalidate the old protection that had formerly been guaranteed to slave-owners and to emancipate all the slaves (the Thirteenth, which was not ratified until December, 1865).

Lincoln at this point, says Stephens, "after pausing for some time, his head rather bent down, as if in deep reflection, while all were silent . . . rose up and used these words, almost, if not, quite identical: 'Stephens, if I were in Georgia, and entertained the sentiments I do – though, I suppose, I should not be permitted to stay there long with them; but if I resided in Georgia, with my present sentiments, I'll tell you what I would do, if I were in your place: I would go home and get the Governor of the State to call the Legislature together, and get them to recall all the State troops from the war; elect Senators and Members to Congress, and ratify this Constitutional Amendment *prospectively,* so as to take effect – say in five years. Such a ratification would be valid in my opinion. I have looked into the subject, and think such a prospective ratification would be valid. Whatever may have been the views of your people before the war, they must be convinced now, that Slavery is doomed. It cannot last long, in any event, and the best course, it seems to me, for your public men to pursue, would be to adopt such a policy as will avoid, as far as possible, the evils of immediate emancipation. This would be my course, if I were in your place.' He went on to say that he would be willing to be taxed to remunerate the Southern people for their slaves. He believed the people of the North were as responsible for slavery as the people of the South, and if the war should then cease, with the voluntary abolition of slavery by the States, he should be in favor, individually, of the Government paying a fair indemnity for the loss to the owners. He said he believed this feeling had an extensive existence at the North. He knew some who were in favor of an appropriation as high as Four Hundred Millions of Dollars for this purpose." When asked "what position the Confederate States would occupy in relation to the others, if they were then to abandon the war," whether they would be admitted to Congress, "Mr. Lincoln very promptly replied, that his own individual opinion was, they ought to be." But he never would yield by a word or a reticence his position that the Union and the Confederacy were not two countries but one, that with the Southerners he could agree to no armistice nor enter into any treaty: they must simply lay down their arms and recognize the Federal Government. Sherman had just taken Savannah and was about to march up through the Carolinas; Lincoln knew that he was now in a strong position.

Abraham Lincoln and Alexander Stephens, who commanded one another's respect and who in intellect and character were peers, have come by this time to stand, in the crisis of the Civil War, at two opposite moral-political poles. They, in fact, now inhabit two quite different spheres, and their minds are more or less incommensurable. For Lincoln is the "man of destiny" who is also the self-appointed leader; who must decide and discriminate in practical affairs, who must discipline and calculate in action, yet who draws his conviction from non-rational impulse, who responds to popular stresses, who hunts as one of a pack. Stephens, too, of course, belongs to his people, and his convictions — as in the case of slavery — have ultimately non-rational sources; but he differs essentially from Lincoln in being usually at odds with the pack. Though the individuality of Lincoln asserts itself in his firmness with his Cabinet and with the opposition elements of his party, he depends, as President of the United States, on being backed by a body of men who are capable of energy and determination; whereas Stephens, in order to prove his strength, must always pit it against that of others; he must cut a diagonal line, establish a separate axis, as he had done with Governor Brown, that will cause the whole globe to wobble. This is a part of the "revenge" against fate of which he had once written to Linton, the will "to meet the world in all its forces." Though an accomplished parliamentarian, though skilful as a politician, the purity and logic of his principles, the resolve to be himself and nothing but himself, will never, in the long run, allow him to be respectful to contingencies or particularly serious about results. He had carried his idealism so far that it was possible for him to imagine that the rightness of the course of the Confederacy would eventually become plain to everybody and that the other states of the Union would all gradually join the Secessionists. "The process of distintegration in the old Union," he had said in a speech of March 21, 1861, "may be expected to go on with almost *absolute certainty, if we pursue the right course*. We are now the *nucleus* of a growing Power which, if we are true to ourselves, our destiny, and high mission, will become the controlling Power on this Continent." He asserted with complete sincerity, at the end of the *Constitutional View,* that just as the colonists had cried, "The cause of Boston is the cause of us all!", so "another like cry shall hereafter be raised, and go forth from hill-top to valley, from the Coast to the Lakes, from the Atlantic to the Pacific: 'The Cause of the South is the Cause of us all!' "

What, then, is the value, it may well be asked, of the impossibilist Alexander Stephens, who may seem to the casual reader of history not merely to have let down the Union but even to have acted in such a way as to handicap his own cause? The answer is that Stephens's value — the opposite kind to Lincoln's — is such a value as the impossibilist may sometimes have: that, by carrying an ideal to extremes, he may raise certain fundamental issues in a way that the more practical and prudent man could never allow himself to do. In this case, it is the question of the exercise of power, of the backing up of power by force, the issue of the government, the organization, as against the individual, the family group — for the South that fought the war was a family group. This issue presses hard on our time. There are moments when one may wonder today — as one's living becomes more and more hampered by the exactions of centralized bureaucracies of both the state and the federal authorities — whether it may not be true, as Stephens said, that the cause of the South is the cause of us all. It was the renewal of the suspension of habeas corpus at the end of 1864 as well as the results of conscription, which he believed to have been fatal to the army's morale, that impelled him at that time to make efforts for peace; and may we not grant that in a sense he was right? that a society which resists coercion in the defense of local freedom should not acquiesce in coercion by even a new governmental machine which has been chosen from among its own members? Better lay down your arms and collapse than adopt the enemy's methods! They had fought against the British Crown, they had fought against the dictatorship of Lincoln; why should they not repudiate their own President when he sought to become dictator, too? Why should they worry about the Negroes, with whose servitude the English had saddled them, when their own rights as independent whites were endangered?

The Northerner who would understand the Civil War must learn to grasp this point of view. He will otherwise be very much puzzled when, for example, in *The Creed of the Old South* by Basil Gildersleeve, the great Carolinian Greek scholar, he comes upon such a statement as "to us submission meant slavery . . . the cause we fought for and our brothers died for was the cause of civil liberty, and not the cause of human slavery. . . ." Stephens's writings will help us to grasp it, and we can most of us find a key in ourselves. There is in most of us an unreconstructed Southerner who will not accept domination as well as a benevolent despot who wants to mold others for their own good, to assemble them in such a way as to produce a comprehensive unit which will satisfy our own ambition by realizing some vision of our own; and the conflict between these two tendencies — which on a larger scale gave rise to the Civil War — may also break the harmony of families and cause a fissure in the individual.

To the people of Georgia, at any rate, their indeflect-able ex-Vice-President became, when the war was over, a revered and almost sacred figure. He persisted in main-

taining his principles. He and Linton refused to countenance the Fourteenth and Fifteenth Amendments, which
debarred former Confederates from holding office and
gave the Negro the vote, on the ground that in the
Congress which passed them ten states had not been
represented; and they rejected the acts to enforce these
amendments on a variety of other grounds. Alexander
was elected to the Senate in January, 1866, but, on
account of his attitude toward the Fourteenth Amendment — though this contained a proviso that an ex-
Confederate could be qualified by a two-thirds vote in
both Houses — was not allowed to sit. His former col-
laborator, ex-Governor Brown, a practical politician, did
soon accept the Fourteenth Amendment, associate himself
with the Republicans and help to put through the measures of Reconstruction; and Stephens, in the *Constitutional View*, expresses himself as follows to his Unionist
guests: "This . . . is one of the main differences between Governor Brown and myself. To his idea that
we are a conquered people, and as such should make
the best terms we can, my reply is, that this was not the
understanding at the time of the surrender. The States,
as States, were distinctly recognized in that surrender,
as we have seen; nor have, even, the Reconstructionists
at Washington, as yet, acted upon the *avowed* assumption that we are thus conquered. These monstrous measures so proposed by Congress, are acknowledged to be
without authority by those who have passed them, and
can, therefore, be considered as nothing but gross usurpations. The Courts have yet to pass upon them."

Alexander lost Linton in the summer of 1872, but,
in spite of his lonely grief at this separation, he long
survived his younger brother. The disabilities of certain
of the Southern leaders had been removed that spring,
and Stephens ran for Congress the following February.

The three other candidates withdrew, and he was almost unanimously elected. For ten years he served in the House, on crutches or in a wheel chair. A newspaper reporter described him thus: "A little way up the aisle sits a queer-looking bundle. An immense cloak, a high hat, and peering somewhere out of the middle a thin, pale, sad little face. This brain and eyes enrolled in countless thicknesses of flannel and broadcloth wrappings belong to Hon. Alexander H. Stephens, of Georgia. How anything so small and sick and sorrowful could get here all the way from Georgia is a wonder. If he were to draw his last breath any instant you would not be surprised. If he were laid out in his coffin he need not look any different, only then the fires would have gone out in those burning eyes. Set, as they are, in the wax-white face, they seem to burn and blaze. Still, on the countenance is stamped that pathos of long-continued suffering which goes to the heart. That he is here at all to offer the counsels of moderation and patriotism proves how invincible is the soul that dwells in his shrunken and aching frame." It was as if he had shrunk to pure principle, abstract, incandescent, indestructible.

He resigned in 1883, but immediately ran for Governor of Georgia and won. He was now seventy years old, and the duties of his office killed him. He died in March of the following year. In the mutterings of a final stupor, he said suddenly very clearly: "But I carried it individually by six hundred majority," and these were his last words. It was the death of the old political South — the South of Jefferson and Madison, of Randolph, Calhoun and Clay; of the landowners' and merchants' republic, of the balance of power in Congress, of the great collaboration and the great debates.

XII

THE MYTH OF THE OLD SOUTH; SIDNEY LANIER;
THE POETRY OF THE CIVIL WAR; SUT LOVIN-
GOOD

ONE MAY FIND in the writings of Alexander Stephens,
presented with conviction and clarity, the Southerner's
case for secession which he opposed to the authority of
the federal government, and one can study here a perfect
example of the rationalist political theory and the logic
of parliamentary argument of which this case was constructed; but from Stephens one can get no hint of the
headlong intoxication which was generated by secession
in the South and which seemed to dispense many
Southerners from worrying about the South's constitutional case. For the South had a reciprocal myth which
it pitted with equal fanaticism against the North's Ar-
mageddonlike vision, derived from its traditional theology, of the holy crusade which was to liberate the slaves
and to punish their unrighteous masters. If the Northerners were acting the Will of God, the Southerners
were rescuing a hallowed ideal of gallantry, aristocratic
freedom, fine manners and luxurious living from the
materialism and vulgarity of the mercantile Northern
society. And you will find this ideal at its most poetic, its
most fervid and its most pure-hearted in the work of
Sidney Lanier.

But this myth, like the New England one, had long roots in the life of the colonies, and it was stimulated, not created, by the crisis of the Civil War. The Northerner as well as the Southerner is likely to be taken in by an historical optical illusion which makes it appear that the life of the South in the period just before the war was still something majestic and lovely; but we must not forget Olmsted's discovery that the "gentry" of the "colony days" now consisted of a very few families "in a region much larger than the old German Empire," and we find when we go back into the literature of the South, that the nostalgia for a noble past, for a paradise already lost, had been felt from long before the war. The old South which the Southerner idealized, which he may still be found idealizing today and which the Northerner has come to idealize, too, was mostly located in time in the eighteenth century; and in geography especially in eastern Virginia, colonial and post-Revolutionary, that powerful and wealthy society, self-confident and self-contained and ruled by a few hundred families who were themselves pretty nearly autonomous. The situation is strikingly illustrated by the legend in the family of Robert E. Lee that their mansion in Stratford, rather plain and foursquare, had replaced something much more magnificent, which, it seems, had never really existed — a palace with a hundred chambers, four outbuildings of fifteen rooms each and a stable for a hundred horses; and that Queen Caroline, when this had burned down, had sent them money out of her privy purse to enable them to rebuild their country seat.

But already by 1817, when the New York novelist James Kirke Paulding published his *Letters from the South*, the so-called "Tidewater" Virginia of the early days, the civilization of the Eastern waterways from which had come Washington and Jefferson, the Randolphs and Patrick Henry, and which had seen at the Battle of Yorktown the definitive defeat of the British, had been partly deserted in the westward flow that was carrying its inhabitants away beyond the barrier of the Blue Ridge mountains and was eventually to make of Virginia and West Virginia two quite distinctive communities. The reckless exhaustion of the soil encouraged by the use of slave labor and the abolition of entail in the interests of a republican society had dispersed the old governing class. Of the "race of stately planters," says Paulding, there is now very little left. "A few of these ancient establishments are still kept up, but many of the houses are shut; others have passed into the hands of the industrious, or the speculating, whose modes of thinking, feeling, and acting, are totally different; and, with here and there an exception, nothing now remains, but the traditionary details of some aged matron, who lives only in the recollections of the past, of ancient modes, and ancient hospitality." He saw in Virginia "deserted houses" and "wagonloads of men, women, and children, passing along the great roads leading to the westward." It was the cotton states then that were flourishing — Virginia raised mostly tobacco — and these had been settled by people who were also of a different breed and whom the disdainful old inhabitants called "cotton snobs."

The literary legend of the pre-cotton South — according to Mr. William Taylor of Harvard, whose recent book *Cavalier and Yankee* is undoubtedly the most searching study yet made of this subject — seems to date from the same year when *Letters from the South* was published. He says that this myth was first cultivated mainly by parvenu literary men who resided in the large towns and had no actual experience of plantation life. It begins, he believes, in 1817 with the *Sketches of the Life and Character of Patrick Henry* written by William Wirt, the son of a Swiss tavern-keeper, who had been born in Bladensburg, Maryland, but who practised law in Virginia. Thomas Jefferson, who had given Wirt some help, by no means approved of this book. He told Wirt that "it would be a question hereafter whether his work belonged to the shelf of history or of panegyric," and he said of it to Daniel Webster that it was "a poor book, written in bad taste," and gave "an imperfect idea of Patrick Henry," who had been cruder and far less literate than his biographer had made him appear. John Randolph, who admired Henry, described the book as "a wretched piece of fustian." "Wirt's contributions," says Taylor, "to the ingredients of the legend of the old South are actually rather modest. Few of the details which characterized the legend in its full-blown form are to be found anywhere in his book. There is no plantation, no belle, no planter even, no romance, no war, and no discussion of Cavalier ancestry, and no terminology from Sir Walter Scott — no knights or ladies or Southrons. There is scarcely any mention of manners, and there are no invidious remarks about life in the North. The apparent novelty in Wirt's interpretation had chiefly to do with his conscious and flagrant disregard for historical fact — his romanticizing of Henry himself — and his nostalgic portrayal of pre-Revolutionary Virginian society. The most important link between Wirt and the legend makers, however, cannot be traced to any particular detail of plot or historical circumstance. It is to be found, rather, in the tone of his language, his manner of address, the very quality of the appeal which he made to his contemporaries. Virginians were asked to downgrade material success and acquisitive values in favor of an image of high civilization characterized by

the twin ideals of domestic decorum and public service."*
It was complained by non-Virginians that the book
glorified Virginia at the expense of the other communities which had taken an active part in the Revolution;
but it had run into twenty-five editions by 1871.

By this time the romance of the colonial past had
been constantly and thoroughly exploited by a whole
group of Southern novelists — Virginian, Carolinian and
Marylander — whose books began appearing in the middle thirties. The most notable of these are the Virginian
physician William Alexander Caruthers, author of *The
Cavaliers of Virginia, or the Recluse of Jamestown; An
Historical Romance of the Old Dominion* and of *The
Knights of the Horseshoe; A Traditionary Tale of the
Cocked Hat Gentry in the Old Dominion* — the first of
which is supposed to take place in 1676 and the second
in 1714; John Esten Cooke, the Virginia lawyer already
mentioned in connection with his war novels and Sherman's march, who wrote *The Virginia Comedians: or
Old Days in the Old Dominion*, which takes place on
the eve of the Revolution (note the recurrence in these
titles of the much-caressed phrase "Old Dominion," of
which the magic is felt even by the Northerner when he
passes it on the New York dock of the Old Dominion
Line); John Pendleton Kennedy, a Baltimore lawyer,
whose *Horseshoe Robinson* and *Rob of the Bowl* deal
respectively with the Revolution and with Protestants
and Catholics in Maryland in the seventeenth century;
and the voluminous William Gilmore Simms, who more
or less covered in his novels and histories the whole
Carolinian past. These novels for the most part, today,
make tedious and insipid reading; but they are important in showing how completely, by the middle of the

* *William Wirt and the Legend of the Old South* in the *William
and Mary Quarterly*, October, 1957.

last century, a literary convention had been established in regard to the life of the Old South.

You find this convention in its most naïve form in Cooke's novel *The Virginia Comedians*, published in 1854. It is typical of the tone of this literature that the description of a banquet at Williamsburg should move the author to the following elegy:

"And so the brilliant party fled away, as all bright things fly far from us into the west, and dead days of the past. Where are they now, those stalwart cavaliers and lovely dames who filled that former time with so much light, and merriment, and joyous laughter? Where are those good coursers, Selim, Fair Anna and Sir Archy; where are black and white, old and young, all the sporting men and women of the swaying crowd? What do we care for them today? What do we care if the laces are moth-eaten — the cocked hats hung up in the halls of Lethe — the silk stockings laid away in the drawer of oblivion? What does it concern us that the lips no longer move, the faces no longer laugh? What do we care for all those happy maiden faces — gallant inclinations — graceful courtesies — every thing connected with the cavaliers and dames of that old, brilliant, pompous, honest, worthy race?

"They have gone away to the other world; their lips are dumb; their heads have bowed and their backs long bent, and they have carried away their loads and themselves to the happy or the miserable isles. We care so little for them, that the poor chronicler who tries to make them speak again to-day is scarcely heard; but still it is his province, he must speak in spite of all."

Cooke turned out his novels with effortless speed — at the rate sometimes of three a year — in the intervals of practising law. He was a master of that agreeable glibness, that bland and somewhat flimsy charm that is still characteristic of one type of Southerner. His stories have the easy fluidity and sometimes the inconsistency of daydreams. *The Virginia Comedians,* for example, is supposed to open in October, but when the head of the house appears, he remarks that, "These August days are excellent for the corn"; a few pages later the author explains that the October evenings are "becoming chilly." And in a chapter entitled *An Adventure,* one of the novel's most dashing heroes — a soldier who has served in Europe and continually exclaims "Morbleu!" — the moment after swimming a river on horseback and emerging soaked to the waist, is able to perform the feat, at the expense of nothing worse than a bruised arm, of checking a runaway "chariot drawn by four spirited horses," and when asked to dinner by the family he has rescued, he rejects the suggestion of the host that, before sitting down to dinner, he might like to go to "a dressing-room." "No, he did not need it." The author has forgotten that the rescuer has had no chance to get dry since his plunge into the river — or does he mean us to assume that a gentleman of those marvelous days of the Old Dominion could correct, by a miraculous act of courtesy, his very bedrenched condition?

The influence of Walter Scott is much in evidence in all these novels. Its intoxicating effect on the South has been eloquently described by Mark Twain in the second part of *Life on the Mississippi.* He has been praising the work of the French Revolution in "stripping the divinity from royalty." But then, laments Mark Twain, "comes Sir Walter Scott with his enchantments, and by his single might checks this wave of progress, and even turns it back; sets the world in love with dreams and phantoms; with decayed and swinish forms of religion; with decayed and degraded systems of government; with the sillinesses and emptinesses, sham grandeurs, sham gauds, and sham chivalries of a brainless and worthless long-vanished society. He did measureless harm; more real and lasting harm, perhaps, than any other individual that ever wrote. Most of the world has outlived a good part of these harms, though by no means all of them; but in our South they flourish pretty forcefully still. Not so forcefully as half a generation ago, perhaps, but still forcefully. There, the genuine and wholesome civilization of the nineteenth century is curiously confused and commingled with the Walter Scott Middle-Age sham civilization, and so you have practical common sense, progressive ideas, and progressive works, mixed up with the duel, the inflated speech, and the jejune romanticism of an absurd past that is dead, and out of charity ought to be buried. But for the Sir Walter disease, the character of the Southerner — or Southron, according to Sir Walter's starchier way of phrasing it — would be wholly modern, in place of modern and medieval mixed, and the South would be fully a generation further advanced than it is. It was Sir Walter that made every gentleman in the South a major or a colonel, or a general or a judge, before the war; and it was he, also, that made these gentlemen value these bogus decorations. For it was he that created rank and caste down there, and also reverence for rank and caste, and pride and pleasure in them. Enough is laid on slavery, without fathering upon it these creations and contributions of Sir Walter.

"Sir Walter had so large a hand in making Southern character, as it existed before the war, that he is in a great measure responsible for the war. It seems a little harsh toward a dead man to say that we never should have had any war but for Sir Walter; and yet something of a plausible argument might, perhaps, be made in support of that wild proposition. The Southerner of the

American Revolution owned slaves; so did the Southerner of the Civil War; but the former resembles the latter as an Englishman resembles a Frenchman. The change of character can be traced rather more easily to Sir Walter's influence than to that of any other thing or person."

This chivalrous ideal had already long before been satirized by a Southerner who had lived with it, the John Pendelton Kennedy mentioned above as the author of two historical novels. His first novel, called *Swallow Barn; or A Sojourn in the Old Dominion,* published in 1832, also deals with the plantation life of Virginia, but it is set in the contemporary world and a good deal more realistic than Cooke — though in a revised edition of 1851 he somewhat modified the satire and added a nostalgic preface. John Kennedy, whose mother was a Pendelton of Virginia, had a Scotch-Irish merchant for a father, and was born and practised law in Baltimore. In the war he supported the Union. John Kennedy was a cultivated intelligent man, a friend of Thackeray, whom he helped with *The Virginians,* and had a sense of social comedy of a fineness rather unusual in pre-war Southern fiction. There is no dream of princely living in *Swallow Barn:* the Virginia plantation it describes is comfortable, friendly, jolly but in some ways quite rustic and plain. There is something of Jane Austen in the handling of the heroine, whose relations with her rural retainers and with the young man who wants to marry her are deeply influenced by her reading of the Waverley novels:

" 'By the by, Mark,' said Ned, changing his mood, and brightening up into a pleasanter state of feeling, 'did you note Bel's horsemanship, — how light and fearless she rides? And like a fairy, comes at your bidding, too! She reads descriptions of ladies of chivalry, and takes the field in imitation of them. Her head is full of these fancies, and she almost persuades herself that this is the fourteenth century. Did you observe her dainty fist? "miniardly begloved," — as the old minstrels have it? — she longs to have a merlin perched upon it, and is therefore endeavoring to train a hawk, that, when she takes the air, she may go in the guise of an ancient gentlewoman. She should be followed by her falconer.'

" 'And have a pair of greyhounds in her train,' said I.

" 'Aye, and a page in a silk doublet,' added Ned.

" 'And a gallant cavalier,' I rejoined, 'to break a lance for her, instead of breaking jokes upon her.' "

And here is Bel on the subject of a local German fiddler, who sings ballads in a nasal voice:

" 'I wish [she says] we had more like him! for Hafen has a great many ballads that, I assure you, will compare very well with the songs of the troubadours and minnesingers.'

" 'There you go,' cried Harvey, 'with your age of chivalry. I don't know much about your troubadours and minnesingers: but, if there was amongst them as great a scoundrel as Hafen, your age of chivalry was an arrant cheat. Why, this old fellow lives by petty larceny; he hasn't the dignity of a large thief: he is a filcher of caps and napkins from a washerwoman's basket; a robber of hen-roosts; a pocketer of tea-spoons! Now, if there was any romance in him, he would, at least, steal cows and take purses on the highway.'

" 'Pray, cousin,' exclaimed Bel, laughing, 'do not utter such slanders against my old friend Hafen! Here, I have taken the greatest trouble in the world to get me a minstrel. I have encouraged Hafen to learn ditties, and he has even composed some himself at my bidding. Once I gave him a dress which you would have laughed to see. It was made after the most approved fashion of minstrelsy. First, there was a long gown of Kendal green, gathered at the neck with a narrow gorget; it had sleeves that hung as low as the knee, slit from the shoulder to the hand and lined with white cotton; a doublet with sleeves of black worsted; upon these a pair of points of tawny camlet, laced along the wrist with blue thread points, with a welt towards the hand, made of fustian; a pair of red stockings; a red girdle with a knife stuck in it; and, around his neck, a red riband, suitable to the girdle. Now what do you think, cousin, of such a dress as that?'

" 'Where did you get the idea of this trumpery?' cried Harvey.

" 'It is faithfully taken,' said Bel, 'from the exact description of the minstrel's dress, as detailed by Laneham, in his account of the entertainment of Queen Elizabeth at "Killingworth Castle." ' "

Her suitor Ned Hazard, whom she treats as a boor, is goaded at last by her ridicule to make an effort to live up to her requirements: " 'I know I shall make a fool of myself,' said he, 'but that is her look-out, not mine. I'll give her enough of her super-subtle, unimaginable, diabolical dignity! — I will be the very essence of dulness, and the quintessence of decorum! — I will turn myself into an ass of the first water, until I make her so sick of pedantry and sentiment, that a good fellow shall go free with her all the rest of her life.' "

The result is a curious scene which cannot but startle and puzzle Bel. A party of the young people are riding through the woods, and Ned reproves a frivolous friend.

" 'Riggs,' continued Hazard, 'is the most inveterate jester I ever knew. He spreads the contagion of his levity into all societies. For my part, I think there are scenes in nature, as there are passages in life, which ought to repress merriment in the most thoughtless minds; and this is one of them. Such a spot as this kindles a sort of absorbing, superstitious emotion in me that makes me grave.'

" 'I observe that you are grave,' remarked Bel.

" 'Since I left college,' said Ned, 'and particularly since my last return to Swallow Barn, I have devoted a great deal of my time to the study of those sources of poetical thought and association which lurk amongst the majestic landscapes of the country.'

" 'Hear that!' whispered Harvey to me. . . .

" 'The ancients, Bel — I see Harvey does not believe me — but the ancients stocked such a place as this with tutelar deities: they had their nymphs of the wood and grove, of the plain, of the hill, the valley, the fountain, the river, and the ocean. I think they numbered as many as three thousand. I can hardly tell you their different denominations; but there were Oreads and Dryads and Hamadryads, Napeæ, Nereids, Naiads, and — the devil knows what all!'

" 'That was a slip,' said Harvey, aside; 'one more and he is a lost man.'

"Bel opened her eyes with amazement at this volley of learning, and not less at the strange expletive with which he concluded, as if utterly at a loss to understand the meaning of this exhibition."

"Where did you get all that nonsense?" asks Harvey when the ride is over.

"Gad, I once wrote an essay on popular superstition! . . . and had it all at my finger-ends."

The ladies have become quite worried. "His manners were strange," says one of them. "He evidently talked like a man who wanted to conceal his emotions. It was just the way with gentlemen who were going to fight a duel."

There was no irony whatever in Sidney Lanier, a rapturous young man from Georgia, who had been born in 1842 and must have been nourished on these early novels. In Lanier the chivalric romance of the South was to merge with German romanticism and to become inflated and irised, made to drip with the dews of idealism, to a degree that is rather startling even to one who has become familiar with its earlier manifestations. The young Lanier had read Novalis, Jean-Paul Richter and other German writers; he translated and paraphrased German lyrics and even wrote some verse in German. German influence — which was more common in New England than the South — is rampant in his *Tiger-Lilies*, a novel begun when the author was serving in the Confederate Army, in the winter of 1863–4, but not finished and published till after the war, in 1867. The main action of *Tiger-Lilies* is supposed to take place in the South but — though Lanier had never been in Germany — we soon get a flashback to Frankfurt-am-Main, which the villain, John Cranston, has visited in his youth. Trade with a capital T is always the evil force with Sidney Lanier, and John Cranston, an enchanting musician, possessing "an acute intellect . . . but thoroughly selfish, and without even the consciousness that this last was his bad trait," is the son of a dealer in drygoods, very rich, and residing, of course, in the North. In Frankfurt, with the aid of his violin and exercising an hypnotic spell, he seduces a beautiful German girl. Here are passages from the chapter describing this:

" '. . . And so, since I am left alone for the day, if Herr Cranston will bring his violin at six, he will be considered very kind by his friend,   Ottilie'

"To receive such a note as this, from which, as it is opened, a faint violet odor floats up, as if the soul of the sweet writer exhaled from her words; to know that she

is gray-eyed, oval-faced, lissome-limbed, full-souled, rising up to anything beautiful as quickly and as surely
as shadows in water rise to meet their falling flowers; —
this is meat, drink, and raiment to a young, untamed,
venturesome lion, who is currying himself and curling
his mane in the best den of the city, or ere he begins
to rampage over Germany. . . .

" 'I announce myself tired of compliments, Herr Cranston, and I long for some music. See, there is your violin,
which your servant brought an hour ago!'

"Cranston unlocked the case.

" 'Poor violin! Take him up tenderly out of his dark
case, Herr Cranston. Ah, when life has played its long
tune upon me, and locked me up in my grave-case, I
hope the Great Musician will take me out so, and draw
a divine love-melody from me. Is not a violin wonderfully like a man? It can be heavenly, it can be earthy, it
can be fiendish! It can make lark-music that draws our
eye towards heaven, it can make dance-music that keeps
our feet moving upon the earth, and it can make Circe-
music that allures us to —'

" 'To hell, Fraulein?'

" 'Yes.'

" 'Which of these styles does the Fraulein prefer?'
said Cranston, gravely arranging his bow.

" 'O, Mephistopheles! play what pleases thy satanic
fancy.'

"Who, being led to the edge of a precipice, has not
felt the insidious and alluring desire to leap over it rising
stronger and stronger within him, until he draws back,
shuddering?

"There are some unaccountable moments when one is
wild with insane longing to leap from the rock of what is
fixed and known as virtuous, into the terrible mist of the
unknown and bad, floating below.

"It was this desire that sparkled in Ottilie _____'s eyes, and drew her to the very brink.

" 'Sound me,' said she, 'some strains from thy native Hades. I do not want any brimstone and agitato and thunder, and all that traditional infernal-music; but something beautiful and wicked and very sweet.'

" 'As if tawny Cleopatra peered wickedly at you over Godiva's white shoulder?'

" 'So; and play, thou Satan in chains, till I bid thee stay!'

"Let it be said only, that this music which John Cranston improvised was like a rose, with the devil lying perdu in its red heart; was like a soft, gray eye, with a voluptuous sparkle in it; was like a silver star-beam, only not cold, but hot with intoxicating perfumes.

"Ottilie sat at the open window. Presently the sun sank beneath to the horizon.

" 'Stop, Herr Cranston, look yonder!'

"One modest star had stolen out in the east, and stood, with all its dainty silver-soul a-tremble, in the passionate gaze of the sun. And all the west blushed to see the sun stretch out two long beams, like arms, which drew down a cloud towards him for a kiss. A costly caress! For, as the kiss of the heaven-born Zillah consumed his earth-born beloved to ashes before his eyes, so now the cloud, as it neared the sun, caught a-fire, and flamed with unutterable brilliancy.

"Ottilie turned away, with sparkling eyes – into the arms of Lucifer.

"O, Ottilie, thou should'st have looked a little longer at the display in the west, yonder! For, presently, the unpitying sun went on his way down the heaven-slope, and left the poor cloud alone; and the cloud gradually darkened from glowing red to a bruise-purple, and then to ashen-gray, dull and dead.

"So shalt thou fare, Ottilie, thou poor gossamer summer-cloud; so shalt thou be consumed with bliss, and then left in the ashen-gray of grief that changeth not, of regret that blotteth not out its sin, of crime that hateth itself, and stingeth itself; but never to death.

"And that day sank slowly into its night, as into a grave."

Nor was this vein confined to his fiction: it was his natural mode of expression. We find him writing as follows, on June 15, 1867, to his first love, Virginia Hankins, on the occasion of the death of her brother:

"In the still temple of your grief I fear me that my rough man's-tread rang full harshly: — and yet, — O Vestal whose name even when I write it calls all my blood rushing into my heart — and yet, I was but trying to steal silently in, and kneel at your side, and pray with you while you prayed, and offer you my knightly service and knightly love, for life and death, when you had come out of the temple."

And to his brother Clifford A. Lanier — to whom he seems to have been attached only less than Alexander Stephens to Linton — on July 1, 1867:

"O my Tube-Rose and my Red Rose; My King and Queen of all flowers, grow, grow i' the Southwinds only, and under the temperate Suns and the tender rains: The Heavens, which are full faithful to beauty, distill a special and most exquisite dew for you, which shall not fail you at mornings nor evenings nor in the hot middle of your day."

To the girl he was to marry, Mary Day, on September 10 [?], 1867:

"Sweet Vine, how hast thou crept and grown upon me, and wound me round about with blessings of wonderful leaves, and buds, and wreathing tendrils, and faint Solemn perfumes, and sacred wavering shadows, and fleckings of holy lights — between-leaves, and the tender glory of the woods-loneliness in which thou, being one with me, bringest me at once the joy of company and the exaltation of Solitude.

"O Thou Christ that hast trained this vine upon my lonely Soul in the desert. Keep the leaves green with the tears thou hast shed in gardens, and shine with smiles like the Sun to ripen the purple fruit of my Vine, the passionate-purple spheréd Fruit, which is Love!

"This the prayer that I pray for my darling Wife-to-be, and there is no Soul but Christ's that knows the great yearning of my uplifted arms to fold themselves about the only Waist in all the world [that] might fill and rest and satisfy them."

And he writes her as follows on the day of their marriage, December 19, 1867:

"How fares our royal Spouse, this marriage-morn?

"Hath our Queen aught of instruction to give the King?

"Will our fair Queen, if the King (who is hurried) cannot see her immediately, send the King a Prayer-book?

"The King."

He has still not abated this fervor after almost three years of marriage:

"And so, Most Rare Comrade, I got me to my lonely room, in the night, and sat me down by my lonely fire, and fell a-musing of thee; and frequently turned the head thereof at hearing the sweet rustle of thy dress about the sacred room where thou and I have lived: and felt the heart thereof breaking, breaking, breaking for thee: and knew great pangs by reason of the bitter onset of my grief for all the sins I have done, above all, for my great, great sin: and begged thee piteously, by all tender names, 'Child,' and 'Rare Child,' and 'Slender May Lilian,' and 'Fair Yoland' and 'Enid' and Guinevere-

Purer-than-Guinevere and Most Dear Ladye and Liebe and Mignonne and Ninita and Fine Sweetheart and a thousand besides, that thy wonderful loving Soul might invent some fair veil wherewith to cover my woful Fault, and that thou wouldst believe yet in my strength wh. thou hast *not* seen, relying upon my love which thou *hast* in some little measure beheld: and thereupon I fell upon the knees thereof and spoke with my Friend, long, anent the matter: Whereto came Answer, wh. may not be told in a word but only in a life lived for thee."

Still six and a half years later:

"My heart's Heartsease, My sweet Too-sweet, My Heaven of My Heaven, if I could wrap thee in a calyx of tender words still would they seem but like the prickly husk in respect of thee, thou Rose, within."

A year later:

"Soul of my heart, thou wilt see by the enclosed that I am due in Baltimore by next Monday.

"I write this little note to beg that thou wilt come here on Friday. Pray bring with thee my black dress-coat, and the black cloth vest thereunto belonging: also, the thick gloves in my trunk: also the extra flute joint which lieth around somewhere: also my small satchell: also my cards which are in the red Russia-leather pocketbook in the trunk, — bring pocketbook and all. I think I can do without the trunk until I see thee again, and much prefer to do so."

They have been married almost eleven years before he addresses her as *you:*

"Dearest Soul. After watching the last puff of smoke from your locomotive as it rounded the curve I wandered disconsolately back to town, held high converse with the india-rubber man, returned to — to — Jane, hailed a passing apple-vender's wagon, helped the apple-vender to load on the silver-box, got up on the seat with him, rode down to the Bank, deposited my precious wares, returned again to Jane, and buried myself in work for the rest of the day. I slept well, and, after a very gorgeous breakfast for a bachelor, have been writing steadily until now, nearly dinner-time."

What, one wonders, were these young Southerners actually like who wrote and received such letters? You can see them in the photographs included in the Johns Hopkins edition of Sidney Lanier: the burning-eyed strong-willed young girls who spurred on the young men in the Civil War, who flashed their fierce gaze at the Yankees; and Lanier with his eager idealist's eyes and his luminous if less flashing countenance. It was said of Boris Pasternak by his friend the poet Tsvetaeva that he looked like both an Arab and his steed. Sidney Lanier is also equine in a poetic way; not an Arabian steed but a mettlesome cavalry horse of the kind that figured so dashingly in the Civil War — Lee's Traveller, Jeb Stuart's Skylark. An ambrotype of Sidney Lanier, taken when he was fifteen years old, reveals, with the superior clarity of these old non-instantaneous photographs that had to be posed and sat for, the knuckles of hands that seem dropped in repose for only the interval of the sitting, the silk stitching of a vest and cravat that suggest a distinguished elegance, the gleam of light in dark long hair, and in the long eager oval face a look of impulsive eloquence — almost as if you had just heard him speaking — like that of the characters in his novel. James Russell Lowell, on whom Sidney Lanier once paid a call in Cambridge, speaks of his "shining presence."

Lanier was born in Macon, Georgia, on February 3, 1842. He was probably descended from a Huguenot family who came to England from France at the beginning of the seventeenth century and who there distinguished

themselves as musicians. One of these had a place in
Queen Elizabeth's household, and his son, who was
"Master of the King's Music," composed scores for the
masques of Ben Jonson and Thomas Campion. Sidney
Lanier's family had on both sides been quite well off,
and there were large Southern estates in the background.
His mother's father had owned a plantation in Virginia
and named four of his sons after characters in Scott.
Sidney, whose father was a cultivated lawyer, showed
an early interest in poetry and music. "I feel," he once
wrote, "a sense of gratitude to old Nicholas [the Master
of the King's Music] for restoring me, as it were, to the
pure stock of the Laniers." He was to have gone to study
in Germany — like the invincible violinist of his novel;
but the outbreak of the war prevented this, and, instead, at the age of nineteen, he enlisted in the Confederate infantry. For this young Southerner, as may
be supposed, the war was a romantic exploit, in which
a company of gallant knights were defending their country and their honor. Sidney Lanier served for almost four
years, and took part in the Seven Days Battles around
Richmond. While picketing the Virginia beaches, he
came down with "chills and fever," and suffered for
two or three months from what he says were called
"'the dry shakes of the sandhills,' a sort of brilliant
tremolo movement brilliantly executed, upon 'that pan-
pipe, man,' by an invisible but very powerful performer."
Later on, with his brother Clifford, he got himself transferred to the Signal Corps and spent a year and a half
near the mouth of the James. "Our life, during this
period," he says, "was as full of romance as heart could
desire. We had a flute and a guitar, good horses, a beautiful country, splendid residences inhabited by friends
who loved us, and plenty of hair-breadth 'scapes from the
roving bands of Federals who were continually visiting

that Debateable Land. I look back on that as the most delicious period of my life, in many respects: Cliff and I never cease to talk of the beautiful women, the serenades, the moon-light dashes on the beach of fair Burwell's Bay (just above Hampton Roads), and the spirited brushes of our little force with the enemy." But this came to an end when, in 1864, he was assigned as a signal officer to a ship that was running the Yankee blockade. It was captured, and Sidney was sent by the Federals to the prison of Fort Lookout in Maryland. This imprisonment, which lasted till the end of the war, broke down Sidney's health completely. Not only had the war disappointed his musical and literary ambitions: it was to turn him into an invalid and shorten his life.

He had now to work for a living, and he first served as tutor in a plantation family, then as clerk in a hotel in Montgomery, Alabama, then as principal of an Alabama academy. But in this last more desirable position Lanier hardly lasted six months. In January, 1868, he had a hemorrhage of the lungs, and the academy was forced to close. He had to struggle against tuberculosis all the rest of his life, and he died at thirty-nine. But it was not merely by illness that he was handicapped. There was very little of "culture" in that part of the South, which, except for a few families, was even more or less illiterate — only one out of thirteen of the white inhabitants was able to read and write — and Lanier complains much in his letters of the lack of any local encouragement. He writes thus, for example, of the projects of Clifford and himself: "You will laugh at these ambitious schemes, when I tell you that we have not yet offered for print a single thing! But, we have no newspapers here with circulation enough to excite our ambition: and of course the Northern papers are beyond our reach. Our literary life, too, is a lonely and

somewhat cheerless one; for beyond our father, a man
of considerable literary acquirements and exquisite taste,
we have not been able to find a single individual who
sympathized in such pursuits enough to warrant showing
him our little productions. So scarce is 'general cultivation' here! But we work on, and hope to become, at least,
recognized as good orderly citizens in the realm of letters, yet." And a few weeks later to the same correspondent: "I despair of giving you any idea of the mortal
stagnation which paralyzes all business here. On our
streets, Monday is very like Sunday: they show no life,
save late in the afternoon when the girls come out, one
by one, and shine and move, just as the stars do, an hour
later. I don't think there's a man in town who could be
induced to go into his neighbor's store and ask how's
trade: for he would have to atone for such an insult with
his life. Everything is dreamy, and drowsy, and drone-y
— The trees stand like statues: and even when a breeze
comes, the leaves flutter and dangle idly about, as if with
a languid protest against all disturbance of their perfect rest. The mocking-birds absolutely refuse to sing
before twelve o'clock at night, when the air is somewhat cooled: and the fire-flies flicker more slowly than
I ever saw them, before. Our whole world, here, yawns
in a vast and sultry spell of laziness. . . ."

In a letter to Bayard Taylor — one of Lanier's few
literary friends — written in 1875, he speaks of his situation with a pathos in which he seldom indulged: "I
could never describe to you what a mere drought and
famine my life has been, as regards that multitude of
matters which I fancy one absorbs when one is in an
atmosphere of art, or when one is in conversational relation with men of letters, with travellers, with persons
who have either seen, or written, or done large things.
Perhaps you know that with us of the younger genera-

tion in the South since the War, pretty much the whole of life has been merely not-dying."

If one reads very much of Lanier, one is tempted in the long run to lose patience with him. He is at once insipid and florid. He is noble, to be sure, but his nobility is boring; his eloquence comes to seem empty. Yet the world in which he had lived had been desolated, and for one who like Sidney Lanier had given his youth to the Confederacy and who continued to live in the South, there was not only no encouragement to practice the arts, there was no real fermentation of thought — the resistance to the "carpetbaggers" was hardly that — to communicate political excitement. The *Constitutional View of the War between the States* was an isolated backward-looking exploit, the self-assertion of a unique individual mind; and for Sidney Lanier the poet, it was possible, in regard to the present, to take only a negative line, making his protest, as in some of his dialect poems, against the cruel abuses of the Reconstruction or denouncing greedy commercialism which was supposed to be behind them. Base "Trade," as I have said, is always his villain, and though we may sympathize with his scorn for commercial ideals, we may find him rather tiresome about it, as when he writes to his friend Paul Hamilton Hayne, the South Carolina poet, praising "the entire *absence*, in everything you write, of *Trade* in any of its forms."

"Trade, Trade, Trade," he continues. "Pah, are we not all sick? A man cannot walk down a green alley of the woods, in these days, without unawares getting his mouth and nose and eyes covered with some web or other that Trade has stretched across, to catch some gain or other. 'Tis an old spider that has crawled all over our modern life, and covered it with a flimsy web that conceals the Realities. Our religions, our politics, our social life, our charities, our literature, nay, by Heavens, our music and

our lives almost, are all meshed in unsubstantial conceal-
ments and filthy garnitures by it.

"But your poems are not. Here the brooks wimple
down the burn in order to be beautiful, and not in order
to make money by turning mill-wheels: and the trees
wave, and the birds sing, and sweet human emotions
come into the woods and blend therewith: and no money-
changers sit in the still leafy temples.

"It is not necessary for me to explain, to *you*, what I
mean by these hasty metaphors. You know what the
commercial spirit is: you remember that Trade killed
Chivalry and now sits in the throne. It was Trade that
hatched the Jacquerie in the 14th Century: it was Trade
that hatched John Brown, and broke the saintly heart of
Robert Lee, in the 19th."

Lanier's purity is also prudish. Despite the wicked
burst of passion in *Tiger-Lilies,* the Puritan subdues the
Romantic. When Lanier attempts to deal with the English novel in a series of lectures at Johns Hopkins, we discover that all the classic novelists from Fielding and
Smollett to Thackeray are offensive to his moral sense,
that he has also reservations about Dickens, for whom
he does feel some admiration, and that he can only fully
approve of George Eliot, to whom he devotes a dispro-
portionate amount of space. But it was not merely prudery no doubt which made him dislike these authors.
The dream of Arthurian chivalry to which he was so
much addicted must have made them all seem to him
vulgar, and it excluded a sense of humor (his efforts to
be amusing consist mainly of long strings of puns).
Though sensitive, Lanier is limited, sometimes a little
stupid.

And yet there was in Sidney Lanier something that
commands our respect, even our admiration. In his life

he was, in a real sense, heroic; his passion for the arts
was intense, it sustained him through many miseries;
and the work that he was doing at the time of his death
seems to show that he was becoming a first-rate artist.
The closer one gets to him, the more one is disposed to
agree with the opinion of Barrett Wendell, in his *A
Literary History of America,* that Lanier "was among
the truest men of letters that our country has produced."

It was not easy, it was almost unheard of, for a Southerner to drop a profession that would make him a regular living, in order to follow the arts. When Lanier had
recovered from his first serious illness, he studied law
in his father's law office, and for a time he practised law
in Atlanta, but he disliked this and dropped it and
boldly announced that thereafter he would devote himself to literature and music. He eventually established
connections with the literary world of New York. Some
of his poems were accepted by New York magazines, and
he was commissioned to do a series of abridgements —
intended for youthful readers — of the romances of
chivalry he so much loved: *The Boy's King Arthur, The
Boy's Froissart, The Boy's Mabinogion,* etc. The language of his letters from this point on — as he is finding
a place in the contemporary world — becomes noticeably
more sober, less bookish. He moves from Atlanta to Baltimore, and is much better off for the change — for he is
able to make a living there by playing the flute in the
Peabody Orchestra and by lecturing at the Johns Hopkins University. But he was obliged to work beyond his
capacity; and at times, when his disease was menacing
and he had to go away for a cure, he was separated for
long periods from his family — he had several sons —
whom he adored. Yet the poetic (rather, now, than
the musical) vocation had become so strong with Lanier
that we feel, as we read his letters, that it has grown to

be a counter-possession which is battling against the bacillus.

To his wife he writes (March 26, 1876): "I have been on the divine heights of my art for several days and nights, and the poem has grown fast. I hope to finish it in ten days. I work about fourteen hours out of twenty-four. I think Charley [Lanier's son] has his own private idea that I am mildly insane." To his father (May 18, 1876): "In short, my dear Father, my experience in the varying judgements of men about poetry has now become pretty large . . . It has all converged upon one solitary principle, and the experience of the Artist in all ages is reported by history to be of precisely the same direction. That principle is: that the artist shall put forth, humbly and lovingly and without bitterness against any opposition, the very best and highest that is within him, utterly regardless of contemporary criticism. What possible claim can contemporary criticism set up to respect — that contemporary criticism which crucified Jesus Christ, stoned Stephen, hooted Paul for a madman, tried Luther for a criminal, tortured Galileo, bound Columbus in chains, drove Dante into a hell of exile, made Shakespeare write the Sonnet 'when in disgrace with fortune and men's eyes &c.', gave Milton five pounds for *Paradise Lost*, kept Samuel Johnson cooling his heels on Lord Chesterfield's door-step, reviled Shelley as an unclean dog, killed Keats, cracked jokes on Gluck, Schubert, Beethoven, Berlioz and Wagner, and committed so many other impious follies and stupidities that a thousand letters like this could not suffice even to catalogue them?" And again, on August 10, 1880: "For two years past — since I have become in health to study at all — I have had such a rush and storm of ideas demanding immediate expression, and have had to put aside such an enormous proportion of them in favor of small daily duties which physically limited me to a book or two a year, that I have been continually jarred and shaken with ever-recurrent shock and resistance, like a steam-boat's frame with the pull and push of the walking-beam. Especially wearing has it been, to do the work for which I care least, and to be continually crushing back poem after poem — I have several volumes of poems in the form of memoranda on the backs of envelopes, odd slips of paper, and the like! while I addressed myself to such work as seemed to offer more immediate return in the way of money. This may seem intangible; but an amount of nervous strength is given out in mere dumb endurance of this sort which far exceeds that lost in physical labor. If I could write nothing but poetry for the next two years — which means if I had five thousand dollars — I would be in vigorous health by October next!" To his friend Paul Hamilton Hayne (November 19, 1880): "For six months past a ghastly fever has been taking possession of me each day at about twelve M., and holding my head under the surface of indescribable distress for the next twenty hours, subsiding only enough each morning to let me get on my working-harness, but never intermitting. A number of tests show it not to be the 'hectic' so well known in consumption; and to this day it has baffled all the skill I could find in New York, in Philadelphia, and here. I have myself been disposed to think it arose purely from the bitterness of having to spend my time in making academic lectures and boy's books — pot-boilers all — when a thousand songs are singing in my heart that will certainly kill me if I do not utter them soon. But I don't think this diagnosis has found favor with any practical physicians; and mean-time I work day after day in such suffering as is piteous to see."

The early poems of Sidney Lanier had suffered somewhat from peculiarities of style which were not at all characteristic of the facile American verse of the period: a stiffening of the lines with consonants that bristle, impede and deaden and that recall the Anglo-Saxon poetry which Lanier had been at pains to study and the German of his early addiction. Though he had thoroughly mastered music — and perhaps for this very reason — it was precisely in verbal music that his poetry had always been deficient. It is not what one would expect from a flutist and a man who is to write a book — *The Science of English Verse* — in order to demonstrate the musical basis of metrics. But — very late in the day, to be sure: in 1878 — Lanier began producing the poems for which he is chiefly known: the sequence of *Hymns of the Marshes*, of which he lived to finish only a few. In these he displays rather suddenly new colors and new rhythms and, for Lanier, a new way of experiencing life. He has hitherto dealt almost exclusively in imagery of a conventional romantic kind and in allegories and moral abstractions. But now at last, in his relation to the outer world, he is beginning to explore real landscapes and in the inner one to deal with the psychology of emotion. The "high-minded" early Lanier, who has seemed rather remote and monotonous, is turning here into a man and a poet; and his stockade of dental and palatal consonants seems in process of becoming fluidified with the flooding of the Marshes of Glynn.

It is terrible that the bacillus of tuberculosis should have paralyzed the wings of Lanier just at the moment of his emerging from his chrysalis. Up to the very end he was preoccupied with his literary activities. It is touching for a fellow writer to find him, only four days before his death, complaining to Charles Scribner, his publisher, about the proofs of his book on metrics: "I had hoped . . . that by the time we should have reached the point where I stopped four weeks ago — I had then corrected about 150 *pp.* of page-proof — the proof-readers would have caught my very simple system of punctuation so clearly as to make any further supervision by me unnecessary; but I find them still sprinkling commas over the page as these country cooks in North Carolina sprinkle black pepper over their unspeakable chicken-pies, out of pepper-boxes whose holes have run together by liberal use and wont until they often give down three grains for one.

"I shall pull through the present crisis and write many another book, whereof the germs have already been born in this strange and beautiful Tryon Valley."

But he died when he had finished his proofs. We shall return to his poetry later when we can see it in the perspective of his time and place.

The period of the Civil War was not at all a favorable one for poetry. An immense amount of verse was written in connection with the war itself, but today it makes barren reading. One of the best-known poets of the war and one of those who had seen most action was Henry Howard Brownell, a newspaperman from Providence, Rhode Island, who had published in the Hartford *Evening Press,* in 1862, a rhymed version of Admiral David G. Farragut's "General Orders" to his fleet on the eve of his attack on New Orleans. These verses were read by Farragut, who wrote to Brownell about them, and, learning that it was Brownell's ambition — he was then in his early forties — to witness a naval battle, the Admiral gave him a rank, assigned him to duty as his secretary, and took him along on his ship, the *Hartford.* Henry Brownell was present at the battles of Mobile Bay and

Vicksburg, as well as several minor engagements. He was detailed to take notes on the action; and it is said that the officers, at Mobile Bay, were astonished by his coolness in accomplishing this. His notations were sometimes in verse. "I did not," he is supposed to have said, "want any of you picking up my manuscript in case I was shot, and saying I was afraid." Immediately after the battle, he wrote a long poem about it called *The Bay Fight*. In 1864 he published a volume: *Lyrics of a Day, Newspaper Poetry, by a Volunteer in the U.S. Service*. Brownell explains in his preface that "Some of [these poems], rather trivial, are included because of their popularity. Indeed all those on war and polity seem to me but ephemeral expressions — *suspiria, risus, elatio* — of the great national Passion, in its several phases." But they were very much admired in New England, and a more complete edition called *War Lyrics* was brought out in 1866.

One cannot, returning to these verses today, but agree with their author's opinion of them. *The Bay Fight* presents, to be sure, what is evidently an accurate account, blow-by-blow, of what happened in Mobile Bay, but one can hardly accept it as poetry. A typical example of the verse of Brownell is a passage, much admired by Justice Holmes, which he quotes in a letter to Harold Laski:

> Ha, old ship! Do they thrill,
> The brave two hundred scars
> You got in the River Wars?
> That were leeched with clamorous skill,
> (Surgery savage and hard),
> Splintered with bolt and beam,
> Probed in scarfing and seam,
> Rudely linted and tarred

> With oakum and boiling pitch,
> At the Brooklyn Navy-Yard!

"Which," the Justice adds, "seems to me fine." And he returns to this poem of Brownell's in a later letter to Laski, declaring that the poet in this passage has "used oakum and boiling pitch with thrilling effect." It is highly characteristic of the tough old Holmes, with his devotion to ungrateful disciplines, that this celebration of "surgery savage and hard" should so have excited his enthusiasm. *The Bay Fight* ends on a note of hope, but a hope of the utmost bleakness:

> Be strong: already slants the gold
>   Athwart these wild and stormy skies;
> From out this blackened waste, behold,
>   What happy hours shall rise!

One feels that there was something in the New England character which made Brownell — perhaps also Holmes — prefer to get his ray of gold aslant on a blackened waste.

But Brownell is at his strongest in *The Bay Fight*. When he is not describing naval battles, his poems make rather a disagreeable impression: the writing is undistinguished, sometimes slipshod, and they are full of partisan hatred. Of the Southern soldiers, he writes that "The only line on their tomb" is "they died — and they died in vain."

> Gone — ay me! — to the grave,
>   And never one note of song —
> The Muse would weep for the brave,
>   But how shall she chant the wrong?
>
> For a wayward wench is she —
>   One that rather would wait

> With Old John Brown at the tree
> Than Stonewall dying in state.
>
> When, for the wrongs that were,
> Hath she lifted a single stave?
> Know, proud hearts, that, with her,
> 'Tis not enough to be brave.

The implication is that the Southerners were so hopelessly in the wrong that they could not even get the Muse to beat the drum for their cause as she was willing to do through Brownell for their enemies. And yet at that very moment, Henry Timrod, the Charleston poet, was writing very much the same kind of verse as Brownell and writing it a good deal better. His most famous poem *The Cotton Boll* was war propaganda like the *War Lyrics,* an expression of local patriotism; it was a hymn to the power of cotton and an assertion of confidence in the victory of the South. But Timrod has a sense of style of a quality that is lacking in Brownell, and he succeeds, like William Grayson, in conveying, along with his patriotism, the soft atmosphere of South Carolina.

One may also give a specimen here of the poetry written out of his experience of the war by John W. De Forest, the New Haven novelist. The following passage from *Campaigning* in a volume called *Poems: Medley and Palestina* has the documentary value of Brownell with something more of literary power:

> In middle night,
> In dewy silence, ocean-deep,
> The hundred-pounder on the bastioned height
> Awakened from its ponderous sleep
> And poured with all its iron might
> A lion-like, a grandly solemn roar
> That boomed and shuddered on

From horizon to horizon
  Until the lofty frame
  Of darkness shook from roof to floor.
Then rose the bomb a-sky,
  A lurid, crimson, bloody fiend of flame
That mounted swiftly while that awful cry
  Along the rocking welkin fled.
It clomb, it soared, it curved its flight,
  It paused one fearful moment overhead,
A meteor as red as hell;
Then burst in ruins deadly white,
In ghastly shatterings of livid light,
  Magnificent, sublime, and fell;
  While, clanging like a Pandemonic bell,
The great explosion shuddered on
From horizon to horizon;
  And once again the monstrous dome of night
Reeled outward from the roar
And shook from awful peak to boundless floor.

John De Forest, as a novelist, is relatively detached; but most of the poetry of the Civil War, Northern and Southern alike, was in the nature of patriotic journalism. The two war ballads still remembered, Whittier's *Barbara Frietchie* and *Sheridan's Ride* by Thomas Buchanan Read, both belong to this category. As a Quaker, John Greenleaf Whittier was on principle opposed to war, but he had become, since the thirties, when he first met Garrison, so active a fighter for Abolition that, when the North and the South came to blows, he had to accept the combat as a part of the inscrutable designs of God. He was as much a publicist as a poet. He had been several times mobbed in New England, and the building in Philadelphia in which he edited an anti-slavery paper had been burned down by a mob. Though he is sometimes a genuine poet in such of his New England pieces as *Skipper Ireson's Ride* and *Snow-Bound,* he wrote innumerable newspaper pieces, nowadays rarely read, which are simply a department of his political campaigning. It was Whittier's habit to produce a poem in connection with every public event in which the issue of slavery was involved, and this work is today more interesting for its chronicle of the incidents that set him off, as recorded in his prefatory notes, than it is for the merits of the poetry. It would perhaps be incorrect to call this propaganda versifying claptrap, because Whittier was not a crackpot and not a demagogue: he was nothing if not an earnest evangel; but today it has become repellent, for it is bigoted and as full of clichés about Freedom and Massachusetts and God as any collection of political speeches. "New Hampshire thunders an indignant No"; "The Yankee abolitionists" are "grim, stalwart men,/Each face set like a flint of Plymouth Rock"; the Freesoilers, migrating to Kansas, are "Upbearing, like the Ark of old, /The Bible in our van." The Southern planters are always either violating or lashing their female slaves. And the supposedly peace-loving Quaker God, when the North shall have won its victory, will show Himself complaisant with His favorites:

> Oh, small shall seem all sacrifice
> And pain and loss,
> When God shall wipe the weeping eyes,
> For suffering give the victor's prize,
> The crown for cross!

At the same time, Bret Harte, a young man in his twenties, working on a paper in San Francisco, is producing, inspired by his elders in the East, a more venomous if wittier variety of just the same sort of thing. He believes all the slanders about Jefferson Davis, and treats him as a low scoundrel. He has no need for the pious decorum which gives Whittier his solid façade, and he sometimes goes so far in his vilification that — though these pieces were added to his work after his death — one is gratified to find he excluded them from the collected edition of his verse.

The most elaborate and the most famous of all these poems that were written for the glory of the Northern cause is the *Ode* by James Russell Lowell *Recited at the Harvard Commemoration, July 21, 1865*. Lowell here did his very best to provide for his Unionist public the full-scale historic poem which their victory was thought to deserve, and everybody did his best to admire what was meant to be a monument. Even Henry James, looking back, persuaded himself that he had and did. But Lowell, except in satire or dialect, can hardly be called a poet at all. The language of his prose suffers somewhat from a rocky angularity of syntax and a gritty collocation of consonants; but it is pleasanter to read than his verse — except in the departments just mentioned — in which, following accepted practice, he is doomed to be self-consciously literary and, in consequence, mostly banal. I may cite what has always been regarded as the most successful section of the *Ode*, which was added, it appears, as an afterthought and seems, on that account perhaps, more spontaneous.

Such was he, our Martyr-Chief
　　Whom late the Nation he had led,
　　With ashes on her head,
Wept with the passion of an angry grief:
Forgive me, if from present things I turn
To speak what in my heart will beat and burn,

And hang my wreath on his world-honored urn.
  Nature, they say, doth dote,
  And cannot make a man
  Save on some worn-out-plan,
  Repeating us by rote:
For him her Old-World moulds aside she threw
  And, choosing sweet clay from the breast
  Of the unexhausted West,
With stuff untainted shaped a hero new,
Wise, steadfast in the strength of God, and true.
  How beautiful to see
Once more a shepherd of mankind indeed,
Who loved his charge, but never loved to lead;
One whose meek flock the people joyed to be,
  Not lured by any cheat of birth,
  But by his clear-grained human worth,
And brave old wisdom of sincerity!
  They knew that outward grace is dust;
  They could not choose but trust
In that sure-footed mind's unfaltering skill,
  And supple-tempered will
That bent like perfect steel to spring again and thrust.
  His was no lonely mountain-peak of mind,
  Thrusting to thin air o'er our cloudy bars,
  A sea-mark now, now lost in vapors blind;
  Broad prairie rather, genial, level-lined,
  Fruitful and friendly for all human kind,
Yet also nigh to heaven and loved of loftiest stars.
  Nothing of Europe here,
Or, then, of Europe fronting mornward still,
  Ere any names of Serf and Peer
  Could Nature's equal scheme deface
  And thwart her genial will:
  Here was a type of the true elder race,

And one of Plutarch's men talked with us face to face.
  I praise him not; it were too late;
And some innative weakness there must be
In him who condescends to victory
Such as the Present gives, and cannot wait,
    Safe in himself as in a fate.
      So always firmly he:
      He knew to bide his time,
      And can his fame abide,
Still patient in his simple faith sublime,
        Till the wise years decide.
    Great captains, with their guns and drums,
      Disturb our judgment for the hour,
        But at last silence comes;
    These all are gone, and, standing like a tower,
    Our children shall behold his fame,
      The kindly-earnest, brave, foreseeing man,
Sagacious, patient, dreading praise, not blame,
    New birth of our new soil, the first American.

It is a gauge of the mediocre level of the poetry of the
Civil War that Lowell's *Ode* should have been thought
to be one of its summits. One can understand Swinburne's saying of it that, in contrast to Whitman, it did
not leave in his ear "the echo of a single note of song."
This section about Lincoln, however, did eventually
stimulate Henry James to write something much finer
on the subject: a passage in *Notes of a Son and Brother*
which is partly a reworking of Lowell:

"The collective sense of what had occurred was of a
sadness too noble not somehow to inspire, and it was
truly in the air that, whatever we had as a nation produced or failed to produce, we could at least gather
round this perfection of a classic woe. True enough, as
we were to see, the immediate harvest of our loss was

almost too ugly to be borne — for nothing more sharply comes back to me than the tune to which the 'esthetic sense,' if one glanced but from *that* high window (which was after all one of many too), recoiled in dismay from the sight of Mr. Andrew Johnson perched on the stricken scene. We had given ourselves a figure-head, and the figure-head sat there in its habit as it lived, and we were to have it in our eyes for three or four years and to ask ourselves in horror what monstrous thing we had done. I speak but of aspects, those aspects which, under a certain turn of them, may be all but everything; gathered together they become a symbol of what is behind, and it was open to us to waver at shop-windows exposing the new photograph, exposing, that is, *the* photograph, and ask ourselves what we had been guilty of as a people, when all was said, to deserve the infliction of that form. It was vain to say that we had deliberately invoked the 'Common' in authority and must drink the wine we had drawn. No countenance, no salience of aspect nor composed symbol, could superficially have referred itself less than Lincoln's mould-smashing mask to any mere matter-of-course type of propriety; but his admirable unrelated head had itself revealed a type — as if by the very fact that what made in it for roughness of kind looked out only less than what made in it for splendid final stamp, in other words for commanding Style."

But Lowell had become dissatisfied with his own conventional poetic language, a language derived from the literature of England and out of touch with colloquial American speech. He was naturally a vigorous writer, and he was irked by the pallidity and the artificiality of an idiom that had become academic. He was to state the case against this idiom when he came to write the introduction to his second series of *Biglow Papers*. "It is only from its roots in the living generations

of men that a language can be reinforced with fresh
vigor for its needs; what may be called a literate dialect
grows ever more and more pedantic and foreign, till it
becomes at last as unfitting a vehicle for living thought
as monkish Latin. That we should all be made to
talk like books is the danger with which we are threatened by the Universal Schoolmaster, who does his best
to enslave the minds and memories of his victims to what
he esteems the best models of English composition, that
is to say, to the writers whose style is faultily correct and
has no blood-warmth in it."

He had begun, at the time of the Mexican War, with
which the first series of *Biglow Papers* deals, to write
in the New England dialect, and these satires on American aggression in the West achieved such a popular
success that he revived his New England characters,
Parson Wilbur, Hosea Biglow and Birdofredum Sawin,
in order to make them express themselves on the subject of the Civil War; and he is now trying to exploit
this dialect in a more serious poetic way. Lowell, too, had
been active as an Abolitionist, and he had much of the
New England intolerance. His point of view on the rights
of the South is quite different from his earlier one on the
rights of the expropriated Mexicans. The speech made
by Biglow in the final paper is, though Lowell had not
enough insight to know it — he had never been in the
South — exactly the sort of thing to enrage a defeated
enemy and to make him as uncoöperative as possible.
The South is treated here as a delinquent child, and
the policy to be adopted is to render her completely
powerless and to make her confess that she has been in
the wrong:

> Wal, all we ask's to hev it understood
> You'll take his gun away from him for good;

> We don't, wal, not exac'ly, like his play,
> Seein' he allus kin' o' shoots our way.
> You kill your fatted calves to no good end,
> 'thout his fust sayin', Mother, I hev sinned!

The Southerners, even after they have taken the oath, are not to be trusted a minute; and he follows this admonition with a fable about the wolves who had once had "certing rights," who slept with the dogs and guarded the sheep, and how this had worked out badly:

> Ez for their oaths they wun't be wuth a button,
> Long 'z you don't cure 'em o' their taste for mutton;
> Th' ain't but one solid way, howe'er you puzzle:
> Tell they're converted, let 'em wear a muzzle.

And we must see to it that the Southerners are Americanized:

> Give wut they need, an' we shell git 'fore long
> A nation all one piece, rich, peacefle, strong;
> Make 'em Amerikin, an' they'll begin
> To love their country ez they loved their sin;
> Let 'em stay Southun, an' you've kep' a sore
> Ready to fester ez it done afore.

(Lowell, it must be said, was later to moderate this attitude when he saw what Reconstruction was doing to the South: "The whole condition of things at the South is shameful, and I am ready for a movement now to emancipate the whites. No doubt the government is bound to protect the misintelligence of the blacks, but surely not at the expense of the intelligence of men of our own blood.")

But the trimmer Birdofredum Sawin is a really amusing character. He has calculated wrong how the cat will jump and, deserting his girl in New England, has gone to live in the South and married a Southern widow, but

when eventually the Union wins, he decides that he has
been with it all along. And the whole book is full of the
kind of wit with which Lowell has already disported himself in the doggerel *Fable for Critics*, but which is here
more concise and pointed. The concrete detail of New
England life and the imagery based on this are quaint,
vivid and sometimes moving. The dialect liberates Lowell
for a play of imagination that one hardly finds elsewhere
in his writing: for example, such a passage as this on the
current unpopularity of old-fashioned mahogany furniture:

> Once git a smell o' musk into a draw,
> An' it clings hold like precerdents in law:
> Your gra'ma'am put it there, — when good-
>   ness knows, —
> To jes' this-worldify her Sunday-clo'es;
> But the old chist wun't sarve her gran'son's wife,
> (For, 'thout new funnitoor, wut good in life?)
> An' so ole clawfoot, from the precinks dread
> O' the spare chamber, slinks into the shed,
> Where, dim with dust, it fust or last subsides
> To holdin' seeds an' fifty things besides;
> But better days stick fast in heart an' husk,
> An' all you keep in 't gits a scent o' musk.

This whole poem, called *Sunthin' in the Pastoral Line*
and relatively free from politics, is undoubtedly one of
Lowell's best pieces.

It has often been remarked that the rustic Hosea Biglow and his learned friend Parson Wilbur, who is preoccupied with supposed Viking runes and the writing of
An Enquiry Concerning the Tenth Horn of the Beast
of the Apocalypse, are two sides of the same coin. In
the *Papers*, Parson Wilbur dies, and Hosea is left to
carry on. It is curious that in Lowell's own life, this order

should have been reversed. He never developed further the style of the *Biglow Papers*, which certainly contains the best dialect verse ever written in the United States. He was appointed by President Rutherford B. Hayes in 1880 Minister to the Court of St. James and he returned, after five years in England so thoroughly Anglicized that he always wore a silk hat in Cambridge. In some of the fragments of the Yankee *Decameron* that he projected in the fifties and sixties, he had been partly working the same happy vein; but, as he afterwards said in connection with this poem, "something broke my life in two and I cannot piece it together again."

Herman Melville, of the same generation, scarcely saw more of the war at firsthand than Whittier or Lowell did; but his visit to his nephew in the Army of the Potomac inspired *A Scout toward Aldie*, which has already been discussed above. This long piece, a short story in verse, was included by him in a volume called *Battle Pieces*, which otherwise consists of poems of a different kind. Some people admire these poems more than the present writer, and they are certainly more interesting than most of the verse that was written about the war; yet, with the notable exception of the *Scout*, they seem to me not really poetry for the same fundamental reasons. Herman Melville, a New Yorker not a New Englander, had nothing of the vehement animus of Lowell, Brownell and Whittier; but he, too, is writing versified journalism: a chronicle of the patriotic feelings of an anxious middle-aged non-combatant as, day by day, he reads the bulletins from the front. The celebration of current battles by poets who have not taken part in them has produced some of the emptiest verse that exists.

Walt Whitman is a different matter. Whitman, too, came from cosmopolitan New York and had nothing of the crusading New Englander. When the war broke out, he was forty-two. He was very little heard of during the first eighteen months, and has been upbraided by Thomas Wentworth Higginson and others for not having rallied at once to the Union; but when he learned, at the end of 1862, that his brother had been wounded in the slaughter of Fredericksburg, he went to join him, and then, making Washington his headquarters and earning a small living there by working a few hours a day as a copyist, he spent the rest of his time visiting the hospitals, where he dressed wounds, brought presents to the soldiers and otherwise made himself useful. He continued this for a year and a half, exposing himself to gangrene and contagious diseases, until finally his own health broke down, and he began having paralytic strokes. He boasted that he had visited at one time or another between eighty and a hundred thousand soldiers, and that in some cases his special attentions had succeeded in saving their lives — which may be true, since a strange personal magnetism as of a being somehow different from the rest of humanity was sometimes felt by people who met him. He was, in any case, as a result of this hospital experience, in a position to write about a side of the war which was otherwise little reported. One finds some record of it in his letters and his wartime jottings: "These hospitals, so different from all others — these thousands, and tens and twenties of thousands of American young men, badly wounded, all sorts of wounds, operated on, pallid with diarrhœa, languishing, dying with fever, pneumonia, etc., open a new world somehow to me, giving closer insights, new things, exploring deeper mines than any yet, showing our humanity (I sometimes put myself in fancy in the cot, with typhoid, or under the knife), tried by terrible, fearfullest tests, probed deepest, the living soul's, the body's tragedies, bursting the petty bonds of art."

Like everyone who in any war is thrown with the rank and file and is brought to realize their helplessness and the pathos of our common humanity, he develops a certain resentment against those who must manipulate and condemn them. Here is a note on one of the deserters whom Lincoln failed to pardon: "While all this gaud and tinsel shines in people's eyes amid the countless officers' straps, amid all this show of generals' stars and the bars of the captains and lieutenants — amid all the wind and puffing and infidelity — amid the swarms of contractors and their endless contracts and the paper money — and out from all this stalks like a phantom that boy, not yet nineteen years of age, boy who had fought without flinching in twelve battles (no veteran of old wars better or steadier) — stalks forth, I say, that single, simple boy, out of all this huge composite pageant, silently, with a bandage over his eyes — the volley — the smoke — the limpsey falling body and blood streaming in strains and splashes down the breast."

He entertained for some years after the war the idea of writing a book on the subject, but he finally gave this up: "And so good-bye to the war. . . . Future years will never know the seething hell and the black infernal background of countless minor scenes and interiors (not the official surface courteousness of the generals, not the few great battles) of the Secession War; and it is best they should not. The real war will never get in the books."

But Whitman did make his distinguished contribution to the literature of the Civil War in the sequences of poems about it — *Drum-Taps* and *Memories of President Lincoln* — which he added to *Leaves of Grass*. The latter of these groups includes *O Captain! My Captain!* and *When Lilacs Last in the Dooryard Bloom'd* — the first of which, by no means of Whitman's best but more conventional in form and closer to topical journalism than anything else in *Leaves of Grass,* proved for a long time the poet's most popular piece, and the second of which is of course one of his finest. Whitman believed himself, at the time when *Drum-Taps* was published, that it was so far the best thing he had written. It certainly contained the best poetry that was written during the war on the subject of the war. Walt Whitman was committed to the Union cause, yet the flapping of the Stars and Stripes in the *Song of the Banner at Daybreak* sets off not a burst of propaganda but a vision of the people of the country, north and south, east and west, set in motion by the impulse of the war that has them all marching, hurrying, working. Instead of the galloping horsemen derived from romantic ballads, Walt Whitman makes a sketch from the life of *Cavalry Crossing a Ford:*

A line in long array where they wind betwixt green islands,
They take a serpentine course, their arms flash in the sun — hark to the musical clank,
Behold the silvery river, in it the splashing horses loitering stop to drink,
Behold the brown-faced men, each group, each person a picture, the negligent rest on the saddles,
Some emerge on the opposite bank, others are just entering the ford — while,
Scarlet and blue and snowy white,
The guidon flags flutter gayly in the wind.

He does not need the slave in chains who has become a stock property of anti-slavery literature:

Ethiopia Saluting the Colors

Who are you dusky woman, so ancient hardly human,
With your woolly-white and turban'd head, and bare
bony feet?
Why rising by the roadside here, do you the colors greet?
('Tis while our army lines Carolina's sands and pines,
Forth from thy hovel door thou Ethiopia com'st to me,
As under doughty Sherman I march toward the sea.)
Me master years a hundred since from parents sunder'd,
A little child, they caught me as the savage beast is
caught,
Then hither me across the sea the cruel slaver brought.
No further does she say, but lingering all the day,
Her high-borne turban'd head she wags, and rolls her
darkling eye,
And courtesies to the regiments, the guidons moving by.
What is it, fateful woman, so blear, hardly human?
Why wag your head with turban bound, yellow, red,
and green?
Are the things so strange and marvelous you see or have
seen?

He does not write editorials on current events but describes his actual feelings:

Year that Trembled and Reel'd beneath Me.

Year that trembled and reel'd beneath me!
Your summer wind was warm enough, yet the air I
breathed froze me,
A thick gloom fell through the sunshine and darken'd
me,
Must I change my triumphant songs? said I to myself,
Must I indeed learn to chant the cold dirges of the
baffled?
And sullen hymns of defeat?

And the final piece of the sequence is an epitaph which would obliterate partisan hatred:

Reconciliation

Word over all, beautiful as the sky,
Beautiful that war and all its deeds of carnage must in
    time be utterly lost,
That the hands of the sisters Death and Night inces-
    santly softly wash again and ever again, this soil'd
    world;
For my enemy is dead, a man divine as myself is dead,
I look where he lies white-faced and still in the coffin —
    I draw near,
Bend down and touch lightly with my lips the white face
    in the coffin.

In the world of the early America just after the Revolution — loose settlements and pleasant towns growing up
on the banks of great rivers, in the span of enormous
landscapes and on the edge of mysterious wilds — it was
occasionally possible for the arts to take seed and quietly
to flower in a purer and freer form than was easy at a
later date. In Albemarle County, Virginia, it is marvelous to see with how sure a touch Thomas Jefferson has
situated his charming creations on the hospitable little
hills in such a way as to involve the landscape in a
personal work of art. The bubble domes, the candid
façades, the variety of the classical cornices in the "pa-
vilions" that enclose the university "lawn" and in which
the professors live, the delightful white octagon rooms,
with French windows that open on level vistas,
have humanized the Palladian style into something
eclectic and lovely; and the very imperfections of these
buildings — the big clock at Monticello which has to be
off-center in the portico in order to be centered in the

hall, the slight irregularity of the number and spacing of the pillars in the college colonnade — only make them blend more pleasantly with nature.

So the marvelous plates of John James Audubon — the animals and birds of a continent — have come to life among the forests and wastes, the vast plains and the inland waterways, where their recently discovered originals had been living on equal terms with the Indians. The animating power of this artist is seen perhaps even better in his "quadrupeds" than in his birds. His larger animals — his bison and bears and bull moose — sometimes take him beyond his range, but his spermophiles and rodents and moles and other of the smaller animals — which do not exceed the scale of the birds but do not meet the artist halfway by providing so much gay color and obvious grace — are delightful illustrations of his genius for personalizing and dramatizing his subjects and, by the imaginative use of landscape, embodying them in balanced compositions: the black fox with his silver-sleek coat and the bright points of light in his alert yellow eyes; the magnificent striped plume of the mother skunk defending from the vantage of a hollow log her still groping babies inside it; the huge paws and topaz eyes of the staring Canadian lynx; the tusked snouts of Richardson's meadow mice pursuing their obstinate path through the gray bristling winter woodland; the cotton rats of the South, sleazy and blue-eyed poor whites, with their imbecile mouths agape, as, with a primitive log shack in the background, they feed on a prostrate yam; the violet rosettes of the star-nosed moles that delicately vibrate to their prey in the darkness of the burrows or streams where they hunt: a strange contrast with the free-skimming sails on the river in the distance behind them; the scampering family of Sciuridæ in their apparently innumerable variety: the purposive snakelike black squirrel, the kittenlike downy squirrel, the pleased and admiring female of the Oregon flying squirrel, as, seated among the acorns, she watches her mate take off, the self-contained long-haired squirrel tenaciously clutching his nut among yellow-brown autumn leaves that harmonize with his belly's burnt-orange, the red-bellied squirrels with their plum-like blend of rose-orange and purple-gray, one prudently hugging its birch branch while the other, jauntily poised, stands up on its hind legs and leans forward, with forepaws flung wide, as if it saw something of special interest.

The stories and poems of Poe do not, of course, have much in common with this outdoor American world, and yet they are also products of this early thinly-populated America. In those neighborly old-fashioned towns there were also close and lonely frame-houses in which isolated morbid relationships, under the influence of alcohol or laudanum, could give rise to visions and hallucinations that had as little relation to society as the animals and birds of Audubon. The vague background of velvet and silk, heavy portières and plush-covered furniture, remembered or longed-for grandeur, only serves to give sharper focus to those images, at once burning and cold — the pangs of horror or pain, bridled hatred or ingrown desire — which are excreted, in the provincial solitude, under pressure of the narrow rooms. And if these hard compulsive pieces of Poe's are thus crystallized like precious gems, the melodies of Stephen Foster flow as naturally as the dews of evening or the amber of maple sap. From the wistful lament of the slave, the jingle of the minstrel refrain, the romantic piano ballad with which the young ladies of that era were in the habit of charming their beaux, he condensed little drops of emotion that have never lost their freshness and felicity. (Here a trimming of barbershop chords which was added by Foster's "arrangers" sometimes figures as a period equivalent to Poe's rustling curtains and irrelevant plush.)

Now, Audubon and Foster and Poe were all of them to become very popular, yet they did not find much steady support in the loose-strewn communities among which they lived. Poe and Foster, though they found a certain market, were never able to make their earnings keep pace with their living expenses; both took to the bottle and died relatively young, wretchedly and almost anonymously. Audubon, closer to the earth and a scientist absorbed in his subject, lived to be sixty-nine, but he was so little broken to society that, on his visit to Scotland, his sponsors and friends had to make him shear off the primeval growth of his long and bad-smelling hair before they would let him go to London: "This day My Hairs were sacrificed," he wrote in his diary, "and the will of God usurped by the wishes of Man." Yet in their work all these artists had had more spontaneity than was usual with the accepted celebrities who followed them. There was in literature still something of this brightness and freshness in the poems and notebooks of Emerson, in the liquidities and densities of *Walden*, in the vividness of Melville's voyages; but all these writers inhabit the natural world — the countryside, the village, the open sea — and as the cities of the East expand, with their tightening reticulation of railroads, their landscape-annihilating factories, this quality comes to seem more and more a choked leak through the cracks of a hardening surface.

During the years of the Civil War, this more authentic kind of poetry scarcely leaks through at all. It is a striking phenomenon of the period that the declamatory versification of public events should completely have rendered inaudible, should have driven into virtual hiding, the more personal kind of self-expression which had nothing to do with politics or battles, which was not

concocted for any market and which, reflecting the idio-
syncrasies of the writer, was likely to take on an unconventional form. There were poets of real distinction who
were writing all through this period but who were
hardly or never heard of, who were even not published
till after their deaths. Walt Whitman himself, one supposes, would have remained as obscure as the others if
he had not undertaken himself to see that *Leaves of
Grass* was published and put into circulation, setting the
type with his own hands and composing bogus reviews
in order to call the public's attention to it. But Emily
Dickinson is a tragic case of the poet who was never
allowed to emerge. The years of the Civil War were for
Miss Dickinson especially productive, but she never, so
far as I know, refers to the war in her poetry, and there
are very few references to it in her letters: she comments on the deaths of the sons of her friends, alludes
to the arrest of Jefferson Davis and, in writing to Thomas
Wentworth Higginson — who with his colonelcy, his bird-
lidded eyes and his inalienable muttonchop whiskers has
come to be ubiquitous in this chronicle — expresses the
hope that he will come back unharmed from his campaign
with his colored regiment and is distressed to hear later of
his injury. She had written him — on April 15 — in the second year of the war, sending him some of her poems and
asking him to tell her what he thought of them, and she
afterwards sent him more; but when Higginson went to
call upon her in Amherst she seems, as has been said, to
have scared him, and he did not encourage her to publish.
Her desperation, her unexpected images and the vagaries
of her versification were inevitably regarded as unsuitable
for the pages of the *Atlantic Monthly*. Only two of Miss
Dickinson's poems ever got into print in her lifetime, and
these attracted no attention. Her work was not known
till the nineties, when Higginson at last helped toward

its publication and made some effort to defend her ec-
centricities.

Emily Dickinson has become an American classic
(though one that I cannot help thinking a little over-
rated), and there is no point in describing her poetry
here. But I do want in this connection to say something
about another poet — Frederick Goddard Tuckerman —
who was "underground" through most of his lifetime and
who is still not well-known today. The Tuckermans were
rather a brilliant New England family, who distinguished
themselves both in literature and in science. You will
find several columns about them in the *Dictionary of
American Biography*. Frederick Goddard's cousin Henry
T. Tuckerman was in his time a very active journalist;
he also wrote poetry, which was mediocre but which usually got into the anthologies. Frederick Tuckerman published only one volume of verse, the title of which was
simply *Poems* and which was at first — in 1860 — only
privately printed, but which was published four years
later in the regular way and reprinted in 1869. There
had been also an English edition in 1863, which may
have been brought out at the suggestion of Tennyson,
with whom Tuckerman had corresponded and whom he
visited in 1855. "I should tell you," he wrote his brother,
"that at parting Mr. Tennyson gave me the original ms.
of *Locksley Hall*, a favour of which I may be justly
proud, as he says he has never done such a thing in his
life before, for anybody." It was said of one of Tuckerman's poems by Emerson, to whom he had sent his
book, that it "ought to be bound up as a fifth in your
friend Tennyson's *Idyls*," and he included this poem in
his anthology *Parnassus*. A copy was also sent to Longfellow, who complimented the author graciously but without any special enthusiasm. One gets the impression, as
has been noted by Witter Bynner, Tuckerman's latter-

day editor, that neither of these older men had any appreciation of what was really original in Tuckerman's work — which was most evident in two sequences of sonnets. And the book itself was quite forgotten up to the time when Mr. Louis How, a literary man in New York, set out, about 1905, to put together an anthology of American poetry — unfortunately never published — which should avoid the too well-known old favorites and revive some less familiar pieces. He was intending to include two of Tuckerman's sonnets, and these were seen by the late Walter Prichard Eaton, who considered them so remarkable that he looked up the Tuckerman volume. Eaton published an article on Tuckerman in the *Forum* of January, 1909, and this brought a response from the Tuckerman family and stimulated the interest of Witter Bynner. Mr. Bynner thought these poems strangely "modern" — that is, modern in terms of his own generation: he speaks of Robinson, Masefield, Millay. He was allowed by the Tuckerman family to examine the poet's papers, and he found among them three sequences of unpublished sonnets. These he brought out in a volume in 1931, with an admirable introduction, together with the sequences from *Poems* and a selection from the rest of its contents. A further posthumous poem, *The Cricket*, was printed, in 1950, as a leaflet by the Cummington Press of Cummington, Massachusetts. So Tuckerman has emerged at last from the obscurity which the retirement of his life invited.

Or rather, for the first time the public was allowed an incursion into Tuckerman's world, which is almost as special as and more private than that of Emily Dickinson. More private because Emily Dickinson does display a certain coyness which implies an awareness of others: though she came to have a phobia about meeting strangers and eventually refused to leave the family house,

she did really want to have herself noticed: with encouragement, she would certainly have published. But
Tuckerman, after bringing out his volume, seems not
to have wanted to communicate with anyone save the
spirit of his lost wife. He had studied law at Harvard
and had practised for a time in Boston, but he did not
need to earn a living and, after his marriage to his com-
panionable wife, he went to live in Greenfield, Massachusetts. Hannah Tuckerman died in 1857, when Tuckerman was thirty-six, but he continued to live in the
country with his children, and he devoted the rest of
his life to poetry, astronomy and botany. He had a telescope, kept a journal of his observations and published
some papers on eclipses; he was a pioneer student of the
flora of his region and became an authority on it; and
he kept on, from time to time, writing poetry. His wife
had died in bearing her third child after only ten years
of marriage, and she haunts the whole series of his sonnets: a strange journal — almost as secret as Pepys's —
of recollections still heart-breakingly vivid, of "weeping
solitudes," country sights, country weather, which extends into the year before Tuckerman's death. I can find
among Tuckerman's poems only one certain reference to
the Civil War, in connection with a young countryman
who has been killed in it. Mr. Bynner believes that
two of the sonnets, though written a decade later, also
refer to the war; but this seems to me rather dubious:
the army of which Tuckerman speaks seems, rather, a
tumultuous metaphor. To write directly about actual
historical events is not at all Tuckerman's way. He has
even partly invented his own history as well as his own
mythology.

It has been noted by W. H. Auden that the invention
of mythologies is an American specialty. Washington
Irving invented Rip Van Winkle and the legend of

Sleepy Hollow in order to provide the Hudson Valley with folk-lore. Longfellow concocted an Indian myth by combining the already rather garbled legends in the ethnological writings of Schoolcraft. Poe invented the dark tarn of Auber and the ghoul-haunted woodland of Weir. James Branch Cabell created the kingdom of Poictesme with its mélange of all the mythologies. And one of the queerest features of Tuckerman's work is his habit of alluding, not merely to characters from Biblical or classical antiquity so obscure that one cannot believe they are real till one finds them in a concordance or a classical dictionary, but also to personages who cannot be found because their names have been made up by the poet. The most outrageous example of this is the sonnet about one Eponina, whom the poet produces from nowhere but refers to as if her story were as familiar as Antigone's or Esther's:

As Eponina brought, to move the king
In the old day, her children of the tomb
Begotten and brought forth in charnel gloom,
To plead a father's cause, so I too bring
Unto thy feet, my Maker, tearfully,
These offspring of my sorrow, hidden long
And scarcely able to abide the light.
May their deep cry, inaudible, come to thee
Clear through the cloud of words, the sobs of song,
And sharper than that other's pierce thine ears —
That so each thought, aim, utterance, dark or bright,
May find thy pardoning love more blest than she
Who joyfully passed with them to death and night,
With whom she had been buried nine long years!

But he is likely to produce his imaginary name as a climax at the end of the poem rather than thus to make its bearer a theme:

And now he breathes apart, to daily drink
In tears the bitter ashes of his love,
Yet precious-rich and a diviner draught
Than Agria or Artemisia drank!

Artemisia, it seems, is real: she drank up her husband's
ashes by mixing them in her wine; but who was Agria
and what did *she* drink?

Did Manoah's wife doubt ere she showed to him
The angel standing in the golden grain?
Had Deborah fear? Or was that vision vain
That Actia, Arlotte, and Mandané dreamed?

Here Manoah and Deborah are real, but who are the
other three ladies with the improbable-sounding names?
We sometimes suspect Tuckerman of cheating by in-
venting a name to fill in for the rhyme. In one poem he
speaks of "perusing a forgotten sage" and "turning . . .
a dim old page / Of history," and not till the end of the
terminal line do we learn the identity of this author,
whom the poet names in a portentous way but of whose
work one has never heard and of whom one can find no
mention.

The sun was gone, the bird, and bleak and drear
An all but icy breath the balsams stirred.
I turned again and, entering with a groan,
Sat darkly down to Dagoraus Whear.

Was Tuckerman being mischievous? I doubt it: I imagine
that these unrecorded characters had really come to live
with him in the solitude of Greenfield. Whether or not
he had read about them was a matter of no importance.

And it would seem that this dissociated poet also invented words, very much in the manner of Joyce:

The little valley hidden in the pine,
The low-built cottage buried in the vale,

Wooded and over-wooded, bushed about
With holm tree, ople tree, and sycamine.

The holm tree can be found in the dictionary; but the ople tree and sycamine cannot. I think that Mr. Bynner is in general correct in his explanation of this passage. It embodies a nostalgic memory of a cottage and a country girl that the poet had passed once on his way to the city, the noisiness and dreariness of which he dreaded. Mr. Bynner believes that the concluding line involves a combination of "elm and holm, apple and opal, sycamore and mine." (Since a holm tree is a holm oak, it cannot be an elm, but the *holm-home* idea may be there.) And he adds, "an apparently whimsical but really emotional use of words that Edgar Allan Poe might have envied." This poet also handles the sonnet form in a quite irregular way, departing from the ordinary rhyme-schemes, not separating the sestet from the octet and not always filling out the pentameter.

It is easier to give an idea of Frederick Tuckerman's little grotesqueries than to illustrate his peculiar excellence. One has really to read his poems in sequence. If his poetry has a touch of the fantastic, it is in general more realistic than the conventional verse of the period. There are a few *thees* and *thous* and some residue of the stock romantic vocabulary, but the phrasing surprises by its sharpness, by its individual flavor; and no feature of the world around him is too homely or too contemporary to be given a place in his verse. His touch has the freshness and felicity of the earlier artists of whom I have spoken. The common creatures and natural objects of the Berkshires and the Long Island beaches appear to us in poignant glimpses. They have been drawn by the poet into the magic kingdom in which, alive to beauty, he grieves:

We hunted on, from flower to rusty flower,
Tattered and dim the last red butterfly,
Or the old grasshopper molasses-mouthed.

And hard like this I stand, and beaten and blind,
This desolate rock with lichens rusted over
Hoar with salt-sleet and chalkings of the birds.

He observes his country neighbors with a certain sympathy, though they sometimes become confused with the other phenomena of nature:

An awkward youth in the dark angle there,
Dangling and flapping like a maple-key
Caught in a cobweb.

"That boy," — the farmer said, with hazel wand
Pointing him out, half by the haycock hid —
"Though bare sixteen, can work at what he's bid,
From sun till set, — to cradle, reap, or band."
I heard the words but scarce could understand
Whether they claimed a smile or gave me pain.
Or was it aught to me, in that green lane,
That all day yesterday, the briers amid,
He held the plough against the jarring land
Steady, or kept his place among the mowers,
Whilst other fingers, sweeping for the flowers,
Brought from the forest back a crimson stain?
Was it a thorn that touched the flesh, or did
The poke-berry spit purple on my hand?

And he is able to accept and ennoble the incidents that make up his own life in a style that never lapses like Wordsworth's, though it cannot sustain the level of Yeats. Here are the last three sonnets of the final sequence, written evidently not long before Tuckerman's death:

And me my winter's task is drawing over,
Though night and winter shake the drifted door.

Critic or friend, dispraiser or approver,
I come not now nor fain would offer more.
But when buds break and round the fallen limb
The wild weeds crowd in clusters and corymb,
When twilight rings with the red robin's plaint,
Let me give something — though my heart be faint —
To thee, my more than friend! — believer! lover! . . .
The gust has fallen now, and all is mute —
Save pricking on the pane the sleety showers,
The clock that ticks like a belated foot,
Time's hurrying step, the twanging of the hours . . .
Wait for those days, my friend, or get thee fresher
flowers.

Let me give something! — though my spring be done,
Give to the children, ere their summertime!
Though stirred with grief, like rain let fall my rhyme
And tell of one whose aim was much: of one
Whose strife was this, that in his thought should be
Some power of wind, some drenching of the sea,
Some drift of stars across a darkling coast,
Imagination, insight, memory, awe,
And dear New England nature first and last, —
Whose end was high, whose work was well-begun:
Of one who from his window looked and saw
His little hemlocks in the morning sun,
And while he gazed, into his heart almost
The peace that passeth understanding, passed.

Let me give something! — as the years unfold,
Some faint fruition, though not much, my most.
Perhaps a monument of labour lost.
But Thou, who givest all things, give not me
To sink in silence, seared with early cold,
Frost-burnt and blackened, but quick fire for frost! —
As once I saw at a houseside, a tree

Struck scarlet by the lightning, utterly
To its last limb and twig. So strange it seemed,
I stopped to think if this indeed were May.
And were those windflowers? — or had I dreamed? . . .
But there it stood, close by the cottage eaves,
Red-ripened to the heart: shedding its leaves
And autumn sadness on the dim spring day.

Tuckerman's occasional obscurity, like that of Emily
Dickinson, contributes to one's general impression of a so-
liloquy not quite overheard. It is interesting that Emily
Dickinson should have known Frederick's brother Edward, who taught botany at Amherst College, and also
Tuckerman's son and his son's wife. There is a good
deal about the Tuckermans in Emily's letters; but —
though Greenfield is not far from Amherst — there is
no mention of Frederick Goddard. Did Emily know that
the father of her friend, almost as much a recluse as herself, was writing remarkable poetry? Had Tuckerman
ever been told that Emily Dickinson wrote? Colonel
Thomas Wentworth Higginson — though he and Tuckerman had been classmates at Harvard—had no notion of
Tuckerman's talent. Old Higginson was still alive when
Tuckerman was rediscovered, and, in response to an inquiry by Bynner, he explained that he remembered his
contemporary "as a refined and gentlemanly fellow, but
I did not then know him as a poet."

Edgar Allan Poe and Ezra Pound make two convenient
pillars with which to mark off a span during which the
art of poetry in the United States got very little serious
attention. Both these men were attempting to rescue it
from the sloppiness and verbosity of magazine romanticism, to insist on concentration — in Poe's case, on
brevity — on intensity of calculated effect.

Poe has explained his aims in his criticism, and if his

own poems are not always what one would expect from this, it is because, after his early poetry, which derived from the English romantics and really aimed at the quintessential, he came under the influence of that baroque Southern poet Thomas Holley Chivers. Poe's *Poems* appeared in 1831; Chivers began sending his verses to the *Southern Literary Messenger,* of which Poe was the editor, in 1835, and the two men corresponded, read one another's work and eventually met. Chivers was a well-to-do physician from Georgia, who practised little but wrote a good deal. He published eleven volumes of verse of a very peculiar kind, which has moments of something like splendor, moments that are incredibly ridiculous and a good deal that is simply mediocre. Yet Chivers had a certain originality, and his rhythms and refrains were infectious. Swinburne and Rossetti both read him and laughed at him, but felt a real interest in him, and the former seems to have echoed him in *Dolores,* the latter in *The Blessed Damozel.* Certainly he went to the head of Poe. It is true, as has been pointed out, that Chivers was influenced by Poe and took over as a property the Israfel of one of Poe's early poems; but it seems to me that only jealous loyalty to Poe can deny that — as Chivers claimed himself — the evidence of priority shows that such later productions of Poe's as *The Raven* and *Annabel Lee* — usually thought of as his most characteristic — have been imitated from poems by Chivers. This is the near-ridiculous side of Poe; his poetry had been more serious before he discovered Chivers. But Chivers had been incapable of self-criticism: he was throwing his inventions away, and Poe was unable to resist picking them up and making some cleverer use of them at the same time that he let himself in for the contagion of the other poet's trashiness. I think that this is the real explanation of Poe's essay called *The Phi-*

losophy of Composition, in which he tells how he wrote *The Raven* as a mere exercise in poetic contrivance "that should suit at once the popular and the critical taste." One remembers the pathetic preface to *The Raven and Other Poems,* published in 1845, in which Poe says that he ought to explain "that I think nothing in this volume of much value to the public, or very creditable to myself. Events not to be controlled have prevented me from making, at any time, any serious effort in what, under happier circumstances, would have been the field of my choice. With me poetry has been not a purpose, but a passion; and the passions should be held in reverence; they must not — they cannot at will be excited with an eye to the paltry compensations, or the more paltry commendations, of mankind." This is perhaps somewhat inconsistent with the statement quoted above from *The Philosophy of Composition;* but in any case it seems quite possible that Poe did feel a certain cynicism toward the poetry of his Chivers period. It was hardly what he had once dreamed of doing. Surprise has been sometimes felt at the admiration expressed by Poe for extremely inferior writers; but special fashion or special affinities may affect the opinion of any critic, and one cannot read Poe's criticism of contemporary poetry without realizing how much closer attention he gave to the texture of verse than was usual in the America of his day. He is sometimes pedantic and spiteful with writers toward whom he feels hostility; but the ideal which he was trying to serve was really an exacting one. Poe's criticism seems to have had very little effect on the American taste of his time, though it may have acted then and later as a brake on the reputations of the more tepid New England poets; but it was very important in France in its influence on the symbolist school.

Ezra Pound, on the other hand, when his time came,

was able to act as marshal to a movement, a movement that was trying to free itself of Victorianism and its American equivalent and even to some extent of the early romantics themselves. The condition of poetry in the United States in the years during which Pound was growing up "in a half-savage country, out of date" — he was born in 1885 — may be indicated by his coming to the conclusion that "verse ought to be as well written as prose." He thought and wrote a good deal about the methods of verse, and he aimed in his own poetry at hard images and compact language. "It would be a very good exercise," writes Pound in *The ABC of Reading*, "to take parallel passages of these two poets [Wordsworth and Swinburne], the first so very famous, and the second one so very much decried at the present time, and see how many useless words each uses, how many which contribute nothing, how many which contribute nothing very definite."

As Poe became a *chef d'école* in France without much affecting his own country, so Pound, who went to live in Europe, became an international figure, whose influence, in one way or another, was felt wherever English was written. But in Pound's case this influence was felt especially in the United States. We have no concern here with this period in which Pound played so central a role, the only period in our literary history in which poetry can be said to have flourished: we are only concerned with the prairie that extends between Poe and Pound. In this prairie push a few rare growths, a few rather amateur poets, who are moving in Pound's direction.

The two volumes of extremely unconventional verse that were published by Stephen Crane in the nineties, with their unrhymed lines of irregular lengths, their nihilistic fables and their laconic irony, were quite unlike anything else that had ever been written in America — or rather, they resembled nothing except, a little, certain other unconventional writers. Mr. Daniel G. Hoffman, the author of *The Poetry of Stephen Crane,* suggests that Crane as poet may have owed something to Ambrose Bierce's *Fantastic Fables* in prose. It has also been thought that Crane may have been influenced by some poems of Emily Dickinson's that are supposed to have been read to him by William Dean Howells. Mr. Hoffman can find only one line of Crane's which may betray a direct debt to Miss Dickinson: "A man adrift on a slim spar" may echo her "Two swimmers on a spar." How solitary these non-conforming poets are!

Miss Adelaide Crapsey, whose posthumous poems were published in 1915, was the loneliest and saddest of all. The daughter of a well-known Episcopal clergyman, she had spent her life in girls' schools and colleges teaching history and literature, and she wrote part of a study of English versification, which was published after her death. This is not a work of very great interest: an inquiry, rather pedantically presented, into the practice of several poets in their addiction to monosyllables, dissyllables or words of more than two syllables, and the effect of this on their poetic styles; but it shows a sensitivity to the mechanics of verse rather rare at the beginning of the century. Adelaide Crapsey died of tuberculosis at the age of thirty-six, and most of her published poems were written in the Saranac Lake sanitarium during the last year of her life. She had invented a five-line verse-form which she called *cinquain,* evidently derived from the Japanese *hokku,* and when these poems were published the year after her death, she at once acquired a special prestige among the younger American poets who were then trying to get away from stale rhythms and traditional phrases.

November Night

Listen . . .
With faint dry sound,
Like steps of passing ghosts,
The leaves, frost-crisped, break from the trees
And fall.

Amaze

I know
Not these my hands
And yet I think there was
A woman like me once had hands
Like these.

The Warning

Just now,
Out of the strange
Still dusk . . . as strange, as still . . .
A white moth flew. Why am I grown
So cold?

They are mostly about death, these poems. She looked out of her window at the graveyard — which she called "Trudeau's Garden" (Dr. Trudeau was the once famous tuberculosis specialist who had founded the sanitarium), where the former patients were buried, and wrote about it a longer poem, almost unbearable to read, in which she addresses these dead, and rebels against their mute impassivity:

Why are you there in your straight row on row
Where I must ever see you from my bed
That in your mere dumb presence iterate
The text so weary in my ears: "Lie still
And rest; be patient and lie still and rest."
I'll not be patient! I will not lie still!

But in the span between Poe and Pound, the great innovator, of course, was Walt Whitman.* Destroying the conventional idiom as well as the conventional rhythms, he communicated his own rhythm and idiom to the most exquisite as well as the most demotic elements of the movement which reached its climax in the second and third decades of this century. The Whitman influence is obvious in Carl Sandburg and Edgar Lee Masters, but, though less obvious, equally important in Pound. "It was you that broke the new wood," says Pound in his poem to Whitman, "Now is the time for carving. We have one sap and one root — Let there be commerce between us." And although T. S. Eliot insists, in his introduction to Pound's *Selected Poems*, that Whitman was "a great prose writer" rather than a poet, it has been possible for Professor S. Musgrove of the University of New Zealand to identify, in his little monograph *T. S. Eliot and Walt Whitman*, what are evidently reverberations of Whitman in Eliot's *Four Quartets* and in the choruses of his pageant play *The Rock*.

Now, the revolutionary impact of Whitman had produced its first important results in the poetry of Sidney Lanier — though, so very old-fashioned in all his tastes except perhaps an admiration for Wagner, he did not discover Whitman till the beginning of 1878, when, on one of his visits to New York, he borrowed *Leaves of Grass* from Bayard Taylor. "Upon a serious comparison," he wrote Taylor, "I think Walt Whitman's *Leaves of Grass* worth at least a million of *Among My Books* and *Atalanta in Calydon* [which Taylor had also lent him].

* I do not mean to imply that no other first-rate poetry was written in America up to the time of Ezra Pound: there were, of course, Trumbull Stickney and Edwin Arlington Robinson; I am speaking here of innovation only.

In the two latter I could not find anything which has not been much better said before: but *Leaves of Grass* was a real refreshment to me — like rude salt spray in your face — in spite of its enormous fundamental error that a thing is good because it is natural, and in spite of the world-wide difference between my own conceptions of art and its author's." Three months later, he wrote to Walt Whitman to order a copy of the book, which the poet was still selling himself. "How it happened that I had not read this book before — is a story not worth the telling; but . . . I cannot resist the temptation to tender you also my grateful thanks for such large and substantial thoughts uttered at a time when there are, as you say in another connection, so many 'little plentiful manikins skipping about in collars and tailed coats.' Although I entirely disagree with you in all points connected with artistic form, and in so much of the outcome of your doctrine as is involved in those poetic exposures of the person which your pages so unreservedly make, yet I feel sure that I understand you herein, and my dissent in these particulars becomes a very insignificant consideration in the presence of that unbounded delight which I take in the bigness and bravery of all your ways and thoughts. It is not known to me where I can find another modern song at once so large and so naïve: and the time needs to be told few things so much as the absolute personality of the person, the sufficiency of the man's manhood *to* the man, which you have propounded in such strong and beautiful rhythms." It is Lanier the tamed and caged "Southron" who speaks in this last sentence.

When Lanier came to write the lectures — delivered in 1881 — which were published as *The English Novel and the Principle of Its Development*, but which are really not primarily concerned with the novel and are better described by the subtitle later substituted by Mrs. Lanier: *A Study in the Development of Personality* — again the caged Southerner's preoccupation — he devoted a good deal of space to Whitman, but he here makes more serious reservations. He objects to Whitman's "theory of formlessness" without indicating, perhaps not realizing, that — as is proved by Whitman's many revisions — he was a much more conscientious craftsman than his critics sometimes credited him with being; and, as seems rather stupid, though he must be sincere, he declares that "on the one occasion when Whitman has . . . written in form he has made *My Captain, O My Captain* surely one of the most tender and beautiful poems in any language." He points out that the rugged American audience to whom Whitman says he wants to appeal is not at all the public that reads him: "It is only with a few of the most sober and retired thinkers of our time that Whitman has found even a partial acceptance. . . . Whitman's poetry, in spite of his feeling . . . that it is democratic, is really aristocratic to the last degree; and instead of belonging, as he claims, to an early and fresh-thoughted stage of a republic, is really poetry which would be impossible except in a highly civilized state of society." It was still at that time rather daring to praise Whitman from an academic platform; and the Johns Hopkins professor who edited these lectures for the volume of them published after the author's death omitted some of the passages on Whitman of which he thought the public would disapprove. Mrs. Lanier, who had been ill at this time, restored them in a later edition.

The discovery of Whitman, in any case, had been stimulating and liberating for Sidney Lanier. He was the only American poet since Poe who had made any serious study of the mechanics and traditions of his art. His *The*

Science of English Verse is not a book of much real importance (though it contains some acute observations on Shakespeare and other poets, and his precepts for beginners might be useful). Like Poe in *The Rationale of Verse*, he is trying to get rid of that system of scansion which the English have adapted from the Greek and Latin classics to schematize our accentual verse; but the musician in Sidney Lanier here gets the better of the poet, and he forces upon poetry an analogy with music — substituting the musical bar for the foot and writing everything in musical notation — which betrays him into fundamental absurdities. Yet this musical conception of verse led him also to a certain freedom which the revelation of Whitman encouraged — with results that seemed almost as inacceptable in the era of Thomas Bailey Aldrich, Richard Watson Gilder and James Whitcomb Riley as the work of Whitman itself. To what degree this was true is demonstrated by Barrett Wendell's statement in 1900 that "this inarticulate verse [of Lanier's] is of a quality which can never be popular, and perhaps indeed is so eccentric that one should be prudent in choosing adjectives to praise it." Through the thickets of romantic ‚verbiage from which Sidney Lanier had emerged, it was as if his old flute were now guiding him to a music more winding and liquid, like the waters of the marshes of Glynn, and also perhaps to a glimpse of that fresher early world of Audubon:

And the sea lends large, as the marsh: lo, out of his
      plenty the sea
  Pours fast: full soon the time of the flood-tide must be;
    Look how the grace of the sea doth go
  About and about through the intricate channels that
    flow
      Here and there,
      Everywhere,

Till his waters have flooded the uttermost creeks and the
      low-lying lanes,
   And the marsh is meshed with a million veins,
That like as with rosy and silvery essences flow
   In the rose-and-silver evening glow.
      Farewell, my lord Sun!
The creeks overflow: a thousand rivulets run
'Twixt the roots of the sod; the blades of the marsh-
      grass stir;
Passeth a hurrying sound of wings that westward whirr;
Passeth, and all is still; and the currents cease to run;
   And the sea and the marsh are one.

One of the villains of Lanier's novel *Tiger-Lilies* is a
poor white from Tennessee named Gorm Smallin, who
deserts from the Confederate army and becomes a
Yankee agent. He has been forced into the army by the
hero's father, a country gentleman named John Sterling,
and when the Yankees, invading Tennessee, have been
burning down houses there, he swears revenge upon
Sterling for involving him in this disaster. " 'Hit's been
a rich man's war,' " he says to himself, " 'an' a poor
man's fight long enough. A eye fur a eye, an' a tooth fur
a tooth, an' I say a house fur a house, an' a bullet fur a
bullet! John Sterlin's got *my* house *burnt*, I'll get *his'n*
burnt. John Sterlin's made *me* resk bullets, I'll make *him*
resk em! An' ef I don't may God-a-mighty forgit me
forever and ever, amen!' " And he eventually burns down
Sterling's mansion, which has been made by Lanier, in
his fable, to stand for the old way of life in the South.
   The malignant Tennessee "cracker" had already been
introduced into literature by the Tennessee journalist
George Washington Harris, who invented a comic character called Sut Lovingood and exploited him for fifteen
years as a narrator of fantastic stories and as a mouth-

piece for political satire. These sketches, of which the first appeared in 1854, were printed not only in the local press but also in a New York sporting paper. Sidney Lanier may have known Harris: he was something of a public figure in Knoxville, which is only fifteen miles from Montvale Springs, where Sidney Lanier's grandfather Sterling Lanier, whose Christian name he had used for the family name of his hero, possessed the impressive estate which is also made to figure in *Tiger-Lilies;* and he must certainly have known about the Lovingood stories. These stories were collected, in 1867, in a volume called *Sut Lovingood: Yarns Spun by a Nat'ral Born Durn'd Fool,* which was reviewed by Mark Twain in a San Francisco paper and to which he perhaps owed something; but Harris's work, after his death in 1869, seems to have been soon forgotten, and it was only in the thirties of the present century that — in the course of the recent excavations in the field of American literature — such writers as Bernard DeVoto, Constance Rourke and F. O. Matthiessen began to take an interest in Sut Lovingood.

Bernard DeVoto thought that it might be a good idea to have the Lovingood stories "translated" out of the dense hillbilly dialect in which Harris had tried phonetically to write them, and this suggestion was taken up by Professor Brom Weber, who published in 1954 a selection of the Lovingood pieces slightly expurgated and transposed into a more readable language. This version was not, however, an entire success. In attempting to clean up Sut Lovingood and make him attractive to the ordinary reader — an ambition probably hopeless — Mr. Weber has produced something that is not of much value to the student of literature. He is correct in pointing out that Harris, in trying to render Sut's illiterate speech, has inconsistently mixed written misspelling, intended to look funny on the printed page — though Sut has never learned to write — with a phonetic transcription of the way he talks; but the writing does have a coarse texture as well as a rank flavor, and to turn it, as the editor has done, into something that is closer to conventional English, and to dilute it with paragraphs and strings of dots, is to deprive it of a good deal of this. By the time Mr. Weber gets done with him, Sut Lovingood hardly even sounds like a Southerner; it is fatal to the poor-white dialect to turn "naik" and "hit" into "neck" and "it." What is worst, from the scholarly point of view, is to comb out "words [that] are obsolete and others [that] are probably meaningless to all but a handful of contemporary readers." If the book was to be reprinted, the text should have been given intact, and the unfamiliar words as well as the topical allusions explained. Mr. Weber makes no effort to do this, nor — though Harris, at the time of his death, was preparing a second volume — does he add any new material except for three little lampoons on Lincoln. Sut himself is depicted on the jacket as a stalwart and bearded mountaineer, a portrayal that has nothing in common with the dreadful, half-bestial lout of the original illustrations.

One is also rather surprised at the editor's idea of deleting "three lines of an extremely offensive nature." One of the most striking things about *Sut Lovingood* is that it is all as offensive as possible. It takes a pretty strong stomach nowadays — when so much of the disgusting in our fiction is not rural but urban or suburban — to get through it in any version. I should say that, as far as my experience goes, it is by far the most repellent book of any real literary merit in American literature. This kind of crude and brutal humor was something of an American institution all through the nineteenth century. The tradition of the crippling practical joke was carried on almost to the end of the century with *Peck's Bad Boy*, and that of the nasty schoolboy by certain of the writings of Eugene Field, a professional sentimentalist, who, however, when working for the Denver *Tribune*, betrayed a compulsive fondness for puerile and disgusting jokes: cockroaches and boarding-house hash and collywobbles from eating green peaches. But the deadpan murders and corpses of Mark Twain's early Far Western sketches are given an impressive grimness by the imperviousness to horror their tone implies, and the nihilistic butcheries of Ambrose Bierce derive a certain tragic accent from his background of the Civil War. The boorish or macabre joke, as exploited by these Western writers, does perform a kind of purgative function in rendering simply comic stark hardships and disastrous adventures. The exploits of Sut Lovingood, however, have not even this kind of dignity. He is neither a soldier nor a pioneer enduring a cruel ordeal; he is a peasant squatting in his own filth. He is not making a jest of his trials; he is avenging his inferiority by tormenting other people. His impulse is avowedly sadistic. The keynote is struck in the following passage (I give it in the original Tennessean):

"I hates ole Onsightly Peter [so called because he was selling encyclopedias], jis' caze he didn't seem tu like tu hear me narrate las' night; that's human nater the yeath over, an' yeres more univarsal onregenerit human nater: ef ever yu dus enything tu eny body wifout cause, yu hates em allers arterwards, an' sorter wants tu hurt em agin. An' yere's anuther human nater: ef enything happens sum feller, I don't keer ef he's yure bes' frien, an' I don't keer how sorry yu is fur him, thars a streak ove satisfackshun 'bout like a sowin thread a-runnin all thru yer sorrer. Yu may be shamed ove hit, but durn me ef hit ain't thar. Hit will show like the white cottin chain in mean cassinett; brushin hit onder only hides hit. An' yere's a littil more; no odds how good yu is tu yung things, ur how kine yu is in treatin em, when yu sees a littil long laiged lamb a-shakin hits tail, an' a dancin staggerinly onder hits mam a-huntin fur the tit, ontu hits knees, yer fingers *will* itch to seize that ar tail, an' fling the littil ankshus son ove a mutton over the fence amung the blackberry briars, not tu hurt hit, but jis' tu disapint hit. Ur say, a littil calf, a-buttin fus' under the cow's fore-laigs, an' then the hine, wif the pint ove hits tung stuck out, makin suckin moshuns, not yet old enuf tu know the bag aind ove hits mam frum the hookin aind, don't yu want tu kick hit on the snout, hard enough tu send hit backwards, say fifteen foot, jis' tu show hit that buttin won't allers fetch milk? Ur a baby even rubbin hits heels apas' each uther, a-rootin an' a-snifflin arter the breas', an' the mam duin her bes' tu git hit out, over the hem ove her clothes, don't yu feel hungry tu gin hit jis' one 'cussion cap slap, rite ontu the place what sum day'll fit a saddil, ur a sowin cheer, tu show hit what's atwixt hit an' the grave; that hit stans a pow'ful chance not tu be fed every time hits hungry, ur in a hurry?"

In view of this, the comments on Sut Lovingood by our recent academic critics are among the curiosities of American scholarship. We find Mr. Franklin J. Meine, in *Tall Tales of the Southwest*, speaking of this hero's "keen delight for Hallowee'n *fun* [italics the author's] — there is no ulterior motive (except occasionally Sut's desire to 'get even'), no rascality, no gambling, no sharping. . . . Sut is simply the genuine naïve roughneck mountaineer, riotously bent on raising hell," and again, "For vivid imagination, comic plot, Rabelaisian touch and sheer *fun*, the 'Sut Lovingood Yarns' surpass anything else in American humor." "Ultimately," asserts Mr.

Weber, "the mythic universalities such as heroism, fertility, masculinity, and femininity emerge over a bedrock of elemental human values which Sut has carved out in the course of his adventures, values such as love, joy, truth, justice, etc. These are only some of the positive concepts which Sut has admired and championed, and it is no small feat that they emerge from behind a protagonist who has ironically been deprecated by his creator. This is humor on a grand scale."

Now, Sut Lovingood can be called "Rabelaisian" only in the sense that he is often indecent by nineteenth-century standards and that he runs to extravagant language and monstrously distorted descriptions. Unlike Rabelais, he is always malevolent and always excessively sordid. Here is an example of his caricature at its best:

"I seed a well appearin man onst, ax one ove em [the proprietors of taverns, evidently carpetbaggers] what lived ahine a las' year's crap ove red hot brass wire whiskers run tu seed, an' shingled wif har like ontu mildew'd flax, wet wif saffron warter, an' laid smoof wif a hot flat-iron, ef he cud spar him a scrimpshun ove soap? The 'perpryiter' anser'd in soun's es sof an' sweet es a poplar dulcimore, tchuned by a good nater'd she angel in butterfly wings an' cobweb shiff, that he never wer jis' so sorry in all his born'd days tu say no, but the fac' wer the soljers hed stole hit; 'a towil then,' 'the soljers hed stole hit;' 'a tumbler,' 'the soljers hed stole hit;' 'a lookin glass,' 'the soljers hed stole hit;' 'a pitcher ove warter,' 'the soljers hed stole hit;' 'then please give me a cleaner room.' Quick es light com the same dam lie, 'the soljers hed stole hit too.' They buys scalded butter, caze hit crumbles an' yu can't tote much et a load on yer knife; they keeps hit four months so yu won't want to go arter a second load. They stops up the figgers an' flowers in the woffil irons fur hit takes butter tu fill the

holes in the woffils. They makes soup outen dirty towils,
an' jimson burrs; coffee outen niggers' ole wool socks,
roasted; tea frum dorg fennil, and toas' frum ole brogan
insoles. They keeps bugs in yer bed tu make yu rise in
time fur them tu get the sheet fur a tablecloth. They
gins yu a inch ove candil tu go tu bed by, an' a littil
nigger tu fetch back the stump tu make gravy in the
mornin, fur the hunk ove bull naik yu will swaller fur
brekfus, an' they puts the top sheaf ontu thar orful
merlignerty when they menshuns the size ove yer bill,
an' lasly, while yu're gwine thru yer close wif a sarch
warrun arter fodder enuf tu pay hit, they refreshes yer
memory ove other places, an' other times, by tellin yu
ove the orful high price ove turkys, aigs, an' milk. When
the devil takes a likin tu a feller, an' wants tu make a
sure thing ove gittin him he jis' puts hit intu his hed to
open a cat-fish tavern, with a gran' rat attachmint, gong
'cumpanimint, bull's neck variashun, cockroach corus an'
bed-bug refrain, an' dam ef he don't git him es sure es
he rattils the fust gong. An' durn thar onary souls, they
looks like they expected yu tu b'leve that they am pius,
decent, an' fit tu be 'sociated wif, by lookin down on
yu like yu belonged tu the onregenerit, an' keepin' a
cussed ole spindel-shank, rattlin crazy, peaner, wif mud
daubers nestes onder the soundin board, a-bummin out
'Days ove Absins' ur 'the Devil's Dream,' bein druv thar
too, by thar long-waisted, greasey har'd darter, an' listen'd
to by jis' sich durn'd fools es I is."

As for the "fun" of Sut Lovingood, it is true that
Harris explained his aim as merely to revive for the
reader "sich a laugh as is remembered wif his keerless
boyhood," and that he liked to express his nostalgia for
the dances and quiltings of his youth; but even in one
of Harris's pre-Lovingood sketches that deal with one of
these, the fun seems mainly to consist of everybody's

getting beaten to a pulp, and in the Lovingood stories themselves, the fun entirely consists of Sut's spoiling everybody else's fun. He loves to break up such affairs. One of his milder devices is setting bees and hornets on people. In this way, he ruins the wedding of a girl who has refused his advances and dismissed him with an unpleasant practical joke, and puts to rout a Negro revivalist rally — for he runs true to poor-white tradition in despising and persecuting the Negroes. He rejoices when his father, naked, is set upon by "a ball ho'nets nes' ni ontu es big es a hoss's hed" and driven to jump into the water. Sut gloats over "dad's bald hed fur all the yeath like a peeled inyin, a bobbin up an' down an' aroun, an' the ho'nets sailin roun tuckey buzzard fashun, an' every onst in a while one, an' sum times ten, wud take a dip at dad's bald hed." This leaves the old man "a pow'ful curious, vishus, skeery lookin cuss. . . . His hed am as big es a wash pot, an' he hasent the fust durned sign ove an eye — jist two black slits." Sut, who supposes himself to be his mother's only legitimate child, has nothing but contempt for his father as an even greater fool than himself, who has bequeathed to him only misery, ignorance and degradation. Most of all, however, his hatred is directed against anybody who shows any signs of gentility, idealism or education. On such people, under the influence of bad whisky, to which he refers as "kill-devil" or "bald face," he revenges himself by methods that range from humiliation to mayhem. His habit of denouncing his victims as hypocrites, adulterers or pedants is evidently what has convinced Mr. Weber that Sut Lovingood cherishes "values such as love, joy, truth, justice, etc." But he is equally vicious with anyone who happens for any other reason to irritate him. In the case of an old lady who loves to make quilts, he rides into her quilting party with a horse he has driven frantic, ripping up all the quilts and trampling the hostess to death. This is Sut's only recorded human murder, but animals he has more at his mercy, and he loves to kill dogs, cats and frogs. It is not in the least true, as another of Sut's encomiasts has said, that pain does not exist in Sut Lovingood's world. On the contrary, the sufferings of his victims are described with considerable realism, and the furtively snickering Sut enjoys every moment of them. It is good to be reminded by Mr. Meine that his hero is never shown as addicted to gambling or sharping.

Nor is it possible to imagine that Harris is aiming at Swiftian satire. It is plain that he identifies himself with Sut, and his contemporaries referred to him as Sut, just as Anatole France in his day was referred to as M. Bergeret. "Sometimes, George, I wishes," says Sut, addressing his creator, "I could read and write just a little." George Harris himself had had — apparently at intervals — but a year and a half of schooling, and it is obvious that he is able to express himself a good deal better as Sut than he can in his own character. He had been steamboat captain, farmer, metalworker, glassworker, surveyor, sawmill manager, postmaster and railroad man — none of them for very long and none with any great success. It is not known how Harris got along during the years of the Civil War. He seems to have dragged his family from pillar to post in Tennessee, Alabama and Georgia. His wife died in 1867, leaving him with three small children. He is evidently speaking of himself, in his preface to *Sut Lovingood*, when he makes his hero explain that he will "feel he has got his pay in full" if he can rouse to a laugh "jis' one, eny poor misfortinit devil hu's heart is onder a mill-stone, hu's raggid children are hungry, an' no bread in the dresser, hu is down in the mud, an' the lucky ones a-trippin him every time he struggils tu his all fours, hu has fed the famishin an' is now hungry hisself, hu misfortins foller fas' an' foller faster, hu is so foot-sore an' weak that he wishes he wer at the ferry."

George Harris had anticipated both the protest and the plea of Helper's *The Impending Crisis*. He represented the same stratum as Helper: that of the white "non-planter" who had got himself some education. We know nothing of Harris's early life except that he had once been a jeweller's apprentice; but his origins seem to have been humble — it is not known what his father did or what became of his parents — and he shared with what were called the "poor white trash" something of their consciousness of limitation and of their bitterness against those who did not want them to escape from it.

In Unionist eastern Tennessee, George Harris never wavered from his original allegiance to the Democratic party, which in the South represented the artisans and farmers as against the industrializing Whigs. But he failed in an attempt at farming as well as at his several industrial projects — his sawmill, his glass manufactory, his metal working shop — and it is plain that a sense of frustration — "flustratin'" is one of Sut's favorite words — is at the root of the ferocious fantasies in which, in the character of Sut, he likes to indulge himself. Yet he also uses Sut as a spokesman for his own sometimes shrewd observations, and this rather throws the character out as a credible and coherent creation, since he is made to see the world from a level which in reality would be beyond him. The effect of it is more disconcerting than if Sut were simply a comic monster, for it makes one feel that Sut's monstrous doings really express, like his comments on the local life, George Harris's own mentality. It is embarrassing to find Caliban, at moments, thinking like a human being.

But the book is not without its power, the language is often imaginative, and Sut is a Southern type, the envious and mutinous underling, which it is well no doubt to have recorded, and which Harris could do better than Lanier. Mr. Weber says truly that Harris has something in common with Caldwell and Faulkner. He is thinking of the tradition of "folk humor"; but what is more fundamental is that these writers are all attempting to portray various species of the Southern poor white. Sut Lovingood is unmistakably an ancestor of Faulkner's Snopeses, that frightening low-class family (some of them stuck at Sut's level, others on their way up), who, whether in success or in crime or both, are all the more difficult to deal with because they have their own kind of pride — who are prepared, as Mr. Weber points out in connection with their predecessor, to "take on the whole world." All that was lowest in the lowest of the South found expression in Harris's book, and *Sut Lovingood*, like A. B. Longstreet's *Georgia Scenes*, with its grotesqueries of ear-chewing, eye-gouging fights and yokelish hunts and balls, is needed, perhaps, to counterbalance those idyls of the old regime by Kennedy, Caruthers and Cooke and the chivalrous idealism of Sidney Lanier.

The dreamy nobility of a man like Lanier and the murderous clowning of Harris are products of the same society, and the two men have something in common. George Harris did not share Helper's politics: he was all in favor of secession. Nor was his Sut disaffected like Lanier's Gorm Smallin, who burned down his master's mansion. From the moment of Lincoln's nomination, George Harris turned Sut Lovingood loose on the Unionists. Here is a passage from one of his libels on Lincoln — to call them satires would be to give them too much

dignity — of which still another infatuated editor, Mr.
Edd Winfield Parks, has said that "though good-humored,
they reveal his [Harris's] feelings," and of which Mr.
Weber, who includes them in his volume, has said that
Lincoln "might not have enjoyed [them] as much as a
secessionist would" but that "he would have laughed at
the exaggeration of ugliness so customary in frontier
humor." Sut Lovingood is supposed to be accompanying
Lincoln on the latter's incognito journey through Baltimore on his way to the inauguration, and Lincoln is supposed to be terrified by the threats of the Maryland
secessionists: "I kotch a ole bull frog once an druv a nail
through his lips inter a post, tied two rocks ta his hine
toes an stuck a durnin needil inter his tail tu let out the
misture, and lef him there tu dry. I seed him two weeks
arter wurds, and when I seed ole Abe I thot hit were an
orful retribution cum outa me; an that hit were the same
frog, only strutched a little longer, an had tuck tu warin
ove close ta keep me from knowin him, an ketchin him an
nailin him up agin; an natural born durn'd fool es I is, I
swar I seed the same watry skery look in the eyes, and the
same sorter knots on the backbone. I'm feared, George,
sumthin's tu cum ove my nailin up that ar frog. I swar
I am ever since I seed ole Abe, same shape same color,
same feel (cold as ice) an I'm d____ ef hit ain't the
same smell."

Sut's tirades after the defeat of the South are vitupera-
tive on a level that almost makes the passage above seem
the work of a sensitive artist. A new rancor, a new
crushing handicap have been added to his previous ones.
He can only spew abuse at the Yankees. The election
of Grant seems a death-blow. According to Professor
Donald Day, the principal authority on Harris, one of
the last of the Lovingood stories, called *Well! Dad's
Dead*, which appeared in a Tennessee paper on Novem-

ber 19, 1868, was inspired by this event. I am not sure that I can accept Professor Day's idea that Sut Lovingood's moronic father has here come to stand for the Old South. He passes, in any case, without lament: "Nara durn'd one ove 'em [the neighbors] come a nigh the old cuss, to fool 'im into believin' that he stood a chance to live, or even that they wanted him to stay a minit longer than he were obleeged to. . . . That night [after they had buried him], when we were hunker'd round the hearth, sayin' nothin' an' waitin for the taters to roast, mam, she spoke up — 'oughtent we to a scratch'd in a little dirt, say?' 'No need, mam,' sed Sall, 'hits loose yearth, an' will soon cave in enuff.'" Sut has always claimed that his father sired him as "a nat'ral born durn'd fool," and his habitual falling back on this as an excuse for both his oafish inadequacies and his sly calculated crimes strikes the only touching note in these farces.

The creator of Sut himself did not long survive Sut's father. Returning from a trip to Lynchburg, where he had gone on railroad business and to try to arrange for the publication of a second Sut Lovingood book, he became very ill on the train, and so helpless that the conductor at first thought him drunk. He was carried off at Knoxville, and died there. His manuscript disappeared. The cause of his death is not known, but it is reported that just before he died, he whispered the word "Poisoned!"

I have said that Sut Lovingood and Sidney Lanier belong to the same world. They represent, to be sure, its two opposite poles, yet they stood for the same cause and when it lost, in the years after the victory of the North they felt the same resentment. This seems strange in the gentle Lanier, who, at the end of a chapter of *Tiger-Lilies*, makes the cultivators of what he calls the

"war-flower," utter the following cry: "Friends and horti-
culturists. . . . if the war was ever right, then Christ
was always wrong; and war-flowers and the vine of
Christ grow different ways, insomuch that no man may
grow with both!" "But," beginning a new chapter, he
continues, "these sentiments, even if anybody could have
been found patient enough to listen to them, would have
been called sentimentalities, or worse, in the spring of
1861, by the inhabitants of any of those States lying
between Maryland and Mexico. An afflatus of war was
breathed upon us. Like a great wind, it drew on and
blew upon men, women, and children. Its sounds mingled
with the solemnity of the church-organs and arose with
the earnest words of preachers praying for guidance in
the matter. . . .

"This wind blew upon all the vanes of all the churches
of the country, and turned them one way — toward war.
It blew, and shook out, as if by magic, a flag whose device was unknown to soldier or sailor before, but whose
every flap and flutter made the blood bound in our veins.

"Who could have resisted the fair anticipations which
the new war-idea brought? It arrayed the sanctity of a
righteous cause in the brilliant trappings of military display; pleasing, so, the devout and the flippant which in
various proportions are mixed elements in all men. It
challenged the patriotism of the sober citizen, while it
inflamed the dream of the statesman, ambitious for his
country or for himself. It offered test to all allegiances
and loyalties; of church, of state; of private loves, of
public devotion; of personal consanguinity; of social ties.
To obscurity it held out eminence; to poverty, wealth; to
greed, a gorged maw; to speculation, legalized gambling;
to patriotism, a country; to statesmanship, a government;
to virtue, purity; and to love, what all love most desires
— a field wherein to assert itself by action."

And Lanier, having been swept with this wind and having staked his life in the war, could not have escaped being left with something of the same rankling bitterness as his fellows with whom he had fought. This occasionally comes to the surface in his poetry. He started working in 1868 on a long poem called *The Jacquerie*, which was still unfinished at the time of his death. The ostensible subject of this poem was the uprising, in fourteenth-century France, of the common people against the nobility; but it is plain that Lanier had poured into it his most lacerating emotions aroused by the war, and this results in a certain confusion of emphasis. The reader is intended to sympathize with the revolting people of France, yet a monk who speaks as a prophet unrolls a pathetic picture of the eventual fate of the nobility when — presumably after the Great French Revolution — they shall have been despoiled and abased. Here the nobles are identified with the ruined South, yet the feelings of the low-born rebels are also those of the Southerners at the mercy of Northern domination. The poem was to end, said Lanier, "with the most barbarous and altogether historical hanging of Master Jacques Bonhomme, the hero of the tale and the leader of the Jacquerie." Here is a stanza from a song in the poem:

> The hound was cuffed, the hound was kicked.
> O' the ears was cropped, o' the tail was nicked.
>   *Oo-hoo-o*, howled the hound.
> The hound into his kennel crept,
> He rarely wept, he never slept,
> His mouth he always open kept,
>   Licking his bitter wound.
>   The hound,
>   *U-lu-lo*, howled the hound.

Eventually he flies at his master's throat. The poet tries to explain in a letter to a friend — without, one feels, quite understanding himself — the morals to be drawn from the poem: "The peasants learned . . . that a man who could not be a lord by birth, might be one by wealth; & so Trade arose & overthrew Chivalry. Trade has now had possession of the civilized world for four hundred years; it controls all things, it interprets the Bible, it guides our national & almost all our individual life with its maxims; & its oppressions upon the moral existence of man have come to be ten thousand times more grievous than the worst tyrannies of the Feudal System ever were. Thus in the reversals of time, it is *now* the *gentleman* who must arise & overthrow Trade."

In *The Revenge of Hamish,* also — one of Lanier's most ambitious pieces — he projects into another situation the self-annihilating fury of his people. The story itself was taken from an incident which Lanier had found in one of William Black's novels; but the fact that the poet should have chosen this incident and retold it with such passionate power shows, of course, that it had for him a special meaning: the same meaning as the episode of the Jacquerie. The fierce pride of the Scottish henchman, his instant retaliation, at whatever cost to himself, when beaten by his choleric master, really figure the revolt of the South and make one of its most tragic expressions in literature. I shall quote the *Revenge* at length because, although it is one of Lanier's best poems — written just before his death, when at last he was attaining real mastery — it is relatively little known. It is written in logœdic dactyls, an informal kind of classical meter, which permits a loose handling of metrics and is an example of the technical experimentation which appears in Lanier's later poems.

It was three slim does and a ten-tined buck in the
    bracken lay;
  And all of a sudden the sinister smell of a man,
  Awaft on a wind-shift, wavered and ran
Down the hill-side and sifted along through the bracken
    and passed that way.

Then Nan got a-tremble at nostril; she was the daintiest
    doe;
  In the print of her velvet flank on the velvet fern
  She reared, and rounded her ears in turn.
Then the buck leapt up, and his head as a king's to a
    crown did go

Full high in the breeze, and he stood as if Death had
    the form of a deer;
  And the two slim does long lazily stretching arose,
  For their day-dream slowlier came to a close,
Till they woke and were still, breath-bound with waiting
    and wonder and fear.

Then Alan the huntsman sprang over the hillock, the
    hounds shot by,
  The does and the ten-tined buck made a marvellous
    bound,
  The hounds swept after with never a sound,
But Alan loud winded his horn in sign that the quarry
    was nigh.

For at dawn of that day proud Maclean of Lochbuy to
    the hunt had waxed wild,
  And he cursed at old Alan till Alan fared off with the
    hounds
  For to drive him the deer to the lower glen-grounds:
"I will kill a red deer," quoth Maclean, "in the sight of
    the wife and the child."

So gayly he paced with the wife and the child to his
    chosen stand;
    But he hurried tall Hamish the henchman ahead: "Go
      turn," —
    Cried Maclean — "if the deer seek to cross to the burn,
Do thou turn them to me: nor fail, lest thy back be as
    red as thy hand."

Now hard-fortuned Hamish, half blown of his breath
    with the height of the hill,
    Was white in the face when the ten-tined buck and
    the does
    Drew leaping to burn-ward; huskily rose
His shouts, and his nether lip twitched, and his legs were
    o'er-weak for his will.

So the deer darted lightly by Hamish and bounded away
    to the burn.
    But Maclean never bating his watch tarried waiting
    below;
    Still Hamish hung heavy with fear for to go
All the space of an hour; then he went, and his face was
    greenish and stern,

And his eye sat back in the socket, and shrunken the
    eye-balls shone,
    As withdrawn from a vision of deeds it were shame to
    see.
    "Now, now, grim henchman, what is't with thee?"
Brake Maclean, and his wrath rose red as a beacon the
    wind hath upblown.

"Three does and a ten-tined buck made out," spoke
    Hamish, full mild,

"And I ran for to turn, but my breath it was blown,
     and they passed;
  I was weak, for ye called ere I broke me my fast."
Cried Maclean: "Now a ten-tined buck in the sight of
     the wife and the child

I had killed if the gluttonous kern had not wrought me
     a snail's own wrong!"
  Then he sounded, and down came kinsmen and clans-
     men all:
  "Ten blows, for ten tine, on his back let fall,
And reckon no stroke if the blood follow not at the bite
     of the thong!"

So Hamish made bare, and took him his strokes; at the
     last he smiled.
  "Now I'll to the burn," quoth Maclean, "for it still
     may be,
  If a slimmer-paunched henchman will hurry with me,
I shall kill me the ten-tined buck for a gift to the wife
     and the child!"

Then the clansmen departed, by this path and that; and
     over the hill
  Sped Maclean with an outward wrath for an inward
     shame;
  And that place of the lashing full quiet became;
And the wife and the child stood sad; and bloody-backed
     Hamish sat still.

But look! red Hamish has risen; quick about and about
     turns he.
  "There is none betwixt me and the crag-top!" he
     screams under breath.
  Then, livid as Lazarus lately from death,

He snatches the child from the mother, and clambers
    the crag toward the sea.

Now the mother drops breath; she is dumb, and her
    heart goes dead for a space,
    Till the motherhood, mistress of death, shrieks, shrieks
        through the glen,
    And that place of the lashing is live with men,
And Maclean, and the gillie that told him, dash him up
    in a desperate race.

Not a breath's time for asking; an eye-glance reveals all
    the tale untold.
    They follow mad Hamish afar up the crag toward the
        sea,
    And the lady cries: "Clansmen, run for a fee! —
Yon castle and lands to the two first hands that shall
    hook him and hold

Fast Hamish back from the brink!" — and ever she flies
    up the steep,
    And the clansmen pant, and they sweat, and they
        jostle and strain.
    But, mother, 'tis vain; but, father, 'tis vain;
Stern Hamish stands bold on the brink, and dangles the
    child o'er the deep.

Now a faintness falls on the men that run, and they
    all stand still.
    And the wife prays Hamish as if he were God, on her
        knees,
    Crying: "Hamish! O Hamish! but please, but please
For to spare him!" and Hamish still dangles the child,
    with a wavering will.

On a sudden he turns; with a sea-hawk scream, and a
    gibe, and a song,
  Cries: "So; I will spare ye the child if, in sight of ye
    all,
  Ten blows on Maclean's bare back shall fall,
And ye reckon no stroke if the blood follows not at the
    bite of the thong!"

Then Maclean he set hardly his tooth to his lip that his
    tooth was red,
  Breathed short for a space, said: "Nay, but it never
    shall be!
  Let me hurl off the damnable hound in the sea!"
But the wife: "Can Hamish go fish us the child from
    the sea, if dead?

Say yea! — Let them lash *me*, Hamish?" — "Nay!" —
    "Husband, the lashing will heal;
  But, oh, who will heal me the bonny sweet bairn in his
    grave?
  Could ye cure me my heart with the death of a knave?
Quick Love! I will bare thee — so — kneel!" Then Mac-
    lean 'gan slowly to kneel

With never a word, till presently downward he jerked
    to the earth.
  Then the henchman — he that smote Hamish — would
    tremble and lag;
  "Strike hard!" quoth Hamish, full stern, from the crag;
Then he struck him, and "One!" sang Hamish, and
    danced with the child in his mirth.

And no man spake beside Hamish; he counted each
    stroke with a song.

When the last stroke fell, then he moved him a pace
    down the height,
And he held forth the child in the heartaching sight
Of the mother, and looked all pitiful grave, as repenting
    a wrong.

And there as the motherly arms stretched out with the
    thanksgiving prayer —
    And there as the mother crept up with a fearful swift
    pace,
    Till her finger nigh felt of the bairnie's face —
In a flash fierce Hamish turned round and lifted the child
    in the air,

And sprang with the child in his arms from the horrible
    height in the sea,
    Still screeching, "Revenge!" in the wind-rush; and
    pallid Maclean,
    Age-feeble with anger and impotent pain,
Crawled up on the crag, and lay flat, and locked hold
    of dead roots of a tree —

And gazed hungrily o'er, and the blood from his back
    drip-dripped in the brine,
    And a sea-hawk flung down a skeleton fish as he flew,
    And the mother stared white on the waste of blue,
And the wind drove a cloud to seaward, and the sun
    began to shine.

The arrogant suicide of Hamish, leaping with the
child in his arms, is a parable of the action of the South
in recklessly destroying the Union. Like George Harris,
the creator of Sut Livingood, tall Hamish the henchman
dies poisoned — by hatred, by the lust for revenge. Sidney Lanier in this piece is a dramatic poet, and that spirit
has spoken through him.

XIII

NOVELISTS OF THE POST-WAR SOUTH: ALBION W.

TOURGÉE, GEORGE W. CABLE, KATE CHOPIN,

THOMAS NELSON PAGE

ALBION WINEGAR TOURGÉE, the once much-read novelist
of the Reconstruction, represented a mixture of blood:
French Huguenot, German Swiss and British. His ancestors had all come over in the seventeenth or early eighteenth century, and he himself was an impassioned product of the Protestant-Revolutionary tradition. He was
born in Ohio but, at the age of fourteen, when his
mother had died and his father had married again, he
rebelled against his family and took himself off to live
with a Winegar uncle in Lee, Massachusetts. He later,
however, returned and eventually, at twenty-one, attended the University of Rochester. He had thus no real
local attachments nor any strongly held regional point
of view, and all his life he was changing his residence.
His longest periods of sojourn were his fourteen years in
North Carolina (1865–79) as a business man, journalist
and judge, his twelve years (1885–97) as a writer and
unsuccessful politician in his mansion in Chatauqua
County at the extreme tip of western New York, and
the last eight years of his life, when he was consul at
Bordeaux, France. He had seen a good deal of the
American world, and he had got himself a good educa-

tion. The Civil War and its consequences were central to his life and thought, but, after serving in the Federal army and administering justice in the South with something of the Abolitionist's fervor, he began to understand the antagonism between the South and the North — which the victory of the latter, as he realized, had not reduced — in a way that was quite unconventional.

Tourgée was an obstinate man, physically and morally courageous, with bad judgment in practical matters and possessed by an intransigent idealism. He enlisted in the New York Volunteers as soon as the war began — in April, 1861 — and was so seriously wounded in the spine at the first Battle of Bull Run less than two months later that he never entirely recovered; but after a year of incapacitation he obtained a commission as first lieutenant in the Ohio Volunteers and went back to the fighting again. His company lost one-third of its men, and Tourgée was injured in the spine again, so that he had to spend two months in the hospital. At the beginning of the following year, 1863, he was captured at Murfreesboro, Tennessee, in a pursuit of John Hunt Morgan the raider, and spent four months in Southern prisons. When he was freed, he went back to Ohio and married the New England girl, of seventeenth-century Yorkshire stock, of whom he had said at school, "I'm going to marry that girl," to whom he had been engaged for five years and to whom he was to say upon his deathbed, "Emma, you have been the one perfect wife." Eleven days after the wedding, he writes in his diary, "Today I left for the war again." He was in action at the battles of Chickamauga, Lookout Mountain and Missionary Ridge. Tourgée was always getting into trouble for insubordination and improper behavior, and he twice tried to resign his commission because "his rights were not respected and his reputation threatened"; but his resignation was not accepted. He later, however, aggravated his injury by jumping over a ditch and left the army at the beginning of '64.

The twenty-three-year-old Tourgée had carried with him on his first campaign the Greek Testament and Cicero's *De Natura Deorum,* and had for the first time read Balzac's novels. In prison, he studied Spanish and read *Don Quixote.* At nineteen he had composed poems to Emma, and during the year of his recuperation he wrote the first chapters of a novel and squandered all his pension money on publishing a book of verse, of which he put the first two copies into the kitchen stove and later cut the rest into pieces. At this time he also studied law and when he left the army in 1864 was admitted to the Ohio bar. But he presently turns up teaching school in Erie, Pennsylvania, and writing for the Erie *Dispatch,* and just before the end of the war, too late, he was on the point of realizing an earlier ambition by getting himself a commission in a Negro regiment.

Tourgée, in July, 1865 — with a certain bold naïveté, which he afterwards bitterly admitted — decided that he could not do better than take his family to live in the South. He was suffering from a weakness of the lungs as well as his spinal wound, and he needed a milder climate. He loved horses and was an insatiable fisherman, and he wanted a life out of doors to offset his intellectual activities. He chose for his residence Greensboro, North Carolina, where he set out to practise law and to run a nursery garden which he rented. He organized a partnership to manage this latter; but he was always a poor hand at business, and he soon fell out with his partners. The firm was dissolved, the nursery failed, and Tourgée was left in debt. He then started to build a factory for tool-handles, which he was never able to finish and which left him with even heavier liabilities. But the public activities of Tourgée — though here, too, he was eventually defeated — were spectacular and somewhat heroic. Entirely uncritical then of the policy of the Radical Republicans in conferring the vote on the Negroes and excluding the Confederates from office, he resoundingly backed this policy in public speeches and private conversations. Thus he won the warm sympathies of the Negroes and of the minority of white Unionists, but of course provoked the hatred of the planters and made an enemy of the governor of the state, who called him "the meanest Yankee who has ever settled among us." His career in the South was extremely rocky. He was appointed a judge of the Superior Court in 1868, in which character he heard and recorded many complaints against the Ku Klux Klan, and as a result of his championship of its victims an attempt was made to remove him from office in 1874. This failed but the hostile pressure had already the year before compelled him to resign from the board of trustees of the University of North Carolina, and he did not receive the nomination which his supporters had hoped to secure for him as the Republican candidate for Congress. He was elected, however, as a delegate to a Constitutional Convention in Raleigh by the largest majority that had ever been won by a candidate from that county — with the result that one of the Democrats made threats in public to shoot him. Tourgée, after borrowing a revolver, confronted this man in a public place and "remained staring fixedly at him for several minutes," which so unnerved his opponent that no further unpleasantness occurred. But Tourgée's life was constantly in danger, and this existence was trying for his family, because Emma Tourgée never knew whether or not he would come back from one of his trips alive. When Grant, in 1876, had appointed him Pension Agent at Raleigh, the hostility toward him increased, and he was finally compelled to leave. He was by this time convinced of the futility of his mission, but he had accomplished a few constructive things. Remembering his miseries in the Southern jails, he had insisted on having jails heated, something which had never been done before, and he had drawn up for North Carolina a Code of Civil Procedure and had compiled a Digest of Cited Cases.

In the meantime, however — what was Tourgée's real triumph — he had been dramatizing his experiences in fiction and had published one novel under a pseudonym. As soon as he left the South, he brought out two more (in 1879). His first novel — called originally *Toinette* (1874) but, after Tourgée became famous, revised and reprinted as *A Royal Gentleman* — was a tragedy of miscegenation. The point that Tourgée wants to make — and in these novels he always wants to make a point — is that, on the one hand, the Negro slaves were not treated so badly by their masters as the anti-slavery Northerners liked to think, but that, on the other hand, the ban on black blood made normal relations impossible. This is the story of a mulatto mother and daughter who both become their masters' mistresses. The mother is already a quadroon, and when her lover, in serious difficulties, is forced to sell her and their children, though with the intention of buying them back and eventually setting them free, and is about to marry a white woman, she murders him. Her daughter is so white that she is never suspected by the Northerners among whom, when she has been freed by her master, she goes with her child to live. This former master is now fighting for the Confederacy, and when he is wounded and taken prisoner, she is working in an army hospital and "nurses him back to life." But as soon as he has recognized his old slave girl Toinette, he cannot help taking down her pretentions. "She was a nigger, but Lincoln had not freed her.

He had done that years ago. If Toinette had gratitude
to anyone it was to him. . . . She deserved all he could
make her feel for trying to pass for a white woman and
a lady. This rushed through his brain in an instant, and
then, with a voice hoarse with excitement, he cried out,
imperiously: 'I say, you girl, Toinette! Toinette!' Five
years were brushed away in a second. Their months of
toil and study were in vain. The knowledge and accom-
plishments for which she had striven were blotted out.
The snug little home in the free North was forgotten
. . . The free, white, intelligent, interesting, beautiful
Mrs. Hunter was lost for the moment. In her stead was
the poor, abject, timid, pretty 'nigger gal.' . . . She was
a chattel at Lovett Lodge again, and Marse Geoffrey in
the library was calling for her angrily. She started like a
guilty loiterer, and answered instantly, with that in-
imitable and indescribable intonation of the slave: 'Sir?' "
His behavior, however, is regarded as rather caddish by
even his fellow Confederate prisoners. Toinette flees but,
later on, after the defeat of the Confederacy, comes back
to North Carolina to live near her former home. When
she is discovered by Geoffrey, he apologizes, takes for the
first time an interest in their son and is eager to return
to their old relations; but he cannot bring himself to
marry her — since his white friends all know what she
is — and, too proud to accept an inferior status, she
leaves for the North again. There is no happy ending
possible.

A Royal Gentleman is full of Victorian machinery:
murders and attempted murders, secret rooms, the walking of unauthentic ghosts, forced non-recognitions and unlikely coincidences. But the verve of Tourgée as a story-
teller does more or less carry it off. He was also an excellent
observer of types and had considerable skill as a mimic. In
his later novel, *A Fool's Errand*, which is his most important book, this verve is to be seen at its best. The

purpose of this second novel, which was first published anonymously, was to convey to the Northern public what had really been going on during the period of Reconstruction, and even in what appear its most extravagant scenes it seems not to depart very far from the adventures of Tourgée and his family. He wanted to tell his bloodcurdling true story, to put on record his observations of the South and to explain the conclusions he drew from them, and he alternates his exciting episodes with chapters of political and social analysis; yet the latter does not deaden the narrative as happens so often with this kind of book. Tourgée is one of the most readable in this secondary category of writers who aim primarily at social history. His narrative has spirit and movement; his insights are brilliantly revealing, and they are expressed with emotional conviction. We relive Tourgée's audacious exploit, with his apparently dashing daughter and his dignified devoted Emma, the latter identified by the half-anagram Metta: the resentment against the alien Northerner, the embarrassment of the friendly Southerners, the heroism of the local white Unionist who is made to pay with his life, the crushed efforts of the able Negroes to make an independent place for themselves, the rise of the Ku Klux Klan in opposition to all these elements and its triumph through blackmail, bullying, flogging, rape of women, castration of men, contemptuous violence to children, burning of Negro houses and shootings, stabbings, drownings and hangings of anybody who offered serious resistance. Thousands, both black and white — though less, of course, of the latter — were slaughtered by the Ku Klux Klan. Tourgée and his family had been through all this, and the story of the nightmarish movement, gradually making itself felt and closing in on the incredulous Northerners, was the one really valuable book that Tourgée had it in him to write.

A Fool's Errand was received as a sensation in its day, and it ought to be an historical classic in ours — for, aside from its interest as one carpetbagger's narrative, it contains the actual text of many newspaper clippings, threatening letters and firsthand testimony by victims of the Klan, and it was supplemented in later editions by a study called *The Invisible Empire,* which is a purely factual inquiry into the history and activities of the organization, based on the author's court records and on the thirteen volumes of reports submitted by a Congressional committee. *A Fool's Errand* sold two hundred thousand copies, plus piracies, and was compared to *Uncle Tom's Cabin,* of which it did, indeed, have something of the compulsive and explosive force. In 1881 its sales declined steeply from the ten thousands to the thousands. (But it has now — 1961 — been reprinted in the John Harvard Library Series.) As we shall see, the people of the North and West did not by that time want to be worried by these painful intractable problems. And the problem presented by Tourgée was particularly intractable and painful, because this problem was not merely a matter of the villainy or barbarity of the South. He calls his book *A Fool's Errand, by One of the Fools,* and the fool's errand is the Northerner's own mission in believing in, defending and attempting to carry out the policies of the Reconstruction government. The moral is not at all what one might think from my account of the crimes of the Klan. For not only did Tourgée come to see that the policies of the government were mistaken: he came to realize that — given the exclusion from government of the former governing classes in the South and their fear of being governed by the Negroes — the creation of the Klan was inevitable; he even came in certain respects to admire it.

Tourgée was a special case. He was a Northerner who resembled the Southerners: in his insolence, his independence, his readiness to accept a challenge, his recklessness and ineptitude in practical matters, his romantic and chivalrous view of the world in which he was living. Tourgée's love of horses was such that he once started a novel called *My Horses*, and the horses in his other novels are personalities as important as their owners. Tourgée's chivalry was first extended to the innocent and persecuted Negro, but then he found that, as a political opponent, he was really meeting the Southerners on their own ground, that he was playing the same game as they, and he evidently elicited *their* admiration or he could never have survived as so provocative an antagonist fourteen years, as he did, in their midst. He came to understand the Southerner's point of view, not merely from firsthand observation but with a sympathetic intuition such as, so far as I know, was exercised by no other Northern invader who has put himself on record; and this makes him a unique witness whose work is an invaluable source. I may quote as a striking example of his non-partisanship *malgré lui* his listing in parallel columns of the reciprocal misunderstandings between the South and the North:

ANTE BELLUM

NORTHERN IDEA OF SLAVERY	SOUTHERN IDEA OF SLAVERY
Slavery is wrong morally, politically, and economically. It is tolerated only for the sake of peace and quiet. The negro is a man, and has equal inherent rights with the white race.	The negro is fit only for slavery. It is sanctioned by the Bible, and it must be right; or, if not exactly right, is unavoidable, now that the race is among us. We can not live with them in any other condition.

NORTHERN IDEA
OF THE SOUTHERN IDEA

Those Southern fellows know that slavery is wrong, and incompatible with the theory of our government; but it is a good thing for them. They grow fat and rich, and have a good time, on account of it; and no one can blame them for not wanting to give it up.

SOUTHERN IDEA
OF THE NORTHERN IDEA

Those Yankees are jealous because we make slavery profitable, raising cotton and tobacco, and want to deprive us of our slaves from envy. They don't believe a word of what they say about its being wrong, except a few fanatics. The rest are hypocrites.

Post Bellum

THE NORTHERN IDEA
OF THE SITUATION

The Negroes are free now, and must have a fair chance to make themselves something. What is claimed about their inferiority may be true. It is not likely to approve itself; but, true or false, they have a right to equality before the law. That is what the war meant, and this must be secured to them. The rest they must get as they can, or do without, as they choose.

THE SOUTHERN IDEA
OF THE SITUATION

We have lost our slaves, our bank stock, every thing, by the war. We have been beaten, and have honestly surrendered; slavery is gone, of course. The slave is now free, but he is not white. We have no ill will towards the colored man as such and in his place; but he is not our equal, can not be made our equal, and we will not be ruled by him, or admit him as a coördinate with the white race in power. We have no objection to his voting, so long as he votes as his old master, or the man for whom he labors, advises him; but, when he chooses to vote differently, he must take the consequences.

THE NORTHERN IDEA
OF THE SOUTHERN IDEA

Now that the negro is a voter, the Southern people will have to treat him well, because they will need his vote. The negro will remain true to the government and party which gave him liberty, and in order to secure its preservation. Enough of the Southern whites will go with them, for the sake of office and power, to enable them to retain permanent control of those States for an indefinite period. The negroes will go to work, and things will gradually adjust themselves. The South has no right to complain. They would have the negroes as slaves, kept the country in constant turmoil for the sake of them, brought on the war because we would not catch their runaways, killed a million of men; and now they can not complain if the very weapon by which they held power is turned against them, and is made the means of righting the wrongs which they have themselves created. It may be hard; but they will learn to do better hereafter.

THE SOUTHERN IDEA
OF THE NORTHERN IDEA

The negro is made a voter simply to degrade and disgrace the white people of the South. The North cares nothing about the negro as a man, but only enfranchises him in order to humiliate and enfeeble us. Of course, it makes no difference to the people of the North whether he is a voter or not. There are so few colored men there, that there is no fear of one of them being elected to office, going to the Legislature, or sitting on the bench. The whole purpose of the measure is to insult and degrade. But only wait until the States are restored and the "Blue Coats" are out of the way, and we will show them their mistake.

The first stage of Tourgée's enlightenment, as expounded in *A Fool's Errand*, was the realization that the North and the South were virtually two different countries, almost as unsympathetic toward one another and incapable of understanding one another as those other two quarrelsome neighbors France and Germany, and that the outcome of the Civil War had settled their differences as little as the subjugation of Ireland by England or of Poland by Russia. The second stage of Tourgée's enlightenment was a partial self-identification, of a kind to which few Northerners would have been disposed, with the disqualified and dispossessed planters (carrying with them the merchant class dependent on them and intimidating the professional class helpless against them) with whom Tourgée had so much in common. Once this group was removed from authority, who was there, Tourgée came to ask, to manage these still semi-feudal communities? The Negroes? The poor whites? They had no training and no experience. The judges and army officers and heads of the Freedmen's Bureau sent in by the revengeful North? It had not, however, as Tourgée explains in a later novel, *Bricks Without Straw*, been entirely vindictiveness on the part of the North which prompted the policy of the Federal government. The Northerners had taken for granted that all that was needed for the salvation of the South was to arrange for the pro-Union and submissive elements to set up democratic machinery in the townships and counties and states, and they were unable to imagine that the system of town meetings and elections by secret ballot was almost unknown in the South. The Southerners had no such tradition of jealously local self-government. The "Chief Executive," says Tourgée, of every state and the dominant party in the Legislature had controlled the central power of every county and had, through it, appointed every justice of the peace, every member of a school committee and every registrar of elections. There was no real democratic process; and when officials came down from the North to act on their false assumptions, they were taken for rogues or idiots or the mere instruments of Northern malignancy. No wonder, then, that the old class of rulers was driven to restore its authority.

"Yet it was a magnificent sentiment that underlay it all, — an unfaltering determination, an invincible defiance to all that had the seeming of compulsion or tyranny. One can not but regard with pride and sympathy the indomitable men, who, being conquered in war, yet resisted every effort of the conqueror to change their laws, their customs, or even the personnel of their ruling class; and this, too, not only with unyielding stubbornness, but with success. One can not but admire the arrogant boldness with which they charged the nation which had overpowered them — even in the teeth of her legislators — with perfidy, malice, and a spirit of unworthy and contemptible revenge. How they laughed to scorn the Reconstruction Acts of which the Wise Men boasted! How boldly they declared the conflict to be irrepressible, and that white and black could not and should not live together as coördinate ruling elements! How lightly they told the tales of blood, — of the Masked Night-Riders, of the Invisible Empire of Rifle Clubs (all organized for peaceful purposes), of warnings and whippings and slaughters! Ah, it is wonderful!

"And then the organization itself, so complete, and yet so portable and elastic! So perfect in disguise, that, of the thousands of victims, scarce a score could identify one of their persecutors! and among the hundreds of thousands of its members, of the few who confessed and revealed its character, hardly one knew any thing more than had already been discovered; *or, if he knew it, did not disclose it!* It is all amazing, but sad and terrible. Would that it might be blotted out, or disappear as a fevered dream before the brightness of a new day!

"Yet in it we may recognize the elements which should go to make up a grand and kingly people. They felt themselves insulted and oppressed. No matter whether they were or not, be the fact one way or another, it does not affect their conduct. If the Reconstruction which the Wise Men ordained was unjust; if the North was the aggressor and wrongful assailant of the South in war; if, to humiliate and degrade her enemy, the terms of surrender were falsified, and new and irritating conditions imposed; if the outcasts of Northern life were sent or went thither to encourage and induce the former slave to act against his former master, — if all this were true, it would be no more an excuse or justification for the course pursued than would the fact that these things were honestly *believed* to be true by the masses who formed the rank and file of this grotesquely uniformed body of partisan cavalry. In any case, it must be counted but as the desperate effort of a proud, brave, and determined people to secure and hold what they *deemed to be their rights.*

"It is sometimes said, by those who do not comprehend its purpose, to have been a base, cowardly, and cruel barbarism. 'What!' says the Northern man, — who has stood aloof from it all, and with Pharisaic assumption, or comfortable ignorance of facts, denounced 'Ku-Klux,' 'carpet-baggers,' 'scalawags,' and 'niggers' alike, — 'was it a brave thing, worthy of a brave and chivalric people, to assail poor, weak, defenseless men and women with overwhelming forces, to terrify, maltreat, and murder? Is this brave and commendable?'

"Ah, my friend! you quite mistake. If that were all

that was intended and done, no, it was not brave and commendable. But it was not alone the poor colored man whom the daring band of night-riders struck, as the falcon strikes the sparrow; that indeed would have been cowardly: but it was the Nation which had given the victim citizenship and power, on whom their blow fell. It was no brave thing in itself for old John Brown to seize the arsenal at Harper's Ferry; considered as an assault on the almost solitary watchman, it was cowardly in the extreme: but, when we consider what power stood behind that powerless squad, we are amazed at the daring of the Hero of Osawatomie. So it was with this magnificent organization.

"It was not the individual negro, scalawag, or carpet-bagger, against whom the blow was directed, but the power — the Government — the idea which they represented. Not unfrequently, the individual victim was one toward whom the individual members of the Klan who executed its decree upon him had no little of kindly feeling and respect, but whose influence, energy, boldness, or official position, was such as to demand that he should be 'visited.' In most of its assaults, the Klan was not instigated by cruelty, nor a desire for revenge; but these were simply the most direct, perhaps the only, means to secure the end it had in view. The brain, the wealth, the chivalric spirit of the South, was restive under what it deemed degradation and oppression. This association offered a ready and effective method of overturning the hated organization, and throwing off the rule which had been imposed upon them. From the first, therefore, it spread like wildfire. It is said that the first organization was instituted in May, or perhaps as late as the 1st of June, 1868; yet by August of that year it was firmly established in every State of the South. It was builded upon an ineradicable sentiment of hostility to the negro as a *political integer,* and a fierce determination that the white people of the South, or a majority of that race, should rule, — if not by the power of the ballot, then by force of skill, brain, and the habit of domination. The bravest and strongest and best of the South gave it their recognition and support, — in most cases actively, in some passively. Thousands believed it a necessity to prevent anarchy and the destruction of all valuable civilization; others regarded it as a means of retaliating upon the government, which they conceived to have oppressed them; while still others looked to it as a means of acquiring place and power.

"That it outgrew the designs of its originators is more than probable; but the development was a natural and unavoidable one."

The Klan was completely successful. It was difficult for the Federal government to take any effective action or at first to do anything but laugh at the reports of superstitious Negroes intimidated by night riders in hoods and white sheets with false goatees and mustaches. Andrew Johnson was standing up to the Radicals in an effort to be lenient to the Southerners; Grant, who followed him in the Presidency, had thought that the Confederate states should be treated as a conquered province. During Grant's first administration a "Ku Klux" law was passed which made it possible for the President to suspend habeas corpus and put counties or states under martial law, which he presently took advantage of when, in October, 1871, he declared nine counties in South Carolina to be in a state of rebellion; but he gave up this struggle four years later when the radical governor of Mississippi called upon him for Federal troops, and declared that "The whole public are tired out with these annual autumnal outbreaks in the South, and the great majority are ready now to condemn

any interference on the part of the government." Tourgée is extremely bitter about the failure of Washington
to back him by sending him reinforcements at the time
he was fighting the Klan. He was told that he and his
fellows had been put in authority there and that they
would have to depend on themselves. It was difficult for
the Northerners to realize that the Southerners were not
definitely squelched. They never really, in fact, learned
the truth till the appearance of *A Fool's Errand* in 1879,
and then they made haste to forget it. In the meantime,
the former masters had reëstablished themselves in the
South, the Negroes by various devices had been in practice — in defiance of the Fifteenth Amendment — deprived of the right to vote and reduced to a condition
which as little as possible differed from their former
bondage; and the atrocities of the Klan had abated.
Tourgée hits off the situation by calling one of his
last chapters "Peace in Warsaw."

As a result of the success of *A Fool's Errand,* its publishers were very insistent that Tourgée should follow
up this success by supplying them with another novel
about the Reconstruction period. He refused at first on
the ground that he had already said everything he had
to say and did not want to repeat himself. But he yielded
at last to their pressure and wrote *Bricks Without Straw*
(1880), in which he deals with the difficulties of a New
England girl who tries to conduct a Negro school in
North Carolina. At one point, on a marvelous black
horse called Midnight, commanding attention with a
borrowed sword, she averts, singlehanded, a dangerous
riot when armed Negroes are marching to the polls, and
in the end she marries a member of one of the best
Carolinian families — of French blood and with a
French name, like so many of Tourgée's heroes — when
she has made herself acceptable to the local best people

by turning out, through some testamentary hanky-panky of the kind so much in vogue in nineteenth-century fiction, to be actually the owner of his family estate.

It is true that *Bricks Without Straw* is largely a repetition of its predecessor, but it gives Tourgée an opportunity to enlarge on what he regarded as an important subject, upon which he had only touched at the end of *A Fool's Errand*. What, in view of all Tourgée now knew, was to be done about the unfortunate South, which had been beaten but would not submit and which had first been mishandled and then dropped by the North? Tourgée had thought much about this, and had arrived at the conclusion, as others had done — Southerners and Northerners alike — that what the Southerners most needed was education: they could not alter their old habits of behavior, nor, consequently, their institutions, without becoming better informed as to what was going on in the rest of the world — they did not even, as Helper had said, have very much real knowledge of what was going on in their own localities — and, as it was, the sixteen former slave states, which then comprised only a third of the population of the country, made up two-thirds of its total illiteracy, and among the white voters there only twenty-five out of a hundred were able to read their ballots, so that forty-five per cent of the voters of this region (he is counting the Negroes as voters) were unable to read or write. The best thing that the federal government could do, if it really wanted to help the South, would be to establish a fund to be spent for national schools and distributed among the states unequally, in proportion to the degree of illiteracy. This proposal is made by the author to come from the Carolinian hero, who is expounding it to a Northern Congressman. The Congressman objects that the Southerners would resent and refuse to accept such inspection by the federal government as would be necessary for such a system, and, as I write, an education bill which is part of the program of President Kennedy is being opposed by Senator Byrd of Virginia on the ground that the sum appropriated would be apportioned unequally, according to need.

Tourgée did a good deal of work on his project for national education. He campaigned in 1880 for James A. Garfield, a schoolmate and close friend of his childhood in Ohio, and Garfield, after his election to the Presidency, wrote Tourgée that but for his books he "did not think my election would have been possible." He inquired of Tourgée how he thought that the South would take the Republican victory, and the latter replied that the thing to do was to offer it national schools. He and Garfield had a conference on the subject, and the President became convinced of the value of Tourgée's suggestions and asked him to write a book explaining them. This the novelist did, but four months after taking office, the new President was assassinated. The book, *An Appeal to Cæsar,* was published in the autumn of 1884, when Tourgée was expecting that the Republicans would win in the current election and hoping that his ideas might influence them; but the Democrats came in with Grover Cleveland. Later on, in 1901, a letter to Theodore Roosevelt, congratulating him on asking to lunch at the White House the Negro leader Booker T. Washington — a gesture which had outraged the Southerners — makes it clear that Tourgée had now ceased to believe in the efficacy of education as a remedy for racial unfairness. "I realize now," he says, "that . . . education does not eradicate prejudice, but intensifies it."

Tourgée wrote in all six "historical novels," as they were called when published as a series, which cover the national crisis from twenty years before the war till

twelve years after it. He suffered the common fate of
men whose great years had been a part of the war and
who did not quite know what to do afterwards. Like
Mosby and Helper, he lectured, and, like them, he was
assigned a consulship. He spent a good deal of time and
money on futile attempts at invention, and he was
always embarking on business ventures that failed.
"My poor husband!" Emma wrote in her diary — she was
much the more practical of the two and the one who
really kept things running — "How his life was embittered, ruined, by his trying to do what he had no
capacity to do!" The year before he died (1905), he
wrote to a friend that he was feeling much better since
"the doctor made an excavation in my hip and took out
a piece of lead which must have been wandering around
in my anatomy since Perryville."

Tourgée produced an immense amount of journalism,
and he continued to publish novels: semi-melodramas that
carry "messages"; but it will be more instructive to examine in detail the bad popular taste of this period in
its effect upon two men of more talent: George Cable
and John De Forest.

George Washington Cable, Jr., in his origins, represented a mixture of the South, the North and the
West. The family of his father had settled in Virginia
before the Revolution. His mother's family had been
New Englanders since the seventeenth century. But his
grandparents on both sides had moved to Indiana early
in the eighteen hundreds, and his parents were married
there. Later — in 1837 — they went to live in New Orleans. The young George was born in 1844. His father
was by that time on his way to becoming a well-to-do
steamboat owner; but at the end of the forties — for

uncertain reasons — the elder Cable suddenly failed. There was a tradition in the family that two of his steamboats had burned, and these years were in many ways calamitous for New Orleans. There were cholera and yellow fever, and the worst flood in the history of the city, which put two hundred and twenty inhabited blocks under four feet of water. The price of cotton fell from ten to five cents. Cable's property was sold by the sheriff, and he sent his wife, with the children, back to her family in Indiana. While he was making a bare living as a notary public and by irregular work on the river, he wrote her affectionate letters, sometimes in humorous verse. The rest is a dismal record of incapacitating injury, enforced separation, another yellow-fever epidemic, which, like the flood, was the worst in history. The older Cable died of chronic diarrhœa at the beginning of 1859, when George, Jr., was fifteen years old.

The boy was now obliged to leave school and went to work in the custom house. Though there is plenty of "adversity" in Cable's books, plenty of injustice and cruelty and plenty of sympathy for the underdog, there is nothing of harsh reprobation: even when he is showing us specimens of the old regime at its worst, he usually makes a point of noting its special virtues; yet one cannot help feeling that this fairness is a little self-imposed and deliberate, that behind it lies a certain resentment at the pretentions of the old Catholic ruling class. It is no doubt, however, true — as Cable's admirable biographer, Professor Arlin Turner, says — that though the Cables were at this time impoverished, and though George had to work for the support of the family, he would appear to have enjoyed his boyhood as he enjoyed most of the rest of his life. But then the Civil War was upon them, and the next year the Yankees came down the river and Ben Butler occupied New Orleans.

George's mother refused to take the oath of loyalty and declared herself an enemy of the United States; her two daughters also refused; and they were all liable to banishment; but Mrs. Cable was too ill to travel and was allowed to stay behind with a younger son of sixteen. The two young girls, twenty and twenty-two, were sent off into the Confederacy with the eighteen-year-old George, equipped with their lunch but no money. Their mother had hidden a pistol in the loaf of bread they took with them. They were rescued by some soldiers in an ox wagon — one of them an admirer of one of the girls — who took them to Mississippi, where in various plantations they were given homes. The next autumn — 1863 — when George was still not yet quite nineteen, he enlisted in the Confederate cavalry, and he seems to have been slightly wounded in a skirmish the very next day. His comrades reported afterwards that he had manifested throughout the campaign his characteristic steadiness and cheerfulness, and that he had kept a promise to his mother by kneeling to pray every night. He was a wispy little youth and looked frail, and a planter with whom his squad stopped exclaimed on seeing the boy, "Great Heavens! Abe Lincoln told the truth — we *are* robbing the cradle and the grave." He was more seriously wounded in the armpit in February of the following year, in a charge on some ambushed infantry, but quickly recovered and was then assigned to the quartermaster's department. He studied Latin and mathematics when he had the chance, and he regularly read the Bible. When, in March, 1865, all the infantry in Mississippi were sent against Sherman in the Carolinas, Forrest's cavalry was left as the sole defense. Forrest was defeated on April 2 in a battle in which Cable did not take part. "This is not a bad world after all," he wrote his mother in one of his encouraging letters,

"— it only has its failings, which we must humor and overlook." Lee surrendered on April 9, and Forrest on May 4. Before the end of the month, George Cable was back in New Orleans working in a tobacco house as errand boy.

Later he became accountant for various cotton merchants. He married, in 1869, a New Orleans girl whose family, like his mother's, had come from New England and who shared with him a social conscience and a sense of responsibility that involved her in community activities. He began, in 1870, writing a weekly column for the *Picayune*, then threw up his accountant's job and became a full-time journalist, reporting the news of the town. But at this Cable did not last long. He says that the work was repugnant to him. They wanted him to review current plays, but his rigidly puritanical principles forbade him to attend the theater. And this strong moralistic strain further made relations difficult with his bosses by leading him to take an interest in political and social reforms. He attacked the New Orleans lottery, which had a charter from the state legislature and retained it by bribing the members; but the president of the lottery succeeded in having the editor of the *Picayune* removed, and the matter was not mentioned again.

The young journalist had by this time, however, begun to have certain doubts about more fundamental matters. "At sixteen," he was later to write, in his autobiographical sketch *My Politics*, "I was for Union, Slavery, and a White Man's Government. . . . When the war ended, I came back to New Orleans a paroled prisoner, without one spark of loyalty to the United States government." But he had been troubled, in the meantime, at hearing that Georgia was threatening to secede from the Confederacy, for this seemed a *reductio ad absurdum* of the Southern position on secession; and it worried

him, when the war was over, to find people saying that
the right to secede had been settled in the negative by
the victory of the North, since it seemed to him that a
matter of principle should not be affected by defeat.
Had the Confederacy, then, been correct in asserting
its right to secede? Had it even been sincere in this?
He looked up Story on the Constitution and decided
that the South, after all, had had no real constitutional
case, and he came to the conclusion that the actual reason for "wasting three hundred thousand young men's
lives" had been simply to defend the slave system. "Did
that shock me? Not at all. Secession was rebellion and
revolution; but rebellion and revolution might be right,
if only slaveholding was right. *Was* it right?" Again and
again he had heard slavery justified by passages from
the Bible, but when he came to look these passages up,
they seemed to him unsatisfactory. He was incapable of
idealizing the Negro; in his "practical daily experiences,"
he had acquired an unfavorable impression of the freedman "in all his offensiveness — multitudinous, unclean,
stupid, ugly, ignorant, and insolent. Maybe it was not
as bad as it looked to me; I am telling how it looked. If
the much feared 'war of races' should come . . . I was
going to be in the ranks of the white race fighting for
the subjugation of the blacks. And yet I began to see
that these poor fellow-creatures were being treated unfairly." He could not bear to find the Southern papers
talking about "our black peasantry." "I made it my private
maxim, 'There is no room in America for a peasantry.'"
At this point, he was "accepting," he says, "the protection and benefits of a government to which I gave no
hearty allegiance; and yet I privately repudiated the
politics of my 'own people.' Their boasted policy of
'masterly inactivity' meant, in plain English, to withhold
the coöperation of society's best wealth, intelligence and

power from all attempts to reëstablish order and safety on the basis of the amended Constitution, and leave this colossal task to the freedman, with none to aid his clumsy hand save here and there a white man heroic enough and shameless enough to laugh at a complete and ferocious ostracism."

He was one day sent out by the *Picayune* to report the proceedings of a Teachers' Institute convoked by an official of the Republican regime, and he at first wrote resentfully that white and black teachers were being forced by the Republicans to sit together. Then, "when other papers joined the hue and cry," he "suddenly weakened, slackened, ceased." The proprietor of the *Picayune* was much annoyed, and this was the beginning for Cable of the decline of his career as a journalist. When he was sent to report day by day the annual examinations at the public schools, he found "white ladies teaching negro boys; colored women showing the graces and dignity of mental and moral refinement . . . ; children and youth of both races standing in the same classes and giving each other peaceable, friendly, and effective competition; and black classes, with black teachers, pushing intelligently up into the intricacies of high-school mathematics." He recognized that this was highly desirable, and he was also forced to recognize that the Democrats of the South were bent upon preventing the Negroes from enjoying any such opportunities. Later on — in the meantime, he had lost his job — a protest meeting of the students, backed by the press and the public, took place when a mulatto graduate of the École Polytechnique in Paris was appointed teacher of mathematics in one of the high schools for boys. As a result of this, the appointment was at once withdrawn, and, not long afterwards, the boys in the high schools went further and drove all the girls of Negro or part-Negro blood out of the female grammar and high schools. In the winter of 1875, when the Republicans had lost ground in the November elections, a mass meeting was held to denounce mixed schools. Cable wrote to the New Orleans *Bulletin,* which was strongly supporting this movement, a letter of expostulation which was signed simply "A Southern White Man."

This was the beginning of George Cable's campaign for Negro civil rights and of a study of the Negro problem which was unique in Cable's own era and which is of special interest today. He laid down at this time the line that he was later to maintain with such constancy. He asserted that mob interference with the policies of Southern education ought not to be tolerated; that, in view of Southern practice before the war in encouraging white and black children to play together and in entrusting white babies to Negro nurses for suckling as well as for care, it was rather absurd to object that association with Negroes in classrooms would be likely to contaminate the whites; and that relations outside the classroom between white and Negro children would, like other social relations, be always a matter of personal choice. The *Bulletin* printed this letter, but accompanied it with a long refutation; when Cable wrote a rejoinder, this reply was not printed. It would seem to have been rather fiery as well as — what was rare with Cable — lacking in tact: "New Orleans has suffered from this 'foul contact' [of Negroes with whites] at least as little as from the fragrant proximity of the somnolent sons of Gascony, whom she never dreamed of cramping into special, equal, separate accommodations." The editor told him that in ten years' time he would be ashamed of having written such a letter; he retorted that in ten years' time the whole South would believe as he did. What happened was that ten years later he found it necessary to reiterate these views, and to state them even more strongly. But the prospect at that moment seemed hopeful. The freedmen were still voting, and the Democratic party in the South had an interest in winning their favor. The Democratic platform in 1873 had been drawn up by an unprecedented mixed committee of fifty Negroes and fifty whites, the latter including the Creole General Beauregard. This program pledged the Democrats to oppose race prejudice and acknowledged all kinds of equal rights; but certain astute Negro leaders announced that they would vote against the carpetbaggers only after these rights had been granted, and this ended the color coalition.

In the meantime, the ex-reporter had returned to the cotton counting room, but had complied with a request of the *Picayune* that he do some historical sketches of New Orleans "churches and charities." He had read up the old newspapers in the archives and had dug up some curious stories about the interrelations in the past among the various nationalities in Louisiana and the difficult complications resulting from the mixture of black with white blood. Cable began turning these episodes into fiction, exploiting them at first, as he says, mainly for their "romantic value." But he had discovered, in the course of his researches, the brutal old colonial "Black Code" in force in the colonial period, and this had moved him to write, "in sheer indignation," on the basis of an ancient episode that had been told him by the porter in his office, the story of an African prince who had been sold into slavery in Louisiana. This man had risen on his master's estate to a position of a certain ascendancy, but drank too much in celebrating his own wedding and overstepped his servile status — as a result of which he was hunted down and killed like a beast. A visiting New York journalist named Edward King, who had been sent to write up the South, met Cable and read his stories. He took two of these back to New York, and one of them, *'Sieur George,* was printed in *Scribner's Monthly* of October, 1873, but the other, which was then called *Bibi,* the tragedy of the African prince, was not well received by the editor who read it, the mediocre poet and essayist Richard Watson Gilder. "Fear not, O Cable," however, Edward King wrote the author in reassurance, "for your fame is sure if you continue to make Bibis. . . . *Bibi* rode me as a nightmare last night. . . . Bless you, my dear friend, if they don't print it, someone else will. . . . But I am only a worm crawling before the Scribnerian throne." In this case, King was far too hopeful; all the magazines refused the story, probably the most powerful thing that Cable ever wrote. The editor of the *Atlantic Monthly* explained his rejection on the ground of its "unmitigatedly distressful effect." They rejected other pieces, also, but between 1873 and 1876 seven stories of Cable's were printed. It was, however, not till 1879 that he was able to persuade a publisher to bring them out as a collection in book form, with the title *Old Creole Days;* but they then very soon took their place as a kind of contemporary classic, and Cable was compared to Bret Harte and even to Nathaniel Hawthorne. These stories ran through seven editions between 1883 and 1937, and, in a somewhat unfortunate way, established the popular conception of Cable as a purveyor of "local color" that has to some extent persisted to the present time. A later collection of narratives, *Strange True Stories of Louisiana* (published in 1889), seems today perhaps more satisfactory than the partly romantic *Old Creole Days,* since the author is here a mere chronicler and can create at least as much human interest by sticking closer to his real point of view, which is not fundamentally romantic but historical and sociological.*

We shall later return to the subject of the pressures brought to bear on Cable by his popular reputation and by the demands of the Northern editors. At this stage, he was quite able to stand up to them. His work during the seventies and eighties — influenced though it partly was by the more banal conventions of Victorian fiction — is astonishing, in a stuffy period and coming from the demoralized South, for its intelligence, its boldness and its brilliance. George Cable emerges in New Orleans as a phenomenon which could not have been predicted and of which, as a matter of fact, neither Northerners nor Southerners knew what to make. Not merely did the author of *Old Creole Days* possess a remarkable literary gift; he had a kind of all-around intellectual competence that was very unusual at that period in men of letters in the United States. The ups and downs of his early life, the drop from prosperity to poverty and the subsequent necessity of regaining his place, had brought the young Cable into contact with all sorts of conditions and races. He had been through the yellow-fever and the cholera epidemics, and in the former had lost a son (these epidemics figure in several of his stories); he had witnessed the capture of New Orleans (which he describes in two of his novels) and he had fought in

* It ought to be explained that a Creole is a white colonial of French or Spanish blood, whereas the "Creole" language is an Afro-French patois spoken by the Negroes of Louisiana, French Guiana and the French West Indies. The confusion between these two things, complicated even further by the half-French mulatto characters of Cable's early books and by the fact that the pure-white Creoles sometimes spoke the Negro patois, misled Cable's non-Southern audience into thinking that a Creole meant a Frenchman with an admixture of Negro blood. This erroneous impression was one of the things that caused the French Louisianians so indignantly to resent Cable's novels.

the Civil War (also described in two); he had acquired,
through his father's interests, some firsthand knowledge
of steamboating (the subject of another novel called
Gideon's Band); and since he had spent ten years of his
life — 1871-81 — first as manager of finances and head of
the accounting department of a prominent cotton broker
and then as secretary of the Finance Committee of the
New Orleans Cotton Exchange, he had a practical grasp
of business (the complications of which in his novels
occasionally become a bore). From his days as a reporter
for the *Picayune,* he had come to know who lived and
traded and more or less what was going on in every
street in New Orleans, as, from his researches in the
city archives, he had mastered its early history. As
secretary of a grand jury, he had been led to look into
conditions in the prisons and asylums of the state (there
is an episode about this in *Dr. Sevier*), and he organized
a movement to reform these institutions. It has been
said of George Cable that he possessed at that time a
more detailed and comprehensive knowledge of the
state of Louisiana than anybody else alive. He was, in
any case, appointed by the federal government to make
the report on his state for the tenth United States
census, and in connection with this census he carried
out a special study of what must have been the only
element of the population of Louisiana that he did not
already know well — the French-speaking Acadians,
known as "Cajuns," of the southwestern part of the state,
descendants of those French Nova Scotians who had
been expelled from Canada in the seventeen-fifties for
refusing to take the oath of allegiance to the English and
whom Longfellow had idyllized in *Evangeline*. He was
also much interested in folklore, studied African voodoo
and witchcraft, and made a collection of songs in the
Creole language.

But with all Cable's intimate knowledge of his region, there is something quite alien to New Orleans in the temper of mind he brought to it: in his striving for accuracy of observation, his naturalist's interest in varied types, in the eventual objectivity of his judgments. With his feeling for the languorous landscapes and the vivid social contrasts of Louisiana, he combines an intellectual rigor and an instinct for nonpartisan morality that was by that time excessively rare in the South on the part of those Southerners who wrote about it. It was no doubt the New England blood which was mingled in him with that of Virginia. The young Cable was pious and conscientious. A Presbyterian, he had always said his prayers, and he would not travel on Sunday as he never attended the theater. He had, however, been reading novels from an early age, and he defended them on the ground that, like the parables of the Bible, they could at their best teach improving lessons. The strongest criticisms of Cable's piety have been made by Lafcadio Hearn, of whom he had seen a good deal during the latter's residence in New Orleans, and by Mark Twain, with whom, in the winter of 1884-85, he made a long tour of platform readings. "Don't try to conceive how I could sympathize with Cable!" wrote Hearn, in a letter of 1883, "because I never sympathized with him at all. His awful faith — which to me represents an undeveloped mental structure — gives a neutral tint to his whole life among us. There is a Sunday school atmosphere." "It has been a curious experience," Mark Twain, in a letter to Howells, reported at the end of their four months' tour. "It has taught me that Cable's gifts of mind are greater and higher than I had suspected. But — That 'But' is pointing toward his religion. You will never, never know, never divine, guess, imagine, how loathsome a thing the Christian religion can be made until you come to know and study Cable daily and hourly. Mind you, I like him; he is pleasant company; I rage and swear at him sometimes, but we do not quarrel; we get along mighty happily together; but in him and his person I have learned to hate all religions. He has taught me to abhor and detest the Sabbath-day and hunt up new and troublesome ways to dishonor it."

Now, Hearn was part Greek and part Irish; he was primarily a literary impressionist, who was always trying to extricate himself from the harsh Anglo-Saxon civilization and get away to something as unlike it as possible — to New Orleans, to the French West Indies, finally to Japan. He was romantic and atmospheric; he had no scientific interest in social phenomena. Hearn's New Orleans was quite different from Cable's. And as for Mark Twain, he was moody, cantankerous and something of a prima donna. He suffered from a chronic bad conscience and a feeling that he did not have the courage to express his unconventional opinions, and it was natural that the imperturbable Cable, always courteous, always tactful, always fair, always knowing what he thought was right and deliberately acting on principle, should have got on the nerves of the satirist. Though both Hearn and Mark Twain had more poetry, more of the "temperament" of the artist than Cable, George Cable had a stronger intellect and more integration of character than either. He was five feet six inches tall and a good deal shorter than Clemens, and they would come on the platform together because it made the audience laugh. There is a photograph of them posing together, and it is curious to see the towering Mark Twain, coat thrown open and hand in his pocket, gazing out at the responsive public on whose response his self-confidence so much depends, but in moral stature not overtopping the concentrated and tiny Cable, with his trimmed beard and his mandarin mustaches, buttoned up in his frock coat, so good-naturedly sure of himself. Nor did the Puritanism of Cable continue to be so incapable of flexibility as Mark Twain had supposed it to be. It is admitted by Hearn in the letter I have quoted, that "Cable is more liberal-minded than his creed; he has also rare analytical powers on a small scale."

Cable did finally go to the theater — in New York in 1883, when he was thirty-nine years old, and he even assisted later at adaptations of his books for the stage. Though he relentlessly taught Sunday school for many years, he had by 1887 become so liberal that to the orthodox his doctrine seemed suspect and even aroused opposition on the part of the clergy. Cable retorted to this by delivering a lecture called *Cobwebs in the Church,* and he afterwards wrote in his diary that certain of the Boston churches — he was by that time living in New England — "had an average religion that was waterlogged with last century bilgewater." He soon gave up his Bible classes. There is nothing of fundamentalism in the little book called *The Busy Man's Bible* that Cable published in 1891. The discrepancies and inaccuracies of the Scripture, its "seeming contradictions of our scientific knowledge," may be left "to professional scholars, or our own later leisure." The thing is "to see that the fundamental truth and essential part of any sincere utterance remains potentially the same, whether its literary form be mythus, legend, allegory, poetry, song, drama, romance, philosophy or history." By the time he writes *Gideon's Band,* published in 1914, he is able to say of "a parson's wife, who had never seen a play, a game of cards, or a ball, danced a dance, read a novel, tasted wine or worn a jewel," that she "revealed the sweet charities of a soul unwarped by the tyrannous prohibitions under which she had been 'born and

raised' and to which she was still loyal." And in spite of
his early pieties and his rigorous sense of duty, it is impossible at any age to characterize Cable as a prig. It
is hard to be a prig in New Orleans. The courtesy and
grace of a people so convivial and so erotic make the
sterner kind of Puritanism difficult, and it comes to seem
ungentlemanly, boorish, to insist upon moral issues of
a political or social character. George Cable, furthermore,
was an amiable man and — in spite of his critical mind
— really loved the Latin side of the city.

What is unique in the work of this Southerner is the
exercise of a Protestant conscience in a meridional and
partly Catholic community, in which it is, however,
completely at home. The violence and the scandal he
writes about are the conditions of the world he lives in,
but presented from a point of view that is quite distinct from the point of view of those who commit them
or suffer them. It is also undoubtedly true that Cable
had derived certain benefits from growing up in this
mixed milieu. The lucidity and accuracy of French had,
both in style and in thought, served him well, and New
Orleans had a regional culture such as no other Southern city possessed. The New Orleanians loved theater
and opera, and there was a certain amount of literary
activity (which had begun with early writings in French
and was to continue in English through our twenties).
Cable had for his associates in his early days — they
later became his enemies — the Franco-Spanish Creole
historian Charles Gayarré, of an older generation, and
his near-contemporary Lafcadio Hearn. The *Picayune,*
for which he wrote, maintained a literary standard that
was unusually high for the South. And the piquant
variety in New Orleans of races, religions and nationalities had given Cable a kind of international experience

which he could hardly, in the pre-war period, have got anywhere else in the United States.

In George Cable's first novel, *The Grandissimes,* published in 1880, this able and gifted man gets the best out of the elements of his unique experience. *The Grandissimes* is made to take place in 1803-04, and it aims at historical accuracy; but Cable was quite explicit in declaring that its moral applied to the present: "I meant to make *The Grandissimes* as truly a political novel as it has ever been called." The resentment felt by the French and the Spanish, just after the Louisiana Purchase, against "American" domination — that is, against the descent on them of the English and Scottish — suggests an analogy with the Southerners in the period of Reconstruction, humiliated by the presence of the Northerners. But another problem figures in *The Grandissimes.* Though the slaves had been freed at the end of the war, the situation between Negroes and whites was in other ways not very different from what it had been eighty years before. From the moment that the occupying forces withdrew, the Negroes were again suppressed, the mulatto again became an outlaw. The mixture of white and black blood had already been treated by Cable in some of the stories of *Old Creole Days,* but he now attacked the subject on a larger scale and with unprecedented audacity and candor. This subject of miscegenation, so determinedly kept out of sight in the South, had hitherto been written about little and then mainly by outsiders — Mrs. Stowe; the Irishman Mayne Reid, who, in the course of his adventures in this country, had at one time been a plantation overseer and who published in 1856 a novel called *The Quadroon,* which was later (1859) converted by Dion Boucicault into the popular melodrama *The Octaroon,* or *Life in Louisiana;* and Tourgée, whose novel *Toinette* was written in 1868-9. George Cable was the first Southern writer to try to deal in a serious work of fiction with the peculiar relationships created by the mixture of white and Negro blood; and it was not to be till fifty years later, when William Faulkner wrote *Go Down, Moses, Absalom, Absalom!* and *Intruder in the Dust,* that a Southerner who had lived with these situations would have the courage to treat them in fiction again. I do not imagine that Faulkner has been influenced by Cable; but it is interesting to note that their methods are in certain respects rather similar and seem inevitably to have been forced upon them by the nature of the material itself. In Cable and Faulkner both, the truth about family imbroglios in which a mixture of blood is involved is likely at first to be concealed from the reader, then presently in an unobtrusive way implied — allowed to leak out in some confidence of a character or made suddenly to emerge like the cat from the bag. It is treated, in other words, in the way that the Southerners treat it, and in Faulkner and Cable the suspense for the reader is likely to be created by the presence of a secret, and the climax will be a surprise.

There is in Cable's case a certain machinery of the conventional Victorian plot, but the effectiveness of his early fiction depends on the startling relationships, the unexpected courses of action that result from the queer situation of two races living side by side, entangled with one another but habitually ignoring this fact, proceeding more or less at cross-purposes but recurrently brought up short by love, sympathy or consanguinity. Hence the violence, the scandal, the constant frustration — to which is added that other frustration of intervention by an alien power: in the early days the "Americans," in the years after the war the Yankees. The pretense that the past has not happened, that ancient history is not still with us here, makes the terror of this Southern world, the tragic irony of Cable's fiction. That episode unanimously rejected by the editors of the Northern magazine — now given a new title by the author: *The Story of Bras-Coupé* — is embodied in *The Grandissimes,* and reverberates all through the novel. The first version of the story was evidently written — by 1873 — before Cable had read Turgenev, but we know that he did read the Russian in 1874, and he must have reworked it before it was published, in 1880, as a part of the novel. At any rate, it reminds one of such stories of serfdom of Turgenev's as *Mumu* and *The Wayside Inn,* and it hangs over the novel of *The Grandissimes* — being part of the background of the Grandissime family — as a horror, a hideous crime, from the consequences of which they can never escape, a little as Turgenev's memories of the atrocities committed by his mother are felt as a motif of fear that runs through the whole of his work. *The Grandissimes* is Cable's best book, and the other strong things in his work are likely to repeat this theme. So in *The "Haunted House" in Royal Street,* one of the *Strange True Stories of Louisiana,* the terrible Madame Lalaurie, who lived with the utmost elegance in a house full of chained and tormented slaves — we are reminded again of Turgenev's mother — and had to flee for her life from a mob when a fire revealed these infamies, is the real ghost whose presence is felt in the accursed house in Royal Street. This house has been converted by the Reconstruction government into a non-segregated high school for girls, but when the federal ascendancy has weakened, it is invaded by a local white mob, who cross-examine the students and drive away all the girls who cannot prove that they do not have black blood.

We shall see in a moment how Cable was diverted

from following his bent and was never to be able again
to write a novel so good as *The Grandissimes*. His fellow
Southerners were, of course, to repudiate this book, and,
undertaken as the book had been entirely on the author's own initiative, with no arrangements for serial
publication, it was not at all the kind of thing to cap-
tivate the feminine taste that was coming to dominate
our fiction. Yet *The Grandissimes* has gone through several editions, and it still lives and speaks for its author.
One is surprised when one picks it up and finds it —
partly tedious, partly brilliant — so observant, so sharp,
so humane in its handling of the maimings and distor-
tions, the comic and tragic involvements of its complicated embarrassing subject. George Cable can be understood and his work given its value today, as seems
rarely to have been the case in the period for which he
wrote, and there is evidence of new interest in *The
Grandissimes*. It has been recently reprinted as a paperback, with an introduction by Newton Arvin, and there
is a chapter on it by Richard Chase in his book *The
American Novel and Its Tradition*. These discussions
of *The Grandissimes* are a good deal more intelligent, do
more justice to the book's real merits, than even the favorable notice of the age for which Cable wrote.

Old Creole Days and *The Grandissimes* were not especially well received by the Creole population of New
Orleans. They thought Cable had made them ridiculous
by representing them as speaking bad English and even
dropping into Negro patois, and they believed that he
had led the public to suppose that all Creoles had Negro
blood. He attempted to counteract this by doing justice
to their Latin virtues in the course of recounting their
history in *The Creoles of Louisiana*, published in 1884.
But when he persisted — through public statements as

well as through his subsequent fiction — in his searching inquiry into Southern affairs, he eventually roused up against him virtually the whole white South. In the eighties, he was publishing as articles or delivering in the form of addresses a whole series of studies of conditions in the states of the late Confederacy, which he later — in 1885 and 1890 — collected in two small books, *The Silent South* and *The Negro Question*. These are among his most valuable writings, and they ought to have been recognized as classics in their field, but they appeared at a time when it happened, for reasons to be noticed later, that neither the North nor the South desired to be harassed further by these problems for which the proposed solutions could never be made to come out right. They were for years almost never read by anyone save the few special students of Cable. The facts and analysis contained in them have, however, become so pertinent to the present crisis in the South that most of the material in them as well as other related writings of Cable's have recently been reprinted, under the editorship of Mr. Arlin Turner, in a volume to which he has given the title of the second of Cable's books, *The Negro Question*.

Fundamental to Cable's position is his valuable formulation — presented in *The Negro Question* — of the attitudes, respectively, of the North and the South at the time of the Civil War. Why, he asks, have the Northerners, who had made so much fuss about liberating the slaves from their bondage, eventually allowed the freedmen to be reduced by the Southern whites to a condition not much better than their previous one? And how is it that the Southerners, who at the time of the war were in tantrums about state rights, are now willing to drop this grievance and be reconciled to accepting a place in the Union? The answers to these questions are complementary. The Northerners, with the exception of a few Abolitionists, would never actually have gone to war over slavery; it was vital to them to maintain the Union, and that was what they were fighting for. With the Southerners, state rights were a pretext: what they fought for was really slavery, on which they thought that their economy and their society depended. As soon as they had largely succeeded in putting the Negro back in his place and knew that they would not be much interfered with, they showed little concern about Constitutional rights. George Cable, who, when secretary of the New Orleans grand jury, had been led to investigate the Southern prisons, had discovered still another effective method besides those described by Tourgée by which it had been possible for the Southerners surreptitiously to reënslave Negroes. This was what was called the Convict Lease System. The device was to arrest as many Negroes as possible and to give them heavy sentences on the pretext of petty crimes, such as hogstealing, engaging in fist-fights or carrying concealed weapons, then to rent them out in gangs as forced labor. This was done on an enormous scale. In Georgia, a long sentence meant certain death. Cable gives the statistics for eleven states.

The first step in Cable's campaign to call attention to these practices in the South was an article called *The Freedman's Case in Equity*, which was published in the *Century Magazine* of January, 1885. (*Scribner's* had changed its name in 1881, but the magazine had still the same editors.) It was the first time, outside his fiction, that he had expressed himself on black and white problems since his ten-years-earlier letter to the *Bulletin*, but he had been moved at last to break his silence by an incident he had recently witnessed on a railroad train in Alabama. His account of this occurrence is as follows: "At rather late bed-time there came aboard the train a young mother and her little daughter of three or four years. They were neatly and tastefully dressed in cool, fresh muslins, and as the train went on its way they sat together very still and quiet. At the next station there came aboard a most melancholy and revolting company. In filthy rags, with vile odors and the clanking of shackles and chains, nine penitentiary convicts chained to one chain, and ten more chained to another, dragged labori-ously into the compartment of the car where in one corner sat this mother and child, and packed it full, and the train moved on. The keeper of the convicts told me he should take them in that car two hundred miles that night. They were going to the mines. My seat was not in that car, and I stayed in it but a moment. It stank insufferably. I returned to my own place in the coach behind, where there was, and had all the time been, plenty of room. But the mother and child sat on in silence in that foul hole, the conductor having distinctly re-fused them admission elsewhere because they were of African blood, and not because the mother was, but because she was *not,* engaged at the moment in menial service. Had the child been white, and the mother not its natural but its hired guardian, she could have sat anywhere in the train, and no one would have ventured to object, even had she been as black as the mouth of the coal-pit to which her loathsome fellow-passengers were being carried in chains."

Cable cut the ground out from under his opponents — though they often paid no attention to this — by de-manding equal civil rights for Negroes, but declaring that social equality was out of the question and inter-marriage between the races undesirable. Social equality, Cable says, is not a *danger,* as so many in the South seem to think; it is simply an impossibility. We are free to choose our own associates, and where the gap between two groups is as wide in education and habits of living as it is for the most part between Negroes and whites, they will rarely be dining together. They are taking, he says, in the South, "diligent and absolutely needless pains to hold apart two races which really have no social affinity at all." As for intermarriage, mixed blood has already made quite enough trouble. He was to elaborate on this later in *Gideon's Band,* in which a big-hearted Californian offers to marry a woman who is technically a slave on account of having a small amount of Negro blood. This is prevented by the counsel of a character who is supposed to be a wise old gentleman. Does he defer, a young girl asks, to Mrs. Grundy? Yes, "But poor, blundering old Mrs. Grundy, always wronging some one, is really fighting hard for a better human race."

Cable was always firm in maintaining that the black and the white should not become amalgamated. He believed, however, that the Negroes were capable of much self-improvement. A group who were sending, as he says, twenty thousand students to normal schools and colleges and supporting eighty newspapers should be able, if given the chance, to provide their own competent leadership, which would guide them in public affairs. "It is widely admitted that we are vastly the superior race in everything — as a race. But is every colored man inferior to every white man in character, intelligence, and property? Is there no 'responsible and steadfast element' at all among a people who furnish 16,000 school-teachers and are assessed for $91,000,000 worth of taxable property? Are there no poor and irresponsible whites? So, the color line and the line of character, intelligence, and property frequently cross each other. Then tell us, gentlemen, which are you really for; the color line or the line of character, intelligence, and property that divides between those who have and those who have not 'the right to rule'? . . . The right to rule: What is it? It is not the right to take any peaceable citizen's civil right from him in whole or in part. It is not the right to decree who may earn or not earn any *status* within the reach of his proper powers. It is not the right to oppress. In America, to rule is to serve."

His point about the "silent South" is that there are many people there who agree with him, and that such people should raise their voices. The essay that bears this title ends with a burst of optimism which makes curious reading today: "Nationalization *by* fusion of bloods is the maxim of barbarous times and peoples. Nationalization *without* racial confusion is ours to profess and procure. . . . We have got to build a nationality as free from all civil estrangement as from social confusion, yet wider than the greatest divergence of human races. This is the meaning of the great revolution upon us today. Daily the number increases of those who grasp it. A little while ago the whole nation rejected it. To reject it today is to be left behind the nation's best thought. How fast that thought is spreading in the South few know. Like the light of kindling watch-fires it is catching from mind to mind. The best men of the South are coming daily into convictions that condemn their own beliefs of yesterday as the antiquated artillery of an outgrown past; and to the present writer, as one who himself found this not easy, but hard, to do, it seems no improbability that our traditionist friends, even before this reply can reach them, may be found ranging themselves among that number, for the promotion of this revolution that everybody knows must come."

The reception of these ideas seemed to Cable at first encouraging. He had already been applauded by the students of the University of Mississippi when he had told them, in a commencement address of June, 1882, that "the plantation idea is a semibarbarism. It is the idea of the old South, with merely the substitution of a Negro tenantry for Negro slaves. . . . Landlordism kept the South poor one century, and just as sure as it survives it will keep her poor another." In September of the following year, he had addressed a National Conference of Charities and Correction at Louisville on the convict lease system, and his address appeared later in the *Century*. "Nothing I have ever written," said Cable, "has gained me so many friends among the best people of the South;" but he was characterized by a senator of his own state as "a Quixotic moral reformer, who, mounted upon the ass of public credulity, rode against the immovable windmills of fixed institutions." And he had said an unfortunate thing on the occasion of writing a letter to explain why he could not be present at a celebration of Harriet Beecher Stowe's birthday. The letter was printed in the Boston *Evening Transcript,* and contained a disloyal passage that the Southerners were never to forgive: "To be in New England would be enough for me. I was there once — a year ago — and it seemed as though I had never been home till then." In July, 1884 — in order to rescue his wife, who was ill, from the prostrating New Orleans summer — he brought his family to Simsbury, Connecticut, where they decided to spend a year. It was in June of that year, before leaving for the North, that he had taken his first bold step in attacking the Negro question. Wanting first to state his views in the South, he had accepted an invitation to deliver a commencement address at the University of Alabama, and what he gave them was *The Freedman's Case in Equity.* He had been hearing a good deal lately of the progressiveness of Alabama, and since the Northerners had largely dropped their interest in the Negro, he imagined that he could hardly be charged with playing up to Yankee ideas. The press was uniformly abusive and called him a "New England Puritan," but Cable had "no lack," he says, of "private expressions of approval," and he "left Alabama more deeply impressed than ever before with the fact that behind all the fierce and resentful conservatism of the South there was a progressive though silent South which needed to be urged to speak and act. To this end somebody must speak first and as I was now out in the storm and, as one may say, wet to the skin, why should it not be I?"

In September of the same year, Cable's second novel, *Dr. Sevier*, was published, and this made the situation worse. He had avoided the Negro problem here, but had included a chapter that was calculated to outrage the whole South. He describes Union soldiers, singing *John Brown's Body*, marching in the streets of New York, and apostrophizes them as follows: "Yea, so, soldiers of the Union, go marching on . . . your cause is just. Lo, now, since nigh twenty-five years have passed, we of the South can say it!" — adding, however, perhaps a little weakly, "'And yet — and yet, we cannot forget' — and we would not." A friend in New Orleans sent Cable a clipping of a review of the book, writing, "Page [Baker, the editor of the paper in which the review appeared] wanted to attack the work viciously, on account of its anti-Southern tone, but Hearn and I persuaded him out of it. Hearn wrote the notice, but does not care for you to know. He is hopelessly down upon you and there is no kind of use trying to argue him out of it. . . . He confessed to me that, but for Page's antagonism, he would have said more in your praise, because he cannot but accord to you marvellous power." Then *The Freedman's Case in Equity* came out in the *Century*, and Page Baker himself attacked Cable, and the eighty-year-old Gayarré — undoubtedly jealous of Cable, who had displaced him as the first man of letters of New Orleans — interrupted a series of historical articles in order to denounce Cable in lectures and print. Gayarré declared in one of his lectures that "Mr. Cable's aim is to degrade, lower in the public opinion the reputation of the population of Louisiana, Creole or not, to put it socially, civilly and politically below the black race, which he considers superior to ours and destined to africanize the whole South. . . . What I am indeed convinced of is that the author of *The Grandissimes* is as deprived of all moral sense as a crocodile." Paul Hamilton Hayne, the South Carolina poet and friend of Sidney Lanier, expressed agreement with Gayarré in reply to his infuriated letters, and added: "Of his books I know nothing; nor do I expect to read them."

Grace King, in her autobiography, *Memories of a Southern Woman of Letters*, tells of a visit to New Orleans in 1884 of Richard Watson Gilder. When Miss King had first met Gilder, he had remarked to her that New Orleans had bad associations for him: his wife's brother had died there, and the funeral had been jeered at by a Southern lady. Miss King, nettled by this, explained that at the time of the occupation she had been playing on her balcony with a child and had happened to be laughing innocently at something the child did. For this the Yankee General ("Beast") Butler had had her sent to Ship Island, a "patch of sand" in Lake Pontchartrain, on which she was the only woman and was guarded by a garrison of Negroes. "After this depressing beginning, he [Gilder] proceeded to ask questions of me about the inimical stand taken by the people of New Orleans against George Cable and his works. I hastened to enlighten him to the effect that Cable proclaimed his preference for colored people over white and assumed the inevitable superiority — according to his theories — of the quadroons over the Creoles. He was a native of New Orleans and had been well treated by its people, and yet he stabbed the city in the back, as we felt, in a dastardly way, to please the Northern press." Unless we bear in mind the embittered context, it may seem to us rather strange that Grace King, the conscientious historian, the admirer of Ernest Renan, should have so misrepresented Cable, should even talk as if she had not read his books. His biographer reveals, however, that much later Miss King met Cable when he was giving, in 1915, a reading before the Louisiana Historical Society and that she afterwards said to an interviewer: "I understand him now. I would say he wrote too well about the Creoles. He wanted to read something of his at a meeting of our Historical Club. Some of the members objected, but we finally made arrangements. He captured the audience. Everyone rushed up and shook hands with him. Many of us never dreamed the day would come when we would shake hands with Cable. He told us a little incident of a Confederate who served in the war and was wounded. It was beautifully written and really the most compelling little incident I have ever heard. The hall was packed. When he finished, everybody stood up, and I never heard such applause. I am so glad that at last he got this compliment from New Orleans. He deserved it, not only as a tribute to his genius, but as compensation for the way we treated him. I am glad. He is an old man, very picturesque, very sad, with beautiful manners." Yet years later, writing her memoirs, she says nothing at all about this, and speaks of Cable in the terms I have quoted. There was evidently in this stubbornness of the Southerner in sticking to an official position even when it must lead to conscious falsity an element of the strategy for which George Orwell, in writing of the modern dictatorships, has coined the word "doublethink." The point of view of the Grace King who read Renan (and who liked to be thought to look like him) existed in a different compartment from that of the loyal upholder of the orthodox Confederate creed, and they moved side by side, simultaneously, along two parallel tracks.

The fierce patriotism and pride of defeat override all mercy and reason. We have seen it in Hitler's Germany. Even Lafcadio Hearn, though he was not himself even a Southerner and although he was particularly attracted to women with dark skins and had at one time been married to a mulatto — even this exotic misfit could not help, as we have seen, being carried along from the moment that the tide began running against Cable. He had even written an editorial against *The Freedman's Case in Equity,* with a title, *Mr. Violet Cable,* which implied that the author had colored blood. When Cable revisited New Orleans in 1886, he found himself more or less ostracized. He had in the meantime made his permanent home in New England. "I must admit," he had written his wife just after his paper on the freedman had been published, "I shall not from choice bring up my daughters in that state of society. The more carefully I study it the less I expect of it; and though there is no reason why I should indulge ungracious feelings toward it I cannot admire it or want my children to be brought up under its influence." He decided to live in Northampton, Massachusetts, where his four girls could go to Smith College; but when he wanted to sell his house in New Orleans, he found that the assessment on his property had been maliciously raised by twenty-five hundred dollars. A lawyer friend in New Orleans brought suit and got this figure reduced. George Cable was now mainly dependent on his readings and did not have much time to write fiction, but he continued his advocacy of justice for the Negro. He made a point of reading everything he wrote on this subject on a public platform in the South before it was published in the North; and he appeared before both black and white audiences.

In 1889, on a visit to Nashville, Tennessee, an incident occurred which made Cable, as Mr. Turner says, "untouchable" in that city and which seems to have had upon him a discouraging effect. He had organized an Open Letter Club for the purpose of exchanging and publishing views among liberals in the South. The membership included Negroes as well as whites, and Cable, having gone to Nashville to talk about the affairs of the Club with a member who was a professor at Vanderbilt University, arranged also to discuss the matter with a group of interested Negroes. Since these could not come to a white man's hotel, Cable met them at the house of a colored lawyer. When the meeting was over and the guests had gone, finding himself alone with the lawyer and his wife and realizing, he says, that they were "in a dilemma between asking a white man to sit at their board and sending him away supperless," he remarked that he had not eaten and accepted their invitation to dinner. He was soon receiving clippings from the Nashville *American* the tone of which may be indicated by the following: "Mr. George W. Cable, just before he took his departure for the East, was entertained by J. C. Napier, colored, where he spent a most agreeable evening in the society of our colored élite. Mr. Cable has often urged social equality of the races, and we are glad to see him following his own advice on the subject. In the South, however, a man must choose the race with which he associates, and Mr. Cable, having signified his preference for the negro race over his own, should be left undisturbed in his choice. We do not mean to say that Cable has lowered himself by accepting the hospitalities of Mr. Napier, colored; on the contrary we think he found his proper level. J. C. Napier is a respectable negro, but, of course, with the prejudices of his race. . . . He probably did not reflect that Mr. Cable is a Southern man who has turned renegade with an eye to Yankee taste and Yankee money, and it is money in his pocket to slander the people among whom he was born."

Cable at once wrote to the editor, and a controversy between them ensued. It was one of the rare occasions when Cable allowed himself to show anger. He said that he had never advocated any blending of the blood of the races (he had also been accused of this). "One may often see gatherings of colored people where in three-fourths of their number the blood of the two races is already mingled. Who has mingled it? Let your Nashville *American* answer that. Probably not one in a thousand owes his or her mixture of blood to anyone suspected of advocating 'social equality.'" On the subject of the dinner with Napier, he said, "If the friendship of any friend of mine, North or South, old or new, hangs on the condition that I must never do again what I did the other day in Nashville, I bid such a friendship a regretful goodbye. I will break bread with the murderer in his cell if I choose. I have no fear that I shall lose all my friends but I know that I shall keep my self-respect." The professor at Vanderbilt wrote that it was impossible for him now, as he had hoped to do, to have Cable come to Nashville for a reading, though, before this incident occurred, Cable could have "filled a house"; he, the professor, had been threatened with physical violence if Cable ever showed himself there again. The Open Letter Club was dissolved.

Cable continued to publish articles on Negro rights

through 1892, but, after this — except when the subject crops up in his later novels — he abandoned his campaign in behalf of them. The cause for the time seemed lost. In the course of the nineties, the Negroes in the South were quietly disfranchised. Mississippi led the way by making the poll tax a prerequisite for voting, and soon added a literacy test. The other Southern states followed suit. The poll taxes became so complicated that it was impossible for the Negroes to work them out, and the literacy tests — entirely, of course, in the hands of the white boards of registry — were administered in such a way as to exclude even Negroes with college degrees.

So much for the response of the South. The influence of the Northern editors was to prove in the long run as lethal. The slow strangulation of Cable as an artist and a serious writer is surely one of the most gruesome episodes in American literary history. We have seen that *The Story of Bras-Coupé* was rejected in its original form, and that the harmless and amusing *Posson Jone'* was refused by four editors before it was accepted by *Appleton's Journal*. It was complained that there was no love interest in *Posson Jone'*, and the editor of *Harper's* objected that "the disagreeable aspects of human nature are made prominent, and the story leaves an unpleasant impression on the mind of the reader." Richard Watson Gilder of *Scribner's* censored a figure of speech in another story, *'Tite Poulette,* and urged Cable to "omit a touch or two of horror in *Café des Exilés."* "Write something intensely interesting," he added, "but without the terrible suggestion you so often make use of." Three stories at this time were refused on account of their political implications, and were never afterwards published. "It is tempting," Mr. Turner well says, "to speculate on the kind of fiction Cable would have produced if from the time he first submitted *Bibi* onward his work had been judged by an editor less fearful of the unpleasant and the touches of horror." Mr. Turner has found two versions of the manuscript of *The Grandissimes,* which came out serially in *Scribner's,* and they show the constant carping and nagging to which the author had to submit. When he suggested doing a sequel to *The Grandissimes,* the editors would not have it at any price, for — even though complaints from the South were not yet making themselves heard — they did not want to publish in their "family magazine" any more uncomfortable stories about people of mixed blood. They really wanted nothing from Cable but little love stories of queer old New Orleans — the romance and charm of the French Quarter, those Creoles with their droll way of talking — and they did not care in the least that Cable had no natural bent for the conventional kind of romance, that his interests and his capabilities all lay in the direction of imaginative history and realistic social observation. He had written a history of New Orleans as an offshoot of his census report, and he tried to make this acceptable to *Scribner's,* but it was not the kind of thing they had hoped for. "The disagreement," says Mr. Turner, "between the author and his editors was simply that he considered the work a history and valued most its completeness and accuracy, whereas they had the needs of the magazine in mind and wanted him to single out the odd and the picturesque for elaboration in the manner of his fiction." He was still, however, in those days obstinately fighting for his own hand, and when he published his compact little history, *The Creoles of Louisiana* (1884), he put back some of the matter that had been taken out. A valuable paper on Creole slave songs and dances and the practice of voodoo in Louisiana had also to be made more amusing and a reference to the Black

Code excised before the editors brought it out as two articles.

It is impossible to know what Cable's second novel, *Dr. Sevier* (1884), would have been like if he had been allowed to publish it as he wrote it. The dreadful conditions in the local prisons were apparently to have played a more important role than they do in the final version. In this case, however, one can sympathize with the advice of Robert Underwood Johnson, at that time an editor of *Century,* when he is trying to persuade Cable of the advisability of dramatizing his social problems rather than lecturing about them. The unsatisfactoriness of *Dr. Sevier* may be due partly to the soft-pedalling of editors and partly to the author's desire to show lovable and worthy characters who would appeal to the Victorian appetite for reading about respectable virtue and humble people with hearts of gold. Here Cable was evidently aiming to supply his readers, also, with a liberal allowance of another product of his which was popular. One of the features of his early fiction had been his scrupulously accurate rendering of the dialects, accents and lingoes of the mixed population of the South, from Negro French and illiterate West Floridian to the English and French of the upper-class Creoles. His skill at this kind of mimicry was one of the things that made his readings successful, and he seems to have set out in this novel to provide a certain number of scenes which would keep his mainly well-schooled audiences in gales of good-natured laughter. You have in *Dr. Sevier* not merely Negro and Creole, but also the imperfect English of Irish, German and Italian Americans, all set down with phonetic precision and stuck full of so many apostrophes that their dialogue becomes an obstacle. This conscientious book suffers, too, from a kind of miscalculation that sometimes occurs with novelists when a curious or striking true story, transposed into a work of fiction, turns out to give an impression of implausibility and, in the case of *Dr. Sevier*, to seem rather pointless as well, and hence uncharacteristic of Cable. *Bonaventure*, which followed in 1888, when Cable had been warned off the subjects that aroused his unwelcome emotions, turned out, in spite of careful descriptions of the "Cajuns" and their rather wild country — the author calls the book a "prose pastoral" and is trying for the poignant-idyllic — to have been rendered completely nonmemorable by a kind of wholesome insipidity and a sentimentality that fails to function.

Cable composed in 1889, as a preface to *The Silent South*, which was about to appear in a new edition, a kind of apologia called *My Politics*, in which he gave an account of his life and the development of his opinions. It was supposed to appear first in the *Century*, but Johnson and Gilder would not have it, and this interesting and important document was never published in full till it was recently included by Professor Turner in the collection called *The Negro Question* mentioned above. Nor would the *Century* run Cable's next novel, *John March, Southerner* — though it was published eventually in book form, in 1895. This story deals with post-war conditions in the imaginary state of Dixie. Richard Watson Gilder, it seems, had by this time decided that the Southerners had been all along perfectly sound in refusing civil rights to the Negroes, and he had therefore been getting out of sympathy with Cable. "I could weep for disappointment," Gilder wrote him about *John March*. "Instead of a return *to* literature, an attempt to fetch everything into literature save and except literature itself. . . . *Beware of the fate of Tolstoy.*" And later: "There is an innate disagreeableness that seems to pertain largely to the conditions described. . . . There is an apparent effort to conceal salutary purpose in the book — but it is there, all the same — running along in a sort of irritating way."

But Gilder was quite right in declaring that there is no literature in *John March* and that its salutary purpose is irritating. For one thing, the novelist had by this time been away from the South too long to be steeped, as he had once been, in the local life, and, furthermore, the locale of the novel is entirely a notebook product, the result of a visit to a small town in Georgia, a state that Cable did not know well. He has tried to invent a community that will serve to show typical situations, but neither characters nor situations can be accepted by the reader as real. Between the Northern characters and the Southern ones and between the blacks and the whites, Cable shrewdly holds the balance as usual: there are good people and bad people on both sides. The hero is an upright and idealistic Southerner, the villain a hypocritical Southerner. The New England businessmen are scrupulously honest and considerate, and the mess that is made of the affairs of the town as a result of its efforts, in the seventies, toward commercial and industrial progress is due largely to Southern crookedness. Lest he be thought to idealize the Negro and invariably to sympathize with men of mixed blood, the author has made a point of having a mulatto for a secondary villain: a bad egg capable of any rascality, who has been brought to the top by the Reconstruction and who, now that the Northerners have gone, remains a nuisance and a menace whom the Southerners can no longer control.

In all this, the novelist has become far too conscious of his social responsibility. Every character, almost every scene, is intended to illustrate some point, and the moral of the whole thing is that the South can be born again only if the decent elements can succeed in disentangling themselves from the corrupt and reactionary ones. The novel is completely synthetic, and it was most unfortunate that Cable, in attempting so serious a book, should have played into the hands of his critics by producing so thorough a bore. The reviewer in the *Atlantic Monthly* expressed his disappointment, says Professor Turner, "because the setting was not in Creole New Orleans, and he missed the earlier 'optimism and hilarity.'" (He was evidently thinking of *Dr. Sevier.*) A book that follows *John March, Strong Hearts* (of 1899), is made up of three stories, two of which show Cable at his sickliest, but the third of which has at least the merit of containing one of the few bright spots of writing to be found in the later Cable. The experiences of a drunkard who reforms himself by escaping to an island in the Gulf of Mexico, destroying his adored sailboat and living alone on the sand, where he barely survives a hurricane, has something of Stephen Crane and something of Ernest Hemingway. It is the old American theme of the isolated man at grips with nature and entirely dependent on his own resources. The Sunday-school Cable is here, but there is also the shrewd psychologist. The drunkard, disappointed in love, can get himself under control only by accepting and intensifying his solitude. *Bylow Hill* (1902), which is laid in New England, is a novelette based on a psychiatric case of Dr. S. Weir Mitchell's, which Mitchell had suggested to Cable as a promising subject for fiction. But Cable had no qualifications — not the right kind of imaginative insight — for a study of pathological jealousy.

The real canon of Cable's books, the five of them that ought to be read by every student of American literature — *Old Creole Days, The Grandissimes, Strange True Stories of Louisiana, The Silent South* and *The Negro*

Question — were all written by 1890. Though somewhat hampered in the novels that immediately follow by the demands of the popular taste, the author of *The Grandissimes* is still trying to maintain his standing on the higher level of literature; but these books show Cable at a serious loss — witness *Bylow Hill* — as to what to do with his talents. And in the interval between *Strong Hearts* and *Bylow Hill,* he had, for the first time in his life, deliberately mustered his powers for a full-scale exploitation of the popular taste.

If one examines the files for the eighties and nineties of the *Century Magazine,* one sees very clearly the falling-off — which becomes at one point precipitous — in the quality of the American reading matter that was provided for the educated public. In 1885, for example, Mark Twain's *Huckleberry Finn,* Henry James's *The Bostonians* and Howells's *The Rise of Silas Lapham* were all running in the *Century Magazine,* as well as Grant's *Personal Memoirs,* the notable series that later appeared as *Battles and Leaders of the Civil War,* the first of Cable's essays on the Negro question, some of Frank R. Stockton's best stories, and papers by Theodore Roosevelt on state legislature and grizzly bear hunting. Nor did these writings, as was to be the case later, come mainly from scattered individuals who were pursuing their different lines in more or less isolation from one another. Henry James had only lately left Boston to take up his permanent residence in Europe, and he and Howells, when both were living in Boston, had seen a good deal of one another, and both were still depicting in a vein that was new the old-fashioned Boston society. Mark Twain, too, was in close touch with Howells, who encouraged him and criticized his manuscripts, and the relations between Mark Twain and Cable were then in their most intimate phase. Mr. Guy A. Cardwell, the author of a book, *Twins of Genius,* on the relations of the latter pair, suggests that it may have been the example of Cable that stimulated Mark Twain to try something more ambitious in his use of his Mississippi material. This — perhaps in conjunction with the example of Howells — would explain the abrupt disparity between *Tom Sawyer* and *Huckleberry Finn;* certainly, it was Cable who persuaded Mark Twain to read the *Morte d'Arthur* and so started the train that soon led to *A Connecticut Yankee in King Arthur's Court.* And it was Clemens, on his side, who suggested to Grant that he ought to write the story of his own career, who gave him confidence in his literary competence and who rescued him from a contract with Century and brought out Grant's book himself.

The editors of the *Century Magazine* were, moreover, at that time, according to their lights, turning out a very creditable monthly. The *Century* was a sound feat of journalism, with substantial informative articles on the arts and sciences and foreign lands cementing the memoirs and the fiction. Yet Howells and Mrs. Clemens were already expurgating Mark Twain, and we may suppose, from their treatment of Cable, that the editors were doing so, too. *The Bostonians,* with its woman's rights Lesbian and its letting-down of Boston idealism, seems to have bored or offended most readers. I was told by the late Frank Crowninshield, who had at one time worked on the *Century,* that *The Bostonians* had long remained a legend of horror, a warning of what to avoid. In addition to its other sins, it had run for an extra instalment beyond the allotted twelve months.

Except for an occasional story or essay, Henry James now disappears from the *Century,* and the drop in his popularity seems to have dated from then. In spite of James's moments of nostalgia and his complaints of the mediocrity of British as well as of American products, there *was* still a literary world and a noble tradition in England, and he was probably better off there. The age of expatriates was well advanced. They were all of them — though James, perhaps, least — somewhat handicapped by their divorce from their American materials; and Cable in a sense was an expatriate, too, but, escaping from the blasted and embittered South, he now found himself stuck in New England, with his market in commercial New York. The "little" magazines, by the middle nineties — *The Chap-Book, The Lark,* etc. — were attempting to get free of this market, and even the established publishers had become so extremely reluctant to take a risk on unconventional books that there came to be a place for an unorthodox publisher: Herbert S. Stone of Chicago, who, besides bringing out *The Chap-Book,* a sort of American equivalent to *The Yellow Book,* took a chance on such outsize, outstyle or outsubject fiction as Henry James's *What Maisie Knew* and *In the Cage,* George Ade's *Fables in Slang* and Kate Chopin's novel *The Awakening.*

Kate Chopin, in this Southern connection, is an attractive and interesting figure. Her maiden name was Katherine O'Flaherty, and her father was an Irish immigrant, but her mother was a Catherine de Reilhe of one of the old French Catholic families of St. Louis, and Kate was born in St. Louis in 1851. She married at nineteen a New Orleans banker, who took her to live on Cane River in Central Louisiana. The village of Cloutierville, where they lived in a galleried mansion, was composed of French-speaking Acadians, and Kate's husband was a French Creole — who brings us back to Simon Legree. For the father of Kate's husband had purchased a Cane River plantation which was still,

when Kate married, in the family, and this Place-du-
Bois Plantation had a sinister history. It had belonged to
a New Englander called Robert McAlpin, who had lived
alone with his slaves and who had become a local legend
for his cruel treatment of them, and it was the stories
of this place of horror — the Cane River is an offshoot
of the Red and runs parallel with it — that Harriet
Beecher Stowe's brother brought back to her from
Louisiana and which inspired the final episode of *Uncle
Tom's Cabin.* The tradition of brutality had been carried
on by Kate Chopin's father-in-law, whose money was
mostly in French railroads and who spent a good deal
of his time in France, so that it touched Kate herself
uncomfortably. There had been even, apparently, a
much-abused slave who was supposed to have suggested
Uncle Tom, and it is amusing that a later Chopin should
have rented his cabin to be shown, at a percentage, at the
Chicago World's Fair of 1893. Kate Chopin explored
this place and introduced a description of it into her
first novel, *At Fault,* published in 1890. She makes her
lovers visit McAlpin's grave, of which the natives
are abjectly afraid and which causes the young man to
shudder and to make the young girl come away. In the
mists that arise from the bayou, Robert McAlpin was said
sometimes to reappear, "stalking down the hill with
threatening stride, crossing the lake in a pirogue or riding across the hills with his bloodhounds in hot pursuit of the slave so long at rest."

Kate Chopin's biographer, Mr. Daniel S. Rankin, insists that she was happy with her husband. She wrote at
nineteen in her diary that she was marrying "the right
man," and she had six children by him; but he died of
"swamp fever" at Cloutierville when they had been
married only twelve years, and the stories which she
afterwards wrote are full of unsatisfactory marriages. In

one of the most interesting of her short stories — a matter of three pages — called *The Dream of an Hour*, a young married woman gets the news that her husband has been killed in a railroad wreck. She suffers from a weak heart, and breaking the news has been carefully handled. When the wife has been told, she has a burst of weeping. Then she goes up to her room, and there she sits silent looking out the window and listening to the sounds from the street. She has the feeling that something is coming to her from the patches of blue in the cloudy sky, from the sounds, the scents, the color outside — something that she is trying to keep away. Then she abandons herself: she whispers over and over: "Free, free, free!" She does not stop to ask whether or not she is possessed by "a monstrous joy"; but "her pulse beats fast, and the coursing blood warmed and relaxed every inch of her body. It was not that she had not loved her husband — sometimes. Often she had not. What did it matter!"; but now she would be able to live for herself, unbowed by that oppressive will which — whether in kindness or cruelty — "men and women believe they have a right to impose . . . upon a fellow creature . . . What could love, the unsolved mystery, count for in face of this possession of self-assertion which she suddenly recognized as the strongest impulse of her being!" She has recently shuddered at the notion that her life might go on a long time; now she wants to live many days — "spring days, and summer days, and all sorts of days that would be her own." But her sister becomes worried about her and is trying to get her to open the door. When she does so and they have gone downstairs, a latchkey is heard in the door of the house, and her husband, who had not been on the train and has not even heard of the accident, enters, "a little travel-stained, composedly carrying his grip-sack and umbrella." The poor young woman falls dead. "When the doctors came they said she had died of heart disease — of joy that kills."

There is a good deal of marital instability in the fiction of Kate Chopin, whether she writes of Acadians or New Orleans Creoles. She was bilingual and translated Maupassant. The situations in her first novel were already rather uncomfortable from the point of view of conventional morality; but in the central one she followed the then standard procedure of getting rid of an undesirable wife by having her accidentally drowned so that the lovers might be finally united. In 1899, however, she published a novel, *The Awakening*, quite uninhibited and beautifully written, which anticipates D. H. Lawrence in its treatment of infidelity. Another attractive young woman, a Kentuckian married to a Creole broker, who is away on a long business trip, falls in love with a young man on a vacation at Grand Isle in the Gulf of Mexico. He is alarmed by the situation and goes away to Mexico. She returns to New Orleans, but she has been transformed. She moves into another house and begins to lead a new social life independent of her husband's circle. She has a love-affair with an experienced Creole. She does not worry about the consequences for her children: she does not want to feel that they possess her; she simply enjoys herself. But the lover does not satisfy her, and when the young man comes back from Mexico, she lets him know that she is now prepared to have with him a serious affair. The scene is interrupted, and he, an all too honorable young fellow, runs away from the situation again, leaving a note to say, "Goodby — because I love you." She goes back to Grand Isle alone, takes off all her clothes on the beach — she had first put on a bathing costume but then "cast the unpleasant, pricking garments from her" — and swims out into the Gulf of Mexico till she tires herself out and drowns. It is a very odd book to have been written in America at the end of the nineteenth century. It is not even a "problem novel." No case for free love or women's rights or the injustice of marriage is argued. The heroine is simply a sensuous woman who follows her inclinations without thinking much about these issues or tormenting herself with her conscience. Even her death is hardly a tragedy, hardly a deliberate suicide. "How strange and awful and delicious!" she thinks, standing naked on the sand, and the description of her fatal swim has the same sensuous beauty as all the rest.

The book was of course a scandal. The St. Louis *Republic* wrote, "In her [Kate Chopin's] creations she commits unutterable crimes against polite society, but in the essentials of her art she never blunders. Like most of her work, however, *The Awakening* is too strong drink for moral babes, and should be labeled 'poison.'" It was taken out of circulation in the St. Louis Mercantile Library — she had returned to her native city — and she was blackballed on being put up for membership in the St. Louis Fine Arts Club. She published in a literary paper a statement which was characteristic in its ironic insouciance: "Having a group of people at my disposal, I thought it might be entertaining (to myself) to throw them together and see what would happen. I never dreamed of Mrs. Pontellier making such a mess of things and working out her own damnation as she did. If I had had the slightest intimation of such a thing I would have excluded her from the company."

From a Lady Janet Young in England Mrs. Chopin received a long letter enclosing another long letter which had been written to her, Lady Janet, by a Dr. Dunrobin Thomson, "the great consulting physician of England" — to whom she has lent the book — both of which remind

one rather of the witnesses for the defense in the trial of
Lady Chatterley's Lover and which make an amusing
contrast with Kate Chopin's serene amoralism. Lady
Janet takes the line that a character in the story, a medical friend of the heroine, should have said to her husband, "Pontellier, like most men you fancy that because
you have possessed your wife hundreds of times she
necessarily long ago came to entire womanly self knowledge — that your embraces have as a matter of course
aroused whatever of passion she may be endowed with.
You are mistaken. She is just becoming conscious of sex
— is just finding herself compelled to take account of
masculinity *as such*. . . . Assist this birth of your wife's
womanliness. Be tender, let her know that you see how
Robert, Arobin affect her. Laugh with her over the evident influence of her womanhood over them." The goal
Lady Janet proposes is that Pontellier shall *trust* his wife
so that he is not afraid to leave her with these other men,
and she, "instead of guiltily saying, 'I fear I love that
man,' . . . shall say within herself with *no* cause of
guilt — 'How that man's masculinity stirs me' — say it
above all to *her husband.*" Dr. Thomson writes Lady
Janet that "this book has stirred me to the soul." He explains that "the especial point of a wife's danger when
her beautiful, God given womanhood awakes, is that she
will save her self-respect by imagining herself in love
with the awakener." She must learn, must be "taught
by her husband, to distinguish between passion and love."
If she knows perfectly well that "that stirring of nature"
is passion not love; "if she esteems and respects her pas-
sional capacity as she does her capacity to be moved by
a song or a sonnet, or a great poem, or a word nobly
said — she is safe. She knows that that thing *is*. She is
no more ashamed of it than of her responsiveness to any
other great appeal. She knows that it does not touch

her wife-life, her mother-life, her self-hood. It is not 'naughty.' "

Kate Chopin never remarried. She died suddenly at fifty-three after a visit to the St. Louis World's Fair which she seems to have particularly enjoyed. What the physical cause of her death was her biographer does not explain, but she seems to have had some sort of stroke.

Kate Chopin had plenty of money and was in a position to write what she chose. But George Cable had to make a living, and he could not solve this problem through small publishers in the West that brought out unusual books. What he did now, for the first and last time in his life, was to blow a big bellows at the forge of sex — keeping, however, as Kate Chopin had not, well within the moral conventions — and, instead of horrifying the public as his predecessor had done, he produced, in *The Cavalier* (1901), his first and his only best-seller. This novel, which was published on October 5, had by Christmas sold a hundred thousand copies.

But how could the model Cable, with his strict piety and his civic conscience, bring himself to turn such a trick? We note with dismay that, in writing this book, the author of *The Grandissimes* is full of exhilaration. He declares that he has come to realize that there are parts of *The Grandissimes* "which sink to a standard of literary workmanship to which I do not believe that one page of *The Cavalier* descends. I never before knew nearly so well just what I want to write or how to write it. I have reached in it the point where my doubts of success are all gone." And when he has finished the first draft: "I certainly think it is far better than *John March*." Professor Turner believes that a part of the author's delight in the book was due to his never having shown partial drafts of it to the ever-scolding Gilder and Johnson. Another factor, no doubt, was that, now in his middle fifties, he was for the first time letting himself go on his youthful adventures in the Civil War. "The author," he exultantly declares, "did not have to read up to write this story." He *had* had to do a great deal of reading-up in order to give his other writings the historical solidity at which he always aimed; he had labored and strained at his responsible thinking; and he had perhaps bored himself with *John March* as much as he bored others. But he was right from one point of view in believing that *The Cavalier* was "far better" than *John March*: it is at least a good deal more readable.

The truth is, however, that this popular novel is almost wholly meretricious. The fundamental thing about it is that Cable has made the decision to give up being a serious writer. He avows this when he says of his later books that he is frankly writing "romances," stories that might "make you feel today that you are entertained, and find tomorrow that you are profited." The moment we open the book and see the frontispiece by Howard Chandler Christy, a wash drawing of impossible young people — imitated raggedly from Gibson — in starchy and crackling clothes that look less like the costumes of the sixties than the long skirts and the stiff suits of the early nineteen-hundreds, we suspect, with something of a shudder, that a base transmutation has taken place. Poor Cable cannot know how pathetic he is when he compares the execution of *The Grandissimes* unfavorably with that of *The Cavalier*. He has actually — in dropping the discipline of his rigorous moral code — become suddenly debauched in an alarming way. It is as if he has gone on a spree. Well, they wanted him to drink with them, and here he is. This is what they had been asking him to give them. Whether or not George Cable "was aware," as Professor Turner says, "of the forces [that were] pushing him toward a new type of fiction, he realized it was a new type for him, and he had evolved a theoretical justification for it."

The result is erotic fantasy that seems not characteristic of Cable, and a deliberate contrivance — not far from Hollywood — of situations that create suspense. But *The Cavalier* does generate excitement. The "love interest" is hot and gasping. The medium of the writing — never employed save in this one book by Cable — is that heightened first-person narrative, a counterfeit of breathless and wondering youth and a conductor of pseudo-emotion, which had made the fortune of *Lorna Doone* and which probably derived more remotely from *David Copperfield* and *Henry Esmond*. A beautiful, witty, audacious girl, capable of the most piquant coquetry — is she a spy or a gallant Confederate? we do not at first know — is married to a ruffian husband, a murderer and a traitor, with whom her marriage has never been consummated, but is in love with a superb young Creole officer, who, unlike Cable's earlier Creoles, speaks English as perfectly as French, is full of resource and daring, and is idolized by his men. The admirer of Cable may be somewhat shocked to note with what conscious competence he has mastered the formulas of the period, how wholeheartedly he is here attempting to satisfy the feminine public that was dictating American taste. One of the primary requirements of the fiction of that time was that events should be presented from a woman's point of view, or, if not through a woman's eyes, in such a way as to appeal to a woman, and the results are often embarrassing. A conspicuous example of this queer transposition is Owen Wister's famous novel *The Virginian*, which came out the year after *The Cavalier* and had an even more sensational success. Here the cowboy hero, so thorough a gentleman, so formidable a man among men, is projected almost entirely in terms of adoring women with whom the author identifies himself: "As we drove by the eating-house, the shade of a side window was raised, and the landlady looked her last upon the Virginian. Her lips were faintly parted, no woman's eyes ever said more plainly, 'I am one of your possessions.'" Then the refined young Vermont schoolteacher takes the Virginian over, and their romance has the following culmination: "The Virginian walked to the hotel, and stood on the threshold of his sweetheart's room. She had heard his step, and was upon her feet. Her lips were parted, and her eyes fixed on him, nor did she move, or speak. 'Yu' have to know it,' said he. 'I have killed Trampas.' 'Oh, thank God!' she said; and he found her in his arms. . . . Thus did her New England conscience battle to the end, and, in the end, capitulate to love. . . . For their bridal camp he chose an island. . . ." This honeymoon goes on for pages, and it must have enchanted its feminine readers. "Was this dreamy boy the man of two days ago? It seemed a distance immeasurable; yet it was two days only since that wedding eve when she had shrunk from him as he stood fierce and implacable."

Poor Cable is not quite up to this, but he makes a terrific effort, and it is distressing to find this fighter for justice going to pieces over the virility of his heroes. The process had begun with John March, a splendid physical specimen, whom the ladylike and reticent heroine devoutly desires to marry. Here is the final passage:

"He started with half-lifted arm, but stopped, turned, and with a hand on his brow, sighed, 'My mother!' But a touch rested on his arm and a voice that was never in life to be strange to him again said, 'If you don't say "our mother," I won't call you John any —'

"Oh! oh! oh! men are so rough sometimes.' "

And now, in *The Cavalier*, not only does the dashing heroine passionately adore Ned Ferry, the perfect young Creole lieutenant, but the narrator, who has served with him as a boy in his teens, is almost equally infatuated: their relations fall little short of the homosexual. The brave Creole's whole command is united in its doting allegiance, and, in fact, most of the characters in the story, male or female, high or low, seem preoccupied, at the expense of the war, with the problem of whether Ned and his hampered sweetheart will win through to the final embrace.

As Professor Turner says, "the issues back of the war are not mentioned"; the only element of social criticism is a caricature of religious bigotry. The only issue in *The Cavalier* is one of the utmost absurdity. How is Charlotte's husband, the villain, to be definitely got out of the way without being killed by her lover — because, of course, if this had occurred, she could not marry her husband's slayer. The scoundrel seems at one point disposed of through the agency of someone else, but then he appears again, and it is necessary to rig up some new device. The manufacture of unlikely obstacles between the young man and young woman who seem destined for one another is another trick of the trade that Cable has carefully acquired and that he will now work and overwork in almost every book. The wicked or insane mate who has to be eliminated is a stock feature of Victorian fiction; but there is also the delicate scruple that gives rise to misunderstandings and prevents or prolongs the betrothal. There is a good deal of this in Howells — *The Rise of Silas Lapham* is a case in point

— and something in Henry James. It is no doubt to the credit of Cable that, in fabricating these book-long barriers, he almost always makes them quite implausible.

In the next of his long novels, *Kincaid's Battery* (1908), also a romance of the war, the lovers are kept apart by the impossible machinations of a devilish Creole woman, who flings herself into the hero's arms in the midst of an extraordinary battle — the chief object of which seems to be to bring about this unlikely situation (illustration by Alonzo Kimball) — while the heroine, lying stunned by a shell and unrecognized by her lover, imagines he is being unfaithful to her. In *The Flower of the Chapdelaines* (1918), a young New Orleanian lawyer passes every morning on his way to his office a beautiful young girl whom he longs to know, but, feeling that his seeing her so often may already be considered rather vulgar, he fears that it would be an impertinence to take steps to meet her socially, that it might even be somewhat embarrassing to meet her correctly by chance. When, however, they are brought together, and he eventually asks her to marry him, she tells him, without giving reasons, that this is completely impossible. The obstacle, it later appears, is the sensitive girl's conviction that marriage to an Anglo-Saxon would shut her off — she is a French Creole — from her dear old French-speaking friends, as to whom she is so obtuse as not to recognize that her admirer adores them. The author, now over seventy, has by this time quite ceased to worry about realism or even about probability.

The Cavalier was a kind of fluke. George Cable was never afterwards to repeat his success in this genre. It may be that his return to the memories of youth had made it easy for him to set off a gusher of adolescent romancing. But its successors are as synthetic as *John*

March, Southerner and have nothing of *The Cavalier's* liveliness. Nothing could be further from the methods of a genuine purveyor of pastry such as the effortless Robert W. Chambers. Cable's intellectual conscience and the complexity of his point of view still forced him to construct, in these potboilers, most elaborate close-fitted machines. *Kincaid's Battery* was as carefully worked out in advance, carried through as systematically, as *Ulysses*. *Gideon's Band* (1914) took Cable as long — six years — as *Madame Bovary* had taken Flaubert. But the expenditure of first-rate powers on situations which are artificial must become, to the admirer of Cable, most depressing and even repellent. When the editors of the *Century*, in 1901, were preparing to give their readers what they advertised as a "Year of Romance" and asked Cable for a Creole story that would have, as they said, "the old charm," he produced for them a piece called *Père Raphaël*, a sequel to the early *Posson Jone'*, which makes an effort to provide the "love interest" that had been missed in the earlier story, but which cannot be anything other than an arid little horror of forced contrivance.*

* The Creole dialect in *Père Raphaël*, as in general in Cable's fiction written after he had left New Orleans, has become rather standardized and labored. It is difficult to tell from Cable's writings exactly what sort of knowledge of French he had. Though he had read a certain amount of French literature and was influenced by Daudet and others, he had had very little schooling and had never been in France, and one wonders whether he was not more familiar with the several varieties of colloquial French spoken in Louisiana than with the classical literary language. In his handling of the dialogue of his Creole characters, he seems to be almost bilingual, but the Gallicized English they speak presents some peculiar features. They are made, for example, habitually to talk of "a difficult," "a possible," "a necessary," "a beautiful," "a dreadful," meaning a difficult matter, a beautiful thing, etc. Now, in contemporary or classical French, one does not know of any such locution; yet Cable is evidently so conscientious in his notation of

Gideon's Band, however, though almost as forced, is not quite so uninteresting as these other later books, because, dealing with steamboating in the fifties, it exploits a new field of interest and because Cable here takes occasion to turn off a few mordant sketches of types he has known in his youth. There are a courteous old fraud of a Southern senator and an insufferable young pair of Southern twins, who, in their insolence, their quarrelling and feuding, and their conviction of inalienable superiority, undoubtedly represented for Cable everything he most disliked in the old plantation South. One of these unpleasant young men is at last accidentally shot by his reckless exhibitionistic brother, and this provides one of the very few scenes in these later novels of Cable's which have anything of his old ironic power. It is a better-done version of the same situation that Tourgée had already exploited in the hospital scene in *Toinette.* The wounded man is being tended by a decent quadroon who looks completely white and who is, in fact, a relation of his. When he orders her to give him his medicine, she answers him, "Yes, sir; where is it?" "Oh, damnation! in my saddle-bags on the washstand. What are you trying to talk white folks' English for?" Doesn't she see the bottle? This time the woman replies, obliging with a darkie accent, "Yass, suh,

---

how people talk that one is bound to assume that he had actually heard the Creoles use it. At other moments, however, his Creoles' wrong choices of words seem queer. In *Père Raphaël,* for example, one of the characters speaks of "a specious Providence," meaning a special Providence. Since *spécial* exists in French as well as *spécieux,* why should he get it wrong? It may be that — being weak, on the one hand, in the use of literary French and having lost touch with his Creoles, on the other — he is now producing a language which is partly artificial. But the public that his editors were aiming at had found this language quaint and delightful, and they counted upon him to keep on supplying it.

but it's full, suh." "Hell! what of that? Fill the glass
and give it to me!" "She filled it but paused. 'It — it looks
like la'danum.' 'Oh, damn you, so did your great-grand-
mother. It's not laudanum. . . . Give it here! God
A'mighty, if I could reach you with my fist — ' " Actually,
the bottle *is* laudanum: too proud to survive as a cripple,
he has decided to extinguish himself. His brother comes
in and so eagerly joins him in browbeating the quadroon
woman — "make that wench give me that glass or mash
her head!" the wounded man is crying — that he pays no
attention to the laudanum and lets his brother take a
fatal dose. When he realizes what he has done, he swal-
lows the rest himself. This scene is, like Lanier's *The
Revenge of Hamish*, a parable for the suicide of secession, the self-doomed demise of the Confederacy through
truculent honor and pride of race.

But, aside from this motif in *Gideon's Band,* it is only
in his last completed book, *Lovers of Louisiana,* published
in 1918, that Cable at last returns, in a more or less
serious way, to the subject of race in the South. This
novel is partly a routine romance, like the others that
Cable has been turning out, but here he for the first
time makes use in his fiction of his experiences with his
Southern compatriots in connection with the Negro question. The story takes place in 1914, and the hero, Philip
Castleton, is a young New Orleanian who has just
graduated from Princeton and is preparing to lecture at
Tulane on American political history. He serves, as
Cable has done, as secretary of a New Orleans grand
jury, and this takes him below the surface of respectable
New Orleans life. He falls in love with a French Creole
girl, but he becomes somewhat suspect to her father,
since the father of the young admirer is known to have
held rather liberal views and the son seems to be going
in the same direction. When a member of her Creole

family remarks that he is quite sure the boy does not believe "some of those things" that his father has written, and the young man inquires what things, " 'Well,' the answer came, 'where yo' father remarks against those Kuklux, those lynchings, and so forth. Biccause now, sinze long time, everybody's find out those things was highly patrio-tique and all for the best for the South and for that — that union, eh?' [Was Cable thinking, perhaps, of the revised views of Richard Watson Gilder?] 'Then, I'm nobody, Mr. Durel,' Philip replied, 'I've stopped trying to believe that.' 'Ah, but even those Yankees, thousands of them . . . they believe that; even Union veterans.' 'Yes, and when I hear a Union veteran say he supposed they'd do the same in our place I'm as thoroughly ashamed of him as of the Kuklux Klan.' "

But what puts an end to Philip's suit is delivering a friendly speech to the literary society of a Negro college. "A radical fault in his discourse was its forlorn futility as coming from a Southerner. 'Friends and fellow-citizens,' he began, 'I can hope for no whole-hearted acceptance of what I have to say unless while I bear in mind that you are colored you kindly forget that I am white.' " A visiting Scottish banker "grunted to [his companion] 'Too Northern to please any Southerner and too Southern to please any Northerner.' " When the word of this gets around, the young fellow finds himself ostracized and is forbidden to see his sweetheart. He has exhorted the Negroes to forget he is white! Philip has been somewhat nettled by the comments of the Scottish visitor, who has said to him, " 'Hark! You're a Southerner, but I'd say this to any American, for ye're all tarred with the same stick, as your saying is. You fancy your race ques tion's a peculiarly American question. Man! —' But here Philip broke in: 'Down South we're narrower than that, Mr. Murray, I'm afraid. We call it a strictly Southern question, which we will take care of if the rest of the country will only let us alone.' 'But it isn't and ye don't. . . . It's a British question and a world question, and it's getting bigger every day.' " Here Cable may well have been thinking of the editor of a Georgia paper named Henry W. Grady, who, in 1885, had replied to *The Freedman's Case in Equity* in substantially the same terms in which Philip replies to the Scot. The latter returns to the subject in delivering a solemn warning to a Creole who tells him that the issue of race is "the deadest queztion in Ammerica": "No, Mr. Durel, it isn't dead, it's merely 'possuming. I say it wi' no vaunting, but wi' drread. Ye may crrack its bones and yet never a whimper yet 'tis but 'possuming. Lorrd! Ye can't *neglect* it to death; the neglect of all America can't kill it. It's in the womb o' the future and bigger than Asia, Africa, and Ammerica combined. Ye'll do well to be friendly wi' its friends and trreat it kindly while it's young and trractable."

In his notes for the novel, Cable had written: "The time will come when the negro will have risen by selection until his story shall be the great romance of American history." The lovers — in spite of obstacles, in this case more probable than in the previous novels — are eventually allowed to marry. The young idealist Philip, though tempted by the offer of a job at Princeton, decides to remain in the South and assist in its transformation. "When the band plays *Dixie* or *Swanee River*," he explains to his girl at the end, "our fancy pictures 'the old folks at home,' doesn't it? The old-time landed squire on the old plantation. . . . The squire was our social unit, the keystone of our whole Southern scheme, was he not? . . . Well, he's vanished. Our keystone's dropped out. He's being industrialized, capitalized, commercialized, modernized out of existence. Now, a revolution may, conceivably, momentarily, go backward; an evolution never. . . . The whole scheme we call 'Dixie' is being superseded, overwhelmed, by an inexorable economic evolution, with our national unity and the world's unity behind it, pushing."

Not long before Cable's death, in January, 1925, the indefatigable old man was working on a new novel which was intended to deal with New Orleans at the time of the first World War. It was to contain — among other things, no doubt — an attack on war profiteering. Did it ever, one wonders, occur to him that hardly a page of the many books he had written since 1890 would ever, in the future, be read with pleasure? At eighty he probably no longer cared. He would only have hoped — as he said at the time of *The Cavalier* — to "make" people "feel" they were "entertained" and at the same time insinuate a lesson. The artist's vocation, with Cable, had always perhaps been weaker than that of the reformer and moralist, but we can leave him with a kind of tribute in the tone of the nineteenth century that has not ceased to be in order in ours:

> They out-talked thee, hissed thee, tore thee?
> Better men fared thus before thee;
> Fired their ringing shot, and passed,
> Hotly charged — and sank at last.
>
> Charge once more, then, and be dumb!
> Let the victors, when they come,
> When the forts of folly fall,
> Find thy body by the wall!

One can trace very clearly in the pages of the *Century* the modulating attitude of the North toward the South. The stories of the Virginian Thomas Nelson Page began appearing in the magazine in 1884, at the moment when the resentment against Cable in the South was reaching its most rabid point. "It is hard to explain in simple terms," says Grace King in her memoirs already mentioned, "what Thomas Nelson Page meant to us in the South at that time. He was the first Southern writer to appear in print as a Southerner, and his stories, short and simple, written in Negro dialect, and, I may say, Southern pronunciation, showed us with ineffable grace that although we were sore bereft, politically, we had now a chance in literature at least." And Page was equally popular in the North. Having devastated the feudal South, the Northerners wanted to be told of its glamor, of its old-time courtesy and grace. That was what they had wanted of Cable. A rush of industrial development had come at the end of the war, and the cities of the North and the West, now the scene of so much energetic enterprise which rendered them uglier and harsher, were losing their old amenities; and the Northerners wanted, besides, a little to make it up to the South for their wartime vituperation. They took over the Southern myth and themselves began to revel in it. This acceptance was to culminate in *Gone With the Wind,* the enormous success of which novel makes a curious counterbalance to that of *Uncle Tom's Cabin.* But it began in the *Century* of the eighties with the stories of Thomas Nelson Page. Though Page had been only twelve at the end of the Civil War, so had had little firsthand experience of the life of the old regime, he really invented for the popular mind Old Massa and Mistis and Meh Lady, with their dusky-skinned adoring retainers. The Northerners, after the shedding of so much blood, illogically found it soothing to be told that slavery had been not so bad, that the Negroes were a lovable but simple race, whose business was to work for the whites. And Page also struck in his stories a note of reconciliation that everybody wanted to hear: he cooked up romances between young Northern officers, as gentlemanly as any Southerner, and spirited plantation beauties who might turn out to be the young men's cousins and who in any case would marry them after the war. To Grace King he gave this advice when she talked to him of a novel which she could not get accepted: "Now I will tell you what to do; for I did it! . . . It is the easiest thing to do in the world. Get a pretty girl and name her Jeanne, that name always takes! Make her fall in love with a Federal officer and your story will be printed at once! The publishers are right; the public wants love stories. Nothing easier than to write them."

In the *Century* of 1891 first appeared *Colonel Carter of Cartersville*, by F. Hopkinson Smith, which, together with its sequel *Colonel Carter's Christmas* (1903), established as a stock figure the mint-julep-drinking Southern gentleman, hospitable, simple-hearted, brimming over with eloquence and gallantry, at sea in commercial New York, where he is ready to fight a duel with anyone whom he believes to have offended his honor, but eventually rescued from penury by the discovery of coal on his property. Hopkinson Smith was a Baltimorean, who was at home on both sides of the Mason-Dixon line, and he presented his dear old gentleman with a good deal of humor and charm. This was a Southerner that the North could love.

As for Miss King, who was grateful to Page for showing the South in a favorable light, she contributed to the *Century* magazine during 1892–93 a series of *Balcony Stories* which was meant as a retort to Cable's but which, contrasted with her announced intention, seems to provide another example of the author's capacity for "doublethink." One of them, and one of the best, *The Little Con-*

vent Girl, deals with the same theme as Cable's *Madame Delphine,* the white-skinned mulatto daughter of a white father and a Negro mother; but it is even more tragic than the other story, for the girl, instead of marrying a white man as Cable's heroine does — Miss King would no doubt have thought this undesirable — is driven to drown herself. (The best known of Kate Chopin's short stories, first published in 1893, *Désirée's Baby,* is an equally tragic tale of mixed blood. Here the girl has married a well-to-do planter, believing herself to be white; he repudiates her when a baby is born that has unmistakable indications of colored blood, and she drowns the child and herself. When the husband is systematically destroying everything in the house that has belonged to his wife, he comes upon a family letter which shows that he is part colored himself.) In another of Grace King's stories, *A Crippled Hope,* the author, who wrote of *Uncle Tom's Cabin* as that "hideous, black, dragonlike book" which the family, in her childhood, had not been allowed to mention, presents a "negro-trader" — the word *slave* is never used — as sinister as anything in *Uncle Tom.* Nor was it true that she made the Creoles more uniformly attractive than had Cable.

Page himself, in 1904, published a book called *The Negro: The Southerner's Problem,* which challenges comparison with Cable and must have been intended to answer him, though Page only mentions him once. Now, Page was a serious-minded, if not exactly a serious, man, and he was making some attempt to deal frankly with the harassing Southern problems; yet his book is full of special pleading. Put beside Cable's clarity and realism, his compact and documented paragraphs, the Virginian seems evasive and rambling. Slavery in America had given the Negro "the only resemblance of civilization" he "had possessed since the dawn of history." (Compare with Cable's careful appraisal, in his essay on *The Dance in Place Congo,* between the varying degrees of development exhibited by the Negroes from the different parts of Africa.) The relations between Negroes and whites had been full of affection and respect. Of course "it was to be expected" that one should find among the Negroes under slavery "an element in whom the instincts of wild life in the jungle and the forests survived. Every large plantation had one or more who had the runaway spirit keenly alive. There were several on our place. They ran away when they were crossed in love or in any other desire of their hearts. They ran away if they were whipped, and, as they were the shirkers and loafers on the plantations, if anybody was whipped, it was likely to be one of them. Yet, curiously enough, if a runaway was caught and was whipped, he was very unlikely to run off again until the spirit seized him." On the Page plantation, he says, only four such young men ran away for good. He dwells on the fewness of the Negroes who had enlisted in the Union army; and he glorifies in a style almost lyrical the clannish loyalty and the sense of responsibility displayed by domestic servants, yet he later describes them as "the pampered class." "House servants," he admits, "were more likely to go than field-hands. Their ears were somehow more attuned to the song of the siren." A son of their wonderful old butler, whose dignity and authority he has just been exalting, "went off at the time of one of Sheridan's raids and was never heard of again until some twenty years after the war, when it was learned that he was a fisherman on the lower James." But this only goes to show, says Page, that the family ties of the Negro are taken even less seriously now than they had been before the war, since, although the young man "lived, and may be living yet, within a hundred miles of his old home, where his father and mother lived, he never took the trouble even to communicate with them once." Another of the old butler's sons followed his brother's example.

"Not the least part," he says, "of the bitterness of the South over the Negro Question . . . grows out of resentment at the destruction of what was once a relation of warm friendship and tender sympathy." It is a ridiculous calumny of the North that the Southerners had not armed the Negroes "because they were afraid to lose their property." (He does not admit a suspicion that the Negroes might turn against their masters.) "Nothing could be more unfounded." The only thing the owners were afraid of was that some harm might come to their servants. Relations between blacks and whites had in general been excellent before the war; but then the Northerners had come among them and made the Negro insolent. "He was taught that the white man was his enemy when he should have been taught to cultivate his friendship." The teachers who were sent from the North, "devoted as many of them were," aroused the hostility of the Southerners by becoming too intimate with the Negroes and presiding in non-segregated schools. The South had made fresh outlays of expenditure for segregated Negro schools, but these Negroes, though well-trained as laborers in their previous servile condition, were at present not good for anything. He is uncomfortable about the methods by which Negroes are prevented from voting: one does not like to put oneself in the position of not complying with the law; but the Negro is not fit to vote, one is forced to come to terms with that fact, and one is forced to find some expedient for dealing with the situation.

As for lynching: the crimes of the Negroes — almost non-existent before the war — have become appalling and frequent. Page notes the high proportions of Negroes to whites among the convicts in Southern jails, but he disregards Cable's findings in connection with the convict lease system. He asserts that the post-war Negro is addicted to murder and rape; yet a table which he quotes from the *Chicago Tribune* shows that, in the course of the four years 1900–1903, Negroes were lynched for "race prejudice" (twenty-four of these), "threats to kill" (six), "burglary" (five), "informing" (two), "robbery (theft)" (fifteen), "suspicion of robbery" (one), "no offence" (one), "cattle and horse stealing" (seven), "quarrel over profit-sharing" (five), "unknown offences" (twelve), "mistaken identity" (five). (These include a few lynchings in the North as well as those in the South, and a few whites as well as blacks.) Yet he maintains, side by side with these absurd statistics, that the innocent are rarely lynched: "The rage of the mob is not directed against the innocent, but against the guilty; and its fury would not be satisfied with any other sacrifice than the death of the real criminal. Nor does the criminal merit any consideration, however terrible the punishment. The real injury is to the perpetrators of the crime of destroying the law, and to the community in which the law is slain." "Lynching as a remedy is a ghastly failure; and its brutalizing effect on the community is incalculable." Burning at the stake is "revolting" and "dreadful." He fights shy of the mulatto problem, but implies that it is absurd of the Northerner to imagine that the plantation owners were capable of "trafficking in their own flesh and blood" — though we know from the Grimké story mentioned above as well as from other evidence that this kind of thing did occur.

He exploits for all it is worth — both here and in one of his fictions — the story of his father's faithful "body-servant," who accompanied the elder Page to the war. "While at Petersburg, where the armies were within a mile of each other, he was punished for getting drunk and he ran away." Instead of making for the Union lines, he started for home, was picked up and sent back to his master in camp, and did not desert again. When the news of the surrender at Appomattox came to the family at home, "through one of the wagon-drivers, who told it weeping," they waited for the master for days. "I seem to see the return now — my father on his gray horse, with his body-servant, Ralph, behind him. I remember the way in which, as he slipped from his horse, he put his hand over his face to hide his tears, and his groan, 'I never expected to come home so.'" All were weeping. "A few minutes later he came out on the porch and said: 'Ralph you are free; take the saddles off and turn the horses out.'" Such scenes did of course occur, and they are moving to read about. But the picture of life they imply — "befo' de war, in ole Virginia" (both phrases are titles of Page's, and it was he who gave them currency in the North) — had become Page's whole stock in trade.

Page's most ambitious novel, published in 1898, was *Red Rock.* This is a story of the Reconstruction — as boring as Cable's *John March,* and for the same conscientious reasons; but it begins before the Civil War and is saturated by memories of the old régime, which Page has now got to the point of treating very much in the vein of his predecessor John Esten Cooke. The South of Cooke's *Virginia Comedians* had been that of colonial Virginia on the eve of the Revolution, and now Page, writing forty-four years later, has brought this lost world of fine living up to the eve of the Civil War:

"No doubt the phrase 'Before the war' is at times somewhat abused. It is just possible that there is a certain Caleb Balderstonism in the speech at times. But for those who knew the old County as it was then, and can contrast it with what it has become since, no wonder it seems that even the moonlight was richer and mellower 'before the war' than it is now. For one thing, the moonlight as well as the sunlight shines brighter in our youth than in mature age; and gold and gossamer amid the rose-bowers reflect it better than serge and crêpe amid myrtles and bays. The great thing is not to despond even though the brilliancy be dimmed: in the new glitter one need not necessarily forget the old radiance. . . .

"Why should not Miss Thomasia in her faded dress, whom you shall meet [as a character in the novel], tell us, if she pleases, of her 'dear father,' and of all her 'dear cousins' to the remotest generation. . . . Do you, young lady, observe Miss Thomasia the next time she enters a room, or addresses a servant; and do you, good sir, polished by travel and a contact with the most fashionable — second-class — society of two continents, watch General Legaie and Dr. Carry when they meet Miss Thomasia, or greet the apple-woman on the corner, or the wagoner on the road. What an air suddenly comes in with them of old Courts and polished halls when all gentlemen bowed low before all ladies, and wore swords to defend their honor. What an odor, as it were, of those gardens which Watteau painted, floats in as they enter! Do not you attempt it. You cannot do it. You are thinking of yourself, they of others and the devoirs they owe them. You are republican and brought up to consider yourself 'as good as any, and better than most.' Sound doctrine for the citizen, no doubt; but it spoils the bow. Even you, Miss or Madam, for all your silks and satins, cannot do it like Miss Thomasia. You are imitating the duchess you saw once, perhaps, in Hyde Park. The duchess would have imitated Miss Thomasia. You are at best an imitation; Miss Thomasia is the reality." But the author himself, having imagined such a paragon, is not up to creating her as a character. When Miss Thomasia appears in the story, she is perfectly commonplace, falls far below the high distinction with which her inventor has credited her.

The whole picture in Page has been blurred. Nobody North or South wanted by that time to be shown the realities. Not only is Virginia before the war made to fuse with the colonial Virginia of Cooke and other writers, so that both hang in the past as a glamorous legend. The attitudes of the North and South themselves have now become somewhat blurred. Animosities must be forgotten; the old issues must be put to sleep with the chloroform of magazine prose.

In *Two Little Confederates*, a story for children, once popular both North and South, a Confederate boy is caught by Federal soldiers, who threaten to shoot him if he refuses to tell where his older brother is hiding. The boy faints, and when he comes to, he finds a "big dragoon" from Delaware tenderly caring for him and is told that they had not really meant to kill him. "The soldier gently set him on his feet, and before he let him go kissed him. 'I've got a curly-headed fellow at home, just the size of you,' he said softly. Frank saw that his eyes were moist. 'I hope you'll get safe back home,' he said." Later, Frank and his little chum find this soldier wounded and begging for water. " 'Willy, it's my Yankee!' exclaimed Frank." But the Federal dies, to the anguish of Frank, before they can do anything for him. The Northerner's mother comes after the war to look for her son's body. Frank shows her the grave in the garden, and she stays several days with his family. Frank's mother commiserates with her: her older son has not come back. But for her the ending is happy, since the young man does later return, and the story is concluded by the mating of two lovers who have been alienated. It was hard to make the Civil War seem cosy, but Thomas Nelson Page did his best.

In another of his sentimental stories — *The Gray Jacket of "No. 4"* — there is a very curious effort in this direction. He describes a parade of veterans on the occasion of the unveiling in Richmond of a monument to the Confederate dead, then comments upon it as follows: "Only a thousand or two of old or aging men riding or tramping along through the dust of the street, under some old flags, dirty and ragged and stained. But they represented the spirit of the South; they represented the spirit which when honor was in question never counted the cost; the spirit that had stood up for the South against overwhelming odds for four years, and until the South had crumbled and perished under the forces of war; the spirit that is the strongest guaranty to us to-day that the Union is and is to be; the spirit that, glorious in victory, had displayed a fortitude yet greater in defeat. They saw in every stain on those tattered standards the blood of their noblest, bravest, and best; in every rent a proof of their glorious courage and sacrifice." Compare this with the scene in *Dr. Sevier* — so offensive to Southern readers — in which Cable makes one of his characters look on while a company of Union soldiers marches in the streets of New York, and the author declares that their "cause is just" — though "we of the South . . . cannot forget — and we would not." Cable — though with tender regret for the heroism of his fellow Southerners — has taken up a definite position: he has decided that the South was mistaken. But Page will not take up a position: he somehow, by ambiguous language, makes it appear that "the spirit of the South," which had "stood up against overwhelming odds . . . until the South had crumbled and perished," was "the strongest guaranty today . . . that the Union is and is to be." What did he mean by this? There was something perhaps of the pre-war pride of the Roman days of the Republic that was common to North and South and has made Northerners claim Lee as a great American. If, however, Page means what he seems to say, it has certainly not proved to be true: that spirit is still resisting its enforced incorporation in the Union. But I believe that what Page was now doing was nothing more than applying soft poultices of words not merely to the suppurating wounds of the South but also to the feelings of guilt of the North; and in New England Thomas Wentworth Higginson, who had subsidized John Brown, served as colonel of a Negro regiment and been present at the burning of Jacksonville, had been weeping over Page's *Marse Chan*, the story of a faithful old Negro stricken by grief at the death of his master, who has fought for the Confederate cause.

In the December issue of the *Forum* of 1888, Albion W. Tourgée, with his experience of the Reconstruction now almost a decade behind him, published a prophetic essay called *The South as a Field for Fiction*. He notes the popularity in the North of such stories as those of Page: "A foreigner studying our current literature, without knowledge of our history, and judging our civilization by our fiction, would undoubtedly conclude that the South was the seat of intellectual empire in America, and the African the chief romantic element of our population." His smoldering admiration for the South comes out in a remarkable prediction, which was certainly to be fulfilled, although not quite so soon as he thought. "To the woefulness of the conquered," he says, "is added the pathos of a myriad of deposed sovereigns. Around them will cluster the halo of romantic glory, and the epoch of their overthrow will live again in American literature." "Because of these things," he concludes, "it is that the South is destined to be the Hesperides Garden of American literature. We cannot foretell the form its product will wear or even guess its character. It may be sorrowful, exultant, aspiring, or perhaps terrible, but it will certainly be great — greater than we have hitherto known, because its causative forces are mightier than those which have shaped the productive energy of the past. That its period of highest excellence will soon be attained there is little room to doubt. The history of literature shows that it is those who were cradled amid the smoke of battle, the sons and daughters of heroes yet red with slaughter, the inheritors of national woe or racial degradation, who have given utterance to the loftiest strains of genius. Because of the exceeding woefulness of a not too recent past, therefore, and the abiding horror of unavoidable conditions which are the sad inheritance of the present, we may confidently look for the children of soldiers and of slaves to advance American literature to the very front rank of that immortal procession whose song is the eternal refrain of remembered agony, before the birth-hour of the twentieth-century shall strike."

XIV

AMBROSE BIERCE ON THE OWL CREEK BRIDGE

AMBROSE GWINETT BIERCE was born in 1842 in a log cabin in Ohio. He is said to have once told a friend that his parents were "unwashed savages," but this was apparently an exaggeration. The family were New Englanders from Barnstable, Massachusetts, of the tough seventeenth-century stock, who eventually reached Indiana by way of Connecticut and Ohio. Though Ambrose's father, Marcus Aurelius, was evidently an unsuccessful farmer, whose large family enjoyed few advantages, he had, on his son's own admission, enough English classics in his bookcase to give Ambrose a sound taste in literature and to inspire him with literary ambition; and it was arranged that the boy should be sent to a military academy in Kentucky by Ambrose's paternal uncle, Lucius Verus Bierce, a man of some local eminence as an orator and a soldier, who attained the rank of general and the office of district attorney. It was he who, at Akron, was to supply John Brown with the short heavy two-edged broadswords which he had used to hack his victims in Kansas.

In 1861, when Fort Sumter was fired on, Ambrose Bierce was the second in his county to enlist. He was then not yet quite twenty. He had three years of active service in the infantry, and the record of his bravery and energy, of which he himself did not boast, is to be found in the reports of his superiors. It was said of Ambrose Bierce by someone in his hometown of Elkhart, Indiana, that "The army seemed to bring out in young Ambrose things that had never been seen in Elkhart." One does not know exactly what this meant, but a photograph of Bierce in uniform shows a fierce-eyed and frowning young lieutenant, with a thick crest of hair and a shaggy mustache. He took part, under General Hazen, in the second day of the battle of Shiloh, advancing, in the teeth of terrific artillery, between Owl Creek and the Tennessee River. The regiment distinguished itself, and the battle, with its blunders and its terrible carnage, made a lasting impression on him. He later wrote a gruesome description of a company of Illinois soldiers, who, refusing to surrender, were completely mowed down and afterwards incinerated in a burning wood. A number of Bierce's short stories were based on real incidents remembered from this battle, and he transposed the Owl Creek from Tennessee to Alabama and made use of a hanging that took place at this time for one of the best of these stories — *An Occurrence at Owl Creek Bridge* — which was to turn out to be an epitome of Bierce's strange doomed and constricted life. In this story, a planter who is being hanged for obstructing the progress of the Union troops is standing on the Owl Creek Bridge with the rope around his neck. He looks down at the current below, then closes his eyes to recall his wife and children. He thinks that if he could only get his hands free, he could jump into the river and escape. The trap is sprung and he falls, then realizes the rope has broken. Under water, he twists the cord off his hands and begins to swim away. He is shot at, but he dives and the bullets miss him. His senses are sharpened by danger, and everything he sees or hears is perceived with a heightened vividness. He finally climbs up a bank and disappears into a forest, through which he walks for a day before he discovers a road that will take him in the direction of his house. At last he finds himself at his own gate in the bright sunshine of morning. His wife, fresh, smiling and cool, is coming down from the verandah to greet him. Then just as he is about to clasp her, "he feels a stunning blow on the back of the neck" and "all is darkness and silence." "Peyton Farquar," writes Bierce, "is dead; his body, with a broken neck, swung gently from side to side beneath the timbers of Owl Creek Bridge."

Bierce's regiment went on to the siege of Corinth; they pursued General Bragg and took part in the battle of Stone River, which lasted for three days and after which they were commended by their general for "perfect discipline, dauntless courage and general fighting abilities." Bierce was made a first lieutenant and transferred to the staff of William B. Hazen as topographical engineer. He took part in the engagements of Chickamauga, Chattanooga and Missionary Ridge. The battle of Chickamauga, in which the Union forces were defeated and which had involved a good deal of slaughter that was thought to have been avoidable, was later to figure in another of the best of Bierce's stories, *Chickamauga*, in which a small boy, a deaf mute, is made to wander through the battlefield just after the battle has taken place, without understanding what has happened — first laughing at the faces daubed with red, because they look like clowns in the circus, then frightened by a man with no jaw, then trying to play what he takes for a game with a line of wounded men who are creeping away — and at last finds his home on fire, with his mother lying dead in the light of the flames, her brains blown out by a shell. In this story, Bierce manages to make us feel the indignity and absurdity of war and at the same time to suggest its nullity from the point of view of a being who should not have any stake in it.

In February, 1864, Ambrose Bierce started out with Sherman on his devastating march toward Atlanta, but was wounded at Kenesaw Mountain. His head, as he said later, was "broken like a walnut," and he was given up for dead. General Hazen, reporting his casualties, mentioned Bierce as "a fearless and trusty man." He went home and took the summer off; but returned to the army in September. Since he now, as the result of his wound, sometimes had fainting fits, he was relieved from marching on foot. He made part of the expedition with Sherman along the Atlantic coast toward Richmond; then, detached from Sherman with a body of troops that was sent to strengthen Thomas in Tennessee, he was present at the battle of Franklin. In a story called *The Major's Tale,* which is known to be autobiographical, he wrote afterwards of the eve of that battle: "On that bleak December morning [actually November 30] . . . when from an hour before dawn till ten o'clock we sat on horseback on those icy hills, waiting for General Smith to open the battle miles away to the right, there were eight of us. At the close of the fighting there were three. There is now one. Bear with him yet a little while, oh, thrifty generation; he is but one of the horrors of war strayed from his era into yours. He is only the harmless skeleton at your feast and peace-dance, responding to your laughter and your footing it featly, with rattling fingers and bobbing skull."

This was the last major engagement in which Bierce took part. The army now went into winter quarters, and he was mustered out early in the following year, when his term of service had expired and the war was nearly won. He had been mentioned in dispatches for gallantry fifteen or sixteen times, and he was later brevetted major.

Ambrose Bierce had found army life so congenial that, after the war was over, he continued to accompany General Hazen, in his capacity of topographical engineer, when Hazen was sent by the government to survey the Indian Territory at a time when the Sioux Indians were still giving trouble, and to inspect the forts of the West which protected the settlers against them. Bierce did not return with the expedition, but stayed on in San Francisco, where he became a successful journalist and spent most of the rest of his life.

In Bierce's writings through the years that followed, he was constantly obsessed with death. This must partly have been due to his experience in the war, as was evidently the somewhat similar though much less exclusive preoccupation of the younger Oliver Wendell Holmes. It was said of Bierce by one of his brothers that he seemed a different person after the war. "The exhilaration of battle was agreeable to him," he was later to write of one of his characters, "but . . . he could not look upon a dead body without a loathing which had in it an element of resentment. . . . [He] was a braver man than anybody knew, for nobody knew his horror of that which he was ever ready to incur." Yet he seems to have been haunted by the idea of death before he had even enlisted. He put on record in later life a significant dream that he had had at sixteen. He had imagined himself, "heartless and hopeless," passing over a "blasted and forbidden plain" and arriving at a gigantic building with "columns of cyclopean masonry," in which, as he wandered through its empty halls, in "awful solitude, conscious of a seeking purpose, yet knowing not what I sought," it was revealed to him that both God and the human race had been "long ages dead." He finally entered a room in which he saw stretched on a bed a "dreadfully decomposed" human body, with black face and grinning lips, which slowly opened its eyes. "Imagine my horror . . . the eyes were my own! That vestigial fragment of a vanished race . . . that hateful and abhorrent scrap of mortality, still sentient after the death of God and the angels, was I!" This dream remained with Bierce all his life, and it recurs in several of his more ambitious poems.

Mr. Paul Fatout, Ambrose Bierce's most recent biographer, asserts — though without producing much positive evidence — that Ambrose, who was the youngest to come to maturity in a family of ten children, had suffered in childhood from his mother's neglect and that he had also been permanently scarred by the rigors of a Congregational home and the hell-fire of camp-meeting Methodism. It is certain, however, that Ambrose Bierce was visited by as many devils as Calvin Stowe, and he did not have Stowe's resources in being able to put them to rout by quoting a text from Ephesians. It may very well be true that the special ferocity and gusto with which Bierce played the Devil's advocate, as well as his readiness to castigate others as "wantons," liars and thieves — that is, blastingly, out of hand, from the point of view of old-fashioned morality — and the curious Puritanism that underlay his San Francisco rakishness, were due to a Calvinist background.

In any case, it is certainly true, not only that, as has been said by Clifton Fadiman, Death itself is Bierce's favorite character, but that, except in *The Monk and the Hangman's Daughter*, a rewriting of a story by someone else, Death may perhaps be said to be Ambrose Bierce's only real character. In all Bierce's fiction, there are no men or women who are interesting as men or women — that is, by reason of their passions, their aspirations or their personalities. They figure only as the helpless butts of sadistic practical jokes, and their higher faculties are so little involved that they might almost as well be trapped animals. But Bierce does succeed in making Death play an almost personal role. His accounts of battles he took part in are among the most attractive of his writings, because here he is able to combine a ceaseless looking Death in the face with a delight in the wonder of the world, as the young man from Elkhart, Indiana, finds himself in a land where "unfamiliar constellations burned in the southern midnights, and the mocking-bird poured out his heart in the moon-gilded magnolia." As in the case of Thomas Wentworth Higginson, the enchantment that Bierce's war memories had for him was partly created by the charms of the South, so different from anything he had previously known. But eventually, in his horror stories, the obsession with death becomes tiresome. If we try to read these stories in bulk, they get to seem not merely disgusting but dull. The horror stories of Poe, with which they have been compared, have always a psychological interest in the sense that the images they summon are metaphors for hidden emotions. The horror stories of Bierce have only in a very few cases such psychological interest as may come from exploiting dramatically some abnormal phenomenon of consciousness. There is, otherwise, merely the Grand Guignol trick repeated again and again. The executioner Death comes to us from outside our human world and, capriciously, gratuitously, cruelly, slices away our lives. It is an unpleasant limitation of Bierce's treatment of violent death that it should seem to him never a tragedy, but merely a bitter jest. He seems rarely to have felt any pity for his dead comrades of the Civil War, and it is characteristic of him that he should write as if in derision, in the passage, already mentioned, of the soldiers who fell at Shiloh and who were burned, some while still alive, in a forest-fire lit by the battle. "I obtained leave," he writes, "to go down into the valley of death and gratify a reprehensible curiosity"; and then, after a description of the corpses, inhumanly swollen or shrunken, "Faugh! I cannot catalogue the charms of these gallant gentlemen who had got what they enlisted for."

Bierce's short stories are often distinguished from the hackwork of the shudder magazines only by the fact that the shudder is an emotion that for the author is genuine, and by the sharp-edged and flexible style, like the ribbon of a wound-up steel tape-measure. He has also a certain real knack for catching, in his stories about the West, the loneliness of solitary cabins, with their roofs partly fallen in and with a grave or two among the trees; of worked-out diggings in Nevada hills with a skeleton at the bottom of the shaft; of empty buildings in San Francisco of which nobody knows the owners but into which some unknown person creeps at night — all places where the visit of Death seems peculiarly blighting and final, where, in pinching out a tiny human spirit, it renders the great waste complete.

In most other departments of Bierce's work — his poetry, his commentary on public events, his satirical and humorous sketches — the reign of Death is only less absolute. He seems interested in denouncing political corruption mainly from the point of view of its giving him an opportunity to imagine macabre scenes in which the miscreants are received in Hell or left to survive alone in a universe divested of life. In his poetry, God and the angels and even the figure of Christ, as well as the Devil and his agents, are sometimes brought on to the scene, but these powers, celestial and infernal alike, act only to reject and to damn. The old apocalyptic note is occasionally struck by Bierce in connection with the Civil War; but more often in this connection he prefers to

make himself disagreeable by inscribing on his list of the
damned those Unionists who defame the Confederate
cause or show a lack of respect for its dead. In his comment on local California affairs, it is the murders and the
hangings that interest him most. His idea of whimsicality
is almost invariably homicidal, as in those stories of his
which begin, "Having murdered my mother under circumstances of singular atrocity, I was arrested and put
upon my trial . . . ," or, "Early one June morning in
1872 I murdered my father – an act which made a deep
impression on me at the time."

As for Bierce's opinions and principles, they were, as
someone said of Voltaire, "a chaos of clear ideas." The
dismay and the doubt which for such men as Bierce, in
the era of big profits and abundant graft, came to cloud
the success of the Union cause is given vehement expression in certain of his poems. And he detested the
melodrama that the Northerners had made of the Civil
War. On one of his visits to the South, he found, in a
little West Virginia valley, a graveyard of Confederate
soldiers who had fallen in one of the battles in which he
had taken part, and he wrote of them – in a piece called
A Bivouac with the Dead – with a tenderness that was
very rare with him: "They were honest and courageous
foemen, having little in common with the political mad-
men who persuaded them to their doom and the literary
bearers of false witness in the aftertime. They did not
live through the period of honorable strife into the period
of vilification – did not pass from the iron age to the
brazen – from the era of the sword to that of the tongue
and pen. Among them is no member of the Southern
Historical Society. Their valor was not the fury of the
non-combatant; they have no voice in the thunder of the
civilians and the shouting. Not by them are impaired the
dignity and infinite pathos of the Lost Cause. Give them,

these blameless gentlemen, their rightful part in all the pomp that fills the circuit of the summer hills." At this time he wrote to his friend, the poet George Sterling: "They found a Confederate soldier the other day with his rifle alongside. I'm going over to beg his pardon."

There are moments when, like Justice Holmes, he is inclined to think that war itself is a purgative and bracing institution: "I favor anything that will quicken our minds, elevate our sentiments and stop our secreting selfishness," he makes a character called the Bald Campaigner say in one of his topical sketches. It is the time of the Russo-Japanese War, and the Campaigner wants to challenge the Japanese. "A quarter-century of peace will make a nation of blockheads and scoundrels. Patriotism is a vice, but it is a larger vice, and a nobler, than the million petty ones which it promotes in peace to swallow up in war. In the thunder of guns it becomes respectable. I favor war, famine, pestilence — anything that will stop the people from cheating and confine that practice to the contractors and statesmen." In Bierce's fantasy *Ashes of the Beacon,* the memory of 1861 gives rise to a nightmare of sectional wars that are to split the United States in even more disastrous earthquakes.

Ambrose Bierce, in the department of religion, was not a militant atheist as he might have been expected to be. Though he baited and made fun of the clergy, he had several clerical friends, and, according to the memoir of Walter Neale, he especially esteemed Jewish rabbis, for their "broad scholarship," their "devotion to the traditions of their religious order" and their "tolerance of other religions." He was respectful toward all the faiths, but conceived them to be all the creations of men. Like Holmes and so many others, he had been influenced by the theory of Evolution. "Evolution accounts for God as it does for you and me," he told his friend Walter Neale.

"Deity — real Deity — must be in process of growth, changing unceasingly, and in this does not violate His own law. As to the man-made God, the Old Testament is studded with the records of His changefulness. Unfortunately, at times He would de-evolute — backslide. . . . There is room for further evolution. . . . And in this He is making excellent progress, since His creators, who are also His worshippers, are themselves being evolved (very, very slowly) from Neanderthaloids into barbarians. Therefore, we may confidently expect in time to worship a nobler God than any of the many that the Jews and Christians have supplied to us." Yet he was haunted by visions of judgment, and he talks about God in a way which, even when he is being facetious, makes one feel that the conception is still real to him, that — remote above the power of Death — it still presides in Bierce's mind.

As for Bierce's political and social views, the disruption of the Republic by the Civil War, in shattering the integrity of the republican ideal, had shaken Bierce's faith in its purpose; yet, like Holmes, he was too much an old-fashioned American to feel himself really at home with the new ideals of social justice — with the socialists or with Henry George. The result was that, in commenting on current affairs in his San Francisco newspaper column, he was often quite inconsistent. It is characteristic of him that he should alternately contend, for example, that the unemployed are all incompetents who deserve to be left to their fate, and that the government ought to do something for them. He once wrote to George Sterling, half joking: "I am something of a Socialist myself"; and in a column of 1894, according to his biographer, Mr. Fatout, he "summarized his politico-economic beliefs in a six-point program that proposed: to abolish private ownership of land; to stop the importation of cheap labor; to check control of property by the dead; to force the state to provide work in time of want; to limit private fortunes by taxation; and to do away with competitive wage systems." But he tended to be anti-democratic. In this he was both the precursor and one of the principal inspirers of the younger writer, H. L. Mencken. There are signs in the later Mark Twain of a reaction against American democracy. The degradation of public life that followed the Civil War and the activities of omnivorous Business which had worried Walt Whitman and others, were now causing younger men to conclude that if this was what democracy meant, there must be something wrong with democracy. The insistence of Ambrose Bierce on discipline, law and order, and on the need for the control of the disorderly mob by an enlightened and well-washed minority has today a familiar fascistic ring. Though Bierce sometimes jeered at the English, he was really — having lived for three years in England (1872–75) — quite distinctly an Anglophile, and he was sympathetic with British imperialism. He seems to have believed that monarchy was the most satisfactory form of government.

At the bottom of all these paradoxes in the thinking of Ambrose Bierce lies the paradox of his strange personality. Let us examine him in terms of his contradictions.

First of all, there is the disconcerting contrast between the somewhat unpleasant impression that we are likely to get of Bierce when we read him or read about him at length, and the attraction which he evidently exercised on those with whom he came in contact. He is said to have been conspicuously handsome: well-built, of soldierly bearing, with a pink fair complexion, golden hair, and blue eyes that fulgurated, to quote Walter Neale, "terror, love, or hate." "Electric" and "vital" are words that seem to come inevitably to those who knew him. Women were mad about him — though his tastes seem to have been peculiar, for Neale tells us that his first mistress was seventy years old (a fact that Mr. Fatout, his biographer, explains — since Ambrose was fifteen at the time — by the need for a substitute mother), and writes that "all those among Bierce's *chères amies* whom I met personally were ugly, even repulsively so, and in every way unattractive." The younger men who became his disciples were evidently hypnotized by him and fantastically overpraised his talent. And it is reported by several persons that Bierce seemed to exert a magnetic power over the animals he kept as pets, and that, by giving a "soft call" in the woods, "half a whisper and half a cry," he could bring the birds to perch on his shoulders and hop about on his uplifted hands; yet there is no love of life in his writings, and barely a flush of responsive warmth toward any other human being. Of the sunlight and flowers and fruit, of the gaiety and good wine and good eating, of the love affairs and friendships that Bierce enjoyed in and about San Francisco for something like thirty years, there is hardly a trace in his work.

Even the best of his fiction is monotonous and almost monomaniacal in its compulsive concentration on death, and the general run of his journalism would seem to have been equally sterile and even more disagreeable in its monotony of personal abuse. Neale says that he never once heard Bierce laugh, that his pleasantries were usually unsmiling, and that his nearest approach to a smile was a "sardonic, macabre" expression that "would cause the onlooker to shiver slightly." He is said to have "abhorred cruelty" — I am still quoting Neale — and to have shown himself "singularly compassionate"; his biographers cite many instances of his kindness and consideration. Yet the impression one gets from his journalism is that of a powerful impulse to denigrate for the lust of destroying. It is only as it were by accident — through the policy of the Hearst newspaper for which he worked — that he for once found in Collis P. Huntington, the California millionaire, an adversary who merited his venom. Bierce was able, in this connection, to perform a real public service by exposing the ingenious devices by which the Southern Pacific Railroad had avoided paying its debts to the government; and, when Huntington, trying to buy him off, asked him baldly to "name your price — every man has his price," Bierce rang the gong, as he rarely did, by firing back the resounding retort: "My price is about seventy-five million dollars, to be handed to the Treasurer of the United States."

His readiness not merely to insult public figures but also to break off relations with friends suggests that the impulse to wound was involved with a vulnerable pride. He obdurately insisted on leaving his wife, whom he declared to be the only woman he had ever loved and who apparently still loved him, over some highfalutin letters from an admirer of hers, with whom, so far as is known, her relations were entirely innocent. He never saw her again except at their son's funeral, and once, by accident, later. And the kind of repulsive or violent death on which he was always brooding and which he finally sought for himself, he seems to have been able to send like a curse upon all who were closest to him. One of his sons, disappointed in love, shot his rival, the girl and himself, killing himself and the other boy, and evoked from his father, when Bierce saw his body lying naked on a marble slab, the tribute, "You are a noble soul, Day — you did just right." His other son died young of pneumonia, as the result of a rather disgraceful spree, after marrying a girl of whom Bierce disapproved and to whom the father refused to speak even at the son's funeral. He had the boy's body cremated and kept the ashes on his desk in a cigar box. He would not allow the graves of his children and wife to be marked in any way. Of the two favorite disciples of his later years, George Sterling and Herman Scheffauer, the former committed suicide and the latter killed his wife and himself. One of Ambrose Bierce's last acts before his disappearance in Mexico was to send to the only one of his brothers with whom he had remained on good terms — and at whose house he had sometimes stayed on long visits — a letter "so harsh," writes George Sterling, "that he [Bierce's brother] complained to me that it kept him from sleeping, and it may have hastened his death, for within five months he had suffered a stroke of apoplexy" — though this may have been Bierce's strange way of trying to diminish the grief that he knew the affectionate Albert would feel at the news of his death.

Walter Neale says that Bierce was embarrassed all his life by his lack of formal education, that he dreaded "the man with the diploma" and "everybody, in whatsoever walk of life, who had won renown — except persons many years his junior." (It may be that a similar principle was at work in his preference for unattractive women; here, also, he would be in the position of conferring the favors on *them* and would not have to fear competition.) It was evidently due to his need to make up for the deficiencies of his education — as well as to the years he had spent as a professional journalist in England — that he developed the standards of literary style that he carried to such pedantic lengths. He abominated dialect literature and wanted to outlaw American colloquialisms. As Mencken says, "It never seems to have occurred to him that language, like literature, is a living thing, not a mere set of rules." It is the hand of death again. The best qualities of Bierce's prose are military — concision, severe order and unequivocal clearness. His diction is the result of training and seems sometimes rather artificial. The soldier commands one's respect, but the queer unsatisfactoriness of Bierce's writing is partly due to the fact that this marble correctitude is made to serve as a mask for a certain vulgarity of mind and feeling. It constitutes no real discrepancy that Neale should write about Bierce, "I should say that he was physically a perfect man," but that another of his biographers, Mr. Carey McWilliams, in remarking that "no one who ever saw Bierce could think him unimportant," notes that his features were "rather coarse." The case of Ambrose Bierce is, in this respect, the opposite of that of Mark Twain, for the homeliness of the Mississippi pilot conveys the perceptions of a sensitive man. Bierce was aware of his crudeness, and it is plain from these books about him that he resolutely struggled against it. But there was something besides the crudeness that hobbled his exceptional talents — an impasse, a numbness, a void, as if some psychological short circuit had blown out an emotional fuse. The obsession with death is the image of this: it is the blank that blocks every vista; and the asthma from which Bierce suffered was evidently its physical aspect. Mr. McWilliams points out that though, as Neale insists, Ambrose Bierce always gave the impression of possessing "the wholesome pink glow of perfect youthful health," he lived, with his periodic seizures, under a threat of suffocation. His writing — with its purged vocabulary, the brevity of the units in which it works and its cramped emotional range — is an art that can hardly breathe.

Ambrose Bierce lacks the tragic dimension; he was unable to surmount his frustration, his contempt for himself and mankind, through work of the stature of Swift's.

Yet his life, like the best of his stories, rises at moments to a bitter nobility. He finished, in the autumn of 1912, the labor of selecting and arranging the twelve volumes of his *Collected Works,* which his friend Walter Neale was to publish, and he announced that his "life's work" was done, that he was "definitely 'out of it'" now. He had already, at sixty, revisited the South and carefully retraced his campaigns. In a letter to a reunion of the veterans of his regiment, he wrote, in a nostalgic vein which was rather unusual with him, of the Cheat River country of West Virginia: ". . . The whole region is wild and grand, and if any one of the men who in his golden youth soldiered through its valleys of sleep and over its gracious mountains will revisit it in the hazy season when it is all aflame with autumn foliage, I promise him sentiments that he will willingly entertain and emotions that he will care to feel. Among them, I fear, will be a haunting envy of those of his comrades whose fall and burial in that enchanted land he once bewailed." Bierce visited it again in 1907, to show it to his friend Percival Pollard, and yet again in 1913, when he set out on his final journey. In this journey, he travelled on from those old battlefields of our Civil War to another civil war which was then taking place in Mexico. "If you hear," he wrote to his niece, "of my being stood up against a Mexican stone wall and shot to rags, please know that I think that a pretty good way to depart this life. It beats old age, disease or falling down the cellar stairs. To be a Gringo in Mexico — ah, that is euthanasia!" With credentials that procured him the privilege of accompanying Pancho Villa's army, he marched with it as "an observer," and he so much impressed the soldiers by picking off one of the enemy with a rifle that they presented him with a sombrero. Nothing further was ever heard from him after a letter in which he told of this incident. He was presumably killed soon after. Like the planter in his famous story who was hanged on the Owl Creek Bridge, he had had, between war and war — in his work and in his personal relations — nothing more than a dream of escape from a paralyzing immutable doom.

XV

THE CHASTENING OF AMERICAN PROSE STYLE; JOHN W. DE FOREST

THE IMPORTANT American literature of the first half of the nineteenth century, the period before the Civil War, was produced by a group of writers who had had the leisure to develop their talent and all of whom had come to maturity and published original books between 1850 and 1860. One of the main elements in this pre-war literature was supplied by the diaries that writers kept; another by the old-fashioned sermon. The diary provided a basis for many of the published books of Emerson, Thoreau and Hawthorne; and Whitman, in *Specimen Days*, reverts to the diary form. The sermon as a literary genre has, it seems to me, been insufficiently appreciated as an influence on American writing. An essay like Emerson's *American Scholar* is practically in sermon form, with the subject considered under numbered heads, and a book like *Representative Men* suggests the loose generalizing treatment of another kind of sermon. Thoreau was also a preacher, though he had never, like his friend, had a pulpit. One of the features of *Moby-Dick* is the sermon of Father Mapple, which Melville gives us at length; and the novels of Mrs. Stowe are full of sermons, both clerical and secular. These elements — the sermon and the diary, the exhortation and the edifying thought — gave our literature a strong moral character, and this tends to disappear after the Civil War. Or rather, it becomes less overt: the moral is embodied in a story or poem. The stories themselves achieve a new kind of form, and the whole style of prose-writing changes.

In the field of prose fiction before the war, the American writers, both North and South, had a verbose untidy model in the novels of Walter Scott. James Fenimore Cooper imitated Scott and wrote even worse than he; Mrs. Stowe, with an admixture of Dickens, belongs to the same school, or non-school, of loose writers. Hawthorne and Melville and Poe were capable of much greater concentration; but Poe sometimes and the other two always embroidered, or, perhaps better, coagulated, their fancies in a peculiar clogged and viscous prose characteristic of the early nineteenth century. This prose, though the product of a more intense art, has something in common with such prose as Scott's: a self-conscious archaizing, a magniloquence which, though sometimes facetious, has little in common with the eighteenth century; and both have some connection with the romantic movement. But the narrative style of Scott, which is animated as well as copious, was rarely carried on by his imitators, whose tempo today seems intolerably slow. We find this in Washington Irving, who combines this slow pace and this plethora of words with the meditative tone of the *Spectator,* and in his follower John Pendleton Kennedy, the author of *Swallow Barn,* who is a much better story-teller than Irving but cannot escape the phlegmatic pace. When this kind of prose is tautened and trimmed, you may get a style like that of Charles Lamb, which is even more static but richer, which pushes archaism to the point of preciosity. This style was at that time an international phenomenon: you find it on the

Continent as well as in England; it even appears in Russia in the writing of Nikolai Gogol at its densest and most elaborate; and the three American writers mentioned above are all examples of this tightening-up combined with refinement or enrichment. There is nothing in the fiction of Hawthorne to carry the reader along: in the narrative proper of *The Scarlet Letter*, the paragraphs and the sentences, so deliberately and fastidiously written, are as sluggish as the introduction with its description of the old custom house. The voyage of the *Pequod* in *Moby-Dick*, for all its variety of incident and its progression to a dramatic end, is a construction of close-knit blocks which have to be surmounted one by one; the huge units of *Billy Budd*, even more clottedly dense, make it one of the most inappropriate works for reading in bed at night, since it is easy to lose consciousness in the middle of one. Poe, of course, can create suspense: he is always moving steadily to a climax, though he may only be writing an inquiry into Maelzel's automatic chess-player or a vision of landscape-gardening, and in *Arthur Gordon Pym* he returns to something like the plain narrative of Defoe and Swift; but in a piece like *The Masque of the Red Death* he is still true to the romantic manner in its more bespangled and bejewelled form.

In the case of all these writers — even Melville and Poe — the relative lack of movement is quite in keeping with the tempo of secluded lives, of men in a position to live by themselves, usually in the country, to write about country manners which they try to think traditional and stable; to idealize historical episodes; to weave fantasies out of their dreams; to reflect upon human life, upon man's relation to Nature, to God and the Universe; to speculate philosophically or euphorically, to burst into impetuous prophecy on the meaning and the promise of the United States.

But a change in American style takes place in the middle of the century. The plethora of words is reduced; the pace becomes firmer and quicker; the language becomes more what was later called "efficient," more what was still later called "functional." Mark Twain was to assert in the eighties in the chapter of *Life on the Mississippi* from which I have already quoted that this change had taken place in the North long before it did in the South, because the North after the Civil War had got away from the influence of Scott, whereas the South had continued to cherish a grandiose and imprecise language along with the legend it clothed:

"One may observe, by one or two signs, how deeply that influence penetrated, and how strongly it holds [in the South]. If one takes up a Northern or Southern literary periodical of forty or fifty years ago, he will find it filled with wordy, windy, flowery 'eloquence,' romanticism, sentimentality — all imitated from Sir Walter, and sufficiently badly done, too — innocent travesties of his style and methods, in fact. This sort of literature being the fashion in both sections of the country, there was opportunity for the fairest competition; and, as a consequence, the South was able to show as many well-known literary names, proportioned to population, as the North could.

"But a change has come, and there is no opportunity now for a fair competition between North and South. For the North has thrown out that old inflated style, whereas the Southern writer still clings to it — clings to it and has a restricted market for his wares, as a consequence. There is as much literary talent in the South, now, as ever there was, of course; but its work can gain but slight currency under present conditions; the authors write for the past, not the present; they use obsolete forms and a dead language. But when a Southerner of genius writes modern English, his book goes upon crutches no longer, but upon wings; and they carry it swiftly all about America and England, and through the great English reprint publishing houses of Germany — as witness the experience of Mr. Cable and *Uncle Remus,* two of the very few Southern authors who do not write in the Southern style. Instead of three or four widely-known literary names, the South ought to have a dozen or two — and will have them when Sir Walter's time is out."

This change may be seen very clearly in the divergence of the style of Lincoln from that of our old-fashioned oratory in the North as well as the South. Such oratory did not, of course, derive from Scott but in its own field it corresponds to the bellelettristic phenomena described above. The florid American rhetoric which flourished in the nineteenth century was, according to Thomas Wentworth Higginson, a typically American product. The speeches of the English Parliament had no longer anything in common with those of Edmund Burke, but exemplified an ideal of good form — the kind of thing parodied by Max Beerbohm in his essay called *The House of Commons Manner* — which eschewed deliberate eloquence and, by vagueness and hesitation, aimed at an opposite effect of gentlemanly inarticulateness that occasionally pulled itself together to deliver a telling point. Nothing could be more different from our public men — after the clear-cut republic-founding era of Washington, Jefferson and the Adamses — who inundated the Senate Chamber with monstrous prepared orations, full of learned allusions to the classics, quotations from Shakespeare and Milton, and long periods of eulogy or invective that had been modelled on Demosthenes and Cicero. But both Higginson, in his series of lectures on *American Orators and Oratory,* and Lowell, in his introduction to the second series of *Biglow Papers,* speak of

Lincoln as the much-needed innovator in a terser less pretentious style.

"Now," says Higginson, "the great step, after all, toward making oratory human is tested, in a degree, by the shortness of the words. As long as words are poly-syllabic and multitudinous you may reach a special class, but you don't reach the human heart.

"I remember, myself, one commencement day, after the Civil War, when a once eminent literary man in Boston, George S. Hilliard, one of the most brilliant of the elder type of men, who had been rather out of sym-pathy with the college during the wartime, came back at last and made an address at the commencement dinner. Dr. Edward Hammond Clarke, of Boston, a classmate of mine, sat beside me as he heard this address, and he turned to me at the end and said:

" 'It is a very strange thing. I can remember a time when that address would have seemed to me the height of eloquence, and yet now it makes no impression upon me at all.' I said to him,

" 'That is just the feeling that has been in my mind.'

"When afterwards Dr. Clarke himself was called upon, a man not then habitually a public speaker, he simply began and went through a perfectly straightforward, up-and-down description of the present condition and pros-pects of the medical school of the university, and swept all hearers with sympathy. Everybody listened to him, everybody delighted in the statement he made.

"The period of the shortening of words and the direct-ness of address had come. It had always come when the learned man of that day was face to face with a plain man, who spoke simply the words that he meant and said the thing in the shortest way. . . ."

And he ends by pointing to the Gettysburg Address

and to John Brown's speech at his trial as "the two high-water marks of our public speaking."

"In choosing the Yankee dialect," says Lowell, "I did not act without forethought. It had long seemed to me that the great vice of American writing and speaking was a studied want of simplicity, that we were in danger of coming to look on our mother-tongue as a dead language, to be sought in the grammar and dictionary rather than in the heart, and that our only chance of escape was by seeking it at its living sources among those who were, as Scottowe says of Major-General Gibbons, 'divinely illiterate.' President Lincoln, the only really great public man whom these latter days have seen, was great also in this, that he was a master — witness his speech at Gettysburg — of a truly masculine English, classic because it was of no special period, and level at once to the highest and lowest of his countrymen. I learn from the highest authority that his favorite reading was in Shakespeare and Milton, to which, of course, the Bible should be added. But whoever should read the debates in Congress might fancy himself present at a meeting of the city council of some city of southern Gaul in the decline of the Empire, where barbarians with a Latin varnish emulated each other in being more than Ciceronian. Whether it be want of culture, for the highest outcome of that is simplicity, or for whatever reason, it is certain that very few American writers or speakers wield their native language with the directness, precision, and force that are common as the day in the mother country." (Lowell, who had not yet been sent to London, was evidently ignorant here of the "House of Commons manner.")

It may be interesting to quote examples of the older American eloquence in order to compare it with Lincoln's. Charles Sumner, the militant Senator from Massachusetts, was one of the most accomplished of the conventional orators. The speech called *The Crime of Kansas* which he detonated against his Southern opponents in May, 1856, was an immensely elaborate oration that had been carefully composed beforehand and that took Sumner two days to deliver. Its heavy and contemptuous sarcasm at the expense of Senator Andrew P. Butler of South Carolina, which does certainly verge on the abusive, so enraged a relative of Butler's, a young Representative from the same state, that, two days later, in the Senate Chamber, he set upon Sumner with a heavy cane and, catching him pinioned behind his desk, beat him about the head so brutally that Sumner was incapacitated for further political life for three and a half years. Here are two of the offensive passages, which are surrounded by a whole apparatus of historical and classical allusions: "The senator from South Carolina has read many books of chivalry, and believes himself a chivalrous knight, with sentiments of honor and courage. Of course he has chosen a mistress to whom he has made his vows, and who, though ugly to others, is always lovely to him; though polluted in the sight of the world, is chaste in his sight; — I mean the harlot Slavery. For her his tongue is always profuse with words. Let her be impeached in character, or any proposition made to shut her out from the extension of her wantonness, and no extravagance of manner or hardihood of assertion is then too great for this senator. The frenzy of Don Quixote in behalf of his wench Dulcinea del Toboso is all surpassed . . .

"With regret, I come again upon the senator from South Carolina [Mr. Butler], who, omnipresent in this debate, overflowed with rage at the simple suggestion that Kansas had applied for admission as a State; and, with incoherent phrases, discharged the loose expectoration of his speech, now upon her representative, and then upon her people. There was no extravagance of the ancient Parliamentary debate which he did not repeat; nor was there any possible deviation from the truth which he did not make, with so much passion, I am glad to add, as to save him from the suspicion of intentional aberration. But the senator touches nothing that he does not disfigure — with error, sometimes of principle, sometimes of fact. He shows an incapacity of accuracy, whether in stating the constitution or in stating the law, whether in the details of statistics or the diversions of scholarship. He cannot ope his mouth, but out there flies a blunder."

This in its way is as gratuitously grandiloquent as the rhetoric of any Southerner, and was sure to exacerbate the situation. Contrast it with the moderate plainspokenness of the speeches of Lincoln in the same year when he is dealing with the same threatening crisis.

But the Gettysburg Address, which is noted as a landmark by Higginson and Lowell both, makes an even sharper contrast with the enormous oration that the then famous Edward Everett of Boston, congressman, preacher and scholar, delivered on the same occasion, the consecration on November 19, 1863, of the National Cemetery at Gettysburg. With the orator's second paragraph, he is well launched in classical Greece: "It was appointed by law in Athens, that the obsequies of the citizens who fell in battle should be performed at the public expense, and in the most honorable manner. Their bones were carefully gathered up from the funeral pyre, where their bodies were consumed, and brought home to the city. There, for three days before the interment, they lay in state, beneath tents of honor, to receive the votive offerings of friends and relatives, — flowers, weapons, precious ornaments, painted vases (wonders of art, which after two thousand years adorn the museums of modern

Europe,) — the last tributes of surviving affection. Ten coffins of funereal cypress received the honorable deposit, one for each of the tribes of the city, and an eleventh in memory of the unrecognized, but not therefore unhonored, dead, and of those whose remains could not be recovered. On the fourth day the mournful procession was formed: mothers, wives, sisters, daughters, led the way, and to them it was permitted by the simplicity of ancient manners to utter aloud their lamentations for the beloved and the lost; the male relatives and friends of the deceased followed; citizens and strangers closed the train. Thus marshalled, they moved to the place of interment in that famous Ceramicus, the most beautiful suburb of Athens, which had been adorned by Cimon, the son of Miltiades, with walks and fountains and columns, — whose groves were filled with altars, shrines, and temples, — whose gardens were kept forever green by the streams from the neighboring hills, and shaded with the trees sacred to Minerva and coeval with the foundation of the city, — whose circuit enclosed

'the olive grove of Academe,
Plato's retirement, where the Attic bird
Trills her thick-warbl'd notes the summer long ' — *

whose pathways gleamed with the monuments of the illustrious dead, the work of the most consummate masters that ever gave life to marble. There, beneath the overarching plane-trees, upon a lofty stage erected for the purpose, it was ordained that a funeral oration should be pronounced by some citizen of Athens, in the presence of the assembled multitude."

A second Grecian paragraph follows; then a thunder-

---

* Everett misquoted recklessly this passage from the Fourth Book of *Paradise Regained*, and I have not been able to refrain from setting it right.

ing rhetorical question of some hundred and eighty words: "And shall I, fellow-citizens, who, after an interval of twenty-three centuries, a youthful pilgrim from the world unknown to ancient Greece, have wandered over that illustrious plain, ready to put off the shoes from off my feet, as one that stands on holy ground, — who have gazed with respectful emotion on the mound which still protects the dust of those who rolled back the tide of Persian invasion, and rescued the land of popular liberty, of letters, and of arts, from the ruthless foe, — stand unmoved over the graves of our dear brethren, who so lately, on three of those all-important days which decide a nation's history, — days on whose issue it depended whether this august republican Union, founded by some of the wisest statesmen that ever lived, cemented with the blood of some of the purest patriots that ever died, should perish or endure, — rolled back the tide of an invasion, not less unprovoked, not less ruthless, than that which came to plant the dark banner of Asiatic despotism and slavery on the free soil of Greece? Heaven forbid! And could I prove so insensible to every prompting of patriotic duty and affection, not only would you, fellow-citizens, gathered many of you from distant States, who have come to take part in these pious offices of gratitude, — you, respected fathers, brethren, matrons, sisters, who surround me, — cry out for shame, but the forms of brave and patriotic men who fill these honored graves would heave with indignation beneath the sod." It is amusing to think of the Federal dead heaving with indignation at the failure of the orator to honor their graves.

Everett, of course, was the speaker of honor; he had not merely to display his eloquence but also to review the battle. Lincoln himself had simply to preside and to "say a few words" at the end. Now, though Lincoln had at moments in his earlier career made attempts at the old

kind of oratory, it was not congenial to him. Note that
Sumner, who was seventeen years younger than Everett,
has been carrying on the Everett tradition, whereas Lincoln, two years older than Sumner, has brought to perfection a style of an entirely different kind:

"Four score and seven years ago our fathers brought
forth on this continent, a new nation, conceived in
Liberty, and dedicated to the proposition that all men
are created equal.

"Now we are engaged in a great civil war, testing
whether that nation, or any nation so conceived and so
dedicated, can long endure. We are met on a great battlefield of that war. We have come to dedicate a portion of
that field, as a final resting place for those who gave their
lives that that nation might live. It is altogether fitting
and proper that we should do this.

"But, in a larger sense, we can not dedicate — we can
not consecrate — we can not hallow — this ground. The
brave men, living and dead, who struggled here, have
consecrated it, far above our poor power to add or detract.
The world will little note, nor long remember what we
say here, but it can never forget what they did here. It
is for us the living, rather, to be dedicated here to the unfinished work which they who fought here have thus far
so nobly advanced. It is rather for us to be here dedicated to the great task remaining before us — that from
these honored dead we take increased devotion to that
cause for which they gave the last full measure of devotion — that we here highly resolve that these dead shall
not have died in vain — that this nation, under God, shall
have a new birth of freedom — and that government of
the people, by the people, for the people, shall not perish
from the earth."

It was partly, no doubt, that the language of the West,
the simple and forceful speech that Lincoln had been

hearing from his boyhood, had made it natural for him to avoid pomposity and ornamentation. The colloquial speech of the West was already, in the work of the Southwestern humorists, having its influence on literary style. Professor Kenneth Lynn of Harvard, in his book *Mark Twain and Southwestern Humor,* has shown how a duality was beginning to appear in the writings of these early humorists, themselves usually educated men, lawyers or physicians or journalists, between the backwoodsman or lout who is supposed to be telling the story and the literary man who reports it and who, while showing off the antics of the clown, always keeps him very firmly in his place. (Even George Harris does this with Sut Lovingood.) The relation I have noted above between Lowell's Parson Wilbur and his rustic friend Hosea Biglow is a duality of a similar sort. But with Mark Twain, the clown and the gentleman are merged in the same person and produce something new that is neither. Though he will sometimes, as in *Huckleberry Finn,* write wholly in the Southwestern vernacular, he is to develop in his own person a style of the utmost limpidity which is clearly an analogue to Lincoln's — Howells called him "the Lincoln of our literature" — and which, without being modified from its original structure of simple declarative sentences, was to find its last sophistication in the work of Ernest Hemingway. (It might be noted here that Faulkner, though he is sometimes affected by the accents or methods of such moderns as Joyce, Conrad and Proust, is also exploiting the traditional clown or carrying on the other tradition, emotional, romantic and fluent, of old-fashioned Southern eloquence.)

Thus, as Higginson and James Russell Lowell were already beginning to see, the necessity of addressing oneself to the "plain man" and of "saying the thing in the shortest way" was making itself felt in literature. But were there no other reasons for this rapid transition from the complex, the flowery, the self-consciously learned, to the direct and the economical? The newspaper writing of the time had no doubt something to do with this shift: the editors were pressing for simplicity and brevity. But undoubtedly the Civil War itself and the great progress in mechanical techniques which followed the victory of the North were important, in the United States, in the development of a kind of prose that was more accurate and swifter in impact.

We had had in English-speaking America from the middle of the eighteenth century a sufficiently sound standard of expository prose. The writings of Lewis Morgan, the "father of American anthropology" — beginning with his *League of the Iroquois,* which appeared in 1851 — are a good example of this, as are the memoirs of those early West Pointers: Sheridan, Sherman and Grant. For such writing no eloquence is needed; decoration would be out of place. But a sobriety, a rigor of logic, was later to impose itself on the writing of essays and fiction, where it had hitherto not been the rule. This is striking in the new kind of craftsmanship that gives its structure to the American story from Ambrose Bierce, let us say, to O. Henry. There had never, before the war, been anything which, in style and form, resembled the short stories of Ambrose Bierce. There were the stories of Poe, of course, which were clear and compact and which sustained suspense, but these were not characteristic of the good American writing of the period. Poe's technique had been evidently acquired in connection with the demand for arresting short pieces on the part of the American magazines, upon which our other first-rate writers of the early years of the century did not depend for their market to the same extent as did the impoverished Poe.

But the magazine market was later to triumph: the American short story was quickly machined to its perfection of sure-fire effectiveness in the period after the Civil War. The cultivation of brevity was no doubt the result of the speeding-up of everything in American life; the ideal of neat contrivance, which is to be seen in the constructions of Henry James as well as the tricks of O. Henry, is the result of a mechanical age in which everything is supposed to work smoothly. The development of the tighter and sharper style is illustrated in a striking way by the difference between the novels of Harriet Beecher Stowe and the short stories of Sarah Orne Jewett. Miss Jewett, who lived in Maine, had as a girl read *The Pearl of Orr's Island,* which takes place on the coast of Maine, and she said that all her fiction was inspired by this. If we read Sarah Jewett's remarks on the carelessness and lack of selection that prevented Mrs. Stowe's Maine novel from being successful as a work of art and if we compare the two writers' renderings of similar seascapes in Maine, we can see how the slack of the earlier writer was taken up by the later. Mrs. Stowe has no sense of proportion and, as I have said, flings out handfuls of words like confetti; *The Country of the Pointed Firs* consists of small finely shaped units in which every word has been weighed.

But the experience of the war itself as well as the mechanical age — and, as Allan Nevins has shown, the conduct of the war gave great stimulus to an increase of Northern efficiency — had its influence on American style. Grant and Lincoln, in writing and speaking, were distinguished by similar qualities: lucidity, precision, terseness. What was it they had in common that gave them the same traits of style? Lincoln was not a West Pointer; he had not been affected by military discipline. Nor was it that both came from the West and had the habit of homely speech. The humor of the West was drawling: its drawl was exploited by Mark Twain in his readings and no doubt in the same way by Lincoln when he was telling his funny stories; and Western eloquence was slow and expansive. But Grant and Lincoln were both quick thinkers: no drawl is to be heard in their writings or in the framing of their reported opinions. Even when Lincoln is debating with Douglas, there is nothing of the spellbinder about him. Though it would seem that he does attempt sometimes, as Douglas accused him of doing, to temper his sentiments to his audience — as he passes, in Illinois, from the North to the South — he avoids the demagogic tricks that make up so much of Douglas's armory; he aims to be direct and cogent, to try to hit the nails on the head. What was it, then, that led Grant and Lincoln to express themselves with equal concision? It was undoubtedly the decisiveness with which they had to speak. They had no time in which to waste words. To temporize or deceive was too dangerous. They are obliged to issue orders and to lay down lines of policy that will immediately be understood. Their role is to convince and direct. This is the language of responsibility, and its accent of decisiveness will be carried on by the younger men who have served in the war: by Ambrose Bierce in his stoical nightmare; by John De Forest in his Roman impassivity; by Justice Holmes in his judicial austerity. One finds this even in Cable when, emerging from the humid bayous and the rich dialects of Louisiana, he comes to present in unequivocal language his analysis of the problems of the South.

In the novels of Lew Wallace, the author of *Ben-Hur* and an exceptionally able soldier, who had served in the Mexican War and who had emerged from its successor a major-general, we usually find Walter Scott at his worst; yet there are moments of something brisker, which suggests giving orders for the movements of troops: "Every soul aboard, even the ship, awoke. Officers went to their quarters. The marines took arms, and were led out, looking in all respects like legionaries. Sheaves of arrows and armfuls of javelins were carried on deck. By the central stairs the oil-tanks and fire-balls were set ready for use. Additional lanterns were lighted. Buckets were filled with water. The rowers in relief assembled under guard in front of the chief. As Providence would have it, Ben-Hur was one of the latter." And when he comes to write his *Autobiography*, with its account of his own campaigns, he strips away the romantic trappings entirely.

In the case of Thomas Wentworth Higginson, who was already thirty-seven when the war broke out and very much a man of letters, with a graceful and elegant style, one cannot say that this style became military, but, stimulated by his Abolitionism combined with Boston assurance, he always knew exactly what he thought and how he wanted to act. The excellent book which he partly based on his diaries of his Southern campaign, *Army Life in a Black Regiment*, is as simple and precise as Grant. He has also, to be sure, some charm: he registers impressions and emotions of a kind that hardly get into Grant's memoirs, though they do sometimes, in a coarser form, into Sherman's. Here, for example, is a passage from Higginson's account of his trip on an armed steamer up the St. John's River in Florida: "Again there was the dreamy delight of ascending an unknown stream, beneath a sinking moon, into a region where peril made fascination. Since the time of the first explorers, I suppose that those Southern waters have known no sensations so dreamy and so bewitching as those which this war has brought forth. I recall, in this case, the faintest sensations of our voyage, as Ponce de Leon may have re-

called those of his wandering search, in the same soft
zone, for the secret of the mystic fountain. I remember
how, during that night, I looked for the first time through
a powerful night-glass. It had always seemed a thing
wholly inconceivable that a mere lens could change darkness into light; and as I turned the instrument on the
preceding gunboat, and actually discerned the man at the
wheel and the officers standing about him, — all relapsing
into vague gloom again at the withdrawal of the glass, —
it gave a feeling of childish delight. Yet it seemed only
in keeping with the whole enchantment of the scene;
and had I been some Aladdin, convoyed by genii or
giants, I could hardly have felt more wholly a denizen of
some world of romance."

It will be seen that Thomas Wentworth Higginson,
who, as a writer was to feel so strongly the need for a
more chastened American prose, had already pretty well
purged his own of the sloppiness and pomposity of his
predecessors. With Higginson, the tone is quite even; the
phrases are shapely and trim; the vocabulary has nothing
of pretentiousness. We shall be caught here in no
Leatherstocking thickets; we shall be bored by no apocalyptic imagery; we shall not have to plod against the clot-
ting of a too long pent-up introspection. There are no
obstacles to the reading of Higginson's prose: one barely
notices, in fact, that one is reading. Yet even in this
chronicle of Higginson's the freezing effect of the war
may be felt. In approaching the Negro character, despite
his Abolitionist sympathy, he shows an exceptional freedom from Northern as well as from Southern preconcep-
tions and observes it a good deal more realistically than
he has ever done that of John Brown, and this of course
inspires respect; but, as a soldier, he cannot be quite free
of a certain insensitivity, and one cannot be surprised that
this callousness, combined with a certain smugness, should

so have enraged James Branch Cabell. It is true that, in Cabell's version of Higginson's account of the taking and burning of Jacksonville, he somewhat distorts this account and misrepresents Higginson's attitude toward the burning, for which the Colonel expresses regret and disclaims responsibility — it was impossible in 1943, as it is, for that matter, today, for the two sides to be fair to one another; but one can sympathize with Cabell's resentment at "the pretty town was our own without a shot" (the last phrase of which Cabell omits), and at his writing of the unauthorized fire, "It made our sorrow at departure no less, though it infinitely enhanced the impressiveness of the scene." One can imagine the Southerner's feelings at reading: "Yet now, in the retrospect, there seems to have been infused into me through every pore the voluptuous charm of the season and the place; and the slightest corresponding sound or odor now calls back the memory of those delicious days [among the Sea Islands of South Carolina]. . . . One escapes at the South that mixture of hunger and avarice which is felt in the Northern summer, counting each hour's joy with the sad consciousness that an hour is gone. The compensating loss is in missing those soft, sweet, liquid sensations of the Northern Spring, that burst of life and joy, those days of heaven that even April brings; and this absence of childhood in the year creates a feeling of hardness in the season, like that I have suggested in the melody of the Southern birds. It seemed to me also that the woods had not those pure, clean, innocent odors which so abound in the New England forest in early Spring; but there was something luscious, voluptuous, almost oppressively fragrant, about the magnolias, as if they belonged not to Hebe, but to Magdelen." In spite of so much pretty writing, it is true, as Cabell says, that one is made a little uncomfortable by the spectacle of Colonel Higginson, the soldier of God, this capable and self-confident New Englander, inflicting his moral principles on his so misguided fellow countrymen of that so delightful South.

All these writers, then, are positive and disciplined, sometimes trenchant and always concise, as if they were sure of themselves, as if they knew exactly what to think. In the case of certain other writers who had not taken part in the war, though they were old enough at the time to serve, but who had undergone the strain of the war years, Henry Adams and Henry James, I believe that the effect of the war may be traced in the development of the opposite qualities — ambiguity, prolixity, irony — that reflect a kind of lack of self-confidence, a diffidence and a mechanism of self-defense.

The case of James is very curious. Neither Henry nor William was involved in the war — their father did not want them to go — though their two younger brothers enlisted. Wilkie James was badly wounded in the assault on Fort Wagner by Colonel Shaw and his Negro regiment; he was brought home and recovered slowly, but returned to his regiment the following year and had been among the Federal troops, as was also his brother Robertson, who entered Charleston after the victory of the Unionists and raised the Stars and Stripes again on Fort Sumter. Henry, in the meantime — he had been only eighteen at the time that the war began — sustained a mysterious injury in the autumn of 1861 while trying to give a hand to the fire company when a Newport stable was burning. The best discussion of this still obscure incident is to be found in *The Untried Years* by Mr. Leon Edel, the first volume of his biography of James. In James's own account of the incident, in his *Notes of a Son and Brother*, he explains that it is closely bound up in his memory with the beginning of the Civil War.

Mr. Edel has been able to show that the fire did not take place, as James believed, in the spring of 1861, but actually on October 28, and that his visit to the doctor in Boston, when the latter refused to take his injury seriously, occurred not in the summer of 1861 but in that of the following year. Here is James's description of the accident. His father, after at first refusing, had eventually given him permission to study at Harvard. "Two things and more had come up — the biggest of which, and very wondrous as bearing on any circumstance of mine, as having a grain of weight to spare for it, was the breaking out of the War. The other, the infinitely small affair in comparison, was a passage of personal history the most entirely personal, but between which, as a private catastrophe or difficulty, bristling with embarrassments, and the great public convulsion that announced itself in bigger terms each day, I felt from the very first an association of the closest, yet withal, I fear, almost of the least clearly expressible. Scarce at all to be stated, to begin with, the queer fusion or confusion established in my consciousness during the soft spring of '61 by the firing on Fort Sumter, Mr. Lincoln's instant first call for volunteers and a physical mishap, already referred to as having overtaken me at the same dark hour, and the effects of which were to draw themselves out incalculably and intolerably. Beyond all present notation the interlaced, undivided way in which what had happened to me, by a turn of fortune's hand, in twenty odious minutes, kept company of the most unnatural — I can call it nothing less — with my view of what was happening, with the question of what might still happen, to everyone about me, to the country at large: it so made of these marked disparities a single vast visitation. One had the sense, I mean, of a huge comprehensive ache, and there were hours at which one could scarcely have told whether it

came most from one's own poor organism, still so young
and so meant for better things, but which had suffered
particular wrong, or from the enclosing social body, a
body rent with a thousand wounds and that thus treated
one to the honour of a sort of tragic fellowship. The
twenty minutes had sufficed, at all events, to establish a
relation — a relation to everything occurring round me
not only for the next four years but for long afterward
— that was at once extraordinarily intimate and quite
awkwardly irrelevant. I must have felt in some befooled
way in presence of a crisis — the smoke of Charleston
Bay still so acrid in the air — at which the likely young
should be up and doing or, as familiarly put, lend a
hand much wanted; the willing youths, all round, were
mostly starting to their feet, and to have trumped up a
lameness at such a juncture could be made to pass in no
light for graceful. Jammed into the acute angle between
two high fences, where the rhythmic play of my arms, in
tune with that of several other pairs, but at a dire disadvantage of position, induced a rural, a rusty, a quasi-
extemporised old engine to work and a saving stream to
flow, I had done myself, in face of a shabby conflagration, a horrid even if an obscure hurt; and what was interesting from the first was my not doubting in the least
its duration — though what seemed equally clear was that
I needn't as a matter of course adopt and appropriate it,
so to speak, or place it for increase of interest on exhibition. The interest of it, I very presently knew, would
certainly be of the greatest, would even in conditions
kept as simple as I might make them become little less
than absorbing. The shortest account of what was to
follow for a long time after is therefore to plead that the
interest never did fail. It was naturally what is called a
painful one, but it consistently declined, as an influence
at play, to drop for a single instant. Circumstances, by

a wonderful chance, overwhelmingly favoured it — *as* an interest, an inexhaustible, I mean; since I also felt in the whole enveloping tonic atmosphere a force promoting its growth. Interest, the interest of life and of death, of our national existence, of the fate of those, the vastly numerous, whom it closely concerned, the interest of the extending war, in fine, the hurrying troops, the transfigured scene, formed a cover for every sort of intensity, made tension itself in fact contagious — so that almost any tension would do, would serve for one's share.

"I have here, I allow, not a little to foreshorten — have to skip sundry particulars, certain of the steps by which I came to think of my relation to my injury as a *modus vivendi* workable for the time. These steps had after the first flush of reaction inevitably *had* to be communications of my state, recognitions and admissions; which had the effect, I hasten to add, of producing sympathies, supports and reassurances. I gladly took these things, I perfectly remember, at that value; distinct to me as it still is nevertheless that the indulgence they conveyed lost part of its balm by involving a degree of publication. Direfully distinct have remained to me the conditions of a pilgrimage to Boston made that summer under my father's care for consultation of a great surgeon, the head of his profession there; whose opinion and advice — the more that he was a guaranteed friend of my father's — had seemed the best light to invoke on the less and less bearable affliction with which I had been for three or four months seeking to strike some sort of bargain: mainly, up to that time, under protection of a theory of temporary supine 'rest' against which everything inward and outward tended equally to conspire. Agitated scraps of rest, snatched, to my consciousness, by the liveliest violence, were to show for futile almost to the degree in which the effort of our interview with the high expert

was afterwards so to show; the truth being that this interview settled my sad business, settled it just in that saddest sense, for ever so long to come. This was so much
the case that, as the mere scene of our main appeal, the
house from which we had after its making dejectedly
emerged put forth to me as I passed it in many a subsequent season an ironic smug symbolism of its action on
my fate. That action had come from the complete failure
of our approached oracle either to warn, to comfort or to
command — to do anything but make quite unassistingly
light of the bewilderment exposed to him. In default of
other attention or suggestion he might by a mere warning as to gravities only too possible, and already well
advanced, have made such a difference; but I have little
forgotten how I felt myself, the warning absent, treated
but to a comparative pooh-pooh — an impression I long
looked back to as a sharp parting of the ways, with an
adoption of the wrong one distinctly determined. It was
not simply small comfort, it was only a mystification the
more, that the inconvenience of my state had to reckon
with the strange fact of there being nothing to speak of
the matter with me. The graceful course, on the whole
ground again (and where moreover was delicacy, the
proposed, the intended, without grace?) was to behave
accordingly, in good set terms, as if the assurance were
true; since the time left no margin at all for one's gain-
saying with the right confidence so high an authority.
There were a hundred ways to behave — in the general
sense so freely suggested, I mean; and I think of the
second half of that summer of '62 as my attempt at selection of the best. The best still remained, under closer
comparisons, very much what it had at first seemed, and
there was in fact this charm in it that to prepare for an
ordeal essentially intellectual, as I surmised, might justly
involve, in the public eye, a season of some retirement.

The beauty was — I can fairly see it now, through the haze of time, even as beauty! — that studious retirement and preparatory hours did after all supply the supine attitude, did invest the ruefulness, did deck out the cynicism of lying down book in hand with a certain fine plausibility. This was at least a negative of combat, an organised, not a loose and empty one, something definitely and firmly parallel to action in the tented field; and I well recall, for that matter, how, when early in the autumn I had in fact become the queerest of forensic recruits, the bristling horde of my Law School comrades fairly produced the illusion of a mustered army. The Cambridge campus was tented field enough for a conscript starting so compromised; and I can scarce say moreover how easily it let me down that when it came to the point one had still fine fierce young men, in great numbers, for company, there being at the worst so many such who hadn't flown to arms. I was to find my fancy of the merely relative right in any way to figure, or even on such terms just to exist, I was to find it in due course quite drop from me as the Cambridge year played itself out, leaving me all aware that, full though the air might be of stiffer realities, one had yet a handful of one's own to face and deal with."

Mr. Edel suggests that this ailment, of which no further particulars have ever been given, was of a neurotic or semi-neurotic character, and that the idea of incapacitation for military service was to become involved in James's mind with sexual incapacity. This is borne out by the three early stories of James that are concerned with the Civil War: *The Story of a Year* (1865), *Poor Richard* (1867) and *A Most Extraordinary Case* (1868).

In the first of these stories, which appeared in the *Atlantic Monthly* just before the end of the war, a young man who is serving in the Union army becomes engaged to a girl who lives in the house with his mother. His mother is the girl's guardian, and she dominates both the son and her. Inhibited evidently by his fear of his mother, he will not allow Lizzie to announce their engagement, and when Jack has returned to his regiment, the mother sends her off on a visit, in the course of which, as the mother has undoubtedly hoped, she attracts and is attracted by another young man more sophisticated and of more decided character. When the news comes that Jack has been wounded, the mother goes off to nurse him. She has been writing her son that his fiancée is now seriously interested in another man, and in her letters from Jack's bedside she now gives Lizzie the impression that her lover is dying. The young girl, as a result of this, more or less accepts her second admirer; but then Jack is brought back not dead, and Lizzie has to regret her disloyalty. Jack, however, now convinced by his mother that the matter has already been settled, gives his rival his blessing and dies. Lizzie is now filled with remorse and makes the gesture of repudiating her second fiancé; but we know that he is resolute and will marry her.

In the second story, *Poor Richard*, a young farmer of passionate but unstable character and more or less given to drink, is in love with a Yankee heiress but finds himself at a disadvantage in competition with two Union officers. He is weak enough to deceive the one of these young men whom the girl is hoping to marry and who is actually, though unavowedly, in love with her, in such a way as to make it impossible for him to see her before he returns to duty. The Colonel is killed, and Richard confesses. (I do not understand, however — unless it is a case of neurotic guilt — why Richard should declare he has *killed* the Colonel.) The heiress has, in desperation, engaged herself to the other of the two officers, who is quietly interested in her money, but in the end she does not marry anybody and goes to live the life of a spinster in Florence. Mr. Edel believes that this story had its germ in an uncomfortable situation, just after the Civil War, in which James and his cousin Minnie Temple, with whom he seems to have thought himself in love, were thrown together in the New Hampshire hills with the future Justice Oliver Wendell Holmes and another young man, also an ex-soldier, both of whom were still in uniform. In the story, Poor Richard enlists, "on a captain's commission, obtained with some difficulty. He saw a great deal of fighting, but has no scars to show." After the war, he moderates his drinking and wants to try his fortune in St. Louis but cannot raise enough money to get there.

The third story, *A Most Extraordinary Case,* is perhaps psychologically the most interesting. A young officer comes back from the war — which is now over — suffering from some sort of "disorder" which is described as "deeply seated and virulent" but the precise nature of which we are never told. He is taken in by an aunt, who nurses him and sees that he gets medical attention. She has a beautiful niece living with her, and the nephew falls in love with this niece; but three years of the war have so worn him down, so used up his physical and moral energy, that before he was rescued by his aunt, he had almost lost the will to live, and now, although he seems to be improving, he cannot surmount his invalidism sufficiently to make a serious play for the girl. He retreats from a country excursion with her when she expresses a fear that for him to stay out longer may have a bad effect on his health — though before giving in to her anxiety, he declares that "there are moments when this perpetual self-coddling seems beneath the dignity of a man, and I'm tempted to purchase one short hour of enjoyment, of happiness — well, at the cost of my life if necessary!," and he performs the symbolic gesture of thrusting his stick, with "a certain graceless *brusquerie*," into a tear in a fold of her muslin dress. He has been further discouraged, in the meantime, by the presence of a vigorous young army surgeon, with whom, though he considers the doctor's a nature less deep than his own, he has been on very friendly terms. The doctor and Caroline are both splendidly healthy, and they are naturally attracted to one another. When, unaware of the emotions of the invalid, they announce that they are going to marry, the sensitive patient remakes his will, leaving the bulk of his patrimony to the doctor, and regretfully but resignedly expires. Now, James had observed in others the destructive effects of the war even on those who succeeded in surviving it. Sidney Lanier, as we have seen, was such a case, though he rallied without wholly recovering, and there were others with less talent and stamina who went to pieces or faded out. But the invalidism half-acquiesced-in, the inveterate disassociation, of James's *Most Extraordinary Case* is certainly James's own.

James does not, I think, revert to the war in any serious way in his fiction, though in one of his late short stories we find what I take to be a significant reference to it. In *The Jolly Corner*, an expatriate American returns to an empty New York house which he has inherited from his family. He prowls around it at night and is eventually confronted by a phantom who represents an alternate self: the man he would have been if he had stayed in America and become a business success. The phantom covers its eyes with its "splendid . . . strong" hands, and he sees that there are two fingers missing, "as if accidentally shot away." Then the specter reveals its true aspect, "evil, odious, blatant, vulgar," and advances as if "for aggression, and he knew himself give ground. Then harder pressed still, sick with the force of his shock, and falling back as under the hot breath and the roused passion of a life larger than his own, a rage of personality before which his own collapsed, he felt the whole vision turn to darkness and his very feet gave way." I take it that the missing fingers are supposed to have been lost in the Civil War, and that "commitment," as we now say, to the war is supposed to have implied commitment to the commercialized society that followed it.

But it is only when James, toward the end of his life, comes to write about his own early memories, that he deals at any length with the war. We are told by Mr. Edel, however — what we should not have been able to guess — that he liked to read military memoirs and books about Napoleon. When an English Field Marshal sent James his memoirs, he wrote: "To a poor worm of peace and quiet like me — yet with some intelligence — the interest of communicating so with the military temper and type is irresistible — of getting so close (comparatively!) to the qualities that make the brilliant man of action. Those are the qualities, unlike one's own, that are romantic, that you have lived all your days by and with them and for them, I feel as if I had never questioned you nor sounded you enough . . . I would give all I have (including Lamb House) for an hour of your retrospective consciousness, one of your more crowded memories — that for instance of your watch, before your quarters, during the big fight in Ashantee — when the fellow was eyeing you to see if you wouldn't get out of it." And he planned, it seems, his conquest of the literary field as if it were a military campaign: the publication of *The Portrait of a Lady* was to figure for him as a major battle which would put him, as a marshal of letters, in a commanding, a key position. The outbreak of the first

World War, when Henry James was over seventy, again renewed his memories of 1861: "The first sense of it all to me after the first shock and horror was that of a sudden leap back into life of the violence with which the American Civil War broke upon us, at the North, fifty-four years ago, when I had a consciousness of youth which perhaps equalled in vivacity my present consciousness of age. The illusion was complete, in its immediate rush; everything quite exactly matched in the two cases; the tension of the hours after the flag of the Union had been fired upon in South Carolina living again, with a tragic strangeness of recurrence, in the interval during which the fate of Belgium hung in the scales and the possibilities of that of France looked this country harder in the face, one recognised, than any possibility, even that of the England of the Armada, even that of the long Napoleonic menace, could be imagined to have looked her. The analogy quickened and deepened with every elapsing hour; the drop of the balance under the invasion of Belgium reproduced with intensity the agitation of the New England air by Mr. Lincoln's call to arms, and I went about for a short space as with the queer secret locked in my breast of at least already knowing how such occasions helped and what a big war was going to mean."

He volunteered to do what he could and composed appeals for contributions for the Belgian refugees in London and for the American Volunteer Ambulance Corps. He became a British subject. Was he trying to make up in old age for the non-participation of his youth — at a time when his very writings intended to help the cause would be unlikely to succeed in their purpose on account of their unreadability for the public at which they were aimed? For the fact of his not having taken part with his brothers in the Civil War had no doubt in its turn driven further a tendency toward detachment, inaction, which had disposed him in his young manhood to this not taking part; and the tendency to dream and to brood, to be content to note personal impressions not acquired in the clash of conflict but experienced on the periphery within himself, was to result in that personal style, which becomes, as James still further withdraws from the asperities of American life, less decisive and more elusive, less directly communicative, more idiosyncratic. This style, from the beginning, was characterized by a looping of circumlocution and by a meaningless insertion of phrases — of *as it were*'s and *so to speak*'s — as padding to fill out the rhythms. The rhythms of the early James are old-fashioned, almost eighteenth-century — the kind of thing that, after the war, as I have said above, was being pulled in, knitted tight. It is true that in his middle period he came to write this style more crisply, and he had also — in imitating French dramaturgy for the purposes of his own ineffective plays — arrived at a kind of construction, well-planned, well-wound-up and well-oiled, which reflected perhaps also the mechanical age and which sometimes — for example, in *The Spoils of Poynton* — is made to violate human probabilities. But in the end James completely succumbs — his lyric Irish eloquence emerging — to a weaving and swathing of language which gets further and further away from the direct presentation of the actual world but which makes possible a poetic richness that his previous work has not had. What has happened is that, in keeping the old-fashioned long rhythms — now impossible for a De Forest or an Ambrose Bierce or even for a William Dean Howells — he has used them for a new kind of impressionism; in returning to the old embroidery, he has varied it with an imagery less formal.

In the case of Henry Adams, there seems hardly to have been any question of his serving in the Civil War.

When the attack on Fort Sumter occurred, his father, Charles Francis Adams, had already been appointed Minister to England and asked Henry to be his private secretary. Henry remained in England from 1861 to 1868, so missed all but the commencement of the war. He says that, during his first year in London, when a third of his classmates at Harvard had enlisted, he thought of going home and enlisting, too, but he never got to the point of doing so. The Adamses were moderate Republicans, who opposed the policies of the Reconstruction, antagonized the ferocious Sumner and eventually found that they had no place in the Republican Party at all. Henry Adams's eldest brother John, in 1867, ran for Governor of Massachusetts on the Democratic ticket; and the attitude of Henry himself toward the Republican administration was to become as detached and skeptical as his attitude toward everything else. We have seen his opinion of Grant; and here is his description of Lincoln as he appeared to the young Bostonian on the only occasion he met him — "at the melancholy function called an Inaugural Ball": "Of course he [Henry Adams] looked anxiously for a sign of character. He saw a long, awkward figure; a plain, ploughed face; a mind, absent in part, and in part evidently worried by white kid gloves; features that expressed neither self-satisfaction nor any other familiar Americanism, but rather the same painful sense of becoming educated and of needing education that tormented a private secretary, above all a lack of apparent force. Any private secretary in the least fit for his business would have thought, as Adams did, that no man living needed so much education as the new President but that all the education he could get would not be enough." Adams did not seem to want to admit that he had been on this occasion mistaken both as to the President's lack of force and as to his not having enough education — for Lincoln did have quite enough to be, as we have seen, very much aware of the role he was playing in history. Henry Adams had apparently come to doubt — as by that time was rarely confessed — the wisdom of Lincoln's decision to commit the federal government to war.

As in the case of Henry James, the long period that Adams had spent abroad — he had had two years on the Continent as well as his seven in England — had made him very critical of the United States: he began to ask fundamental questions about American society and government, to be dubious about our future. And his literary style, like James's, becomes anything but sharp and decisive. You feel that he is constantly shifting between a mood of ironic malice at the expense of the sordid era to which Grant's Presidency has given free rein and the consciousness of a personal inadequacy that he fears is his own fault. His writing looks clear on the page, but when we begin to read one of his books, we soon realize how sinuous his style is and how uncertain are the ideas it conveys; how treacherous its irony becomes, since, in narrating the history of the United States or in discussing its current problems, this descendant of two able Presidents seems sometimes to be undermining the Republic itself; and, in examining his own career or describing his favorite friends, to be sapping their moral dignity, casting doubts on their actual merit. Now, Ambrose Bierce, a man of the war, is just as critical of America as Adams; he, too, has the special perspective acquired during residence abroad; but he always stands up for himself though he knows in his heart he is doomed, as he always writes as if he had the answers to the questions that Adams is asking, though actually he does not have them.

What Adams and Bierce have in common, and what

they share with John De Forest and Holmes, is a certain aridity and bleakness which come not only from their New England heritage but also from their lack of a compelling faith. A Lincoln or a Harriet Beecher Stowe was impassioned by a vision, a purpose. The one sought to obtain for his nation that it should have, under God, a new birth of freedom and prove to the sneering old world that such a government as the Revolution had tried to establish could survive internal dissension; Mrs. Stowe, who had been read to in her childhood from Cotton Mather's history of New England, still believed that America was "consecrated by some special dealing of God's providence." But neither Henry Adams nor Ambrose Bierce, once the Civil War was over, was in a position to dedicate himself to any such whole-souled endeavor. And Mark Twain, in his later years, finding himself more and more out of harmony with our democratic-commercial society and devoid of religious faith, becomes bleak and uncomfortable, too.

The men who had been soldiers in the war generation give the impression of speaking with certainty; yet what seems to be certainty is often mere rigidity. It is a costume, a uniform, still worn after the crisis no longer decrees it, a relic preserved from their battles like a well-cleaned old rifle or sword. It may even have cribbed or constrained them, have kept them from responding to life. Neither Holmes nor De Forest nor Bierce is remarkable for a warm interest in human beings. Certainly Henry James was to become the greatest writer of this war generation. He had not given himself to the cause, so he did not have to adjust himself to a disillusion. He had acknowledged the demands of the war by suffering his dubious injury. This obliged him in later years to spend long periods of rest on his back, but even that was a small enough price. He had chosen his vocation early, and he was free all his life to follow it. Fine talent, strongly felt vocation, tenacity of moral character enabled him to escape both the rock of the war and the whirlpool of popular fiction. And certainly Henry Adams throws more light on the politics and society of nineteenth-century America than any of these other writers, for he is able to study it as a special case in the development of the human breed as only a detached observer and a student with leisure can do. They also serve who only stand and watch. The men of action make history, but the spectators make most of the histories, and these histories may influence the action.

The novels of John William De Forest had little popular success during his lifetime, and after his death in 1906, they were for thirty years almost completely ignored. But they had been highly praised by William Dean Howells, and that later led students of American literature to look De Forest up. This New England writer was first restored to his place in the history of our fiction by Mr. Van Wyck Brooks in his second New England volume. Brooks found when he looked up De Forest's books in the Yale University Library — the only one, so far as I know, where all the writings of De Forest are accessible — that many of his books had not been taken out since sometime in the eighteen-nineties. But at about the same time, 1939, the one of De Forest's novels which is usually considered the most important, *Miss Ravenel's Conversion from Secession to Loyalty,* was reprinted with an introduction by Professor Gordon S. Haight of Yale, and it has since been brought out in paperback; and De Forest has been given the attention he deserves in the chapter called *The Beginnings of Realism* contributed by Professor Haight to the *Literary*

History of the United States edited by Professor Willard Thorp. Another of De Forest's more interesting novels, *Honest John Vane*, has recently been republished with an introduction by Professor Joseph Jay Rubin of Pennsylvania, and a third, *Playing the Mischief*, has been announced. De Forest has thus now come to be recognized as a precursor of realism in American fiction: his first novel was published in 1857, and Howells and Henry James, as novelists, did not emerge till the seventies; but now that De Forest has been rescued and accepted, he seems to me a little in danger — in the current rather overwrought cultivation of our earlier literature — of having his actual merits exaggerated. And yet, though he is often boring and though his novels never quite come off, he is an honest and an informative writer, and his career as a whole has a certain interest. He is the first of our writers of fiction to deal seriously with the events of the Civil War.

John De Forest was born in 1826, so was thirty-five years old when the war began. Unlike Bierce and Lanier, both born in 1842, and Cable, born in 1844, he had seen a good deal of the world and had already got well started as a writer. De Forest was born in Connecticut, and his headquarters were always New Haven; but, though his father was quite well-to-do — a cotton manufacturer — the son did not go to Yale. An attack of typhoid fever in his teens was thought to have left him too frail for college. When he was twenty, however, he travelled to Syria, where his brother Henry, a missionary, was the head of a girls' school in Beirut, and he spent something less than two years there, in the course of which he explored the Syrian ruins and made a trip to Jerusalem. When he came back to the United States, he wrote a book called *History of the Indians of Connecti-*

cut from the Earliest Known Period to 1851, which was published by the Connecticut Historical Society, when De Forest was twenty-five. This is a work of some historical value, which, in tone and method, seems more mature than one would be likely to expect from so young a man. De Forest's characteristic objectivity is already here well developed: he regards the Connecticut Indians as savages who had inevitably to be displaced by the superior civilization of the white man, yet he coldly condemns the whites for the cruelty and dishonesty of their dealings with the Indians. And one feels also in this book already that curious dull and chill touch which, through the whole of De Forest's career, was to have had the fatal effect of partially deadening the interest of subjects which, intelligently chosen, seemed to offer much greater possibilities. His failure to attract the public was, I am sure, due as much to this as to the reason assigned by Howells: his failure to appeal to the feminine market — or rather, this failure was one aspect of a fundamental non-radiation. It is true that his portraits of women are less flattering than was common in his day, that he recognizes that love is an appetite as well as an elevating sentiment; but if this makes him exceedingly bad at exploiting the then conventional vein of romance, it also makes him unsuccessful at investing the relations between his men and his women with any sort of heat or excitement. It is significant that in his second novel, *Seacliff*, the character he identifies with himself should be reproached by a "susceptible" Southern friend with "being an unloving man, incapable of earnest affection for woman," and that the hero of *Miss Ravenel's Conversion*, whom he also identifies with himself, should at first fail to attract Lillie Ravenel, for the reason that, though "very pleasant, lively and good," "she felt that he was not magnetic." The aspect of De Forest's insensi-

bility which is, however, most in evidence in his study
of the Connecticut Indians, is an attitude toward killing
and torture which cannot properly be called sadistic because it would be more truly described as the result of
a disposition not to flinch in the presence of ferocity that
verges on an attraction toward such spectacles as challenges to iron nerve. De Forest has moral indignation,
but no fury and no real compassion.

In the meantime, after finishing this work on the Indians, he left New Haven and spent four years in
Europe. It is usual to say of De Forest that he was remarkably cosmopolitan for an American of his period,
and to invoke his Huguenot ancestry in explanation of
this; but a reading of his two books of travel — *Oriental
Acquaintance* (1856) and *European Acquaintance* (1858)
— makes one realize his limitations. He is observant, but
only moderately sensitive. He does not respond emotion-
ally to experience; the restraints of New England conduct
seem to keep an unwavering rein on the exercise of his
curiosity. In his account of the Syrian ruins, the abandoned towns of the Seleucids, he measures the walls and
columns and gives you their exact dimensions, but he
does not evoke very vividly the dead world that they
represent. When he attends the Miracle of the Holy
Fire in the Church of the Holy Sepulchre in Jerusalem, of which so turbulent a description had been written
by Robert Curzon in his *Visits to Monasteries in the
Levant* — true, Curzon was present at a murderous riot
— De Forest's indurated Protestantism prevents him from
entering into the spirit of the occasion or even from
being sufficiently interested to speculate as to how the
strange trick is performed. "We witnessed the hocus-
pocus of the Holy Fire, while a host of fanatics stamped
and screamed in a kind of lunatic war-dance around the
Sepulchre. One thing about the ceremony had an air

of the miraculous; that was the rapidity with which the fire was diffused through every nook and cranny of the huge rambling edifice. From torch to torch it leaped like lightning; clomb the walls on cords let down from above, and darted like will-o'-the-wisps to the height of every dome and gallery. Everybody had a taper in his hand, passing fingers, beard, and face through its flames, and pretending to purify his very garments by its sacred unconsuming heat. 'It wo'nt burn! it wo'nt burn!' shrieked an old Greek *papa* by my side, as he charitably offered his candle for the benefit of my soul, skin, and raiment. I tried to make him hold his fingers in the blaze, but the old fellow dodged them through dexterously, and, to my disappointment, got off without a scorch. If the church had a morsel of wood about it, the holy fire would have burnt it up ere this, and perhaps roasted its fanatical admirers into a suspicion that it came from some other place than Heaven."

In Europe, still "pursued," as he says, "by the fretting enmity of a monotonous invalidism," he lingers only briefly in Florence and Venice, then consigns himself to a terrible cure, self-mortifying as the ceremonies of the Penitentes, at Graefenberg in Austrian Lombardy. Of his first bath at Graefenberg De Forest writes, "He [the presiding doctor] then ordered the wet sheet to be spread, and signed me to stretch myself in it. As soon as I had measured my length on the dripping linen, Franz folded me up rapidly, and then packed me thickly in blankets and coverlets, as if I were a batch of dough set away to rise. Neuville followed my damp example, and our teeth were soon chattering in chilly sympathy. Having noted the intensity of our ague, as if it were a means of judging what degree of vigor in the treatment we could bear, Priessnitz [the doctor director] marched off to survey the agonies of Irwine and Burroughs . . .

Franz now engineered me into a side room, and halted me alongside of an oblong cistern, brimming with black water, supplied by a brooklet, which fell into it with a perpetual chilly gurgal. In a moment his practiced fingers had peeled me like an orange, only far quicker than any orange was ever yet stripped of its envelope. As I shuffled off the last tag of that humid coil, the steam coiled up from my body as from an acceptable sacrifice, or an ear of hot boiled corn. Priessnitz pointed to the cistern, like an angel of destiny signing to my tomb, and I bolted into it in a hurry, as wise people always bolt out of the frying-pan into the fire, when there is no help for it. In a minute my whole surface was so perfectly iced that it felt hard, smooth, and glossy, like a skin of marble. I got out on the first symptom of permission, when Franz set about rubbing me down with a new linen sheet, still possessed of all its native asperity . . . Once more in the double-bedded chamber, I gave myself a few hurried rubs of supererogation, and was about dressing, when Neuville and Franz reappeared from the lower regions. With shivering fingers I seized my thick under-wrapper, and proceeded to don it, with a glorious sense of anticipatory comfort. But that atrocious Franz saw it, snatched it, tucked it under his arm, made a grab next at my drawers and stockings, and then signified, by menacing signs, that I was to leave my cloak on its nail. No luckless urchin in Dotheboys Hall was ever stripped half so pitilessly. . . . It was a raw, misty morning, as are nearly all Graefenberg mornings, and the chill humidity crept like a breath of ice through our thin remainder of raiment. Loose and shaky, from our coat skirts to our teeth, we ambled up the hill back of the Establishment, in hopes of sheltering ourselves in its woods from an ill-dispositioned wind, which blows, year in and year out, over those unfortunate landscapes." One is reminded of that other taut New Englander, the historian Francis Parkman, tormenting and subduing his flesh through his travels among the Indians.

De Forest did not, however, complete this heroic cure. "The climate," he says, "was detestable. It rained nearly half the time, even when it was fair weather. The winds were as cold as if they slept in wet sheets, and blew all the while, without pause or punctuation. The food was an insult to the palate and an injury to the stomach." He passes on to another sanitarium at Divonne in south-eastern France, where the treatment was not quite so rugged but where the weather seems to have been quite as bad. He and one other patient were, De Forest records, the "only two braves" — note the Indian identification — who "remained to encounter the inclemency of January packings and douches. The climate of the Valley of Geneva is not at any season of the year a very perfect one, except in two or three sheltered nooks like Montreuil; while in winter it is boisterous and glacial enough to make a white bear curse the north pole, and wish himself at the equator." He had been trained in the austerity of New England, but this was a more stringent ordeal. "Notwithstanding atmospheric observations and linguistic studies," he says, "I sometimes felt dreadfully lonely and unemployed in my hydropathic seclusion."

When he emerges from this seclusion, he visits Switzerland and then proceeds to Paris. "I shall make short work of Paris," he begins his chapter on this capital. Then he goes on to Florence, for which he feels a decided enthusiasm. "Florence!" the chapters on the city begin. "I seldom hear the word without at least a faint semblance of that emotion with which a man hears the name of the mistress of his heart." Florence, of course, is more sober, more like a university town; yet to De Forest even the social life of Tuscany proves too frivolous and unfettered for his temperament. At an informal evening party, "The eldest sister, a gay, good-hearted creature, lively and boisterous for an Italian lady, sat down to the piano, and played the choicest parts of Robert the Devil. The others moved through a pantomime of that wild opera with a facility, a grace, and an expression which would have done honor to long artistic experience. Very unwillingly did I allow myself to be forced into the game, for I felt as if my northern stiffness jarred harshly with the flexile movement and power of personification instinctive in these southern natures. So let them fly away now from my memory, treading on skies of music and interwinding through a dance of poesy!" He seems to have expected Italy to have fortified him with its antique virtue, but he finds it only seduces him toward sensuality:

"Into Italy, therefore, I entered as into a Valley of Vision, where I should behold glories little less than unutterable. Memorable and humiliating was my disappointment. Despite of strong effort to realize the historic value of the scenes around me, despite of dutiful pilgrimages to countless classic shrines, I remained the same being that I had been in America, the spirit equally clogged by the body, the wings of the imagination as easily wearied as ever, and the terrestrial nature which they have to upbear as ponderous.

"More than this, the very beauty of Italy, the finish of its scenery, and the luxury of its climate, seemed to lap me into an unusual sensuousness of enjoyment. Particularly was this noticeable at Florence, where I staid longest and fought my earthliness hardest. I wondered how Galileo could have been intellectual there, how Dante and Michel Angelo could have been sublime there. It was in vain, for the most part, that I tried to study the art which was around me, or tried to call up the antiquity which crouched mysteriously behind it, and I returned forever to the starlight on the Arno, to the sunlight on the green hills, to the whispering groves of the Cascine, as to the immemorial and rightful deities of the locality."

He occupied himself for a time by translating into Italian, with difficulty, *The House of the Seven Gables.*

When De Forest returned from Europe, he wrote two novels: *Witching Times,* a story of the Salem witch trials, which appeared as a serial in *Putnam's Magazine* in 1856–57 but was never brought out in book-form, and *Seacliff,* which was published in 1859. The first of these may come as a surprise if one has not got around to reading it till after one has explored De Forest's better-known novels, for in certain ways it is more nearly satisfactory than many of those that came later. It has nothing of the mistiness of Hawthorne (whose ancestor, the judge, appears in it) in dealing with similar subjects, and it reduces to a prosaic minimum the inevitable element of Scott romance. De Forest was subjecting to a scrutiny that for its time may be called scientific and presenting in terms of what was to be called realism those half-legendary happenings of the seventeenth century which had lurked as a hideous scandal in the background of American history. He has scrupulously studied the record, and he has embodied in his narrative certain insights into the phenomena of mass mania which sometimes suggest analogies with the hysterias of our own time. We have a twisted little girl who informs against her mother and then terrorizes the household into which she has been adopted by bedevilling it with poltergeist tricks; the breakdown under questioning and imprisonment of those who have been arrested as witches to the point that they are ready to confess to crimes which they have never committed; the assumption that protest or criticism must invariably imply a complicity with the witches: "The Devil put that into your mouth!"; the fascination of the idea of Satan and the formidable power he wields, which seduces the weakminded Deacon Bowson from an abject terror of witchcraft to a conversion to "the Devil's party" and the conviction that he himself is possessed of supernatural powers; the demagogic playing on ignorant fears of the vulgar and ambitious Elder Parris; the grovelling moral struggles of the somewhat superior Elder Noyse, who succumbs to the temptation to exploit popular panic for personal revenge and advantage and to help destroy an innocent man, with the result — one of De Forest's unexpected strokes — that, after "many fits of remorse, when all danger seemed to be over [the danger of his losing his position in the reaction against the witch persecution] . . . he became spiritually calm again, and went on peaceably preaching very orthodox sermons; although he thought that he never quite recovered his former inward fervor and tranquillity. What a shabby, feeble, inane termination to that tragedy of soul which he had passed through; to all those subtle temptations, those fierce desires, those lengthened apostasies; to his deep-laid wicked plots, his bloodguiltiness and his keen consciousness of damnation! Yet, so it was; for such was his coward mind that he could not inflict any terrible punishment on himself; dared not become a warning to mankind by openly bearing the cross of utter condemnation." Cotton Mather, whose relation to the witch trials was one of central importance and who would seem to offer dramatic opportunities, is relegated by De Forest to a role that is almost peripheral; yet he touches on the strong motivation, later emphasized by Brooks Adams, of the professional and class interests of the Mathers, supported by Governor Phips, in arresting, through red-her-ring technique, the threatened subversion by the congregations of the priesthood's autocratic authority.

In so far as *Witching Times* is a fable intended by De Forest to be applied to the contemporary world of the fifties, it is designed, as is intimated by the author in an occasional aside to the reader, to discourage that atmosphere of the supernatural of which I have spoken above in connection with Francis Grierson and Calvin Stowe — an atmosphere, peculiar to the North and ridiculed by the Virginian Fitzhugh, to which had contributed, as De Forest notes, the supposed revelations of Joseph Smith and the growth of the Mormon Church, the Millerites or Seventh-Day Adventists, who repaired "to midnight churchyards, in white robes, to be in at the resurrection," the spirit rappings of the Fox sisters of Rochester and the believers in animal magnetism. And if it is a question, says De Forest, of unwarranted executions, what about the lynching of Negroes? The subject gives De Forest an excellent field for the exercise of his non-romantic, of his strictly non-sensational, grimness. The reader cannot help expecting that the enlightened English gentleman, Henry More, the central and most sympathetic male character, will triumph over the forces of superstition; but De Forest, without compunction, gives these forces of darkness their head, and the reader becomes rather appalled as what the author refers to as "the Juggernaut" of the witch-exterminators mows down one innocent victim after the other: first Henry More's old Irish nurse along with the other humble suspects; then the reluctant executioner, who decides he has had enough and tries to run away; then, finally, Henry More himself, a man of almost superhuman strength, whom the reader, accustomed to modern films, may expect to make a last-minute getaway but whose prowess is ascribed to the Devil by a man he has knocked about and whom the author allows to be brought to the scaffold. For it is not really congenial to De Forest to deal in melodramatic values. His protagonist's defense in court, though it is supposed to impress the spectators, has no virtue to save him from the gallows and his daughter, in the role of heroine, is very soon convicted, too. Only here does the author relent. Her husband arranges a jailbreak, and they manage to escape to Virginia.

It is quite understandable that the publishers of the fifties should not have felt any inducement to bring out *Witching Times* in book-form: De Forest was scarcely known, and the novel had been published anonymously, like all the contributions to *Putnam's;* as it is also understandable that his later novels should have been sometimes so obscurely and unattractively published — in paperback, in double columns, anonymously in the "No Name" series. But today when this writer has been rediscovered and his novels are being reprinted, it might be worth while for some university press to retrieve this forgotten work, which shows certain of his qualities at their strongest.

The second of these pre-war novels, *Seacliff; or the Mystery of the Westervelts,* goes much further than *Witching Times* in the direction of conciliating the popular taste. It is, in fact, deliberately contrived as a Victorian melodrama in the fashionable Gothic style, for which De Forest had no gift whatever. Here a well-read well-travelled young man of very high moral principles, who has just returned from abroad and is about to publish a book of travels — much, in fact, like De Forest himself — falls in love with the daughter of a well-to-do family who inhabit a large mansion on Long Island Sound, and gradually becomes involved in the affairs of their complicated household. This is quite an ambitious work and, given the absurd plot, is carried through with complete conscientiousness. De Forest, in the course of his travels, had discovered Balzac and Stendhal and had been influenced by the methods of French fiction as well as by Trollope and Thackeray, and he is trying to make his characters as faithful as possible to American society as he knows it. The novel, like its predecessor, gives evidence of the seriousness of De Forest's first attempts to establish a new realism in American fiction, but also, more conspicuously than *Witching Times*, of a certain lack of talent for writing it. There is accurate observation in *Seacliff*, and some of the characters are original conceptions: the giddy young college boy Hunter, who is always boasting of vices and scandals that turn out to be non-existent, and Somerville, a variation on the traditional aristocratic villain, who is a genuinely distinguished and cultivated man and who, amusingly, while committing his unimaginable crimes, improves the whole tone of the household which he is dominating and undermining.

But these characters are conceptions, not creations. It is one of the weaknesses of De Forest that he lacks a sense of his audience, that even when, as happens fairly often, he hits upon a good idea, he is likely to make the puppet who embodies it a monotonous and mechanical bore. One feature of this otherwise uninteresting book may be mentioned as anticipating in a striking way one of the typical situations in Henry James. All the events of the story — as is so common with James — are witnessed through the eyes of a single observer, the young man just returned from Europe; and this witness becomes so much interested in the mysteries by which he is surrounded — gratuitously, so far as one can see, since his relations with the girl he is in love with are at first in no way imperilled by them — that he puts himself to an immense amount of trouble, even making an expedition to

New York, in order to ferret out the relationships of the other members of the family. Now, we know that Henry James had read De Forest, for in a review of one of De Forest's later books, he refers to his earlier productions as "entertaining novels"; and we cannot but be reminded by *Seacliff* of such a *tour de force* as *The Sacred Fount*, in which a guest at an English house party is engaged in a similar exploit. I do not know whether Henry James had originally picked up this theme from De Forest or whether they got it from a common source. The convention of the curious guest who turns into an amateur detective may well have derived from such Victorian devices as the narratives of Esther Summerson in *Bleak House* and of the witnesses who report the strange happenings in *The Moonstone* of Wilkie Collins.

De Forest had married in 1855 the daughter of a professor of mineralogy, who taught his subject both in Amherst and in Charleston. De Forest, before his marriage, spent a winter with the family in Charleston and, afterwards, at least two more winters there; and he thus came to know something of the South. He had entered into a partnership with his brother, who was in the lumber business — a silent partnership, which involved no responsibility — and he does not seem to have needed to earn a living. He was in Europe when the war broke out, and he soon returned to America. The Union defeat at Bull Run convinced him that the war was more serious than he had at first thought it was going to be, and he set about recruiting in New Haven a company of volunteers. Though he never rose to higher rank than captain, he spent six and a half years in the army. "I was," he says, "in three storming parties, six days of field engagement, and thirty-seven days of siege duty, making forty-six days under fire." He served in Louisiana and was

present at the taking of Port Hudson; and he afterwards
fought with Sheridan in the Shenandoah Valley campaign. After the war, during the Reconstruction, he
worked in the Freedmen's Bureau in Greenville, South
Carolina. De Forest was finally mustered out in January,
1868.

In the meantime, through the whole of this period, he
had been writing long letters to his wife, and he later
put together out of these and some articles for magazines
in which he had described his experiences two volumes
called *A Volunteer's Adventures* and *A Union Officer in
the Reconstruction*. These books were, however, for un-
explained reasons, not published till 1946 and 1948, when
they were printed by the Yale University Press. Though
De Forest came out of the service in worse health than
when he had entered it, the man who appears in these
records is hardheaded, clear-sighted, quite sure of himself; he has been tempered now by ordeals that have required more fortitude than even those of the cold baths
and wet towels of that murderous Austrian clinic. His
style, always rather impassive, has now hardened into
something quite Roman, and one finds it rather odd to
remember that these journals were sent to his wife. What
is surprising is not only that he should spare her so little
of the hardship and brutality of war but that he should
always seem to find it possible, in illness, privation or
disaster, to write her with fulness and precision about
everything that is going on. He is as dispassionate in
noting the phenomena of his own thoughts and feelings
in battle as he is in his account of the punishments
which, in the course of his court-martial duties, he is
obliged to inflict upon soldiers who have been guilty of
violating discipline, and he sets down his personal impressions of Sheridan, Butler and Grant in the same imperturbable way. What dignifies and elevates his writing

is his sense of his own competence, his pride, which is, however, quite without ostentation, in his principles, his abilities and his stamina. It is said that De Forest's wife was an excellent classical scholar, and this may have had something to do with the stoically noble tone in which he finds it natural to write to her.

During an interval in 1864, when De Forest was in such bad health that he had himself mustered out and returned for four months to New Haven, he began writing a novel about the war, which he afterwards finished and published — in 1867 — as *Miss Ravenel's Conversion from Secession to Loyalty*. The military parts of this novel dealt with more or less the same campaigns as the journals of *A Volunteer's Adventures*, and they constituted a real piece of pioneering in the treatment of war in fiction. De Forest seems to have read *La Chartreuse de Parme*, with its realistic description, in its time unconventional because totally non-heroic, of the battle of Waterloo, in which Stendhal had taken part; but Tolstoy, who had also been influenced by this, only started on *War and Peace* after De Forest had begun *Miss Ravenel*. When *War and Peace* appeared in English in 1886 and Howells got De Forest to read it, he wrote to Howells: "Let me tell you that nobody but he has written the whole truth about war and battle. *I* tried, and I told all I dared, and perhaps all I could. But there was one thing I did not dare tell, lest the world should infer that I was naturally a coward, and so could not know the feelings of a brave man. I actually did not dare state the extreme horror of battle, and the anguish with which the bravest soldiers struggle through it." Stephen Crane, in *The Red Badge of Courage*, was influenced by Tolstoy's *Sevastopol*, though he had apparently not yet read *War and Peace*, and he may also have been influenced by De Forest. It had already been suspected that Crane had read *Miss Ravenel's Conversion,* and the probability has now been made stronger by a paper by Mr. Thomas F. O'Donnell of Syracuse University in the issue of *American Literature* of January, 1956 — *De Forest, Van Petten, and Stephen Crane* — in which he shows that the Reverend John B. Van Petten, who was Crane's teacher of history at school, had been a fellow campaigner of De Forest's and is mentioned by him often in *A Volunteer's Adventures.* It is assumed — though there is no real evidence — that Van Petten would have talked to his students about his old friend De Forest's book.

In any case, the war scenes in *Miss Ravenel's Conversion* were the first of their kind in fiction in English, and it would be more than a decade, so far as I know, before any other writer of talent who had taken an active part in the war would describe it with equal realism. Tourgée's *Figs and Thistles,* with its first-hand account of Bull Run, did not appear till 1879; Ambrose Bierce's *Tales of Soldiers and Civilians* and Joseph Kirkland's *The Captain of Company K* were published in 1891; and Horace Porter's *Campaigning with General Grant* in 1897. Though the stoical De Forest cannot bring himself, as he wrote to Howells, to admit any quailing on the part of his hero, he does allow himself — while this hero "smiles grimly" — a description of general panic: "The unusually horrible clamor and the many-sided nature of the danger had an evident effect on the soldiers, hardened as they were to scenes of ordinary battle. Grim faces turned in every direction with hasty stares of alarm, looking aloft and on every side as well as to the front for destruction. Pallid stragglers who had dropped out of the leading brigade drifted by the Tenth, dodging from trunk to trunk in an instinctive search for cover, although it was visible that the forest was no protection but rather an additional peril. Every regiment has its two or three cowards, or perhaps its half-dozen, weakly-

nerved creatures, whom nothing can make fight, and who
never do fight. One abject hound, a corporal with his
disgraced stripes upon his arm, came by with a ghastly
backward glare of horror, his face colorless, his eyes pro-
jecting, and his chin shaking. Colburne cursed him for a
poltroon, struck him with the flat of his sabre, and
dragged him into the ranks of his own regiment; but
the miserable creature was too thoroughly unmanned by
the great horror of death to be moved to any show of
resentment or even of courage by the indignity; he only
gave an idiotic stare with outstretched neck toward the
front, then turned with a nervous jerk like that of a
scared beast, and rushed rearward. Further on, six men
were standing in single file behind a large beech, holding
each other by the shoulders when with a stunning crash
the entire top of the tree flew off and came down among
them butt foremost, sending out a cloud of dust and
splinters. Colburne smiled grimly to see the paralyzed
terror of their upward stare and the frantic flight which
barely saved them from being crushed to jelly. A man
who keeps the ranks hates a skulker, and wishes that he
may be killed the same as any other enemy." And there
is a scene in one of those primitive field hospitals which
Grant could not bear to visit, in which a wounded man,
just arrived, has made himself raving drunk in order to
face its horrors. One of the characters, who shares with
the author a certain *sang-froid* in writing to his wife, reports to her — "although not given to noting with much
interest the minor and personal incidents of war" — the
following ironic mishap: "I had just finished breakfast
and was lying on my back smoking. A bullet whistled so
unusually low as to attract my attention and struck with
a loud smash in a tree about twenty feet from me. Between me and the tree a soldier with his greatcoat rolled
under his head for a pillow lay on his back reading a

newspaper which he held in both hands. I remember smiling to myself to see this man start as the bullet passed. Some of his comrades left off playing cards and looked for it. The man who was reading remained perfectly still, his eyes fixed on the paper with a steadiness which I thought curious, considering the bustle around him. Presently I noticed that there were a few drops of blood on his neck, and that his face was paling. Calling to the card players, who had resumed their game, I said, 'See to that man with the paper.' They went to him, spoke to him, touched him, and found him perfectly dead. The ball had struck him under the chin, traversed the neck, and cut the spinal column where it joins the brain, making a fearful hole through which the blood had already soaked his greatcoat. It was this man's head and not the tree which had been struck with such a report. There he lay, still holding the New York *Independent,* with his eyes fixed on a sermon by Henry Ward Beecher. It was really quite a remarkable circumstance."

Miss Ravenel was originally intended to appear as a serial in *Harper's Monthly,* which had been publishing De Forest's war articles, but its harshness made the editor jib. "I make no objection," wrote De Forest, "to your moral reform of the story. If it goes into the *Monthly* of course it ought to be made proper for families. Only I think it ought to be understood, for the sake of *vraisemblance,* that the Colonel did frequently swear and that the Louisiana lady was not quite as good as she should be." Even the admiring Howells, writing thirty-four years after the book had been published, complains that this Louisiana lady is "very lurid" and says that he cannot think of her "without shuddering." It has been claimed as an achievement for De Forest that he was the first American novelist who dared to let a "bad woman" go unpunished. Mrs. Larue is left happily living under the protection of a high Southern official, who hands over to her several thousand bales of cotton with a permit to sell them in the North and so to restore her fallen fortunes. It is true that, at a time when our fiction had been quite played off the stage by the national drama, De Forest made a brave new beginning in his attempt to rescue war from heroics and sexual relations from sentimentality, and it is true that he suffered, like Cable, from the censorship of publishers and editors. The editor of *Harper's* decided that *Miss Ravenel* could never be serialized, and, though it was brought out by the house of Harper in book-form, the publishers took so little interest in it that the proofs were never corrected — De Forest was still stationed in South Carolina and was counting on the editor to attend to this — so that the book came out with hundreds of errors. But today such audacities as De Forest commits seem mild enough when we compare them with the French naturalism of the nineteenth century or what we are getting in America and England today. And one even finds *Miss Ravenel's Conversion*, De Forest's most ambitious work, a little disappointing, a little dull. The characters are correctly described, but one never feels the least excitement as to what is going to happen to them.

We are confronted at the beginning of *Miss Ravenel* with a sketch of New Haven — which is called New Boston — as it appeared to De Forest in the middle of the century, with its solemn and self-conscious hierarchy that is at once theological and academic, and De Forest, with his knowledge of the larger world, can judge it and gently make fun of it; but his weakness as a novelist is that he himself carried into his fiction a little too much of New Haven: its coldness and sternness and stiffness. It is not only in those parts of the story which take place in this Connecticut stronghold that we seem to find ourselves enclosed in the high-ceilinged boxlike compartments of the formal old New Haven mansions, with their square bulks and bleak façades. De Forest, in another of his books, has a description of one of his characters, returning like him from a sojourn in the Middle East, "driving soberly among the rectangles of New Haven," and the author, for all his long travels, has never really left these behind.

De Forest's style, though firm, sure and accurate, now an excellent style in its way — it has improved since his earlier writings — is of a kind that almost completely excludes, not only the nuances of atmosphere and the vibrations of unspoken feeling, but also the real pulse of emotion. And though he is interested in different sorts of people and is able to present a whisky-drinking Virginian or a promiscuous Creole lady with a detachment that is not provincial, the structure of his moral world is built upon Puritan girders. He is able to see human beings quite clearly in their proper dimensions, he has a sharp practical eye for their motives, and he is not afraid to write what he sees. Yet he cannot get into his narrative very much of the color or movement of life. The incidents of *Miss Ravenel's Conversion* do not pass before the reader with the unexpected naturalness of *War and Peace*. The tempo is deliberate, the tone unperturbed. The moral is very confident. De Forest never has any doubt of the correctness of the Northern position nor has he any real sympathy with the Southerners. Lillie's father, a South Carolinian who has been for twenty years a professor in a New Orleans medical college but who, rather than betray the Union, has come north at the beginning of the war, replies at the end of the book, when Colburne, as the author says, "moralizes," that "In the long run the right conquers": "Yes, as that pure and wise martyr to the cause of freedom, President

Lincoln, said four years ago, right makes might. A just system of labor has produced power, and an unjust system has produced weakness. The North, living by free industry, has twenty millions of people, and wealth inexhaustible. The South, living by slavery, has twelve millions, one half of whom are paupers and secret enemies. The right always conquers because it always becomes the strongest. In that sense 'the hand of God' is identical with 'the heaviest battalions.'" . . . "The Southern character," says Colburne, "will be sweetened by adversity as their persimmons are by frost. Besides, it is such a calming thing to have one's fight out! It draws off the bad blood. But what are we to do about punishing the masses? I go for punishing only the leaders." " 'Yes,' coincided the Doctor. 'They are the responsible criminals. It is astonishing how imperiously strong characters govern weak ones. You will often meet with a man who absolutely enters into and possesses other men, making them talk, act, and feel as if they were himself. He puts them on and wears them as a soldier crab puts on and wears an empty shell. For instance, you hear a man talking treason; you look at him and say, 'It is that poor fool, Cracker!' But all the while it is Planter, who, being stronger minded than Cracker, dwells in him and blasphemes out of his windows. Planter is the living crab, and Cracker is the dead shell. The question comes up, 'which shall we hang and which shall we pardon?' I say, hang Planter and tell Cracker to get to work. Planter gone, some better man will occupy Cracker and make him speak and live virtuously."

These predictions and moral judgments are typical of the complacency of the cockily victorious North. Their divergence from the opinions of Tourgée is extreme. But they are partly to be explained by the time at which they were written. De Forest had not yet at this time had his

intimate experience of the post-war South as an agent
of the Freedmen's Bureau; and, in any case, he left South
Carolina in January, 1868, at the time when the Ku Klux
Klan was only just coming into prominence. He had
furthermore been posted in a part of the state where, as
he says, there were as yet no carpetbaggers. As the result of his later observation, he became aware, like
Tourgée, that the planters who had supported the Confederacy were the ablest group of men in the South and
regretted that they were being excluded from the management of public affairs. But in the chapters on what
De Forest calls "Chivalrous Southrons" and "Semi-
Chivalrous Southrons," which first appeared as magazine
articles in 1869, though he attempts to be just to this
class and to appreciate the Southern qualities, these
qualities were not of a kind particularly to appeal to De
Forest. It is interesting to find him noting the old-
fashioned "individuality of character" of the Southerner:
"He had [note the past tense] salient virtues, vices, and
oddities; he had that rich, practical humor which is
totally unconscious of being humoristic; he in the gravest manner decorated his life with ludicrous and romantic
adventures; in short, he was a prize for the anecdotist
and novelist. . . . In that land of romance you will find
Uncle Toby, Squire Western and Sir Pitt Crawley and
Colonel Newcome and Mr. Pickwick and Le Chourineur,
all moving in the best society and quite sure that they
are Admirable Crichtons." It is precisely this sort of
character with whom, though he regularly attempts it,
De Forest the novelist always fails, and the sarcasm of
the final sentence above betrays his lack of respect for
such characters. Like the younger Oliver Wendell
Holmes, who was to say that he had never met a Southerner whom he regarded as really a gentleman, De Forest
can never conceal a basic contempt for the "Southrons";

and Lillie Ravenel, the beauty from Louisiana who has taken the opposite side from her father and sympathizes with the Southern cause, who has married a sensual Southron rather than the non-magnetic Colburne, must at last, when her husband has betrayed her with the scandalous Mrs. Larue, be made to prefer the North and to acknowledge the rightness of the Northern cause, must come back to sound and sure old New England and — her husband having perished with the Confederacy — be married to the upright Colburne, who has weathered and won the war.

Before going on to consider the rest of De Forest's work, one should mention the remarkable essay on the past and the prospects of American fiction which, just after the publication of *Miss Ravenel*, he brought out anonymously as a kind of manifesto in the issue of the *Nation* of January 9, 1868. This is called *The Great American Novel*, and it is said to have first given currency to this still all too current phrase. It is at any rate a kind of landmark, a candid and mordant summary that marks the moment of a new departure in the development of American fiction.

"A friend of ours," De Forest begins, "a fairly clever person, and by no means lacking in common sense on common subjects, has the craze in his head that he will someday write a great American novel." "Will he produce it?" De Forest asks. "Will any one of this generation produce it? It is very doubtful, for the obstacles are immense." The kind of novel that De Forest is thinking of is a "picture of the ordinary emotions and manners of American existence." "This task," he says, "of painting the American soul within the framework of a novel has seldom been attempted, and has never been accomplished further than very partially — in the production of a few outlines. Washington Irving was too cautious to make the trial; he went back to fictions of Knickerbockers and Rip Van Winkles and Ichabod Cranes; these he did well, and we may thank him for not attempting more and failing in the attempt. With the same consciousness of incapacity Cooper shirked the experiment; he devoted himself to Indians, of whom he knew next to nothing, and to backwoodsmen and sailors, whom he idealized; or where he attempted civilized groups, he produced something less natural than the wax figures of Barnum's old museum. If all Americans were like the heros and heroines of Cooper, Carlyle might well enough call us 'eighteen millions of bores.' As for a tableau of American society, as for anything resembling the tableaux of English society by Thackeray and Trollope, or the tableaux of French society by Balzac and George Sand, we had better not trouble ourselves with looking for it in Cooper.

"There come to us from the deserts of the past certain voices which 'syllable men's names' — names that seem to sound like 'Paulding,' 'Brown,' 'Kennedy' — and we catch nothing further. These are ghosts, and they wrote about ghosts, and the ghosts have vanished utterly. Another of these shadowy mediums, still living, if we are not misinformed, is W. Gilmore Simms, of whom the best and the worst thing to be said is this — that he is nearly as good as Cooper, and deserves fame nearly as much.

"Thus do we arrive, without frequent stoppage, at our own times. Hawthorne, the greatest of American imaginations, staggered under the load of the American novel. In *The Scarlet Letter*, *The House of the Seven Gables*, and *The Blithedale Romance* we have three delightful romances, full of acute spiritual analysis, of the light of other worlds, but also characterized by only a vague consciousness of this life, and by graspings that catch little but the subjective of humanity. Such personages as Hawthorne creates belong to the wide realm of art rather than to our nationality. They are as probably natives of the further mountains of Cathay or of the moon as of the United States of America. They are what Yankees might come to be who should shut themselves up for life to meditate in old manses. They have no sympathy with this eager and laborious people, which takes so many newspapers, builds so many railroads, does the most business on a given capital, wages the biggest war in proportion to its population, believes in the physically impossible and does some of it. Hawthorne's characters cannot talk? Certainly not in the style of this western world; rather in the language of men who never expressed themselves but on paper, and on paper in dreams. There is a curious lack of natural dialogue in Hawthorne's books, and with this, of course, a lack of almost all other signs of the dramatic faculty. Besides, his company is so limited. New Englanders they profess to be: to be sure, they are of the queerest; men and women of the oddest, shyest, most recluse nature, and often creatures purely ideal; but they never profess to be other than New Englanders. The profoundest reverence for this great man need prevent no one from saying that he has not written 'the Great American Novel.'

"The nearest approach to the desired phenomenon is *Uncle Tom's Cabin.* There were very noticeable faults in that story; there was a very faulty plot; there was (if idealism be a fault) a black man painted whiter than the angels, and a girl such as girls are to be, perhaps, but are not yet; there was a little village twaddle. But there was also a national breadth to the picture, truthful outlining of character, natural speaking, and plenty of strong feeling. Though comeliness of form was lacking, the material of the work was in many respects admirable. Such Northerners as Mrs. Stowe painted we have seen; and we have seen such Southerners, no matter what the people south of Mason and Dixon's line may protest; we have seen such negroes, barring, of course, the impeccable Uncle Tom — uncle of no extant nephews, so far as we know. It was a picture of American life, drawn with a few strong and passionate strokes, not filled in thoroughly, but still a portrait. It seemed, then, when that book was published, easy to have more American novels. But in *Dred* it became clear that the soul which a throb of emotion had enabled to grasp this whole people was losing its hold on the vast subject which had so stirred us. Then, stricken with timidity, the author shrank into her native shell of New England."

The novels of Oliver Wendell Holmes — which De Forest regards as rather half-baked — have, like Hawthorne's, the disadvantage of dealing only with the New England world. The difficulty, according to De Forest, of writing an American novel is the "variety" of our regional life and the "antagonism" between the different sections. "When you have made your picture of petrified New England life, left aground like a boulder near the banks of the Merrimac, does the Mississippian or the Minnesotian or the Pennsylvanian recognize it as American society? We are a nation of provinces, and each province claims to be the court." Then, American society has been changing so rapidly that it has never been possible to take it for granted, to grow up in it, to study it, to transfer it to paper. (I have heard M. André Malraux give the same sort of explanation for the unsatisfactoriness of Soviet fiction.) "Ask a portrait-painter," De Forest propounds, "if he can make a good likeness of a baby, and he will tell you that the features are not sufficiently marked nor the expression sufficiently personal. Is there not the same difficulty in limning this continental infant of American society, who is changing every year not only in physical attributes, but in the characteristics of his soul? Fifteen years ago it was morality to return fugitive slaves to their owners — and now? Five years ago everybody swore to pay the national debt in specie — and now? Our aristocracy flies through the phases of Knickerbocker, codfish, shoddy and petroleum. Where are the 'high-toned gentlemen' whom North and South gloried in a quarter of a century since? Where are the Congressmen who could write *The Federalist?* Where is everything that was? Can a society which is changing so rapidly be painted except in the daily newspapers? Has anyone photographed fireworks or the shooting-stars? . . . When Mr. Anthony Trollope commences a novel, he is perplexed by no such kaleidoscopic transformations and no such conflicting claims of sections."

At the end of this article of De Forest's, which I read in a volume of the *Nation* in the Harvard University Library, I found that some modern reader had not been able to restrain himself from writing: "Poor Melville, not a word for him!" But the allegories and fantasies of Melville were not at all the kind of thing that would have answered to De Forest's ideal of the great American novel. In the first place, what De Forest wanted was realism. There were already when De Forest wrote the beginnings in the United States of a kind of realistic movement. William Dean Howells was its great promoter. He had come back to the United States in 1865, after his four years of consulship in Venice, during which he had read a good deal of Italian fiction and realized that, though Goldoni, "the first of the realists," had established a tradition in the theater, the Italians "had no novels which treated of their contemporary life; that they had no modern fiction but the historical romance."

He had not yet discovered the Spaniards Valdés and Galdós, nor the Russians Turgenev and Tolstoy; he had apparently not even yet read Zola. But on his return to his native country, he discovered *Miss Ravenel's Conversion*. "Among the first books that came to my hand was a novel of J. W. De Forest, which I think the best novel suggested by the civil war. If this is not saying very much for *Miss Ravenel's Conversion*, I will go farther and say it was one of the best American novels that I had known, and was of an advanced realism, before realism was known by name. I had a passion for that book, and for all the books of that author; and if I have never been able to make the public care for them as much as I did it has not been for want of trying." And he also discovered James, when, as reader for the *Atlantic Monthly*, he came upon the manuscript of one of his first short stories. The Jameses were then living in Boston, and he and Henry saw a good deal of one another: they took long walks and discussed current fiction. Howells, at first as subeditor, then as editor-in-chief of the *Atlantic*, was publishing, all through the seventies, as much as possible of both James and De Forest, and he acted as a link between them. He evidently persuaded James that he ought to look into De Forest, and James, as we shall see in a moment, was much less enthusiastic than Howells; but De Forest, though he, too, later had his own reservations, regarded the success of James as a victory in a common cause. "I don't understand," he writes Howells in 1879, "why you and I haven't sold monstrously except on the theory that our novel-reading public is mainly a female or a very juvenile public, and wants something nearer to its own mark of intellect and taste, as, for instance, *Helen's Babies* and *That Husband of Mine*. There is James, to be sure, who belongs to our school, and who yet seems to be forging ahead. But I think that is because he has crossed the ocean and appealed to the maturer public of the old world. At home I suppose that he has only had a *'succès d'estime,'* or rather, perhaps, a *'succès de haine,'* for the women are very mad about his *Daisy Miller."* And Howells never wavered in his loyalty to either of his realist allies. He did his best, through his whole career as an editor and a reviewer, to advertize and encourage De Forest, though the latter never "caught on" with the public, and, soon after taking over the direction of the *Atlantic,* he printed – had no doubt commissioned – an article on De Forest by one Clarence Gordon, which, like De Forest's own essay on the American novel, is striking for the barrenness of its backward view.

When Howells, in 1901, came to sum up De Forest's career in one of the chapters of his *Heroines of Fiction,* he attributed, as I have mentioned, De Forest's unpopularity mainly to his failure in charming, his liability in fact to antagonizing, the novel-reading feminine public. "He is distinctly," Howells wrote, "a man's novelist, and as men do not need novelists so much apparently as women, his usefulness has been limited. When he was writing the novels which, like *Kate Beaumont,* commanded for him the admiration of those among his countrymen best fitted to know good work, it seemed reasonable that he should be lastingly recognized as one of the masters of American fiction; and I for one shall never be willing to own him less, though I cannot read many pages of his without wishing that he had done this or that differently. It is not only the master who chooses to leave things in the rough; it is sometimes the 'prentice who has not yet learned how to shape them perfectly. Still, in spite of all this I remember and I feel his strenuous imaginative gift working with a sort of disdainful honesty to the effects of art. Finer, not stronger workmen succeeded him, and a delicate realism, more responsive to the claims and appeals of the feminine over-soul, replaced his inexorable veracity. In the fate of his fiction, whether final or provisional, it is as if this sensitive spirit had avenged the slight it felt, and, as the habit of women is, over-avenged itself. It had revealed itself to him as it does only to the masters of fiction, and he had seemed not to prize the confidence — had mocked at it, or what was worse, had made it the text for dramatic censures far more cutting and insufferable than sermons."

De Forest had long been complaining, as had even Henry James, about the stupid limitations imposed by a market which insisted upon prudery and demanded sentimentality. We find him writing to Howells on December 6, 1886, after reading the latter's novel, *The Minister's Charge; or the Apprenticeship of Lemuel Barker*: "You will meet hostile criticism enough from allies, and you deserve (all the more) eulogy from a man who knows something of your business. . . . I admire most of all your honesty and courage. How dare you speak out your beliefs as you do? You spare neither manhood nor womanhood, and especially not the latter, though it furnishes four fifths of *our* novel-reading public. It is a wonder that the females of America, at least the common born and bred of them, do not stone you in the street." And in a letter of January 24, 1887, he brackets Howells with Zola and deplores the defection of James: "I am glad to have found Tolstoi. I had been reduced, in the matter of novels, to Zola and you; and two men can't write fast enough for one reader. There are other good story writers, such as James, Cable, Craddock. But they are not to me satisfactory and instructing novelists. I now want somebody from whom

I can learn both the what and the how. Isn't it odd that the creator of Daisy Miller fails somewhat in larger paintings of human nature."

But it was not merely contemporary realism at which these three pioneers were aiming. Both De Forest and James had read Balzac, and both were ambitious to live up to the role that Balzac had announced for himself: that of "secretary of society." It is evident from the essay I have quoted above that De Forest's ideal for the "American novel" was a work that would cover a great deal of ground, a variety of localities and classes. It was the range of *Uncle Tom's Cabin,* with its Southerners and Northerners and Westerners, its dramatization of a national issue, that made De Forest regard it as up to date, the nearest approach to this; and De Forest's own extensive range will be evident in this survey of his work. Henry James, though he had not travelled widely at home, nevertheless knew both New York and New England — which presented at that time stronger contrasts than are likely to appear today — as well as a little of Washington, and had lived a good deal in Europe, and he set out with a similar intention of describing and contrasting manners in different parts of the western world. Howells himself, though he does not, in *My Literary Passions,* mention Balzac among the writers who influenced him, is also — with his business and professional men, his Bohemians, rural types and members of religious cults, his transference of his interest from Boston to New York and his return in his late novels to his native Ohio — exerting himself, like the other two, to cover a considerable area, to observe and report at firsthand.

That both Henry James and De Forest should have expressed such admiration for Howells as, in their letters and articles, they constantly did, that they should both have applauded *The Minister's Charge* as a coming to grips with the raw reality of ordinary American life in a way of which they thought that they themselves would not have been capable may appear to us today rather strange, but the theme of this novel itself shows the problem with which all three were struggling. Just as the Bostonian Reverend Sewell in *The Minister's Charge* has embarrassing demands made upon him by the clumsy young country boy Lemuel Barker, who wants to become a poet and awakens the minister's sympathy but who gets himself arrested for theft and puts a strain on his protector's conscience in its conflict with his genteel professional life, so Howells, the admirer of Zola who was nevertheless always shocked by the language of his friend Mark Twain, the mild-mannered preacher of realism, must have found himself embarrassed when, years later, in the nineties, he was confronted with such an outlaw as Stephen Crane, who had set out to make this realism harsher. Yet Howells, in his mid-fifties, had taken on Crane as the Reverend Sewell had taken on Lemuel Barker; had gone the rounds of the New York booksellers in an attempt to get them to stock the young man's *Maggie,* the then horrifying story of a prostitute which Crane had had printed at his own expense. The spreading sordidness, the inundating vulgarity of post-war American life was coming, as the century went on, to dismay all three of these realists.

John De Forest had been through more rough living and had had more experience of practical affairs than either of the other two writers. Let us see how he sustained his effort to carry through his Balzacian program.

De Forest, after *Miss Ravenel's Conversion,* further dealt with the life of the South, in two novels the scene of both of which is laid in South Carolina: *Kate Beaumont* (1872), which is supposed to take place before the war, and *The Bloody Chasm* (1881), which is supposed to take place just after it. These are even more pedestrian than *Miss Ravenel*. De Forest, as usual, makes an honest attempt to be fair to the Southern character and, as usual, can never quite succeed in conveying his appreciation without sounding a little patronizing, even hostile. *Kate Beaumont* is made to center on one of those pre-war Southern feuds that were likely to cost so many lives and that could not but seem to a New Englander completely idiotic; and De Forest brings out aspects of Southern life that a John Esten Cooke or a Thomas Nelson Page would never have admitted to his fiction. There is a scene in which a Southern lady visits a gentleman alone in his house and mixes drinks for him and drinks herself till they have both of them become quite tipsy; and another in which another Carolinian gentleman carouses with the white Crackers and comes home and beats his wife, who has hidden the whisky from him. But the book is neither tragic nor amusing nor does it communicate in any convincing way the passions supposed to be felt by the characters. Even the scenes that are meant to be most animated do not shake off that pall of ennui which De Forest spreads over his subjects. He really succeeds better with the "Southrons" in his chapters on them in his book on the Reconstruction.

In the second of these novels, *The Bloody Chasm*, a New Englander, an ex-Abolitionist, who has lived in his youth in Charleston, returns there after the war. Silas Mather has formerly been tutor in a Charleston first family, the Beauforts, and has married a daughter of this family. Now his wife is dead. Coming back, he still feels resentment as he remembers the horror of the Beauforts at the prospect of their daughter's marrying a

Yankee, and he notes with the satisfaction of a former anti-slavery moralist the abasement to which Charleston has been reduced. Here De Forest is treating ironically the complacency of the winning North which he had seemed in some degree to share at the time of his writing *Miss Ravenel*, and what follows might have been made effective if De Forest had had the knack of drama. The visitor from New England, while walking about, first comes upon a shabby old gentleman, "a man over sixty, thin in figure and haggard in countenance, with long, white neglected hair," who "glanced sadly around the field of ruins, and then, setting his gaze upon the shattered Huguenot Church, folded his arms with an air of submission to final and crushing calamity." He turns out to be the minister who presided at the wedding of Silas Mather and his South Carolinian wife. A conversation takes place between them, in which the self-righteous ex-Abolitionist is made to play a somewhat odious role. The old man tells Mather that he is glad to see him — so many of the people he once knew are dead:

"Mr. Mather realized all at once, and for the first time, that he was in a land of bereavement and mourning. His instant impulse was to resist this unexpected claim upon his pity. 'It is the usual experience of men of our age,' he said. 'Death is everywhere.'

"Mr. Roget shook his head — shook it pensively and repeatedly — as if seeking to repulse many sad recollections. 'But here,' he sighed, 'it has been a whirlwind of death.'

"Mather shook his head also, but somewhat with an air of sternness, as if dispensing judgement. 'You sowed the wind,' he said, 'and you reaped the whirlwind.'

"The clergyman made no response in words. He merely glanced in a meek, troubled way about the field of ruins. He had the air of thinking that the whirlwind

was enough, without joining to it the exultation of a
foe. Mather followed his wandering, sorrowful gaze,
and then looked at the shattered, tattered man himself.
'I don't reproach you, sir,' he added. 'I think I heard that
you personally did not accord with the fiendish madness
of secession. I was thinking of the wicked leaders in the
movement and their crazed followers. They brought their
doom — the doom of this destruction — upon their own
heads. You surely owe *them* no sympathy.'

" 'I could not help suffering with them,' groaned Mr.
Roget. 'I can not help grieving with them.' "

But the New Englander's self-satisfaction returns when
he has parted from the minister. "Left to himself amid
the ruins of Charleston, Mr. Mather soon recovered his
equanimity. The widespread spectacle of that flame-
blackened desolation was very comforting and exhilarat-
ing to him. In all honesty and purity of spirit he compared himself to a prophet walking among the ruins of
Babylon.

" 'I knew it would come,' he said aloud. 'I knew that
slavery and treason and unprovoked rebellion could not
conquer in the end. I felt and asserted that, so sure as
there is a God above — a God of justice and holiness
and awful power — just so surely would the violent
South be brought to destruction. This spectacle is the
most striking proof that I have ever seen of the might
of a good cause, and of the overruling watchfulness of a
holy Creator and Governor.' "

He now meets another old friend, an ex-general in
the Confederate army, whose face has "lost its old plump-
ness and air of confidence" and whose figure "looked
bony and wasted through his mean raiment." The insufferable Mather begins on the note of "I told you so."
His first words are, "As I was saying, sir, it can't be
done." "I beg your pardon, sir," answers the General.

"You have the advantage of me. . . ." " 'Four years ago,' said Mather slowly, 'in my office in Boston I told you it could *not* be done.' . . . 'I see it can't,' bowed the Southerner. He laughed but not blithely, and then shook his head very sadly. 'We did our best,' he added. 'Your worst.' 'Ah, sir! You are victors.' This was uttered with a sigh. 'You have the right to exult. I would simply ask, my dear sir, is it magnanimous?' " What is the news, inquires Mather, of the Beauforts? "There's not a man of that noble race," says the General, "on the face of this miserable earth. . . . It had furnished many gentlemen to South Carolina, and it ended as a race of gentlemen should. Every one of those four Beaufort boys fell in the fore-front of battle, with his back to the field and his face to the foe." " 'May God forgive them,' said Mather solemnly. 'They have gone to their account.' For a moment the General seemed to forget his elaborate Southern urbanity. 'It strikes me, sir,' he observed dryly, 'that God may find it easier to forgive than a New England Puritan can.' "

There are other good things in *The Bloody Chasm* — things, at least, that are well-observed if not very well presented: the effect of emancipation on colored Aunt Chloe, "the last faithful remnant of the feminine property of the Beauforts," who remains devoted to the family but who now dares to speak and behave with a good deal more independence; the demoralizing effect of poverty on one of the Charleston ladies, who has been living in a ruined shanty, and her resumption of her former dignity on acquiring some money again. The main theme of the novel is the strained relation that is established between a fierce embittered Beaufort girl, the niece of Mather's wife, and a young Yankee colonel, Mather's nephew, who is in love with her and who will receive a large gift from his uncle — more afflicted by the tragedy of the war than has appeared on his first arrival — if the young man will marry the girl and thus reunite the two families. This reunion through marriage of North and South is not, as has somewhere been said, the first appearance in fiction of this comforting resolution which was afterwards to be so much overworked, since De Forest himself had used it in *Miss Ravenel*, and Tourgée in both *A Fool's Errand* and *Bricks Without Straw*.

Two points are worth noting here in connection with these novels of De Forest's written after *Miss Ravenel's Conversion*. I have spoken of the sober propriety of the style of the earlier story. The style of *Kate Beaumont*, which follows it (after one intervening novel), surprises by a certain colloquialism that jars on the former almost classical decorum. Thus you find such expressions as the following: "But this strange courtship must have the go-by for the present."; "It is worthy of note . . . that she promptly dismissed her interest in the Gilyard courtship, on discovering that it might interfere with her Washington whimwham." And he sometimes writes *laid* for *lay* — as, however, was not then uncommon on the part of American writers, even of those whose grammar was otherwise perfect — in such sentences as "He laid down to rest." I believe that the explanation of this change in De Forest's style is to be found in a passage in *Playing the Mischief*, a book written after *Kate Beaumont*: "Mr. Hollowbread," says the author, "perceived (to use one of those picturesque idioms which give so much pain to critics of a certain bore and penetration) that he had put his foot in it." De Forest's editors had no doubt been at work on him. Howells, who published *Kate Beaumont* as a serial in the *Atlantic Monthly*, may have left him a freer hand than certain of his other supervisors. What has evidently been happening here is that De Forest, in his role of realist, has, like Lowell and Mark Twain and others, been feeling the necessity of getting away from conventional literary English and expressing himself in a language that is closer to common American speech. He was not, in a literary way, so well-bred as the Boston writers, who did not allow this kind of thing, but he, too, had been frozen in the standard mold, so his lapses always give one a shock.

A second feature of De Forest's novels to be remarked for its sociological interest is the compulsion that he seems to have felt, in spite of his realist principles, to conform on occasion to the popular formula. The accepted indispensable axis of the ordinary American novel had come, as we have seen in Cable, to be a love story treated in a certain way: the lovers must eventually marry, but in the meantime they must be kept apart by obstacles. Sometimes, as in *The Cavalier*, the woman is first married to a villain, who has to be got rid of by the author in order that she may marry her proper mate, and *Miss Ravenel* had more or less run true to this formula, though it somewhat departed from convention in that the wrong man whom Lillie first marries is not even so much of a villain as the husband of Isabel Archer in Henry James's *The Portrait of A Lady*: he is a man she has had reason for loving and whose sins against her she is ready to forgive. But De Forest, after writing *Miss Ravenel* — in an attempt to meet the public halfway — fell back from time to time on the expected thing and was put to as much labored contrivance as poor Cable was later to be. The device that De Forest most favored was to manœuver either the hero or the heroine into the danger of marrying some inferior person; and, in spite of his disposition, in dealing with any such relationship, to emphasize the masculine side, one finds that his heroines, in the seventies and eighties, are steadily moving up-stage, so that the other characters have to turn toward them, and one finds him adopting toward these heroines the correct current fictional tone. Such passages as the following, from, respectively, *Kate Beaumont* and *The Bloody Chasm*, normal enough though they may appear when thus excerpted, are significant of a special situation which prevailed at that period in American fiction: "She rustled forward, put one of her large arms around *the girl's* waist and kissed her in an eagerly petting way, as a mother kisses her baby"; " 'Ah, well!' responded *the girl*, drawing another sigh, a slightly weary one . . . *The girl* read the letter aloud."

The point is that this figure "the girl" has taken her place, in the last quarter of the century, at the center of almost every American novel. "The girl" has become the ideal, the touchstone, the democratic princess, who may turn up in any household and keep the family in breath-less suspense as to whom she is going to marry. She represents maidenly modesty combined with common sense and a will of her own, instinctive good taste and good manners even if this is not always combined with good breeding (which, if necessary, will be supplied by the well-bred young man she marries). In the novels of James and Howells, "the girl" has come to be the cyno-sure, and not merely of her eager admirers but of all the other characters, too. You have only to turn a few pages of *The Rise of Silas Lapham* to light upon, " 'No. It's the end,' said the girl, resuming at last something of the hoarse drawl which the tumult of her feeling had broken into those half-articulate appeals"; or a few pages of *The Portrait of A Lady* to encounter some such passage as, "The girl had a certain nobleness of imagination which rendered her a good many services and played her a great many tricks." Which suitor of several will "the girl" end by choosing? Or in the case of her being engaged, will she marry the man she is engaged to; if it is clear that she ought not to marry him, how will she manage to escape from the engagement?

Now, De Forest was not terribly good with "the girl" and the insipid situations she gave rise to. When he wants to manufacture "love interest," he is likely to fall back on the banality, very uncharacteristic of him, of simply remarking, "It was the old, old story." The generous Howells included Kate Beaumont in his gallery of "Heroines of Fiction," but he admitted that "the want of something salient in her appearances unfits her for quotation," and actually she is not much more real than the Victorian heroine of *Seacliff*. Yet De Forest did have some success with the women of a less maidenly type that are a feature of his later more satirical novels and that give some color to Howells's belief that he was distasteful to feminine readers.

Kate Beaumont was followed by *Honest John Vane*, published in 1873, and *Playing the Mischief*, of 1876. These novels, which are more or less comic, take for their field the fantastic· corruption that was rampant under the Grant administrations. De Forest, who, in spite of his war record, had never risen higher than a captaincy, came to realize by the end of the war that promotions were being procured by influence or bribery in Washington. He exposes this scandal in these Washington novels, but only as one element in a whole disgusting picture of what was happening to our public life. Like certain other serious Unionist writers who had believed in their country before the war, he was beginning to lose his faith in democracy. "In every civilized land on this planet," he writes in *Honest John Vane*, "thoughtful souls are seeking to divine, by the light of these and other similar dolorous revelations, whether it is possible for a democracy to save itself from the corrupting tyranny of capital. Within our own borders sadder spirits are asking which is the most alluring spectacle, — a free America falling into squandering and bribery, or a monarchical Prussia ruled by economy and honesty." (Note the admiration for Bismarck's Germany so common in the North in that era.) John Vane is a country bumpkin married to a vulgar ambitious wife; he gets himself elected to Congress on the basis of his reputation for honesty, and on this account he tries for a time to resist the temptation, omnipresent in Washington, to make money by dishonest means. But he eventually succumbs to his wife's insistence on a higher standard of living, and from that moment finds himself compromised. In the interest of their social career, he even winks at her affair — or flirtation: such matters in our novels were then left rather vague — with a silly old lady-killing senator, and in order to avoid being ruined is forced to borrow a large sum of money from him. There is nothing left now of his honesty but a boyish face and oafish manners, behind which acquired slyness has come to override stirrings of conscience; but 'his reputation as Honest John Vane is still a political asset. He recognizes fully now that "the lobby was a cleverer and more formidable assemblage than either of those two chambers which nominally give laws to the nation," and he takes part in a gigantic fraud, a parody of the Crédit Mobilier swindle which was perpetrated under Grant in connection with the Union Pacific railroad: a great Subfluvial Tunnel Road (in the novel) which, running under the Mississippi, is to unite Lake Superior with the Gulf of Mexico. As in the case of the Crédit Mobilier, when the danger of exposure threatens, the Congressmen are bribed with slices of stock. There is at last an investigation, but Vane acts the part of a booby and escapes without public discredit.

This is one of John De Forest's more interesting novels, certainly his most amusing. It is something like *The Gilded Age* by Mark Twain and Charles Dudley Warner, which was published three years before it, and, like *The Gilded Age*, it is in some way not really good literature. It seems hard to get a first-rate novel out of political corruption alone — I cannot think of a single example. Henry James, in reviewing the book, concluded with the following observation: "Whether accidentally or intentionally we hardly know, *Honest John Vane* exhales a penetrating aroma of what in plain English one must call vulgarity. Every note the author strikes reverberates with a peculiarly vulgar tone; vulgarity pervades the suggestions, the atmosphere of his volume." I am not, however, sure that, in the case of such a book as this, such a criticism as James's is valid. Good novels have been made out of vulgar materials: those of Sinclair Lewis, for example. And the kind of thing that De Forest is doing here is an anticipation of Lewis. The complaint should be rather that De Forest is not enough of an imaginative artist to exploit the possibilities of his vulgar material. His characters are caricatured but not by a caricaturist. On the other hand, he will not allow them to possess any real human interest. We may identify ourselves with Vane when he stands up to his first temptation and will not yield to the demands of his wife, but when he has run himself into debt and is well on the road to damnation, his creator will not even let us pity him; calls him "simian" and says with contempt that he "comes of a low genus." But the voice of the old theology is made to sound, nevertheless, in this simian world. The lobbyist Darius Dorman, who is Vane's original tempter — with his

smirched and scorched appearance, as if permeated with
soot and cinders, "his haggard, ghastly features, his lean,
griping claws" — is soon recognized as the Devil in
person. Mysterious chucklings are heard when he has
finally bought up John Vane's soul, and at the end he
announces simply — his mission presumably accomplished
— that he is now "going back." The book concludes like
a pamphlet: "Such men as John Vane will inevitably
find their way in numbers to the desks of the Capitol.
Better and wiser men than he will be corrupted by a
lobby which has thoroughly learned the easy trick of
paying a hundred thousand out of every stolen million.
Nothing in the future is more certain than that, if this
huge 'special legislation' machine for bribery is not
broken up, our Congress will surely and quickly become
what some sad souls claim it already is, a den of thieves."

The second of these Washington novels, which carries along some of the figures of the first, presents a
feminine scoundrel, a kind of counterpart to Honest
John Vane. Josie Murray, a pretty young widow, comes
to Washington to press a claim. The payment out of
government funds of huge sums for fraudulent claims
was, it seems, one of the features of the Grant administrations; and Josie Murray has discovered that a barn
which belonged to her husband's family was burned
down by American troops in the War of 1812. Although
claims for destruction in war were not supposed to be
honored, and though two thousand dollars had already
been paid on a previous application, she succeeds, by the
end of the story, in obtaining a further hundred thousand. This has involved her becoming engaged to two
politicians at once, both of whom she throws over when
they have served their turn, and resorting to a professional lobbyist, whom she sends away with ladylike
indignation when he comes to claim the cut she has

promised him. In the meantime, she has been sponging
on and scandalizing an uncle and aunt of her husband's,
a pious old couple who become so upset by the incubus
that has settled upon them and is dishonoring the family
name, that she reduces them to prostration and hastens
their deaths.

This is the story of *Playing the Mischief*, and it might
have been telling if De Forest had done it on the
moderate scale of *Honest John Vane*; but, with his lack
of the artist's instinct, he stretches it out till — creating
no suspense: it is simply a long string of intrigues — it
becomes insupportably tedious. Josie Murray is of interest as a prototype of the voracious and unscrupulous
American siren who was later to be satirized with brilliance — after many intermediate appearances — in Anita
Loos's *Gentlemen Prefer Blondes*. But Josie Murray, unlike Lorelei Lee, is always well-mannered and decorous
as well as seductive and clever. De Forest understands
her well, and he is psychologically, I think, at his best
when he is showing how a certain admiration for an
attractive young man whom Josie cannot use, and the
physical distaste she feels for the men that she finds she
can, somewhat complicate her inner life but fail to de-
flect her from her purpose.

De Forest, at the end of the story, is visited by one of
those dramatic inspirations which he never quite knows
how to handle. Josie Murray, having plundered the
public funds and having kicked her helpers downstairs,
is for the first time invited to dinner at the house of the
banker Allchin who has been hovering in the background of her operations. This signalizes Josie's admission to the society of a more important set than that
which she has hitherto known. These are the big railroad magnates and financiers, with the brokers and
lawyers who serve them, beside whom the lobbyists and

Congressmen are actually very small fry. There is also the Queen of the Claimants, a great personage quite out of Josie's class: "a superb woman of thirty-five," who is supposed to have nineteen million in gold due her and who is borrowing money from the financiers at 100 per cent interest. They are all there in the house of the banker, ready to welcome Josie, and Josie is immensely delighted to find herself received among them. But what Josie has failed to grasp is that these predators are waiting to eat her up. An excellent idea, but it ought to have been staged, and De Forest does not know how to stage it. He tells you who the people are, but, except for a few quite perfunctory strokes, he does not really show them to us. We ought to see them, we ought to hear what they say, we ought to hear what Josie says. How Edith Wharton would have done it! One remembers a scene somewhat similar at the end of *The Custom of the Country,* which dramatizes the culminating phase of the career of the beautiful Undine Spragg, a greedy and destructive heroine in Josie Murray's tradition.

The story of Josie was followed — in 1879 — by *Irene the Missionary.* Here De Forest returns to Syria, and he is now — with the free hand of fiction — able to make the Middle East more interesting than he was in *Oriental Acquaintance.* This is, in fact, one of the most readable of De Forest's novels. His account of the Americans in Syria — the consulate, the mission, the tourists — brings to light an odd corner of our history, and it is presented, as must have been uncommon, quite without any pious idealism, as the element of exotic adventure is, for its period, treated quite unromantically. The Sinclair Lewis-ish characters are better done: the consul from the American West who knows nothing whatever about Syria and makes no effort to try to learn, the visitors from Vermont who have been to Jerusalem but were much disappointed in it: "We are on the way back to Vermont, you see," the lady explains to the mission residents; "and you won't wonder when you go to Jerusalem yourselves, for it's out of the question to lead a spiritual life where there are so many insects of one kind and another, and, as Mr. Brann says, no man can look up to God in a right spirit when he's bitten from head to foot."

The thoroughbred hero from Albany is allowed by De Forest to be seriously tempted by a Syrian girl who falls at his feet, and his lack of religious faith has made him unacceptable to Irene, who has come to the Middle East with the intention of becoming a missionary. "I do believe that woman isn't quite right in the head," says Irene of another American. "She is a millenarian now." "Oh, very likely," answers the sophisticated De Vries. "It's quite common for old belles to turn religionists." "The student of the Scriptures," says the author, "looked at the student of Balzac with an expression of trouble amounting to pain." But De Forest now falls back on the familiar device — which had been ridiculed by the plot-scorning Howells — of having De Vries win the heart of Irene by rescuing her from grave danger at the hands of natives, and, in spite of his unbelief, she renounces her mission and marries him. (The attitude of De Forest toward De Vries may be contrasted with his attitude toward Somerville, the sophisticated villain of *Seacliff*, who is treated with an honest manly scorn, not untinctured, however, with admiration. The creator of Fitz Hugh and Colburne, the good quiet plain young men of his earlier novels, now identifies himself with Hubertsen De Vries — like Somerville, a skeptical man of the world, whose aplomb, like his, is always perfect but whose decency is also impeccable. For De Forest, as had already been apparent from the doubts expressed in *Honest John Vane,* the stock of democracy is going down.)

Three later novels of De Forest's are, however, of little interest. *Overland* (1871) is a story of Western adventure — covered wagons, Apaches, etc. — which is supposed to take place in the middle eighteen-fifties. It was one of the first pieces of fiction that exploited the Far West, but De Forest had never been there and relied on such documentation as he could find in the Yale University Library and that of his father-in-law, who had been interested in the Southwest from a geological point of view. The story has a scaffolding of conventional melodrama, as has also *The Wetherel Affair* of 1873, the old-fashioned setting of which is similar to that of *Seacliff* — a Victorian house on Long Island Sound. It is touching, but also exasperating, to find De Forest writing to Howells, apropos of a newspaper article in which it has been said that the former has been "doing good work 'almost unnoticed,' " that if Howells thinks well of the idea, he "will try [in his fiction] to put in more stimulus, or that failing, to be much briefer. Perhaps, however," he adds, "the coming volume publication of *Overland* will help." *Justine's Lovers* (1897), which begins in New York City, returns soon to the Washington setting of *Playing the Mischief* and *Honest John Vane,* and to some extent continues their satire. Here "the girl" is made to tell her own story, and the result, although truthful no doubt as a record of the hardships and coldness encountered by a once-rich young lady who has suddenly lost her money at a time when the great new fortunes were determining social status, may well have been found forbidding by an audience that subsisted on sentiment. Five years after the book's publication, the publishers still had sixteen hundred copies unsold.

It may, however, be worthwhile to do justice to its

author by rescuing from *Justine* and from *The Wetherel Affair* — both hard to get hold of nowadays and unlikely to be read in the future by anyone except literary historians — a few memorable character sketches. They are the better for being Eakins-like portraits in dark and neutral tints of the kind with which De Forest is so much more successful than with anything that demands vivid color.

Here is a description from *The Wetherel Affair* of a distinguished old Connecticut judge, as he appears to a young lady, a missionary's daughter, who has just arrived from Erzeroum:

"A circumstance . . . which added much to his air of stiffness, was a high, old-fashioned black stock, which completely hid his emaciated neck, and seemed to be the only support of his head. This head he turned rarely to right or left, frequently addressing people without looking at them, or bringing himself to face them by slowly wheeling his whole body, as if he were a battalion changing front to open fire. It was with his eyes set straight before him that he carried on a conversation with Nestoria as he escorted her into his parlor . . .

"A dictatorial soul by nature, and capable of being very grimly authoritative under a consciousness of duty, so that he was an absolute terror to all evil-doers whom circumstances placed under his thumb, he had at the same time a most mellow streak of considerate, old-fashioned courtesy in him, and knew how to be gentleness itself with the gentle.

" 'A Christian,' he was accustomed to say, 'ought to be the most perfect gentleman on earth'; and in his secret heart he could not help feeling that this rule was especially binding on Wetherels. All his ancestors, as far back as the days of the *Mayflower,* had been not only Puritans, but Puritans of good social position and of

high breeding. In spite of his earnest yearnings after a
humble spirit, he was proud of his descent from such
men; and because of this pride he considered himself
bound to emulate their graces and virtues. Furthermore,
his judicial mind, partly the gift of nature and partly
the result of a long habit of examining both sides of
weighty questions, enabled or rather forced him to be
deliberate, considerate, and delicate even in matters
which concerned his strong prejudices. . . .

"At half-past six in the morning, as virtuously brisk
and punctual as the early bird that catches the worm, a
servant maid skipped through the house, and, applying
her knuckles to every bedroom door, pecked up the
slumberer within. If Alice or her mother — both dilatory
persons, and occasionally averse to duties — proffered any
remonstrance against this clamor, this maid, by the
Judge's express orders, put her mouth to the keyhole
and said in a monotonous, official tone, 'Go to the ant,
thou sluggard; consider her ways and be wise.'

"An hour later, precisely at half-past seven, the old
gentleman entered his parlor, marched with the deliberation and gravity of a procession up to a large Bible which
occupied a table by itself, took it deferentially in his
meagre arms, seated himself, opened the book upon his
knees, wiped his spectacles, and rang a little bell. This
bell, by the way, was of bronze; and when Alice once
substituted for it a silver one which she had bought with
her own money, her grave relative put it aside and
called for the plainer instrument; at the same time remarking, with his characteristic solemn humor, that
silver was a noble metal and worthy of the New Jerusalem, but brass was good enough to call sinners together.

"It was expected that at the sound of this bell all the
family, including the domestics, should appear immediately. If one lingered, that one was sent for; but mean-

while the Judge showed no annoyance or even impatience; he waited in solemn silence and with an air of abstracted meditation; his sunken, glassy eyes were never lifted from the sacred page. On the advent of the loiterer he invariably said, 'The king's business requires haste,' and then proceeded with his service. . . .

"He then read, very slowly, the eleventh chapter of Hebrews, pausing occasionally to utter brief comments, some of the ordinary type of Biblical exegesis, and others of an originality which bordered on humor. But whatever his thoughts might have been, his countenance remained grave; not even a comic incident could ruffle the icy surface of its solemnity. After he had read of the faith of Abraham, Isaac, and Jacob, etc., he paused over the inquiry, 'And what shall I more say?' Here the elderly cook, who took it that this was a question of Judge Wetherel's own asking, and that he was hard bested to answer it, came to his relief.

" 'Say?' she repeated in a prompt, confident treble; 'why, say they were good men and ought to go to heaven.'

" 'Sarah,' tranquilly remarked the old man, 'there is a wisdom which is profitable,' and continued his reading.

"Sarah, obtusely conscious of approval, glanced cheerfully at her juniors in domestic travail, and then, curbing her spiritual pride, bent her loose eyes upon the floor. A sparkle of amusement danced under Mrs. Dinneford's lashes, and the rattle-headed Alice barely prevented a smile. Nestoria, educated in habits of the profoundest respect for devotional matters, exhibited not the slightest change of countenance. Nor was she at all diverted when a sportive kitten mounted the Judge's back while he was on his knees, and played with the silver locks which hung over his high coat collar. The old gentleman, too, was equally indifferent to the feline disturbance; he touched upon all his customary 'topics' with his customary deliberation.

"At last the service ended; the Judge rose with effort to his feet; and now he allowed himself to salute his guest."

And here, from *Justine's Lovers*, is the mother of Justine's New York fiancé — a highly successful young lawyer, who will drop her when she loses her money. It is the girl who is telling the story:

"With Mrs. Starkenburgh I was delighted at the first glance, she was so obviously the mother of her magnificent son. She was a very tall lady, with just Henry's imposing carriage, his dark complexion and impressive eyes, too, and a deep contralto voice which seemed the echo of his noble bass. When she rose and advanced to greet us, there was such a dignity in her gait, notwithstanding a noticeable limp, that I was reminded of the Venus de Milo.

"But her conversation was something in the way of a disappointment. It had not a sparkle of her husband's wit, nor the glow of his sympathy and geniality. Of course she said some kind things to me; it would have been brutal to omit them: no woman could have done it, I suppose. But she did not put me entirely at ease, nor adopt me at once into the family, as Mr. Starkenburgh had done.

" 'I do not wonder in the least, now that I have the pleasure of seeing you, at the fact that Henry found his fate in Boston,' were her very first words to me, pronounced in the tone of a professor of rhetoric.

"I would not look at mamma, although I knew that she gave me a glance. It was so like the letter of invitation, and so like Henry's own oratory and music! No wonder that Mr. Starkenburgh, senior, had been interested in Galton's *Hereditary Descent of Genius*. I had to drive away a feeling that the resemblance between mother and son was little less than comical; and I also had to struggle with another and much uglier idea which just then broke in upon my sensitiveness. It occurred to me, for the first time, that there was some egoism, some lack of sympathy with others, inside of this careful diction and elaborate intonation. These suspicions I fought with like a tiger, while doing my best to be sweet and interesting.

" 'You are too flattering, Mrs. Starkenburgh,' I stammered. 'I hope, however, that I shall make you like me as much as I should wish and do wish.'

" 'I make no question of it,' she replied, in a voice that would have fitted a Lady Macbeth. 'My husband and my son have both prepared me to believe that there is no alternative for me but to like you extremely.'

" 'The preparation was a pity,' observed mamma. 'Perhaps your expectations have been raised too high.'

" 'I am accustomed to rely implicitly upon the judgement of my son,' intoned Mrs. Starkenburgh.

" 'I think I should rely on your husband's also,' I said.

"Mrs. Starkenburgh made no reply.

" 'Your son has the good-fortune to have inherited a vast deal of talent, and he has improved it to great advantage,' ventured mamma.

" 'He is a true Dickerman,' answered Mrs. Starkenburgh, referring of course to her own family. 'He is a Dickerman in body and in spirit.'

" 'We are all more or less a reproduction of our ancestors,' observed mamma, plagiarizing from Mr. Starkenburgh, senior.

"It was amazing how stilted we had become. Moreover, mamma and I were talking contralto, in unconscious, helpless imitation of our hostess. We both had soprano voices, and yet there we were orating contralto, just as deep as we could draw it. It is wonderful what an influence, what an imperative magnetism, there is in an unusual physical gift. I suspect, for instance, that a little man rarely converses with a tall one without standing an inch higher on his toes than usual.

"By-the-way, also, these dazzling peculiarities are not always good for manners, or even for character. A person who possesses an unusually powerful and musical voice is generally addicted to running it up and down the scale and dinning the company with it, as if it were an ophicleide. In the course of time I came to admit that Henry had this habit. I would have said *defect*, only that it did not seem to make him the less agreeable, that is, to people in general. Almost everybody listened to him with pleasure, even if he were obviously in the wrong, so delightful was that *basso profondo*.

"But I am forgetting Mrs. Starkenburgh. She soon dropped me as a subject, and commenced on her ailments. I never heard from any other person such a long and detailed statement of symptoms, delivered, too, in tones that never forgot themselves, and in what Blair calls 'full periods.' How flat and yet how sensible mamma seemed when she at last replied with that wretched commonplace, 'You have been a great sufferer!'

" 'I am gratified with your sympathy,' tromboned Mrs. Starkenburgh. 'It is the sweetest boon which can be offered to stricken humanity. What a woman needs, and almost all that a woman needs, is sympathy.'

" 'Some bread-and-butter,' smiled mamma, half scared at her own boldness.

"Mrs. Starkenburgh took no notice of the suggestion.

" 'I get so little of it, except from my son,' she continued, evidently referring to sympathy, and not to bread-and-butter, which she probably got from her husband. 'Mr. Starkenburgh lacks that chord — the mightiest of all. He is a genial, light-hearted, jocose person, very different indeed from the Dickermans. We think ourselves a remarkable family, Mrs. Vane. I wish much that you could have known my father. I will venture to say that no other man of his generation was his superior, if even his equal. He was the very embodiment of Dickerman character and manner. I never knew him to speak but with such an air that any one who did not hear what he said would have supposed that he was deciding the interests of the nation. Ah, he was a terrible loss to me, and to Goshen County, and to the world. But you shall see my brother, Mrs. Vane; you shall not leave New York without that pleasure. He is his father over again. The republic doesn't at all know what a son it has in him, or he would be filling its highest offices and transacting its mightiest affairs. It is dreadful — is it not? to think that such men must some day be taken from a land which so needs them? My brother is poorly at present, and seldom leaves his house. Whenever he does take that risk, I tremble for the consequences.'

" 'Your son is growing up to fill his place,' said mamma, without in the least knowing what that place might be. 'I should judge that he inherits the talent of his race.'

" 'Yes, Henry is a Dickerman to the backbone,' replied Mrs. Starkenburgh, with a really angelic smile of satisfaction. 'Not a fibre of his father is there in him. He is of *our* family. So serious, so reserved, so resolute, so ambitious! I must be allowed, my dear Miss Vane, to congratulate you on your prospects. You may laugh at me, if you will; you may call it a mother's vanity, if you will; but I trust that time will see Henry in lofty and potent places. I do not despair of seeing him all that he aspires to be; I am not afraid to say chief-justice, or even president. There! I have made my prediction, absurd though it may seem. Time will pass judgement upon it.'

"Now, I agreed with her as to Henry; at least, I thoroughly believed that he would win wealth and fame. I did not see how, with his talents and industry, he could fail of it. Had I been alone with this doting mother, I could have listened gladly to her hymn of praise, and joined heartily in the chorus. But there was mamma, who was neither Henry's parent nor his sweetheart, and who, as I knew, had a wicked tendency to satire. The interview began to be just a little bit dreadful. So I stirred in my chair and said,

" 'Perhaps we are tiring you, Mrs. Starkenburgh.'

" 'Not in the least, my dear,' she replied energetically, looking quite annoyed at the suggestion of departure. 'If it were not for my lameness, I should be capable of any exertion, and never know the sensation of lassitude. I despise idleness and adore labor, and hate the very word "tired." You do not as yet know me, nor the Dickerman nature. By-the-way, I must show you the family portraits. It is one method of making our acquaintance.'

"She touched a bell, and a maid appeared.

" 'Jane,' said Mrs. Starkenburgh, 'prepare the library for an exhibition of the family portraits.'

"If she had been announcing the opening of a parliament, she could not have had a grander air or a more sonorous utterance.

"Presently Jane returned from her errand, and showed us meekly into the library. It was a large, fine room, richly carved in oak and black-walnut, with a thousand or two of books, scores of bronze gimcracks, and four full-length portraits. The blinds were tightly closed, and we could see nothing plainly.

" 'Take seats, ladies,' said Mrs. Starkenburgh. 'No, not there; pray excuse me. You will not obtain the correct angle of vision. May I beg you to go into that farther corner and occupy those two ottomans? They are consecrated to this purpose.'

"So we went submissively and sat down in the corner, like little girls playing school under the orders of a big one. I could see that mamma was biting her lips, and I gave her a really savage shake of the head. Mrs. Starkenburgh placed herself in a huge arm-chair, with her back toward us, and said, in a truly startling voice, 'Jane, bring the pictures into exhibition.'

"The girl took something out of a closet, and then closed the door of the library, leaving us in total darkness. It was perfectly incomprehensible; I couldn't imagine what would come next. Mamma, too, was rustling and shaking by my side as though she would burst out in a giggle.

"I was just wondering whether New-Yorkers generally showed their picture-galleries in this way when a vivid stream of light shot through the gloom. It was so sudden and supernatural that I uttered an exclamation. Then I dimly perceived Jane seated upon the floor and holding a dark lantern, out of which a long red cataract flamed over portrait number one.

"The effect was so unexpected and striking that it put me in mind of the stories about spiritualistic manifestations. The painting came out with furious distinctness and energy, as though it had made up its mind never to go in again. We beheld a tall, stout, dark, clean-shaven, gray-haired gentleman of perhaps seventy, standing at his full height on a green carpet, with rows on rows of law-books for a background.

" 'That,' said Mrs. Starkenburgh, in a sepulchral tone, 'is my honored and lamented father, Judge Henry Peters Dickerman. Do you retain your positions, ladies? If you will have the kindness to retain your positions, and to pass your eyes slowly from the feet of the figure up to the reverend gray hair, you will gradually discover a wonderfully life-like portrait, and will, as it were, see my father in the flesh.'

"We did as we were told; at all events, I suppose so. I could not see mamma, and, in fact, did not want to. In solemn silence we looked successively at the feet, the pantaloons, the vest, the face, the gray hair, and said, 'Wonderful!'

" 'Is it not?' reverberated Mrs. Starkenburgh. 'Jane!'

"Jane turned the red cataract on picture number two, beginning as before at the bottom.

" 'That,' said Mrs. Starkenburgh, 'is my brother, William Peters Dickerman, Esquire. Do you retain your positions, ladies? If you will have the kindness to retain your positions, and to pass your eyes deliberately from the feet of the figure up to the forehead, you will see my brother as he is, and as I trust you will shortly behold him. The accuracy of the likeness you may readily infer from its wonderful family similarity to the portrait of my father. Do you see it, ladies?'

" 'Wonderful!' we both murmured.

"Mamma found voice and steadiness of nerve enough to add, 'There is no doubt but he is a Dickerman.'

" 'Is he not?' replied Mrs. Starkenburgh. 'Jane!'

"The girl turned the light on picture number three. By this time the exhibition had become very trying to me. Mamma, although struggling not to laugh, was shaking hysterically, and I felt that, if I did not get away from her, I should catch the infection.

" 'Do excuse me if I change my place,' I said. 'It seems to me that I shall see better if I come nearer.'

" 'My dear child, you are mistaken,' cried Mrs. Starkenburgh. 'I beg you to pardon me for insisting that you are mistaken. Many experiments have convinced me that that corner is the only position from whence the portraits can be inspected to advantage. Oblige me by resuming your seat.'

"I was already back on my ottoman, dreadfully scared

and humbled, like a child who has been set down hard.

" 'That,' continued Mrs. Starkenburgh, 'is myself. Will you have the kindness to pass your eyes steadily upward as before, and then say whether the likeness is tolerable.'

"It was a good portrait; considerably flattered, to be sure; but all the more fervently we said, 'Wonderful! perfect!'

"Then came the turn of the fourth painting; and we saw a fearfully illuminated Henry.

" 'I will not go through the farce of telling Miss Vane who that is,' intoned Mrs. Starkenburgh. 'Undoubtedly she knows.'

"Of course I knew, but of course I could say nothing about it, except that one stupid word, 'Wonderful!'

" 'Not yet,' interrupted Mrs. Starkenburgh. 'You have not had time to pass your eyes upward from the feet of the figure. You must do that before you are qualified to judge of the merit of the portrait. Now, have you done it?'

" 'Yes,' I whispered, miserably subdued by all this governing and tutoring. I could have worshipped the picture, if she would have let me alone. It was a noble portrait; it showed all the young man's grandeur of height and carriage and countenance; it made me remember vividly that I adored him. Even mamma was quiet here, perhaps guessing my feelings. Then Mrs. Starkenburgh half spoiled everything by saying, 'Is he not a true Dickerman?'

"We made our proper response of 'Oh, wonderfully so!' Then mamma, in a tone very near to sharpness, added, 'But where is Mr. Starkenburgh?'

" 'In the garret,' answered Mrs. S., with sternness. 'We can obtain no satisfactory presentation of him. Mr. Starkenburgh is not laborious; he has not the patience to be a good sitter. Moreover, his irregularity of feature unfits him for portraiture. I at last decided that I would have no likeness of him about, rather than endure the presence of a poor one.' "

The men of the Dickerman family have had actually, as the visitors eventually discover, entirely mediocre careers. Mrs. Starkenburgh's "honored and lamented" father had never risen beyond the dignity of a probate judge. The only Dickerman who has really been successful is a business man who has made a fortune. When Justine comes eventually to meet him, she discovers that this brother of Mrs. Starkenburgh is "the corpulent and fat-witted member of the family. He was a heavier man in body and soul by a hundred pounds or so than his portrait made him out to be. If he was really the image of his father, as his sister constantly averred, the departed judge must have made the bench creak smartly. To my surprise I found that he was a retired dry-goods merchant, and had never done anything more conspicuous than standing behind a counter, except that he had once served some village as justice of the peace. But he was very rich; had gone out of business years ago; owned a handsome house in Fifth Avenue.

" 'There has always been a moneyman in the Dickerman family,' Mrs. Starkenburgh explained to me. 'William felt it to be his duty to amass a fortune for the benefit of the rest of the blood. And he did it so easily! It was a mere by-play to him. If he had turned his talents toward any other career, no matter how lofty and difficult, he would have succeeded equally. He has the most wonderful knowledge of finance and the tariff! If he were Secretary of the Treasury, the administration would indeed have a policy, instead of getting on from hand to mouth like a hard-up grocer, as William pithily expresses it.' "

To a reader whose memory extends to the threshold

of the present century, both these figures from the sub-
fusc nineteenth, Judge Wetherel and Mrs. Starkenburgh,
will be recognizable and dismally amusing; but De
Forest, as is usual with him, does not know, after these
first introductions, how to create real roles for his actors.
Old Wetherel, for the sake of the plot, must immediately
be made the victim of a murder, and the novel becomes
one of those tiresome affairs that depend on mistaken
identity — those implausible two men who look exactly
alike — with the secret quite plain to the reader from the
moment the murder occurs. One finds also in *The Wetherel Affair* another character who might have had possibilities — a devoted disciple of Emerson, who pretends,
through a touselled robustiousness and an urban adoration of Nature, to live up to the ideal of the Master; but
he becomes one of the very worst examples of the labored
and monotonous puppetry that almost always results
from De Forest's attempts to contribute to the comedy
of "humours." He would have done better to stick to
Stendhal rather than follow Dickens. Even the more
successful Mrs. Starkenburgh — whom Dickens would
have known how to develop, always varying her remarks
in connection with the portraits instead of making them
all the same and having her turn up again to utter even
more fantastic absurdities — is allowed, after this first
appearance, almost entirely to drop out of the story.

De Forest made an effort at sixty — like Cable in his
final years — to take some cognizance of the new situations that were presenting themselves in America. "I have
written," he announced to Howells in a letter of June
24, 1886, "a novel called *A Daughter of Toil*, sketching
the struggle of a city working girl for life and respectability, and dealing rather freely with such subjects as
rate of wages, cost of living, details of labor, humble

lodgings, etc." But this novel was never published, and the manuscript has disappeared. He brought out through a New Haven printer — no doubt at his own expense — two volumes of verse: *The Downing Legends* (1901) and *Medley and Palestina* (1902). The second of these has already been mentioned in the section on the poetry of the Civil War; but it should also be noted here that one of these poems has a special personal interest. The ferocity in De Forest's novels is always kept so firmly under the gelid surface, the wildness of diabolical visions so rationalistically or satirically held off at arm's-length, that we are never allowed any glimpse of the sources from which these arise. But there is a poem which does give some suggestion. In the piece called *The Dark Comrade,* he tells us that he has walked with a "Shadow of Madness," "a mournful fiend" who was "the friend of my bosom" and for whom he now sometimes longs, "though seraphim beckon and chide." *The Downing Legends* is full of these fiends. This strange work is a characteristically ambitious and characteristically labored epic which De Forest tries, rather pathetically, to commend to the indifferent public by explaining to the reader that its cantos should be regarded as "rhymed 'magazine stories' " — a description which could hardly be further from the truth. He has invented here an American folk hero, the Yankee superman Adam Downing, who is supposed, he explains, to embody "American 'manifest destiny' in a whimsical guise":

> "A demiurge, a type, a fate,
> Percursor of a coming nation,
> His heart was pure, his aim was straight,
> His sabre-stroke, predestination."

This hero takes on in titanic struggles all the enemies of the early Americans: the Indians, the Satan of the Salem witches, the Tories and their Hessian mercenaries.

But De Forest now sees in the attitude of the Yankees toward the Indians and the witches a relationship more complex than he had when he had originally studied these matters. In both cases, a beautiful woman lures the Yankee into their alien realms — in the case of the witches, a demon sylph who represents the glamor of the pagan world locked out by Puritanism; in the case of the Indians, a solitary maiden in a "wizard-built canoe," who draws Downing ever on to the wonders of the West: Niagara, the Mississippi, the "Painted Land" and the petrified forest. A youthful New England parson who has danced in the woods with the *diablesse* is last seen by Downing united with her and "hurried swift as lightning," on account of their sin, "through a fiery rift of Eblis," while, on the contrary, to Downing's sympathetic daughter it seems that, "winged with love" and "on beaming clouds," they are floating "to meet the dawn." The Indian girl, at last overtaken and dragged by Downing into his own canoe, turns pale and quickly expires, but not before she has poured out a "death-song," in which she tells how her people have had their revenge on the whites by "filling New England earth with graves," and declares that she would rather die free than live as a slave to Downing or even than be "honored in his power." Downing "raised his hand to stay / A tear from sliding down his cheek"; "He felt like one who journeys slow / In some funereal train of woe, / And cannot find a bitter word, / Although the corpse to be interred / Was once his hated, harmful foe." In the case of the English Tories, the attraction is the other way: an aristocratic young officer of the redcoats falls in love with Downing's daughter Esther:

> So presently this English earl
> Began to love our Yankee girl,
> And strove with every tender art

To reach the heaven within her heart . . .
    But how could Esther think of love?
Her mind was drawn to things above;
Her heart was otherworldly pure.
She knew no girlish guess or lure;
And when she lifted up her eyes
Of azure light to azure skies
She purposed not to dazzle men,
Nor guessed that she was comely then;
She only lifted them to pray
That worldly thoughts might pass away.

The young earl rescues Esther from the Indians, but is himself picked off by a Yankee sniper. Esther never knows of his love, but her father does and weeps when the young man dies.

De Forest is not much of a poet — as will have been gathered from the above quotations — when he is writing in the conventional romantic language; but he becomes somewhat better when, following Lowell, he is making Downing tell his story in his own New England dialect. Here is Downing's encounter with a mammoth:

"The monster give me lots of trouble,"
Says Downing in his pictured page;
"He allays charged upon the double,
In spite of his unusyal age.
I had to skip like forty crickets
To dodge his vicious pokes an' hits;
For, as to skulkin' 'mongst the thickets,
He'd ripped a wilderness to bits.

"He charged an' charged an' kep' a-chargin',
As full of friskiness as spunk,
An' onst there warn't a finger's margin
Betwixt my bacon an' his trunk.
I used the powwow's bow an' arrer,

Bewitched to kill at every lick;
An' every time he passed, I'd harrer
His highness with a whizzin' stick.
But, all the same, the pesky creetur
Would face about an' buck agin,
Nor didn't show in limb or feetur
The slightest sign of givin' in.
I had an awful lengthy battle
Afore I fetched a drop of blood,
An' want no more to do with cattle
Who orter drowned in Noah's flood.

   "At last I sorter recollected,
While restin' on my twentieth pull,
How finely mammoths are purtected
By that tremenjous clip of wool.
So when the obstinate old bison
Discharged another cannon-roar,
I sent a yard of powwow-pizen
Full-chisel down his yawnin' bore.
The venom took like scarlet fever;
He stopped his rush an' stood aghast,
An' presently begun to weever
An' tremble like a fallin' mast.
His awful sasser-eyes were glassy,
His tongue was furred, his trotters sagged;
Then down he slammed! good lordamassy!
The biggest game I ever bagged!"

De Forest had hoped to be able to see an edition of
his collected works, to leave, as he said, "a small monument" for himself, and he revised them with this in
view; but he was unable to persuade any publisher to
bring out such an edition, and the texts he prepared —
with the exception of the two novels that have been
reprinted — lie uncirculated in the Yale University Li-

brary. He wrote only one more novel – in 1898: *A Lover's Revolt*. The tide of historical romances which was to threaten to swamp the nineteen-hundreds had already by that time risen high, and De Forest evidently hoped to take advantage of this by writing a story of the Revolution. It appears from a letter to Howells that he thought it had a chance of success. But De Forest was entirely incapable of concocting the kind of novel that would have been popular in that second-rate era.

A Lover's Revolt is historical, and exceptionally so in the author's striving for accuracy, but it is not romantic at all. This book, rather unexpectedly, is a return to the historical realism of De Forest's earliest novel *Witching Times,* and it is curious that the first and the last of his novels, the least read of all his little-read fictions, should today have come to seem among the most interesting. He was undoubtedly more at home in New England, where these first and last stories are made to take place, than in either the South or Washington, with both of which he was unsympathetic, or in the West, which he did not even know at firsthand; and the old soldier of New Orleans and Cedar Creek has reverted to the asperities of wartime, the barbarities of the battlefield, in an attempt to dispel the revolutionary legend and to try to see how Concord and Lexington, Bunker Hill and Dorchester Heights, must really have looked and felt in the acting, before the legend had begun to transform them. What, for example, were the actual relations between, on the one hand, the rebelling veterans of the French and Indian wars in combination with the raw unruly farmers whom they led and, on the other hand, the loyalist shopkeepers, who still adored everything from England, and the exiled British officers and their hired troops? What was their fighting like in those battles, which were mainly improvisations, between such incongruous opponents, in which the uniformed troops of Europe, drawn up in regular formation, advanced upon ambushed natives who had learned their tactics from the Indians and who could not afford to waste a shot. And how did the colonials live and talk? De Forest returns here to the practice he had adopted in his Salem novel of reproducing the differences of class in manners and language and accent — aristocratic, middle class, cockney and Scottish — by which these transplanted Britishers must still have reflected the society at home, as well as the new variations which had developed in the new environment. And how did the women behave? The title of the novel, *A Lover's Revolt,* is misleading in the sense that the lovers of the story are by no means the main source of interest; they become, in fact — and not tragically — non-lovers. Here De Forest, who has evidently become bored with "the girl," allows her to go plumb to blazes. She jilts her young patriot admirer of years for an arrogant red-faced English captain, who is known to have noble connections and of whom she becomes enamored for reasons that are purely snobbish. She hopes he will marry her and take her away, but the Captain only hopes to seduce her. Nor does Huldah ever recognize her error and return to her fighting American. He himself has come to despise her and has put her out of his mind. She has a breakdown when the Captain drops her; and when he gets himself sent back to England, she goes completely insane — tries to smuggle herself aboard his ship and, failing in this, wanders through the countryside, inquiring for his whereabouts. At one point, she looks on at a gruesome scene: a loyalist uncle of hers is being tarred and feathered by the patriots (there is no real bias of partisanship in De Forest's approach to the Revolution: the brutalities of neither side are spared); but, not recognizing him, she only shrieks with laughter. She now finds an old canoe that has been left on the beach of an inlet, and, still pursuing her lover, she paddles it off with her hands. She is later found dead on the shore. Huldah's family, divided in their loyalties, are by this time in such consternation under a heavy bombardment by the British that the news of their daughter's death only adds to the general confusion.

A Lover's Revolt, without doubt, is De Forest's most genuinely searching novel. Going back into the Revolution, he evidently feels freer, dares go further, than with the people and events of his own period — his Washington lobbyists and politicians are mostly two-dimensional demons. He enjoys trying to visualize — which he can do without offense to anyone except idealizers of the Revolution — exactly what was happening in America at the end of the eighteenth century, and he can bring to the Revolution the insights he has learned from the Civil War. He knows that the rebellious patriots must have experienced, like the soldiers of the sixties, the irrational exhilaration, the irresTible momentum of war:

"He wondered," he writes of a patriot squire, "that this blood-stained dream should not be horrible to him. It was not; not even strange. All at once he was wonted, brutalized, to war. He felt as much at home in it as though he had passed his life in being shot at and in shooting others. Why had he never done it before? Merely from lack of opportunity. Apparently combat was the natural state of man, and peace an enforced episode, the result of untoward circumstances. It did not take long to become a fighter and a veteran. Of course there were disagreeable moments in battle, although at *this* moment he was ashamed to admit it. He had cringed at Lexington when the British muskets blazed, and their bullets whistled over him. But what a pleasure it had been to fire back and see one of his enemies drop!

"Why did he fight and slay? an inner self (a self of other days) kept on enquiring. Was it for God and conscience? he asked, remembering Warren's high sounding phrase. To his astonishment the words seemed to have no relation to his present feelings and conduct. Was it for revenge? He had not thought of it; all that morning he had scarcely once remembered that Englishmen were overbearing to provincials; and, if he had brooded over Huldah Oakbridge's preference for Moorcastle, it was only at intervals. Because Britons shot at him he shot at them, and was glad when they fell. Moreover (and this was another powerful motive) he was ashamed to desert his comrades, and so forfeit their respect and his own."

Another old Union soldier — Joseph Kirkland of Chicago — had published in 1891 an interesting Civil War novel called *The Captain of Company K*. Kirkland is best known for his stories, also pioneer attempts at realism, of Middle-Western rural and village life: *Zury, the Meanest Man in Spring County* and its sequel, *The Mc-Veys* — which were something of a novelty in the eighties; but he went on to apply his methods to Middle Westerners in the Civil War. Kirkland had first served as a private, then as aide-de-camp to McClellan, then as captain on the staff of Fitz-John Porter. He was much further away from his experience than De Forest had been when he wrote *Miss Ravenel,* and his picture does not have the solidity of De Forest's immediate record; but Kirkland is temperamentally rather different from De Forest and is trying to do something different. He has departed even further than his predecessor from the old conventions of writing about battle, which he parodies in an amusing passage: "Gen. Rearview, now observing a wavering on the left, led forward the brigades of the reserve, and right gallantly did they spring to the rescue. Passing through the decimated ranks of their comrades, and over the bodies of the fallen, lying so close together that it was difficult to avoid stepping on them, they soon crossed bayonets with the foe." For Kirkland is much more interested than De Forest — as Stendhal and Tolstoy had been — in the reactions of individuals.* What he shows us of the unexpected surrender of Fort Donelson and the confusions of the Battle of Shiloh are the comradeships and animosities, the blunders and fatigues and frights, the humiliations, fevers and woundings of the small group of characters he follows; and he sometimes strikes a humane and questioning note which contrasts with the passage on the compulsions of war quoted above from *A Lover's Revolt* and which is, in fact, nowhere to be found in De Forest:

"Who am I?" asks Kirkland's hero. "Am I Will Fargeon, or am I a Sabbath-breaking, tobacco-smoking, swearing, drinking, murdering ruffian? Who was it storming up and down that man's corn-field, glad to see my friends killing other people's friends? Glad Chipstone's bullet plowed through the lung of that splendid old man's splendid son! Glad my men fired low and sure while theirs fired high and wild! Glad about those corpses with flies sucking the unshed tears from their eye sockets!"

* Tourgée, in his novel *Figs and Thistles*, is somewhat less interested in personal relationships, but in his account of the Battle of Bull Run, based on his own experience, he sticks to the adventures of his hero's regiment and makes no attempt to tinge them with glory. "When the fighting ceased . . . ," he writes, "our men began to look around. Then came an overwhelming sense of isolation. Each regiment felt that it was by itself. We had not been associated in brigades, so as to know our comrades in battle. . . . nor did we know our commander. It was rumored that we were under General Hunter, but he was a myth. None of the soldiers knew him." They did not even know they were being defeated. The hero, like Tourgée, is wounded, and "through the long hours of the night, crawling, clambering, hobbling," drags himself inside the Federal lines.

And later on we have the following conversation:

"As they walked back, Chip said: 'What did the doctor say about Clint?'

" 'Very doubtful.'

" 'Which, leg or life?'

" 'Both. If the fever goes off, the leg must probably *come* off; and if they amputate the leg, he'll have a poor chance to get over it.'

" 'Great God! Is that so?'

" 'Yes. Likely that bullet has silenced Clinton Thrush's singing for good.'

" 'Curse the bullet — and the man that fired it!'

" 'And those who sent him to fire it,' added Fargeon."

One cannot but feel respect for the hard and clear mind of De Forest; and one cannot but regret that — De Forest having lost his original religious faith — it never attained to anything like a real point of view, to any sort of general philosophy of society, politics, morals. For the lack of this, De Forest's observation of the American life of his time, accurate and shrewd though it is, has less value as criticism than one feels it ought. And, on the other hand, he is hardly an artist. In spite of his Balzacian ambitions, he has not enough imaginative genius to create a world of his own. One wonders whether the background of Calvinist theology may not have had something to do with De Forest's deficiencies as a novelist. He believed, as we have seen, that an American was handicapped in writing fiction by the instability of American society. But for success in this kind of fiction one needs to have a very strong interest in the personalities of individuals, and Calvin had no interest in the individual: there were simply the Elect and the damned, and among the vital elements that Calvin squeezes out of the Gospels are the daily contacts of Jesus with a variety of individuals and the illustrative stories he tells that always hinge on particular situations. You could hardly get a Shakespeare or a Balzac or a Tolstoy or a Dostoevsky out of a mind that had been molded by this doctrine.

In the Greek and Roman Catholic Churches, the priest, in the confessional and otherwise, must always be dealing with individuals, and is himself, though accountable to God, a man of like passions with the penitents he confesses, while the typical Calvinist pastor presumably belonged to the Elect, and addressed his congregation from a pulpit that was set very high above them. The medieval world of Dante is populated by individuals who, though classified according to a system worked out by a completely non-personalized God — in close collaboration, however, with that irreducible individual Dante — are all quite distinct from one another; whereas Milton is quite incapable, in this sense, of creating an individual: his best realized character is Satan, who is an equivocal figure of Protestant theology: at once an heroic rebel against the established authority and a victim who is doomed to be expelled by it. The love of Paolo and Francesca provides a personal drama, as do the hatreds of Ugolino and his cruel Archbishop, and these dramas pose moral problems which are not entirely easy to deal with. They do not provide melodramas, but Catholicism at its least subtle may allow for a melodrama as between the Devil and God. This clear opposition between God and the Devil on the part of the Catholic Church was regarded by Calvin as a damnable lapse into the pagan doctrine of Manichæism, and he somehow makes the Devil a part of God, who has been pleased to create him and to use him. Which persons will be damned — what the Devil will do — has all been arranged beforehand, so no real confrontation of forces is possible.

The Calvinistic view of the world is thus even less stimulating to drama not merely than the Catholic one but even than that of Marxism, which also tries to ignore the individual and which in other ways it somewhat resembles but which at least involves the conflict of classes. "History," the Dialectic, is sure to win out in the end, yet an element of dramatic suspense may arise through the possibility that any particular battle may result in either triumph or defeat for the proletarian "Antithesis" of the dialectical process. But in Calvinism there is no dialectic: no conflict can exist within God, who is infinite, who includes the whole universe and who has not even the dimension of time. But since the Devil is one of His aspects, He is bound to seem double-faced. Is the "angry God" of Jonathan Edwards, in whose hands "the sinner" is writhing, a God of mercy or an unrestrained fiend? The only real dramatic subject possible is to be found in the relation of man to this God: is the Deity a friend or an enemy? what fate has He fixed for one? has one been chosen or not? Hence Dimmesdale of *The Scarlet Letter*, who has thought himself a man of God but is actually one of the damned. Hence the strange situations in Melville as to which we do not know whether the objects of pursuit are drawing the pursuers on to ecstasy or to damnation. Hence the Satan of Mark Twain's *The Mysterious Stranger*, who helps or ruins human beings in a way that is entirely capricious since he can feel for them nothing but contempt, and who keeps the young narrator to whom he has revealed his identity in a state of agonized uncertainty. Never to be sure where one stands with God makes life extremely uncomfortable, and the constant obsession with infinite power makes it difficult to be interested in one's neighbor. It is pointless, besides, in a Calvinist world, to try to put oneself in another's skin, live his life in imagination. Why should one who has been appointed a member of the "Communion of Saints" try to imagine the lives of the predestinated damned? and how are the predestinated damned to imagine the lives of the "Saints"? And if so much of the American fiction which attempted in the nineteenth century to chronicle social types or to develop picturesque characters is cold, pale and mediocre, while the few really powerful novels that have endured from the post-Calvinist period, when it had for the first time become possible for writers of Calvinist training to indulge themselves in fiction at all, are in the nature of moral fables or allegories, the chief cause is no doubt to be found in the tyranny of the Calvinist tradition.

Henry James, who was a Protestant but an Irishman, a New Yorker and not a New Englander, whose father had rejected with revulsion the stiff orthodox Calvinist doctrine of the Princeton Theological Seminary and invented for his spiritual needs his own benevolent brand of Swedenborgianism, did retain some Presbyterian traits — his plain and virtuous people are likely to triumph morally over the beautiful and worldly ones — but he did create a fictional world as De Forest was unable to do. This world takes one under its spell; one forms a taste for it, enjoys revisiting it as one could never do with that of De Forest. And it is inhabited by real individuals. Even from such a queer production as *The Awkward Age* — so abstract, so systematically contrived — one remembers the personalities quite clearly. In any case, as Howells, in his *Heroines of Fiction*, concludes in his chapter on De Forest, "Mr. De Forest's books are a part of our literary history; Mr. James's are a part of our literature."

XVI

JUSTICE OLIVER WENDELL HOLMES

WITH THE OLIVER WENDELL HOLMESES, father and son, the theology of Calvinism has faded, but its habits of mind persist. The father of Dr. Holmes was Abiel Holmes, a Connecticut preacher, who came to occupy in Cambridge, Massachusetts, the pulpit of the First Congregational Church. He had been educated at the Yale Divinity School, which at that time stood somewhat to the left of the fundamentalist Princeton Theological Seminary but still kept closer to Calvinist orthodoxy than the Harvard Divinity School, already infected in the twenties with the fashionable Unitarianism. Abiel Holmes was himself not severe in the matter of doctrine: he appears in the novels of his son in the characters of the Congregational ministers who are surreptitiously humanizing their creed. But he found himself, in his Cambridge church, between a new liberalizing party and the still powerful old orthodox Calvinists. Under pressure of an orthodox newspaper and especially, among the clergy, of Lyman Beecher, the father of Harriet Beecher Stowe, he abandoned the now common practice of exchanging Sunday pulpits with other Congregationalist ministers, regardless of their theological views. But his parish was attainted with liberalism and did not care to have Dr. Beecher, with whom Holmes had been led to exchange, assailing them from the pulpit with the menace that if they should yield to the Unitarian heresy, a "moral desolation" would "sweep over the land." Dr. Holmes in his novels made his kindly old ministers escape from the pressures of orthodoxy, but the contrary had been true in the case of his father, who barred liberal preachers from his pulpit and was forced to resign by his congregation and to set up a Second Congregational Church.

The effect of this on Abiel's son, at that time a student at Harvard, was to stir in him a strong opposition to the traditional Puritan theology, which he came to feel was wholly monstrous and a hindrance to human progress. He said that his whole conception of the place of man in the universe had been upset at some point in his childhood by seeing the planet Venus through a telescope. Through the study and practice of medicine, he tried to substitute the discipline of science for the discipline of the old morality. I have spoken of his *One-Hoss Shay* as a parable of the break-up of Calvinism; and his novels are intended to show that destructive or peculiar tendencies on the part of an individual are due not to Original Sin but to "prenatal influence" (at that time taken seriously even by the medical profession), special heredity or early trauma. The first of these novels, *Elsie Venner*, published in 1861, so outraged the Protestant clergy that one religious paper as far away as Chicago made a point of denouncing each instalment as the story came out in the *Atlantic Monthly*. Yet Holmes himself, as he tells us, was never to succeed completely in freeing himself from the Calvinist inculcations: he could never, to the end of his life, allow himself to read novels till sundown on the Sabbath, and there always went on in his mind a dialogue between the inherited doctrine and the new scientific point of view.

The young Wendell, who could start from the point to

which his father had succeeded in advancing, was not
troubled by these hauntings from the past and put the
old New England God behind him — though, as we
shall see, in his temperament and his type of mind, he
was much closer to the Puritan breed than his father.
He had read Herbert Spencer at Harvard and had incurred a rebuke from the President for answering back
a professor who was teaching a course on the Evidences
of Religion. But during his service in the Civil War, he
was subjected to a desperate ordeal, which, instead of
having the effect, as such ordeals sometimes do, of impelling him to turn to God, caused him definitely to dismiss this Deity. He had enlisted when he was only just
twenty, in April, 1861, and he had been badly wounded
in the chest at the Battle of Ball's Bluff in October. "I
thought I was a gone coon," he wrote to Frederick Pollock long afterwards, and he was actually not expected
to live. "I happened to have a bottle of laudanum in my
pocket and resolved if the anguish became unbearable
to do the needful. A doctor (I suppose) removed the
bottle and in the morning I resolved to live." But in the
meantime the crisis had occurred. Here is his own account of it, written down almost immediately afterwards, an effort at self-observation — very remarkable
on the part of so young a man — which shows his courage
and the strength of his intellect:

"Much more vivid [than his recollection of what was
actually happening] is my memory of my thoughts and
state of mind for though I may have been light-headed
my reason was working — even if through a cloud. Of
course when I thought I was dying the reflection that
the majority vote of the civilized world declared that with
my opinions I was *en route* for Hell came up with painful distinctness — Perhaps the first impulse was tremulous — but then I said — by Jove, I die like a soldier any-

how — I was shot in the breast doing my duty up to the hub — afraid? No, I am proud — then I thought I couldn't be guilty of a deathbed recantation — father and I had talked of that and were agreed that it generally meant nothing but a cowardly giving way to fear — Besides, thought I, can I recant if I want to, has the approach of death changed my beliefs much? & to this I answered — No — Then came in my Philosophy — I am to take a leap in the dark — but now as ever I believe that whatever shall happen is best — for it is in accordance with a general law — and *good* & *universal* (or *general law*) are synonymous terms in the universe — (I can now add that our phrase *good* only means certain general truths seen through the heart & will instead of being merely contemplated intellectually — I doubt if the intellect accepts or recognizes that classification of good and bad). Would the complex forces which made a still more complex unit in *Me* resolve themselves back into simpler forms or would my angel be still winging his way onward when eternities had passed? I could not tell — But all was doubtless well — and so with a 'God forgive me if I'm wrong' I slept — But while I was debating with myself Harry Sturgis bulged upon the scene — I don't remember what I said — I know what I wanted — it was the cool opinion of an outsider — a looker-on — as a *point d'appui* for resistance or a που στω from which to spring aloft, as the case might be; at any rate a foreign substance round which my thoughts could crystallize — Sturge I hear says I was very profane, to this effect — 'Well Harry I'm dying but I'll be G. d'd if I know where I'm going' — But I doubt it although a little later I swore frightfully — to the great horror of John O'S. who tried to stop me thinking I was booking myself for Hell rapidly. Sturge thereat with about his usual tact, begun 'Why — Homey — you believe in Christ, don't

you' etc. with a brief exposition of doctrine argumenta-
tively set forth — I gave him my love for Pen whom I'd
not yet seen, & the same message home which I subse-
quently gave the Fire Zouave Surgeon and Sturge departed." He had denied God and still survived, and that
was the end of God in the cosmogony of Oliver Wendell
Holmes, who was never again tempted to believe and
who lived to be over ninety.

The young Holmes's experience of the Civil War, besides settling for him the problem of faith, also cured
him, and cured him for life, of apocalyptic social illusions. Perhaps no one had enlisted at the beginning
of the war with a more devoted ardor than Holmes. "It
is almost impossible here," says Higginson in his *Cheerful Yesterdays*, "to reproduce the emotions of that period
of early war enlistments. . . . To call it a sense of
novelty was nothing; it was as if one had learned to swim
in air, and were striking out for some new planet. All
the methods, standards, habits, and aims of ordinary
life were reversed, and the intrinsic and traditional
charm of the soldier's life was mingled in my own case
with the firm faith that the death-knell of slavery itself
was being sounded." The memory of that early exaltation was to remain with Holmes all his life. He had
been almost as much carried away by the novels of
Walter Scott as any of his Southern contemporaries, and,
as late as 1911 we find him writing to the Baroness
Moncheur, wife of the Belgian ambassador: "Just now
I am having one of my periodic wallows in Scott. He also
is dear to most people, I suppose — but the old order in
which the sword and the gentleman were beliefs, is near
enough to me to make this their last voice enchanting in
spite of the common sense of commerce. The same belief
was what gave interest to the South, but they paid for it

by their ignorance of all the ideas that make life worth living to us. But when you see it in costume, with people who could not have heard of evolution, belated but in its last and therefore articulate moment, Oh what a delight it is." This spirit of romantic chivalry he brought to the Abolitionist cause, by which he afterwards said he was "moved . . . so deeply that a Negro minstrel show shocked me and the morality of *Pickwick* seemed to me painfully blunt," and he had acted as a bodyguard to Wendell Phillips when there was a threat of his being mobbed at an anti-slavery meeting. He had left college in his senior year and forfeited graduation in order at once to enlist.

He thus accepted the war as a crusade, and, even in the April of 1864, when he had been through some of the worst of the fighting, he forced himself to continue to do so. "I have long wanted to know more of Joinville's *Chronicle* than I did," he writes to Charles Eliot Norton apropos of an article of his, "but the story seems to come up most opportunely now when we need all the examples of chivalry to help us bind our rebellious desires to steadfastness in the Christian Crusade of the 19th century. If one didn't believe that this was such a crusade, in the cause of the whole civilized world, it would be hard indeed to keep the hand to the sword; and one who is rather compelled unwillingly to the work by abstract conviction than borne along on the flood of some passionate enthusiasm, must feel his ardor rekindled by stories like this."

For this cause and in this crusade, the young Oliver Wendell Holmes, as we have already seen, had faced death at the very beginning: "It is curious," he wrote in the account of his wounding from which I have already quoted, "how rapidly the mind adjusts itself under some circumstances to entirely new relations — I thought for a while that I was dying, and it seemed the most natural thing in the world – the moment the hope of life returned it seemed as abhorrent to nature as ever that I should die." He went home on leave to recover, but returned to his regiment the following March (in the second year of the war). He was wounded again at Antietam in September: the bullet went through his neck and just missed his windpipe and jugular vein. He was shipped home again for six weeks; then, in the middle of November, was ordered back. He had a moment of extreme discouragement. From Virginia, three days later, he writes: ". . . with the crack brained Dreher & obstinate ignoramus Shepherd as act'g Col & Lt. Col. the Regt is going to H — L as fast as ever it can or at least no thanks to them if it isn't – I wouldn't trust it under them for a brass tuppence in a fight – They'd send it to the devil quicker even than Gen. Sumner and I've pretty much made up my mind that the South have achieved their independence & I am almost ready to hope spring will see an end – I prefer intervention to save our credit but believe me, we never shall lick 'em. – The Army is tired with its hard [work?], and its terrible experience & still more with its mismanagement & I think before long the majority will say that we are vainly working to effect what never happens – the subjugation (for that is it) of a great civilized nation. We shan't do it – at least the Army can't –" In December he writes to his father: ". . . – I never I believe have shown, as you seemed to hint, any wavering in my belief in the right of our cause – it is my disbelief in our success by arms in wh. I differ from you . . . – I think in that matter I have better chances of judging than you – and I believe I represent the conviction of the army – & not the least of the most intelligent part of it – The successes of wh. you spoke were to be anticipated as necessary if we entered into the struggle — But I see no farther progress — I don't think either of you realize the unity or the determination of the South. I think you are hopeful because (excuse me) you are ignorant. But if it is true that we represent civilization wh. is in its nature, as well as slavery, diffusive & aggressive, and if civ. & progress are the better things why they will conquer in the long run, we may be sure, and will stand a better chance in their proper province — peace — than in war, the brother of slavery — brother — it is slavery's parent, child and sustainer at once — At any rate dear Father don't because I say these things imply or think that I am the meaner for saying them — I am, to be sure, heartily tired and half worn out body and mind by this life, but I believe I am as ready as ever to do my duty — " He had dysentery that winter and was wounded in the heel at Fredericksburg on May 1 of the following year.

The young soldier now spent ten months at home; but he returned to the army again in January, 1864. He had become a lieutenant-colonel and was made aide-de-camp to Major General Horatio Wright, who was stationed above the Rapidan. In Wright's corps there were only the remnants of Holmes's Massachusetts Twentieth Regiment. The friends with whom he had graduated from Harvard, the officers he had fought beside, were mostly dead. Some thought that he himself was not fit to serve; but he went through the terrible battles of the Wilderness: Spottsylvania, North Anna, Cold Harbor. In May, he performed an exploit of which he was rather proud. He describes it as follows in a letter to his parents: "The afternoon of the 29th I had my narrowest escape — Dispatch to carry — important — don't spare y'r horse — gallop — 1 mile — small boy (one well known as Col. Upton's scout) retreating at a run — reports fired at 2 reb. cav^y — looked round for forces — one straggler

(infty) one (unarmed) man on mule, one sick officer —
& boy — I spy 4 of our cav^y foraging dismiss former
forces & order them with me — trot — when boy was shot
at gallop — bend in road — woods cease — bang — bang —
whiz — whiz — about 20 reb^s in line — 'Halt. Surrender'
I pulled up & sung out 'friends' deceived by number
and darkness of their clothes — They keep on shooting
then I saw & put in licks for straight ahead — Anon a
fellow comes riding down the road — I think I'll gobble
him — he to me 'Halt Surrender' I see others on R. of
road — he is unslinging his carbine as I get to him, I
put my pistol to his breast & pull — enclosed cap snaps —
then I run the gauntlet — bang — whiz — Halt — Surrender lying along the neck of my horse — Got my dispatch through & return in triumph to find myself given
over for lost — " But in spite of a certain exuberance
here, we have come a long way from the boyish exhibi-
tionism of the days just before Ball's Bluff. His diaries and
letters, both, become more and more confused and dis-
jointed. The action is moving so fast that we hardly
know where we are: yells and firing, shells bursting,
brains spattering. The dead are piled in trenches at the
edge of the wood, and the trees have been shot to
splinters.

"Before you get this," he writes to his parents on May
16, 1864, "you will know how immense the butchers
bill has been — And the labor has been incessant — I
have not been & am not likely to be in the mood for writing details. I have kept brief notes in my diary wh. I
hope you may see some day — Enough, that these nearly
two weeks have contained all of fatigue & horror that
war can furnish — The advantage has been on our side
but nothing decisive has occurred & the enemy is in front
of us strongly intrenched — I doubt if the decisive battle
is to be fought between here and Richmond — nearly

every Regimental off — I knew or cared for is dead or wounded —

"I have made up my mind to stay on the staff if possible till the end of the campaign & then if I am alive, I shall resign — I have felt for sometime that I didn't any longer believe in this being a duty & so I mean to leave at the end of the campaign as I said if I'm not killed before."

He was later annoyed with his father — the natural annoyance of the man in the field with the immoderate belligerence of the people at home — for misunderstanding this letter. He had long ago, however, grown used to the slaughter. "It's odd," he had written fifteen months before, "how indifferent one gets to the sight of death — perhaps, because one gets aristocratic and don't value much a common life. Then they are apt to be so dirty it seems natural — 'Dust to Dust' — I would do anything that lay in my power but it doesn't much affect my feelings." But he has just been through much of the worst of the war. He has constantly expected to be killed, and we gather that he wrote notes to his parents before he went into battle, and no doubt, as many soldiers at Cold Harbor did, pinned them onto his clothes. He seems to have destroyed them later when he was going over these papers. But in the meantime, he writes as follows: "rec^d y'r letters of 21d 22d the latter fr. dad, stupid — I wish you'd take the trouble to read my letters before answering — I am sure I cannot have conveyed the idea, rightfully, that I intended resigning before the campaign was over (i.e. next winter just near the end of my term of service) — then I probably shall for reasons satisfactory to myself — I must say I dislike such a misunderstanding, so discreditable to my feeling of soldierly honor, when I don't believe there was a necessity for it — I shall stay on the staff and wish you'd notify the Governor to commission new field officers to the 20th I waive promotion — I am convinced from my late experience that if I can stand the wear and tear (body & mind) of regimental duty that it is a greater strain on both than I am called on to endure — If I am satisfied I don't really see that anyone else has a call to be otherwise — I talked with Hayward the mentor of the Regt & told him my views on the matter — I am not the same man (may not have quite the same ideas) & certainly am not so elastic as I was and I *will not acknowledge the same claims upon me under those circumstances* that existed formerly — a day & a half have passed since I wrote last word — it is quarter to 12 between May 31 & June 1 I have just been riding through black woods after some H^dQrs — and we are going to have another of those killing night marches as soon as we can start out of a country worse than the wilderness if possible — I have hardly known what a good night's sleep was since the campaign opened — constantly having, as tonight, to be up all night — "

"I started in this thing a boy," he later — in June — wrote his parents. "I am now a man and I have been coming to the conclusion for the last six months that my duty has changed." In July he was mustered out: his three years' enlistment was over.

The conclusions to which Holmes had been brought under pressure of his service in the Civil War were to effect in fundamental ways the whole of his subsequent thinking. But his relation to the war was peculiar. He did not like to refight its battles; he did not care to read about it. Over and over to his correspondents, he reiterates this reluctance to revert to the years of the war, making exceptions only for Lord Charnwood's *Lincoln* and for John S. Mosby's memoirs, which had been sent him by "old Mosby," as he calls him, "the famous guerilla man on the Southern side." He even extends this disinclination to Thucydides, of which, when he gets around to it at the age of eighty-three, he writes to Sir Frederick Pollock: "It isn't the kind of thing I like to read — just as I hate to read of our Civil War." Nor is he concerned with the consequences of the war. By that summer of 1864, he had had quite enough of the army and was eager to embark on a learned career. He started in at Harvard Law School that autumn and graduated in 1866. By this time Lincoln was dead, and there had died with him any possibility of a clear and decent policy toward the South. The struggle had commenced in Congress which was to culminate in the attempt on the part of the Radical Republicans to drive President Andrew Johnson from office. During the years when Holmes was first practising law in Boston and editing the *American Law Review,* the exposures of the squalid scandals of the Grant administrations were being one after another exposed in the papers. But Holmes, who was later deliberately to make a practice of not reading the newspapers, seems already to have adopted the policy of dissociating himself from current events. An account of the impeachment of Andrew Johnson confines itself, says his biographer, Mr. Mark De Wolfe Howe, to the purely legal aspects of the trial without giving any intimation of approval or disapproval. Holmes was solely intent on his own success, a success for which he was quite prepared to pay any cost in effort it demanded.

The young Holmes had brought out of the war a tough character, purposive, disciplined and not a little hard, a clearly defined personality, of which his humor and affable manners, his air of being a man of the world and the ready susceptibility to feminine attraction which he sometimes a little paraded,* could never quite embellish the bleakness. His concentration on his work, his grim industry, were astonishing to those who knew him at the time when his career was still to make. It was said of him by one friend that he knew more law than anybody else in Boston and by another that he, the friend, had "never known of anyone in the law who studied anything as hard as Wendell." He had been worried at first by a feeling that this profession was unrewarding and sterile. Like his father, he had always had a strong taste for literature and had even once thought of becoming a poet. A sonnet that he wrote in the army has a throb of the emotional power of which I have spoken above as redeeming in that period the verse of the amateur in contrast to the rhymed editorial. He was to speak of his early forebodings in regard to the career he had chosen in an address to a college audience in 1897: "There were few," he says, "of the charts and lights for which one longed when I began. One found oneself plunged in a thick fog of details — in a black and frozen night, in which were no flowers, no spring, no easy joys. Voices of authority warned that in the crush of that ice any craft might sink. One heard Burke saying that law sharpens the mind by narrowing it. One heard in Thackeray of a lawyer bending all the powers of a great mind to a mean profession. One saw that artists and poets shrank from it as from an alien world. One doubted oneself how it could be worthy of the interest of an intelligent mind. And yet one said to oneself, law is human — it is a part of man, and of one world with all the rest." And working hard and working uphill, stubborn tension of the will and the intellect, were natural, even necessary, for Holmes; they were a part of his Puritan heritage.

* "Oh, to be eighty again!" he is said to have exclaimed at ninety when passing a pretty woman on the street.

He produced his great book *The Common Law* — in 1880, when he was thirty-nine — by dint of dogged application in the evenings. "I can assure you," he wrote his friend Pollock, "it takes courage and perseverance to keep at a task which has to be performed at night and after making one's living by day." He told a friend that he hoped by this book to supersede Blackstone and Kent and that he aimed to become, first, Chief Justice of the Supreme Court of Massachusetts, then Justice of the Supreme Court of the United States.

This ambition and his relentless pursuit of it were dismaying to some of his friends. A man who knew him well, James Bradley Thayer, a partner in the law firm for which Holmes first worked, said of him that, in spite of his "attractive qualities and solid merits," he was "wanting sadly in the noblest region of human character, — selfish, vain, thoughtless of others;" and one of his ex-secretaries, not himself a New Englander, once said to me that Holmes had a streak of "the mean Yankee."

His relations with William and Henry James are, in this connection, particularly significant. Holmes and William, as young men, were extremely close. Holmes's mind was fundamentally philosophical, rather than either legal or literary, and they had discussed the great problems together; but Holmes, in his later years, when, in spite of his professions of skepticism, his negative convictions had become quite rigid, felt that James had gone rather soft, that he was giving in to religion and leaving a loophole for the supernatural. Their sympathies became more and more imperfect, and William James, in his letters to Henry, makes his own feelings almost ferociously clear: "The more I live in the world," he wrote in 1869, "the more the cold-blooded, conscious egotism and conceit of people afflict me. . . . All the noble qualities of Wendell Holmes, for instance, are poisoned by them, and friendly as I want to be towards him, as yet the good he has done me is more in presenting me something to kick away from or react against than to follow and embrace." And years later (1876), when he has been to visit the Holmeses at Mattapoisett, he writes Henry that Wendell "is a powerful battery, formed like a planing machine to gouge a deep self-beneficial groove through life; and his virtues and his faults," James adds, "were thrown into singular relief by the lonesomeness of the shore, which as it makes every object, rock or shrub, stand out so vividly, seemed also to put him and his wife under a sort of lens for you. . . ."

In the case of Henry James, I have been told on good authority that when Holmes went to see him on his visits to England, he was in the habit rather brutally of baiting him on account of his expatriation, as if he were shrinking from the dust and heat of life in his native country; and it is evident from James's correspondence with Holmes that when the former revisited the United States in 1910–11, the latter was not quite sure that the former would want to see him. The intimation of this in a letter brought out all that was most feminine in Henry James, and one is reminded of James's story *Poor Richard*, published forty-four years before, and evidently inspired by the holiday that he and Holmes and another ex-soldier had spent in North Conway, New Hampshire, with James's cousin Minnie Temple. "I ask myself frankly today, dear Wendell, — or rather, still more frankly, ask *you* — why you should 'feel a doubt' as to whether I should care to see you again and what ground I ever for a moment gave you for the supposition that the 'difference in the sphere of our dominant interests' might have made 'a gulf that we cannot cross.' As I look back at any moment of our contact — which began so long ago — I find myself crossing and crossing with a devotedness that took no smallest account of gulfs, or, more truly, hovering and circling and sitting on your side of the chasm altogether (if chasm there were!) — with a complete suspension, as far as you were concerned, of the question of any other side. Such was my pleasure and my affection and my homage — and when and where in the world did you ever see any symptom of anything else?" But Henry James, too, had his reservations. When Holmes had sent him a Memorial Day address delivered at Harvard in 1895, he wrote William: "It must have been rarely beautiful as delivered. It is ever so fine to read, but with the always strange something unreal or meager his things have for me — unreal in connection with his own remainder, as it were, and not *wholly* artful in expression. But they are 'very unique' — and I shall write to him in a high key about this one."

This address — *The Soldier's Faith* — illustrates in a striking way the paradox of Holmes's attitude toward the Civil War. Though he did not want to hear about it, though he seems to have felt little interest in it as an episode in American history, he had it with him, nevertheless, all his life. That he has managed to survive his regiment has become for him a source of pride, and in writing to correspondents, even to those whom he does not know well and even as late as 1927, he rarely fails to signalize the dates of the Battles of Ball's Bluff and Antietam, at both of which he had been wounded, by some such note as "31 years and one day after Antietam," "Antietam was 65 years ago yesterday," "We are celebrating Antietam, where if a bullet had gone one eighth of an inch differently the chances are that I should not be writing to you." It is as if he were preening on paper his formidable military mustaches, for the trimming of which, he mentions to Pollock, he depends upon a favorite Washington barber. (John De Forest wore a similar pair, and Ambrose Bierce's, although not of the handlebar type, had also the military bristle. Neither of these, however, was at all on the scale of Holmes's.) "It may well be," says Mr. Howe, "that of the two wars, the war in fact and the war in retrospect, it was the latter which was dominantly formative of [Holmes's] philosophy." He seems now to have completely lost sight of the angry young man who had once rebelled against the butcheries of Cold Harbor and the Wilderness. He comes finally to insist on the dignity of war as an exercise in personal virtue. "I do not know what is true," he wrote in *The Soldier's Faith*. "I do not know the meaning of the universe. But in the midst of doubt, in the collapse of creeds, there is one thing I do not doubt, that no man who lives in the same world with most of us can doubt, and that is that the faith is true and adorable which leads a soldier to throw away his life in obedience to a blindly accepted duty, in a cause which he little understands, in a plan of campaign of which he has no notion, under tactics of which he does not see the use."

He seems now to approve of all wars — at least those in which the English-speaking peoples take part. At the time of our war with Spain, he writes Pollock that the sound of a military band recalls to him "old days": "It gives one a certain ache. It always seems to me that if one's body moved parallel to one's soul, one would mind campaigning less as an elderly man than as a young man"; and he "confesses to pleasure" in hearing, on the part of his friend Brooks Adams, "some rattling jingo talk after the self-righteous and preaching discourse, which has prevailed to some extent at Harvard College and elsewhere." Writing to Pollock when the Boer War is going on, he wishes the British "a speedy success"; and writing to Harold Laski in 1916, he assures him of the ancient

Romans that, "It did those chaps a lot of good to live expecting some day to die by the sword." When Pollock,
after World War I, visiting France in 1928, writes
Holmes of his indignation at the idea of "preaching to
the French" that they ought to forget what the Germans have done to them, he replies, "I agree with your
condemnation of armchair pacifists on the general ground
that until the world has got farther along war not only
is not absurd but is inevitable and rational — although of
course I would make great sacrifices to avoid one." A
saying of Rufus Choate's about John Quincy Adams that
the latter "had the instinct for the jugular" — Holmes's
own having been barely missed when he was shot
through the neck at Antietam — was to become one of
his favorite phrases.

These evidences of abiding pugnacity, when piled up
as I have done with them above, may give the impression
that Holmes was a tiresome old professional veteran, always ready to rattle his saber; but actually he was much
too well-bred and much too serious-minded ever to let
himself become boring or ridiculous. With his essentially philosophic mind, which was speculative but also
very rigorous, he must account for the war and his part
in it in terms of a general philosophy, and it is here
that his honesty as a thinker is to be seen at its most
impressive. There is no cant about the war in Holmes;
for a Northerner of his generation, he permits himself a
minimum indulgence in conventional special pleading
and obscuration of actuality by myth. It is true that
although at one point in the war he had come to believe that the Union was aiming at "the subjugation . . .
of a great civilized nation," he was to become, when the
war was over, distinctly contemptuous of the Southerners and to write to Senator Albert J. Beveridge: "I hope
that time will explode the humbug of the Southern
Gentleman in your mind — not that there weren't a few

— and not that their comparatively primitive intellectual condition didn't sometimes give a sort of religious purity of type, rarer in the more civilized and therefore more sceptical northerner. But the southern gentlemen generally were an arrogant crew who knew nothing of the ideas that make the life of the few thousands that may be called civilized." Elsewhere he goes even further and declares that he has never known a Southerner whom he considered to be a gentleman. But he always accepts realistically and indeed makes the basis of his system — legal as well as historical, since law, in Holmes's conception, is always molded by history — the action of the Union and its consequences.

He has repudiated the gospel of the militant God; he thinks that God has had nothing to do with it. The New England theocracy is gone forever. "I can't help an occasional semi-shudder," he says in a letter to Laski of May 8, 1918, "as I remember that millions of intelligent men think that I am barred from the face of God unless I change. But how can one pretend to believe what seems to him childish and devoid alike of historical and rational foundations? I suppose such thoughts would be as likely to occur to you about Valhalla or the Mahometan hell as about this. Felix [Frankfurter] said so himself the other night — but I was brought up in Boston — and though I didn't get Hell talk from my parents it was in the air. Oh — the *ennui* of those Sunday morning church bells, and hymn tunes, and the sound of the citizen's feet on the pavement — not heard on other days. I hardly have recovered from it now. I am glad to remember that when I was dying after Ball's Bluff I remembered my father's saying that death-bed repentances generally meant only that the man was scared and reflected that if I wanted to I couldn't, because I still thought the same."

That Holmes had begun to think early about the problem of moral relativity and actually to formulate the conceptions which were to govern his thinking in later life we have seen from his reflections on his escape from death after his wounding at Ball's Bluff. He had decided already at twenty that "good" and "general law" were "synonymous terms in the universe," that "good only means certain general truths seen through the heart and will instead of being merely contemplated intellectually," and that he doubted "if the intellect accepts or recognizes that classification of good and bad."

What is left, without God's direction, is simply a conflict of forces, in which the party that wins rules the roost. Mr. Howe, in his searching biography, has shown how Holmes's point of view owed a good deal to Darwin's theory of the survival of the fittest and to the positivism of Auguste Comte, as well as to the pragmatism of Charles S. Peirce, who had been one of Holmes's circle in Boston. Such thinkers as Peirce had rejected the authority of both divine and "natural" law. Moral values could not be decided in any objective way, and if two sets of values conflicted, the question of which should prevail could only be decisively settled by one side's suppressing the other. "Pleasures are ultimates," Holmes writes to Laski on August 5, 1926, "and in cases of difference between ourself and another there is nothing to do except in unimportant matters to think ill of him and in important ones to kill him. Until you have remade the world I can class as important only those that have an international sanction in war." It is amusing but very characteristic that this dictum about fundamentals should have been prompted by a difference of opinion between Holmes and his British correspondent as to the merits of Jane Austen's novels, for which Holmes, like Mark Twain, did not care; but it was none the less a serious expression of the Justice's fundamental

ideas. The question of the dulness of Jane Austen leads
him to argue his pragmatic position, and this pragmatic
position implies his attitude toward the Civil War. The
Unionists and the Southern secessionists had had, from
Holmes's point of view, a serious difference of opinion
about matters sufficiently important to warrant their resorting to arms. The Northerners had had to kill the
Southerners in order to keep the South in the Union.
And thus, at least, Holmes is never misleading. He does
not idealize Lincoln; he does not shed tears about slavery.
He does not call the planters wicked; he merely says
that they are not truly "civilized." In his opinions on
cases in the South in which the court has been intimidated by a mob, he will censure its legal procedure, but
he never, even off the bench, gives way to moral indignation.

The rights, then, in any society, are determined, after
a struggle to the death, by the group that comes out on
top. Holmes is always insisting on the right to kill, to
establish authority by violent means, to suppress in a
crisis, as Lincoln did, subversive or obstructive speech.
In peacetime, the sovereign power has the right to impose its policies, and the function of the laws that it passes
is to see that these are carried out.

Quotations from Holmes could be multiplied to demonstrate his philosophy of *force majeure* — as they could
be on any other point of his thinking, for in his papers
and correspondence he repeated his opinions again and
again, often in the same words. One may quote from his
letters to Laski and Pollock such passages as the following. To Laski, October 26, 1919: "I fear we have less
freedom of speech here than they have in England.
Little as I believe in it as a theory, I hope I would die
for it and I go as far as anyone whom I regard as competent to form an opinion in favor of it. Of course when I

say I don't believe in it as a theory I don't mean that I do believe in the opposite as a theory. But on their premises it seems to me logical in the Catholic Church to kill heretics and [for] the Puritans to whip Quakers — and I see nothing more wrong in it from our ultimate standards than I do in killing Germans when we are at war. When you are thoroughly convinced that you are right — wholeheartedly desire an end — and have no doubt of your power to accomplish it — I see nothing but municipal regulations to interfere with your using your power to accomplish it. The sacredness of human life is a formula that is good only inside a system of law." There is of course on Holmes's part a certain inconsistency here, to which we shall return in a moment. To Laski, January 14, 1920: "I repeat my old aphorism that everything is founded on the death of men — society, which only changes the modes of killing — romance, to which centuries, that is generations, of dead, on the memorial tablets of a great war, are necessary." And on the following February 1, he expressed the same idea to Frederick Pollock: "I loathe war — which I described when at home with a wound in our Civil War as an organized bore — to the scandal of the young women of the day who thought that Captain Holmes was wanting in patriotism. But I do think that man at present is a predatory animal. I think that the sacredness of human life is a purely municipal ideal of no validity outside the jurisdiction. I believe that force, mitigated so far as may be by good manners, is the *ultima ratio,* and between two groups that want to make inconsistent kinds of world I see no remedy except force. I may add what I no doubt have said often enough, that it seems to me that every society rests on the death of men . . ." And to Laski on May 20 of the same year: "Perhaps you respect the self-assertion a little more than I do," he writes apropos of

Randolph Bourne, who had opposed our intervention in the first World War. "If I may quote my favorite author (as Thackeray says) with regard to his objections to treating a man as a thing — a means — and not as an end in himself, 'If a man lives in society, he is liable to find himself so treated!' I have no scruples about a draft or the death penalty."

I do not mean at all to depreciate Holmes by pointing out the special emphasis that he put upon killing. This was the heritage of the Civil War. Ambrose Bierce, as we have seen, after a similar experience, was obsessed by the idea of death, and he succumbed to its morbidity as Holmes did not. Holmes's long and hard service as a soldier had, besides, given him something else which was to become excessively rare in the period after the war, when most Northerners wanted to forget or to disguise what had happened. For a young man who has always lived comfortably and accepted the security of convention, it may be an educational advantage for him to see his society with the bottom knocked out, its most honored institutions threatened and its members, irrespective of class, thrown together in conflict to the death or in obligatory coöperation. The law had broken down in America; the Constitution had gone to pieces. It was impossible for an honest man of Holmes's probing intelligence to pretend that the law was a sacred code, which had simply to be read correctly. He always saw it as a complex accretion, a varied assortment of rules that had been drawn up through more than a thousand years and which represented the needs and demands of people existing in particular places at particular periods of history. He was not the first writer to examine the law from an historical point of view, and he must have been influenced by *Ancient Law*, the pioneering book by Sir Henry Maine, which was published in 1861. But in his treatise on *The Common Law* he, too, was a pioneer in examining our legal code in the light of its historical origins. The book begins with a statement of the attitude and method of the author which has now become a classical formulation: "The life of the law has not been logic: it has been experience. The felt necessities of the time, the prevalent moral and political theories, intuitions of public policy, avowed or unconscious, even the prejudices which judges share with their fellow-men, have had a good deal more to do than the syllogism in determining the rules by which men should be governed. The law embodies the story of a nation's development through many centuries, and it cannot be dealt with as if it contained only the axioms and corollaries of a book of mathematics." He unravels with subtlety and coolness many curious misunderstandings by which antiquated statutes have been carried along and have been made to mean something quite different from what they did in their remote beginnings. He shows, also, how ancient ideas of morality still color the language of modern law and how modern ideas of morality are read back into language where they do not belong. Holmes's interest in the law, as he often says, is anthropological and sociological as well as philosophical. He likes to treat tradition lightly, to insist that a law's long existence is no reason for not repealing it tomorrow; yet, skeptical though he is, he believes in the general validity of any corpus of law as the expression of the dominant will of any considerable social group.

How, then, in view of this philosophy, was it possible for Oliver Wendell Holmes to become, in the nineteen-twenties, a great hero of the American "liberals," who were intent upon social reforms and who leaned sometimes pretty far to the Left?

There was a certain element of comedy in this situation. Besides believing that might made "rights," Holmes could not, in his economic views, have been further from Harold Laski and the editors of the *New Republic,* and he was as contemptuous of what he called "the upward and onward" as H. L. Mencken was of what he called "the uplift." He was actually, in certain ways, intellectually closer to Mencken than to his favorite young friend Laski, to whom he writes (February 10, 1920): "I took malevolent pleasure in Mencken's *Prejudices,* which devotes a chapter to speaking ill of [Thorstein Veblen]. Do you know that writer [Mencken]? With various foibles, he has a sense of reality and most of his prejudices I share." The economic views of Holmes did not admit of redistribution of wealth, and they had never, as has been said by Mr. Francis Biddle, changed at all since he was twenty-five. "On the economic side," he writes to Laski on January 8, 1917, "I am mighty skeptical of hours of labor and minimum wages regulation, but it may be that a somewhat monotonous standardized mode of life is coming. Of course it only means shifting the burden to a different point of incidence, if I be right, as I think I be, that every community rests on the death of men. If the people who can't get the minimum are to be supported, you take out of one pocket to put into the other. I think the courageous thing to say to the crowd, though perhaps the Brandeis school don't believe it, is, you now have all there is — and you'd better face it instead of trying to lift yourselves by the slack of your own breeches. But all our present teaching is hate and envy for those who have any luxury, as social wrongdoers." He had a conception of "the stream of products," as he called it, as something with which one should not try to tamper. "For instance, take taxation — ," he writes Laski, May 17, 1917, "if you stop with preliminary machinery you think of breaking up great estates and old families by an inheritance tax or of cutting down great profits by an income tax — if you pass by means to ends you see that any form of considerable taxation means withdrawing so much of the stream to feed, clothe, and house those whom the Government elects to feed, clothe, and house — and that the rest of the crowd must have so much less." And he had been permanently influenced by Malthus. "To my mind," he says in a letter of May 24, 1919, "the notion that any rearrangement of property, while any part of the world propagates freely, will prevent civilization from killing its weaker members, is absurd. I think that the crowd now has substantially all there is — and that every mitigation of the lot of any body of men has to be paid for by some other or the same body of men — and I don't think that cutting off the luxuries of the few would make an appreciable difference in the situation."

The only possibility for human improvement that he seems to have been able to envisage is some process of breeding a "selected race." He mentions this in a letter to Pollock of February 1, 1920; and he seems to be referring to a theory which he has already rather remotely invoked without elaborating upon it in a paper of five years before, *Ideals and Doubts* (reprinted in *Collected Legal Papers*): "I believe that the wholesale social regeneration which so many now seem to expect, if it can be helped by conscious, coördinated human effort, cannot be affected appreciably by tinkering with the institution of property, but only by taking in hand life and trying to build a race." This last reference to building a race is illuminated by passages in unpublished letters. To Lady Leslie Scott he had written in 1912: "As to eugenics I don't exactly know what your government could undertake if they wanted to tackle it. But, as you probably know, I have thought from before the days of Galton that it was the true beginning, theoretically, of all improvement. The folly, to my mind, of socialism is that it begins with property instead of with life. I remember saying to Arthur McLellan in the Army — the day will come when the boss will say we shall be wanting some statesmen (artists, manufacturers or whatnot) in thirty years — John A376 and M2 — which I think embodied the principles in sufficiently concrete form." And to another correspondent, in 1917, he professes a profound contempt for any variety of socialism which does not try to remold life rather than rearrange property and to put to death all the people who do not come up to a certain standard. But he does not, so far as I have been able to find, enlarge on this proposed solution. One cannot be sure whether Holmes is thinking of eugenics or education.

There were, however, two important matters as to which the opinions of Holmes seemed to be often on the same side as those of the liberals: labor and free speech. In the course of his twenty years — 1882-1902 — as a judge of the Massachusetts Supreme Court (and Chief Justice from 1899), he had sometimes dissented in cases where the right to strike or to picket was being denied by his colleagues, and this had horrified conservative Boston and gained him the reputation of being rather a dangerous man, a reputation which provoked some strong protests when in 1902 he was appointed by Theodore Roosevelt to the Supreme Court of the United States. "They don't know much more," he wrote Pollock, "than that I took the labor side in *Vegelahn v. Gunther* and as that frightened some money interests, and as such interests count for a good deal as soon as one gets out of the cloister, it is easy to suggest that the judge has partial views, is brilliant but not very sound . . ." In the United States Supreme Court itself, he continued to pursue this policy of not hesitating to decide against the "money interests." He dissented, for example, with Louis Brandeis, from a majority decision which declared unconstitutional an Act of Congress that prohibited the transportation from one state to another of the products of factories in which children were employed, contending that if Congress had the power to regulate interstate commerce in such matters as fraudulent drugs and the transportation of girls for purposes of prostitution, it had also the power to prohibit the transportation of "the product of ruined lives." In writing this dissenting opinion, he evidently feels some sympathy for the children; but he had no special feeling for labor. He seems instinctively to have turned away from the dingy industrial world with which these opinions dealt. He said once that his only firsthand contact with Massachusetts industrial life had been occasionally taking out, in his youth, the girls from the Lawrence factories. It is true that his long friendship with Louis D. Brandeis, whom he had known when the latter taught at Harvard Law School and with whom he was later associated when Brandeis, in 1916, was appointed to the Supreme Court by Wilson, did something to call his attention to the badness of working conditions and the odds against which labor was struggling. He writes at the same time to Pollock and to Laski, in May 1919, when he is already seventy-eight years old — using in both cases the same murderous metaphor — that "Brandeis the other day [I quote from the letter to Pollock] drove a harpoon into my midriff with reference to my summer occupations. He said you talk about improving your mind, you only exercise it on the subjects with which you are familiar. Why don't you try something new, study some domain of fact. Take up the textile industries in Massachusetts and after reading the reports sufficiently you can go to

Lawrence and get a human notion of how it really is." But, Holmes goes on to say, "I hate facts. I always say the chief end of man is to form general propositions — adding that no general proposition is worth a damn. Of course a general proposition is simply a string of facts and I have little doubt that it would be good for my immortal soul to plunge into them, good also for the performance of my duties, but I shrink from the bore — or rather I hate to give up the chance to read this and that, that a gentleman should have read before he dies. I don't remember that I ever read Machiavelli's *Prince* — and I think of the day of Judgment." And to Laski, in June of the following year: "In consideration of my age and moral infirmities he [Brandeis] absolved me from facts for the vacation and allowed me my customary sport with ideas." In his attitude toward any dispute at law between working class and "money interests," Holmes felt himself so incomparably superior to the common run of either that it cost him no struggle of conscience to announce what he thought was just, and, in writing certain opinions, he even felt, I think, a certain lofty relish, *"le plaisir aristocratique de déplaire."*

In the matter of free speech, he was perhaps somewhat inconsistent, in philosophy, if not in practice. We have seen this in one of the quotations above. He does not like to hear people talk about the "class war" in the United States, and he is reluctant to extend to a dominant group *inside* an established society the same authority that he willingly assumes for a conquering over a conquered nation: "When I talk of law I talk as a cynic," he writes Laski (December 3, 1917). "I don't care a damn if twenty professors tell me that a decision is not law if I know that the courts will enforce it. . . . And I understand by human rights what a given crowd will fight for (successfully)." He had already expressed similar opinions in a letter of September 15, 1916, but had added: "All my life I have sneered at the natural rights of man — and at times I have thought that the bills of rights in Constitutions were overworked — but these chaps [Faguet and Hazlitt, whom he has just been reading] remind me, if I needed it . . . that they embody principles that men have died for, and that it is well not to forget in our haste to secure our notion of general welfare." (Note that what justifies these principles is that men have allowed themselves to be killed for them.)

It may be that the influence of his new friends the liberals counted for something with Holmes in his opinions after the first World War in cases in which the issue of free speech was involved. In the cases of Schenck and Debs, he had upheld, under the wartime Espionage Act, convictions for obstructing the draft. But he had reacted to the wartime intolerance against any sort of expression of radical opinion, as he invariably did, after the Civil War, to fanaticism of the Left or the Right. He writes Laski in connection with Debs on March 16, 1919: "The federal judges seem to me (again between ourselves) to have got hysterical about the war. I should think that the President when he gets through with his present amusements [Wilson's visit to Europe in the interests of the League of Nations] might do a little pardoning." And to Pollock on April 5: "I am beginning to get stupid letters of protest against a decision that Debs, a noted agitator, was rightly convicted of obstructing the recruiting service so far as the law was concerned. I wondered that the Government should press the case to a hearing before us, as the inevitable result was that fools, knaves, and ignorant persons were bound to say he was convicted because he was a dangerous agitator and that obstructing the draft was a pretence. How it was with the Jury of course I don't know, but of course the talk is silly as to us." In the Abrams case, which followed in the same year, dissenting with Brandeis from the majority opinion, Holmes took a strong line in favor of Civil Rights and tried to square the right to free speech with his philosophy of the rights of power. Russian immigrants had scattered some leaflets in which — though the authors made plain that they were not opposed to the war against Germany — the munition workers were urged to strike against the armed intervention by the United States in opposition to the Russian Revolution. Holmes held that even this exhortation did not constitute "resistance to the United States." "In this case," he goes on, "sentences of twenty years' imprisonment have been imposed for the publishing of two leaflets that I believe the defendants had as much right to publish as the Government has to publish the Constitution of the United States now vainly invoked by them. Even if I am technically wrong and enough can be squeezed from these poor and puny anonymities to turn the color of legal litmus paper — I will add, even if what I think the necessary intent were shown — the most nominal punishment seems to me all that possibly could be inflicted, unless the defendants are to be made to suffer not for what the indictment alleges but for the creed that they avow — a creed that I believe to be the creed of ignorance and immaturity when honestly held, as I see no reason to doubt that it was held here, but which, although made the subject of examination at the trial, no one has a right even to consider in dealing with the charges before the Court." He now, in his final paragraph, reverts to his theory that repression is the prerogative of established power: "Persecution for the expression of opinions seems to me perfectly logical. If you have no doubt of your premises or your power and want a certain result with all your heart you naturally express your wishes in law and sweep away all opposition. . . . But when men have realized that time has upset many fighting faiths, they may come to believe even more than they believe the very foundations of their own conduct that the ultimate good desired is better reached by free trade in ideas — that the best test of truth is the power of the thought to get itself accepted in the competition of the market, and that truth is the only ground upon which their wishes can safely be carried out. That, at any rate, is the theory of our Constitution. It is an experiment, as all life is an experiment. Every year if not every day we have to wager our salvation upon some prophecy based upon imperfect knowledge. While that experiment is part of our system I think that we should be eternally vigilant against attempts to check the expression of opinions that we loathe and believe to be fraught with death, unless they so imminently threaten immediate interference with the lawful and pressing purposes of the law that an immediate check is required to save the country. I wholly disagree with the argument of the Government that the First Amendment left the common law as to seditious libel in force. History seems to me against the notion. I had conceived that the United States through many years had shown its repentance for the Sedition Act of 1798 by repaying fines that it imposed. Only the emergency that makes it immediately dangerous to leave the correction of evil counsels to time warrants making any exception to the sweeping command, 'Congress shall make no law . . . abridging the freedom of speech.' Of course I am speaking only of expressions of opinion and exhortations, which were all that were uttered here, but I regret that I cannot put into more impressive words my belief that in their conviction upon this indictment the defendants were deprived of their rights under the Constitution of the United States."

The important point here is that, in firm disregard of the panic created by the Russian Revolution, he is giving the foreign radicals the benefit of a doubt. This opinion provoked a fierce outburst on the part of John Henry Wigmore, the Dean of Northwestern Law School, which Holmes characterized as "bosh," but it brought from Harold Laski a paean of praise. It may be that in the climate of appreciation provided by the liberal group the spirit of Puritan protest was coming to life in Holmes after the paralyzing stroke to his idealism administered by the Civil War, in which the Abolitionist protest against slavery had been discredited by his practical experience, and his incipient sympathy with the protest of the South had been killed by the victory of the North and by a realistic recognition of the power of the latter to impose its will. But the liberals of the post-World War period were now slaking Holmes's thirst for intercourse with men of ideas. They stimulated and entertained him as well as gave him the admiration he craved. He had always been rather lonely, since the days of the Harvard philosophers, for the intellectual companionship of equals. His long correspondence with Sir Frederick Pollock, a sort of English opposite number, like Holmes a great legal scholar with wide-ranging historical and literary interests — which began in the middle seventies and continued to the end of Holmes's life — shows how eager he was for this. "I . . . must vent a line of unreasoning — rage I was going to say — dissatisfaction is nearer . . ." he writes to Pollock of the newspaper comments on his appointment to the United States Supreme Court. "They are so favorable that they make my nomination a popular success but they have the flabbiness of American ignorance. I had to get appreciation for my book in England before they dared say anything here except in one or two quarters. . . . It makes one sick when he has broken his heart in trying to make every word living and real to see a lot of duffers, generally I think not even lawyers, talking with the sanctity of print in a way that at once discloses to the knowing eye that literally they don't know anything about it. . . . If I haven't done my share in the way of putting in new and remodeling old thought for the last 20 years then I delude myself. Occasionally some one has a glimpse — but in the main damn the lot of them." Later on, in 1917, he writes enthusiastically about Laski, the brilliant young Jew from Manchester then lecturing on politics and history at Harvard: "He goes with some of the younger men like Frankfurter and the *New Republic* lot, who make much of your venerable uncle and not only so, but by bringing an atmosphere of intellectual freedom in which one can breathe, make life to him a good deal more pleasant."

But the further these liberals incline toward the Left, the less can Holmes accept their conclusions. "I have begun Karl Marx's book," he had written Pollock in 1893, "but although he strikes me as a great man I can't imagine a combination less to my taste than Hegel and political economy"; and he writes later, in 1912, that Proudhon was "a man of insights, who ends by boring you as all men with issues and panaceas in their head do, especially if you think you know the answer," and that "I liked to have him walk into Karl Marx as a plagiarist and a humbug, after K. M.'s bullying everybody else as a bourgeois intelligence." Of "the accursed Trotsky's" autobiography he writes to Laski (July 10, 1930): "I am interested enough not to throw the book aside but I shall be glad when I am done with it. I don't like him and the book seems to have a dominant purpose to blow his own horn at the expense of Stalin. I feel the tone that I became familiar with in my youth among the abolitionists. He to be sure takes his principles for granted. I should like to see them stated. If he still believes in

Marx I thought that *Capital* showed chasms of unconscious error and sophistries that might be conscious."
The certainty of one's moral rightness, the absolute confidence in one's system always set up in him the old
antagonism. "He seems to me," he writes Harold Laski in
September, 1918, of the pacifist activities of Bertrand
Russell, "in the emotional state not unlike that of the
abolitionists in former days, which then I shared and
now much dislike — as it catches postulates like the in-
fluenza"; and in October, 1930, when he has been reading Maurice Hindus's *Humanity Uprooted*, "His account
of the Communists shows in the most extreme form what
I came to loathe in the abolitionists — the conviction that
anyone who did not agree with them was a knave or a
fool. You see the same in some Catholics and some of
the 'Drys' apropos of the 18th amendment. I detest a man
who knows that he knows." The agitation over the Sacco-
Vanzetti case had the same effect on Holmes. He received an appeal by counsel for the defendants for a
writ of habeas corpus on August 10, 1927, in the week
when the two Italian anarchists were condemned to be
executed for a supposed murder, and ten days later an
appeal for an extension of time in order to apply to the
Supreme Court for writs of *certiorari* and for a stay of
execution while the application was pending. Both of
these Holmes denied on the ground, in the first instance,
that he "had no authority to take the prisoners out of
the custody of a State Court having jurisdiction over the
persons and dealing with the crime under a State law,"
and in the second, because, as he says, he "thought no
shadow of a ground could be shown on which the writ
could be granted." These appeals had been made in the
hope that the Justice would recognize an analogy between the Sacco-Vanzetti case and a Southern Negro
case of a few years before in which he had formulated

the majority decision in granting a writ of habeas corpus
for five men convicted of murder in a court which, as
Holmes says, was dominated by a mob, "ready to lynch
the prisoner, jury, counsel and possibly the judges if
they did not convict"; but he declined to accept this
analogy: the prejudices alleged in the Massachusetts
court were not really the same thing; in any trial some
prejudice could be alleged. And why so much fuss over
Sacco and Vanzetti when "a thousand-fold worse cases
of Negroes come up from time to time, but the world
does not worry about them." The demonstrations at home
and abroad, a shower of denunciatory or pleading letters
and the blowing-up of the house of one of the jurors
had the effect of getting the old Justice's back up. "My
prejudices," he writes Laski, after the executions, "are
against the convictions, but they are still stronger against
the run of the shriekers. . . . The *New Republic* had an
article that seemed to me hysterical. . . . So far as one
who has not read the evidence has a right to an opinion
I think the row that has been made idiotical, if considered on its merits, but of course it is not on the merits
that the row is made, but because it gives the ex-
tremists a chance to yell." In December of the following
year: "[Felix Frankfurter] is convinced of their innocence — but I was not convinced that too much talk had
not been made on the theme. The *New Republic* recurs
to it from time to time. But the *New Republic* strikes
me as having become partisan in tone of late judging
from an occasional glance. It seemed to nag at Coolidge
— and I rather think believes a number of things that I
don't. I come nearer to reading it than I do reading any
other newspaper — but I can't be said to read that."

The extent to which Holmes was a "liberal" has therefore been considerably exaggerated; but it is true that

the "American Renascence," which began first to stir
under Theodore Roosevelt, which was manifesting itself
quite vividly when our armies got back from France and
which reached in the course of the twenties at least almost
the dignity of an Enlightenment, did make Holmes a conspicuous figure and cause him to be generally recognized
in the intellectual world as the truly great man he was.
His prestige at the Harvard Law School seems steadily
to have increased with the years, and in the same year,
1914, that the *New Republic* was founded, Felix Frankfurter, a sort of disciple of Holmes, or at least in certain
respects a continuator of the Holmes tradition, became
a professor there. Holmes had always been fond of
young people — he had no children of his own, and he
was now much sought after and honored by younger
men of congenial tastes. Every year he was supplied with
a secretary who had graduated from Harvard Law School
— a post for which the qualifications were not only special competence in legal studies but historical and cultural interests which would make him a companion for
Holmes. The old Justice begins to appear — as he has
never in his life done before — in the light of an established sage, a god of the national pantheon. His books
are reprinted and read; his minor papers collected and
published. In following his correspondence, one feels that
he smiles more and growls less. He knows, and the public
knows, that Justice Holmes has become a classic. In the
reaction against the gentility, the timidity, the sentimentality of American cultural life, he is seen to have
been a humanist, a realist, a bold and independent
thinker, who has required of himself from the first to
meet the highest intellectual standards and who has
even, with little public encouragement, succeeded in
training himself to become also a distinguished writer.
The Common Law, though lucid in intention, is so

compact and so closely reasoned that it is sometimes opaque to the layman, and one is relieved to hear even from lawyers that they sometimes find it difficult reading. But in general Holmes's legal studies are so elegantly and clearly presented, so free from the cumbersome formulas and the obsolete jargon of jurists, that, though only an expert can judge them, they may profitably be read by the layman.

As for the speeches and non-legal essays, they ought to be read by everyone. One guesses that it is only Holmes's atheism, his lack of conventional patriotism and his complete incapacity for the optimism which, in that period of national self-congratulation, had become almost obligatory for public figures — Holmes thought that even William James was too open-minded and exuberant — which have kept them out of school and college text-books. The younger Holmes was not, like his father, a fluently felicitous writer; but his literary sense was developed in a remarkable, if limited, way. One feels sometimes that this sense is quite subtle, as when, in a letter to Owen Wister, he compares the effects of light on light in Dante's *Paradiso* with Andrew Marvell's "green thought in a green shade," or when he comments, in a letter to Laski, on Alfred de Musset's stories: "He is like the flowering of an apple tree and hardly lives beyond the moment of copulation, but I can't believe that knowing but essentially second-rate Remy de Gourmont that we now know that A. de M's phrase is empty. Charm is one of the few things that survive." But there is also a certain unwillingness to let himself go with the poets. He firmly maintains that Macbeth, on hearing of the death of his lady, would hardly have been likely to soar into the "Out, out, brief candle" speech; and, having put himself through the *Odyssey* in Greek, he doubts whether it has been really worth while. He is torn between a moral obligation to make himself acquainted with the classics and a feeling that they are out of date, that it is more profitable to read something modern. But he developed, for his occasional pieces, a literary style of his own which conforms to the same austere ideal as his professional legal papers. He worked very hard over writing, and he gave to these short pieces a crystalline form as hard and bright as Pater's flame. They are perfect, and they are undoubtedly enduring — since their value lies not merely in the style, by means of which he "makes every word tell": it is almost impossible for Holmes even to touch upon any problem of legal interpretation or to compose a brief memorial for some old colleague of the Boston bench or bar without assigning it or him to a place in a larger scheme.

It is Holmes's special distinction — which perhaps makes him unique among judges — that he never dissociates himself from the great world of thought and art, and that all his decisions are written with awareness of both their wider implications and the importance of their literary form. He was not merely a cultivated judge who enjoyed dipping into belles lettres or amusing himself with speculation: he was a real concentrator of thought who had specialized in the law but who was trying to determine man's place, to define his satisfactions and duties, to try to understand what humanity is. It is this that makes Holmes's correspondence, as well as his more formal writings, so absorbing and so fortifying and a very important part of his "œuvre." In spite of his strong negative predispositions, he will not relinquish a fundamental skepticism as to human convictions and systems, and he is always alert and attentive, always inquiring and searching, to find out some further answers. "The book is pretty thick with suggestions, . . ." he writes Pollock when he is reading Spengler. "I don't value his conclusion, but do his *aperçus*. Isn't that so of all theorists and system makers. . . . Yet when one suspects that a man knows something about life that one hasn't heard before one is uneasy until one has found out what he has to say." Through his long lifetime — Holmes died at ninety-four — he seems never to falter or to become fatigued in the discharge of his professional duties or in the eager intellectual life which occupied him beyond his profession. Among the sequences of correspondence so far published, Holmes is to be seen at his best in his long exchange of letters with Pollock. With Laski, a much younger man, whom he did not know till 1916, there is never the same intimate relationship; and Laski sometimes falsifies his side, in his effort to keep the old man amused, by resorting to a certain amount of flim-flam. But in the correspondence with Pollock, in which both are as free as was possible for men of their generation from common nineteenth-century prejudices, as they discuss their professional interests and boundlessly range beyond them — Frederick Pollock was a great linguist and traveller — through a friendship that lasted six decades, we see Holmes on his highest level.

Of his generation that fought in the Civil War and among the really gifted men whose characters and subsequent careers were profoundly modified by it, Holmes the younger perhaps stands alone as one who was never corrupted, never discouraged or broken, by the alien conditions that the war had prepared. How was it that he managed to survive, to function as a first-rate intellect, to escape the democratic erosion?

He was indeed a very special case. It is plain that his unshakable self-confidence, his carapace of impenetrable indifference to current pressures and public opinion was due partly to the impregnable security of belonging to the Boston "Brahmin" caste. This term had been invented by Dr. Holmes, and the peculiar position of the caste, its conception of its own special function, is explained in the opening chapters of his novel *Elsie Venner*. The Boston Brahmins, says Dr. Holmes, are not only distinct from any other group in New England, they differ from any other aristocracy in the world. There are, to be sure, in New England, families who seem to rise by suddenly making money, but they lose it in the third generation, and they cannot become Brahmins. The distinguishing mark of the Brahmin is that, from generation to generation, he maintains a high tradition of scholarship: the Brahmins are all preachers, lawyers, doctors, professors and men of letters. Some rough ambitious young boy may come to college from the New England countryside and prove able to compete with a Brahmin, but this is rather an exceptional event, and if one finds a young man with an unknown name, not "coarse" and "uncouth" like the countryman, but slender, with a face smooth and pallid, features "regular and of a certain delicacy," whose eye is "bright and quick," whose lips "play over the thought he utters as a pianist's fingers dance over their music," whose "whole air, though it may be timid, and even awkward, has nothing clownish," you may be sure that his mother was a Brahmin. There must of course at some point have been money to supplement the aptitude for learning. The author of *Elsie Venner* does not say this in so many words, but he admits that it is sometimes possible for a Brahmin to become impoverished and that in that case he may marry property. Now, Oliver Wendell Holmes the elder had himself married the daughter of a Jackson, a justice of the Massachusetts Supreme Court, whose family, successful merchants, owned most of the large town of Pittsfield (where

Oliver, Jr., spent his boyhood summers), and the son married Fanny Bowditch Dixwell, the granddaughter of the celebrated author of that Bible of the New England sea trade, the *Practical Navigator,* and the daughter of Epes Sargent Dixwell, who had read law in Judge Jackson's office and later, with a reputation as the best classical scholar in Boston, been headmaster of the Boston Latin School, at which Oliver, Jr., had studied.

It would be easy, by appropriate quotation, to create the impression that Holmes was an egregious social snob of a peculiarly provincial kind. His contempt for the common run of men had come out very strongly at the time of the war, when for the first time he had had to have some contact with it. "While I'm living *en aristocrate,*" he had written his sister on his way back from furlough to rejoin his regiment, "I'm an out-and-outer of a democrat in theory, but for contact, except at the polls, I loathe the thick-fingered clowns we call the people — especially as the beasts are represented at political centres — vulgar, selfish and base." We have seen his opinion of Southerners and their pretentions to be considered gentlemen. Of even the Philadelphians he writes Pollock that, "While not infrequently having the manners of the great world," they have "somehow . . . always . . . struck me as hopelessly injected with the second rate, when I have seen them in their law, on which they pride themselves — but I would not breathe this aloud." He hardly ever mentions the Jameses without referring to the fact that they are Irish, with, in Henry's case, an intimation of underbreeding in comparison to the Anglo-Saxon and, in William's, an implication that, though lively and full of eloquence, he is not quite to be taken seriously. (His attitude toward the Jews is quite different. Through his intelligence and his love of learning, his sharpness of mind and his humor, he has obviously more

in common with certain of his Jewish colleagues than with
most of his Gentile ones; and there is also no doubt the
traditional prestige which the Jews have had in New
England, due to the self-identification of the Puritans
with the Old Testament Israelites. Holmes is said to
have believed that the Wendells were Jewish — they were
originally Vondals from Holland; and he seems to have
regarded the intellectual Jew as a special variety of
Brahmin.)

Holmes's attitude toward the ablest of the Presidents
under whom, as a soldier or a judge, he had served was
invariably patronizing. He was not at first impressed by
Lincoln: "Few men in baggy pants and bad hats," he
wrote to one correspondent, "are recognized as great by
those who see them." And to Beveridge: "Until I was
middle-aged I never doubted that I was witnessing the
growth of a myth. Then the revelation of some facts and
the greatness of some of his speeches — helped perhaps
by the environing conviction of the later world — led me
to accept the popular judgement — which I do, without a
great deal of ardor or very great interest in the man." Of
Theodore Roosevelt, by whom he had been appointed to
the Supreme Court, he writes Pollock that he "was very
likeable, a big figure, a rather ordinary intellect, with
extraordinary gifts, a shrewd and I think pretty unscrupulous politician. He played all his cards — if not
more." Roosevelt had apparently expected Holmes, in
return for his appointment to the Court, to vote in support of the President's measures, and when Holmes had
soon failed to do this in dissenting from a majority decision, in the Northern Securities case, which held that
this company had violated the Sherman Anti-Trust Act,
the President — by way of third parties — emphatically
expressed his displeasure. The response of the Brahmin
judge to such an explosion of pique on the part of a

successful New York politician was a lofty New England contempt. In the same letter quoted above, he tells Pollock that "a Senator in his [Roosevelt's] day" had said that "What the boys like about Roosevelt is that he doesn't care a damn for the law." Holmes continues, "It broke up our incipient friendship . . . as he looked on my dissent to the *Northern Securities Case* as a political departure (or, I suspect, more truly, couldn't forgive anyone who stood in his way). We talked freely later but it never was the same after that, and if he had not been restrained by his friends, I am told that he would have made a fool of himself and would have excluded me from the White House — and as in his case about the law, so in mine about that, I never cared a damn whether I went there or not." It is amusing, in view of this, to remember the acute sensitivity — the Coolidges being an old Massachusetts family — of his suspicion that the *New Republic* is "nagging" at the pygmy Coolidge. It has been thought that his reluctance to intervene in the Sacco-Vanzetti case was due to a stubborn unwillingness to impugn the Massachusetts bench, on which he himself no longer sat — a reluctance which he had not felt, in the Negro and the Leo Frank cases, in regard to the Southern judiciary.

It will, however, be seen that there runs all through this the special ideal of the Brahmin, whose superiority is not merely social. The Philadelphians, though sometimes good-mannered, are decidedly second-rate at law; the Irish, though gifted, lack rigor; Lincoln, though he wore baggy trousers and though he could hardly be interesting to a Brahmin, did in his speeches have moments of greatness. And it is greatness, not a polished complacency — though, to be sure, a better turned-out greatness than that of which Lincoln was capable — at which Holmes himself always aims. When he says — it is a favorite phrase — that someone is "a great swell," he never means that he is socially brilliant but always that he is preëminent intellectually — a top expert in some department or a profound and original thinker. When he speaks of "touching the superlative" — another favorite phrase — he always means excelling in one's work. After the funeral of Mahlon Pitney, one of his Supreme Court colleagues, he writes Pollock, "He could not touch the superlative, and when he first came to the bench riled me by excessive discourse. But he took his work seriously, was untiring in industry, had had some experience of life, and as Brandeis always said and, I came to think, truly had intellectual honesty that sometimes brought him out against his prejudices and first judgment." And elsewhere in a letter to Pollock: "I am looking forward with curiosity to the new Chief Justice [William Howard Taft]. He marked a fundamental difference in our way of thinking by saying that this office always had been his ambition. I don't understand ambition for an office. The only one that I feel is to believe when the end comes, for till then it is always in doubt, that one has touched the superlative. No outsider can give you that, although the judgment of the competent, of course, helps to confidence — or at least to hope. Between ourselves I doubt if Mr. T. can do that."

It was not true, as we have seen, that Holmes had never been ambitious for office; but it *was* true that, having attained it, he wanted to feel that he stood in the highest rank of a non-official scale of values. How eager he was for assurance of this appears in a letter to Pollock just after his eighty-first birthday: "I have had some letters and one or two notices in the paper that have touched me deeply. They have said what I longed to hear said and would almost willingly have died to hear twenty years ago" — that is, in 1902, when Roosevelt had appointed him to the Supreme Court and when Holmes had complained to Pollock of the lack of recognition of his merits, as he was later sometimes to complain that he was not fully accepted as "a great judge." "The only thing an internal man cares for," he writes Dean Wigmore in 1910, "is to believe he is taking the right track for intellectual mastery. Only a few men in this world . . . can do anything to assure one's ever-doubting soul about that." There is surely something of Calvinism in this: the anxiety, the undermining doubt as to whether one has really been Elected. Holmes is Calvinist in his concentration on making certain of his own élite status, as well as in his almost complete lack of interest in other people as individuals. There is no gossip in Holmes's letters, very little discussion of personalities; when he expresses an opinion of somebody, it is always in terms of his abilities, that is, of his eligibility to be counted among the Elect. He read a good many novels — he seems to have had a special liking for French ones — and in Washington he and his wife went to the theater every Thursday night; but he did not care much for biographies. His reading is dominated by a sense of duty and a Puritanical fear of idleness. He feels that he must grapple with certain works, quite apart from any pleasure they give him, and, once having begun a book, no matter how dull or verbose it is, he must read every word to the end. He is always imagining — this is humorous, of course, but it shows a habit of mind — that God, at the Judgment Day, will ask him to report on the books which he ought to have read but hasn't. Yet in all this he shows a humility which redeems a certain narcissism. He likes to believe of others, whatever their reputations, that they have not really touched the superlative, and his biographer says that he is grudging in acknowledging his debt to his predecessors; but of certain people — Pollock, for example — he seems somewhat to stand in awe, and he is always confessing his deficiencies. One feels that he is not very far from Calvin's conception of "the Communion of Saints." Calvin readily admitted that his clergy on the earth were not free from non-Elect elements; but this alloy did not impair the true church, which consisted of those who were saved, whether living or already in Heaven, and who constituted a kind of club from which everyone not saved was excluded. So Holmes finds his only solidarity with the classical "great swells" of the past and with the few possible "great swells" of the present and future.

Now, despite the fact that Holmes as a judge is dealing constantly with concrete cases of men in relation to men and in spite of his insistence that "the life of the law" has been not logic but historical experience, in spite of the common sense that he brings to the application of his principles — in spite of all this, it would seem that dedication to an ideal of excellence which is not to save others but to justify oneself must cut one off from the rest of society. He had no children to bring to his notice the problems of the contemporary world, and is said not to have wanted any, since he feared they would distract him from his great objective. In Holmes's effort to touch the superlative by practising his juristic profession with all its drudgery and its hard limitations, he evolves the conception of the "jobbist" and even forms a kind of jobbists' club, which, however, except by correspondence, may not involve personal contacts. The jobbist is one who works at his job without trying to improve the world or to make a public impression. He tries to accomplish this professional job as well as it can be accomplished, to give it everything of which he is capable. The jobbist is alone with his job and with the ideal of touching the superlative — which in his grandfather Abiel Holmes's time would have been called being chosen for salvation.

The extent to which the grandson succeeded, after his service in the Civil War, in remaining aloof and detached from the life of the United States was a phenomenon of a very uncommon kind. He is at first, when appointed to the Supreme Court, as he writes Pollock, "more absorbed, interested and impressed than ever I had dreamed I might be. The work of the past seems a finished book — locked up far away, and a new and solemn volume opens. The variety and novelty to me of the questions, the remote spaces from which they come, the amount of work they require, all help the effect. I have written on the constitutionality of part of the Constitution of California, on the powers of the Railroad Commissioners of Arkansas, on the question whether a law of Wisconsin impairs the obligation of the plaintiff's contract. I have to consider a question between a grant of the U.S. in aid of a military road and an Indian reservation on the Pacific coast. I have heard conflicting mining claims in Arizona and whether a granite quarry is 'Minerals' within an exception in a Railway land grant and fifty other things as remote from each other as these." But though the Holmeses had made one trip to the Coast in 1888 and spent two weeks at Niagara Falls, it would never have occurred to the Justice to pay a visit to any of these places or even to read them up. And not only does he resist the suggestion that he look into the conditions of American labor, he even makes it a rule not to see the papers, which he feels are a waste of time. "I don't read the papers," he writes Pollock, in 1905, "or otherwise feel the pulse of the machine." It was mainly through Mrs. Holmes that he acquired any knowledge of current events. Of American business he knew almost nothing, only as much as his cases compelled him to learn. "We are sitting and having cases that I dislike about rates and the Interstate Commission. I listen with respect but without envy to questions by Brandeis and Butler using the words of railroading that I imperfectly understand" (to Laski, 1929). But he tried to give the business man his due, and he cherished a strange idealization of James J. Hill, the Western railroad magnate, against whose monopolistic operations the government had intervened in the Northern Securities suit and whose case had been supported by Holmes in the dissent which had infuriated Roosevelt. "I regard a man like Hill," he tells Pollock in 1910, "as representing one of the greatest forms of human power, an immense mastery of economic details, an equal grasp of general principles, and ability and courage to put his conclusions into practice with brilliant success when all the knowing ones said he would fail. Yet the intense external activity that calls for such powers does not especially delight me." And to Laski in 1923: "I . . . don't sympathize with your artist friends in their loathing for business men. It seems to me merely an illustration of the inability of men to appreciate other forms of energy than that which is natural to them. I am not, and I fear could not be a business man — but the types that I have in mind seem to me among the greatest. This is a disinterested appreciation of what generally is disagreeable to me." He had been in fact almost as little prepared as Lincoln or Grant or Lee to understand the social-economic developments that followed the Civil War, and he seems to have had as little to do personally with the tycoons whom he tries to praise as with the factory workers of Lawrence. If he *had* known them from personal contact, as had that other Boston Brahmin, the younger Charles Francis Adams, who became an expert on railroads and eventually President of the Union Pacific, Holmes would no doubt have agreed with him when he said, in his testy New England way: "A less interesting crowd I do not care to encounter. Not one that I have ever known would I care to meet again, either in this world or the next; nor is one of them associated in my mind with the idea of humor, thought or refinement." (This reference to the next world would seem to have something to do with the New England assimilation of the Communion of Saints to a kind of superior club.)

The real key to Holmes's attitude to business, as to many other aspects of life, is to be found in the distaste for facts and the preference for "general propositions" which he expresses, in the quotation above, in connection with Brandeis's efforts to interest him in factory conditions. This is one of his recurrent themes. He tells Laski, in a letter of January 16, 1918: "My difficulty in writing about business is that all my interest is in theory and that I care a damn sight more for ideas than for facts." And so he further confesses to the same correspondent (October 9, 1921) that his conception of Jim Hill as his "favorite" man of action has been derived "not from knowledge of Hill but from a theoretic construction of what he might have been." To Pollock he writes in 1904: "I never knew any facts about anything and always am gravelled when your countrymen ask some informal intelligent question about our institutions or the state of politics or anything else. My intellectual furniture consists of an assortment of general propositions which grow fewer and more general as I grow older. I always say that the chief end of man is to frame them and that no general proposition is worth a damn." He repeats this in a letter to Pollock seventeen years later, adding, "We are not sure of many things and those are not so."

Though he is still always inquiring into the destiny of man, he can no longer believe that the human race is necessarily of any importance. He writes to Pollock when he is seventy-eight: "I have just read Marvin, *The Century of Hope,* an interesting conspectus of the modern period inspired by a rather deeper belief in the spiritual significance of man than I am able to entertain and a consequently greater faith in the upward and onward destiny of the race." This readiness to conceive of the human race as an insignificant detail of the universe seems also to be traceable to Calvin, who believed that mankind was nothing in comparison with the omnipotence and infinity of God. In the letter just quoted and another that follows, Holmes even allows himself the concession of using the word *God:* "I only don't believe, i.e. have no affirmative belief, that man was necessary to God, in order to find out that he existed (if the cosmos wears a beard, as to which I have no opinion). It seems to me probable that the only cosmic significance of man is that he is part of the cosmos, but that seems to me enough. . . . It strikes me that these philosophers [such as Ralph Barton Perry of Harvard] have gone round the globe to get to the spot close to which they stood before they began to philosophise — also that they still show their theological inheritance by assuming the special cosmic importance of man. I see no reason to believe that God needed him otherwise than as he may need all that is." But he usually speaks in terms of a beardless universe, and it is one of his recurring contentions that it is foolish to revolt against this universe — in the manner of the angry romantics — because man is a part of this universe and cannot differentiate himself from it in such a way as to create an issue as between himself and it.

As for transforming human society, the old Justice — having lost in the war the high hopes of the Northern crusade and fallen back on a Calvinist position which will not admit the realization of the Kingdom of God on earth — must simply, as a jurist and a jobbist, submit to the dominant will of the society he has sworn to serve. He sometimes detested the laws that this society made him enforce and would, as we have seen, sometimes seize upon the benefit of a doubt to declare himself in the opposite sense. He did not approve of the Sherman Anti-Trust Act and had no sympathy with the Volstead Act, which deprived him of the bottle of champagne which it had always been his ritual to drink with his wife on the occasion of their wedding anniversary. If the business men made the laws, he would have to accept their authority; if the people should decide to vote for socialism, he would have to accept that, too — and it was always from the point of view of assessing this latter possibility that he did his occasional reading in the literature of socialism.

So Holmes achieved isolation, remaining unperturbed and lucid, through the whole turbid blatant period that followed the Civil War — with its miseries of an industrial life that was reducing white factory workers to the slavery which George Fitzhugh had predicted, with its millionaires as arrogant and brutal as any Carolina planters, with the violent clashes between them as bloody as Nat Turner's rebellion or John Brown's raid upon Kansas, with its wars in Cuba and Europe that were our next uncontrollable moves after the war by which we had wrested California from the Mexicans and the war by which we had compelled the South to submit to the Washington government. These events touched him only at secondhand in the cases that came up before his tribunal and which elicited his crystalline opinions. His Brahminism, his high-minded egoism and his philosophic temper of mind had equipped him with an impenetrable integument.

Eventually the country at large came to join Holmes's colleagues in the law and his later-coming liberal admirers in assigning to him a consecrated authoritative role, though certainly the public in general knew as little about his work and ideas as they had when he was appointed to the Supreme Court. It was partly, no doubt, the prestige of longevity when the ancient has retained his faculties, partly the feeling of awe — of which I have spoken in connection with Lee — inspired by the rare survival of the type of the republican Roman, irrespective of what he now stands for: Justice Holmes was perhaps the last Roman. But there was also, I think, something more which was not inconsistent with these. The popular feeling about Holmes was illustrated in a striking and touching way in the reception by Eastern audiences, sixteen years after Holmes's death (in 1951), of a rubbishy film about him with the title *The Magnificent Yankee*. It was significant that what most moved these audiences were not the parts that were personal and sentimental but the scenes, all too few and inept, in which the hero's moral courage was shown. They seemed to be responding to these with a special enthusiasm of reassurance because they were made to feel — at a moment of the national life particularly uncertain and uncomfortable: the end of Truman's second administration — the Korean War, the Hiss trial, the rise of McCarthy — that here was a just man, a man of the old America who, having proved himself early in the Civil War, had persisted and continued to function through everything that had happened since, and had triumphed in remaining faithful to some kind of traditional ideal. But what *was* this ideal they applauded? I have tried to make out what Holmes meant to them. Independence and fair-dealing, no doubt; rectitude and courage as a public official; and a conviction that the United States had a special meaning and mission to devote one's whole life to which was a sufficient dedication for the highest gifts.

Was this Holmes's own understanding of the "job" to which he found himself committed? When he died in 1935 at the age of ninety-four, it appeared that he had left bequests of $25,000 each to Harvard and to the Boston Museum of Fine Arts, but all the rest of his very modest fortune — something over $270,000 — to the government of the United States. There was much speculation over this. It was true that his wife was dead, that, childless, he had not even any relatives to whom such a sum might have been useful. But why had he not bequeathed it to Harvard Law School or some other institution to be used for some specific purpose? I have heard two quite different explanations, both suggested by younger men who had seen a good deal of Holmes. One felt that his failure to do this was due simply to a lack of imagination. Having rarely, so far as is known, given a penny to a cause or a charity, indifferent to the improvement of others while preoccupied with the improvement of himself, it never came into Holmes's head to contribute to the usefulness of an institution. The other of Holmes's friends believed that, on the contrary, there was a definite point in Holmes's disposal of his money. He had fought for the Union; he had mastered its laws; he had served in its highest court through a period of three decades. The American Constitution was, as he came to declare, an "experiment" — what was to come of our democratic society it was impossible for a philosopher to tell — but he had taken responsibility for its working, he had subsisted and achieved his fame through his tenure of the place it had given him; and he returned to the treasury of the Union the little that he had to leave.

INDEX

BY FRANCES S. RADLEY